More
WATERLO

"A beautifully written account of the arrival of trattorias, Carnaby Street, tower blocks and gentrification, as the capital was developed after the destruction of the war."
—SIMON HEFFER, *Daily Telegraph*

"I absolutely love this book. It is wonderfully wide-ranging, urbane and amusing, and so clearly the result of exceptionally deep research. I am confident it will be a classic of London history, and ought to have a very wide readership."
—OTTO SAUMAREZ SMITH, author of *Boom Cities: Architect Planners and the Politics of Radical Urban Renewal in 1960s Britain*

"This is an engrossing, scholarly account of a time when London was in transformation . . . and one that will interest Londoners and non-Londoners alike."
—MARTIN CHILTON, *The Independent*

"A vivid, ambitious and comprehensive history of two crucial decades in the formation of modern London told through fifteen different studies that capture the city as a totality. *Waterloo Sunrise* is a sensational and extremely compelling work of history, beautifully written and incredibly rich."
—SAM WETHERELL, author of *Foundations: How the Built Environment Made Twentieth-Century Britain*

"Like the Kinks classic to which the title playfully alludes, *Waterloo Sunrise* is infectious, full of human detail, and generous in its narrative sweep."
—MATTHEW D'ANCONA, *Tortoise Media*

"Davis weaves two decades of social, physical, economic, cultural, and political change into a coherent tapestry. . . . A welcome, well-written resource."
—*Choice Reviews*

Waterloo Sunrise

Waterloo Sunrise

LONDON FROM THE SIXTIES TO THATCHER

JOHN DAVIS

PRINCETON UNIVERSITY PRESS
PRINCETON & OXFORD

Published by Princeton University Press
41 William Street, Princeton, New Jersey 08540
99 Banbury Road, Oxford OX2 6JX

press.princeton.edu

First paperback printing, 2024
Paperback ISBN 9780691223797

The Library of Congress has cataloged the cloth edition as follows:

Names: Davis, John, 1955– author.
Title: Waterloo sunrise : London from the sixties to Thatcher / John Davis.
Description: Princeton ; Oxford : Princeton University Press, [2022] |
    Includes bibliographical references and index.
Identifiers: LCCN 2021041511 (print) | LCCN 2021041512 (ebook) |
    ISBN 9780691220529 (hardback) | ISBN 9780691220581 (ebook)
Subjects: LCSH: London (England)—History—1951– | London (England)—
    Social life and customs—20th century. | London (England)—Social conditions—
    20th century. | Social change—England—London—History—20th century.
Classification: LCC DA688 .D26 2022 (print) | LCC DA688 (ebook) |
    DDC 942.1—dc23
LC record available at https://lccn.loc.gov/2021041511
LC ebook record available at https://lccn.loc.gov/2021041512

British Library Cataloging-in-Publication Data is available

Editorial: Ben Tate, Josh Drake
Jacket/Cover Design: Lauren Smith
Production: Danielle Amatucci
Publicity: Alyssa Sanford, Carmen Jimenez

Jacket/Cover Credit: Pedestrians on London Bridge, London, ca. 1960s. Photo: John Gay. Heritage Image Partnerships / Alamy Stock Photo

This book has been composed in Arno Pro

CONTENTS

PREFACE

Unlikely as it might appear, the impetus for this book came from a drive through the recently unified East Germany in 1991, when I spent two nights in Rostock. Rostock was then still essentially a DDR city, and though prosperous by East German standards, its slow development since 1945 meant that it still bore some of the scars of war—unrepaired bomb damage, buildings still marked by fire, and so on. It was also a working port with an obviously polluted river. In these ways it proved powerfully and unexpectedly evocative of a London which I had known only fleetingly as a small child in the early sixties and which largely disappeared during the following twenty years. Thoughts about London's transformation in the sixties led me to convert myself from a nineteenth-century London historian into a postwar London historian, and this book is the product of that move.

It is not a conventional narrative history. Rather, it consists of sixteen essays on aspects of London in the two decades covered by the book. Chapter 1 serves in part as an introduction, chapter 16 in part as a conclusion, but both are research-based essays in their own right. Each of the sixteen essays is free-standing. I recognise that this might make the work appear rather episodic, but I have long had misgivings about attempting a linear history of a city as complex, diverse and multifaceted as London, and I believe that working in a relatively limited period allows the historian to explore parallel themes in the way that I have attempted to do here. More importantly, there is an overarching theme to the work, which would not necessarily be evident from reading any of the essays in isolation but which is teased out towards the end of the book—that London in these years anticipates in various, often unrelated, ways many of the features of 'Thatcher's Britain' in the 1980s.

The Governing Body of The Queen's College, Oxford and the Oxford University History Faculty assisted me both financially and by granting me sabbatical leave, for which I am especially grateful. In addition, I have inevitably drawn on the help of many individuals in putting this book together. Having visited the local studies centres of all the thirty-two London boroughs in the course of my research, I hope that the many archivists who have helped me will accept a collective acknowledgement, though I wish to thank specifically Robert Jones and Sanjida Alam of Tower Hamlets, Simon Donoghue of Havering, Sarah Gould of Merton for dealing with particular research queries. The London Metropolitan Archives has been the indispensable focal point for me as for every historian of London, and Sally Bevan has been unfailingly helpful in dealing with all my LMA-related demands. The staff at the National Archives have made that essential repository a very user-friendly place in which to carry out research. A substantial part of my research has entailed work on the metropolitan and local press, much of which would have been infinitely more difficult without the expertise of the British Library staff at, first, Colindale and later the St Pancras Newsroom. Sarah Garrod of the George Padmore Institute helped greatly with my work on Chapter 12. I am also grateful to those who have assisted my picture research—Luci Gosling at the Mary Evans Picture Library, Erin Quigley at Alamy, Junior Cunningham at Getty Images and Steph Eeles at the London Picture Archive. Mike Pretious deployed deft detective skills in identifying the location in the photograph of Kelly Street, Kentish Town (chapter 5). Finally I must thank all those who have helped me by giving me references or simply airing their own ideas in seminars, tutorials or conversation: Aaron Andrews, Katharina Boehmer, Duncan Bowie, Phil Childs, Joana Duyster Borredà, Jed Fazakarley, Nick Garland, Peter Ghosh, Joanna Godfrey, Ian Gordon, Matthew Grimley, Simon Gunn, Jose Harris, Michael Hebbert, Karin Hofmeester, Janet Howarth, Ben Jackson, Alistair Kefford, Peter Mandler, Graham Marshall, Ross McKibbin, Anna Minton, Pip Monk, Holger Nehring, Nick Owen, Susan Pennybacker, Harriet Rudden, Otto Saumarez Smith, Delyth Scudamore, Florence Sutcliffe-Braithwaite, Rachael Takens-Milne, Natalie Thomlinson, Selina Todd, Jim Tomlinson, Tony Travers, Philip Waller, Christine Whitehead and Cornelia Wilde. Ben Tate at Princeton has been an excellent editor to work with, tolerant and accommodating. I wish also to thank Oxford University Press for permission to republish, in amended versions, chapters 6, 9 and 13, Manchester University Press for permission to republish the revised chapter 14 and Palgrave for permission to republish chapter 11.

And above all I must thank Carolyne Larrington for putting up with this seemingly endless project—and with me.

ABBREVIATIONS

BTA British Tourist Authority
CDA Comprehensive Development Area
CDP Community Development Project
CND Campaign for Nuclear Disarmament
COS Charity Organisation Society
CPF City Parochial Foundation
DJC Docklands Joint Committee
EEC European Economic Community
EEDAG East End Docklands Action Group
ELA *East London Advertiser*
ES *Evening Standard*
GLC Greater London Council
GLDP Greater London Development Plan
GMC General Management Committee
HO *Harrow Observer*
ILEA Inner London Education Authority
IRR Institute of Race Relations
JDAG Joint Docklands Action Group
LB London Borough
LCC London County Council
LCSS London Council of Social Service
LMA London Metropolitan Archives
LPL *London Property Letter*

'Why London? Why Now?'

THE SWINGING MOMENT

London was repeatedly discovered in the mid-1960s. More accurately, the West End of London was discovered by several writers and journalists, most of them from overseas. They were looking for the source of the British innovations in fashion and popular music which had recently permeated North America and western Europe. They found a metropolitan centre less straight-laced than they had taken Britain to be, with cutting-edge popular culture and a vibrant nightlife enjoyed by young pleasure-seekers. They concluded that London was 'the most swinging city in the world at the moment.'[1]

Britain's pop-music revolution—by now centred in London—was the principal reason for the fixation, but this new bout of Anglomania was driven by a comprehensive enthusiasm for London's innovative culture, embracing fashion, design, food and lifestyle generally, as well as music. Across the Atlantic, at least, London fashion had been noticed before Beatlemania arrived. *Glamour* magazine of New York featured the British model Jean Shrimpton on its cover as early as April 1963, and Mod women's fashion became a staple of US women's magazines over the following months. A feature in US *Vogue* in September 1964 focused specifically on the 'new rush of Bright Young People in Britain'—'Britain' meaning London, a city 'filled with these young women, their right-up-to-the-minute look, their passion for doing things, their absolute talent for fun.'[2] Six months later the US teenage magazine *Seventeen*, responsible for introducing the designer

Mary Quant to American fashion followers in 1961, produced a special issue promoting 'The London Look.'[3]

Seventeen's readership consisted largely of American teenage girls, most of whom would have had little prospect of visiting London in the near future. Its immediate aim was to promote sales of London designs in the US, strengthening the tie-up that the magazine had established with a manufacturer; it did so by 'capitaliz[ing] on the British fever the magazine helped to induce.'[4] In August 1965 the Hamburg teen periodical *Star Club News* published a well-informed piece on the London youth scene for readers who stood a better chance of experiencing it than did American teens, concentrating on Mod style and entertainment and describing in detail a performance by The Who at the Marquee Club.[5] The German teenage magazine *Bravo* carried a feature on the Mod fashion fulcrum Carnaby Street, in West Soho, in February 1966.[6] *Bravo* was a teenage lifestyle publication, chiefly concerned with pop music. It was the fusion of fashion and pop which produced the 'youthquake' in British popular culture in the sixties, and a similar effect became evident internationally as the Beatles and other British groups became global brands during 1964. It produced an interest in Britain and British modernity which focused on London as the world's 'only truly modern city.'[7]

The American columnist John Crosby, working as London correspondent of the *New York Herald Tribune*, did more than most to project the city to Americans as a 'place to be', though he eventually distilled his impressions of 'The Most Exciting City' not in the *Tribune* but in the London *Daily Telegraph*'s new weekend magazine in April 1965. 'London is where the action is', he wrote, as Paris and New York had been after the war and Rome in the midfifties. He identified a new magnetism in Britain's capital city, as a young, vibrant London pulled Britain out of the 'long Dark Age' which had begun in the thirties and continued through the years of war and austerity. It was being led by a self-confident generation of young creatives, fun-loving and irreverent but still driven by 'a steady pulse of serious purpose.' Crosby interviewed several of them, including thirty-year-old John Stephen, who had effectively created Carnaby Street as the world's hippest menswear centre; Rupert Lycett Green, twenty-six-year-old creator of the expensive but modishly elegant clothes sold in the Dover Street boutique Blades; the Mod designer Caroline Charles, already a millionaire having started her own label little more than a year earlier at the age of twenty-one; Mark Birley, a veteran of thirty-four, who had founded the up-market Annabel's nightclub in Berkeley Square two years earlier; and

Brian Morris, aged thirty, the manager of the exclusive and fashionable Ad Lib Club off Leicester Square. Morris told Crosby that 'this is a young people's town. The young have suddenly become visible.' Observing an Oxford graduate swathing himself in brown corduroy in Blades and working-class boys 'splurging on suede jackets' in Carnaby Street, Crosby concluded that youth had trumped class in the new England and that 'the caste system is breaking down at both ends.'[8]

Crosby's was an American view of London, carried in a British publication. It was not until a year later that London was projected directly across the Atlantic in the encomium to the city by Piri Halasz in *Time* magazine's issue for 15 April 1966. The feature would become one of *Time*'s most famous pieces, but it was the result of a spur-of-the-moment editorial decision and was researched and written in nine days, with material supplied by the magazine's London bureau. At its core were five vignettes, or 'scenes', depicting an evening at the Clermont gaming club in Berkeley Square, during which 'the handsome son of a peer' lost $450,000; a Saturday afternoon in Chelsea's King's Road, featuring Mick Jagger and the Mod queen Cathy McGowan in the Guys and Dolls coffee bar; an 'in-crowd' lunch at Le Rêve restaurant in Chelsea, involving Terence Stamp, Michael Caine, David Bailey and the Chelsea tailor Doug Hayward; an account of the recreational life of the twenty-three-year-old fashion writer and stylist Jane Ormsby Gore; and a Kensington house party given by the actress Leslie Caron for Marlon Brando, Barbra Streisand, Warren Beatty and others ('Dame Margot Fonteyn is due'). Halasz in New York then worked up the story to incorporate some of her own ideas—that the young were becoming more influential in the modern world and that people from humble backgrounds, with provincial accents, were becoming more influential in London. The colour illustrations helped complete the image of 'the Swinging City': vinyl-clad girls in the King's Road, fashionable youth in Carnaby Street, a striptease artiste at the Sunset Strip club in Soho, revellers at the exclusive Scotch of St James nightclub, a *chemin de fer* session at the still more exclusive Crockford's gaming club. The result was, as Halasz acknowledged, 'a collage, pastiche, composite, or synthesis of words and ideas contributed by many people', but it was a pastiche which produced a lasting image.[9]

A 'passionate Anglophile',[10] Halasz saw London as an optimistic place and its youth as a force for good. Aged thirty herself, she had recently filed reports on youth movements in Cuba, the Netherlands and Indonesia, and she warmed to London as 'yet another situation where a new generation was playing a key role.' During the midsixties lull in youth activism in Britain, however, between the waning of the Campaign for Nuclear Disarmament (CND) and the explosion of student protest later in the decade, it was difficult to present a similar degree of political engagement in London. Instead the article's emphasis on consumerism and clubbing reinforced another of Halasz's convictions—that the retreat from empire 'had enabled England to regain the free and easy spirit that had been crushed out of it by the weight of commanding the globe', liberating London in particular 'to share pleasure with its workers and its youth.' A reference to the 'pot parties of Chelsea' was removed before publication, but *Time*'s London appeared unserious, an impression reinforced by the illustration of a bowler-hatted City type forging across London Bridge 'to manage the affairs of a suddenly frivolous city.'[11]

Halasz's editor urged her 'to be sure and get that good stuff about decadence into the story.'[12] As the Wilson government struggled to defend the pound in the summer of 1966, external commentators drew easy connections between London's self-indulgence and Britain's economic plight. Two weeks before the *Time* article, Pierre Joffroy in *Paris Match* had written a sympathetic piece on London, which nonetheless ended by asking (quoting the *Times* and ultimately Oscar Wilde) whether Britain was dying beyond its means.[13] The American evangelist Billy Graham launched his month-long Greater London Crusade in May, 'bent on saving this city from its excesses.'[14] Like many tourists, he made his way to Soho—'the sleazy "Square Mile of Sin"'—though police, concerned about the crowds, stopped him bringing Jesus's love to Old Compton Street.[15] As the summer's sterling crisis mounted, the treatment of London's swingers became increasingly censorious. 'The pound trembles, the gold runs out, Britain's ships stand in the docks', wrote Anthony Lewis in the *New York Times* in June, 'but at Annabel's they come and go, talking of how short the skirts can go. The atmosphere in London today can be almost eerie in its quality of relentless frivolity. There can rarely have been a greater contrast between a country's objective situation and the mood of its people.'[16] The US men's magazine *Esquire* published an enthusiastic set of pieces on the 'London Charivari 1966' in July, but many observers saw the austerity package imposed in that month as calling time on the city's self-indulgence. '"Swinging London" swings on, but the swinging lacks conviction', Dana Adams Schmidt told *New York Times* readers in October.[17] At the end of the year Gene Farmer wrote a lachrymose 'Special Report' in *Life*, yearning for the poor but honest London he had known in the early fifties, when meat and eggs were almost unobtainable and people burned 'nutty slack' to fend off the cold. By contrast, London's new incontinence was illustrated by underdressed bunny-girls serving blackjack-playing gamblers at the recently opened Playboy Club in Park Lane. '"Swinging", Farmer wrote, 'has got out of hand because it is the kind of fun only a rich nation can afford—and England is no longer a rich nation.'[18]

Londoners, 'partly appalled by the speciousness, partly amused by the attention',[19] reacted with knowing scepticism to what the journalist Maureen Cleave called 'the tedious swinging London that foreigners are always going on about.'[20] This picture of relentless hedonism, constructed largely by outsiders, was at best unreal, at worst offensive. It was based almost entirely on the West End, which was, for many Londoners, a place to visit rather than the focus of their lives. As the *Evening Standard*'s theatre critic Milton Shulman noted in October 1966, local television news programmes depicted a very different urbanity, portraying London as 'a vast suburb where rows about rates, higher rents, snarls, and grocery prices . . . dominate the souls and imaginations of the capital's inhabitants'—a metropolis as mundane as 'Swinging London' was exotic.[21] This might have been just as myopic a view—Shulman thought so—but it is true that a researcher today, reading only the local newspapers covering the London beyond the glossy centre, would struggle to recognise the world's 'most exciting city.' Sixties London was a place in which most public transport stopped by 11.00 P.M. and many West End stores closed for the weekend at 1.00 P.M. on Saturday.[22] Sundays were so inert that the author Betty James wrote a guide in 1964 to help Londoners relieve the tedium of their Sabbath.[23] It is routine now for memoirs of Londoners who grew up in the sixties to stress that their part of the capital—whether comfortable suburb or decaying inner-city area—was not really very swinging at all.

But to point out that 'Swinging London' meant little to the average Londoner is not to say much. Of course Swinging London, as depicted, was largely mythical, just as the received images of 'belle époque' Paris, Weimar Berlin, *la dolce vita* Rome and the two analogues suggested by both Crosby and Joffroy—1920s Paris and post-1945 New York—were mythical. The myth emerged from stylised accounts which privileged the exotic over the routine, leisure over work, the centre over the periphery, producing a city portrait which was inevitably overdrawn. The question is why it was drawn at all: What magnetism made London an 'in' city, however briefly? We should be asking not whether 'Swinging London' was real but rather the question posed by the author of the *Esquire* piece: 'Why London, why now?'

The Unswinging City

In the early sixties much of London—and most of its Victorian core—could best be described as an ageing industrial city scarred by war. Only in 1963 was the last bomb site in the City of London built over.[24] Outer London was still pockmarked by bomb damage, while the East End and other targeted industrial areas remained disfigured throughout the decade. The prefab units introduced in the last year of the war to provide emergency—and supposedly temporary—housing were still a common feature of inner London in the sixties: indeed, the London County Council (LCC) initiated a new four-year prefab-building programme in 1964 to plug some of the gaps in South and East London's housing stock.[25] Much of the regular housing was substandard, enfeebled by decades of rent control.[26]

London displayed the familiar environmental problems of an industrial city, which were being tackled by the sixties but would not be dispelled before they were exacerbated by those of the modern age. Thus the Thames was cleaner than it had been in the 1950s, when it had officially been declared 'biologically dead', but the Thames estuary still received some five hundred million gallons of sewage effluents every day in 1962. Only a tenth of that amount entered the river above London Bridge, but that was enough to ensure that the Thames did not smell very swinging even in the centre of town. The growing volume of household detergents in waste water meant that parts of the river surface carried a regular 'head' of foam; the effect on the oxygen balance was equivalent to the discharge of crude sewage from a million people.[27] Industrial pollution and domestic coal fires had combined to take four thousand lives in the smog of 1952, and although that catastrophe prompted the 1956 Clean Air Act, which mitigated the problem, the smog reappeared, albeit on a smaller scale, in 1960 and particularly in December 1962, when visibility fell to less than five yards, the concentration of smoke and sulphur dioxide in the atmosphere rose to fourteen times normal levels and bronchitis deaths increased.[28] In any case, the 1956 act did nothing to combat the growth of hydrocarbon pollution caused by rising traffic volumes.[29] Even by 1967 a quart of London air was said to contain 'about 10 million particles of soot or dust in addition to various unhealthy gases.'[30] It left its mark on the urban fabric: the two million or so tourists coming to London annually in the mid-1960s gazed on 'some of the scruffiest buildings in the world.'[31] In December 1966

A bomb site in the Harrow Road area of Paddington, still undeveloped in 1960. (Roger Mayne Archive/Mary Evans Picture Library)

the *Standard*'s planning correspondent, Judy Hillman, assessed the condition of several public buildings, awarding 'black hand' ratings to the worst afflicted—the Palace of Westminster, Westminster Abbey, the nearby Middlesex Guildhall and the church of St Clement Danes, exposed to traffic exhaust on two sides on its island site.[32] Traffic also exacerbated noise pollution: in 1961 one in six Londoners claimed that traffic noise had made their house shake, one in four that it kept them awake.[33] Cars and lorries were the main culprits, transforming what had once been a domestic problem into an environmental one and creating an ambient noise nuisance: where once householders had been as much disturbed by noise from neighbours as from outside, 'it has been found now [1963] that only 14 per cent notice indoor noises, while 50 per cent complain about the traffic.'[34]

In the nineteenth century such disamenities in urban Britain had been accepted as the price payable for the higher standard of living that manufacturing cities offered. Since the outbreak of war in 1939, however, inner London had seen a steady outflow of people looking to escape the drawbacks of the inner city and enabled to do so by a similar outward movement of employment, to outer London, to the postwar New Towns or beyond.

Unswinging London. Hampden Street, LB Camden, early sixties. (John Gay/English Heritage NMR/Mary Evans Picture Library)

Greater London in the 1960s was in fact only halfway through a population fall which had begun on the outbreak of war and would continue until the late 1980s. The capital was shedding cockneys. Initially the postwar decentralisation of population was public policy, rooted in prewar concerns about London's strategic vulnerability and more recent anxiety about congestion of the central area and pressure on the housing stock and public transport. Only in the 1970s would depopulation become a matter of public concern; before then the assumption was that movement out of the inner city—and perhaps out of London altogether—offered the most reliable means of securing an improved quality of life.

Those who left London were replaced by incomers who ranged from people driven from their previous homes by war, political upheaval or economic collapse to those for whom a move to London was necessary to develop their careers, with a large group in the middle who had judged, rightly or wrongly, that their prospects would be better in the city. The geopolitical upheavals of the mid-twentieth century accounted for the

The first day of London's last great smog, 4 December 1962. That day and the next brought fifty-five deaths from respiratory disease. (Mirrorpix/Alamy Stock Photo)

arrival of German and central European refugees from Nazism, for the postwar Polish refugees from communism, for the Chinese who came, via Hong Kong, during and after the Chinese Civil War and for the Cypriots— Greek and Turkish—who left their island to escape the communal hostilities of the fifties and sixties. Other ethnic minority communities were augmented by assisted migration schemes: London's Maltese population expanded from the late forties, prompted by financial assistance from the British government.[35] Migrants from South Asia and, particularly, the West Indies were encouraged to move to Britain from the late forties to offset labour shortages on public transport and in the National Health Service.

These were all arrivals from overseas, contributing to London's developing diversity. They were the mid-twentieth-century equivalents of the men

Working river. Lightermen on barges moored on the south bank of the Thames, opposite Queen-hithe in the City, late fifties. (The John Turner Photographic Collection/Mary Evans)

and women who had migrated from country to town during the industrial revolution, seeking and generally gaining an improved standard of living at the cost of often squalid living conditions, with the added drawback of receiving frequently uninhibited racist hostility from those who were longer established in London. Perhaps the most misleading aspect of the 'Swinging London' stereotype was the undiverse nature of the city that it depicted. Crosby noted briefly that 'the Flamingo [Club], a beat spot, caters to the West Indians',[36] but otherwise the American commentators, who might have been expected to be alert to urban racial issues in the midsixties, were so set on projecting London as a carefree place that the possible recurrence of racial tension in a city that had seen serious race riots as recently as 1958 passed unmentioned.

Nonetheless, most of London's in-migrants had come, as always, from the British Isles, including the Republic of Ireland, which was still exporting around forty thousand people to London annually in the late 1950s.[37] Many of these British or Irish migrants had come to London with less assured prospects than, for example, the West Indians recruited to work on the buses, and many found themselves consigned to the lower reaches of London's employment and housing markets. The journalist Melanie

Phillips interviewed the residents of what was then a slum in Cambridge Street, Pimlico, shortly before their eviction in 1977. Of the eight whose origins were specified, all came from the British Isles, but only three were Londoners. The others were a twenty-four-year-old from Bangor who had briefly worked as a waitress, an unemployed porter from Tipperary, an unemployed baker from the Isle of Wight, a casual catering worker from a village in the Trossachs and his partner, from Stirling, who had just walked out of a job as a cinema usherette.[38] To them and many similar incomers London offered only 'insecure, non-unionised, low-paid work combined with insecure, low-standard accommodation.'[39]

'Is only rubbish-people come to this town', claimed a Greek Cypriot coffee grinder in Camden Town, interviewed by Jonathan Raban in 1973. He had come to London in 1956 so that his children could receive an English education: 'next year, maybe year after, I go home.' A compatriot, Helena Petrou, had found herself alone in London after her husband divorced her, with a child, little English and no money. She lived by making up twenty dresses a day by artificial light in her basement flat in Tufnell Park. In the city but not of it, she nonetheless clung to London: 'I want to stay here for a moment. Life changes from today to tomorrow. Who knows?' Her memory of Cyprus—'the Eden from which, long ago . . . she was expelled'—became steadily more distant and more rosy.[40]

London's diverse and complex economy had always absorbed large numbers of such people without conferring security or comfort on them. Helena Petrou experienced Tufnell Park in much the same way as sweated immigrant tailors had experienced Whitechapel in the 1880s. If anything, the position of the most precarious worsened during the years covered by this book; in 1977 one of Phillips's Pimlico subjects spoke of his London life as 'a question of survival', weeks before he lost his home.[41] Overall, though, London was a prosperous city and one in which an evolving 'growth services' sector offered opportunities not to be found—or not to be found in such abundance and offering such rewards—elsewhere.

In a 1966 *Evening Standard* piece about the allure of London, Angus McGill interviewed four incomers from points north: a market researcher from Middlesbrough, a public relations man from South Shields, a BBC producer from Sheffield and the Carnaby Street mogul John Stephen, from Glasgow. All were representatives of the new London, benefiting from opportunities which they could not have enjoyed in the London of twenty years earlier. None wished to return. Stephen, who had arrived from Glasgow in 1952 with '£13 in a burgundy leather wallet and nowhere to go', exemplified those who were enriched by London's new economy. 'London is where the opportunities are', he told McGill.[42] Similarly Tom Benson, who rode from Liverpool on his scooter to take a job washing up in Ray Parkes's Chelsea restaurant, ended up cooking the food and eventually running Parkes at its fashionable sixties peak.[43]

There were many more, though, who, though not exactly rich, were comfortable enough to enjoy experiencing the city in a way that a Cypriot seamstress trapped in a Tufnell Park basement could not. The novelist A. S. Byatt, Sheffield-born, who 'likes to think of herself as a northerner, although she prefers living in London', enjoyed the diversity of the mothers' group at her children's nursery in Bloomsbury, where she encountered 'doctors' wives, actors' wives, a striptease artist, university wives, Indians, Italians, Cypriots.' Her previous home in Durham had been beautiful, but 'the orderliness of society weighed on [her].'[44] Martin Holmes, market researcher from Middlesbrough, told McGill, '[Back home] I'd have a far higher standard of living. I'd live in a house with a garden rather than a flat without one. But London holds you. You feel that you are closer to things happening.'[45] An anonymous stripper interviewed by Anne Sharpley in 1965 explained that she had come to London from Yorkshire with a job offer as an assistant manageress, which she had rapidly dropped, feeling that 'this is not like London': 'I wanted something more glamorous, wanted to get into the West End.'[46] The gays who spoke to Sharpley in a groundbreaking series of articles in 1964 expressed 'the relief they have at first coming to London from country districts to find "there were hundreds like me, all more than understanding"'; the prosecution rate for what was still an illegal act was only half that in the rest of the United Kingdom.[47] Sharpley herself, from Cheshire, appreciated the 'stiff course in urbanisation' that cosmopolitan Balcombe Street, near Dorset Square, gave her: 'it has become an engrossment, an arena, a listening post, a liability, an insight—and an everlasting instruction that people, after all, are more important than trees.'[48] Anne Ward, a twenty-four-year-old personal assistant, loved 'the feel of the town' and got 'a tremendous kick out of merely walking around on those fabulous misty days': 'It's so romantic—the bomb sites and the church spires looming up. It sounds very provincial, but I walk down Fleet Street and I think: "I wouldn't go back to Chesterfield for the world."'[49] Valerie Warden, a twenty-six-year-old fashion artist from Liverpool, believed that had she stayed at home, she would have drifted into marriage rather than a career; 'just when she thinks she's had enough of London, something happens to convince her she can never

Aerial view of the City by night, November 1964, showing the concentration of offices in the formerly blitzed area surrounding St Paul's Cathedral. (Mirrorpix/Alamy Stock Photo)

leave it.'[50] For Mary Taylor, a nineteen-year-old secretary, 'things are much more exhilarating in London. Even the top jobs in Bristol go at half the speed.' Taylor, who had left Bristol at fifteen because she thought she might as well 'join the herd', explained that 'girls come to London to have a good social life, two holidays a year and earn a lot of money.'[51]

Secretaries like Taylor were beneficiaries of the office boom that was transforming the capital. The Conservative government had lifted controls over commercial development in 1954, enriching a small group of men who had had the foresight and nerve to buy Central London property during the war.[52] Their efforts reshaped the face of the capital, providing most Londoners with their first—and starkest—illustration of the changing nature of the metropolitan economy, as office towers sprouted in what had always been a low-rise city. Few welcomed their assault on London's fabric. Most postwar building in the West End and, particularly, the City did little to capture public imagination. Observing the first signs of the City's postwar transformation in 1954, Harold Macmillan feared that 'a lot of very confused and unworthy building will ultimately replace what the Germans destroyed.'[53] Tension built up until 1959, when public anger was vented at the clumsy stump designed by John Poulson for the developer

Jack Cotton on the Monico site at Piccadilly Circus. Poulson's design was approved by the LCC but subsequently shot down after a public inquiry.[54] Though Cotton responded by engaging Walter Gropius as a kind of consultant,[55] there was not the incentive that exists today for developers to use prestige architects as a means of gaining planning permission. Generally permission was gained as a result of hole-and-corner negotiation with the LCC in which developers agreed in return to help the LCC attain one of its own development objectives. The indispensable skill of the architect consisted rather of extracting the most profitable outcome from the LCC's system of plot ratios and height restrictions rather than endeavouring to beautify London; the arcane and clandestine nature of these negotiations meant that the London public became aware of most projects only when they began to be built.[56]

As the supply of bomb sites dwindled from the late 1950s, much development entailed the destruction of familiar landmarks. These included West End theatres and railway termini, targeted in the late fifties and early sixties by private developers promoting the replacement of an existing Victorian building by a supposedly more efficient successor, buried under an office tower.[57] The bomb-damaged stations at Holborn Viaduct and Cannon Street and, more controversially, the Doric Arch and Great Hall at Euston and the St James's Theatre in King Street were victims of these initiatives;[58] many more buildings were threatened. It is hard to convey today the unsettling effect on Londoners of the constant threats to and recurrent removal of a familiar townscape. Byatt, conscious that 'things are disappearing and decaying' in Georgian Bloomsbury in the early 1960s, described it guardedly as a good place to live 'for now.'[59] Bette Spektorov, an Oxford graduate interviewed by Maureen Cleave for the *Standard* in 1964, had come to London for its theatres, exhibitions and museums but thought it 'fearfully ugly': 'And what beautiful things there are, they are pulling down. It brings tears to my eyes. Very soon it will be ghastly to live here.'[60]

But the office boom brought jobs. Companies sought mostly to recruit school leavers: the director of one plastics company was said to have declined to rent a new block outside London because 'there isn't even a pop record shop nearby.' Sixty-five percent of office staff were women, most of them secretaries.[61] Many of them found secretarial employment unstimulating.[62] It displayed many of the features of a casual trade. Skill levels were low—a 1960 survey found that the average London typist averaged only 1,648 words a day[63]—and training was often limited or nonexistent.

Typing pool in a City office, 1978. (Homer Sykes/Alamy Stock Photo)

Turnover rates were high, with both the women and their bosses assuming that their employment would end upon marriage. Few secretaries remained in the job beyond their twenties—nearly 70 percent of London secretaries were aged twenty-nine or younger. Opportunities for career development were limited, and promotion was more likely to arise from a transfer to a higher-status boss than from any enhancement of professional expertise. Old-school secretaries, with learned skills, feared that their trade was being debased by the flood of new entrants. A 'secretary' in sixties London might be anything 'from shorthand-typist to private scribe to glorified personal assistant':[64] indeed, the term 'personal assistant' was said to have been adopted by senior secretaries as a means of distinguishing themselves from the unskilled mass. For all that, though, the rapid expansion of London's commercial sector meant that unlike most casual workers, secretaries were in demand and startlingly well paid. 'These days a good secretary can virtually write her own ticket', Karin Hart wrote in 1966; by then around a quarter of the secretaries in the City were earning more than £1,000 a year, when the national average wage for all employment was below £900.[65] Even sixteen-year-old school leavers could command £9 a week in the City.[66] The Town and Country Planning Association found in 1962 that the pay for an unskilled female office worker had risen by 180 percent since 1950, against a 60 percent increase in the price level.[67] 'The worst economic freeze does not touch the pockets of secretaries', as Jonathan Aitken put it.[68]

There were approaching half a million secretaries in London by the midsixties.[69] Most came from London, and many continued to live at home, earning well and paying little or nothing in rent.[70] But many came from outside—'typists from Bradford and Hull, secretaries from Newcastle, audio-typists from Leeds and female clerks from Doncaster come hotfooting to London as fast as their parents will allow.'[71] Many lived in bedsits—single rooms, usually in houses shared with other young women. Barbara Griggs described this milieu in 1963: 'This home from home will be furnished with a divan bed in one corner, a minute electric cooker in another corner, assorted bits of uninspired secondhand furniture, and a decoration scheme that you loathe at sight but can't afford to modify by any more decisive means than the introduction of a couple of jolly red and orange cushions on the divan to counteract the prevailing note of smoggy fawn and fern green, and an Impressionist print on the walls.' For most young women in the city, this was merely a base in which an outgoing social life could be planned: 'bedsitter life makes you gregarious from necessity.'[72]

Gregariousness could lead to babies. Lamenting the number of illegitimate births to London teenagers in 1964, the London Diocesan Council for Moral Welfare noted that 'a large proportion of the girls are commercial or office workers who live alone in bedsitters.'[73] London's illegitimacy rate grew steadily from the mid-1950s. It became a talking point in the early 1960s, when it was usually attributed to pregnant girls coming from the countryside or, stereotypically, Ireland, to give birth in the anonymous setting of the big city.[74] Over the course of the decade, though, it became evident that the rise reflected changing conditions in London more than circumstances elsewhere. In 1969 James Weir, medical officer for Kensington and Chelsea, advanced a sociological explanation for his borough having the highest illegitimacy rate in Britain: it was characterised by a large number of people living in lodgings, an extraordinarily high percentage of women in the 'at risk' years of fifteen to twenty-nine, 'abundant temptation' and the social pressures pushing young people into extramarital sex.[75] Weir's counterpart in Redbridge noted in 1969 that a rise in illegitimacy had been accompanied by a fall in the occupancy of homes for unmarried mothers, suggesting that as 'society is becoming more permissive, unmarried mothers can remain with their parents.' The Greenwich medical officer observed in his 1971 report that illegitimacy could no longer be assumed to reflect 'low social standards.' It was 'to be found in all walks of life. Indeed, on occasions, it would appear to be sought by certain types.'[76]

'London is the easiest city in the world to find a partner', the English writer Al Alvarez told American readers in September 1967.[77] If the partner sought was young and female, he may have been right. Women formed 55 percent of the population between fifteen and twenty-four in the 'Greater London Central Conurbation' identified in the 1966 Sample Census.[78] The idea that these women had turned London into the global capital of recreational sex owed much to Crosby and his male interviewees. A January 1964 piece in the *New York Herald Tribune* described seductively sassy 'Chelsea girls' empowered by fashion, 'striding along in their black leather boots, their capes, their fur hats, their black stockings with wild designs.'[79] In the *Weekend Telegraph* fifteen months later Crosby suggested that 'young English girls take to sex as if it's candy and it's delicious.'[80] Interviewed in 1967, Helen Brook, who had founded the Brook Advisory Service in 1962 to advise young Londoners in matters of sex and contraception, painted a different picture, of widespread ignorance and insecurity about sex, noting that neither innate intelligence nor an educated family guaranteed sexual awareness.[81] Inner London's numerous young women had to gain wisdom in an environment where sexual opportunity was greater and social constraints weaker than anywhere else in Britain. 'What I hate to see is a young girl coming to London and hopping from bed to bed just because her friends do. It happens to a lot of young girls', Jenny Randall, a secretary sharing a Belsize Park flat with five other young women, told Maureen Cleave in 1964.[82] Randall's six years in London had instilled caution, but as Cleave pointed out, 'for what [young single women] suffer in loneliness, shortage of money, horrible food and terror of the big city, they are rewarded in freedom'[83]—and freedom might include sexual freedom.

Six anonymised but unusually frank interviews in the magazine *Look of London* in February 1968 give an idea of the variety of strategies adopted by young single women in the capital's sexual jungle. One respondent had avoided sex until she was twenty but after embarking on a serious relationship felt free to have affairs with men she believed could 'help her with her natural development.' After ending the relationship and going onto the pill, she became more eclectic and claimed to have had forty partners—some of them women—by the time of the interview. Another, who had jettisoned her virginity at the age of sixteen 'because she felt that it was time

to do something about it', had had about ten men since, on a serial mo-
nogamy basis, ending each relationship herself, and only when a replacement had been identified. One, admitting that 'she is very keen on sex and
finds it beneficial to her health', nonetheless 'found great pleasure in leading people right to the brink and then refusing them'; 'she found herself
easily infatuated but just as easily bored by a man.' One, initially repelled
by sex after being 'half-raped' at fifteen, had subsequently had flings with
men she found physically attractive, but 'now realises she cannot go to bed
with men casually.' Another had had two lengthy relationships during
which she was not entirely faithful, admitting that she had practised casual
flings 'partly in order to run a check on the physical prowess of her main
partner.' The peer pressure felt by young single women is suggested by one
who had resisted sleeping with her boyfriend for three years until she was
eighteen but admitted that before then 'she used to pretend she'd had fantastic affairs to anyone who happened to be interested' and by another who
'feels shame at admitting that she is still a virgin.'[84] Even she, though, was
evidently prepared to countenance sex outside marriage, like most in her
generation.

Randall's view was clear: 'I disapprove very strongly of adultery and
divorce. Once you're married, that's it. But I disapprove of the attitude of
the women's magazines that sex is a miracle that happens the moment you
get a gold band on your finger, and before that it's disgusting and filthy.'
The very finality of marriage made sexual experimentation beforehand
acceptable. We cannot know how widely Randall's attitude was shared, but
we can see it as a rational response of a young woman to London's opportunities and pitfalls. It may well be that young men were more predatory,
as Randall suggested,[85] but the result was to diminish the number of young
people of both genders believing that premarital sex was wrong. A 1970
survey of Londoners' sexual attitudes for the *Standard* showed a pronounced generational divergence in attitudes to premarital sex, with
60 percent of those aged between sixteen and twenty-four believing that
'young people today should . . . have sex before marriage', compared to
29 percent in all age groups.[86]

Men were less evident beneficiaries of the office boom, but they were
beneficiaries nonetheless. The median wage for young male clerical staff
in the lowest grade rose by 142 percent between 1950 and 1960, against a

52 percent increase in the price level.[87] 'The young office workers who filled the new office towers rising around the city' sustained the thirty-six betting shops which sprang up in the City of London (a square mile with a minuscule resident population and expensive rents) within three years of the legalisation of gambling in 1960.[88] They fuelled the menswear boom of the early sixties: 'You could be a bank clerk and people would think "There's a smart young lad," but you could also be fashionable', Pete Townshend told Shawn Levy.[89] But there was also an indirect effect. Office expansion widened the horizons of working-class boys entering the labour market. In the early 1950s, as the East End community activist Patrick Hanshaw later recounted, jobs had been plentiful close to home, but the local economy offered 'full employment with only a restricted choice of direction': 'We were what loosely could be described as "factory fodder"', and 'as they had done for generations, the Docks were already lifting that beckoning finger.'[90] The singer Tommy Steele remembered being summoned to see the headmaster on leaving his Bermondsey school in 1952 to find 'a grumpy old soul': '[His] one object was to put us off what we wanted to do and stick us into a factory.'[91]

Ten years later, however, 15–20 percent of boys and the majority of girls leaving East End schools went into office work: 'The office seems to be regarded as the acme of working life', as Poplar's Youth Employment Officer put it.[92] This undermined traditional industrial recruitment and the idea of the heritable trade. The Thames lighterman Dick Fagan noted in his 1966 memoir that 'fewer and fewer recruits to the trade come from lightering families. . . . This is the reason why there are so many "nonnies", that is to say, men from non-lightering families, to be found on barges today.' He regretted the change but understood the reason for it: 'Why put a boy into it—even if he was prepared to go—when there's so much other work going with higher pay, better conditions, more security, a more certain future?'[93] During the 1962 postal workers' strike, J. W. M. Thompson of the *Standard*, noting that the union leader, Ron Smith, had followed his father into the service, asked, 'How many boys are eager to do the same today?' and answered, 'Very few.' He concluded that 'the loss of that tradition of esteem and continuity' would continue to damage the service even after the dispute had been settled.[94] Nevertheless, the pull of office work created labour shortages and high wages for those who chose to remain in industry. The memoirs of Alfred Gardner, describing his life in the East End garment trade, are illustrated by two views of Stepney factories in the late fifties, plastered with posters advertising jobs for machinists. On leaving school in 1956, Gardner felt sufficiently confident to turn down work in a cabinet maker's modern factory because its production-line techniques would have been 'too tedious, ... the atmosphere was too depressing.'[95] Within a few years the shortage of skilled workers would accelerate the deindustrialisation of Gardner's East End,[96] but in the early 1960s general affluence kept many inner-London industries afloat. Those benefiting from the tides of fashion, such as the garment trade, were buoyant.

In April 1962, as Teddy Boys evolved into Mods, the *Standard*'s Angus McGill spoke to some of 'the modernists [who] earn more money than teenagers have ever earned before—and ... spend it with frank enjoyment on themselves.' Roy Pope, a nineteen-year-old plumber from Battersea, earning £15 a week, bought three new suits a year and had shirts made to measure. Pete Smith, an eighteen-year-old butcher from Wandsworth earning up to £30 a week, owned eight suits. Keith Smith, earning around £20 per week, also bought three suits a year, 'each different from the last to keep abreast of the mutations of modernist fashion.' They were dressed by two Clapham tailors, Brian Hoddinot and Richard Press—'the Diors of the modernist set'—who had devised a suit known as the Sackville in response to the Mod demand.[97] This direct relationship between young working-class men and responsive tailors—as close as that between any Savile Row couturier and his clients—had begun with the Teddy Boys, whose prescribed mode of dress had formed a kind of uniform, devised on the street. By extension, as Jane Wilson described, 'Mod fashions evolved in a curious untraceable way, mostly in the south and east of London where there were enterprising tailors and shoemakers who had once catered for the Teddy Boys and could still produce goods to order from customers' own messy sketches. The kids had the money and they knew what they wanted.'[98] John Stephen's dominance of the youth menswear market owed much to his readiness to produce to order in this way, getting goods made up overnight in the workshops of the small tailors who had moved to Soho from the East End during the Blitz.[99] 'Mod fashions can change overnight', McGill explained, 'but mods know that John Stephen will be there next morning with the new thing.'[100] In 1964 Stephen opened the John Stephen Custom Made shop as part of his Carnaby Street empire, where customers could bring in their own designs to be made up on the premises.[101]

The revolution in women's fashion did not as clearly come from the streets, but it did derive from young, freelance designers' frustration with established couturiers. Barbara Hulanicki, who would found Biba in Kensington in 1964, explained that 'the shops in England at this time [1960]

Caps and ties for sale in the John Stephen store, Carnaby Street, April 1966. (PA/Alamy Stock Photo)

were full of matronly clothes—either direct copies of Paris clothes or deeply influenced by the Paris collections. There was little specifically designed for the young.'[102] Mary Quant believed that 'the young were tired of wearing essentially the same as their mothers.'[103] She had initially envisaged her Bazaar boutique, opened in the King's Road in 1955, purely as a retail operation and only began to design her own goods when she could not find enough off-the-peg stock that appealed to her.[104] What started as the recognition of a gap in the market became, though, a kind of generational battle cry: 'the young must never *on any account* look like the old.' In a 1967 interview Quant described with candid horror what the old looked like: 'Women . . . wore stiletto heels and corsets. They had no bottoms, you remember, but seats. They didn't have nipples but great appendages of bosom and none of these things fitted together: the bosom came into the room first and the woman would follow. They looked like tarts really, with their bottoms all over their toes because of the stilettos. And you

Mary Quant in her flat in Draycott Place, Chelsea, November 1965. (Keystone Pictures USA/ZUMAPRESS.com/Mary Evans)

never wanted to touch their hair because it might sting or burn. On my thirteenth birthday I cried because this horror was getting closer to me.'[105] Her creations consequently came in gamine form, to the discomfort of even moderately buxom customers, but with sales rising more than elevenfold (passing £4 million in 1966), it became clear that Quant had found a gap in the market.[106]

Quant had a difficult relationship with the 'frankly beastly' fashion industry.[107] So did most cutting-edge designers, both in women's wear and menswear. As Stanley Adams, who opened in Kingly Street in 1965, put it, 'Buyers don't know their arse from their elbow. They have no identity with, or understanding of, the sort of people they are attempting to provide for.'[108] Designers could, though, function with a fair degree of autonomy, hoping that hard work and the serendipity of public taste would see them succeed. Quant initially put together her designs in her own bedsit; Biba began as a mail-order business, with a single design.[109] Premises suitable for boutiques—characteristically intimate and underlit—could be rented relatively cheaply even in Central London at least until the middle of the decade. Most boutiques began with very little capital—a weakness which would undermine many of them in the harsher climate of the 1970s, but which mattered little during fashion's boom years.[110]

Barriers were higher in the music industry. At the grassroots, music was characterised by a do-it-yourself approach similar to that in menswear. The skiffle boom of the 1950s involved homemade instruments in the hands of amateurs. The autobiography of Alan Johnson, growing up poor in Notting Hill in the 1950s, has a subplot recounting a musical career which began with his mother buying him a Spanish guitar from the proceeds of a pools win and ends with him performing in a band before sizeable audiences in pubs and clubs.[111] Many trod a similar path, particularly as the rewards of pop stardom became clear. 'There's so many groups it's getting ridiculous', the manager of the Tiger's Head dance hall in Catford told Jane Wilson in November 1965: 'we've had three in already this evening looking for work.'[112] Most would fail for lack of talent, but some were blocked by the industry's innate conservatism. Eddie Rogers's 1964 account of London's Tin Pan Alley (Denmark Street, off the Charing Cross Road) lamented that the street, once the home of the professional songwriter, was now 'a Mecca for the unskilled amateur' and that 'the old hands . . . either cannot get the feel of the songs that are selling today, or else they don't want to try.'[113] Though Rogers himself spoke warmly of the Beatles, many of those whom he interviewed evidently saw the new generation of pop musicians as charlatans—'amateurs' heedless of the industry's standards. To judge from the book's illustrations, few of Rogers's interviewees would see fifty again; arguments over the value of new music were sharpened by generational hostility. 'I don't like the old people in this teenage business because they don't know what it's about', the prolific twenty-six-year-old producer Mickie Most complained to Maureen Cleave in 1964: 'I don't interfere with Bing Crosby records.' Noting that the establishment had sought to warn him off producing the Animals' number-one "House of the Rising Sun," he aspired to make the charts with 'a record that only dogs can hear.'[114]

Two years earlier, Decca had rejected the Beatles. The idea of a middle-aged establishment blind to trends in youth taste is now a commonplace, both in fashion and in music. In reality it is unsurprising that the more iconoclastic aspects of the new culture disturbed those who saw their job as to target the median customer rather than the trendsetter and nationwide rather than just in London. Not every woman, after all, felt comfortable in a miniskirt. John Stephen was 'designing essentially gay clothes for straight men',[115] with his use of colour and tight-fitting designs, which many straight men thought risqué. When Decca turned down the Beatles, the company was in good commercial health, with profits generated by Tommy Steele, Anthony Newley and Mantovani.[116] Neither industry was oblivious to the power of the teenage pocket: the difficulty lay in reading the trends in teen taste. In the spring of 1966 Carnaby Street was said to be full of 'buyers from the more staid clothes retailers who have come to spy out what the young are buying next. They must often leave completely baffled.'[117] Even Mary Quant, who shaped fashion far more than she was shaped by it, admitted as she entered her thirties that she and her husband watched 'all the young television programmes' and that they went 'to places like the Ad Lib where you can see the early signs of some new fad or craze beginning to develop amongst the most up-and-coming trend-setters.'[118] Both Dick Rowe, who turned down the Beatles for Decca, and George Martin, who signed the group for EMI/Parlophone, were men in early middle age trying to gauge teenage musical appetites. 'The young will not be dictated to', as Quant put it: it was difficult to 'anticipate a mood before people realize that they are bored with what they have already got.'[119]

Inevitably the advantage lay with those who were closer to the age group in question, which accounts for one distinctive feature of sixties London, the twenty-something plutocrat. Andrew Loog Oldham was in fact only nineteen when he became manager of the Rolling Stones in 1963: 'Five years ago', he told Maureen Cleave in 1964, 'they wouldn't have let me make tea, let alone records.'[120] Still more striking, perhaps, was the trajectory of Oldham's onetime bodyguard, Reg King, who rose from working as a butcher's slaughterman to managing the group Thee. This group made no great mark on musical history, but King could still afford at the age of twenty-two to drive a white Lincoln convertible round Stanmore, where he lived with his mother.[121] Mickie Most, installed in a new house in Wembley Park by 1964, drove a Porsche and claimed to have been making at least £100 per week since he was seventeen.[122] In 1962 the twenty-eight-year-old John Stephen became the youngest man in Britain to own a Rolls Royce, but luxury cars soon became standard issue for the Carnaby Street moguls: 'we each have a Rolls-Royce as a status symbol', the twenty-eight-year-old Warren Gold, co-owner of the boutique Lord John, told Rodney Bennett-England in 1967.[123] By then Stephen had bought his second car, a Cadillac.[124]

Such opulence elevated these men to the swinging aristocracy. More significant, though, was the evidence it provided that youth culture was becoming commercially and socially pervasive. In the 1950s Teddy Boy gangs had been aggressively exclusive. In the early sixties Mods and Rockers were tribal and territorial. McGill described in 1963 their finely delineated

Two Mods in Brixton, 1963. (Roger Mayne Archive/Mary Evans Picture Library)

Rockers and bikes, Brixton, 1963. (Roger Mayne Archive/Mary Evans Picture Library)

pitches in Northeast London: 'Mod strongholds are Dagenham, Ilford, Tottenham, Manor Park, Hackney, Stratford East, Mile End, East Ham, Stoke Newington, Stamford Hill. Rocker strongholds are Finsbury Park, Highbury, Holloway, Enfield, Bethnal Green, Dalston, Finchley Road, Hoxton Market. "No Mod would dare walk through Hoxton Market on his own", one rocker told me this week.'[125] Mods, like Teds before them, helped broaden the range of men's fashion, but clothes were tokens of their exclusivity. Music produced its own, less violent, tribes: trad jazz, modern jazz, folk revival and even early rock and roll were essentially cultish, but by the midsixties these distinctions were being blurred. The Beatles' development of a widely accessible musical idiom had much to do with that. They have been targets of a revisionism bent on depicting the 1960s as the least culturally eventful decade of the century, but to suggest that they 'appealed primarily to girls between 10 and 14' is to understate their appeal to almost everybody else below the age of thirty.[126] 'Beatlemania' was in itself an adolescent cult, but the Beatles were instrumental in developing musical modes which—in many hands—had an extraordinary appeal to teenagers and young adults. The same effect became apparent in menswear. McGill reported in 1962 that Stephen's customers were 'entirely teenagers', but two years later he noted 'a growing number of adult customers' in

Stephen's shops.[127] 'Two years ago in 1965 we were just catering for the kids', said Warren Gold: 'Today everyone comes here.'[128]

The New Boy Network

As Frank Mort has argued, 'the social elites were more than simply a residual presence in post-war London: they featured as active and frequently dynamic players in metropolitan culture.'[129] London's aristocracy had not been 'levelled' by the years of war and welfare. It had evolved, but the effect of that evolution had been to root the elites more firmly in metropolitan society.

In London's Victorian heyday, its aristocracy had been a caste. It lived an insular existence, focused on the noble mansions of Mayfair and limited to the months of the Parliamentary sessions. The London 'Season' was a tightly programmed series of social occasions designed to insulate the elite from wider metropolitan society.[130] Its schedule of events covered much of the Home Counties, with some of them—the Derby, Royal Ascot, Henley Regatta—not in London at all. By contrast the Season's parties and dances were restricted to a very limited area of Mayfair, centred on Park Lane, Brook Street, Grosvenor Street and Grosvenor Square.[131] This world began to crumble after the First World War, when higher direct taxation and death duties undermined the financial security of the 'upper ten', and Mayfair's mansions began to pass from residential into commercial use.[132] The proportion of the Grosvenor estate in private occupation peaked in 1914;[133] thereafter the commercial penetration of the West End proceeded steadily, bringing the demolition of the grander houses, from Devonshire House in 1924 to Londonderry House in 1965.[134] London lost its Marais.[135] By 1960 Berkeley Square had 'finally lost a long battle with Big Business', and none of its houses remained in private occupation; five years later one estate agent declared Mayfair 'finished' as a residential area.[136]

The cost of maintaining a London establishment was the force behind this collapse, and many aristocratic families simply abandoned their London base altogether.[137] Those who stayed moved south and westwards, to Belgravia or to Chelsea, where the number of peers rose from twelve in 1935 to forty-three in 1965 despite a drop in the resident peerage in London as a whole in that period.[138] Chelsea particularly attracted what Peter Thorold calls 'the young—the expectant rich', drawn by the area's unpretentious but elegant early nineteenth-century town houses and the smaller cottages built for working-class occupation. The latter 'provided exactly the right amount of accommodation for young families, with an au pair and probably someone to do the cleaning, but without traditional servants.'[139]

Those who moved into Chelsea were occupying London's Montmartre, an area with an artistic tradition running from J. M. W. Turner to Augustus John. The fusion of artistic Bohemianism and aristocratic libertinism gave birth to what became known as the 'Chelsea Set' in the 1950s. In a valedictory 1965 account of twenty years in Chelsea, the King's Road bookseller Francis Marsden described the coalescence of the 'Set' in the Fantasie coffee bar, opened by Quant's backer Archie McNair in 1955, after which 'the night air was soon loud with the richly modulated cries of the "debs" and their "delights" as, clutching bottles of red wine, they sped to parties in their noisy little cars.' These were the figures whose antics intrigued the *Evening Standard*, the *Daily Mirror* and any other paper with a gossip column to fill, but they were a noisy minority. More significant was the evolution of the area's young middle class. Marsden described the change in street style as the war receded, with 'long black Civil Defence greatcoats and ex-Navy duffel coats' yielding to 'duffel coats . . . that had never been nearer the sea than the Charing Cross Road. These were worn with the *New Statesman* and the *Times Literary Supplement* tucked under one arm.'[140] The Canadian sculptor Maryon Kantaroff, arriving in Oakley Street in January 1958, found that the people she met in Chelsea 'were all very, very busy being writers or painters or would-be intellectuals', while 'passing sleeping partners around. "You must meet so and so, he's a fantastic lover."' They lived off baked potatoes because 'nobody had any money.'[141] In the spring of 1959, though, Robin Douglas-Home observed that 'the artists, sculptors and musicians living simply in their studios and attics' were retreating before well-heeled invaders from Belgravia and Mayfair.[142] Soon Chelsea ceased to be a haven for penniless creatives. By 1961 'property prices had risen with obscene regularity since 1945, causing great hardship to artists', as the sculptor Anthony Grey told a public meeting called to form a Chelsea Studio Protection Society.[143] The society was formed but had no discernible effect in shielding poor artists from rising rents.[144] They would move down the road to Fulham, beginning that area's overspill gentrification,[145] or across the river to Putney, where Edna O'Brien described in 1964 an 'outpost for Bohemians' that had formed in the quirky houses of Deodar Road, comprising the painter Sidney Nolan, the sculptor Anthea Alley and the writers Nell Dunn, Jeremy Sandford and O'Brien herself.[146]

'The only artists likely to be found in Chelsea today are . . . interior decorators', as one local noted in 1961.[147] Priced out of Bohemia, Chelsea's artists gave way to successful and fashionable practitioners of what Anne Sharpley called 'the near-arts of photography, interior decoration, journalism, stage and dress design.' They conformed to a now familiar gentrifier image—well-heeled, liberal in outlook and aesthetically aware, 'spend[ing] their money on holidays, food, paintings, not on large houses, big cars, servants or gadgets.'[148] They could afford to live in sixties Chelsea—and, indeed, contributed to house-price inflation there—because these 'near-arts' were lucrative to those who had founded their success on the expansion of London's creative economy. The fashion boom enriched not only designers but also fashion photographers. The rise in TV ownership—naturally most marked in the capital—and the arrival of commercial television benefited not only telejournalists, editors and presenters but also the advertising industry, with 'London's Madison Avenue' developing in Eastbourne Terrace near Paddington.[149] Gentrification itself stimulated the demand for interior designers since, as the designer David Mlinaric explained, 'people have no self-confidence about their decorating. They don't mind risking a bold seven-guinea dress and chucking it away if their friends don't like it, but they can't chuck away a room.'[150]

The melding of this 'new aristocracy' with the old one, creating a 'new boy network' or 'new class', became clear to the world in February 1960 when Buckingham Palace announced the engagement of Princess Margaret to a commoner. Antony Armstrong-Jones—a barrister's son, Belgravia born, Eton and Cambridge educated—was not actually very common, but he cultivated classlessness. His friends had never seen him wearing an Old Etonian tie: 'he prefers denim trousers and a suede jacket.'[151] As a fashion and portrait photographer who had once operated from Archie McNair's King's Road studio, he was a representative member of London's 'near-arts' corps. His engagement helped place this group in the public eye. Within days of the announcement, the *Evening Standard* produced a series of five profiles of members of what it called 'The New Elite.'[152] All the subjects were exponents of the arts or 'near-arts': the theatre director Peter Hall, the choreographer John Cranko, the interior decorator David Hicks, the art director of *Queen* magazine Mark Boxer and Armstrong-Jones himself. Apart from the South African Cranko, all went to English public schools (Hall as a scholarship boy). Hall, Boxer and Armstrong-Jones went to Cambridge. At the time of Armstrong-Jones's engagement, he was living in a gentrified house in 'a somewhat run down area of Pimlico', affording 'an excellent view of the working-class flats at the bottom of the Armstrong-Jones back yard.'[153] Boxer was one of the colonisers of World's End, the shabby extremity of the King's Road; his home, Sharpley noted without further comment, 'formerly housed four working-class families.'[154] Hicks was described as 'not unique' but rather 'a very successful example of a type that has moved elegantly into Belgravia and Chelsea in the last 10 years.'[155]

By the midsixties these people needed less introduction, many being celebrities in their own right. Collectively they formed what Anthony Haden-Guest labelled the 'New Class' ('bred from the Affluent Arts out of the Consumer State') in a caustic, insightful semiparody in *Queen* in 1965.[156] They provided the core of Jonathan Aitken's interviews for his 1967 study *The Young Meteors*. They clustered in the young professions. Television was 'stuffed with highly ambitious and talented young men who will be contemptuously discarded or rapidly elevated between 30 and 35'; Desmond Wilcox, editor of the BBC's current affairs programme *Man Alive*, felt 'incredibly old and defeated' when he turned thirty in 1961.[157] Interior design had expanded so rapidly as to be effectively a new industry in the sixties. Mlinaric had founded his own firm at the age of twenty-five in 1964 and had twenty jobs under way when *London Life* interviewed him in 1965. His staff of five were all aged under twenty-seven.[158] Journalism, though hardly new, was also turning to youth at the time. Several of the opinion formers prominent in the *Evening Standard* in its late-sixties heyday under Charles Wintour were in their twenties: Jonathan Aitken (born 1942), Valerie Grove (née Jenkins, 1946), Max Hastings (1945), Simon Jenkins (1943).

The twenty-nine-year-old film director Michael Winner told Haden-Guest that a 'medium-good film script writer should turn in £50,000 a year', at a time when the prime minister's salary was only £14,000.[159] The nine fashion and advertising photographers whom Aitken interviewed for *The Young Meteors* claimed to be making between £25,000 and £60,000 a year. The writer Nik Cohn made £10,000 from freelance journalism at the age of twenty, while Haden-Guest himself made the same amount at the age of twenty-nine.[160] In the 'near-arts' few starved. Few made the kind of money claimed by the photographers, of course, but careers in these young or rapidly expanding industries also offered responsibility at a young age and the chance to be creative. Michael Beaumont, a twenty-six-year-old account executive for the advertisers Mather and Crowther, was interviewed by Maureen Cleave for an *Evening Standard* series on London's bachelors in 1964. As he was a product of Eton, Oxford and the Coldstream Guards, his trajectory might have been expected to have carried him into the City. He chose advertising instead because 'it sounded tough and therefore exciting', though it paid him a relatively modest £1,300 a year.[161]

The City itself, conservative and clannish,[162] was no place for the ambitious young. Michael Burns left his stockbroking firm after receiving a Christmas bonus equivalent only to the expenses claimed by one senior partner in a weekend. Tellingly, he became a TV cameraman and later a producer and, like Beaumont, a Labour voter.[163] 'Don't be young', Diana Mallory warned in a hostile account of the City in 1963; 'you can just about get away with 35.'[164] Aitken found few 'meteors' in the square mile. An entrenched 'bias in favour of the gentleman amateur' deterred them, particularly when reinforced by insistence on the kind of outmoded dress code that offended the swinging: at Cazenove's throughout the decade 'all partners still wore bowlers, almost all men still wore stiff collars and no female member of staff dared to wear either trousers or too provocatively short a skirt.'[165] Aitken saw not only the City but also medicine, the civil service and the church as professions tainted in the eyes of the young meritocracy by their inbuilt barriers to talent.[166] In the law, the Inns of Court had long imposed a protracted impecunious traineeship on would-be barristers, while the system of articled clerkships for solicitors was creaking in the midsixties, creating 'a permanent pool of young trainees who cannot find articled vacancies.' A twenty-four-year-old trainee solicitor could expect to earn only £1,200 a year—little more than a competent secretary—and many looked elsewhere.[167] Just as career-path dependency was disappearing for postmen and lightermen, so it was for those who were once destined for the conservative professions.

Women had never found plentiful openings in these old worlds—a 'woman is tolerated in the City only as a handmaiden', as Mary Murry, a typist-translator for one of the big banks, wrote in 1961.[168] But they benefited from the greater flexibility of the younger trades. Journalism, broadcasting, advertising and the media all offered openings to career-minded young women, with glass ceilings still pitched some way above the heads of their generation. The TV producer Elizabeth Cowley had arrived in Britain from Canada in 1952, working in Harrods' advertising department and for *Woman* magazine before landing a BBC job simply by writing to the producer Donald Baverstock. Josephine Douglas, producer of the first TV chart show, the *Six-Five Special*, maintained firmly that 'it is no tougher being a woman in television than it is being a man.'[169] Cowley and Douglas were career women in their thirties.

The career of Lucy Bartlett, daughter of another TV woman, the announcer Mary Malcolm, reveals the more happy-go-lucky approach of a well-connected twenty-four-year-old in the midsixties, sampling all that

Queen Charlotte's Ball, 1967. Queen Charlotte's Ball, considered the centrepiece of the London Season, was instituted in 1780 on the birthday of Queen Charlotte, wife of George III. Debutantes were required to curtsey to the queen and to a large birthday cake. The ball—and the cake— survived the end of presentations at court in 1958, after which debutantes curtseyed to the guest of honour. The last ball (before the Season's recent revival) was held in 1976. (© David Hurn/Magnum Photos)

Swinging London offered. After art school, Bartlett worked briefly as a restorer for an antique dealer and a public relations officer for a wine company, before writing for *Teen Scene* on the BBC's Light Programme. A walk-on part in Richard Lester's film *The Knack* and an appearance on the TV pop show *Juke Box Jury* followed before she borrowed £100 from her father, the actor Sir Basil Bartlett, to start an interior-design company. She drove a Mini Cooper and spent £15 a week on clothes. In London, she felt, 'you push all the doors marked pull, and you get what you want.' Jack Wilton, who profiled Bartlett for *London Life*, believed that this type of new woman 'thinks of herself as an *entrepreneuse*' with a 'candidly mercenary' attitude to money. Her friends would be writers, artists and photographers rather than stockbrokers, barristers, merchant bankers or young Tories, 'all of whom she will find gruesomely boring.' She 'would far rather make £10,000 for herself than marry a man with £50,000 in stocks' and would augment her regular income from office work by occasional modelling or by designing clothes for a boutique.[170]

Fiona MacCarthy's account of the last debutantes to be presented at court (in 1958) indicates a consistent aspiration, even among those who did marry men with £50,000 in stocks, to lead independent lives. The group included the first woman on the board of Anglia TV, a future editor of the *Times Higher Education Supplement*, a deputy secretary of the Royal Academy, a professional interior decorator working with David Hicks, the fashion editor of the *London Evening News*, one of the founders of the classy Kensington boutique Annacat and a record-breaking helicopter pilot, as well as MacCarthy herself, a distinguished journalist and author.[171] Most of them remained within the general 'creative' milieu but rejected the life which the London Season conventionally prescribed, of 'arranging another bowl of flowers and organising another dinner party *ad infinitum*.'[172] In the early sixties debutantes began to distance themselves from the principal purpose of the Season ('Debdom is a marriage market. Ugh!'),[173] routinely expressing their disenchantment with the constricting etiquette and repetitive parties and balls that its rituals prescribed. 'The season is ridiculous, idiotic, complete nonsense and a waste of time,' pronounced seventeen-year-old Angela Berkeley-Owen in 1961, adding, 'I am going to take part in it because my mother wants me to.'[174] In fact the Duke of Kent's engagement earlier that year to Katherine Worsley, 'the country girl who has never been a deb', dampened many mothers' enthusiasm for the substantial expenditure that the Season entailed.[175] By 1967, as the journalist Godfrey Smith wrote bluntly, 'the London Season carries on but no longer matters.'[176]

The Season at its peak had enforced a finely calibrated definition of the social elite. Daughters of barristers but not of solicitors, of surgeons but not of general practitioners, could be presented at court.[177] By the 1960s respect for such distinctions had dwindled; by the seventies it was even suggested that 'the occasional well-born foreign name and the not-so-lofty merchant classes' had infiltrated the Season.[178] Haden-Guest stressed that his 'New Class' saw no need to ape the existing establishment, as 'they have numbers, money, status' already.[179] As is well known, the profusion of new ways of getting rich in London allowed some working-class men and women to enter swinging society—the actors Michael Caine and Terence Stamp; the hairdresser Vidal Sassoon; the photographers David Bailey, Terence Donovan and Brian Duffy; those members of pop royalty willing to be initiated—but such upward mobility was unusual. A 1966 *London Life* feature on the photographer Patrick Lichfield, the queen's cousin, with his assistant Viscount Encombe, his secretary Lady Elizabeth Ramsay and his model, former 'Deb of the Year' Rory Davis, reminds us that status and money were advantageous even in the new trades.[180] The slightest glance at *Queen* and *London Life*—'the hymnal and psalter of the switched-on cult', as Aitken called them,[181] with their accounts of society weddings, expensive restaurants and foreign travel, and their adverts for country house property—indicates that these magazines did not court the unwashed. What they also show, though, is the easy absorption of the principal elements of the new popular culture. High culture was not displaced but augmented in this milieu: London's new woman, Jack Wilton suggested, 'will feel the same intensity of interest in, say, a new Beatles record and a visiting exhibition at the Tate.'[182] So would London's new man.

The West End leisure culture that *Time* and the other outside observers documented in 1965–67 had been forged in the previous ten years, founded on a determination to spurn the 'square.' The gentlemen's clubs of Pall Mall, with firm dress codes and no women, were shunned. By the sixties several were reduced to offering lower subscriptions to men aged under thirty, but with so little success that they were forced to accept 'all sorts of people who would have been contemptuously rejected in the high days of clubland' in order to stay afloat.[183] The nightclub-cum-discotheque emerged instead, such as the short-lived Ad Lib, the very exclusive Annabel's or, above all, Sibylla's, founded by two advertising copywriters and a property developer in Swallow Street in 1966. Sibylla's was partly funded by Beatle George Harrison and intended as a refuge for 'the current young meritocracy of style, taste and sensitivity.'[184]

Just as nightclubs supplanted gentlemen's clubs, Italian trattorie became modish in these circles at the expense of haute cuisine French restaurants. The Trattoria Terrazza, opened by Mario Cassandro and Franco Lagattolla in Romilly Street, Soho, in 1959, became stiflingly fashionable in a city striving to find new ways to eat.[185] Similarly, boutiques threatened the fashion departments of the great stores: by the early 1960s it had become clear that boutiques provided 'scope for the shopping individualist' in women's fashion which the stores were slow to match. *Queen*'s survey in July 1962 shows the wide range of boutiques available even by then, in Mayfair as well as Chelsea, catering for 'those with a smart but straightforward approach', for those 'with more taste than money' or simply 'for the very few.'[186] The smart-modern tailoring of the menswear boutique John Michael, opened by John Michael Ingram in the King's Road in 1957, was trendsetting in a way that Oxford Street recognised only slowly and Savile Row initially eschewed. Ingram acknowledged his initial uncertainty about whom he was targeting—'I suppose it was my own age group—between twenty and thirty'—but he knew that he could not have started out any-where other than in Chelsea.[187]

In 1960 Antony Armstrong-Jones, newly ennobled as Lord Snowdon, turned up at the Trattoria Terrazza in a roll-neck shirt and without a tie. Initially reluctant, the coproprietor, Mario Cassandro, admitted him, hav-ing received a briefing on the dress etiquette of London's new élite. There-after 'Mario would hardly let in anyone wearing a tie.'[188] This seismic mo-ment in London's social history heralded a general rejection by the 'new élite' of the class-coded trappings of West End convention. In a 1971 study of postwar men's fashion, Nik Cohn noted that from the midfifties the sons of gentlemen stopped going automatically to the same tailors as their fathers: 'They thought Savile Row humbug, all those fittings and adjustments, all that obsequience, and at the end of it, what? Another dark grey suit.'[189] Received pronunciation was another rejected inheritance. 'Now public schoolboys talk with a Cliff Richard accent', Simon Napier-Bell remarked in 1966;[190] Haden-Guest saw 'disc-jockey's mid-Atlantic and David Frost-Midlands' as 'the two great voices of the television age.'[191] Outside observers interpreted this and other elements of inverted snobbery as a sign that the English class system had been subverted in modern London, which was to mistake gen-erational sparring for social levelling. The impression was reinforced, though, by the coming together of London's new tribes in the West End.

Convergence

In 1960 Tommy Steele recalled that as a teenager in early 1950s Bermond-sey he had 'never ventured into the West End': 'We had heard rumours about getting lost and never coming back. The bus in our street said Pic-cadilly, but we thought that was miles away and we never got on it.'[192] The office boom ended that, drawing young Londoners into the City and the West End to work and, by extension, to play. The introduction of the espresso machine to the Italian quarter of South Soho in 1953 established the coffee bar as a modish social venue for those who were too young to enter pubs legally (though coffee bars were said frequently to offer clan-destine alcohol and amphetamines).[193] Soho subsequently became a mag-net for London youth: Steele himself launched his career performing at the 2is coffee bar in Old Compton Street ('London's most powerful teen magnet' in the late 1950s).[194] London's first two skiffle clubs were in Soho, in Wardour Street and Gerrard Street.[195] The 1950s transformation of

Soho, an area ever reinventing itself, was serendipitous. Proximity to the-atreland accounted for the presence of a long-established gay commu-nity,[196] which in turn provided the market for the adventurous menswear sold in Bill Green's Vince Man's Shop, where John Stephen was an em-ployee. Soho's Italian community nurtured the coffee-bar craze, which at-tracted clothes-conscious Mods to the area. The relocation of East End tailors to the streets behind Oxford Street after the Blitz allowed Stephen to have his own designs made up locally, undercutting Green's imports,[197] and to cultivate a Mod market large enough to obscure the original gay connotations of his designs. Thus established, Stephen became the 'King' of his new territory, the West Soho backwater of Carnaby Street, owning nine shops in the short street at his peak. By around 1962 a Carnaby Street location had become such an indispensable asset in the menswear business that Ste-phen's rivals were ready to lease property for which he owned the freehold, paying rents which, by the midsixties, had risen tenfold over five years.[198] The Gold brothers, Irvine Sellar, Sidney Brent and Stanley Adams, all moved from the outer East End into shops in or near Carnaby Street.[199]

Every week the Mod invasion would begin on Thursday or Friday, after payday. On Saturdays Carnaby Street was 'a kind of teenagers' Play Street when the mods arrive from all over London.'[200] A Mod-oriented club scene grew up to accommodate them, centred farther east, in Wardour Street—'the most peachy place. The most Modernist street in the world', as one eighteen-year-old told Anne Sharpley in February 1964.[201] The Mar-quee Club's move from Oxford Street to Wardour Street in the following month completed its evolution from a jazz to a pop venue and a celebrated Mod centre.[202] The management of Tiles Club, at 79 Oxford Street, just north of Soho Square, was said to have discouraged anyone aged over twenty-five from entering.[203] The development of this West End 'scene' undermined suburban dance venues, just as the rise of Carnaby Street had weakened the 'Diors of Clapham.' Surveying the suburban dance halls in November 1965, Jane Wilson found that while the Streatham Locarno and the Wimbledon Palais still prospered, lesser venues provided a picture of cavernous, underoccupied interwar halls, unknown bands and an anach-ronistically restrictive dress code. 'I reckon they come specially to have a miserable time', the lead singer of 'Mr Bean and his Runners' suggested of his audience at the Tiger's Head, Catford.[204] Suburban cinemas suffered a similar decline. Norwood lost all its film houses between 1956 and 1971, as a host of interwar picture-palace names—the Royal, the Central, the Astoria, the Albany, the Regal, the Rialto and the Odeon—passed into oblivion.[205] The principal cause was, of course, the spread of television, but the effect was again to underline the primacy of the West End even where a cinema did survive.[206]

The separate development of Chelsea's leisure scene had reflected the social composition of the area. What became famous as Mary Quant's Bazaar was not originally envisaged as a showcase for her designs but as part of a venture uniting boutique and restaurant in the same building—a combination carefully aimed at West London's *jeunesse dorée*. John Michael, whose men's boutique opened two years after Bazaar, '[did] for the young executive what John Stephen had done for the working-class boy.'[207] The profusion of restaurants opening in or near the King's Road in the late 1950s and early 1960s—the tally of eating places in Chelsea was estimated to have risen from a dozen to around two hundred in these years[208]— clearly signified opulence. So did the plethora of antique shops: significant as the King's Road obviously was as a platform for new fashion, by weight of numbers it was primarily an antiques centre, sporting forty-one antique shops by 1966.[209]

The two poles of the new London were thus initially comparable but distinct: Soho was a Mod gathering ground and a melting pot for the capital's European immigrant groups. Although the gang warfare of the 1950s had subsided, it remained an edgy area, where at night the police patrolled in pairs with Alsatians and where, according to the A6 murderer James Hanratty in his 1962 trial, '[you] can get a gun for £10 or £12 any day of the week.'[210] Chelsea and Kensington, by contrast, catered to the young, well-heeled fashion-conscious: '[Mary Quant's] Bazaar was for rich girls', in the model Twiggy's blunt words. A pinafore dress featured in *Vogue* in 1960 cost three weeks' wages for an office girl.[211] In menswear the *Standard*'s Angus McGill distinguished between '*le style* King's Road', meaning 'the leisure clothes that we have suddenly become so good at—handsome, beautifully made and rather expensive'—and '*le style* Carnaby Street': 'cheap, stylish, sexy clobber for the kids.'[212] Each had its place.

By the midsixties, though, the distinction between the two areas was being blurred. The trattoria craze had drawn all and sundry into Soho, making it less outré: 'Opera singers, princesses, hairdressers, crooks, boxers, surgeons, parsons, they all dine in Soho at some stage of the year', and few of the customers of Soho restaurants came from Soho itself.[213] In 1966 Alvaro Maccioni, manager at the Terrazza, led the Italian escape from Soho by establishing Alvaro's trattoria in Chelsea, where Italian restaurants had been thin on the ground: 'Something new was happening, every time I

went down the King's Road', he explained; 'Soho was for the older generation, a continuation of the fifties and I was younger.'[214] Barbara Hulanicki's
first Biba shop, which opened in Abingdon Road, Kensington, in August 1964, brought affordable, imaginative women's wear to West London
and, like Stephen's shops, became popular with both the classes and the
masses. In the space of a few pages in her autobiography, Hulanicki listed
the celebrities who patronised her second (Church Street) shop at its
height—Mia Farrow, Princess Anne, Brigitte Bardot, Marianne Faithfull,
Yoko Ono and others—while also complaining that 'the glossy establishment press' ignored her because her shop 'sold to real people and not just
jet setters.'[215] The juxtaposition appears jarring but was not misleading:
like Stephen, Hulanicki demonstrated that the key to success lay in combining modishness with affordability. By the midsixties several cheaper
boutiques had appeared in the King's Road. John Stephen himself opened
two branches there in 1963–64, combining Soho style and Chelsea décor—
'it's all coach lamps, brass and quality.'[216] Meanwhile the modishness of
Carnaby Street attracted fashionable customers to mingle with the teens:
at the eponymous John Stephen boutique in 1967 'the clientele includes
all the usual pop personalities, and you may see such celebrities as Lord
Snowdon, The Duke of Bedford and Peter Sellers.'[217] In consequence Mod
dominance of the street was diluted; indeed Stephen's biographer sees
1967 as the point at which Mods began 'to do a vanishing trick from main-
stream fashion.'[218] This was accelerated by the spread of hippie eclecticism
in menswear. The eccentric purveyor of ex-military uniforms I Was Lord
Kitchener's Valet, founded in the Portobello Road in 1966, moved to form
branches in both the King's Road and Carnaby Street.[219] Rodney Bennett-
England argued in 1967 that events had overtaken Carnaby Street, which
now 'cater[ed] for tourists with frivolous and poor quality merchandise
resembling fancy dress.' 'We are not trying to dress exhibitionists', Bill
Green of the Vince Man's Shop in Newburgh Street told him: 'they can go
to Carnaby Street.'[220]

Rave magazine's April 1966 map of 'in' places depicted a London consisting entirely of Soho/Piccadilly and Chelsea/Kensington.[221] Halasz's
Time piece in the same month was accompanied by a map showing virtually the same London, and neither magazine suggested that one area was
less accessible than the other. By the midsixties, differentiation within the
'scene' depended less on locale and more on price or less tangible forms of
social filtration. Thus even within Stephen's Carnaby Street empire, a two-
piece suit at 'John Stephen's Man's Shop' (49 Carnaby Street) could cost

Swinging London mapped by *Rave* magazine, April 1966, showing the clubs, boutiques and other venues of 'the scene.' (Rave/future content hub.com)

up to sixty guineas, while an off-the-peg suit at 'John Stephen' (52–55 Carnaby Street) could be had for twelve guineas.[222] While the Trattoria Terrazza established itself as one of the most chic restaurants in early sixties London, cheaper Soho restaurants such as Bianchi's, La Capannina and the Trattoria Da Otello provided younger, poorer gourmands with what was probably very similar food.[223] Even within the Terrazza, the proprietors encouraged the notion that the downstairs Positano Room was more exclusive than the rest of the restaurant.[224] Their former manager, Maccioni, at his new King's Road restaurant, deployed a 'skilful exploitation of the hideous snobbery of the English', as Quentin Crewe put it, suggesting that the phone number for reservations was ex-directory and known to only around two hundred people in London, although it was actually freely published in restaurant reviews.[225] Similarly, Kevin Macdonald, one of the promoters of Sibylla's discotheque, told Aitken that 'anyone who had to ask how to get into Sibylla's wouldn't be a member'—the strategy of the gentlemen's club through the ages.[226] Discotheques *were* in fact quite exclusive in the midsixties, charging five pounds for admission and a further pound as cover charge. Jane Wilson suggested in 1967 that 'it's possible to live through several days in London without encountering a single soul who has ever set foot in a discothèque.'[227] The former Mod Ken Browne, interviewed by Terry Rawlings in 2000, remembered that while 'the upper-class kids' might set foot in the affordable Tiles ('they had the moves, and they could afford to dress a bit better'), the average Mod would not be seen in such chic spots as the Scotch of St James or the Cromwellian—'it was also about seven quid to get in or something ridiculous which was unbe-lievable in those days. There was a whole different scene going on in those places.'[228]

Swinging London thus had its pecking orders. They are best seen, though, as social responses to the homogenising potential of a commer-cialised youth culture which appeared to transcend social divisions and which was increasingly concentrated in a relatively small area of Central London. By the midsixties the West End had developed an elaborate rec-reational 'scene', focused on music, clubs, fashion and eating out and domi-nated by young adults and teenagers. Nothing quite like it had existed in 1960. It was what foreign observers came to observe.

'Why London? Why Now?'

The subeditor for John Crosby's *Weekend Telegraph* piece suggested, 'We [Londoners] may be living too close to the revolution to recognise it, we need a foreigner to do that.'[229] It was a compelling suggestion but uncon-vincing. The 'revolution' that London's many overseas observers recog-nised in the midsixties was largely conveyed as pastiche. They were jour-nalists rather than social anthropologists, and they followed a journalistic imperative to produce a coherent story from the random material they had to hand: Halasz saw her job for *Time* as 'the presentation of "Swinging London" as a single unified phenomenon.'[230] Taken as they were by the idea of dukes shopping in Carnaby Street and secretaries shopping in Chelsea, they constructed an image of classlessness that could not stand very close scrutiny. Taken as some of them were by the idea of young Lon-don 'chicks' taking to sex like candy, they developed a picture of sexual eclecticism that was misguided even in this relatively liberal milieu. Almost all their accounts were shaped by presuppositions about Britain's condition—first the benign view that London was providing a colourful escape from the nation's natural grey austerity but later, as financial and industrial problems mounted in the summer of 1966, that the city displayed feckless escapism in the face of economic crisis. Both the benign and the censorious reading of Swinging London assumed a degree of self-indulgence at odds with the lived experience of most 'real' Londoners who had to eat, sleep, commute and work in the city. The writers' understandable emphasis on the West End then reinforced this effect by drawing in two minority leisure pursuits that happened to be concentrated there, in the strip clubs of Soho and the casinos of Mayfair.

Both phenomena were real enough. Soho was already well established as London's erogenous zone, but its seedy reputation was reinforced from the late 1950s as Paul Raymond and others exploited the ambiguity of controls over public nudity.[231] This development comprehensively thwarted the efforts of local traders in the Soho Association to make the area more respectable;[232] in 1963 the writer Wolf Mankowitz, a native and resident, described Soho appositely as 'an industrial centre for the manufacture of strip and trattoria.'[233] The Metropolitan Police were sufficiently concerned about the impression made on tourists coming to London for the 1966 World Cup to mount a cleanup of Soho clip joints before the tournament,[234] but striptease in itself continued to be treated as risqué but harmless in the midsixties. Halasz's piece in *Time* included an illustration of a performer at the Sunset Strip club in Dean Street: she posited as a selling point that 'dozens of nightclubs offer totally uninhibited striptease.'[235] And while betting shops sprang up everywhere, the casinos had their origins in gentlemen's gaming circles and were consequently fixed in aristocratic London, mostly in Mayfair. Crockford's Club—another of Halasz's 'Scenes'—was in St James's Street, Quent's in Hill Street, Curzon House in Curzon Street, Les Ambassadeurs in Hamilton Place and John Aspinall's Clermont Club in Berkeley Square. Both striptease and casinos depended significantly on overseas visitors, whether tourist voyeurs or high-rolling gamblers, who were drawn more readily to the West End than to Enfield or Lewisham. The casino world, in which 'a famous peer' could lose £125,000 in a single session at Les Ambassadeurs, was hardly typical even of the affluent society. It was an exclusive milieu, with entry tightly controlled[236] and conduct governed by the quasi-chivalric codes of honour that came to light in 1974 when the Lord Lucan affair opened a window on the Clermont Club. 'Membership compulsory and very exclusive', *London Life*'s listing for Curzon House announced: 'prospective members vetted before joining.'[237] The strip clubs and the casinos appealed to limited—and almost entirely male—clienteles, but they were rooted in the West End and shared that limited space with the nightclubs, the trattorias and the boutiques. Outside observers, inevitably focusing on the West End, conflated them all, creating a composite picture of a London recreational life—a trip down the King's Road to blow half a week's wage on clothes, followed by a flutter in a black-tie casino and an evening in a strip club—that no Londoner actually lived.

Faced with this image of decadence, 'real' Londoners, at the time and since, have constructed a counterorthodoxy to the effect that the sixties cultural revolution, if it happened at all, was limited to the Chelsea set or similar hedonists and that 'nothing very swinging happened in Streatham.' To dismiss the 'revolution' altogether, though, is as dangerous as to take it at face value. Aitken's 1967 verdict remains valid: 'The changes in tastes, behaviour and attitudes of the younger generation over the last few years have at least to a small extent influenced the lives of every Londoner under the age of 35. Whether these changes have anything to do with "swinging" is a matter of semantics, but the fact remains that without these changes today's younger generation would be imperceptibly different from their parents, whereas in fact they are enormously different.'[238] When pressed, most of those who claim today that the swinging sixties passed them by will acknowledge having owned Beatles records or, indeed, heard the group live—in their touring days they played several unprepossessing suburban venues as well as grander central ones.[239] They may have shopped in one of John Stephen's boutiques or in Hulanicki's 'exclusive, inexpensive' Biba.[240] They may have danced at the Marquee or eaten at Fiddlers Three in Chelsea or Cranks in Soho. These pleasures were accessible and affordable in a way that many of those depicted by Crosby and Halasz—the nightclub Annabel's, the Ad Lib Club, where one table was 'more or less permanently reserved for the Beatles'[241]—were not. The new popular culture *was* indisputably popular, even if its delights were almost exclusively enjoyed by teenagers and young adults.

Halasz's instinctive belief in the influence of youth in London was not misplaced. In 1966 almost a quarter of all residents in what the Census called the 'Conurbation Centre' were aged between fifteen and twenty-nine. In Greater London as a whole, the proportion of residents aged between fifteen and twenty-four was, at 15 percent, higher than in any Census since 1931. The young of 1966 were, of course, significantly more opulent than the young of 1931, and without reducing the cultural phenomenon of Swinging London purely to a matter of purchasing power, it was the youth pound which created the new aristocracy whose antics so fascinated foreign observers. 'In the early 1960s,' as an otherwise rather close-focused

Greater London Council (GLC) research report on Carnaby Street put it in 1975, 'the affluent young were beginning to assert their economic power, a power to make world celebrities out of pop groups, fashion models and clothes designers.'[242] If these world celebrities then lived at a level of self-indulgence unimaginable to the young consumers who had made them, that does not mean that Swinging London was completely elitist or negate its foundations in broadly based youth affluence. It reflected an age structure—particularly in inner London—skewed towards youth and, above all, the sheer prosperity of the city in the early sixties.

Seen in a longer-term perspective, London's economy was undergoing a process of change by which the newer service industries described earlier expanded and much of its traditional manufacturing industry declined. These two processes did not occur in step, though. For a decade or so from the midfifties, the office economy grew rapidly with little effect on manufacturing beyond creating labour shortages which raised wages. As a result, if anywhere epitomised the affluent society, it was midsixties London. Looking back from the turbulent midseventies, one GLC research report concluded that in London 1966 had been 'an extremely prosperous year when the demand for labour was unusually high'; all but two of the thirty-two boroughs showed increased economic activity from the already high levels of 1961.[243] This was strikingly demonstrated by Colin Crofts's 1983 analysis of Family Expenditure Survey returns for London, which depicts the movement of the top and bottom income quartiles, and of median incomes, over the period 1961–79, in constant (1980) prices.[244] The early sixties emerge as years of steady improvement for all groups. If Londoners were indeed guilty of ignoring the nation's balance-of-payments problems while they partied, it was probably because most of them had never had it so good.

Thereafter, though, the situation became more complex. The balance of payments caught up with London's pleasure-seekers with the Wilson government's credit squeeze in the winter of 1966–67. In October Charles Lyte in the *Standard* noted a drop in discretionary spending in London: sales of pop records had fallen, and there was 'a general decline in the restaurant trade.'[245] Jonathan Aitken looked specifically at 'Swinging London' in November. Though he was not entirely pessimistic, concluding that 'unless things get very much worse, the talented and hard working swingers will survive easily, and only the floss will have been removed from the candy floss society', he recognised that there was much floss to remove. On the club scene, while expensive venues like Annabel's and cheap ones like the Marquee still flourished, there was 'an embarrassing acreage of empty tables' in many

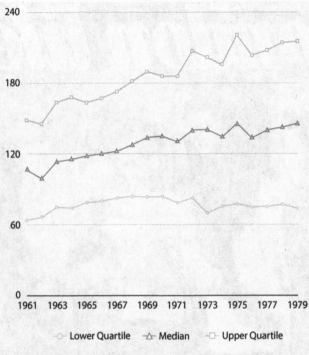

Household real incomes in Greater London, 1961–79 (£/week at 1980 prices)

once-buoyant clubs. The overstretched gambling world was inevitably vulnerable: Aitken recorded the collapse of 'dozens of smaller gaming clubs' and even contraction at the Clermont. Fashion was struggling. The previously lucrative market for fashion photography had collapsed, and the designer Alice Pollock told him that 'everybody's miserable in the King's Road. . . . The scene has quietened down and everyone feels low.'[246]

The 1966–67 'squeeze'—a belt-tightening exercise by which the Wilson government sought to stave off the devaluation of sterling—in itself said little about the strengths and weaknesses of the London economy. That winter would, though, bring early hints of the process of deindustrialisation that would transform inner London over the next two decades. The two boroughs which had fallen back between 1961 and 1966 were Newham and Tower Hamlets, presaging—even before the dock closures of the late sixties—the industrial contraction that would eviscerate the East End in

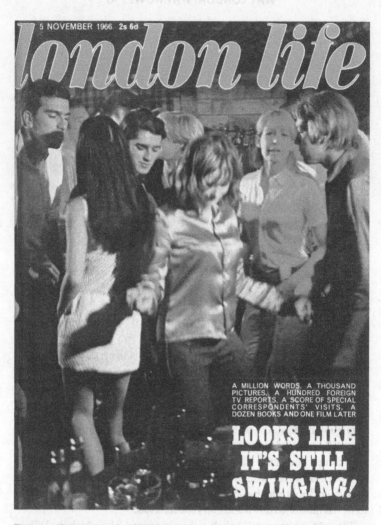

5 NOVEMBER 1966 2s 6d

london life

A MILLION WORDS, A THOUSAND
PICTURES, A HUNDRED FOREIGN
TV REPORTS, A SCORE OF SPECIAL
CORRESPONDENTS' VISITS, A
DOZEN BOOKS AND ONE FILM LATER

LOOKS LIKE
IT'S STILL
SWINGING!

The 'in-crowd' magazine *London Life* smiling in the face of the Wilson government's economic 'freeze'
in November 1966, barely six months after *Time* christened London 'the Swinging City.' (Illustrated
London News Ltd/Mary Evans)

the next few years. From 1967, in fact, unemployment rose across the inner-London boroughs.

For almost a decade the London economy had been stimulated by the boom in office and commercial employment, without being greatly afflicted by the decline in traditional manufacturing industry that was its natural concomitant. From the late sixties, though, deindustrialisation proceeded apace. Between 1971 and 1974 manufacturing employment fell by 14 percent in Greater London, against a drop of only 2 percent in Great Britain as a whole.[247] The most visible victims were those of upper-middle age who had spent their lives in the docks or ancillary riverside trades and could not retool, but industrial contraction also hit the young hard. By 1971 the economic inactivity rate for persons aged between fifteen and nineteen in London had more than trebled, against a doubling of the rate for the working-age population as a whole.[248] The exuberance of the midsixties, fuelled as it had been by youth spending power, was a thing of the past.

This development made London's traditional industrial areas highly vulnerable to the severe economic turbulence that followed the oil shock of 1973–74. Crofts's analysis shows the results. Between 1970 and 1979 London's lowest quartile suffered a startling 12 percent drop in real incomes, as the combination of unemployment and very high inflation rates hit those who were least able to resist—mostly pensioners, school leavers and the unemployed. In these years the capital's inner-city problem became inescapable, and the London press and much business opinion was suffused with pessimism, as a declinist orthodoxy took root concerning the city's future.[249] What Crofts's figures also show, though, is a 16 percent rise in the real incomes of the top quartile across the decade. The seventies brought not general decline to London but growing inequality. And in the midst of that inequality, median real incomes rose by 6 percent, buffeted by the alarming inflation rate but not permanently depressed. Despite everything, the 'median Londoner' was becoming steadily more comfortable, as the rich grew richer and the poor poorer.

Conclusion

Although London's fabric had obviously been battered during the Second World War, the London of the late fifties had been, in its patterns and processes, a city which the late Victorians would have recognised. London had been the nation's principal manufacturing centre in the Victorian age, and it still was. The port of London had been a global entrepôt, and it still was. London's social topography was broadly that of the classic industrial city, with a working-class core around the Central Business District and affluence levels rising the farther one got from the centre. The private landlord still accommodated around half the city's households—significantly more in the older parts of the city, where the quality of much of the housing stock was low. Late-Victorian London had been ethnically complex but overwhelmingly white, which was still the case. Most people then had traversed the city by means of public transport: in 1960 they still did.

By the late seventies much had changed. The upriver docks had closed or were about to close. London's manufacturing industries had suffered an unexpectedly sharp contraction. Though the office boom had slowed after 1966, the faster contraction of industry meant that offices accounted for 40 percent of London's employment in 1976. London's economy could no longer be said to rest on its industry, and the capital was more evidently a city of consumers than of producers. The private rental market was shrinking, and the owner-occupied house was fast becoming the ultimate consumer durable. Gentrification had refreshed much of the older housing stock while making London's social map more complicated. While car-ownership levels were still slightly below those of the rest of the United Kingdom, at around 50 percent of London households, they were sufficient to call into question the appropriate balance between public and private transport in the modern city. The characteristically postindustrial creeds of urban environmentalism and building conservation coloured this debate, but other consequences of the contraction of traditional industry were less benign. London's inner-city problem had intensified during the 1970s, with conventional poverty morphing into multideprivation and something akin to social exclusion. Within the inner city racial tension had been intensified by new commonwealth immigration and by the coincidence of deindustrialisation with the coming of age of the first generation of British-born Blacks, who were consequently alienated as profoundly as any minority ethnic group in London's history.

London's 'swinging moment' should be seen in this context—as a transient element in a deeper and broader transformation of the metropolis, played out over two decades. That transformation is described by means of a series of case studies in the chapters that follow. This approach might appear episodic, and this work does not claim to be a comprehensive history of London in the sixties and seventies; but the cumulative impression created by the sixteen chapters is, it is argued, that of a city evolving in these decades in ways which anticipated strikingly the Britain of the 1980s. The foundations of 'Thatcher's Britain' were laid in the nation's dominant economic centre and opinion former before Margaret Thatcher came into power. They owed virtually nothing to her.

2

The Death of the Sixties, Part 1

SOHO—SIXTIES LONDON'S EROGENOUS ZONE

Prominent amongst the attractions of the exciting London which John Crosby described in his *Weekend Telegraph* piece of April 1965 was the newfound permissiveness of a city in which pretty girls had discovered sex and taken to it 'like candy.'[1] Underlying most accounts of 'Swinging London' produced in the next two years was an assumption that the capital was leading Britain out of its earlier suffocating prudishness. One of the team at *Time* magazine that compiled the celebrated Swinging City piece in April 1966 had decided in advance that England was no longer 'a fussy, Victorian sort of place . . . but real he-man country, as it had been back in Elizabethan times, with lusty lads and lasses tumbling in the hay.'[2] The article's guiding notion—that London was a young person's town, busy discarding the moralism of older generations—carried within it at least the hint of sexual permissiveness. *Time*'s piece was not as preoccupied with sexual licence as Crosby's had been, but it was illustrated by a dim rear view of a naked stripper at the Sunset Strip club in Dean Street, Soho. The caption, announcing in a matter-of-fact way that 'most London strip clubs open in the afternoon' and that 'Sunset Strip caters to a noonish crowd',[3] seemed to present strip clubs as a regular public facility in the new, sexually enlightened metropolis.

Like much of the Swinging London image, the suggestion misled as much as it informed. Striptease *was* a feature of sixties London which had proliferated in recent years. The Sunset Strip, like other clubs in Soho, operated openly and profitably in the heart of the West End. Midsixties London probably was more relaxed about sexual behaviour than it had been a decade earlier or than most provincial towns were still. Those who applied the term 'permissive society' to sixties Britain doubtless had London in mind. In fact the transformation of Soho into a sex centre in these years tells us little about Britain's supposed permissiveness in the wider sense—a readiness to dispense with previously dominant restrictive taboos concerning premarital sex, homosexuality, and so on. Even in the narrower sense of public regulation of sexual display, the true lessons of Soho's emergence remain unclear. London's authorities and much of the London public were long uncertain about how to respond to it: in practice much would depend on the pressure of events.

Soho and the Revuebar

Time's writers would have needed few detective skills to identify Soho as London's sex centre: the area's racy reputation was decades old. It consisted of a handful of streets grouped around Soho Square, containing mainly eighteenth-century houses, shops and small workshops, framed by the nineteenth-century developments of Regent Street and the Charing Cross Road and bisected by the Metropolitan Board of Works' Shaftesbury Avenue in the 1880s. It had been a reception area for the early waves of migrants to London—Huguenot, Jewish, German, Italian—whose restaurants and delicatessens still provided one of the area's most distinctive features. Another was its bohemian reputation, reinforced in the 1950s by a cluster of bibulous eccentrics whose antics have been lavishly chronicled.[4] By the 1960s they were already being supplanted by a wave of young gentrifiers, drawn by the area's proximity to the West End and, in part, by its risqué image.

Soho had always been associated with sex. Forming Piccadilly's hinterland, it was a traditional centre for street prostitution before the 1959 Street Offences Act drove the tarts indoors. So-called near-beer clubs or clip joints (in which hostesses induced men to pay inflated prices for nonalcoholic drinks in the hope of sexual reward) were said to date back to the mid-1920s in Soho and had multiplied there from the early 1950s.[5] From the 1890s, when the widening of the Strand had destroyed the original centre of London's sex trade in Holywell Street, the pornographic book trade had drifted

Italian delicatessen in Soho, 1972. (Alain Le Garsmeur London 1972/Alamy Stock Photo)

to Soho, and from the 1930s the area emerged as London's centre of erotica.[6] By 1960 it had established itself as Britain's capital of striptease.

This happened, in large part, because of the absence of any clear legal directive to prevent it happening. The law on nudity in public performances was elusive. A tradition of nude *tableaux vivants* had been established in interwar London, most effectively commercialised by the Windmill Theatre, off Shaftesbury Avenue. As a theatre, the Windmill was regulated by the Lord Chamberlain under the Theatres Act: nude revues were permitted under this normally censorious regime provided that the performers remained static while naked. Lesser venues were not, though, subject to the Lord Chamberlain's jurisdiction. Public dance halls were licensed by the London County Council, while private clubs did not need a licence from any public authority. During the war an alleged trend towards risqué performance in dance halls exercised the Lord Chamberlain, who, in Britain's darkest hour, found time to exhort a meeting of licensing authorities and entertainment industry chiefs in April 1940 to remove 'objectionable business and gags and "strip-tease acts" ... from the stage.' A voluntary agreement produced a short-lived cleanup, but by 1951 the LCC contemplated imposing more direct control.[7] In 1952 it resolved to refuse a music and dancing licence to any club offering striptease, defined as 'the removal of garments while the performer ... is within the view of the audience.' Interestingly, the proposal from the Council's Public Control Committee proposed explicitly to insist that 'the private parts of the body cannot be seen from any position in the auditorium', even in still nude poses, was not adopted by the full Council.[8] While banning erotic dancing, the Council declined to go further than the state in curbing nudity itself.

That even static nudes could pull in the crowds had been shown by the success of the Windmill's revues, which attracted an aggregate audience estimated at ten million before the theatre closed in 1964.[9] It closed because it had 'been beaten at its own game ... by the strip clubs.'[10] The first of these in London is said to have been the Irving Strip Club, in Irving Street, between Leicester Square and the Charing Cross Road, where the proprietor, D. P. Chaudhuri, offered from some point in the midfifties 'the only theatre in London where the nudes can move.' By enrolling his clientele of 'bowler-hatted businessmen on long lunch breaks' as members, full membership to be confirmed twenty-four hours later, Chaudhuri claimed the privileges of a private club—most significantly freedom from the LCC's licensing regime—and his customers 'could watch a naked girl go "bu-bu-bu-bu!" to the rhythm of a drum roll, with her breasts and hips this way and that.'[11] Her audience consisted entirely of paying customers: the Irving was not a private club as the term was generally understood, with a formal, registered membership, and it incurred repeated fines as a result. They were not so heavy, though, as to dent seriously the profits made by selling membership and drinks, and Chaudhuri regarded them as a business expense.[12] This was the model followed by the other clubs which began to appear in the late 1950s, the Gargoyle Club in 1957 and, in particular, Paul Raymond's Revuebar, which opened in Walker's Court, Soho, in April 1958.[13]

'As this will be a private club,' the Revuebar's launch publicity explained, 'the nudes can move about.'[14] Raymond, Liverpool-born, was a small-time entertainer who had exploited the potential of the static female nude in shows like his *Festival of Nudes* (1951) throughout the 1950s.[15] Aware that the traditional revue was in decline, he had been alerted to the commercial appeal of striptease proper by his public relations agent, following a visit to the Folies Bergère in 1957.[16] Raymond envisaged the Revuebar as 'a place where a man can take his wife, have a meal in pleasant surroundings and see a first-class show. Just like the nude clubs of Gay Paree!'[17] Whilst it might not have been exactly 'a luxurious West End Club', as claimed in its initial publicity,[18] the Revuebar was less hole-and-corner than its predecessors. Raymond's approach hinged on the calculation that genteel audiences might feel less uncomfortable about watching a risqué show if the venue was well appointed: he emphasised in his relentless early promotions the distinction between the Revuebar and 'some of these tiny one-room backstreet clubs' which threatened to 'give the properly run, bona fide clubs a bad name.'[19] To emphasise his club's bona fides, Raymond appointed a Church of England chaplain to the Revuebar, arguing that every strip club should have one.[20]

Such window dressing could not alter the inherent legal weakness in the Revuebar's situation—that while claiming to be a private club, it was operating as something akin to a commercial theatre. It was obvious to the police investigating the Revuebar a fortnight after its opening that membership carried little of the commitment and less of the scrutiny to be expected in a conventional private club. Of 715 membership forms examined by the Metropolitan Police a month after the club opened, 392 had no proposer or seconder and a further 319 had been proposed by the box office manager. Though the Revuebar boasted, quaintly, a General Committee and a Wine Committee, Superintendent Strath of the Metropolitan Police concluded that 'no general meeting of members has ever been called and the general body of patrons have no say whatever in the conduct of the business.'[21] The inevitable prosecution for permitting unlicensed dancing demonstrated, though, the law's toothlessness. Raymond was fined a total of £30, though £20 of this was for the separate offence of selling drinks without a licence. With the Revuebar said to be earning around £250,000 per annum,[22] a £10 fine was bearable.

Raymond told the press that 'there are at least four other similar clubs in London that will also benefit' from this outcome.[23] By 1961 there were said, in fact, to be about two dozen strip clubs in the West End.[24] All were, to all intents and purposes, open to the paying public: a licensing system which aimed to exclude striptease from premises licensed for dancing had clearly failed to stop the strip trade's expansion. As the number of clubs increased, the need to, literally, outstrip the competition became all the greater. Neil Lyall, the Revuebar's promotions manager, told the *People* in 1961 of management conferences 'where [Raymond] and his executives decided just how far they would go to outdo their rivals.' These rivals having started inviting their audiences to help girls undress, Raymond supposedly responded by encouraging his strippers to fall over into customers' laps and by introducing Julie Mendez's notorious snake act.[25]

Snakes had become regular props for Soho performers in the late fifties. Publicity-conscious artistes occasionally 'lost' them in the West End: in 1958 'blonde showgirl' Eve Richardson contrived to mislay 'Khrushchev',

a five-foot-long boa constrictor, in the Piccadilly Hotel, while in the following year a python was found in a Soho taxi.[26] Mendez was the custo-
dian of three constrictors and a python.[27] Her creative relationship with
these animals ('snakes are deaf and they live by smell and vibrations, so
there is a special way of becoming friendly with them')[28] produced the
most striking part of the performance that led to the 1961 prosecution of
the Revuebar under the Disorderly Houses Act of 1751. The contents of the
show were culled by a Greater London Council inspector from police reports when the Council reassessed its striptease policy five years later:

> A woman stripped on stage and stood naked, with legs apart. She placed
> her hands between her legs, one on top of the other, so that she was
> touching her vagina. She then moved her hands about quickly making
> suggestive body movements. She then rubbed her hand over her face.
> The [sic] let out a piercing scream. Replaced her hand between her legs
> and continued massage. . . . Girl came on stage with a live snake six feet
> long. She then made snake crawl over her body. The [sic] put tail be-
> tween her legs and stuck it out behind. She appeared to be coaxing tail
> towards her vagina. Stroked snake between her legs and encouraged it
> to move backwards and forwards causing friction between her legs.
> Then changed her position and snake's tail came out in front of her legs.
> Stroked tail and moved provocatively.

'After the show', the report concluded, 'the national anthem was played',
but this piety did not protect Raymond from a second prosecution.[29] This
time the offence lay more explicitly than before in the content of the performance. The 1751 act, still the governing statute for entertainment licensing, had been passed in response to Henry Fielding's pamphlet of the previous year, 'An Inquiry into the Increase of Robbers in London', which had
claimed that the multiplication of places of public entertainment 'for the
lower sort of people' had caused an increase in robberies to enable the lower
sort to pay their entrance money.[30] Entertainment regulation was therefore
linked to the prevention of public nuisance and of the disturbance of the
peace. By an extension of this argument, Raymond was alleged to have out-
raged public decency by staging provocative performances at the Revuebar,
and the chairman of the Inner London Sessions invited the jury to convict
him if they concluded that 'what was taking place night after night in that club
was a filthy, obscene, lewd, disgusting, corrupting and depraving show.'[31] Raymond incurred a heavy fine—£5,000—when he was convicted in April 1961.
This fine still made only a dent in the Revuebar's profits, but the risk of

flouting the law was made clear by the fate of Samuel Bloom, proprietor of the Keyhole Club in Old Compton Street. Bloom had been prosecuted in January 1961 for what appears to have been a less provocative performance and fined £2,500. His appeal, heard with Raymond's, failed in June 1961, and he unwisely sought to raise money to pay his fine and costs by putting on 'an even more indecent show',[32] in which one performer 'grasped the edge of the curtain and undulated her body against it as if having sexual intercourse' and another 'came on stage with an electric massage machine.'[33] For this demonstration that London striptease had moved a long way from 'the nude clubs of Gay Paree'—a second offence for good measure—Bloom received a three-year prison sentence.[34]

These prosecutions from 1958 to 1962 clarified the clubs' freedom of movement. Although the law governing the content of strip performances was hazy, a two-hundred-year-old statute relating only to London had proved sufficient for the successful prosecution of Raymond and Bloom and had resulted in heavy penalties. Competitive obscenity onstage was risky. Simple striptease—undressing to music—was legal only if the venue could claim to be a private club and thus beyond the reach of the LCC's licensing provisions. As strip was a competitive business, and no club actually wished to confine its custom to a limited group of identified members, most clubs either resorted to sham membership schemes or simply decided to take their chance with the law.

A club—open or private—could stay within the law if the artistes did not move at all, provided that music did not form a substantial part of the performance.[35] This sanctioned nude posing clubs, such as that at 9 Berwick Street, where individual naked models sat still, ostensibly to be sketched. The audience generally showed little interest in developing their drawing skills, shunning the easels and sketching materials provided. Indeed, with an entry fee of ten shillings, significantly more than they would have paid for an LCC life-drawing evening class, the men were effectively paying *not* to have to draw—and for the guarantee that the models would always be female. Posing was, though, seldom more than a last resort. The artistes themselves hated it. Many aspired to be dancers, and none enjoyed sitting still to be gawped at—Richard Wortley's protégée Tina, a stripper at the Naked City club in Tisbury Court, had found in her posing days that she 'wanted to get up and jig about all the time.'[36] Prohibiting movement meant that there could be neither strip nor tease, and it was hard to draw a crowd when Soho offered so much more excitement: 'we are ... too proud of our reputation to present anything as unexciting as a posing show', one unidentified club proclaimed.[37] Inspector Yeoman of the Met found an audience of nine on his visit to Berwick Street in September 1963.[38]

Most proprietors simply decided to break the law and risk the consequences. The scale of fines was increased from the earlier nugatory levels by the London Government Act of 1963, which repealed the entertainment licensing sections of the 1751 act.[39] The threat of prosecution could no longer be treated lightly, but for most club owners fines were just another overhead.[40] After one conviction owners generally took the precaution of employing front men to protect them from the heavier fines imposed on repeat offenders: 'the guv'nor pays a man fifty pounds a week to stand up in court', as the Naked City stripper Tina explained to Richard Wortley; 'that's how he does it, but he can't afford too many fines.'[41] Neither the police nor the LCC could, though, spare the manpower for very frequent investigations, and the Council in particular became loath to do so if there was little prospect that prosecutions would change anything. During a four-month period in the winter of 1962–63, the Carnival Club was fined a total of over £1,000 for unlicensed dancing, in addition to £1,350 for liquor-licensing offences, but the stripping never stopped.[42]

In the 1960s and early 1970s heyday of London striptease it was clearly extremely profitable. The *Empire News* estimated in 1960 that the twelve clubs then operating in Soho grossed £48,000 per week; Raymond claimed in the same year that he might take as much as £9,500 a week at the Revuebar.[43] The early entrants to the market made easy money. Don Short, founder of the Sunset Strip in Dean Street, was mesmerised by the profits in striptease when performing as a comedian in a strip club: 'I was just a makeweight, but I suddenly realised how much money was pouring through the doors to see the girls. I got a few girls, trained them for a few days, and then opened up a club. I had four quid in my pocket that afternoon. If someone had asked for change for a fiver I'd have been very embarrassed. But at the end of an hour or two I had £68 in my hand. I was on my way.'[44] The proliferation of clubs in the early sixties must have limited this bonanza, though by how much is unknowable. Clare, who dabbled in stripping for a few months after leaving university, sought information on the profitability of the clubs she worked for in 1971–72 but found that 'everyone is so afraid of the taxman and refused to divulge anything.' With entrance fees ranging from 50p to £25, depending on the club, she was surely right, though, to conclude that each club had a weekly turnover running into thousands of pounds. It is clear that many clubs carried very substantial outgoings with a nonchalance suggesting that they took high profit levels for granted. Clare was soon able to earn a healthy £120 a week,[45] and many similar examples suggest that few clubs blanched at paying even novice girls amply.

It seems clear that most clubs also allowed for regular payments to police officers, to minimise harassment. With fines for licence evasion relatively bearable, bribery on a very large scale made little sense, but it was widely believed, for instance, that the Maltese 'Syndicate' run by the Mifsud brothers, which controlled the majority of the Soho clubs by the late sixties, had the Met in its pockets. In 1966 the manager of the Pelican Club claimed in open court that 'the Maltese clubs were in a position of privilege due to their readiness to bribe the police and . . . the readiness of the police to be bribed.'[46] Seven years later a GLC inspector recorded that the manageress of the Playboy Club, Eva Winn, 'spent most of the time while she was on the phone complaining that she had been unjustly convicted and implying that criminals who were still allowed to hold ent. licences bribed the police.'[47] Still hazier is the money paid to criminal gangs for protection. Raymond established a profit-sharing relationship with the Richardson brothers and their hard man, Frankie Fraser, to shield his empire from protection racketeers.[48] Explosions in two of the Mifsud clubs, the Gigi and the Keyhole, within the space of three weeks in November 1966 showed the need for protective deals of some sort.

Punters and Performers

These outgoings—whether to the police or to criminals—were tolerable because there was an enormous and very dependable demand for striptease. Raymond's insistence that the Revuebar's regulars included many pillars of society may or may not have been valid—his claim in his 1961 trial that the membership included at least thirty practising solicitors must have provoked a frisson in court[49]—but even the limited evidence we have of the numbers attending strip shows suggests that they were not confined to the 'dirty mac brigade.' The stripper Nickie Roberts had expected her audiences to consist of 'pathetic "sick" creatures in scruffy wankers' macs' but found instead that 'most of the men were Mr Norman Normals.' Her early shows, from midday to 4.00 P.M., would be attended by the 'office-types'; 'brollies and rolled-up copies of the *Financial Times* were wielded like clubs' if a front-row seat became vacant.[50] We do not know how normal were the customers at the Nell Gwynne Theatre in Dean Street, whose

Punters outside the Naked City strip club, Tisbury Court, Soho, 1966. To overcome any language barrier the club, perhaps unnecessarily, informed Continental visitors that it offered 'Schöne Mädchen, Jollies [sic] Filles, Belle Ragazze.' (Philip Harrington/Alamy Stock Photo)

details were recorded by the police, for whatever reason, in December 1970, but we do know their names, addresses and ages.[51] Of the forty-nine questioned, twenty-nine were below the age of forty, and only two were older than sixty, challenging the 'dirty old man' image. Only twenty came from the Greater London area, reinforcing the picture of Soho as a magnet to outsiders, but although one was an Indian immigrant, none was a foreign tourist, casting some doubt on the frequent claim that the strip trade was easing Britain's balance-of-payments problem. All were male. Ray Durgnat spoke of 'a sprinkling of wives' at the Revuebar, while a *Sunday Times* account of Soho in 1968 claimed that 40 percent of the audience at the Revuebar's late-night shows were women;[52] but the standard audience at a run-of-the-mill club was overwhelmingly male: Roberts's chief memory of her debut at El Paradiso was of the heat rising from the packed audience 'like a mist, thick and clogged, smelling of men.'[53]

Men often came in boisterous groups. At Naked City Tina did not 'know whether the pigs had come in or the farmers' during the Smithfield Show.[54] Out-of-town football fans descended on Soho after away games in London, the Cup Final or, particularly, during the 1966 World Cup Finals, when England played all its games at Wembley. Roberts's impression of football-crowd nights was of 'a strip club jam packed with drunken slobs all howling in unison: "WE WANT TO SEE PUSSY."'[55] In the quieter weekday turns, though, strippers faced audiences composed of individual men, perhaps feeling sheepish about what they were doing and reluctant to draw attention to themselves. In an age of growing consumer power, club owners enjoyed the unusual advantage that few of their customers would complain, however disappointing their experience. Customers were vulnerable to various scams, the most familiar being the 'box office', resembling a regular club but in fact existing only to relieve customers of cash in return for leading them to a proper club, perhaps only a few doors away, where they would be relieved of more. This was a frequent means by which customers were directed to posing clubs, which would have struggled to attract custom otherwise.[56] A similar experience of bilking was described in unusual detail in 1979 by a Singaporean visitor to the Moulin Rouge 2 club in Great Windmill Street, sufficiently frustrated to complain to the GLC:

> I wish to complain that the abovementioned Club had cheated me. When I passed the abovementioned Club, I noticed the signboard saying "LIFE SHOW", it was also printed on the ticket, for which I attached it for your perusal. I was told that it cost £2.00 to see the life show, but

as soon I had paid the money, they issued a ticket, but insisted that I have to pay additional £10.00 as membership fee. I told them if they had said before that I had to pay additional £10.00 I would not have paid the £2.00 for admission fee, but nothing was mention about membership fee untill [sic] you had paid the £2.00. I objected and they slashed the membership fee by half to £5.00. But to my disappointment, they were NO LIFE SHOW, only 1 hour Sex film show of very poor quality, which I could see better in Amsterdam, Holland, of better quality, no time limit for equav [sic] £0.75. This kind of cheating give a very bad impression to the tourist visiting London.[57]

Occasionally the punter fought back, as when George Caruana, one of the Maltese 'circuit' and proprietor of the Keyhole Club, was fined £25 by the Bow Street magistrates in 1969 for obtaining ten shillings from one Mashrif Ali. Caruana had promised a live show with sixteen girls when all that was on offer, it being a Sunday, was a film.[58] The evidence was clear enough, but it required much courage to take on club owners in this way.

Proprietors were more ready to alienate their customers than to alienate their girls. Don Short at the Sunset Strip gave his performers advice on house purchase; James Humphreys at the Queen's Club was said to have paid his girls' National Insurance stamps and was remembered by one of his dancers as 'her most considerate employer ever'.[59] In general the fringe benefits were less important than the actual pay. From the early days, when Raymond had run amateur striptease competitions with a prize of £2,000 for the winner, strip had offered expansive rewards to those who were prepared to shed their inhibitions. At the top of the range, the Revuebar artistes earned staggering amounts: the £1,000 per week said to have been earned in 1960 by Tempest Storm, the best paid stripper in the world, equates to a Premier League footballer's wage today.[60] 'I could make more money paying some raw girl £20 a week to pay her clothes off, but I prefer artistic standards', Raymond explained in 1969.[61] Believing that English girls were not up to the mark ('listen, as showgirls they are *fantastic*, but as strippers they don't know what their bodies are for'),[62] he preferred to recruit established professionals from overseas, and paid accordingly. His star performers were said to earn £450 per week in 1967—'a marvellous way of saving the deposit for a mortgage', as Jan Carson, 'one of stripdom's superstars', explained: 'I could never have done it as a secretary.'[63]

That sort of reward required considerable dedication and professionalism on the part of the performer; with lower but still significant pay to be gained at the unrefined end of the market, many girls settled for less taxing careers. 'Cathy, a Peepshow Dancer' interviewed by Nickie Roberts in 1986, had spurned the Sunset Strip in the 1970s for the Carnival and the Dolls House: 'It was meant to be like the poor man's Paul Raymond's—and all that crap about rehearsing. But at the end of the day . . . they weren't there to see an "up-market" show, they were just there to see tit'n'arse and everything else.'[64] Clare was able to earn £120 a week after a few weeks, with no previous experience and minimal training. Tina estimated that an ordinary stripper could earn anything from £20 to £100 per week, 'given the stamina.'[65] Stamina was, in fact, the critical variable, as the punishing schedule—'it's an eleven-hour day in the West End', as the stripper Suzy Dalrymple told *Frendz* in 1971[66]—would take its toll on those who worked flat out for six days. Roberts was considered lazy by her colleagues for limiting herself to a three-day week when she started;[67] many of them worked the full six days, keeping themselves going by liberal use of amphetamines.[68]

'Twenty-six strips a day is hard work', an anonymous eighteen-year-old stripper told Anne Sharpley of the *Evening Standard* in 1965. She had lost a stone in six weeks. She endured the regime because it allowed her to save for a house: 'I know a lot of girls [in regular jobs] who've worked five or six years and still have nothing.'[69] Many strippers saw their work as a step up from jobs that were neither inspiring nor rewarding. Roberts left a mill job in Burnley to come to London; Julie, one of the girls interviewed for the striptease documentary film *Carousella* in 1965, found stripping 'more satisfying and entertaining than the more conventional jobs she has from time to time taken up and dropped—factory hand, shop assistant, etc.' She hoped to visit Hawaii. Her colleague Katy 'would like to mingle with Bohemians and wander through primitive areas of South America for a time':[70] strip might allow ordinary girls to join the middle-class hippie trail. Wortley's Tina, 'bright, lazy, widely read, a good secretary for several years', simply 'want[ed] money quickly.'[71]

Clare discovered that she 'really enjoyed stripping, with the result that the punters seemed to enjoy [her] act.'[72] The stripper interviewed by Anne Sharpley in 1965 claimed, 'When men look at you, I like it. It makes me feel more important. Wherever I have worked before, I have always been a junior, a mug, always looked down on.'[73] She was unusual in claiming to enjoy being gazed at. Roberts's attitude was more common: she openly 'despised the men who used [the] clubs' but assumed 'that men were "like that" to some degree or another' and got on with the show. 'Just pretend they aren't there', she was told by 'Big Linda' when she started: 'I always

Dressing room at the Casino de Paris strip club, Denman Street, Soho, 1970s. (Mary Evans
Picture Library/David Lewis Hodgson)

look over their stupid heads, at the lights. And all the time I am thinking,
what colour shall I do the bed-room?'[74] Sharpley's interviewee was not
alone, though, in suggesting that stripping gave a sense of empowerment:
none of those who have left testimony appears to have felt demeaned by
her work. Self-confidence was bolstered by the evident camaraderie of the

girls, forged in claustrophobic dressing rooms in conditions of collective undress. Clare carried from her brief spell as a stripper the memory of her colleagues, 'shrewd, independent, cheerful and tough, with a trouper-like loyalty that comes from being in a hard-working minority.'[75]

Once strippers were habituated to the practice of exposing themselves, most felt less uncomfortable about what they were doing than did many in their audiences, which conferred both confidence and power. Vexatious customers were handled with a robustness unusual in a service industry. 'When a boisterous fellow daringly touched a girl's foot,' Ray Durgnat recounted, 'she muttered through gritted teeth, "Do that again and I'll kick your fucking face in."' 'To wankers you would say loudly "You enjoying yourself, love? Put it away, there's a dear"', Clare recalled. 'Twat gazers', as Roberts called them, who stared obsessively at performers' crotches throughout their acts, might prompt a 'pussy strike', in which G-strings were removed only at the last second. Tina was used to snatching cameras out of the hands of would-be photographers, who generally sat in the front row, and removing the film. Like many strippers, Clare reserved a particular animus for any women in the audience; 'Want to come and have a go, love? Like to see *you* try.' Roberts felt that 'it adds insult to injury when your own sex tries to demean you.' In the last resort, the audiences could not do without the performers, and misbehaviour could safely be punished by the withdrawal of their labour. Tina's colleague Maggie 'will just stop the show if she gets annoyed; she'll place a chair on the ramp, sit down on it and say, "Now it's my turn to look at you."'[76]

Performers were protected to some extent by the understanding of the law after the 1961 prosecutions and Bloom's imprisonment: 'the salutary penalties imposed in these cases put a stop to the low-class type of striptease entertainment', the Metropolitan Police commissioner reported in 1963.[77] In fact the competitive nature of the trade meant that the temptation to go to the limits of the law could never be entirely removed, particularly when the Lord Chamberlain's censorship of theatres was abolished in 1968. Don Short, of the Sunset Strip, acknowledged in that year that his girls 'play up to all these codgers who come along. They are not obscene, but they go as near the knuckle as possible.'[78] In 1970 it was alleged, admittedly by a rival, that the Sunset Strip's show 'has lesbian leanings, nude double acts, etc',[79] and Nickie Roberts found herself plunged into a countess-and-maid bath routine, followed by lesbian groping on the floor, at the El Paradiso in Brewer Street.[80] But a rash of prosecutions between 1969 and 1972, culminating in a £300 fine and a suspended prison sentence for the owner of the Playboy Club, served notice that the obscenity laws remained in operation. One Home Office official attempting to summarise the situation in 1972 concluded that prosecution would result if artistes committed indecent acts *and* audience participation was involved:[81] in the Playboy Club case one artiste admitted throwing her knickers into the audience and inviting the patrons to throw them back, 'with her vagina as the target.'[82]

In practice the police decided who should be prosecuted, but clubs operated according to broadly acknowledged guidelines. One result of the judicial deliberations on obscenity during 1961–62 was the gradual acknowledgement that full frontal nudity was not in itself obscene. Initially, many clubs had played safe in this respect. In one attempt at self-regulation by a group of *soi distant* respectable clubs in 1960, it had been laid down that they would 'not allow an entirely nude girl to appear—she'll have to wear either sequins or a G-string';[83] early performers at the Revuebar and elsewhere had generally worn G-strings or, with whatever discomfort, covered their pubic hair with sticking plaster.[84] These fig leaves were apparently abandoned around 1964; by the midsixties there was 'no nonsense about keeping on a G-string.'[85] A distinction emerged between the upmarket clubs, where the emphasis was on nude dancing and the performers shaved their crotches, and the rest, in which the whole object of the performance was to display 'the piece de resistance, pubic hair.'[86] 'I must emphasise this, no G-string worn in this establishment', Jeremy Sandford was promised at an unnamed club in 1967: 'These girls show you the lot. They stand before you naked. Nothing is hidden.'[87]

In these clubs—the majority—the culmination of the standard routine of the 1960s became the 'flash': a moment of statuesque frontal nudity before the lights dimmed and the stripper scampered from the stage. The principal skill in what was largely an unskilled trade lay in spinning out the process of removing clothing to fill the time taken by the recorded music. Clare recalled reaching complete nudity five minutes too early in her first performance, 'prancing' and 'giggling hysterically' for what felt like hours before the stage manager put out the lights.[88] To protect against the danger that overenthusiastic performers or audiences might slip into obscenity, many club managers imposed a kind of 'Windmill rule'—no movement when completely naked—on themselves. "At the end of the third record, you take off the knickers and *stand still*," one of Roberts's colleagues was told by her choreographer, and Roberts herself believed that 'it was illegal to move with no G-string on.'[89] The promotion of the 'flash' as the grand climax of a strip act—'without a flash they just sit there with long faces', as Jane of Sunset Strip explained[90]—underlined the objectification of the body that strippers disliked,[91] but it may have spared them more degrading exercises before the rules began to loosen in the mid-1970s. As Ray Durgnat noted in 1966, 'the men seemed solaced, rather than stirred, by contemplating, coveting and/or worshipping the varied totems of female nudity',[92] but they would react vigorously if denied their eyeful. 'Are you mental or what?', Roberts was asked by her 'fat Maltese choreographer' when once she forgot to remove her bra during her act: 'they want to see your tits; you have tit-men out there, you know.'[93]

Policy Dilemmas

At first sight, the strip explosion appears to be one facet of the supposed permissive society of the 1960s. On closer examination, though, very little had been actively permitted—by the law, by the police, by public authorities or even by public opinion. Rather, an existing tradition of naked display had been amplified enormously by commercialisation, leaving public agencies uncertain as to how they could or should respond. Even what appeared an unambiguously permissive step—the GLC's decision in December 1966 to revoke its 1952 decision to deny music and dancing licences to establishments staging striptease shows—was in reality more complex.[94]

The logic behind the GLC's change of heart was clear enough. The increase in the maximum fine leviable for unlicensed dancing to £200 under the 1963 London Government Act came into force when the Council was created in 1965. It was, though, less a prohibition than a means of taxing a highly profitable industry, which raised significant sums of money—more than £20,000 in fines and costs between April 1965 and September 1966[95]—but offered no prospect of suppressing the strip trade. Fines had always helped push marginal clubs over the edge ('How much will it cost me?', the owner of the Original Geisha Club asked when informed that he would be prosecuted for unlicensed dancing in 1963. 'The place has already cost me a bomb'; 'I thought these clubs would be an easy way of making money, but they are just one big headache'),[96] but the big players were largely impervious to them, even after the increase. The use of front men was so well established that it was 'rare for more than two or three convictions to be recorded against the same person.'[97] As early as January 1963 the Metropolitan Police had indicated to the LCC that it 'could not pay [the clubs] as much attention as they would like, due to pressure of work, etc', inviting the Council itself to undertake more frequent observation, but the Council was understandably reluctant to transfer its 'few inspectors onto intensive inspection of bogus clubs' merely to relieve the Met.[98] By 1966 the GLC, inheriting the LCC's licensing powers, had also become relaxed about the likely public response to a change of policy. E. W. Newberry, the chief officer of the Licensing Department, stressed in his reports of October and November 1966 that 'the Soho activities have occasioned little complaint to the Council.' He pointed out that the 'in some respects revolting' performances which had brought the prosecutions of the Keyhole and the Revuebar in 1961 were 'in no way representative of the entertainment regularly provided in Soho strip-tease clubs.'[99] Alec Grant, the Labour chairman of the Licensing Committee, agreed that the Disorderly Houses legislation should continue to catch obscenity and that the licensing regulations had clearly proved ineffective in stamping out strip. 'In any case', he added, 'I am not sure that it is our job to stop all striptease.'[100]

Above all the Council was concerned about safety. With thirty or so strip clubs operating unlicensed, many in small basement rooms, there was no means of ensuring that they met even minimal safety requirements. Smaller operators, used to offering regular tributes to the authorities in fines for licence evasion, were seldom eager to add safety expenditure to their burdens. One who did, Jimmy Jacobs of the Gargoyle Club, a reasonably well-appointed establishment with a strip club on its fourth floor, hoped to recoup his investment by shopping his rivals, warning the Council in 1965,

> It has, on numerous occasions, been drawn to our attention by various of our members that there are dozens of little striptease clubs in the surrounding area that have not even an elementary form of fire precaution or emergency exits. We must admit that these remarks were made, in many instances, quite jocularly, quote 'God knows what they would do if there was ever a fire there', etc. . . . Now that we have acquainted you with the facts we are certain that you will feel as we do regarding the necessity of bringing these places into line with your public safety regulations.[101]

He had a point. In the basement club at 11 Greek Street, for example, two hundred men might be crammed into a space fit for fifty, so that 'the stairway was crowded, the fire exit was open but blocked by persons seeking better viewing positions.'[102] Fire safety was a GLC concern at all places of public entertainment, but the problem was more intense at a strip show than at a performance of *Hamlet* or *The Mousetrap*. The Council was in fact well aware that 'many of the clubs are operating in basements where a secondary means of escape is unlikely to exist and [that] the decorations in such places are likely to be flammable',[103] but it was hard to tackle the problem when no unlicensed club would welcome GLC scrutiny. The core of the new policy was therefore that 'for reasons of public safety . . . it seems that the Council should seek to control these premises through its licensing powers.'[104] Once the policy had been approved, the Council issued a circular inviting clubs to submit to a structural survey with a view to being licensed when any necessary work had been carried out.[105] Some found the prospect of legality hard to cope with after years of clandestine operation: the owner of the premises containing the Playboy Club simply refused to believe the manager, Mrs Winn ('who was "an old boiler" and "a bloody liar"') when she conveyed news of the policy change.[106] By May 1968, though, seven clubs had been licensed, and another eleven were to be licensed when structural work was complete.[107]

Among other effects, the new policy brought four clubs to light which the Council had not known to exist,[108] and it is entirely possible that a major tragedy was avoided by the Council's change of direction. The new policy nonetheless carried disadvantages, played down during the Council's deliberations but soon obvious. Critically, the new works demanded by the Council often entailed substantial expenditure, and as the Council soon realised, 'there has been a reluctance to incur such expense without an assurance that a licence wld be granted on completion of works.'[109] In effect the GLC found itself morally obliged, once structural improvements had been carried out to its satisfaction, to favour strip-club licence applications, even in the face of objections from local residents or the police.

The police watched frustrated as a succession of dubious licence applicants received the GLC's approval. Most, of course, had form for previous unlicensed dancing, but some had more serious convictions. Benny Caruana of the Keyhole Club had been sentenced to three months' imprisonment for possession of an offensive weapon in 1966.[110] Wilfred Gardiner, the applicant for 9 Berwick Street in 1969, had tax problems and sixteen convictions stretching back to 1944, but the licence was granted.[111] Most spectacular was the case of the Carnival Club in Old Compton Street, in 1968. The nominal applicant, Manuel Cauchi, had two unspecified convictions dating from 1951 and was employed by Anthony Cauchi, one of the people convicted of the 1966 bombings, and Romeo Saliba. Cauchi had sixteen criminal convictions dating back to 1941, including malicious wounding in 1947 and brothel keeping in 1955, as well as the explosions cases, while Saliba had amassed eighteen convictions in sixteen years, including two of actual bodily harm. The Met took the matter seriously enough for a letter detailing the applicants' track records and drawn up at assistant commissioner level to be sent to the GLC's director-general.[112] The Council's consideration of the case spelled out the dilemma: 'This is a strip-tease establishment, and since the Council's policy is that these places should be brought under control, the Committee may wish to consider how far they are prepared to accept unsuitable applicants— presumably all strip-tease proprietors are likely to be a bit shady—though Mr Cauchi seems an extreme case.'[113] But the Council was effectively constrained by its own policy, and the application was approved.

Official sanction for a semicriminal trade also concerned local residents, already anxious that the Soho area was coming to be dominated by strip. The strip trade naturally clustered rather in the way that the artisan trades in nineteenth-century London had clustered—the jewellers in Clerkenwell or the furniture makers in Bethnal Green. The reasons were similar: the pooling of resources and the knowledge that the area's reputation would attract custom. The main 'resources' that were pooled were the girls. Although the most up-market clubs engaged professional dancers—the Casino de Paris had a permanent troupe of trained dancers by 1968, one of whom had worked there for five years[114]—most strippers worked for any establishment ready to engage them and dashed from club to club, throwing a fur coat over their stage uniform, to maintain a schedule defined with military precision. Darlene of the Sunset Strip saw 'almost as much of Soho in a day as Soho sees of her' in 1968: '1.25 P.M. Taboo strip-club, Dean Street; 1.40 Folies Bergere strip-club, Green's Court; 2.7 [sic] Red Mill strip-club, Macclesfield Street; 3.25 Taboo; 3.40 Folies; 4.7 Red Mill; 5.25 Taboo; 5.40 Folies; 6.7 Red Mill; 7.25 Taboo; 7.40 Folies; 8.7 Red Mill; 8.48 Hawaii Club, off Windmill Street, Soho; 10.7 Red Mill; 10.48 Hawaii; 11.25 Taboo; 11.40 Folies; 12.7 A.M. Red Mill; 12.48 Hawaii . . . and so to bed.'[115] At any point in the stripping day, from lunchtime to the small hours of the morning, girls with fur coats and makeup bags could be observed traversing the streets of Soho. According to one German guide to London in the 1970s, one mark of a bad club would be the long pauses between acts as the manager left the premises to try and recruit a passing performer on the streets.[116] The main reason for clustering, though, was the area's reputation—time-honoured, of course, but massively reinforced by the publicity given to the Revuebar in its early years. James Humphreys, proprietor of the Queen's Theatre Club in Berwick Street, established a 'booking office' for his club in Walkers Court precisely because of 'its proximity to the Raymond Revuebar' and 'thought a loss of trade inevitable' if he moved.[117] Most of the hole-and-corner clubs in Soho depended essentially on hooking the casual punters drifting around the area, which was why formal membership arrangements were unrealistic for most of them and why they had remained vulnerable to prosecution. 'You should be a member for 24 hours before you are entitled to see the private show but I will give you a ticket which will get you in', the doorman at the Phoenix Club, Old Compton Street, artlessly told passing punters in 1966, one of whom was a plainclothes policeman.[118]

With the creation of a licensing procedure for clubs, local residents and regular businesses were able to voice their anxiety about the area's changing tone. In particular they feared that the licensing authorities had decided that 'this is a "West End area"' and therefore strip has paramount rights': the 1970 inquiry into the Sunset Strip's licence application, for instance, would bring a laconic acknowledgement from the Westminster planning officials that 'the City Council considers that the proposed use, which conforms to the zoning of the area, is in keeping with the existing character of Dean Street.'[119] The Sunset Strip was also 'opposed by local commercial interests' in 1970, because the club would 'tend to bring about a degrading atmosphere in the eyes of visiting clients', but to no effect.[120] At the very first licence application hearing under the new regime, for the Dolls House club in Carlisle Street in October 1967, objections had come from 'businessmen and traders in Carlisle Street', which were duly 'overruled by the Council's 15-member licensing committee.'[121] In 1969 the residents of Kemp House, Soho's only tower block, petitioned against a proposal for a dance hall with striptease at the 9 Berwick Street site: 'We can well enough do without that, for we have enough with Stripp-Tease [sic] around us with fights nightly.' The GLC's apparent determination to sanction an application that was not obviously calculated to improve the area puzzled the residents and did not enhance their respect for the Council: 'if these are the type of people who have the authority to issue or refuse licences, well God help us!'[122]

Such concerns were intensified in the late 1960s, when the relaxation of laws controlling the publication of pornography in Sweden and Denmark between 1965 and 1969 released an unlimited supply of explicit material which could be sold at a premium in any country with stricter laws. Soho had long had its dirty bookshops, of course, but with this new mass of material available, porn shops expanded at a still more rapid rate than had strip clubs a decade earlier: 128 shops existed in Soho by 1969.[123] Posing fewer organisational challenges than strip clubs, porn shops offered immense returns to those who were ready to risk breaking the law. That risk disappeared for those who were ready and able to suborn the police—in this case the Met's Obscene Publication Squad (OPS). The long-established porn merchants Bernie Silver and Ronald ('John') Mason, along with the strip-club owner James Humphreys, who entered the porn trade in 1969 and teamed up with Silver, paid the dominant figures in the OPS, Wallace Virgo and Alfred ('Bill') Moody, to ensure that potential competitors received particular police attention, suffering repeated raids in which their stock would be confiscated. Humphreys was said to have paid £1,000 or more per month to members of the OPS, as well as paying half his takings to Silver, but so lucrative was the trade that he could still make £216,000 in two years in the early 1970s.[124] Virgo, claiming his share, allegedly collected nearly £60,000 from pornography dealers in two years.[125]

This corrupt restraint of trade diminished the number of shops to a mere sixty-one in Soho's square mile, whilst guaranteeing the profits of most of those which survived. It would prove short-lived. The appointment of Robert Mark as a 'new broom' Metropolitan Police commissioner in April 1972 indicated Whitehall's intention to clean the Met's various shabby stables, and the opportunity was provided by Humphreys, who released diaries describing his dealings with the OPS in order to gain revenge on the police after his jailing for grievous bodily harm in 1973.[126] The diaries formed the basis of the case against Virgo, Moody and nine other members of the 'dirty squad', convicted in Old Bailey trials in 1976–77, when Humphreys was the principal prosecution witness.[127]

Ironically, though, the attack on police corruption removed the constraints on the porn trade that these arrangements had imposed. The result was a tidal wave of sex shops, which devastated Soho's fragile local network of delicatessens, small workshops and the like, businesses which were in any case finding it difficult to pay rising West End rents and which stood no chance of competing with the sex trade. The transformation became chronic in 1975 when, facing perhaps tenfold rent increases, Isow's restaurant, the poulterers Hammett's, Madam Cadee's copper saucepan shop and Lipton's bacon merchants made way for the Paradise Sex Gardens and Doc Johnson's Love Shop.[128] In 1977 Leslie Hardcastle of the Soho Society estimated that between thirty and forty restaurants and small shops had disappeared in the previous two years.[129] The onslaught continued until the end of the decade, with particular press attention being given to the closure of the 'Épicerie Française' in Wardour Street. This was a family business founded in 1873 and run by two sisters for forty-five years, which was 'priced out by the sex industry' in December 1980.[130] 'The vice' were unrepentant: 'people may say it is a pity shops like this are declining,' said David Reed, of Conegate, the investment company established by the pornographer David Sullivan, which had acquired the freehold of the 'Épicerie Française' site, 'but if they supported them they would not decline. We believe in a free market economy.'[131]

The rapid conquest of old Soho by the sex trade catalysed public opinion to a degree not previously evident. In particular it brought together the Soho Society and the Conservatives who took over the GLC in 1977. The Soho Society was a rather Bohemian variant of the standard residents association, whose regular protests against the spread of 'the vice' were usually prefaced by a disclaimer of any wish to appear prudish or moralistic. It advocated the municipalisation of the sex industry 'as a means of control, and to stop racketeering.'[132] Of 124 readers of the Society's newsletter surveyed in 1977, 70 approved of sex establishments in principle and 61 claimed that they would find sex shops more acceptable if their displays were less explicit. Nonetheless, only 5 of the 124 respondents approved of the sex trade as it now appeared in Soho.[133] A rampant trade, apparently heedless of all planning regulations, mocked Soho's status, since 1969, as a conservation area. Above all, the Society was concerned that 'Soho should not automatically be considered the capital's main repository for book shops and sex shops, which would cause a scandal if they were situated in such profusion half a mile nearer to Westminster.'[134] 'Emphatically, we are not involved in a moral campaign', the Society's secretary protested: the intense concentration of the sex trade in Soho's square mile had rendered questions of individual moral conduct redundant, as the area threatened to become 'London's erogenous zone.'[135]

Whereas postwar Soho had combined crime, vice and literary Bohemianism in a mix that gained a nostalgic appeal, the Soho of the 1970s appeared destined to be given over entirely to sex. This proved intolerable. Soho's residents were more liberal than most and had often seen the area's risqué tone as part of its appeal, but the idea of being effectively zoned for the sex trade disturbed many even in the late 1960s. By the mid-1970s, when the mass importation of foreign pornography threatened to turn every delicatessen or small workshop into a porn bookshop or nude-encounter venue, the area faced comprehensive conversion to sleaze. 'Soho used to be a rather naughty place, but never the sleazy place it is now',[136] one resident wrote in 1981; the idea that Soho could be treated indefinitely as a risqué but harmless enclave in the West End became unsustainable.

Cleanup

In the late 1970s Bohemian Soho combined with the forces of moral purity in a cleanup campaign that demonstrated the weakness of permissive sentiment when it came to the peddling of sexual fantasy. The GLC Tories, returned to power in 1977, became unlikely allies for the Soho Society. Their leading crusaders on this issue represented the moral wing of the 1970s new Right. The campaign was led by Bryan Cassidy, the new vice chairman of the Public Services and Safety Committee (which now dealt with licensing issues), and Bernard Brooke-Partridge, who would become chairman of that committee in 1978. Brooke-Partridge had earlier resigned from the GLC's Film Viewing Board not because of any misdemeanour but for fear that 'he was becoming corrupted by the sights he saw.'[137] Permissiveness was, in his view, a symptom of a lack of self-discipline which he attributed to intrusive government: 'it was over-government and over-taxation which bred the moral collapse of Rome.'[138] He imparted these insights to the evangelical journal *New Tomorrow*; Cassidy's motivation was also in part evangelical. He believed that the Tories had regained control of the GLC because 'the voice of God had spoken through the people and there had been a change of administration.'[139] He had, though, the political sense not to ally the cleanup campaign too closely with the overtly Christian Festival of Light.[140]

The cleanup campaign sought to regulate the sex industry rather than obliterate it, an emphasis which disturbed some churchmen.[141] Cassidy impressed on the shadow home secretary, William Whitelaw, in 1978, 'the only way we can deal with this problem is to have a comprehensive new Act of Parliament which will bring the whole range of sexual establishments under control in the way that betting shops and offices are tightly controlled', adding that the transparent regulation of off-course betting had limited the opportunities for police corruption in that area.[142] Legislation duly followed from the first Thatcher government in 1981–82, controlling indecent displays outside cinemas and clubs, regulating the activities of sex shops and cinemas and allowing local authorities to control the number of sex shops in their areas. The City of Westminster eventually licensed six out of twenty-seven licence applicants in 1983.[143] Between 1982 and 1985 the total number of sex establishments in Soho was halved.[144] Though striptease was not the principal target of the cleanup, the stricter licensing conditions already in force for strip meant that it suffered heavily from the change of climate: licences were renewed less readily and licence evaders chased more vigorously. By the mid-1980s the number of strip clubs had fallen to low single figures.[145]

In the early 1980s Paul Raymond moved into property. Believing that 'it was only a matter of time before most of the existing sex shops, porn cinemas and clip joints closed down', he considered Soho's future to lie in becoming 'another Covent Garden before too long.'[146] He was broadly right. Once pornography displaced performance as the main focus of the sex trade, there was little reason for operators to pay the high rents that their earlier activities had generated in Soho—no reason to operate from the heart of the West End or, indeed, from London at all. The emerging porn entrepreneur David Sullivan owed his success to his development of a mail-order business, and the future development of the sex trade would hinge more on videos and the internet than on shops in the West End. The shop on the old Épicerie Française site would remain Sullivan's only Soho outlet. His mail-order business moved its centre of operations to south Yorkshire, and his publishing director promised to 'turn Barnsley into a sex shop centre until the town becomes synonymous with Soho.'[147]

Conclusion

It is tempting to see what Raymond called the 'stampede into sensuality'[148] unleashed by the Revuebar and other strip clubs in the sixties as reflecting the emerging 'permissive society' in that decade. To question that is not to challenge the idea that London became more permissive in these years but rather to ask whether this kind of brazen advertisement of the female body had anything to do with changing views of sexual relationships and sexual conduct amongst the general public. There is little in the account given here to suggest that it did. What emerges is a different picture. Erotic dancing had been available in the West End since at least the turn of the century. Static female nudes had been available since the 1930s. What happened in the 1950s was that several entrepreneurs found that it was possible to combine the two by describing their establishments as private clubs and that the substantial profits delivered by this deceit allowed them to treat recurrent fines for licence evasion as no more than running costs. This discovery might surely have been made at any point: it bore no obvious relationship to any emergent permissiveness. There was no 'Lady Chatterley moment' in this saga—no point at which society scrutinised its moral code and resolved to shed its Victorian shackles. Instead it was content to regulate the content of strip acts by means of a two-hundred-year-old statute with only inferential relevance to striptease. Once Raymond and others had succeeded in deriving spectacular profits from the commercialisation of the male sex drive, the authorities decided pragmatically that the combination of commercial muscle and the male libido was irresistible. The GLC concluded that if strip clubs could not be prevented, they should at least be stopped from becoming fire traps. The police concluded that if strip clubs could not be prevented, they could at least be 'skimmed' by bribery. The Westminster City Council decided that if strip clubs could not be prevented, they should at least be confined to Soho.

The result of all this pragmatism was that the sex trade was confined to a limited area, but within that area it was all-powerful and threatened to transform the landscape. In the process the whole question of regulation changed. At issue by the late seventies was less whether the authorities could legitimately curb the risqué pleasures of the private individual and more whether it was desirable for a section of the West End to be transformed into a sex *quartier*. Was London really eager to project itself as a 'sin city', in the manner of Amsterdam or, latterly, Bangkok? It took twenty years' development of the commercialised sex trade for the question to assume that form, but when it did, the answer given was, inevitably, not a permissive but a conservative one.

3

The Death of the Sixties, Part 2

THE FALL OF THE HOUSE OF BIBA

The death sentence was finally passed on swinging London this week', the *Economist* declared in August 1975.[1] The occasion was the announcement of the closure of the boutique-turned-department-store Biba by its parent company, British Land, with a view to making better use of the seven-storey Kensington High Street emporium which Biba occupied. Part of the building—built in 1933 for the drapery store Derry and Toms—was let to Marks and Spencer. Despite some speculation that Biba might continue to trade in the remainder, it closed for good at the end of September 1975. The closure of a clothes shop was hardly a rare event in 1970s London, but Biba's demise attracted national attention. In its original boutique form, Biba had offered affordable, stylish clothes to the young women of 1960s London. Retro and dusky where most King's Road fashion was modern and brash, 'the Biba look was unmistakably urban and unique.'[2] Its strangulation by a property company and partial replacement by that most sensible of stores, M&S, symbolised the suppression of sixties fantasy by seventies functionalism. If the fashion revolution had been at the heart of 'Swinging London', the fall of Biba did indeed mark its end.

Fashion: A Frightening Business

Asked in 1963 by an unusually curious policeman to explain the difference between Mods and Rockers, seventeen-year-old John Henry Hassall, shoe

The interior of an unidentified Carnaby Street boutique, photographed in a convex mirror in 1967, with a customer contemplating buying a tomato-red shirt. (Mary Evans Picture Library)

salesman, of Manor Park, replied, 'only that they dress differently.' At Hassall's trial for insulting behaviour, the policeman, Anthony Brady, told the Guildhall magistrate Sir Bernard Waley-Cohen that 'the "Moderns" wore Italian-cut suits, chisel-toed shoes, slim ties and college boy haircuts. The "rockers" wore long coats, black jackets—some leather—jeans, heavy suede chukka boots and Tony Curtis hair styling.'[3] Hassall was a Mod, and as Angus McGill explained to *Evening Standard* readers four months later, 'the Mod is a bit of a dandy. He thinks about clothes, talks about clothes, spends most of his wages on clothes.'[4] The Mod propensity to dispose of much of his disposable income on clothes is now familiar; what is evident from Hassall's account is the particularity of his style. Further, his very specific prescription represented only one stage of an evolution later captured by Nik Cohn, as, from the late fifties to the midsixties, 'Moderns' sported 'a whole sequence of similar styles, all based on short jackets and narrow pants: first the Italian Look itself, then the round-collared Cardin suit, later revived as the Beatle suit; and finally the Mod suit, the first stand-by of Carnaby Street.'[5] The menswear boutiques of Carnaby Street emerged to provide a kind of flexible response to the precise, fast-moving demands of Mod fashion—one which could not or would not be provided by conventional retailers.

The sixties fashion revolution in London was initially driven not by department stores or multiples but by boutiques. The sixties boutique was a development of a type of small shop suited to the modest, low-key architecture of much of Central London—in Bronwen Edwards's words, 'part of a tradition of small, jewel-like, fashionable and luxury shops which drew on a French model' and 'flourished in the smaller streets of the West End in the interwar years.'[6] Their small scale encouraged informality in both exterior and interior décor—sometimes carried to the point of extravagance in the uninhibited sixties—and allowed for more 'niche' retailing than larger stores cared to explore. Both Dale Cavana's shop in Kinnerton Street, Belgravia—established in the late 1940s and identified by McGill as London's first boutique[7]—and Bill Green's Vince's Manshop in Soho catered more or less explicitly for young gay customers. John Stephen in Carnaby Street made his fortune by producing gay-derived menswear—figure-hugging and rich in colour—to a young straight market, responsive to adventurous design.

The secretary of the National Association of Outfitters defined boutiques as 'shops that cater for the man who doesn't want to conform. . . . They aim at the individualist.'[8] As such, they encouraged the individualistic designer: John Michael Ingram, who opened the first significant menswear shop in the King's Road, Chelsea, in 1957, two years after Mary Quant's Bazaar, defined the boutique as 'a menswear shop run by designers, not by buyers.'[9] Ingram, then twenty-six, was advantaged by being 'the first shopkeeper to be the same age as his customers.'[10] Likewise in womenswear: Quant herself spoke of being motivated to first sell and then design clothes that appealed to her by an awareness that 'there was a real need for fashion accessories for young people chosen by people of their own age'; Barbara Hulanicki, the founder of Biba, began to design clothes in the early 1960s because 'the shops in England at this time [1960] were full of matronly clothes—either direct copies of Paris clothes or deeply influenced by the Paris collections.'[11] This first generation of entrepreneur-designers benefited from the tardiness of traditional clothiers in recognising the depth of young pockets and their failure, even when they had recognised it, to create the infrastructure necessary to exploit it. As Victoria Brittain noted in an early assessment of the Carnaby Street phenomenon, 'the majors can never compete with the street in the creation of fashion, as they lack the vital flexibility of small, closely controlled production lines, and the close touch with the market.'[12] Dependent on nineteenth-century mills geared to the production of large runs of any given design,[13] they could not adapt swiftly to changes in taste and had relied on imposing fashion on the consumer by means of regimented seasonal production.

In a prescriptive, demanding but promisingly affluent youth market this proved inadequate.

Of the original Carnaby Street magnates, David and Warren Gold and Irvine Sellar gained their understanding of the emerging menswear market from street trading, as did Stanley Adams in nearby Kingly Street and Sidney Brent in Wardour Street and Great Marlborough Street. John Stephen, the 'King of Carnaby Street', would 'test reaction with a few dozens' of any design, which he had made up quickly by the tailors in the hinterland of Oxford Street: having established the taste of the market, 'it is easy to repeat successes.'[14] Mary Quant began by making small runs of her own designs in her flat—'I don't think that bedsitter of mine will ever recover from its spell as a factory'—relying on immediate sales to purchase the material for her next production.[15] Hulanicki's career took off when a gingham dress of her design was featured in the *Daily Mirror* in 1964; seventeen thousand examples were sold from what was still operating as 'Biba's Postal Boutique.'[16]

All these figures prospered on the strength of their entrepreneurial talent and their ability to gauge the youth market. In truth, though, this was not a difficult market in which to flourish, provided that one entered early enough. The demand for adventurous clothes—male and female—was evidently enormous in the early sixties. Hulanicki believed that the typical Biba customer was a working girl earning £10 to £15 per week, who would spend £6 to £7 of that on clothes.[17] The Carnaby Street retailers interviewed by Victoria Brittain told her that 'an average customer will . . . spend £10 a week on clothes while a wad of £50 in fivers is not an uncommon sight on boys who look about 15–17 at the most.'[18] This level of expenditure suggests that many of the young consumers were still living at home and paying little or nothing in rent. There were many such consumers in London, but the case of Pauline Hazell from Hendon, interviewed by Jenny Dingemans for the *Standard* in 1965, suggests that careful budgeting could allow for sporadic self-indulgence even among the more rooted. Married for a year, she earned £12 a week as a receptionist at a Chelsea hair salon and set aside half of that for housekeeping. She and her husband were saving to buy a house, but she still bought 'her clothes on impulse': '"If I see something I like," she says, "I buy it if I can possibly afford it."' She would spend up to £6 on shoes and £20 on a coat—a sum which would have enabled her to shop at Foale and Tuffin.[19]

Brittain found the Carnaby Street moguls coy about their own turnover figures but happy to estimate their rivals' takings to the last £5. 'A figure of £1000 a week is thought fair by some, poor by others and laughable by one,

Barbara Hulanicki and her husband, Stephen Fitz-Simon, 1975. (David Montgomery/Premium Archive/ Getty Images)

who reckoned he could take that in one good day.' This was despite the fact that Carnaby Street, previously a West Soho backwater, 'breaks all the rules of retailing: it's hard to find, you can't park, all the shops depend on the same market, compete directly, there is no conventional advertising.'[20] The belief that a boutique provided a licence to print money inevitably drew large numbers—mostly unqualified—into the business by the middle of the decade.

In May 1967 the *Financial Times* carried an advertisement in its 'Business Opportunities' section from Fanny Boutiques of Pimlico, headed, 'Have You Ever Thought of Opening a Boutique but Hesitated Because of Lack of Experience?'[21] The firm was looking to attract managers with enthusiasm and time but also £2,000 in capital. Many who lacked experience were tempted by such opportunities. Jonathan Aitken noted that seven new boutiques opened in one small section of the King's Road between November 1966 and January 1967; by that time there were around two thousand boutiques in Greater London.[22] An early sign of oversupply was the ennui evinced by fashion writers forced to investigate a myriad of near-identical shops. By April 1966—just when *Time* magazine discovered young London—Barbara Griggs of the *Standard* felt reluctant to sample yet another boutique:

> Not if it's been started up by an 18-year-old amateur who's been designing her own kooky clothes ever since she chucked secretarial college. Not if the place has been merrily decorated by chums with witty junk and stripped pine and lots of bright paint. Not if the shop assistants are the designer's girl-friends giggling into a telephone and yawning their pretty heads off because they were dancing till 4 A.M. Not if the clothes are mainly trouser-suits, six-inch-long skirts and cut-out dresses in clashy colours, all run up any which way by a private army of chums of chums of chums. And not if there's non-stop pop to keep the customers happy.[23]

This was the frustration of a jaded professional, but her depiction of the customer experience was a familiar one. Angela Ince wrote in a similar vein in *London Life* three months later: 'Boutique' was 'French for Little Shop, and far too often it's English for inefficiency, rudeness and Who Cares About the Customer Anyway? . . . What is a boutique? Far too often it tends to be a small airless room, decorated "amusingly" or "wittily" (or frankly, "grubbily")', with cramped and crowded changing rooms, staffed by inattentive assistants and offering 'unlined skirts that split at the first dinner party you wear them to.'[24]

The reputation for producing showy but shoddy clothes would dog the London fashion trade for years. Hulanicki denied the charge with some vigour so far as Biba was concerned: 'We were told that our clothes fell apart! We knew that our quality was good, if not better than anybody's'. This may have been true in the firm's mature years, but she had been ready in 1966 to accept that 'until recently Biba had dash, style and some of the worst-made clothes in town.'[25] In truth, shops catering for the 'bulk' end of the market, where competition was intense and new styles came and went with dizzying rapidity, had little incentive to invest in quality. Much women's wear was notoriously shoddy. A survey by Sidney Brent's boutique Take 6 in 1968 found that 70 percent of female customers in its menswear stores actually came to buy for themselves—mostly shirts and sweaters—rather than for a man, because they 'felt that the men's clothes fitted better and they thought they were better quality than women's garments.'[26] Customers ready to buy on impulse and eager not to wear the same clothes for months showed a tolerance that might not have been offered to other types of retailer, but over time—and in the gloomier climate of the late sixties—the boutique image was tarnished. In November 1968 no fewer than 86 percent of owners of 'trendy fashion shops' surveyed by the shopfitting firm City Industrial Ltd gave 'a definite "no" to the question "would you describe your shop as a "boutique"?' The investigator concluded that 'shop owners . . . have suddenly become very touchy about the term boutiques.'[27]

Reflecting on a decade of running the smart and successful Kensington boutique Annacat at the time of the shop's closure in 1976, Janet Lyle acknowledged the naivety with which she and co-owner Maggie Keswick had embarked on their retailing adventure: 'The day after the [opening] party we went to our shop and sort of wondered what to do next. Then suddenly a *customer* came in and *bought* something. We were quite taken aback. We had no bags or receipt book, we had no change and nowhere to put the money. Later we acquired a cash box which was, needless to say, stolen.' She attributed the shop's survival to the fact that they had learned from their mistakes before the business became impossibly competitive: 'so by the time the market was crowded with shops like ours we really knew what went on.'[28] Later entrants missed this opportunity, and the pages of the trade press in the late 1960s and early 1970s are freighted with accounts of hopeful amateurs stumbling into insolvency. Most common were the cases of owners gulled by agents into buying more stock than they could sell before tastes changed: 'I didn't buy the wrong things. I bought too much'; 'She had bought badly, as well as overbought, and she was left with stock she could not clear. She lacked capital to buy new lines, and her regular customers drifted away when they found the same garments on sale week after week.'[29] Some simply failed to anticipate the more restrained demand for youth fashion in the difficult economic climate of the early 1970s: 'Trading in Hampstead during 1971 was very bad and, in fact, the company's turnover was diabolical and money just did not come in. The position was eventually reached where the company had a large stock and, with fashion changes, had to be sold at the best price possible.'[30] Some underestimated the importance of location, such as the women's wear retailer in the City who committed himself to a weighty £3,000-a-year rent in Victoria only to come—oddly late—to realise in 1968 that 'King's Road, Chelsea . . . has taken a lot of business away from the Victoria area.'[31] Examples abounded of failures with liabilities far in excess of assets (the Official Receiver told creditors of Escalade, Ltd, Brompton Road, in 1973 that the company's debts were '"probably rather more than £400,000." . . . He knew of no assets.').[32] Many owners—like housewife Muriel Daniels, who opened the Needlecraft boutique in Hammersmith in 1971—had simply entered the business with a 'tiny bit of capital and a lot of hope.'[33]

Most of the boutique owners filing for bankruptcy in these years had been ill equipped to flourish in the trade in any but the euphoric conditions of the midsixties. More significant, perhaps, is the evident strain felt even by the stars of the business in their efforts to sustain what was effectively a cottage industry in the face of economic fluctuations and better-resourced competitors. Quant learned quickly that 'it was one long battle all the time.'[34] John Stephen worked a seventy-two-hour week even at the height of his success. He took to drink with increasing frequency and suffered a breakdown in 1965.[35] Both Quant and her husband, Alexander Plunket Greene, sought psychiatric help as their business grew.[36] Quant's 1966 autobiography contained much cautionary advice about the pitfalls of operating in a business in which the failure even of a single design might prove damaging and 'one is surrounded by vast quantities of risk money all the time.'[37] When Vanessa Frye's Sloane Street boutique sought voluntary liquidation in 1972, the creditors included Mary Quant and the Mary Quant Ginger Group, Foale and Tuffin and Caroline Charles, owed amounts up to £1,400.[38] An unnamed wholesaler told journalist Angela Ince in 1966, 'There are so many new boutiques. . . . They come in here every week wanting to buy stuff—but you know only too well they won't pay'; as Hulanicki's husband, Stephen Fitz-Simon, put it, 'boutique is a dirty word to wholesalers or cloth manufacturers.' 'The whole rag trade runs on a series of credit', Fitz-Simon explained, 'and all this credit depends on the final outlet—at some stage a customer has to hand over pound notes to the retailer, who passes them back along the chain.'[39] The first challenge was to persuade the customer to part with the notes at all. The whole trade was vulnerable to shoplifting, but boutiques, often with untrained staff, subdued lighting and crowds of shoppers, were in particular danger. One unidentified West End boutique apprehended 328 suspected shoplifters in a four-month period in 1973, prosecuting half of them. Nearly 90 percent of thieves operated simply by slipping garments into a bag, taking advantage of the modish dim lighting in many boutiques.[40] The trade believed that shoplifters were most likely to be young, which again made boutiques more vulnerable: a 1968 London School of Economics (LSE) survey found that 13 percent of London boys aged between thirteen and sixteen had been caught stealing by police, and 16 percent of self-professed thieves claimed never to have been caught. Over half of them had stolen from shops.[41] The three teenage thieves interviewed by Anne Sharpley for the *Standard* in 1966 saw shoplifting as a functional necessity: 'We don't have the money to buy clothes, things like Mary Quant. I mean that skinny rib we saw costs £3 10s, didn't it? I mean how are you going to get your clothes, you just have to go on the nick?'[42]

Designer-owners faced the particular problem of bootleg versions of their more successful products appearing almost as soon as their popularity was clear. Hulanicki wrote of one 'well-known lady proprietor of a big dress company' who would buy her dresses in order to copy them before returning them and asking for her money back.[43] Stephen convinced himself that 'when people stop copying [his] ideas the time will come to worry' and responded to plagiarism by lowering his prices,[44] but few designers could afford his relaxed attitude. John Michael Ingram's response was more common: 'We introduce a new fashion—like the colour purple for men, the striped shirt or denim, and within a few months every other shop in London is marketing a copy. That's when we know we have to drop it and search around for something else.'[45] In a fast-moving business, where no design could expect a long shelf life, this made more sense than attempts to chase the bootleggers through the courts, but it imposed a frustrating penalty for success.

There was, of course, no legal redress for the appropriation of the boutique concept by the larger stores, which represented the biggest threat to small retailers. Simpsons of Piccadilly had opened a department called 'Trend' in 1965.[46] In 1966 Selfridge devoted twenty thousand square feet on the ground floor of its Oxford Street store to the new Miss Selfridge shop, 'frankly geared to wooing 17- to 25-year-old girls away from the boutiques.'[47] By the summer of 1967 several major London stores had followed suit.[48] In that year even the normally staid Harrods joined the game, with its Way In boutique, with later opening and closing hours than the main store, a separate entrance and prices in pounds rather than guineas. The staff—presumably less obsequious than the Harrods regulars of that time—were to be no older than twenty-four and to 'wear the kind of clothes they are selling.' As if to set the tone, at the launch of Way In in June 1967 the company chairman, Sir Hugh Fraser, wore a 'cinnamon belted corduroy

Shoula Tevet modelling stock on offer at the Way In boutique on the fourth floor of Harrods, two days before its opening in June 1967. (Mirrorpix/Alamy Stock Photo)

suit and suede boots.'[49] The larger stores could carry larger overheads than individual boutiques could afford, even running to computerisation to help them 'stay profitably attuned to changes of fashion and fancy.'[50] They could, like Miss Selfridge, offer easy credit terms, whereas the boutiques, plagued as they were by shoplifting and suppliers' bad debts, were reluctant to expose themselves to credit defaults: Stephen's businesses, in contrast, were all 'cash only.'[51]

'You can't just be a little exclusive shop any more, run with little business experience', Sue Locke, who had established the Susan Locke boutique at the World's End extremity of the King's Road, told the *Drapers Record* in 1967: 'So many of this type of boutique have died, and others will follow.' Alistair Cowin, founder of Grade One, off Kensington High Street, used his boutique 'like a showroom': 'If a line sells well in the shop, odds-on it will go well for the mass market.'[52] Those who had read correctly the lessons for retailers of the Wilson government's 'freeze' in 1966–67 looked to protect themselves if possible by wholesaling, manufacturing and exporting. All these responses made commercial sense but carried new risks. Stephen owned factories in Glasgow and Kilburn, which produced 20 percent of his sales by 1966, even though Carnaby Street in general 'fights shy of manufacturing',[53] but not every boutique owner was cut out to run a factory, engaging with possible attendant labour-relations problems and other difficulties of management. A successful export business was the ultimate prize. Stephen, Ingram, Quant and some of the other market leaders established links with department stores in the United States, and Quant was instrumental in the establishment of an Italian 'Carnaby Street' in the Via Margutta in Rome in 1967.[54] In general, though, British exporters suffered for the cheap and cheerful nature of much of their produce: after a burst of American interest in 'Swinging London' in 1966, 'the high duty on these terribly produced clothes made the New York selling price ridiculous.'[55] British fashion came to be seen overseas as offering 'little in between dullness . . . and somewhat shoddy high-style swinging gear', and British fashion exports enjoyed only patchy success.[56] It was perhaps for this reason that the Board of Trade appeared cagey in responding to repeated requests for help from would-be exporters, despite Britain's late-sixties fixation with its balance of payments.[57]

In all, as Quant wrote, 'fashion is a frightening business to be in.'[58] Just how frightening was shown by the spectacular collapse in 1972 of Tommy Roberts's Freedom Group. The Group had contrived to lose £150,000 in twelve months, and creditors learned to their dismay that its assets of around £35,000 were likely to be claimed entirely by the Inland Revenue.[59] Roberts, a former used-car salesman from Catford, had opened the Mr Freedom boutique in World's End in 1969, moving to more opulent premises in Kensington Church Street in 1970.[60] His reputation as one of London's more inventive, if idiosyncratic, designers would be rebuilt after his 1972 difficulties, but the account of those problems at the winding-up hearing provides an epitome of all that could go wrong in the popular fashion business:

Mr David Andre Morgan, a director, had said the companies suffered from not being able to get economically long production runs. The designs were also difficult to make up and involved high labour costs. He had said the complicated designs and materials also needed careful making up and it was difficult to get Odd One Out's factory into full production as a result. Another problem was the sizing of garments. Mr Morgan had said export clothes needed different sizing to the home market. Some of the materials used, such as black velvet, were not always available in sufficient quantities for outstanding orders. Mr Morgan had said these shortages sometimes meant the factory was not working to capacity, and hitting a proper balance became a major problem. Overheads, particularly wages, were also very high at the factory. This was because skilled labour was needed to produce the garments and those workers demanded good wages. Other manufacturers were not interested in making up for the companies unless vast quantities were ordered.[61]

On top of all these problems came the substantial cost of converting the Kensington premises, formerly used as a restaurant. Fashion truly was a frightening business to be in.

Big Biba

Even at the height of the fashion boom, in January 1966, Victoria Brittain had argued that boutiques 'cannot stand still. To expand they must either go really big with branches in every likely provincial town and export divisions as well (John Stephen's probable pattern); or, like the efficient Mr Ingram of John Michael, they must trade up into an exclusive market.'[62] In the event, though many of the designer-owners looked for export markets, few sought to multiply within Britain. The principal exception was Irvine Sellar, one of the Carnaby Street moguls, whose Mates shops proliferated in the late 1960s. Many of his new stores marked a departure from the boutique concept, most obviously the shops opened in Regent Street and Oxford Street—the latter with five thousand square feet of floor space—in the second half of 1968. Asked if the proximity of the Regent Street store to Carnaby Street would be problematic, Sellar replied—correctly—that 'from a trading point of view, it is a million miles away.' He added that 'Carnaby Street has a specialised type of trading'; the new store would carry a much more comprehensive range of men's and women's clothes as well as evening wear, rainwear, millinery and perhaps underwear.[63]

Mates was, though, still a clothes shop. The most comprehensive development of the boutique concept came from Barbara Hulanicki, who had told her bank manager in 1967 that 'Biba would one day be like Harrods.'[64]

Having started as a 'postal boutique' in 1963, Biba acquired its first premises, in Abingdon Road, Kensington, in the following year. In 1966 it moved to larger premises in Kensington Church Street, but the Harrods ambition really began to take shape with a further move, to 120 Kensington High Street, in 1969. This emporium was less a boutique than a department store, selling men's as well as women's clothes, cosmetics, jewellery and furnishings, all in Hulanicki's idiosyncratic style. It necessarily brought a step away from the boutique tradition of frenzied intimacy, with nine thousand square feet of floor space.

To fund this expansion, Hulanicki and Fitz-Simon had ceded 75 percent of their business to the women's wear firm Dorothy Perkins. There was a commercial logic to this step. Dorothy Perkins had until the mid-sixties been a 'strictly stockings-and-undies' brand, and at a time of increasingly adventurous innovation in fashion, it wished to shed its rather staid image. It hoped to draw on Hulanicki's flair and, in particular, her 'blackly Satanic and plummily coloured' cosmetics, to be sold across the chain. Biba, in return, would gain the retailing know-how of the Perkins management.[65] The marriage does indeed appear to have been a happy one, which allowed Biba to move from a loss of £40,000 in 1969 to a profit of £300,000 in 1973,[66] but it entailed sacrificing the independence integral to a buccaneering enterprise like Biba.

The implications would become clearer in time, as Dorothy Perkins's own independence was diluted by its relationship with the property company, British Land, but in the short term this arrangement facilitated still further Biba expansion. The first fruit of Dorothy Perkins's relationship with British Land was the formation of a joint subsidiary—Dorothy Perkins Properties—to manage and develop the company's estate. Its first venture was the purchase of the former Derry and Toms building from the House of Fraser in 1971, a move clearly intended to provide a new home for Biba.[67]

Hulanicki had supposedly long dreamed of occupying this building. It stood only across the road from the third Biba store, but contained four hundred thousand square feet of floor space, of which around one hundred thousand square feet would be offered to Biba—more than ten times the area of the existing shop—with the possibility of more to come. It would provide the venue for perhaps the most ambitious British retail venture of the period: what would become known as 'Big Biba.' The firm's origins in women's fashion were almost obscured in what was now unambiguously a department store. Its seven floors contained a food hall, a book store, a children's store, a restaurant, a maternity store and other departments selling sportswear, household goods, cosmetics, shoes, jewellery, leather goods, and both regular and irregular lingerie in the 'Mistress Room' (where 'a girl can pick her jewelled bra'),[68] all in addition to the men's and women's clothing.

The first major new department store in Britain for decades, Big Biba sold a whole lifestyle—one designed almost entirely by Hulanicki herself. The stock consisted very largely of own-brand goods, including Biba soap and baked beans. The setting, designed by Tim Whitmore and Steven Thomas, was similarly distinctive. Hulanicki later wrote that the interior of each of the four Biba shops was designed to reflect the period of the building itself, and in her new art deco temple she imagined 'Garbo-esque figures floating in vast spaces in languid clothes and murky lighting.'[69] This produced the touches of the 1930s United States—giving rise to the frequent charge that Big Biba reeked of Hollywood—interspersed with incongruous but striking ancient Egyptian motifs in the communal changing room on the 'Biba Floor'—the women's wear section. More than a quarter of the floorspace—twenty-six thousand square feet—was laid in marble.[70] Many of the fittings were tongue-in-cheek—a display of soup cans contained in a giant replica can in Campbell's red and white and labelled 'Warhol's Condensed', pet food cans displayed in the cutaway stomach of a model Great Dane.[71] The whole store was an exercise in ostentatious display: 'the Big Biba', as Hulanicki intended, 'was going to be an Oscar-winning performance.'[72]

The store certainly drew the crowds, with an initial one million visitors per week after its opening in September 1973. But if Big Biba was, as Hulanicki claimed, the second most visited tourist attraction in London after the Tower,[73] the concern remained that more people were coming for the spectacle than the shopping. A loss of £364,000 in the forty-eight weeks to the end of March 1974 reinforced this concern, not least because the figure was diminished by profits made by the first High Street Kensington store for five months before the move.[74]

Whatever Big Biba's potential, the timing of its arrival was unfortunate. Only weeks after its opening Western economies were crippled by the OPEC crisis, leading in Britain to accelerating inflation, an energy shortage exacerbated by the 1974 miners' strike and, in January and February 1974, Edward Heath's emergency Three-Day Week. Consumer confidence was hit hard, and there can have been few worse points in the twentieth century at which to launch an innovative retail experiment. The economic crisis not only damaged Biba directly but also intensified the pressures resulting

The food hall in Big Biba, with shelves encased in giant replica cans of Heinz beans and 'Warhol' condensed soup. (ewastock cc/Alamy Stock Photo)

from its surrender of autonomous control four years earlier. In the summer of 1973 British Land had taken over Dorothy Perkins; Biba had thus become directly owned by a property company.

'It is every retailer's nightmare to be controlled by a property developer', Hulanicki wrote in 1983.[75] Property developers as a class had gained an antisocial image in the years from the midsixties to the bursting of the property bubble in 1973, as a small group of men who had acquired Central London land during or shortly after the war exploited their monopoly possession to prosper from the office boom, playing the planning system and often blighting the urban landscape in the process. Particular animus was directed at Harry Hyams and his company Oldham Estates, which built the conspicuous Centre Point at Tottenham Court Road only to keep it empty in anticipation of higher future rents. British Land was by no means as cynical in its approach to its buildings, but its strategic approach of acquiring property with a long-term reversionary potential left it vulnerable to short-term fluctuations. When the steam went out of the property market in 1973, British Land, with an unusually high proportion—for a property company—of its borrowing in the form of short-term and floating-rate loans, was very exposed. Its current income was inadequate

and was effectively capped by the business rent freeze imposed as a coun-
terinflationary measure by the Heath government in November 1972. A
profit of £3.8 million in 1972–73 was transformed into a loss of £398,000 in
1973–74, with the second half of that year bringing a massive loss of £1.5
million.[76] Under such circumstances, it could not ignore the continuing
losses at Big Biba, which reported a pretax loss of £1.46 million in its first
full year of trading, 1974–75.[77]

What followed was a battle between retailing as understood by a Swinging London entrepreneuse and retailing as understood by a property company. 'Swinging London retailing' deployed many of the informal methods
carried over by Biba from its boutique days—a relaxed approach to paper-
work ('for the past eight years it had never been necessary to write a memo
to anyone')[78] and the notoriously casual demeanour of the staff, 'inattentive, except to their fingernails.'[79] Claire Alexander of the *Drapers Record*
noted with regret that 'the merchandise was too limited in scope; sizes
were haphazard and badly marked; fit was poor and there was nothing for
larger girls or anyone who was not already a Biba customer.' She observed
that 'attention to this kind of detail is, to the creative mind, probably the
boring part of retailing which can be overlooked; experience has shown
that this is not so, and that the bread-and-butter part of merchandising is
an essential underpinning to originality.'[80] The longer-serving staff acknowledged that the employees 'used to be very casual' but maintained
that 'everything would get done and the staff had pride.' They resented the
diktats from the new management prohibiting smoking, eating or drinking
on the shop floor and the 'bloody awful' regime by which they had all their
'responsibility taken away and almost become robots.'[81] 'Property company retailing', on the other hand, meant constant supervision of staff, an
accountant's approach to costs and strategic direction by a 'think tank',
which especially irked Hulanicki and Fitz-Simon.[82] They were removed
from all involvement in the management of the company from the autumn
of 1974, to their distress. 'I wouldn't say they're happy about the affair', one
codirector of British Land told the *Guardian*, 'but then I wouldn't expect
them to be happy. We're dealing with artistic people.'[83]

The conflict came to a head, appropriately, over the artistic use of space.
Though the first High Street Kensington shop had been large by boutique
standards, its '9,000 cluttered square feet' offered an inadequate setting for
Hulanicki's ambition.[84] Sixties boutiques—at least successful ones—were
classically small and crowded. This had diminished the scope to apply the
often powerful imaginations of the designer-owners to their interior

decoration, even as they became increasingly inventive with window displays and shop exteriors—the controversial mural on the Beatles' short-lived Apple Boutique in Baker Street, for instance, or the successive facades of Nigel Waymouth's Granny Takes a Trip in World's End, culminating in the installation of the front half of a 1948 Dodge car projecting from the wall.[85] There was no appetite for covering the art deco Derry and Toms building in psychedelia, and Hulanicki eschewed window displays in all her shops; but her consistent interest in interior décor—'from day one of the first Biba I was never quite certain which came first, the clothes or the interiors'[86]—found an unparalleled opportunity in the vast expanses of floor space in Big Biba. In the work of the Whitmore/Thomas partnership much hinged on the creative use of space, particularly on the ground floor, designed to beguile as much as to sell, with each department 'unmistakeably defined since there are vast areas of empty space in between.'[87] In contrast to the claustrophobic changing rooms of traditional boutiques, the Egyptian-themed rooms on the Biba floor resembled 'the inner chambers of one of the great pyramids after they had been looted.'[88] Only one-sixth of the floor space was actually used for selling.[89]

Property companies, in contrast, lived or died by their efficient use of space. In the planned environment of the central city, commercial architects built their careers on the skill of maximising remunerative office space within the local authority's prescribed plot ratios.[90] Although the previous Biba store had made unusually lucrative use of floor space, with a turnover of £200 per square foot, against an average for department stores of £50, even at the time of Big Biba's opening, analysts asked 'how any store in central London can operate successfully on a less than 50 per cent space utilisation.'[91] The store's poor commercial performance suggested that it could not, and British Land became steadily less indulgent of its loss-making flagship. The expansive ground-floor design was abandoned as an indefensible luxury, and 'every inch of spare marble was now covered by supermarket-like units and dump bins.'[92] Six months before full closure, the household and menswear floors were closed 'to make the store function more efficiently'[93]—a portent of the end. When the lease of part of the store to Marks and Spencer was announced in July 1975, British Land emphasised that it was a response to Biba's 'extravagant' use of space, suggesting that it should be possible for the truncated store to achieve the same turnover in the seventy-five thousand square feet that remained to it.[94]

Marks and Spencer was an attractive tenant because the substantial footfall that it generated attracted other retailers to neighbouring sites.[95]

With the lifting of the cap on commercial rents in March 1975, it was widely anticipated that British Land would look for new tenants for the rest of the building. In these circumstances, as the journalist Elinor Goodman put it, Biba was 'as disposable as the clothes it sells.'[96]

A Failed Experiment

Goodman concluded that Biba's demise should alarm all businesses dependent on 'the fickle tastes of the under-25s.'[97] The pop fashion trade that had developed in London since the midfifties was obviously vulnerable on that count. It had rested heavily on the affluence of teenagers and young adults in the sixties, and that age group had been hit severely by the worsening unemployment of the seventies. This chapter has been a catalogue of the difficulties encountered by small-scale operators tempted into the fashion business in the prosperous sixties but ill equipped to cope with a colder economic climate. Those that were best equipped to weather the storm of the midseventies were, as Goodman observed, the fashion chains, with the cash flow to withstand economic squalls. The designs they sold, as the trade press noted with some relish, were more cautious than before: 'the new sedate London look' meant 'forsaking gimmicks, freaks and revivals of fashions past' in favour of 'lots of pretty clothes', as 'gimmicks and swift fashion changes please no-one and certainly don't make for good business.'[98] The individualists retreated from the boutique business: Mary Quant had closed her three Bazaar shops by 1969, having been advised by her 'business nanny', Archie McNair, that income from licensing her brand name was more dependable.[99] John Stephen sold his company to the clothing manufacturers Raybeck, which also bought the Gold brothers' Lord John shops, in 1975. The innovative Michael Fish closed his Mr Fish boutique in Mayfair in the same year because his backers 'decided that there are no great profits to be made retailing fancy silk shirts and cashmere sweaters in today's economic climate.'[100] Others—like Annacat—simply went under.

At first glance, the fall of Biba appears part of this process. Accounts which took it to symbolise the 'death of the sixties' evoked the image created by the first two Biba stores, epitomising to many people the sixties boutique. The store that failed in 1975, though—'Big Biba'—was not just an overgrown boutique. Hulanicki, a resourceful and imaginative businesswoman, had registered the flaws in the boutique model. In Big Biba she created something very different, and effectively seeking to tap into the emerging 'experience economy' of seventies London—a point missed by those who were critical of its 'Hollywood theatricality.'[101] The experience economy was christened and academically analysed by the American economists Joseph Pine and James Gilmore in the late 1990s, though the concept had been understood for as long as the affluent society had been recognised. Pine and Gilmore's argument was that consumers in an affluent age sought more from their purchases than the simple provision of goods and services. They identified a distinction within the service sector in modern economies—and predominantly in modern urban economies[102]— between routine services such as laundry or car repair and those discretionary services which were consumed for the pleasure that they brought.[103] In creating her 'wonderland of escapism' in Kensington,[104] Hulanicki sought to introduce 'experience' into retailing. Most directly, the generous use of space that the Derry and Toms building made possible contrasted with the positively uncomfortable consumer experience in cramped sixties boutiques. Design, colour and exoticism were applied to the interior of Big Biba in order to make the business of shopping an adventure in itself. As Philip Norman wrote in the *Sunday Times*, the atmosphere of Big Biba served 'the unusual object of giving enjoyment at no charge to its customers',[105] but however invigorating the experience on offer, it was not clear that experience alone could promote sales of baked beans or dog food. Innovative and imaginative as the store was, it offered no solution to the fundamental difficulty of compelling anyone who visited a shop actually to purchase anything; as Fitz-Simon recognised, there was no guaranteed way to 'convert spectators into customers.'[106] It was certainly questionable whether Kensington High Street, one of London's more expensive retail centres, was the best place to experiment in this way. The pillars of the urban experience economy would be those operations which could charge more directly for the experience they offered: entertainment venues, the new type of coffee shop (the first Costa opened in London in 1978) and, above all, restaurants.

4

'Now That Londoners Have Discovered the Delights of the Palate'

EATING OUT IN 1960S AND 1970S LONDON

In the mid-1950s Beauchamp Place, off the Brompton Road, was a centre of ladies' couture, with tailors, dressmakers, milliners, furriers and the like accounting for 48 of the 118 businesses in the 1955 *Post Office Directory*. Other enterprises comprised what passed for the service sector in Kensington, including twelve antique dealers, a naturopath and a provider of 'dogs' baths and requisites.' There were three restaurants, none well known. By 1966, though, Beauchamp Place offered 'more restaurants per hundred yards than almost any street outside Soho.'[1] By the late 1970s it contained sixteen restaurants and was one of London's culinary centres.

Beauchamp Place's reputation owed most to the success of the restaurant Parkes, established by the Yorkshire-born Ray Parkes in 1960 and carried on after his death three years later by his protégé Tom Benson. Parkes was considered by the food critic Egon Ronay to be 'a true creator of dishes such as has never existed before', while Benson's idiosyncratic cooking was compared to 'the fantastic buildings by Gaudi in Barcelona.'[2] Dishes like melon with blackcurrants or chicken with cider had little in common with West End haute cuisine but reflected the undeferential tone of the time; Parkes became among the most sought-after restaurants of sixties London, putting Beauchamp Place on London's culinary map. The street's

Beauchamp Place, SW3: restaurants, 1960–79.

1960 1961 1962 1963 1964 1965 1966 1967 1968 1969 1970 1971 1972 1973 1974 1975 1976 1977 1978 1979

- 1a — Parkes
- 4 — Parkes
- 5 — Benson's / Bistro d'Agran
- 6 — Beauchamp's Mulligatawny and Song / Taming of a Stew / Shahzada Tandoori
- 7 — Miss S. Liddell Restaurant
- 9 — Octopus / Il Regalo / Chez Noel
- 11 — Caravela
- 13a — Cantina Marchigiana
- 15 — Osteria San Lorenzo / Fiddlers Three / Greek Bouzouki Restaurant By Night
- 22 — Verbanella
- 30 — Bentley's
- 31 — Borshtch'n'Tears
- 38 — Massey's Chop House / Cossacks
- 39 — Beauchamp Buttery / Trattoria La Bocca
- 46 — O Fado
- 50 — Lisboa / Luso / Algarve
- 51 — Paraguay / Pizza Oven

development over two decades, shown graphically opposite, exemplifies much that was characteristic of the trade's evolution. At number 15, Fiddlers Three, with 'whitewashed walls, scrubbed tables and a blackboard menu', predated Parkes and anticipated many similar English-style eateries, proving that 'one can eat in London very modestly, yet have decent food that is properly cooked.'[3] The Bistro d'Agran (no. 1a) had been one of the first Chelsea 'bistros' on its original site in Pavilion Road, offering 'spaghetti Bolognese, corn on the cob, whitebait' when such items were delicacies.[4] Massey's Chop House (no. 38) had pioneered the charcoal grill in London. The creation of a former wing commander, it exemplified the adventurous amateurism that would drive much of the 1960s restaurant expansion, though by the late 1960s it belonged to the Forte group.[5] Verbanella (no. 30) and the Great American Disaster (no. 9) also belonged to chains, the latter being, in the early 1970s, one of the first to offer the 'genuine' American burger to a community disenchanted with Wimpy Bars.[6] The Osteria San Lorenzo (no. 22) had opened in 1963, seeking to emulate the small-scale Italian trattoria in a city whose experience of Italian cuisine had previously been largely confined to Soho.[7] By the late 1970s, though, Italian was only one among many varieties of national cuisine evident in this one street, which offered Greek, Indian, Russian, Portuguese and, briefly, Paraguayan food. The Paraguay, like the similarly short-lived Cossacks, Mulligatawny and Song, and Il Regalo, demonstrate the precarious existence of many restaurants, but the overall picture is one of sustained expansion, even in the face of the economic difficulties of the 1970s.

With bistros cheap and dear, trattorie, a burger house and several ethnic restaurants, Beauchamp Place epitomised the growth of the catering trade in London over two decades. Restaurants characterised 'the swinging city' just as boutiques and discotheques did, sustained generally by the affluence of the time but dependent individually on consumer whim. Thus the pattern exemplified at Beauchamp Place was not just one of expansion but also one of diversification, as a previously rather staid trade sought to keep pace with the dictates of fashion. Restaurateurs responded not just to 'demand' but to an unpredictable variety of demands. The process by which London's restaurant scene assumed in these years a shape recognisable today was not straightforward, but underlying it all was the consumer power characteristic of the modern affluent city.

New Directions

In 1964 the journalist Quentin Crewe took the pop singer Sandie Shaw to dine at the Mirabelle in Mayfair—a place 'for birds of passage rich enough not to mind the number of feathers they leave behind them.' The ensuing Eliza Doolittle episode gave Crewe good copy. Shaw had been brought up in working-class Dagenham and worked as a clerk at Ford's before her singing career took off. Unsophisticated but unimpressionable, she scrutinised the menu undeferentially, questioning the concept of caviar in a manner unfamiliar at the Mirabelle: she did not want to eat 'fishes' eggs', and 'in any case, it's silly to pay all that.' She also observed that nobody appeared happy: 'Don't the waiters ever smile? Aren't they allowed to? Or the other people?' Even in the sixties, dinner at a leading West End restaurant was no laughing matter.[8]

If Shaw felt out of place, it was because London's élite diners did indeed form something of a closed circle. Mario Gallati, proprietor of the Caprice in St James's, compared his restaurant to a club: 'most of our patrons have been coming here for years, and everybody seems to know everybody else.'[9] Simone Prunier, who had presided over the establishment of the London branch of the Parisian Maison Prunier in 1935, saw her customers in 1970 as 'an élite. A small section of the population with very definite tastes, habits and demands.'[10] Those demands might be quite traditional. Gallati, who was one of the people responsible for the return of haute cuisine to postwar London, recalled that many of his celebrity customers insisted on English staples: 'Christina Foyle['s] favourite dish is steak and kidney pie. . . . Jack Hylton adores tripe and onions. . . . Baron Rothschild . . . loves treacle tart and roly-poly pudding.'[11] As this suggests, austerity had eroded London's standing as an international culinary centre, but its élite restaurants retained the formality and snobbery of prewar dining: as one anonymous diner put it, 'in London you put on formal dress to have Welsh Rarebit.'[12] Dress codes were applied with varying degrees of moral suasion, particularly to women,[13] along with often arbitrary rules about the food itself ('"The lobster is never hot," [Crewe] was told in tones which a duchess might use if she saw someone polishing the gold plate with Vim').[14] In a withering review in the midsixties, generally held to have initiated the modern practice of restaurant criticism, Crewe depicted the combination of opulence and infantilisation involved in lunch at Wilton's

Franco Lagattolla (*left*) and Mario Cassandro, who opened the Trattoria Terrazza in Romilly Street, Soho, in 1959. (Illustrated London News, Ltd/Mary Evans Picture Library)

in St James, where 'waitresses dressed like nannies' served 'nursery food plus caviar, oysters and lobsters' to the aristocracy.[15]

Unsurprisingly, when the trade did expand on the back of postwar affluence, the growth in number of restaurants went hand in hand with a rejection of old modes of dining—including by younger members of the élite—in favour of informality and innovation. The most heralded part of this upheaval was the 'trattoria revolution' initiated by Mario Cassandro and Franco Lagattolla with the Trattoria Terrazza, opened in Romilly Street, Soho, in 1959. The small-scale Italian restaurant is now so familiar in Britain that it is hard to comprehend the originality of Mario and Franco's (as they were usually known) enterprise or the enthusiasm surrounding the Terrazza in the early 1960s. It rested on the relative novelty of Italian cuisine, but not only on the food. The entire 'offer' contributed to its success: the light and colourful interior designed by Enzo Apicella, a liberal etiquette—inaugurated serendipitously when Anthony Armstrong-Jones was admitted without a tie—a sense of attainable exclusivity and, as success bred success, the chance to glimpse Princess Margaret, Elizabeth Taylor or a Beatle.[16]

On the back of the Terrazza's success, Mario and Franco opened the Trattoo in Kensington followed by trattorie in Chancery Lane and the Edgware Road.[17] Their empire spread to Leeds and Manchester, and they contemplated expansion in the United States. They had, like many of their

Pioneer of the sixties 'Trattoria Boom', the Trattoria da Otello in Dean Street, Soho, pictured in 1960. (Mary Evans/Glasshouse Images)

compatriots, worked their way up the West End restaurant ladder, and several of *their* employees sought to emulate their success. By the 1970s seven of them ran London trattorie,[18] the best known being Alvaro Maccioni, whose Alvaro's opened in the King's Road in 1966. So fashionable were trattorie by then that Maccioni could promote his new enterprise by advertising the very exclusivity of his 'nonmembership club'—most notoriously by letting it be known that pressure of demand had forced him to go ex-directory.[19]

While the small number of fashionable trattorie caught the public eye, more representative of the trade's expansion in the early 1960s was the 'bistro'. As John Ardagh argued in 1968, 'If this city has succeeded recently in establishing a "typically London" style of restaurant, it is a "bistro"—not a bistro in the true French sense, which means a cheap workmen's café, but a small informal restaurant, usually with self-conscious décor, candlelight and tables close together, serving more or less French food to a young Chelsea style clientele.'[20] *Queen* identified a 'boom in bistros' in 1961. Fay Maschler, restaurant critic of the *Evening Standard* from 1972, remembered waitressing ten years earlier in 'one of those many bistros that were springing up then like mushrooms à la grecque.'[21] They were disproportionately located in Kensington and Chelsea, helping set the area's tone. In 1964, for

The Chelsea bistro: diners at Au Père de Nico, Lincoln Street, Chelsea, 1966. In its late-sixties/
early-seventies heyday, the bistro's known patrons included—among many other luminaries—Mick
Jagger, John Betjeman, Laurence Olivier, Malcolm Sargent, Rudolph Nureyev, Brian Rix, Susannah York,
Harold Pinter and Diana Rigg. Quentin Crewe described it as 'a friendly old joint, where the
customers are not too querulous about such things as having all their food overcooked.' (*Evening
Standard* 29 December 1971). (Illustrated London News, Ltd/Mary Evans Picture Library)

instance, Crewe depicted the 'eminently sensible new restaurant' 235 King's
in the King's Road, providing 'somewhere to eat for not much in anti-precious
surroundings.' Jokey retro décor—'oddments on the walls such as five old-
fashioned wall telephones and advertisements from pubs'—underlined this,
as did 'waiters polite without subservience and gratefully normal.' 'Anyone
in a hat would look rather ridiculous.'[22]

The 'more or less French food' in these places was frequently more English than French: Fiddlers Three in Beauchamp Place offered 'duck soup, stuffed marrow, Norfolk stew with dumplings, baked wood pigeon and . . . various fruit pies.'[23] At the Bistro d'Agran in Pavilion Road, a pioneer Chelsea bistro which Maschler thought 'largely responsible for the upsurge in eating out' in the early 1960s, the 'numerous meals . . . of paté or egg mayonnaise [were] followed by what seemed like the cheapest steak in London . . . with chips and peas and a hunk of French bread.'[24] London's bistros were small but traded on their 'intimacy.' Wedged into the interstices of the city, in basements or down alleyways, they were easy to set up. Whereas the trattorie were generally run by men who had served a traditional apprenticeship in West End hotels or restaurants, bistro proprietors, animated by what Crewe called the 'curious passion which those who are successful in other fields have for opening restaurants',[25] often had little catering experience. Nick Clarke, who founded the successful Nick's Diner in Chelsea, was a former guardsman; Ray Parkes had trained as an architect. The bistro 235 King's, with 'Victorian-cum-French-surrealist' décor and 'vivacious and mini-skirted' waitresses, was founded 'for the fun of it' in 1965 by a twenty-five-year-old ex-Gurkha officer.[26] The Chelsea bistros were the culinary equivalent of the King's Road boutiques, mushrooming because they required little capital or prior experience and sustained, for most of the sixties, by an apparently unlimited demand.

Precarious Expansion

In 1974, Joseph Berkmann, of the Genevieve group, looked back wistfully to the previous decade, when restaurateurs had had a 'licence to print money.'[27] It had been evident even then, though, that easy entry to the trade placed most establishments under constant pressure. In January 1965 Crewe had warned of London's 'almost ridiculous proliferation of restaurants.' 'There are certainly far more of them than makes economic sense', John Ardagh wrote in 1968: 'now that Londoners have discovered the delights of the palate, every would-be restaurateur is keen to make hay.'[28] Crewe's in-tray was 'piled with eager letters from people who have just opened "what we think is the answer to a long-felt need—an intimate little place, with all the trimmings of *haute cuisine*, with unusual dishes to satisfy jaded palates and slender purses."' In practice, he knew, 'it will be something for which no-one feels a need—another cramped little joint', hoping to convince Chelsea's gourmands that 'a banana, some chunks of pineapple and a few nuts [could] make drab old veal palatable.'[29] Three years later, still more jaded, Crewe suggested that 'the multiplicity of restaurants makes one feel that instead of there being 1500 little places, London is served by about six enormous restaurants chopped up into small rooms', identical in décor and cuisine.[30]

The effects of competition were aggravated by problems specific to the late 1960s. The Wilson government's Selective Employment Tax in 1966 was widely resented in the trade.[31] The swelling London property bubble left restaurants vulnerable if leases fell in or they found themselves in a redevelopment area: the *Evening Standard*'s Simon Jenkins pointed out that small businesses like restaurants lacked the protection enjoyed by the individual tenant against the vagaries of the property market, with rent likely to rise tenfold on the expiry of a ten-year lease.[32]

Above all, restaurants faced growing difficulty in recruiting and retaining qualified staff. The British hotel and catering industry was said to lack fifty thousand skilled workers—from chefs to chambermaids—in 1970.[33] Richard Kotas, studying restaurant economics in these years, found staff turnover to be three times higher in catering than in manufacturing industry.[34] Catering-school students wished to go straight into management—few aspired to be chefs and none waiters.[35] Simone Prunier, one of the instigators of the London Restaurants Training Group in the midsixties, described how both the trainees sponsored by her restaurant in 1968 had rapidly left the industry—one to become a farmhand, the other a shop assistant.[36]

Competition impeded attempts to pass on costs. Kotas's study of seventy-four restaurants across Britain showed that while provincial restaurants had raised prices by 71.2 percent between 1962 and 1971, London prices had risen by only 55.3 percent.[37] Hence restaurateurs' efforts to be distinctive. They knew that restaurants which became 'in' could flourish while they remained fashionable. There was, though, no recipe for fashionability. Celebrity customers might help: Gallati's autobiography is a catalogue of the famous whom he had fed. The unpretentious Polish bistro 555 in Battersea started as a South London *restaurant du quartier*, but once discovered by the pacesetters from north of the river, it acquired a cachet which attracted Vivien Leigh, Jane Asher and the Beatles. Their patronage further reinforced the place's magnetism.[38]

Inventive cooking might help. Peter Langan, Robert Carrier and Justin de Blank all made their names in 1960s London. But the scope for shaping taste was limited. Admittedly London's culinary revolution had produced a market for transient fads, as Maschler suggested in a 1973 review: 'Anything made with kippers is *de rigueur*.... Steak au poivre has made a comeback, but it must be with *green* peppercorns. In fact any dish made with green peppercorns is smart but beginning to be a little predictable. Up-and-coming numbers: deep-fried mushrooms; cassoulet; venison and a wider use of pickled herrings.'[39] Restaurateurs tried to ride this whirlwind—'no matter what the current food gimmick is we have it on our menu', one of the co-owners of the Bistro d'Agran admitted guilelessly in 1974[40]—but aping modish menus would not necessarily guarantee a competitive edge. Too many chefs experimented with dishes more quirky than appealing. Crewe noted in 1971 that British cuisine had responded to affluence not by emulating French sophistication but by courting novelty through improbable combinations: 'mutton and marshmallow, pheasant and gorgonzola, mayonnaise and coffee, haddock and gooseberries. Every wretched place made its already nauseating cooking that much nastier by adding what it fancied was an exotic touch.'[41] By 1972 even the inventive Tom Benson had vexed *The Good Food Guide* with 'food more original-for-originality's sake than delicious.'[42]

Designers were similarly torn between catching a trend and offering something distinctive. It was well known that Apicella's unmistakeable style—'the rough terracotta floor; the heavy hewn monastic chairs; the white vaulted ceilings, splashed with sunlight'—had contributed to the appeal of the new trattorie.[43] By contrast, the sombre red and purple interiors of David Mlinaric targeted another distinct clientele, as at the suggestively named Rupert in Chelsea, patronised by 'dashing blades, tally-hos and stiff collars.'[44] Linda Blandford, reviewing for *Queen* in 1968, saw the ascetic exterior of the short-lived Cramps in the New King's Road as a pitch to 'the almost-in-crowd' of Parsons Green: 'the outside is a blank brown wall with red lettering. It gives nothing away—not even how to get in.'[45] Gradually sixties bistro style yielded to a more homely look, 'symbolised by a potted palm, a bentwood chair or a William Morris print.' By the midseventies 'every hairdressers' shop, restaurant and Hampstead living room looked like a conservatory.'[46] Flip names like 'Cramps' were another element of sixties restaurant branding. Jabberwocky, which opened in Belgravia in 1959, resembled 'many establishments which supply good, French-influenced food in rather cramped quarters',[47] but it stood out for its name alone, highly idiosyncratic for that time. By the early seventies 'restaurants with names like Gulpers and Knackers', Maschler suggested, were de rigueur, replacing the cosy French titles—'Au Petit Coin de Vieux Provence'—of the bistro wave.[48]

A distinctive niche market might offer some security, most obviously in the burgeoning demand for vegetarian or health food. Patrons might be less flighty than most if they had been attracted by, for instance, an aversion to factory farming or specifically drawn to South Asian vegetarian cooking by the hippie spiritual enthusiasms of the sixties, as at Guru Nanak's

Conscious Cookery in Notting Hill (where a group of American Sikh converts offered 'mystical-vegetarian food to hip Londoners') or the Hindu vegetarian Hare Krishna Curry House in Hanway Street.[49] But the economics of vegetarian restaurants made it difficult to enlarge the core market. Diners were frequently reluctant to pay much for vegetables, even though the overheads which comprised the bulk of a restaurant's costs were no lower for vegetarian establishments than for anybody else, and those ascetics who spurned meat often spurned alcohol, which provided most restaurants with their profits.[50]

In the last resort there remained the pure gimmick. Some Italian restaurants rejected the conventional 'Chianti-bottle fishing-net syndrome' in favour of spurious antiquity.[51] The Roman Room, in the Brompton Road, was 'aggressively Roman with pillars, statues, enormous candles burning on the tables, waiters clad in the appropriate style and one delectable girl slave', who was said (unusually for a slave girl) to be 'a real Roman Citizen.'[52] SPQR in Dean Street offered hors d'oeuvres Brutus and Avocado Julius Caesar. 'If ancient Rome was like this', Crewe mused, 'one can see why the Greeks thought it vulgar.'[53] The crudest marketing initiative, in a trade fast losing its reputation for finesse, was that of the club-restaurant Brush and Palette in Queensway, which engaged 'a group of delectable girls who pose very decently and properly in the nude for the amateur artists in the restaurant to paint or draw.' The proprietor claimed that Picasso had eaten there, though he left no sketches.[54]

The alchemy ensuring success was impossible to specify. It depended, as Maschler put it, on 'a combination of decor, location, staff, the customers who are attracted, prices and, to a varying (and sometimes small) extent, the food.'[55] 'There is nothing strikingly evident to make Daphne's [in South Kensington] into a fashionable restaurant', Crewe wrote in 1966, two years after it opened. The food, though good, was expensive, and the place was cramped; 'yet the restaurant is packed every night with just the people restaurants like to attract. It is just that Daphne knows she is going to succeed.'[56] Daphne Ainley's confidence was justified: she was able to sell the restaurant within two years,[57] and it survives today. But fashion could be fickle. Linda Blandford remembered that when she had arrived in London in 1961, the grill house Charco's, off the King's Road, was 'the place every girl yearned to be taken to as proof that she had Made It.' In 1959 The Good Food Guide had indeed noted that Charco's 'bursts its bonds onto the pavement whenever the weather permits, and is still crowded', but by 1968 Blandford found the food dry and the service casual, and it scarcely figures in guides from the late sixties.[58]

Surviving the Seventies

Put simply, the trade was overstocked, and by the late 1960s costs were rising still faster than demand.[59] Many restaurateurs underestimated catering's perils, and the trade was characterised by recurrent openings and closures. In 1975 Maschler described the recent history of Langton Street, Chelsea:

> At no 5 . . . there's a restaurant called La Famiglia. It used to be called Le Routier. Le Routier is now at no 7 . . . where, if you had popped in a year or so ago, you would have found De Marco's. If De Marco's means nothing to you, perhaps the Chelsea Nuthouse rings a bell. That's what De Marco's used to be called. At 1a . . . there's a place called Zia Sophia. The residents can tell you about a time when this was called World's End One. Some recollect the days (numbered) of Bumbles "B". And old-timers reminisce about that period when it was called, appropriately some thought, Get Stuffed. Langton Street SW10 has seen more restaurants than you have had hot dinners.[60]

By 1975 the problems afflicting the London trade in the late sixties had been compounded by inflation and economic upheaval: Mike Bygrave and Joan Goodman listed thirteen new restaurants in the second edition of their *Fuel Food* in 1975, only to find that two of the additions had folded before it appeared.[61] Restaurants could only attempt to contain costs. The trade press, aimed at institutional caterers as much as restaurants, championed frozen or even canned vegetables,[62] and many restaurants evidently succumbed, even though cheap ingredients invited scathing reviews. Meanwhile waiting became largely casualised, as Kotas pointed out, with restaurateurs employing 'retired persons, students, married women, casual employees, etc', and skimping on pay and fringe benefits. When Justin de Blank wanted to staff his new restaurant in Duke Street in 1973, he approached the Universities Appointments Board for names of undergraduates who had failed their exams.[63] 'We certainly get what we pay for', Kotas concluded;[64] increasingly astringent reviewers castigated service that was 'more willing than efficient', particularly when the use of migrant labour added a language barrier to the regular drawbacks ('at the moment fluent Spanish helps').[65]

Even the élite establishments felt the pinch in the seventies. As Simone Prunier lamented, 'unlike the mass caterer we have no room for manoeuvre, no convenience foods to turn to, no gimmicks, no real labour-saving methods.'[66] The rapporteurs for James Sherwood's London guide in 1975 noted 'suspiciously brilliant orange carrots' served by the Connaught Hotel restaurant near Grosvenor Square, generally reckoned to serve the best haute cuisine in London.[67] La Toque Blanche, created by the Kensington French community and the first English restaurant to gain a Michelin star, made a virtue of necessity by using asterisks in its menu to distinguish fresh from frozen or canned vegetables.[68] The cost of dining in such places ensured that any corner-cutting brought loud criticism. The 1977 edition of *The Good Food Guide*, compiled, as always, from reports by members of the dining public, caused a stir by attacking L'Étoile, Rules and the 'glorified chop house' of Simpson's-in-the-Strand, along with the Savoy for its 'overcooked gigot and "foul" jugged hare.'[69] Prunier had been lauded for its efforts to maintain Parisian standards, but it folded in 1976. 'Many fine restaurants were swept away in the financial downpour', as Christopher Driver noted in *The Good Food Guide*.[70]

Nonetheless, élite restaurants were best placed to weather the storm. They attracted a clientele whose conception of dining out was an opulent one and who would linger over a meal. 'More leisured meals promote conversation, a sense of well being', Prunier explained in 1970, 'which in turn means more "extras" sold—wines, liqueurs, cigars, coffee. And it is here where the extra profit lies.'[71] Affluent customers paid larger tips, subsidising wages and helping restaurants to retain skilled staff. In a trade characterised by casualisation and high labour turnover, fifteen of the staff at Scott's seafood restaurant in Piccadilly in 1968 were said to have worked there for twenty years.[72] Kotas's work on London restaurants in the midsixties demonstrated a positive correlation between the spending power of customers and turnover per seat. He noted in 1975 that restaurants with richer patrons could raise prices by even 10 percent without deterring clients.[73] A 10 percent rise might still have been inadequate at a time when inflation stood at twice that level and food prices rose by more than 18 percent,[74] but places with less well-heeled clients found difficulty raising prices at all.

Crewe suggested in 1968 that with competition forcing the 'old monsters' of the restaurant world to raise their game, their intrinsic advantages would see them prevail.[75] The Caprice, the Connaught, L'Escargot, Kettner's, Rules, the Savoy, Scott's, Simpson's and Wilton's survive today, having long outlived Parkes and the Trattoria Terrazza. By the late sixties, indeed, reviewers were disenchanted with the chic trattorie. Crewe maintained that their fashionability had turned them into 'highly expensive, pretentious, snobbish restaurants', betraying their original aims.[76] The ambition of Mario and Franco to instil a taste for their native cuisine encountered twin obstacles: the critical consensus that 'Italian cooking, being basically bourgeois and simple, is not suited to this treatment'[77] and the culinary conservatism of many of those who were able to afford the trendier trattorie. Surveying in 1974 the selections made by customers at the Terrazza in the fifteen years of its operation, Lagattolla acknowledged the limits to the restaurant's educative efforts. While cauliflower and other English vegetables were being gradually supplanted by aubergines and courgettes (in 1959, Lagattolla said, 'we could not sell a courgette to save our lives'), customers remained wedded to beef—35 percent of all main-course orders—and Dover sole, despite the predominance of veal and chicken dishes on the menu.[78] Just as Jack Hylton had once gone to the Caprice to eat tripe and onions, so diners drawn by the allure of the Terrazza asked chefs from the Amalfi Coast to produce beef and roast potatoes. Eventually many doubtless concluded that they might have fared better at the Savoy. Going public in 1968 made Cassandro and Lagattolla millionaires, but a fall in the group's profits in 1969 foreshadowed problems to come.[79] The 1970s proved difficult for the chic trattorie; tellingly, James Sherwood's *Guide* noted in 1975 that Alvaro's—ostentatiously ex-directory in 1966—had shed its previous 'arrogant and unwelcoming' approach,[80] unable to risk alienating custom.

Parkes also fell from favour. Unanimously praised in the sixties, it incurred sharp criticism in the 1972 *Good Food Guide*. In 1977 the restaurant often credited as the British pioneer of *cuisine minceur* received a damning review in the French Gault-Millau London guide.[81] Parkes had epitomised the bistro wave of the 1960s, and its problems were amplified in the numerous Chelsea eateries offering similar food in similarly restricted premises, catering for young couples and young lovers more than business lunchers or big spenders. Economically the small bistro was a flawed model, characterised by a high ratio of staff to turnover without the long hours or the rapid throughput of customers that benefited fast-food establishments. By the mid-1970s the bistro was in decline, 'too expensive for a casual visit', Maschler argued, 'and not quite good enough . . . for a special occasion.'[82]

Fast Food

In 1974 Langan described restaurant economics as a matter of the survival of the fittest.[83] Survival often entailed loss of independence, as restaurants were absorbed by chains.[84] The Wheeler's chain, for instance, 'specialise[d] in taking on restaurants that are doing poorly and making them pay.' It owned eleven establishments by 1970, expanding from the original oyster bar in Old Compton Street. It centralised the purchase of all food and the manufacture of restaurant fittings and recruited Chinese chefs and kitchen staff.[85] The cheaper restaurant chains, devoted to the dependable provision of a single type of food, operated on similar lines—the Angus Steak Houses, the various components of the Spaghetti House brand and the rapidly proliferating pizza chains (by 1977 there were six branches of Pizza Hut, thirteen of Pizza Express and twenty-three of Pizzaland in London).[86] At Pizza Express, 'They all produce identical pizzas, which is not too difficult because the dough is made at a central kitchen; the cooks in each restaurant weigh it out in equal amounts, press it into pie tins, sprinkle handfuls of prescribed fillings on top and bake them, thirty at a time if need be, at incredible speed.'[87] London's burger houses likewise obtained their meat from the same butcher in the 1970s, G. W. Biggs in York Way, so that, as Bygrave commented, 'the search for the "best hamburger in London" is an elusive one.'[88]

Burger houses, 'as much meeting places as places to eat', as Bygrave noted, had 'become for the 1970s what bistros were for the 1960s—cheap, reliable places for young people to go, somewhere between a café and a real restaurant.'[89] And as bistros dwindled, the 'good traditional English chop houses, tea houses or restaurants with dinners of roasts, grills and steak and kidney puddings for under £2 have absolutely vanished.'[90] This silent revolution, as Bygrave hinted, partly reflected a generational shift of taste: young Londoners found chop houses passé until they became so rare as to be interesting again.[91] The chains also profited, though, by providing food of a dependable quality previously lacking in cheap catering. As early as 1959 Raymond Postgate had explained the success of the first Angus Steak Houses: 'the proprietors have merely secured a supply of the best Scotch beef, hung it properly, and grilled it correctly.' It was 'disgraceful that [this] should be regarded as a new principle in catering . . . but it is so.'[92] According to The Good Food Guide to London in 1968, if you 'squeeze yourself down at a shared table among the medical students and typists' at the Pizza House in Goodge Street, 'a swift, red-jacketed ragazza will slap in front of you a very good pizza.'[93] Nine years later Bygrave praised the first Burger King, in Coventry Street, and similar American arrivals, including McDonald's; Irene Pylypec, a Canadian landing in London in 1975, soon learned that 'according to Londoners, it's worth it to splurge on McDonald's rather than buying Britain's own tasteless Wimpy Burger.'[94] Dependent on rapid turnover, such places emphasised the takeaway trade, so that those who wished to linger faced 'plastic, spartan discomfort', but 'they achieve their basic aims: excellent value at rock bottom prices, total cleanliness and speed of service.'[95] If reviewers felt uncomfortable about the chains' predictability, they seldom disparaged their food.

Reviewers' concern was rather that however worthy the cheap pizza or burger houses might be, the process of commercialisation behind their rise also threatened standards in conventional restaurants. Maschler described a 'disastrous meal' at the previously well-regarded Le Carrosse in Chelsea after its takeover by Empire Foods, owners of the Wimpy Bar chain. As she pointed out, restaurants' ultimate owners might not even be primarily catering concerns: 'probing into the ownerships of innocent looking places in London can reveal Dog Food Manufacturers or Record Companies in the background.'[96] She lamented an 'almost inevitable relaxation of standards' when 'a company rather than a dedicated individual is in control.'[97] Christopher Driver, editor of *The Good Food Guide* in the 1970s, associated this drop in quality with chains' centralising methods. The managers of the Wheeler's restaurants, he noted, could not answer the *Guide*'s questionnaire without referring it to head office, 'so it is not surprising that few local initiatives are taken with the cooking.'[98] Many reviewers feared a homogenisation similar to that developing in the cartelised brewing industry.

In reality this standardisation was less of a threat than it appeared. Formulaic production methods worked well in fast-food outlets where they were justified by cheapness and convenience, but they were out of place anywhere more sophisticated. Moreover, the capital's size produced local variations working against standardisation. Crewe described perceptively the failure of the Bienvenue chain's branch in the Brompton Road in 1965. The parent company had hoped to establish thirty-two restaurants across the country, with identical menus, so that 'faithful patrons of the Liverpool one will feel at home in the Glasgow one.' The food was good, but Crewe explained why it shut after five months: 'Each district of London can support a seemingly enormous number of restaurants. But they must conform to the customs of the district. Chelsea and Kensington do not like large restaurants. The *Bienvenue* was too big. Diners go to Chelsea for intimacy. They require that a restaurant should have a proprietor who is always there. . . . On the whole if people want to spend more money they will go to the West End. The food may be no better, but they are consciously living it up.'[99] Culinary conservatism in the City allowed restaurants to serve 'barely edible food'—'the punishment that British financiers take for being rich',

Driver believed.[100] Humphrey Lyttelton, reviewing for *Queen*, concluded that 'the inhabitants of Hampstead will indeed eat anything so long as it is presented in a pretentious way',[101] which at least ensured that they remained wedded to culinary individualism; they would maintain a decade-long resistance to McDonald's in the 1980s.

Diversity

Gradually, too, individual parts of London gained discernible ethnic identities. Soho had been dominated by Italian restaurants for half a century or more.[102] The first cluster of Indian restaurants appeared in Whitfield Street and neighbouring parts of Fitzrovia in the early 1960s, while the beginnings of the modern Asian concentration in Brick Lane were evident by the mid-1970s.[103] The two most visible clusters emerging in the 1960s, though, were the Greek-Cypriots in Charlotte Street and the new Chinatown which came together almost overnight after 1966 in South Soho, centred on Gerrard Street.

Charlotte Street in Fitzrovia had long been a magnet for southern European migrants. Mario Gallati, himself a settler there in 1903, remembered it providing 'the immigrant Italians [with] a constant reminder of home', with English rarely spoken.[104] It had also long boasted Continental restaurants—Schmidt's German restaurant, 'like one of those vast caverns that surround somewhere like Munich Station', and Bertorelli's, serving Italian meals to 'minor authors, publishers and other Bloomsburians'.[105] The Italian-run French restaurant L'Etoile, at number 30, offered dowdy décor and high-quality food.[106] In 1963 the Spaghetti House chain sought to cash in on the trattoria boom by opening its Trattoria dei Pescatori at number 57. By then, though, Charlotte Street was predominantly Greek, the transformation having begun during the Second World War as Soho's Italians were interned.[107] The chart on page 112 shows the emergence of a cluster of Greek restaurants in the 1960s, 'casual, cheap, friendly',[108] with an ambience appreciated by the host community. 'The English love it', Bygrave and Goodman wrote of Anemos, at number 34, in 1973; even with a reservation, 'you need to be prepared to wait—standing—for up to forty-five minutes for a table.'[109] Greek restaurants' un-English habit of placing tables on the street in summer reminded patrons that this was one of London's quirkier, more cosmopolitan locales: 'watching Charlotte Street pass is still London's best cabaret', Simon Jenkins observed.[110]

Charlotte Street scene in 1969. The Venus Kebab House, like several of Fitzrovia's Greek restaurants, encouraged diners with vivid imaginations to eat outside and dream that they were in the Mediterranean. Schmidt's German restaurant is on the left-hand side of the street. The Post Office Tower (now BT Tower) was among the modern buildings most favoured by the London public. (Mary Evans Picture Library)

Gerrard Street was the heart of the new Soho Chinatown.[111] The postwar Chinese community was produced by emigration from Hong Kong following the collapse of agriculture there in the 1950s, and many of the émigrés entered catering. Chinese restaurateurs initially settled in the suburbs, safely distant from one another. London had around two hundred Chinese restaurants in the early 1960s,[112] but they were scattered, as were its five thousand or so Chinese. The formation of the Soho Chinatown represented a spontaneous attempt to provide a gathering place for this community, with Chinese supermarkets, hairdressers, a travel agency, a dentist, minicab operators, clubs and, of course, restaurants, which served as the principal foci.[113] The first 'truly authentic Cantonese restaurant' in London—the Canton— had opened in neighbouring Newport Place in the late 1950s.[114] Twenty years later there were eight Chinese restaurants in Gerrard Street alone, with others in nearby Lisle Street, Rupert Street and Shaftesbury Avenue. The chart on page 113 plots the transformation of Gerrard Street.

It had long been possible to find exotic or unfamiliar cuisines in London: diversity predated postwar immigration. The first West End Chinese restaurant, the Cathay in Glasshouse Street, opened in 1908.[115] London's first Indian restaurant, Salut e Hind in Holborn, opened in 1911, followed by the Shafi in 1920 and Veeraswamy in Regent Street in 1926.[116] The first German restaurant on the site eventually occupied by Schmidt's in Charlotte Street opened in 1901.[117] Spanish restaurants became popular in the 1920s; one of the pioneers, Martinez in Swallow Street, would survive until 1988.[118] London's best-known Greek restaurant, the White Tower in Percy Street, was founded in 1938. Russian and eastern European restaurants spread after 1945. They were usually patronised by émigrés or refugees from communism (Maschler found London's Russian restaurants in 'perpetual mourning for the demise of Czar Nicholas', while *Time Out*'s Sue Miles encountered 'the last of the Free Polish Army' at Daquise in South Kensington),[119] though the best-known central European restaurant, the Gay Hussar in Greek Street, was created by the Swiss/Welsh Hungarophile Victor Sassie, moved by the belief that '*coq au vin* is the worst dish in the world.'[120]

Catering attracted immigrants; it had long been an entry trade. It offered an outlet for the entrepreneurial talent of those like the flamboyant Latvian Benny Taylor, who came to England in 1945 and, after dabbling with ice cream parlours and junk shops, struck gold with the eastern European restaurant Borshtch'n'Tears in Beauchamp Place in 1965.[121] Others took up catering *faute de mieux*, like Cheng Looi, proprietor of the Chinese

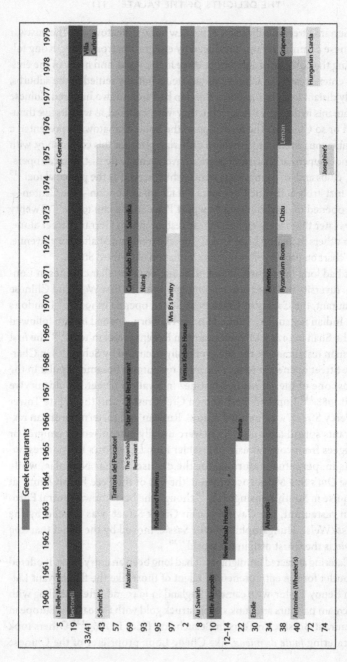

Charlotte Street, W1: restaurants (Greek restaurants in red).

Gerrard Street, W1: restaurants, 1960–1979 (Chinese restaurants in blue).

The chart shows, by street number, the following restaurants and years of operation:

No.	Restaurant	Years
7	Champagne Inn	1970
7	Gerrard Chinese restaurant	1976
7	Dragongate	1978
8	Curry Centre	1960
8	Trattoria Grotta Azurra	1963
8	Halal Centre	1978
11	Tin Luk	1966
13	Mandarin	1961
13	Sun Wah	1965
13	Far East	1966
15a	Luigi's	1960
15a	Dumpling Inn	1967
16	El Morocco	1965
16	Lee Ho Fook	1968
18	Shaffi's Indian Restaurant	1962
22	Chu Chin Chow	1968
22	Kowloon	1971
22	Lucky	1974
27	Boulogne	1961
27	Loon Fung	1968
27	Kowloon	1977
37/8	La Reserve	1960
37/8	Cunningham's Oyster Bar	1964
40	Cafe Portugal	1964
40	Ganges	1966
41	Lido	1970
42	Peter Mario	1960

Lantern in Thackeray Street, who had aspired to become a film producer but concluded that "that is not so much a calling for a Oriental person."[122] For decades, though, most of these immigrants had attempted to replicate familiar culinary traditions. Thus the Greek-Cypriots frequently running workmen's cafés in the 1950s 'aimed to please British tastes with British food like liver and onions.'[123] The many Italian immigrants working in London's élite establishments generally accepted that theirs was a French milieu. 'Being an Italian, I like Italian food', Gallati admitted, but 'any restaurant in the world which aspires to give its clients *haute cuisine* must serve French food.'[124] At the Etoile in Charlotte Street, 'a classic French restaurant with a Portuguese chef', the eight waiters were German, Cypriot and Italian, but the lingua franca of the kitchen was French.[125]

Thus while London had long had a smattering of foreign restaurants, and many of its immigrants had long sought to make a living in catering, these two realities had not combined to produce the culinary diversity that might have been anticipated. This was what Mario and Franco had sought to change when they first contemplated starting an authentic Italian restaurant in the early 1950s, 'to compete in cuisine, wines and prices with the finest French haute cuisine restaurants in London.'[126] This proved overambitious, as has been argued, but the sixties vogue for the chic trattorie did encourage both the spread of middlebrow Italian restaurants in London and the understanding that a meal out did not have to be 'franglais' in origin.

British diners were not as insular as many people believed: 51 percent of respondents in the 1966 National Catering Inquiry claimed to have eaten in a 'foreign' restaurant.[127] But the belief that unfamiliar dishes would have to be 'anglicised' to appeal to the host community took a long time to die. The early Chinese restaurateurs felt that their suburban customers would feel more comfortable with pseudo-Chinese dishes such as chop suey— 'not so much Chinese as San Francisco, this dish with vegetables topped with an omelette, but no worse for it', as the reviewer for *Where to Go* gamely reported in 1967.[128] In the 1960s many restaurants offered mixed menus. The fundamentally English offering in Italian-run workmen's cafés might be augmented by basic Italian dishes, as at Alfonso Ruocco's Frank's Café in Neal Street, where 'ravioli, spaghetti and risotto . . . figure on the menu, which also offers very good British working man's fare.'[129] Genuinely 'ethnic' restaurants continued to offer dishes assumed to be congenial to timid English diners: in 1967, for example, John West sampled chicken Maryland and mixed grill at Au Caprice des Dieux, a Cypriot-owned restaurant with a French name, offering, as he charitably put it, 'basically Greek food, with a slight continental ambience.'[130]

This approach was undermined by the growing sophistication of London diners. Those wedded to conventional British food were unlikely to find it at its best in restaurants unversed in producing it: 'I don't see the point of going to a Turkish place to eat steak', as Sue Miles wrote in *Time Out* in 1975.[131] And London's *bon viveurs* were becoming increasingly curious about unfamiliar food. Reviewing the Dania in Brixton in 1966, *London Life* advised its readers to 'stick to the national [i.e., Danish] dishes', since 'there are few enough Scandinavian restaurants in this country', even if this one offered 'chips with everything.'[132] 'A new awareness is breaking down barriers and making people more adventurous in what they choose to eat', the manager of the China Garden in Brewer Street told Christopher Gower in 1968.[133] Restaurateurs gradually responded by phasing out mundane English dishes: 'one item that is beginning to disappear from the menus of Indian restaurants is Omelette, Chips and Peas', Maschler noted in 1973, a development she attributed to 'the huge improvement in quality and appeal of what has been a much misunderstood cuisine.'[134]

In 1974 Stavros Georgiou renovated the 'working man's caff' that he had run in Shaftesbury Avenue since 1947. It was 'enlarged, redecorated and went Greek.'[135] Six years earlier, 'Tino', proprietor of the Costa del Sol in the Fulham Road, had transformed his snack bar into 'an elegant dining place with distinctive Spanish cuisine', including the 'Basque country delicacy of hake fish gills.' By then an ethnic eatery made better commercial sense than a 'greasy spoon', as the exotic was recognised as marketable.[136] Tino dressed his waiters in matador costumes costing, he claimed, £200 each in 1968.[137] The (British) Golden Egg Group bolstered its risky entry into Indian cuisine at the Mumtaz in Haymarket with abundant cultural clichés: 'a turbaned doorman, a dark entrance lined with Indian silk, a terracotta statue of an Indian lady and a temple frieze. All this before you get into the restaurant.'[138] The Busabong Thai, in the Fulham Road, hoped that 'Thai classical dances and sword fighting' would attract customers to a still unfamiliar cuisine.[139]

If ethnic food was marketed by parody, the food itself was initially something of a pastiche. Although the trattoria pioneers in the late 1950s had aimed to introduce authentic Italian food to Britain, when Antonio Carluccio arrived in the 1970s, he found that 'Italian food here was very much "Britalian" food.'[140] In particular, regional differences within Italian cuisine were smothered, as an unvarying 'Britalian' culinary identity emerged. Retiring as the *Evening Standard*'s restaurant critic in 1972, Crewe felt that the hardest part of his job had been 'thinking of some new thing to say about the 15th little Italian restaurant with white arches and a red-tiled floor, which cooks very nice spaghetti alle vongole and veal pizzaiola.'[141] Similarly with Indian food. The days when 'curry' amounted to a routine meat stew doused in curry powder passed in the mid-1960s with the introduction of the tandoori oven.[142] This improved Indian restaurant food significantly, so that 'even Indians eat it now',[143] but also had a homogenising effect: Bygrave and Goodman thought it 'pretty profitless to try to track London's Indian restaurants to their Indian roots.'[144] English assumptions that Indian food should be hot meant that restaurants used 'much more spicing" in Britain than in India, as the manager of the Standard in Westbourne Grove told Bygrave in 1973,[145] while Asian views of the English as meat eaters marginalised India's subtle vegetarian cuisine.[146]

Authenticity

The tide turned first in the Chinese sector. The trend towards what Ardagh identified as '"Anglo-Chinese mish-mash" adapted to English tastes' was halted by the emergence of the Soho Chinatown.[147] The suburbs had already seen the introduction of authentic Pekinese cuisine in T. H. Young's Richmond Rendezvous and Kuo Teh-Lu's Kuo Yuan in Willesden,[148] but the point of Chinatown was to service the growing Chinese community not only of London but of Britain as a whole. Whereas so many ethnic restaurants targeted English diners with idealised images of the homeland, the Dumpling Inn, displacing Luigi's Italian restaurant in Gerrard Street in 1967, left the former restaurant's murals of Venice untouched.[149] That Chinatown's eateries were intended for Chinese diners was evident in the early years from menus written only in Chinese characters and from famously offhand service: English diners might be left to find their own tables or censured for not using chopsticks.[150] Loon Fung, in Gerrard Street, gained credit from *The Good Food Guide* for 'the least hostile set of waiters [in Chinatown]', the most hostile being those at the Michelin-garlanded Lee Ho Fook.[151] Maschler felt 'many excellent Chinese restaurants make it so unpleasant for the non-Chinese diner that we will settle for less good food but less overt contempt.'[152] As her comment suggests, though, the standard of the food was high, and London's culinary explorers were already hunting down authentic Chinese cooking, with the '*beau monde* oscillating ... between Limehouse and Willesden in pursuit of their spare ribs and lobster balls.'[153] Aggressive service and drab décor merely enhanced the edgy pleasure of eating 'real' Chinese food surrounded by real Chinese people.

Chinatown's explorers were briefed as if travelling in the developing world: 'None of the waiters speaks much English, so be prepared to order by number'; 'Eat like they do and what they do. Just point and ask for "some of that."'[154] The belief that these hardships represented a just price for a new culinary experience points to one advantage enjoyed by ethnic restaurants in the 1970s. The London diner, or one type of London diner—young, comfortable but not opulent, a *Time Out* rather than a *Times* reader—would allow a latitude to 'authentic' ethnic restaurants not generally extended to other places. When the Satay House in Sussex Gardens advertised itself in 1973 as the only Malaysian restaurant in London offering traditional Kelantan food, most English customers were in no position to argue. The Andalucia in Hampstead even traded on the claim that 'one of the glories of Spanish eating is waiting for what you have ordered.'[155]

One early Thai restaurant, the Siam in Kensington, explained that it offered only set menus because if it 'were to offer a choice people wouldn't know which things combine well.'[156] Reviews of ethnic restaurants were as much educative as critical: '[Satay] is meat on a skewer—a kind of kebab, in fact'; 'Sashimi is raw fish, but it's delicious'; Thai food was 'a cross between Indian and Chinese cooking and better than each of them'; 'Don't confuse Japanese cooking with Chinese.'[157] Reviewers were often educating themselves. Crewe admitted in 1966, 'Few of us have the least idea what standards oriental food should conform to. I have a vague notion that there are various entirely separate *cuisines* in China—Cantonese, Peking and so on'; by 1971, he said, 'while I am learning about Chinese food, I do not pretend to know anything about Indian.'[158] Even the more streetwise Maschler admitted to being 'beguiled by . . . something called lemon grass' in 1978.[159] Reviewers fearless in offering their opinions on French or English meals clung to the received opinion that significant numbers of customers from the relevant community proved an ethnic restaurant's quality—'their large Chinese clientele must attest to something'; 'packed with families of Orientals every evening which is an indication that the food is good',[160] and so on—although minority communities were often a captive market and, as Maschler pointed out, 'even they have their equivalent of egg and chip fanciers.'[161]

Whether or not a core of 'regulars' from a minority community testified to quality, they did help protect ethnic restaurants from the winds of fashion. In the years after the establishment of the Tokkos restaurant in Maple Street in 1958, it had seen Greek restaurants proliferate around it in Fitzrovia, but, as the proprietor's son argued in 1975, 'I don't know of any restaurant in this area which lives off passing trade. We are all dependent on our regular customers, so really there's no need for any jealousy.'[162] This advantage was enjoyed most obviously by restaurateurs from the larger minority communities—South Asians, Greek Cypriots, Hong Kong Chinese—but in a highly cosmopolitan city not only by them. Clusters of students formed the original clientele for London's first Burmese restaurant, the New Burma Orient in St Giles High Street, and for the Rasa Sayang in Bateman Street.[163] Diplomats from Kensington's embassy-land sustained several national cuisines in that area: the only Vietnamese and Bulgarian restaurants in London, for instance, and the only Romanian restaurant in Britain in 1970.[164]

Affordability

Above all, ethnic restaurants offered good value. Not all were cheap, of course. The early Japanese restaurants, beginning with Hiroko in St Christopher's Place, were 'much patronised by senior Japanese businessmen', a fact reflected in prices which deterred London's hipsters and delayed the spread of Japanese cuisine until the midseventies.[165] There were, of course, upmarket options even in normally cheap cuisines, such as Michael Chow's Cantonese restaurant in Knightsbridge. The White Tower in Percy Street had been founded in 1938 as a moussaka and kebab café before its owner, John Stais, decided to 'go for quality' with an à la carte menu and expensive specials, advertising genuine Greek food in 'papers read by intellectuals.'[166] It became in Peter Langan's view 'London's greatest restaurant', attracting film stars, politicians and the ubiquitous Princess Margaret.[167] This was, though, the exception among Greek restaurants, which were normally 'the cheapest "real" restaurants in London, where you can linger over a meal, take guests and generally feel you've had a "night out."'[168] In a gentrifying city, they offered a substitute for, and an improvement on, the workmen's café. The conversion of one Cypriot-owned café in the Pentonville Road (where '99% of the cafes are the usual egg and chips variety') into a Greek restaurant, with plastic vine leaves hanging from the roof, provided 'a prayer's answer' for the beleaguered nearby journalists of *Time Out*.[169]

The economic traumas of the midseventies placed a premium on affordability. *Time Out*—aimed at the young metropolitan middle class—in its early years did not carry regular restaurant reviews, concentrating instead on home cooking. When its restaurant listings began in 1970, the emphasis was placed on value-for-money places; briefly from the summer of 1971 it graded restaurants by price.[170] Two paperback guides to affordable eateries in London appeared in these years—Bygrave and Goodman's *Fuel Food*

(1973) and Campbell and Towle's *Cheap Eats in London* (1975)—both underlining the appeal of ethnic cuisine to people with limited budgets. In 1975 *Where to Go* suggested that Indian, Chinese and Greek restaurants were 'the only ones left where two people can have a reasonable meal with a bottle of plonk for around a fiver.'[171] 'At the lower end of the price scale', Maschler argued, 'you will almost always be better off at an ethnic restaurant.'[172]

'At the end of the meal you gasp, "But how do they do it at this price?",' Valerie Jenkins of the *Evening Standard* mused apropos Greek restaurants in 1972.[173] The answer was that they were better able to contain labour costs without losing staff. Speaking in 1966, the catering industry analyst John Fuller remembered being advised decades earlier that 'the only way to succeed in this game was to marry early and have a large family to work for you.'[174] This was essentially what many ethnic restaurateurs had done. As Maschler noted, 'Chinese and Indian restaurants . . . are frequently family-run affairs, or are based on other relationships of obligation, and the overhead of staff wages is consequently lower.'[175] Family employment was implicitly exploitative, 'other relationships of obligation' more blatantly so, when staff spoke limited English, were unfamiliar with their employment rights and feared contact with officialdom. In the 1980s generational warfare would erupt within London's Chinese community as its sons and daughters, well educated and often conversant with the law, challenged the Dickensian treatment of their parents by Chinese restaurateurs—crippling working hours in steamy kitchens, nonpayment of national insurance contributions and redundancy, physically broken, in middle age.[176]

Doubtless many of London's *bien pensant* diners would have been uncomfortable to learn of the employment conditions in restaurants they patronised, but the ethnic sectors provided them with adventurous and affordable meals. Whilst these meals were generally Chinese, Indian or Greek, there was a restless consumer imperative to seek out new varieties of cuisine. Spanish, Turkish, Mexican, Russian, Polish, Thai, Malaysian, Indonesian and Japanese restaurants were relatively easy to find by the 1970s, and the properly briefed explorer could eat, for example, Korean, North African, Armenian, Afghan, Sri Lankan, Hungarian, Brazilian, Portuguese, South African, Lebanese, Iranian or Israeli food if prepared to travel around London. By the end of 1971 *Where to Go* listed restaurants representing nearly forty different national cuisines.[177] One of those cuisines was 'English'—effectively just another ethnic option. When Peter Evans's Eating House opened in 1961, claiming that 'plain English cooking [was] equal to the best anywhere',[178] some people had anticipated an English culinary renaissance, but by 1973 *Time Out* could note the scarcity of English restaurants in London.[179] Those that did not adopt such spuriosities as the 'Tudor-style banqueting room complete with a King Henry VIII' in the Tudor Room, AD 1520 in St Martin's Lane, or similar gimmickry in King Henry's Restaurant in Warwick Street,[180] generally offered 'Jorrocks food'— game pie or steak and kidney pudding, followed by treacle pudding or 'other old school ties that bind', as Maschler put it—in rooms adorned with 'all the clobber of coaching England.'[181] It is hard to imagine a French restaurant in Paris resorting to semiparodic national stereotyping in this way.

Culinary Consumerism

According to Quentin Crewe, Raymond Postgate, the Marxist founder of *The Good Food Guide*, had believed that 'socialism would mean *haute cuisine* for everybody.'[182] In the event, the culinary revolution of these years was less a socialist than a consumerist one, by which restaurants became established as a key component of the urban experience economy. The diffusion of affluence was at the root of it: as Anne Lorentzen has noted, 'the profitable trade with experiences requires a mass market.'[183] The restaurant trade had accordingly expanded rapidly on the back of sixties prosperity. The economic troubles of the midseventies culled many individual establishments, but whereas the boutique boom had been effectively extinguished by those traumas, the habit of eating out, once acquired, proved unquenchable. As Maschler noted in 1975, 'I'm always being asked if restaurants in these harsh times are nearly empty, but the answer is that, with some exceptions, of course, they are not. Eating out is a pastime and a pleasure that people seem loathe to sacrifice. And even if they have to do it once a month rather than twice, or at an Indian restaurant rather than a French one, they still do it.'[184] It was, indeed, in the seventies that eating out became firmly established as a feature of metropolitan lifestyle for even the moderately affluent.

This consumer revolution had two principal features: the raising of standards at the affordable end of the market and the dilution of the exclusivity associated with fine dining. In the first place, consumer demand for affordable meals of a higher quality than was provided in 'greasy spoons' or fish-and-chip shops had driven the expansion of the burger, pizza and pasta chains. Maschler identified in 1974 the way in which they had successfully blurred the boundary between restaurant and snack bar: 'The Golden Egg restaurants should be credited with being the first people here to spend a great deal on the decoration of premises that offered only a snack meal. But it was The Great American Disaster, its imitators and the Pizza chains who perfected the formula and hit upon the key—classlessness.'[185] Certainly these places were hard to label socially. They were also clearly popular. Great American Disaster was selling six hundred burgers a day in its original Fulham Road restaurant shortly after its opening in 1970,[186] succeeding—like the other 'authentic' American burger places that appeared in the seventies—because 'the [burger-eating] public have been fed on soya beans and fat for too long.'[187]

The ability of the chains to offer a good evening out was limited, though—not just because so many of them prioritised the takeaway trade but also because their model relied on a standardisation of meals that was somewhat out of place in the 'experience economy' of eating out. In the classic treatment of the experience economy, restaurants were taken to promote themselves by gimmickry,[188] but there is little to suggest that Tudor serving wenches, Roman slave girls or nude models won over many of London's diners. The experience that those diners sought was rather that of new, exotic tastes in a city with a previously limited culinary range. The proliferation of different cuisines on offer in an ethnically diverse city was a response to this demand: the consumerist revolution did not bring 'haute cuisine for everybody' but rather instilled an inquisitive eclecticism in the dining public.

The trade's growing diversity was in its way a democratising force. This had been somewhat obscured in the early days of the trattoria revolution— the 'swinging' phase of London's culinary evolution—when proprietors sought to cultivate their own snobberies and distinctions even as they abandoned the formality of more traditional establishments. Maccioni's claim that his restaurant was ex-directory, its number known only to an initiate élite, typified this approach. Speaking candidly in 1968, he acknowledged his anxiety two years earlier, when building delays had threatened the opening of Alvaro's: 'I almost went crazy. . . . I sat at home and I thought "have I lost all the beautiful people? Will I just get people off the streets who you never see again?" I couldn't have borne it.'[189] Ultimately, though, the trattorie could not sustain indefinitely the illusion that rustic Italian cuisine represented the peak of fine dining, however beautiful their clientele, and they too succumbed to the twists of fashion, as restaurants offering new and less familiar cuisines proliferated in London.

These restaurants' very unfamiliarity acted as a kind of leveller, dispelling any concern that eating out required culinary knowledge shared only by aficionados. In 1976 the *Standard*'s Angus McGill looked back without regret to the days when West End restaurants had been staffed by 'Olympian persons, haughty of mien, . . . barely concealing their impatience as you wondered what *blanquette de veau* could possibly be.'[190] If Crewe had found his lunch with Sandie Shaw uncomfortable, it was less because of her unfamiliarity with the Mirabelle's etiquette than her unfamiliarity with its menu—'what do you order for someone who hasn't ever tasted even a melon?'[191] Knowledge was power in those circumstances, but the balance of power shifted with the introduction of new cuisines. Even the sophisticated and widely travelled Crewe admitted that he lacked the expertise to review Chinese or Indian restaurants. Such uncertainty was widespread in a generation unfamiliar even with the courgette: Londoners initially took the presence of Chinese diners in Chinese restaurants as a guarantee of quality precisely because they felt unable to make that judgement for themselves. But this was a learning curve which anybody could ascend: the capital's culinary adventurers learned to make their way to Willesden for authentic Szechuanese, and by 1973 'there can be few Londoners who don't know what a kebab is.'[192] Indeed, the chef of the fashionable Doner Kebab House in Wardour Street recognised in 1977 that he was a beneficiary of Londoners' restless search for the unfamiliar: Turkish food had taken off because 'after the curry and Chinese novelties have worn off, it seems different.' An immigrant from Bolu, between Istanbul and Ankara, he acknowledged that London had treated him well.[193] It would continue to do so. Turkish cuisine would eventually lose its novelty, but it held its place in an eclectic repertoire which continued to expand.

Conclusion

In April 1976, after the *Michelin Guide* had produced its umpteenth annual essay in condescension towards London's cuisine, *Time Out* hit back, suggesting that the *Guide*'s 'total Frenchness' had blinded it to the quality of the capital's ethnic restaurants: 'How can they believe there are no good Italian, Indian, Chinese or Middle European places in London?'[194] The magazine was right to suggest that the *Guide* was asking the wrong question. The assumption that a good restaurant had to be French, and to devote itself to the endless refinement of the Escoffier tradition, had been rendered redundant in London by the city's particular culinary evolution. That evolution had launched a complex process of natural selection that left London with three principal restaurant types: a small but well-rooted group of élite establishments, many trading more on tradition and snob appeal than real quality; a bedrock group of affordable places, ranging from the burger and pizza places to chains like Wheeler's or Spaghetti House, trading on good basic standards and the dependability that came with predictability; and a large diaspora of ethnic restaurants, trading on their customers' enthusiasm for 'experience' and 'authenticity.' In an ethnically diverse city with a wide and expanding consumer base, that outcome made economic and social sense. The development of London's cuisine reflected the nature of the city itself.

5

'Hot Property—It's Mine!'

THE LURE AND THE LIMITS
OF HOME OWNERSHIP

To modern eyes, the most striking finding of the Government Social Survey's 1960 investigation into housing in England and Wales was the ambiguous attitude of many respondents towards owner occupation. There was a widespread feeling that property ownership was 'too much of a tie or responsibility.' A significant proportion of those who *did* own their homes professed to having bought only because they had failed to find suitable property to rent. Around one-third of owner-occupiers claimed that they would actually have preferred to rent. Responses in London were similar to those in the country as a whole, though, unsurprisingly, the aversion to ownership was stronger in the lowest income group. A sixth of London owner-occupiers who were actively seeking to move would only consider renting their next home. The property-owning democracy had still to take root.[1]

London in 1960 was really a rental city. More accurately, inner London was a rental city. The 1961 Census, the first to record details of tenure, revealed the contrast between inner London,[2] where most pre-1914 housing had been built for rent, and outer London, which reflected the interwar shift towards building for sale. In outer London it was normal to own, in inner London to rent: the owner-occupation rate in such outer suburbs as Beckenham, Sutton, Bexley or Wembley was, at 70 percent or more, as high as anywhere in Britain, whereas in the LCC area it was, at 19 percent, less than half the national average.[3] The next twenty years, though, would bring

London closer to that average, as an increasing proportion of Londoners took to home ownership.

Ironically, the initial stimulus to owner occupation came from the Conservatives' concern to rescue the private rental sector in the 1950s. For much of the period since the First World War, renters had been favoured by a statutory cap on the rent that they paid, imposed initially in 1915 with an eye to wartime morale and reimposed in 1939 for similar reasons. These ad hoc origins left rent control open to criticism both from those who believed that housing for low-income groups should be provided by the state and from those who argued that rent-capping prevented the housing market from functioning properly. A situation in which, in extremis, it might cost scarcely more to rent a house than to rent a television had become hard to defend,[4] as had the damaging effect of rent control on landlords' capacity to maintain their often ageing property. The private rental sector accounted for around 40 percent of the Greater London housing stock but almost three-quarters of the accommodation classified as 'unfit.'[5] In the 1950s both major political parties had adopted remedies rooted in their separate ideologies: Labour called for the municipalisation of the private rental sector from 1954, while the Conservatives sought to liberate the private landlord from state regulation of rents.[6] With the Conservatives in power through the 1950s, it was the latter path which was followed, but with an important proviso to soften the impact of liberalisation. The 1957 Rent Act removed from control (after a three-year transitional period) all rented property assessed for the rates at over £40 in London, but property below that level would pass out of control only when its current tenancy ended.

The effect of the legislation was greater in London than elsewhere. In February 1957, as the Rent Bill made its way through the Commons, the Conservatives lost a by-election in Lewisham North after a campaign dominated by the rent issue. In 1961, when the act took full effect, the London Labour Party hoped to mount a mass campaign against decontrol. In the event their efforts were blunted by the retention of control, pro tem, for cheaper property,[7] and the strongest protests came from the suburbs, where Labour was otherwise weak and the rental sector was relatively small.

Where decontrol threatened a sharp rent increase, tension might be eased by the sale of the property to the sitting tenant. Rent control had never been the only drawback faced by landlords, who also suffered from a disadvantageous tax position and the burden of maintaining their property;[8]

A slum street in the Harrow Road area, awaiting redevelopment, 1960. (Roger Mayne Archive/Mary Evans Picture Library)

decontrol did not necessarily make landlords more enthusiastic about letting. Tenants had often been held back from purchasing only by the benefits of artificially low rent and security of tenure.[9] When these disappeared, the advantages of ownership might appear incontestable. Indeed, tax relief on mortgage interest payments usually made it cheaper to buy than to rent a decontrolled property: 'the very taxes which have made the life of a landlord so difficult have enhanced the benefits of being an owner occupier.'[10] Purchase was also encouraged by the provision of relatively easy credit by building societies in the early sixties. Prices accordingly rose steeply, and more so in London than in the provinces: the 53 percent real terms increase in London house prices between 1959 and 1965 established a differential between London and the regions which has lasted ever since.[11] 'There comes a time in every landlord's life', as the Peachey Property Corporation put it, 'when it is realised that the market value of his asset is more than the investment value based on the yield he is then obtaining.'[12] The rising market meant that the end of a controlled tenancy—allowing the landlord to sell with vacant possession—might provide the owner of a previously burdensome property with a windfall gain. One witness before the Committee on Housing in Greater London (Milner Holland Committee) estimated that vacant possession would add 'four to six thousand pounds' to the value of property even in unfashionable Kentish Town.[13]

Sixteen percent of dwellings still under rent control in 1960 had passed into owner occupation by the end of 1963.[14] In perhaps two-thirds of these cases the property had been vacated by a tenant dying or voluntarily moving.[15] In most of the remaining cases the tenant was likely to have been paid to leave, but in some it was clear that persuasion or coercion had been applied to encourage tenants to shift. One in ten of the tenants surveyed for the Milner Holland Committee in 1963 claimed that their landlord had urged them to move out.[16] 'Urging' might turn to harassment or intimidation which, with London private tenants four times more likely to occupy the same premises as their landlords than those elsewhere,[17] might prove highly unsettling. Such methods could be at best disruptive and could at worst force people onto the streets: the most authoritative report on London homelessness concluded that the rapid rise in admissions to temporary accommodation in 1959 'was undoubtedly due to a sudden increase in evictions by private landlords after the 1957 Rent Act.' The steady postwar fall in homelessness in London was reversed in 1958; thereafter the figure would rise relentlessly.[18]

This was the context for the eruption of public concern in 1963 over the activities of the slum landlord Peter Rachman, who came, even after his death, to represent the figure of the exploitative and socially irresponsible slum landlord, 'winkling' out tenants by intimidation in order to free up a property for sale.[19] Landlordism was discredited as a whole. The Milner Holland Committee, appointed in response to the housing crisis, would lucidly explain in its 1965 report the need for a functioning private rental sector in a large and dynamic city, but the press and public reception focused on the evidence it provided of landlord wickedness: 'A dead rat, . . . itching powder, . . . live snakes, . . . a juke box, . . . threats that a tenant's life was in danger. These are some of the "weapons" used by unscrupulous London landlords to drive tenants out of their homes. . . . The report estimates that AT LEAST 3000 families in London alone suffer this sort of treatment— and worse—each year.'[20] Where the Labour Party had failed to mobilise a mass protest against rising rents, it benefited unexpectedly from a press

Graffiti reflecting the reaction against the private landlord in the early sixties, Kentish Town.
(John Gay/English Heritage NMR/Mary Evans Picture Library)

furore over the very concept of landlordism. The 1957 Rent Act, intended
to revive private renting, proved instead to have boosted owner occupation
and provoked the public vilification of the private landlord. Both effects
would influence the subsequent evolution of London's housing.

Gentrification and the Transformation
of the Inner City

Gentrification was first identified in London, where it had been recognised
well before Ruth Glass coined the term in 1964, and was usually called
'Chelseafication' by the estate agents who prospered from it. The roots of

Kelly Street, Kentish Town, early 1960s. (John Gay/English Heritage NMR/Mary Evans Picture Library)

Chelsea's postwar transformation lay in the granting of business licences in Mayfair before the war, forcing the opulent residential population west-wards.[21] Chelsea's elegant late-Georgian and early-Victorian housing con-tained a substantial working-class population alongside an artistic and literary community. 'The combination of money and artiness' lay behind the area's fashionability in the mid-1950s,[22] when the 'Chelsea set' became arbiters of modern taste. By the early 1960s, though, when 'Chelsea prices amaze even estate agents',[23] it was becoming clear that money was under-mining Bohemia, as artists were priced out of the area.[24]

It was inevitable that Chelsea's quaint if run-down early nineteenth-century artisans' cottages would be carried on this moneyed tide. The roots of London's gentrification lay in the 'crooked little streets and shaggy houses' off the King's Road.[25] Godfrey Street, for instance, had been 'not exactly a slum, but . . . not much brighter than one' before the war; its 'little houses . . . had no electricity or baths. . . . It took a pioneer with a little imagination and money in the 1930s to paint and convert his little house and start the street's new lease of life.'[26] By 1950 similar Chelsea cottage property was being offered at the substantial price of £7,000, and by the end of that decade 'you have to be very fashionable, and to have a lot of money in your pocket to live in Godfrey Street.'[27]

'Chelseafication' meant the refurbishment and embellishment of generally run-down property of the type and vintage prominent in Chelsea, normally two-storey cottages or three-storey terraced houses, dating from the late eighteenth or early nineteenth centuries. By the early 1960s there were few sales and no bargains to be had in Chelsea itself,[28] and gentrifiers had to look elsewhere, to areas like Notting Hill, where early Victorian 'houses that go for £16,000 in Chelsea sell for £5,000–£7,000.'[29] There were many parts of London where such property was to be found—in Notting Hill and Paddington,[30] in Kennington and Elephant and Castle,[31] in Canonbury and Barnsbury,[32] in Camden and Kentish Town,[33] in riverside Greenwich[34]—even in parts of Wimbledon, Barnes and Richmond.[35] The *London Property Letter*, the privately circulated bible for speculators in London residential property in the sixties, described the likely purchasers in consistent terms: 'the more fashionable professionals' in Paddington,[36] 'young professional men—architects, solicitors, doctors, actors and an artist or two'—in the quainter parts of Camberwell,[37] 'artists, TV actors and politicians' in Blackheath,[38] 'intellectuals' in Camden Town,[39] 'the advance wave of artists, actors and architects that usually preludes the stampede' in Greenwich.[40] They were the pacesetters of London's service economy—'a new moneyed class on the look out for houses.'[41] For 'creatives' they were markedly unoriginal: the symbols of 'Chelseafication' were the same across London—pastel colours for doors and window frames, brass door knockers, window boxes and carriage lamps. The Labour leader of Lambeth Council described with some distaste in 1964 the process by which the incomers marked their territory in a working-class area: 'You close the basement, put a girder across to hold the rest up, you paint the front door yellow and buy a coach lamp for 30/- and it immediately becomes rather, I would call it, lower middle class.' He was describing Cleaver Square, a 1790s enclave in Kennington.[42] Its potential had been spotted in the early fifties by a chartered surveyor, P. J. Broomhall, who had urged his clients to buy there despite its dilapidation, prompting a speedy and relatively uniform renovation. By 1963, 'The address, in the heart of this doggedly down-to-earth borough, is now as socially acceptable as Chelsea, Hampstead and Highgate. There are pastel-painted doors, wrought-iron gates, and even an old coach lamp or two. Some of the homes in the square have been featured in the glossy magazines and others recently visited by burglars. A few yards away houses built more recently are being demolished as slums.'[43]

A similar transformation occurred in the still edgy district of Notting Hill. 'We're really an overspill of Chelsea here', one incomer told the *Evening Standard* in 1965, 'and slightly pleased with ourselves for slumming.'[44] Slumming required fortitude. 'The easily daunted don't survive, nor the squeamish', Barbara Anne Taylor told the *Standard*'s readers earlier that year. She recounted the experience of Daphne Weston who, at the age of twenty-four, had bought a house in Pimlico lacking electricity, a lavatory and running water, 'impregnated with filth and inhabited by a clique of tramps.' It took 'twelve months and many agonies' to transform the place, along with £7,000 for the purchase and £3,000 for the conversion. But the rewards were tangible. The 'awesomely energetic' Weston and her husband not only completed the house's metamorphosis but also started their own firm of building contractors on the basis of their experience.[45]

The investment of 'sweat equity' in this way was characteristic of first-wave gentrification in London,[46] where purchasers were characteristically young and energetic, with firm ideas about domestic taste—'young couples with Chelsea ideas but Notting Hill Gate pockets', as the *London Property Letter* put it.[47] Increasingly, though, gentrifiers preferred to buy their conversions off the peg, and these years saw the proliferation of small companies seeking to profit from the gap between the prices of derelict and of rehabilitated property in fashionable districts. These 'questionable investment companies' were depicted as generally disreputable by witnesses before the Milner Holland Committee, which contrasted their rapacity with the paternalism of 'traditional' landlords.[48] This probably underestimated traditional landlords' lust for profit in a bull market, but the new companies undoubtedly were commercial operations, forcing the pace of transformation in many working-class districts. Sitting tenants, usually enjoying controlled rents and security of tenure in property below the £40 threshold, were the principal obstacle to their operations.

Although the Labour government elected in 1964 was no longer committed to municipalising private rental housing, it had pledged a crash programme of council-house building and the introduction of a modernised form of rent control. The latter materialised in the 1965 Rent Act, which introduced a system of arbitration between landlord and tenant in the unfurnished sector, by which 'fair rents' could be determined and a degree of security of tenure conferred. A system of arbitration was created, allowing tenants and landlords to bring their grievances to borough-level panels consisting of a lawyer, a valuer and a layman. In Kensington and Chelsea, for instance, the senior rent officer was Colonel Harry Phillips, an estate agent, who sought to bring landlord and tenant together in 'relaxed and informal' meetings, 'as if they were in their own drawing rooms.' Phillips believed that the 1957 legislation had been 'too sudden' and 'took this job because the concept of a fair rent has always appealed" to him.[49] The fair rent was to be assessed in the manner of a 'just price', with no account taken of market forces in the area. As a result, some 80 percent of the market rents reached after 1957 were lowered by local borough panels in the system's first six months.

From a landlord's perspective any cap on rents would erode returns in an inflationary age. By May 1967 the *London Property Letter* was reporting that 'the unfurnished market has virtually shut down since the coming of the Rent Act', with landlords selling where they could and converting their property to furnished accommodation—more lightly regulated by the 1965 act—where they could not.[50] The depletion of the whole rental sector by sales meant that although the supply of furnished rented accommodation increased as a result, the demand rose still more quickly: a 1969 study found that furnished property in London cost on average three to four times more than a GLC flat to rent, although it was usually far inferior accommodation. Furnished lettings became conflict sites, with four-fifths of landlords finding their tenants unreasonable and two-thirds of tenants feeling similarly about their landlords.[51] By the end of the decade the private rental sector in London had entered a rapid, embittered decline.

Even the most optimistic advocates of rent liberalisation had not expected the 1957 legislation to rejuvenate London's most run-down areas, where much property remained controlled. In 1963 the Ministry of Housing instead considered regenerating 'twilight' areas through public-private partnerships, along lines pioneered in the United States by the construction firm Taylor Woodrow. The local authority would assemble by compulsory purchase large-scale sites, which would then be developed by private enterprise to provide private housing for rent or sale. Social housing would be offered to those who were displaced by the clearance. Taylor Woodrow was engaged to conduct a pilot study in London. It focused on a part of

Fulham, a choice which made more sense for the developer than for the Ministry. Fulham had been one of London's fastest risers from the late 1950s, as neighbouring Chelsea became unaffordable, but the area's late-Victorian terraces lacked the period charm behind Chelsea's magnetism. The prospect of providing modern town houses in an upwardly mobile neighbourhood kept Taylor Woodrow engaged, though it feared that the social housing obligation would make the scheme unprofitable. The Ministry, aware that Fulham 'was not by any means the "darkest" twilight area in the county' and that its houses were not slums,[52] indulged the project for two years in the hope of finding a cheaper model for area regeneration than local authority redevelopment. Even the Labour-controlled Fulham Borough Council, reluctant to deploy its compulsory purchase powers to promote middle-class private housing, acknowledged that 'comprehensive redevelopment is essential if an environment capable of sustaining modern urban life is to be created.'[53]

Taylor Woodrow's eventual proposals did indeed raise tricky questions about modern urban life, though they hinged on the technical issue of residential density. Taylor Woodrow suggested that an overall density of 250 persons per acre was needed to make the scheme viable. This was far above the normal limit of 136 persons per acre—a figure reflecting planners' ingrained belief that higher densities would diminish green space, play space and privacy and 'repeat the social errors of Victorian tenements.'[54]

Taylor Woodrow responded that 'current planning standards seem to stem from an ideology which denigrates urbanism and seeks to create Utopias based on the ideals of the garden suburb and the city-beautiful', claiming that such restrictions in earlier centuries would have suppressed Bloomsbury and Belgravia.[55] Unrestricted, the company could 'rebuild the decaying inner ring of the capital so that the enormous potential talent of the Metropolis is harnessed and exploited to produce a coherent and truly modern solution.'[56] The Ministry considered this special pleading, doubting that a new Bloomsbury was likely to emerge in Fulham,[57] and the prospects for this experiment in area regeneration were dwindling even before the return of a Labour government in October 1964 signalled a return to municipal building. The vision of area renewal by public-private partnership receded, leaving the replenishment of London's housing dependent on the two processes already at work: local authority clearance for redevelopment and private-sector rehabilitation of the existing stock.

In fact, with both slum clearance and gentrification quickening in the early 1960s, there was more scope for public-private conflict than

Susannah York decorating her flat in Seaton Street, Chelsea, 1960. (Popperfoto/Getty Images)

cooperation. Open class warfare had erupted in Chelsea in 1962 over the borough council's scheme to redevelop the World's End area, in the western reaches of the King's Road. The scheme had first been mooted in 1946, but after a decade and a half of inactivity, gentrifiers had put down roots in the area, either ignorant of the development proposal or confident that it would never happen. 'Film stars and millionaires outnumbered the dustmen and pensioners' in some of the scheduled streets.[58] Their campaign against the scheme was mobilised by two residents of threatened Seaton Street, the novelist Robin Maugham and the actress Susannah York. Maugham had bought a 'decrepit little house' on his father's death in 1957 and spent £8,000 to create 'the most expensive slum in London'; Chelsea-born York's talent had elevated her from a bedsit in Lots Road to a Seaton Street house on which she spent £5,000, treasuring the neighbourhood's 'healthy, scruffy atmosphere which is awfully nice.'[59] There were, though, less appetising conditions in an area that was only on the cusp of transformation:[60] 'Mrs Battle showed a gaping hole in the roof of her kitchen ... where the wood had rotted away and the rain flooded in'; 'no water, dry rot, beetles, gaping cracks in the floors'; collapsed ceiling plaster patched up with cardboard; and so on.[61]

Clearance promised modern council flats to slum residents, who were unmoved by conservationist arguments which threatened to trap them in their decaying homes. The debate rehearsed the pros and cons of gentrification, with an unmistakeable class edge. The objectors maintained that redevelopment implied the 'wholesale slaughter of a part of London that is acquiring character . . . to build a lot of shoe boxes': 'I don't want to live under the council. I had enough of that sort of thing in the army'; 'the people who own houses round here are not the gilded rich.'[62] Their opponents alleged that Maugham and his colleagues *were* the gilded rich, or at least 'the ones who can "get away from it all" for weeks on end', who could pay for repairs when necessary rather than wait for a landlord to act, who would never 'trot up and down five steps every time they have to get water, and in this day and age boil clothes in a bucket.' With some justification they suggested that money devoted to 'pricey alterations' might have been better spent on a more diligent legal search to reveal the plans for redevelopment.[63] For all the prestige and resources of the objectors, the World's End development went ahead.

Such confrontations occurred across gentrifying London, but their frequency diminished. While freelance modernisers like Maugham continued to be caught out, property companies normally observed the industry's first 'commandment'—to check with the authorities before purchase that a house did not fall within a slum clearance area.[64] Similarly, local authorities became more attuned to the spread of gentrification and more wary of conflicts with combative middle-class occupiers: the Georgian houses in Kennington Park Road, for example, were spared demolition for Lambeth's Braganza Street estate by 'some of the progressives already in there who are smartly persuading the authorities to place their terrace on the list of preserved properties.'[65] London in the 1960s offered much scope for *both* slum clearance and rehabilitation.

In September 1965 the housing minister, Robert Mellish, announced a programme to build 125,000 new houses for Londoners by 1968. In the brief period before the Wilson administration was consumed by worries over the balance of payments, money was available in relative abundance. 'The nation has got to afford it. . . . Germany can afford it. . . . So must we', Mellish maintained.[66] Given Labour's manifesto commitment to build 500,000 houses per annum nationally, 125,000 over three years appeared modest, but their presentational effect was significant, coming months after the creation of the new London boroughs. Many of the new authorities wanted landmark projects to establish their identities, and many, at least in the inner city, had inherited extensive housing programmes. Thus in Newham the expansionist housing policy of the former West Ham borough trumped the more cautious approach of East Ham, and the new council embarked on a building spree 'considerably larger than the combined programmes of the two old Boroughs.'[67] There, as elsewhere, the pace of the programme dictated high-rise construction using system-building techniques which had shown teething troubles in earlier projects. In 1966 alone the proportion of new council houses in London built by industrial methods rose from 23 percent to 48 percent.[68] By 1968 London had more than seven hundred high towers—defined as ten storeys or more—with almost four hundred more under construction. Wandsworth alone planned thirty-two new blocks, while Barking, Hammersmith and Hackney each planned twenty or more.[69]

As the dramatic transformation of inner London by council building gathered pace, the less ostentatious improvement of the existing housing stock by private developers slowed somewhat. The late-fifties price surge slowed in 1963 as private landlords sought to sell their houses in anticipation of a Labour government restoring rent control.[70] Building societies and other lenders became more suspicious of 'secondhand' houses in the light of press exposure of their frailty. Their responses to the *Evening Standard* writer Angus McGill's efforts to borrow on a Georgian house in Islington in 1963 revealed the persistence of attitudes formed in the years of rent control, when older properties often fell into dilapidation and larger ones into multi-occupation: 'anything older than 50 years gets very short shrift'; 'NEVER lend on property with more than two floors'; 'basements and attics are RIGHT out. . . . I don't know why.'[71] At the beginning of 1967 the *Standard*'s property correspondent, William Roland, noted that prices had been flat since 1964, concluding that 'the days of fancy prices and a seller's market were over.'[72] Slowdown did not mean slump, though. 'We used to be reasonably pleased if we sold three houses a day. Now we're happy if we can sell three a week', one South London estate agent acknowledged in 1965,[73] but the sales continued, supported by the buoyant London economy, the influx of young high-earners into the capital and the continuing shrinkage of the rental sector.

In particular, the decanting of run-down rental property onto the market following the partial reimposition of rent control in 1965 meant that there remained a substantial gap between the price of a dilapidated shell with controlled tenants and its value after rehabilitation. Tenants of run-down property were often willing to be paid to leave, the developer adding the cost of this bribe to the cost of renovation. In 1967 the *London Property Letter* recounted the tale of an investor who had bought a number of houses in Charlton Place, Islington, 'for a song' five years earlier. 'Slowly and systematically' he bought out the sitting tenants, paying £750 per floor. The houses then sold at £5,000 unmodernised and as much as £11,500 fully modernised.[74] This market sustained the numerous small property enterprises that flourished in the capital, generally run by young men with money who resembled the young entrepreneurs found elsewhere in the 'Swinging City': men like John Birrane, 'a youthful figure with blue eyes and a razor look'; like John White, who had attended Bedford School, rowed at Henley, skipped university and worked briefly for the family joinery firm before forming his own development company in 1963; or like Michael Beardmore, previously a district commissioner in East Africa and a venerable thirty-five in 1966 when, with his twenty-six-year-old colleague Hugo Jeune, he effected several lucrative flat conversions in Westbourne Terrace, Paddington.[75]

Birrane helped make Kennington's Georgian houses fashionable, while White promoted the transformation of W11, justly confident that Notting Hill 'is well placed for a whole wave of fashion.'[76] They facilitated the culturally freighted gentrification so conspicuous in the 1960s. After Chelsea, parts of Notting Hill, Islington, Camden Town, Kennington and elsewhere developed middle-class enclaves, housed in suitably humble late-Georgian or early-Victorian property. In a satirical age, they invited such parody as the cartoonist Mark Boxer's 'Life and Times' strip in the *Listener*, depicting Camden Town's literati. Predictable lifestyle markers became modish in these ghettoes, comprising the 'style of elegant austerity' described by Jonathan Raban in his account of the transformation of Arundel Square, Islington, in the late 1960s: 'Japanese lampshades, *House and Garden*, French baby cars, white paint, asparagus tips, Earl Grey tea and stripped pine stereo systems.'[77] Usually left-leaning, Raban's colonisers—'Nigel and Pamela, Jeremy and Nicola'—permeated the local Labour Party with their 'honourable theories of workers' control', unable to understand how 'acres of white paint [could] be construed as a vulgar exhibition of financial power?'[78] But parody could yield to hostility in the face of a social takeover, however friendly. Gentrifiers often occupied areas less genteel than those they had left: one Notting Hill incomer told the *Standard*'s Anne Sharpley in 1965 that she witnessed a knifing in her first weekend in the area: 'We got so used to frightening things going on at night that in time . . . we stopped getting up to look out of the windows.'[79] The settlers' frontier mentality produced associational organisations stronger and more determined than those to be found in the rest of London, 'getting up little campaigns to preserve this and demolish that', as Raban put it.[80] Deploying 'a few sharp middle-class cries of distress over the telephone' to get the streets of Notting Hill swept more carefully caused little offence,[81] but when residents' power was used to remodel the urban environment to their own benefit—most notoriously with the promotion of a scheme to divert through traffic away from the more select parts of Barnsbury in 1965[82]—gentrification became controversial.

These trendsetters promised riches for developers. The *London Property Letter* suggested that 'middle-class householders need an inner London area to colonise almost every year,'[83] and previously unremarkable areas were touted as 'new Chelseas.' Confidence persisted that 'you only have to improve one house well and it's never long before someone says "that's a nice house. Let's go and live next door." Then the whole street goes like a rocket',[84] but it was not always possible to invent demand in this way. In 1970 the *Letter* warned that merely improving one house would do little to raise the value of a semiderelict area: it would take the renovation of whole streets and squares at once, a task normally beyond the small companies dominating the market.[85] Dereliction and a century and a half's soot might conceal the qualities of the most elegant quarters. The LCC actually proposed Barnsbury—later the epitome of gentrified chic—as a twilight zone better suited for Taylor Woodrow's attention than Fulham in 1963;[86] four years later the sternly classical Milner Square still bore the scars of decades of multi-occupation: 'cracked windows, blackened rendering, blistering and peeling paintwork.'[87] Purchasers and lenders might consider such buildings beyond salvation—Milner Square was only rescued by Islington Council's rehabilitation programme in the 1970s—as many developers learned to their cost.

'Slope off into the unknown and the snakes will get you', the *London Property Letter* warned developers.[88] It was safer to buy on the fringe of already-rising areas, in the hope of attracting purchasers priced out of those areas. This lesson came from Fulham, whose freeholders had prospered on the back of Chelsea's rise. Fulham's buoyant property prices had helped undermine the Taylor Woodrow proposals in 1963: buying out owners in a rising market would threaten the project's viability.[89] Fulham, displaying slow but steady renewal, represented the evolution of inner-London housing in these years better than such sites of overnight middle-class takeover as Canonbury or Cleaver Square. It offered late-Victorian terraces rather than Georgian cottages. In 1963 its 'shopkeepers continue to boggle at requests . . . for a Camembert or a carton of sour cream', and as one incomer lamented, 'if I want tarragon vinegar or cranberries or a modern light fitting I have to go all the way to the King's Road.'[90] By 1968 the Moore Park district of Fulham had sprouted a couple of antique shops;[91] the area's gentrifying future was emerging, but it would take time to materialise. As in much of inner London, a core of working-class owner-occupiers had bought their homes as sitting tenants following the 1957 Rent Act and stayed put until house-price inflation made the temptation to sell irresistible. By 1979, when Max Hastings looked at the transformation of Britannia Road, Moore Park, for the *Evening Standard*, many owner-occupiers had banked their winnings in the property lottery—'Mr Scott the plumber from no 11 had retired to Littlehampton, and another plumber higher up the road moved to Raynes Park'—but a dozen old-timers remained. Though the transformation had begun in the late 1950s, Hastings concluded that it would take another decade until Britannia Road had 'bettered itself into uniformity.'[92]

There *were* killings to be made from developing London residential property in the 1960s, but they were seldom guaranteed. Anybody who followed the *London Property Letter*'s advice to invest in Deptford or Stockwell in 1963 faced a long wait for returns.[93] Even Islington 'only caught on in patches' in the early sixties, with 'fortunes being made in one street and fingers being burned just round the corner.'[94] The reasoning behind the 'fringe law'—for investing on the edge of established areas—was the likelihood of an unsatisfied demand in those areas. The most obvious unsatisfied demand in the owner-occupier market, though, was for property compact enough to be affordable for small households. As the Milner Holland report emphasised, much of London's housing stress was caused by the mismatch between houses and households, with property built for large Victorian families ill suited for the smaller households of the 1960s.[95] For that reason it was the conversion of larger houses into flats that provided the bread-and-butter returns for developers in the 1960s. The artisans' cottages central to 'Chelseafication' were unsuited for that work, being small and 'not easy to slice.'[96] Houses disparaged as 'Victorian monstrosities'—the large, divisible properties in places like New Cross or Ealing[97]—proved a better prospect for developers: in 1966, for instance, the *Letter* estimated returns of up to 65 percent on conversions of the 'not particularly sophisticated' six-bedroom semis overlooking Wandsworth Common.[98] Such property was more plentiful than the dwindling supply of Georgian gems, ensuring that the developers' reach extended across the capital, to areas unlikely ever to become fashionable. Insofar as such activity replaced lower-income renters with higher-income purchasers, it could be categorised as gentrification, but it differed greatly from what had happened in Chelsea, Islington or Notting Hill.

Old Houses into New Homes

Speaking to the *Evening Standard* in 1977, one long-term Barnsbury resident admitted that she found her new middle-class neighbours 'highbrow', but 'mind you, the place wanted a lot of doing up and they did it.'[99] The work of individual occupiers varied in quality, but the renovation and conversion work carried out by property companies in the sixties was generally sound. The *London Property Letter* warned its developer readers in 1967 that the recent abundance of flat conversions had produced a buyers' market in which it was unwise to botch a conversion, particularly given building societies' reluctance to lend on older property.[100] Appraising the Taylor Woodrow Fulham scheme in 1963, the Ministry of Housing had noted that spreading owner occupation meant that 'a lot of the area is regenerating itself.'[101]

At the same time, public expenditure constraints from the midsixties threatened councils' redevelopment schemes. The issue was forced by the GLC's 1967 survey of London's housing stock, which showed that 150,000 houses in inner London—some 16 percent of the total—had a useful life of fifteen years or less. In Lambeth, Newham, Southwark and Tower Hamlets more than a quarter of all dwellings came into that category.[102] This evidence of the state of London housing came as the National House Condition Survey, also conducted in 1967, suggested that 14 percent of dwellings in England and Wales were unfit and that 'they were not so much concentrated as had been believed before, but more spread out.'[103] These discoveries made the Ministry more eager to harness the potential of private rehabilitation and less concerned by its piecemeal nature. The result was the policy shift embodied in the 1968 white paper *Old Houses into New Homes* and the 1969 Housing Act.

The 1969 act empowered local authorities to designate General Improvement Areas, in the hope that improvement of the general environment by, for example, traffic regulation or the provision of play spaces

would encourage individual owners to improve their houses.[104] This optimistic prescription was generally considered 'a flop' in London and was
certainly slow to get off the ground, with only 7 percent of designated
schemes having received any financial support by the beginning of 1973.[105]
More significant was the distinctly liberal provision for home-improvement
grants. Grants for rehabilitating older houses had been introduced in 1949
and extended in 1954, 1959 and 1964. In practice the grants had been taken
up overwhelmingly by owner-occupiers, and the latter two acts effectively
limited payments to those living in the property to be improved.[106] In
1969, though, not only was the maximum grant level almost trebled, but
there was no requirement for the improver either to live in the property or
to refrain from selling it after improvement.[107]

More than half the improvement grants paid out in Islington went to
the gentrifying areas of Canonbury and Barnsbury.[108] At a time of curbs
on welfare expenditure, open-handed grants of public money to enable
home owners to improve their own homes struck a jarring note. Descriptions of what was done with the money do have a certain 'ideal home'
flavour to them, as with this Fulham householder interviewed by the *Evening Standard* in 1972: 'I spent hours with every kitchen catalogue, trying
to make up my mind as to what style of cooking and eating I was going to
have. In the end I opted for the semi-open plan.'[109] Yet more contentious
was the generosity of the 1969 act—a Labour-government measure, after
all—towards property developers, many of whom were 'rubbing their eyes
in disbelief that . . . Government grants would be available on conversions
for sale.'[110] The House of Commons Expenditure Committee investigated
this drain on the public purse in 1973, and the developers giving evidence
admitted that improvement grants simply augmented the profit on operations which were normally profitable anyway.[111] The explanation was that
Whitehall was preoccupied with preventing further housing decay and saw
private developers as its best allies. Though this was not a Treasury measure, the Treasury's representative on the group constructing the 1969 bill
described succinctly its purpose, alluding to his department's 'indirect interest in ensuring that the older houses do not slide into further decay and
become slums which have to be replaced at public expense.'[112] This sentiment was expressed openly by Conservative Housing Minister Julian
Amery in 1972: 'it's less damaging that a few people should make a profit
than [that] the momentum for improvements should be held up.'[113]

Ultimately this indulgence towards *residential* property speculators was
unsustainable at a time of widespread public hostility towards their

commercial counterparts; indeed the *London Property Letter* had urged its readers in 1969 to apply for this unexpected bounty as soon as possible, as 'the Government will nobble this sort of grant as soon as the money involved gets big.'[114] So it did, with a new Housing Act in 1974, requiring grant recipients who resold their property within five years to repay the grant with compound interest.[115] By then, though, it would appear that much of what could profitably be renovated and converted in London had been. Many of the areas promoted by the *London Property Letter* in the early 1970s had a marginal look to them—Balham, Finsbury Park, Peckham, even Brixton and Kilburn ('not that anybody in his right mind would ever say that they'll turn into second Islingtons').[116] In the spring of 1974 the *London Property Letter*, chronicle of the capital's gentrification since 1963, renamed itself the *Property Letter*, reducing its London content.

In April 1972 the *Evening Standard* carried a piece on improvement grants—'Get a "New Home" from the Town Hall'—promising that 'there is still lots of money in the kitty and they are longing to give it to you.'[117] In fact, although councils were normally reimbursed by central government for three-quarters of the cost of the grants, many of them resented paying even the remaining 25 percent. When the 1969 act came into force, the Tory landslide in the 1968 borough council elections meant that almost all London boroughs were in Conservative control, ensuring a relatively easy ride for a measure subsidising owner-occupiers and property developers. In 1971, though, Labour regained most of its inner-city strongholds, and improvement grants came under closer scrutiny. It had long been recognised that the improvement of a run-down area seldom benefited the original residents and that where houses had been in multi-occupation, improvement was likely to bring mass evictions: as the research officer of the Notting Hill Housing Trust wrote in 1972, 'homelessness and displacement may increase at the same time as the area appears to "improve."'[118] The price paid for the beautification of Barnsbury and Canonbury in the 1960s, for instance, was the degradation of the area around Westbourne Road in Islington, where 1,150 families occupied 350 houses in 1968, in conditions of 'multi-occupancy, poor sanitation and overcrowding.'[119] The 1969 act intensified this problem. Department of the Environment research suggested that where grants were paid to landlords and developers rather than owner-occupiers, 60 percent of tenants were displaced.[120] Councils found themselves expected to partially fund the creation of a homelessness problem which would eventually land on the desks of their housing and social service departments. In protest, some imposed restrictions of doubtful legality on developers.[121]

The Retreat from Council Housing

Behind these concerns lay a deeper apprehension that the 1969 exercise in state-sponsored gentrification reflected wider uncertainty over council housing as a social service. During the 1960s many people in decaying private accommodation had pined for a council house, believing that municipal housing offered affordable, well-built accommodation, with de facto security of tenure, under a responsible landlord attentive to maintenance and repairs. The shift to high-rise blocks in the 1960s changed the nature of the municipal 'offer', but it was not immediately clear that tower blocks were unpopular. A 1963 LCC survey of housewives living in blocks of more than ten storeys found 86 percent of them happy with their conditions, appreciating the views, the absence of noise, the privacy, the cleaner air and the light. Of those seeking to move within their block, two-thirds wished to move higher. Dissatisfaction was expressed with lift breakdowns and blocked rubbish chutes, though,[122] and a 1969 survey underlined that resident satisfaction depended in large part on the quality of the building.[123] Some borough architects had their misgivings from the start about system building: Lambeth's Edward Hollamby, for instance, warned in 1965 that it 'may be quick and efficient, but it's almost all extremely bad architecture. If industrialised building means this, then it isn't going to produce an environment which is acceptable.'[124] The 1969 survey suggested that the very tall blocks that system building made possible—twenty-two storeys rather than fifteen—were generally unpopular.

The responses in 1969 would have been influenced by the disaster occurring a year earlier, when an entire corner of a system-built block in Newham, Ronan Point, collapsed following a gas explosion, killing four people. This horror owed as much to the poor construction of the block itself as to weaknesses in the Larson-Neilson technology behind the building, but in the public mind it demonstrated the evils of high-rise. In Newham it produced what Patrick Dunleavy has called 'a crisis of legitimacy', where the council ignored local fears about high-rise living, telling people at the head of the waiting list to take or leave accommodation on offer in the tower blocks approaching completion.[125] Such was the level of housing stress in the East End that the council knew that it would readily find volunteers even for Ronan Point's sister block, Merritt Point, but Newham's heavy-handed attitude towards its residents' legitimate anxieties reflected a wider inflexibility on the part of housing authorities.

Architect Erno Goldfinger (*left*), leader of the Greater London Council Desmond Plummer (*centre*) and GLC Housing Committee chairman Horace Cutler take in the view from the flat which Goldfinger had moved into in his Balfron Tower, Poplar, August 1968. Goldfinger was conducting 'a sociological experiment' for two months to test the living conditions which he had created. (PA/Alamy Stock Photo)

In 1965 the Islington councillor Harry Brack had been expelled from his local Labour Party for arguing that 'too many councils have imposed low housing standards, due perhaps to cost considerations', on 'people who are emerging from the slums and will accept any improvement offered', producing what Brack called 'the slums of tomorrow.'[126] Council housing regimes had always displayed a degree of coercive paternalism, but this had previously seemed an acceptable price for accommodation superior to that which most tenants had left. Once councils appeared to be forcing people into accommodation that was itself substandard, or requiring families with

Mrs Ingeborg Paine and her daughter look out at the scaffolded Ronan Point tower block in January 1969, eight months after its partial collapse killed four people. Mrs Paine and other occupiers of blocks similar to Ronan Point were about to be moved to blocks of traditional construction. (Keystone Pictures USA/Alamy Stock Photo)

small children to accept flats at the top of high blocks,[127] the image of the local authority as benign provider was dented. Ann Holmes's 1970 investigation for the campaigning homelessness charity Shelter of housing-stress areas in Islington revealed a widespread distrust of the council's actions: 'I wouldn't like to live in Islington in 50 years' time, they're not building houses, they're building rabbit hutches'; 'they're pulling down the wrong

High-rise protest: residents at the twenty-three-storey Sporle Court, near Clapham Junction station, protest against Wandsworth Council's failure to find them alternative accommodation, 1979. (Mary Evans/Marx Memorial Library)

houses—the local authority sends the Compulsory Purchase Order by post, and they don't give any explanation of why they're doing it'; 'it's a great pity they're pulling so many old places down and building new blocks when they could improve the old.'[128] By the midseventies many local authorities were finding that their rehousing programmes were being delayed by increasingly choosy applicants, who refused initial offers of rehousing to hold out for 'a tenancy in a house of a modern low-rise development.'[129]

Councils' reputation as housing authorities was dented further by their handling of the unyielding problem of homelessness. The 1948 National Assistance Act had imposed on local authorities an ill-defined obligation (reinforced in 1977) to provide temporary shelter for those who were made homeless by unforeseen circumstances, which could include eviction.[130] They generally became the responsibility of social service rather than housing departments, so that policy towards homelessness developed separately from councils' wider housing aims.[131] Nonetheless, homelessness was a symptom of the worsening housing situation in London in the 1960s, both in its direct sense—the number living in temporary accommodation in inner London rose fivefold between 1957 and 1970[132]—and in respect of the 'hidden homeless': those who were reluctantly living with parents, those doubling up with friends, or families living in single rooms.

Public concern about evictions revived in 1972, posing new challenges for housing authorities. Most inner-London councils already had lengthy waiting lists which they sought to reduce by their building programmes. In practice, though, their reluctance to build at densities approaching those of the slum areas they had cleared made it difficult to achieve a substantial housing gain, given the obligation to rehouse those who were displaced by clearance. The Southwark Community Development Project's researchers claimed that the ambitious redevelopment programme embarked on by Southwark Council from 1965 brought virtually no housing gain to a borough with a waiting list of nine thousand.[133] The CDP was a hostile witness, but it does appear that large-scale redevelopment scarcely diminished council waiting lists, which would only fall with the exodus of inner London's population in the 1970s: Tower Hamlets was responsible for a third of all the demolitions in inner London between 1965 and 1970, but in 1968 it was estimated that it would take the borough forty-two years to clear its waiting list at the current rate of progress.[134] Waiting lists became inert obstacles to change, used by councils to justify refusing to deal with the newly homeless. Council officials emulated the fictional but plausible stonewalling bureaucrats depicted in the 1966 TV drama *Cathy Come Home*, their insensitive explanations of their inability to provide—'well, people are passed on like a ping pong ball until they disappear'; 'oh we use our manipulative powers to persuade relatives to take them'—furnishing ammunition to Shelter.[135]

While it was generally true that local authorities lacked the temporary accommodation needed to handle the swelling numbers of homeless, their case was weakened by the large number of houses compulsorily purchased for redevelopment schemes but left empty for years. Several councils had been spurred by the 1967 house-condition survey to acquire large amounts of short-life property at just the point when the Wilson government restricted central support for local housing projects. The indefensible reality of houses kept empty at a time of accommodation shortage fuelled the squatting explosion of the early 1970s. By 1975 there were at least twenty thousand squatters in London, probably more.[136] Despite contemporary fears of squatters colonising private property left temporarily unattended, there was so much genuinely empty property in local authority hands that such provocation was generally unnecessary. In Lambeth, with as many squatters as any borough, 'the council's present "problem" over squatting, can in the main be directly attributed to empty houses created via the C[ompulsory] P[urchase] O[rder] programme.'[137] By 1970, when Lambeth's waiting list stood at 12,500, only about 15 percent of those who were eligible to join it actually attempted to do so, the rest judging correctly that their prospects were minimal.[138] Those who did not have a medical or similar special case stood little chance of council accommodation; squatter groups were dominated by healthy twenty-somethings,[139] spurred to take direct action by the knowledge that public policy offered them nothing.

Councils reacted with varying degrees of intolerance to the squatter challenge, but Labour authorities with long waiting lists tended to dismiss it as 'the worst form of queue-jumping.'[140] Some resorted to vandalising their own property, sending in council workmen to block or smash up toilets in order to make serviceable houses uninhabitable. In the late 1970s Camden, Islington and Lambeth deployed the Metropolitan Police to effect often-violent mass evictions. In the eyes of the new urban Left, which had come to see squatting as an expression of community self-defence, 'old Labour' councils had aligned themselves with the defenders of social inequity, becoming another sinister interest attacking London's weakest citizens. Given the centrality of council housing to the narrative of municipal socialism since the 1880s, this represented a striking transformation.

Ultimately, though, the critique from the Right was more damaging. When disenchantment with the Wilson government produced a near clean sweep of inner-London boroughs for the Conservatives in 1968, many of the new Tory-led councils began to consider alternatives to the ambitious housing programmes that they had inherited. It was, though, the Conservative Greater London Council elected in the previous year that produced the most coherent challenge to social housing orthodoxy, when the new Housing Committee chairman, Horace Cutler, promoted a twin policy of selling council houses and limiting rent subsidies.

The sales policy was based on that developed by the Conservatives on Birmingham City Council.[141] The ninety-four thousand tenants of houses on GLC cottage estates were offered the chance to buy their own homes, at discounts reflecting the time they had lived in the property, with mortgages available to would-be purchasers.[142] The first sale was completed in October 1967. Take-up proved sporadic. Many tenants could not afford the mortgage repayments, and many of those who could felt that if they 'did buy a house it would be a new up-to-date one with all mod-cons on a private estate.'[143] Some older tenants simply felt, 'at my time of life it's too late to think of buying a house.'[144] Tenants' associations and some individual tenants were hostile in principle to an unambiguously Tory policy.[145] Of the sixty-two thousand tenants circulated by July 1968, fewer than seventeen thousand inquired about a price, and fewer than three thousand agreed to proceed.[146] Sales were healthiest in what had been out-county LCC estates before the expansion of the county in 1965, where the property was spacious and generally well built. More than seventeen hundred tenants on the enormous Becontree Estate—always a showpiece—had bought their houses by August 1972. They proceeded to 'Chelseafy' their council homes: 'The dull brown pebbledashing goes gay with bright colour. . . . Coach lamps appear at the side of the front doors.' One house in Boxhall Street acquired 'a porch supported by Grecian columns' as well as the inevitable coach lamps; a photograph of this creation was hung in County Hall 'as an example of what can be done.'[147] In July 1972 one Becontree resident became the ten thousandth GLC tenant to acquire his own home; another seventy-four hundred sales were said to be in the pipeline, though only forty-three hundred had been completed by the time that the incoming Labour administration suspended the programme in June 1973.[148]

The GLC's ten thousandth purchaser suggested that imminent rent increases would eventually make buying no more burdensome than renting.[149] This was unlikely, but the sense that the council tenant was helpless in the face of ever-rising rents was one of the principal motives to buy.[150] This view was reinforced by the controversy surrounding the Conservative GLC's 'fair rent' policy of 1968 and the Conservative government's application of the same principle nationally by the Housing Finance Act of 1972. The Tory GLC elected in 1967 had calculated that its rents were on average 70 percent lower than tribunal-assessed fair rents for comparable privately rented property and had resolved in October 1968 to implement a 70 percent increase over three years. The first year's 25 percent increase was reduced to 16 percent by the Ministry but still provoked a rent strike by eleven thousand tenants, of whom around five thousand, almost all in the East End, were still on strike in the summer of 1969.[151] The action fizzled out during 1970, but the rent issue revived in the following year, with the introduction of what would become the 1972 act. Many Labour-controlled borough councils toyed with the thought of refusing to impose the new enhanced rents, but the risks inherent in such defiance—massive surcharges on dissident councillors and the loss of central-government subsidies for their authorities—soon concentrated minds. By the spring of 1972 only four 'refusenik' London authorities were still holding out, the last to fold being Camden in January 1973.[152]

Conservatives' 'fair rents' policies, whether local or national, derived from their belief that Labour authorities had entered into a corrupt bargain with their tenants, buying votes with artificially low rents. This was a long-standing concern, but it had acquired a fresh intensity in inner London, where, if votes *were* being bought, high land prices and building costs made the outlay expensive. The deficit on Lambeth's Housing Revenue Account rose by 74 percent between 1967 and 1969, forcing the Labour council to impose sharp increases in council rents before the Conservative administration of 1968 introduced its own 'fair rents' scheme.[153] The Tory GLC's 1968 increase followed a 23 percent increase in 1963 and a 25 percent increase in 1965 under Labour administrations.[154] The economist Marion Bowley, commissioned by Camden Council to analyse its own housing finance problems in 1968, calculated that sixteen London housing authorities' accounts showed a deficit per dwelling more than four times the average of the seventeen largest provincial authorities.[155] In these circumstances, a free-thinking Tory like Cutler gained licence to change fundamentally the relationship between council and tenant: no Labour housing chairman could have proposed 70 percent rent increases, however serious their council's financial situation. The Labour councillors across London forced to implement the Housing Finance Act may privately have been relieved to blame a Tory government for increases they recognised as inescapable.

Nonetheless, the 1972 increases did little to offset the cost of building in London. In 1975–76 rent receipts after rebates covered less than a third of councils' housing expenditure in London, compared with just over a half in the rest of England and Wales.[156] After the furore generated by the GLC's and the Heath government's attempts to raise rents, it was clear that the London council tenant could never be made to bear the full cost of their housing. London ratepayers were increasingly reluctant to bear it for them, though, given the severe rate increases of the mid-1970s. This prompted a fundamental reappraisal of the whole concept of social housing in London, which climaxed in 1976. In that year Richard Balfe, Labour chairman of the GLC Housing Development Committee, called for 'a new socialist perspective' on London housing, urging councils to diminish the barriers between council and owner-occupied housing by helping people to move within their tenure group and from one tenure group to another. Authorities would be encouraged to lend to would-be purchasers and to build for sale, acknowledging the failure of estates built in 'the heyday of architectural folly' and the desire of 'the average working man' to own his own home.[157] In August the *Evening Standard*'s Simon Jenkins attacked the 'liberal housing establishment' and in particular the homelessness charity Shelter for its unstinting advocacy of municipal building. He argued that council housing had largely failed to cater for the truly needy: 'the immigrant, the vagrant homeless family, the student, the battered wife, the single person newly arrived in London': 'It is no good saying that one day the State will provide. It will not, and has increasingly shown that it cannot.'[158] In the same month the Department of the Environment's Action Group on London Housing drew attention to the time taken not just to build but even to plan London council housing: the preconstruction stage accounting for seven years in the boroughs and ten years for GLC houses, against three years in the provinces.[159] In October the academic geographer and GLC planner David Eversley argued that the sums involved in London housing did not compute: £76 million of London housing expenditure was falling on the rates; 'government will not, cannot, increase its subsidies for London housing. London tenants will not pay rents which are higher than their mortgage repayments on "proper" housing would be, for what they consider to be inferior property.'[160]

This line of argument was developed by local politicians on the increasingly confident New Right. The radical Conservative group which regained control at County Hall in 1977 was set on ending the GLC's housing role by transferring estates to the boroughs and by reviving sales to tenants.[161] In the summer of 1978 it sought to coordinate efforts in Tory-controlled boroughs to sell off half a million council houses across the capital. A meeting of sympathetic council leaders was summoned in June, with Margaret Thatcher present.[162] The case was made for a counterrevolution in housing, to prevent London being turned into 'councilville.'[163] Every borough, it was claimed, had increased its municipal stock during the seventies: more than half the new houses scheduled for completion by 1983 would be council-owned.[164]

George Tremlett, the GLC's Housing Policy Committee chair, associated council building with the deepening inner-city crisis: 'What one has now found is that particular areas of London for 40, 50, 60 years have believed that the solution is to have massive council house building programmes, and those have become the poorest areas in London, the employers have left, the educational attainment is very, very poor indeed, and those particular boroughs have effectively cut away the life supply to their communities.'[165] Once seen as the only conceivable solution to London's most pressing social problem, the council house was being depicted as a symptom of the corrosive influence of the local state.

In August 1976 the *Sunday Times* summarised a leaked memorandum indicating that such ideas were also gaining ground within the Department of the Environment.[166] It was written by Alex Henney, formerly housing coordinator in Haringey, who had been seconded to the department to work on its Housing Finance Review. Henney noted that London accounted for half the capital expenditure on new council housing in England and Wales but only a fifth of the output. This expenditure was producing 'a Glaswegian spectre of south, east and north east inner London girded by a ring of generally gruesome high density council housing with severe vandalism and vacancies.' A construction programme aimed at the inner-London working class took no account of the collapse of manufacturing industry in the inner city or the desire of so many people to escape. Henney argued that 'no case of substance has been made on economic grounds for maintaining [inner London's] population, let alone a case for spending considerable sums of money achieving that end with unusually expensive public housing. . . . It makes no sense to crowd more people into the most densely populated part of the country, . . . the more so as so many wish to leave it.' Drawing on the unpublished work of the Lambeth Inner Area Study, which drew attention to the difficulties faced by inner-London council tenants wishing to move away,[167] Henney argued that many people were effectively trapped by council housing in a declining inner city. The outward movement of population was already reducing London's housing deficiency, he suggested, so that 'the inner borough building programme could be stopped now without undue housing consequences.'[168]

This last claim was optimistic, and the department officials questioned some of Henney's assumptions, but they acknowledged that 'he has a valid and worrying point which cannot be ignored.'[169] Any reservations were in any case overwhelmed by the financial crisis which hit Britain at the end of 1976. Council housing programmes were vulnerable under the austerity programme imposed by the International Monetary Fund, and with the capital consuming a third of England's public-sector housing investment,[170] London's programmes were the most vulnerable of all. The Treasury, inevitably, queried the excessive cost of London schemes: 'The Treasury formulation of these issues was as follows: "What are we getting for the money that goes into housing investment in London? If we were meeting the same need elsewhere it would cost less; what are we getting for this money, and is it worth it?"'[171] A joint inquiry into London housing investment was mounted in some secrecy by the Treasury and the Environment

Department in the winter of 1978–79. The Environment Department was less sceptical than the Treasury but was nonetheless critical of authorities such as Brent, Lambeth and Islington which were committed to 'public sector housing at almost any cost' and those like Camden which were accused of deliberately exceeding cost guidelines.[172] By 1978, though, such councils were in a minority. The adventurous use of compulsory purchase to expand the council sector had greatly diminished, and most councils concentrated on improvement of the stock they already owned, upgrading interwar estates and rehabilitating houses purchased in the late sixties.[173] The shift from redevelopment to rehabilitation was in line with an increasingly conservationist public opinion by that point, but the cost of refurbishing what might be listed Georgian terraces in Islington or Lambeth—95 percent of London's rehabilitation schemes exceeded the department's cost limits[174]—only strengthened the perception that London's public-sector housing was intrinsically expensive. Housing projects in the pipeline continued to boost London's total social housing stock until it peaked at just over 30 percent of households in the early 1980s, but there was little chance of the programme regaining its sixties vigour. The contraction of the council housing sector was signalled before Margaret Thatcher's 'right to buy' programme and the other blows dealt in the 1980s. It represented a significant step towards the dismantling of the welfare state, but by the 1970s the combination of social, architectural and financial problems surrounding the sector meant that its containment produced few protests.

Owner Occupation by Default

The attack on council housing coincided with the continued shrinkage of the private rental sector. The rent control applied to unfurnished lettings in 1965 was extended to furnished rentals in 1974. At the bottom end of the rental market, most landlords abandoned hope of a worthwhile return and tried to sell. One claimed to the *Standard* in 1970 that his ten unfurnished houses in Waltham Forest yielded little more than his old-age pension, which was 'much less trouble to collect.' He persisted in the hope of eventually gaining vacant possession, which would enable him to sell; aware of that, his tenants demanded up to £1,000 to leave.[175] As Charlotte Gray wrote in 1974, rent control trapped landlord and tenant in each other's company, working 'to fasten together people who have cause to dislike each other.'[176] The 'flitting' tenant now held no terrors for the landlord: it was those who stayed and paid who were resented. 'It's an awful thing to say, but I often wish my tenants would die', as one Thornton Heath landlady put it in 1978.[177]

Landlords who were unable to sell increasingly sought to evade the law by dressing up their properties as company lets, which carried no security of tenure, or as spurious bed-and-breakfast hotels, in which 'board' might constitute a box of groceries provided by the landlord. Holiday lets also lay outside the legislation if shorter than eight months. As Richard Northedge wrote in the *Standard*, 'holiday lettings in Hackney or Wandsworth are likely to be bogus.'[178] In the West End they might provide genuine accommodation for tourists, but at the cost of depleting further the rental stock. Those landlords who were genuinely letting in marketable areas competed for overseas tenants—employees of foreign companies or embassy staff—who were less concerned about security of tenure and far less likely to resort to rent tribunals than their local counterparts were. 'Owners are ringing up and saying "Have you got any foreigners?"', the *Standard*'s correspondent Kevin Murphy was told by one Kensington letting agency in 1974: 'They know foreigners won't stay.'[179] Such competition pushed up prices at the top end of the rental sector. In 1975 the director of one housing-aid charity reported that 'self-contained flats are almost impossible to find in London except at rents paid by embassy staff and visitors'—meaning at least £50 per week.[180] The number of dwellings in London's private rental sector fell by over one hundred thousand between 1971 and 1976.[181] Even bedsits, symbols of cheap-and-cheerful living for London's newcomers in the sixties, were renting for £10 per week in fashionable areas by 1975. Three years later they were said to be so thin on the ground that two people might pay £15 each to share one.[182]

The *London Property Letter* had suggested as early as 1963 that it might become cheaper to buy than to rent,[183] as the shrinkage of the private rental sector first became apparent. By the late 1970s this had become a commonplace, at least among those whose horizons were limited to the top end of the rental market. In 1977 Robert Langton of the *Standard* spoke to a Harrods employee who was purchasing in Baron's Court because 'she had worked out just what she had paid in rent over the years [in South Kensington] and was shocked.'[184] A year later the *Standard* described a young couple whose house hunt ended in a maisonette in Harlesden, costing them £97 a month after tax relief, whereas their one-bed rented flat in Kentish Town had cost £114.[185] They had, though, been attempting to buy for over two years, in an increasingly hostile and frenetic market.

With the supply of new property for sale limited by planning constraints, a steady upward pressure on property prices developed, with sporadic bubbles. In 1972 the *London Property Letter* noted that rising prices were actually fuelling demand, as would-be purchasers decided that the trend would continue indefinitely and first-time buyers feared being left out of the market altogether.[186] The experience of one young Harrow couple in 1972 has a modern ring:

> Getting their spacious semi-detached house in St Ursula Grove was quite hectic. They bought it in February when the buying and selling spiral of rising house prices was at its height. They were living in Chamberlain Way, Pinner, and had circulated all the estate agents with the type of house they wanted. The estate agent told them at 10 P.M. one Saturday that the house was on the market. At nine next morning they were on the doorstep of their new home and after a quick look round decided to buy it in case the price went up in the next hour. They sold their maisonette in less than half an hour of its being on the market.[187]

The intense miniboom of the late seventies brought similar stories of a panicky market, with first-time buyers taking whatever they could find in order to get into the market and incomers from the provinces particularly disadvantaged.[188] In 1978 the *Standard*'s Lynda Murdin described leaving 'the comfort' of her rented flat to occupy a single room in De Beauvoir Town, while 'Alf the builder' worked around her on the overdue conversion of the rest of the building. She lived 'surrounded by pots and paint, plaster boards and putty': 'It may sound like hell—but it's heaven, because it's mine, all mine.' Having made 'a snap decision on a purchase costing more money than you had ever set eyes on', she trusted that the market would continue rising: 'at least all we property owners hope it will.'[189]

Murdin's account—of moving from rented comfort to a building site in order to call it her own, paying heavily for it and looking to future price rises to vindicate her purchase—echoed the experience of a generation of buyers in 1970s London. The savage increase in the cost of living in that decade made the house more an inflation hedge than the endlessly appreciating investment that it would become in the 1980s, but the image of the owned home as part sanctuary, part asset, dates from these years. Critically, it *was* attainable for many people, for all the recurrent panics and concern for first-time buyers. Between the booms, London house prices fell more steeply in real terms than did house prices in the rest of the United Kingdom,[190] and by the end of the decade almost half the capital's households lived in homes they owned. Soon home owners would be in the majority.

London's 'Mixed Economy of Housing'

At the height of the Rachman scandal, the North Paddington Labour MP Ben Parkin, who had been principally responsible for bringing exploitative landlordism to light, called for 'a basic rethink of Beveridge' to bring housing properly into the ambit of the welfare state. He argued that 'private property in houses was not an absolute and eternal thing.'[191] Twenty years later Horace Cutler, principal architect of the Conservative GLC's assault on social housing, complained in his autobiography that 'housing has become a social service, which it should certainly never be.'[192] Each of these fundamentalist sentiments appeared optimistic when voiced: over 80 percent of Greater London housing was privately owned or rented when Parkin spoke in the early sixties, while social renting accounted for around 30 percent of London's housing stock when Cutler published his memoir, but we still find left-wing councils proposing to municipalise privately rented property in the midseventies and a renewed assault on social ownership from the GLC and some Tory boroughs a few years later. Ultimately nobody planned London's mixed economy of housing: it emerged as the resultant of largely independent forces—policy prescriptions on left and right and the autonomous trend towards owner occupation.

The last of these was probably the most important. At the start of our period London had a lower owner-occupation rate than the country as a whole, and as the 1960 Social Survey report showed, many of those who did own their homes did so reluctantly. This reluctance was most evident in inner London, reflecting the age and poor condition of so much of the older housing stock, which at first glance did not appear tempting either as investment or asset. Enough of it was intrinsically appealing, though, to spark the phenomenon of gentrification, which quickened the pace of purchase. By the midsixties the Milner Holland Committee could note that owner occupation was becoming the favoured means of acquiring accommodation in inner London.[193] Between 1959 and 1965 London house prices rose by 53 percent in real terms—an increase significantly more rapid than in the United Kingdom as a whole, establishing a price gap between London and the regions 'which was never subsequently reversed.'[194] By 1970 lenders were advising first-time buyers, 'try to find something you can afford—even if you don't like it', in order to enter a rising market.[195] In that year Ann Holmes noted that owner-occupiers in the housing stress areas that she studied in Islington displayed high levels of satisfaction with their accommodation even though it was essentially slum property, cramped and lacking in amenities: 'satisfaction seems, in large part, to relate to the nature of the tenure itself'.[196] During the seventies, as the minority Labour group on the GLC noted in 1980, owner occupation expanded rapidly, 'in spite of more rapid inflation, worse economic performance and real wages rising more slowly.'[197] Though those who bought at the top of the market might have found repayments burdensome, few would have contemplated a return to renting. The prize of ownership was too valuable to surrender.

In the 1964 follow-up to the 1960 Social Survey, Myra Woolf noted that ownership was clearly associated with high incomes only amongst those who had purchased since 1960. Earlier purchasers were more likely to be in lower-income groups—'probably the widow and pensioner households'—which doubtless explains why early-sixties London contained so many reluctant owner-occupiers.[198] The spread of owner occupation from 1960 clearly was a reflection of the capital's growing affluence, though: the owned home became the ultimate consumer durable in modern London.

That was predictable. Less so was the way in which owner-occupiers, and the army of converters and developers who serviced them, became agents of housing policy, effecting the overdue refurbishment of a large proportion of London's housing stock, nearly half of which in 1960 dated from before the First World War. This was where gentrification was most significant. Much of the property targeted by early gentrifiers, in Chelsea, Notting Hill or Islington, had been considered slum housing and assumed to be beyond correction. In fact very little London housing was entirely beyond correction if a purchaser was prepared to spend enough on renovation, and many of the early nineteenth-century houses in question possessed an aesthetic appeal which—in addition to a central location and good transport links—justified the gamble of refurbishment. Over time, rising demand and the growth of the conversion business extended the market in 'secondhand' houses—as they tended still to be called in the sixties literature—to cover more ordinary property and purchasers, until 'gentrification', with all its connotations, was no longer an adequate term to describe the process.

This development was always likely to prompt some sort of reappraisal of housing policy in London. From the dawn of municipal housing in the 1880s, public policy had aimed not only at improving the health and quality of life of lower-income groups but also at effecting environmental improvement through slum clearance. Each objective was considered intrinsically desirable, and the two were seen as interlinked; but comprehensive redevelopment was always forbiddingly expensive in inner London. The moment in 1963 when the Ministry of Housing recognised that the area of Fulham chosen as a pilot for area improvement was 'regenerating itself'[199]—that private capital was spontaneously funding urban improvement—was perhaps more significant than was obvious at the time. By 1969 a Labour government was prepared to subsidise the ad hoc improvement of existing houses not only by their owner-occupiers, who were increasingly likely to be affluent, but even by profit-seeking developers. The objective of physical improvement was being pursued for its own sake, to the likely benefit of middle-class occupiers.

Labour-controlled inner-city authorities were inevitably suspicious of this redirection of policy. Most pressed on with traditional redevelopment programmes which offered some protection against the embourgeoisement of their areas. In London's most 'labourist' borough, Tower Hamlets, 82 percent of dwellings were municipally owned by 1981, as were two-thirds of Southwark dwellings.[200] Such statistics fired concerns on the right that parts of inner London were becoming 'councilville.' The proportion of London dwellings accounted for by social housing continued to rise until the early 1980s, but the tide had really turned against council housing in the midseventies, when the sector came under sustained critical fire. Such evidence as we have suggests, in fact, that council tenants were not widely unhappy with their accommodation, even if most would have preferred to own,[201] but the wider public discourse in these years highlighted the problems caused by overrapid building in the sixties, while attempts to improve standards—most imaginatively in the designer estates produced by Camden Council—invited charges of extravagance.[202] As the sociologist Ray Pahl put it in 1974, 'Local authority housing lacks its champions: our educational system and the National Health Service have their respective supporters and admirers but "council housing" has become more an indication of "problems", "trouble" or poverty.'[203] Critically, the charges made against council housing in the 1976 Henney memorandum were never entirely countered, at least to the satisfaction of the Environment Department, which controlled local government's purse strings.

The council sector would peak in the early eighties at around a third of London households. At that level, or below, it was something of a closed shop, with most new accommodation filled by the victims of slum clearance and waiting lists slow to shrink. This underlined the significance of the contraction of the private rental sector. The reimposition of rent control in 1965 and 1974 was sanctioned politically on the strength of the poor image of the landlordism following the Rachman scandal, but one suspects that in a welfarist age, policy makers instinctively assumed that the state could and would provide, offering a more efficient and benign service than the private landlord. This had always been questionable. As the Milner Holland Committee pointed out in 1965, a city like London required a functioning rental sector to accommodate 'particular groups, especially the newly formed households, migrant newcomers, single and childless people, many of the aged and some of the rich,'[204] who stood little chance of securing council accommodation. The Milner Holland Committee had brought to light the abuses perpetrated by many private landlords in conditions of housing shortage; closely read, though, its report demonstrated the indispensability of a flexible rental sector in a city as diverse as London. The private rental sector was still larger in London than in England and Wales as a whole;[205] but it was much smaller than it had been, and many in it—landlords and tenants alike—wished to escape.

Conclusion

In 1970 Father Paul Byrne, of the Shelter Housing Advice Centre, had described giving housing advice to inner-city schoolchildren, apparently contemplating early marriage: 'If they come from a council home background, they half expect that there will be a nice new council flat for them at the end of the honeymoon. We have to tell them that this is nothing short of a miracle—and that saving towards a home of their own is the answer.'[206] These were prescient words, some years before council housing really fell out of favour, but one suspects that few of those who heard them were on the property ladder by the end of the decade. Many must have had to choose between staying with their parents, passing a long stint on a council waiting list, trying their luck in a shrinking rental sector and leaving London altogether. It was not easy for those on low incomes to put money aside, and the obstacles to their becoming home owners had not disappeared. Affluence had made owner occupation more widespread, but with few new houses being built, rising demand tended to make London property less and less affordable until each bubble burst, which made houses affordable again but did nothing to solve the problem of supply.

Those who had a plausible chance of purchase took it, even at the cost of squatting in their own property while 'Alf the builder' did his worst. Owner-occupation levels would move steadily upwards until the early 1990s, but they would never surpass 60 percent and have been falling since the turn of the century. All could not own.

These developments sharpened critically the distinction between the haves and the have-nots in London's housing market. In chapter 1 it was argued that the 1970s brought greater income inequality in London, as the poorest lost ground, but that the 'median Londoner' gained in real terms over the decade as a whole. There was no automatic relationship between income distribution and housing tenure, but by the end of the decade there was a similarity of outcome. Outside the rather insular council sector, around 70 percent of households owned their homes; the comparable figure in 1961 had been around 45 percent. Home ownership brought independence and security. It was demonstrably the preference of householders nationally,[207] and there is no reason to believe that Londoners differed. Whatever misgivings some owner-occupiers had expressed in the 1960 survey, and whatever difficulties faced those who had purchased at the top of the late-seventies boom, very few new entrants to the property market by 1979 would willingly have returned to renting. But ownership levels in London remained comfortably below the national average, and with council housing reaching its peak, those who were stuck outside both sectors faced considerable difficulties in a shrinking, deteriorating and expensive private rental sector. Developments over the previous twenty years had ensured that by 1981 many more Londoners enjoyed the benefits that home ownership conferred, but at the cost of marginalising many others and creating the affordable-housing problem that has plagued the capital ever since.

6

'You Only Have to Look at Westway'

THE END OF THE URBAN MOTORWAY IN LONDON

In June 1966 officials from the Greater London Council revealed to their counterparts in the Ministry of Housing and Local Government what the men from Whitehall considered 'almost a revolution in planning techniques.'[1] The GLC had come into being barely a year earlier, replacing the London County Council and governing a far higher proportion of London's current built-up area than the LCC had done. Though the GLC retained many of the powers that the LCC had possessed, it was intended to act as a 'strategic' planning authority, shaping the development of London as a whole rather than governing in detail. The preparation of a new strategic plan for the capital was its principal statutory duty. To fulfil that duty, it sought to recapture something of the holistic vision that had inspired the classic wartime plans constructed by Patrick Abercrombie. Abercrombie's plans had attempted both to reflect and to shape the vital forces of a city. He had engendered a public eagerness to see rational and beautiful urban environments rise from the ashes of blitzed cities and provided the impetus for the Attlee government to enhance the planning powers and duties of local authorities in legislation of 1947. The 1947 act proved to be a somewhat pale reflection of Abercrombiean aspirations, though, largely limiting itself to the regulatory side of planning—the curbing of random and antisocial development. A national planning system emerged, with local authorities producing quinquennial development plans, but the emphasis was placed on land-use planning and development control. By the time this modern Domesday was completed, in 1961, a new generation of professional planners questioned the limited vision of the 1947 system. In 1965 the Ministry of Housing's Planning Advisory Group addressed the question of 'how the planning system can be made a better vehicle for planning policies.'[2] Arguing that existing development plans were often clogged by detail, it called for a separation of strategic and local planning. For larger urban areas it advocated 'a new type of urban plan which concentrates on the broad pattern of future development and redevelopment and deals with the land use/transport relationships in an integrated way, but which excludes the detailed land use allocations of the present town maps'[3] Details could be left to the local planning process, leavened in future by more extensive public consultation and participation.[4] The concept of the 'structure plan'—more comprehensive and less close-focused than existing development plans, emerged from this process, and the creation of the GLC offered an early opportunity to devise one.

The result was the Greater London Development Plan, published in full in 1969. It was the most ambitious exercise in British urban planning since Abercrombie's 1944 plan, covering the demography, economy, mobility, housing, recreation and environment of the London of the future. One of its architects, Peter Stott, the GLC's director of highways and transportation, had been a member of the Planning Advisory Group, and the GLDP reflected the group's concern for strategy and flexibility in assessing the way in which a large urban society functioned. It sought 'an equilibrium between houses-work-movement', based on empirical study of London life, in a plan flexible enough to be amended on the strength of current knowledge and future trends, rather than devoted to fixed objectives: 'housing + work + movement = the way that Londoners live.'[5]

In seeking to understand the workings of the metropolis, the GLC planners had been able to draw on a wealth of existing survey material. They collated, inter alia, the Ministry of Transport's London Traffic Survey of 1964,[6] the central-area land-use survey of 1962, workplace tabulations from the 1961 Census, surveys of office floor space in new buildings, Factory Inspectorate statistics on central-area industries, 1948 and 1959 surveys of canal and riverside premises, London Transport's annual journey-to-work surveys, a 1962 central-area car-parking survey, a sample survey of business trip generation from 666 central-area firms, work on housing stress areas, a 1964 survey of department stores in the centre and the West End, a 1964 analysis of central hotel accommodation, information on the seating capacity of cinemas and theatres and even interviews with the users of Lincoln's Inn Fields and the Victoria Embankment.[7]

This empirical emphasis carried the risk of destroying the flexibility claimed for the new system, but the GLDP was not, taken as a whole, unduly prescriptive. In one vital respect, though, it could not avoid a degree of dirigisme. The 'movement' that Stott sought to plan for, in addition to 'houses' and 'work', would require investment in fixed transport infrastructure, addressing the question of increasing concern to urban managers in the early sixties: how to accommodate the rising level of car ownership and use. This had, of course, been a matter of concern in London for decades, and the favoured solution, in the eyes of traffic planning professionals, had also long been clear. In the late 1930s and in a seminal work of 1942 Alker Tripp, assistant commissioner of the Metropolitan Police in charge of traffic, had advocated modernising London's 'obsolete' road network to channel through and fast traffic into purpose-built new roads, where neither local traffic nor pedestrians would impede it.[8] In towns, he maintained, 'the aim must always be to give the motor traffic on the main roads such a dominance as will attract it there and keep it there, thus effectively draining it off from other and less desirable routes.'[9] Tripp's arguments were accepted by Abercrombie and incorporated into the latter's *Greater London Plan, 1944*. Abercrombie was an advocate of ring roads and planned five of them for London, as part of a web of arterial roads.[10] In the interstices between these major roads, 'precincts' were envisaged by both Tripp and Abercrombie, depicted as oases free from dangerous, intrusive traffic.

Where main roads were concerned, Tripp argued that 'it is just as necessary to keep [pedestrians] off the tracks provided for vehicles as it is to keep them off railway tracks.' He believed that bridges, with pedestrian walkways at bridge level, were the means to achieve that separation. Shop frontages and front doors would 'of course' also be at that level. This was a prescription for new construction, but he felt that similar principles would be followed 'even in the old towns of the old countries' when the benefits of pedestrian safety became clear.[11] The idea that town planning should seek to separate traffic and pedestrians even in established urban areas was developed by Colin Buchanan in his lauded 1963 report *Traffic in Towns* and developed into a programme for the extensive remodelling of town centres to prevent the car from strangling the city.[12] Buchanan might well have left a greater mark on London than he eventually did. As the inspector who conducted the public inquiry into the proposed redevelopment of

Piccadilly Circus in 1960, he had argued for the physical segregation of traffic and pedestrians in the Circus, which in time gave rise to William Holford's implausible 'Piazzadilly' scheme of 1968, depicting a raised pedestrian piazza with traffic concealed beneath it,[13] and the *Traffic in Towns* report is perhaps best known now for a conjectural—if startling—projection of a space-age Fitzrovia. The GLC traffic planners were clearly taken by Buchanan's arguments, but in their proposals for a primary road network they avoided the central area.[14] The *London Traffic Survey* (*LTS*), commissioned by the Ministry of Transport in 1960 and published in 1964, had suggested that the principal growth area for London traffic would be found in journeys outside the centre.[15] In February 1965, presenting the conclusions drawn from the first two *LTS* volumes, Peter Stott accepted that 90 percent of journeys to work were made by public transport but argued that the real problem lay in the clogging of the existing road network by intraurban journeys that were not easily made by public transport—'journeys of the type Dagenham to Putney, Greenwich to Hampstead.'[16]

Tripp had argued in 1942 that 'at least one good circular road is . . . required within the confines of the town itself, to enable the town's own traffic to by-pass the centre as much as possible.' Such ring roads should be 'so attractive, by virtue of width and absence of checks, as to *induce* traffic to use them, despite any additional mileage.'[17] The GLC's planners therefore proposed to build three orbital motorways outside the central area. The innermost of them, the so-called Motorway Box (later Ringway 1) was unveiled immediately after the GLC came into being in 1965 and would run provocatively through Hampstead, Camden, Barnsbury, Hackney, the Blackwall Tunnel, Kidbrooke, Blackheath, Brockley, Peckham, Clapham, Putney, Chelsea, Holland Park and Willesden. Ringways 2 and 3 were developed as parts of the Greater London Development Plan, completed in 1969. Ringway 2 was intended to replace the 'ludicrous backstreet' that was the South Circular Road,[18] linking it to an upgraded North Circular to form a second circle in inner suburbia. Ringway 3 encircled outer suburbia. The northeastern section, from South Mimms across the river to Swanley, would eventually be built as part of the M25. Much of the route taken by the southern section remained unclear, though it was likely to have passed as close to Keston, Croydon, Esher and Walton-on-Thames as politics allowed. In the west it was planned to run through or near to Sunbury, Northolt, Ruislip, Denham, Bushey and Moor Park.[19]

Two key principles of the Buchanan report had particularly influenced the GLC: the assumption that the rise in car ownership and use was inexorable and had to be catered for and the belief that engineering solutions could be found for most traffic problems.[20] The idea that city centres could be so remodelled as to allow cars and pedestrians to coexist within them appeared to offer an elegant solution to an increasingly pressing urban problem, but ministers recoiled from the cost involved, about which Buchanan—like Abercrombie before him—appeared somewhat insouciant.[21] The GLC avoided the unimaginable cost of extensive road-building in the central area by concentrating on orbital roads outside it, but no infrastructural project in London ever comes cheap. The GLC's own estimate to the eventual public inquiry into the plan costed the Ringways and the new radial roads linking them at almost £1.4 billion, with the Motorway Box (Ringway 1) alone coming in at £480 million.[22] It was primarily the cost of Ringway 1 which led the *Evening Standard*'s Simon Jenkins to predict as early as November 1969 that 'the most lavish public expenditure project ever undertaken in Britain' would never be built.[23]

The rate of growth in car use projected from the *London Traffic Survey* had been called into question even before GLC's final proposals were published. The results of the 1966 Census of Traffic suggested a marked slowing in that rate, convincing one traffic analyst that 'it would be wrong to rush into major decisions merely out of a sense of panic.'[24] In fact, although the Ringways' advocates were given to suggesting that London would grind to a halt without them, the roads were not a panic measure in their eyes but rather an attempt to respond to apparent changes in the nature of motoring. The 1964 *LTS* findings suggested that increasing car use was related to rising household income and that it was growing most rapidly in respect of journeys unconnected with work, a finding echoed nationally by the 1964 Birmingham University study 'The People and the Car.'[25] The Ringways would be 'social roads', offering, in planner-speak, 'the only real opportunity available to secure adequate amenity provision in a modern pattern of living.'[26] The Council inferred from its empirical studies—and particularly the *LTS*—a developing consumerist impetus behind car use that implicitly sanctioned the construction of new roads. 'People's preferences are fairly clear at all income levels', Stott asserted: 'We know that public transport and prohibition represent a lower standard of living than that we have arrived at. . . . We must provide more road capacity.'[27] The belief in a bottled-up public demand for high-grade urban roads lay behind the GLC's initial confidence that the proposed motorways would be welcomed by the London public. In the preparation of the *Report of Studies* volume, accompanying the full GLDP, it was decided that 'the material should state very early on that transport was a major element in determining the development of London, particularly in respect of general amenity—that is, the facility for movement and the quality of the environment.'[28] Anticipating a doubling of car ownership between 1962 and 1981, Stott argued that currently 'the contribution that this personal mobility makes to efficiency and enjoyment is tempered by congestion and environmental deterioration.'[29]

Much rested on the assumption that a city's social evolution could be planned on the strength of empirical evidence-gathering: as J. R. Fitzpatrick, the GLC's assistant director of planning and transportation, put it, 'the prerequisite of planning is information.'[30] This was doubtless true, and so far as traffic planning was concerned, the unprecedentedly comprehensive results of the *London Traffic Survey* provided a firmer evidential basis than any highways authority had possessed before. Nonetheless, in going beyond the measurement of traffic flows and the identification of pinch points, in assuming that public opinion could be inferred from observed public behaviour, the GLC was asking a lot of its empiricism. The embittered debate over the Ringways, and their eventual abandonment, would make this clear.

Reaction

'HOW DO THE GLC KNOW WHAT THE PEOPLE OF LONDON WANT? HAVE THEY EVER ASKED THEM?' demanded one of the thirty thousand objectors to the GLDP before its public inquiry.[31] The short answer was that they had not; the longer one was that they preferred information-gathering to opinion-sampling. If the prerequisite of planning was information, the Council had drawn on plenty of it in compiling the GLDP, but it had tended to rely on the measurement of outcomes rather than attitudes. The GLC planners remained cautious about attitude surveys: market-research techniques might be appropriate when 'a range of simple questions can be asked upon a particular topic', but they 'would not be suitable for complicated major issues of strategy or policy.'[32] If market research confirmed behavioural surveys, it would be redundant; if it conflicted with them, it would be dubious: the GLC planners never entirely shed the assumption that the general public 'just do not understand the nature and purpose of a structure plan. By and large they are concerned with their own back yard.'[33] Such reasoning was comprehensible, but it masked a flaw inherent in the new mode of planning—that the structure created by structure planning was so elaborate that it was very difficult to accommodate public opinion, whether positive or negative, within it. This is to some extent true of all metropolitan planning, but it became a more significant weakness when the plan concerned proposed major construction that threatened to disrupt the urban environment and alienate the people being planned for. In such circumstances it became dangerous to infer public preferences from the Council's voluminous survey material— to assume, as Robert Vigars, chairman of the GLC Planning and Transportation Committee, put it crudely in 1969, that because Londoners would own two million cars by 1980, 'they will want to drive them somewhere.'[34]

There is no doubt that car-ownership levels were rising or that the effects of congestion were irksome, but these facts could not guarantee public support for the Ringways at all costs. While drivers were obviously likely to prefer purpose-built, high-grade roads to old and ill-designed ones, the choice was not made in isolation. Most obviously, those who were sufficiently affluent to own a car were increasingly likely also to be home owners. The years of greatest contention over the GLDP—1969 to 1973—were the years of the property bubble, during which rising house prices made existing owner-occupiers conscious of the value of their principal asset and encouraged others to enter the market. Owner occupation in the suburban areas threatened by Ringways 2 and 3 was already high, and it was rising in several of the gentrifying areas to be invaded by Ringway 1. Home owners were likely to feel rooted in their area and therefore more resistant to any local environmental intrusion even if their own homes were not directly threatened. Even if none of those considerations applied, it was still possible to see the car as a desirable—even essential— possession without wishing to see the urban fabric butchered to accommodate it. In the event, a generalised public acceptance in the early sixties that London needed a more modern road system was rapidly dispelled when the outline of the Motorway Box was published, to persistent apprehension about its effects on the city.[35] A new consensus emerged, which amplified the simple 'nimbyism' that the GLC had always anticipated into a broader concern for the urban environment—and a critique of the car's place within it which challenged all the GLC's assumptions about public preference.

Mobilisation

'It really is ridiculous', complained one objector before the public inquiry. 'People are encouraged to become "property owning democrats." They put a large part of their savings effort throughout their lives into buying a house. Then you come along and make it virtually worthless.'[36] 'I do not wish to live in Council accommodation', protested another; 'all we want is our own home & to leave it at my convenience & not to be pushed out of it by the GLC & other bodies that limit our freedom to live where we choose.'[37] 'Our house is not only to be considered as a property but it is above all a home which took great sacrifices and considerable time to find and to adapt for our families [*sic*] purposes', wrote an objector in Camden.[38] The files of objections to the GLDP bristle with submissions from owner-occupiers who knew or feared that their houses lay in the path of the motorways. Those who attended two of the local meetings held to discuss the GLDP in 1969 were disproportionately owner-occupiers.[39] So were the suburban opponents of Ringways 2 and 3: the Bromley-based Ringway 2 Resistance Group, for instance, found that of 349 people canvassed along the road's proposed route 80 percent were owner-occupiers, and all but three of them opposed the road.[40] 'Why have the GLC said it must be privately owned property that is blighted and not their own?', asked a Bromley woman.[41] The answer was, as the Planning Committee imprudently admitted,[42] that paying an owner sufficient compensation to buy a new house was cheaper than rehousing council tenants, but the political cost was high.

This was a middle-class resistance movement.[43] It is self-evident, though, that only a small proportion of the thirty thousand objectors to the GLDP (mostly private individuals) were directly threatened by the road plans. The motorway protest was not simply a revolt of householders protecting their gardens; it was more accurately seen as an expression of what David Donnison identified in 1973 as the emerging micropolitics of the city.[44] Although the unveiling of the Ringway proposals in 1969 caused almost instant consternation in the areas affected, conventional local politics offered little help to those who were worried. The Labour opposition on the GLC remained somewhat compromised by the party's initial sponsorship of the Motorway Box, only beginning to distance itself 'quietly' from the proposals in 1969,[45] while amongst the borough councils—almost all of them under Conservative control after the party's landslide gains in 1968—only four would submit strategic objections to the primary road proposals at the eventual public inquiry.[46] In any case, as one Ealing objector argued before the public inquiry, the borough councils 'may be so full up with day-to-day business that they haven't got time to consider points of principle. . . . Residents associations such as ours can look at the thing rather more as a matter of principle, consider the background.'[47] Opposition therefore tended to be expressed either through normally unpolitical amenity or other societies or by ad hoc groups formed expressly to oppose the roads. Analysis of those who attended the Camden and Croydon public meetings showed that around a third of those present belonged to civic or amenity groups.[48]

The growth of these groups in London was rapid: by 1973 the seven hundred or so active community groups necessitated the publication of a separate London Community Planning Directory.[49] They varied in kind. Some had been formed in the early 1970s in order to defend working-class communities against the wave of redevelopment associated with the property boom; these groups played little part in the opposition to the GLDP. But the GLC calculated that 83 percent of the first twenty-one thousand objections either came from or were supported by local groups of some kind.[50] Many of the suburban groups were traditional ratepayers associations.[51] Others had clearly been called into existence by the GLDP itself: the London Motorway Action Group, which spearheaded the resistance to the GLDP, included eighteen local antimotorway groups amongst its corporate members. In inner London a number of well-established local societies, such as the Islington Society or the St John's Wood Preservation Society, essentially antiquarian local history groups, became active in the guerrilla campaign against the Ringways. They were joined by newer associations reflecting inner-city gentrification. The Barnsbury Association, formed in 1964, is exemplary. During the 1960s the proportion of professional and managerial families in that rapidly gentrifying area had risen from 4 percent to just over half.[52] The association was formed in August 1964 when news leaked that Barnsbury was threatened by redevelopment. From the summer of 1965 it had advocated an 'environmental plan with local citizen participation', lobbying government and running candidates in local elections.[53]

Such organisations mattered particularly because they embodied the resistance to Ringway 1—the Motorway Box—the most fiercely contested of the three roads. The route plan of Ringway 1 amounts to a gazetteer of gentrification, encompassing Hampstead, Highgate, Islington, riverside Greenwich, Blackheath, Battersea and other parts of the nineteenth-century urban rim, where middle-class colonists were renovating 'characterful' property. The GLC consistently underestimated this phenomenon. It stressed the dereliction of much inner-area property as a selling point for Ringway 1,[54] without any apparent comprehension either of the amount of capital invested in gentrification or of the articulacy and determination of the gentrifiers.

The Barnsbury Association acknowledged its reliance on 'an influx of professional people, many of whom are architects, traffic experts, town-planners and so on.'[55] The eventual public inquiry into the GLDP witnessed a debate on planning technique precisely because the opposition included so many people *au fait* both with current planning theory and with the arguments against it. But this was not just a planners' dispute: it involved a wider circle of informed white-collar laypeople—teachers, lawyers, academics and local government officers—who ensured that the case against road-building was elevated above the mere defence of property.

There is greater uniformity than might be expected in the thirty thousand or so objections to the GLDP. In part this reflects effective organisation by the opposition: many individual objections followed pro forma prescriptions devised by particular groups (GLC analysis identified twenty-six standard forms of objection in multiple use).[56] Many of the arguments advanced in the opposition 'Bible', *Motorways in London*, written by the LSE economist J. M. Thomson for the London Amenity and Transport Association, became common objector currency. The GLC privately acknowledged the force of Thomson's book and urged its inquiry counsel to familiarise themselves with it.[57] Thomson provided a damaging critique of the *LTS* and its methodology. He demonstrated the poor return on capital provided by Ringway 1, provided the clearest exposition of the argument that new roads actually generated traffic and called for a powerful Planning Inquiry Commission, along the lines of the Roskill Inquiry into London's third airport.[58]

In the view of one Ministry of Housing official surveying the amenity group phenomenon in 1969, 'with rising wealth and aspirations, some of the wealth, and more importantly, some of the aspirations, will be turned to the physical environment.'[59] The growth of amenity groups typified an emergent conservation movement concerned less with the preservation of individual buildings than with the defence of familiar locales. 'There are no specific buildings that one can say attract people', explained one objector, referring to riverside Chiswick: 'there is no specific grassy patch or anything like that, but yet the whole build-up of that area, the way that it has been built up, appeals.'[60] The representative of the Grove Park Group in Chiswick challenged the plan's unadventurous approach to conservation, which largely confined itself to predictable national treasures: 'the Plan merely states the obvious and nobody wishes to destroy St Paul's Cathedral and that is specifically mentioned but Oxford Street where it is mentioned is mentioned only as a problem area and yet Londoners who live in Dalston and Sunbury and Kingston make weekly expeditions to Oxford Street, not just St Paul's Cathedral, important though it is.'[61]

Two seminal works on urban living had clearly entered the metropolitan bloodstream, by Steen Eiler Rasmussen and Jane Jacobs. The argument of Rasmussen's *London, the Unique City* (1934), a paean to the diversity and individuality of London villages, became received opinion amongst the GLDP's opponents.[62] 'London is, you know, a number of villages', the inquiry was told, 'each village with its group of suburbs which link together.'[63] Not only nominal villages like Blackheath and Highgate but Chiswick and Barnes, even Lewisham and the Isle of Dogs, were so depicted.[64] Chiswick, for example, was 'one of the few remaining village centres in London where they still play cricket on the Green on Saturdays in summer.'[65] The Ratepayers Association in Beddington, known to many people as the site of the Croydon sewage farm, recited its village's history since the Conquest.[66] 'Villages' nurtured 'community', which the Ringways would destroy. Purpose-built oases like Bedford Park emphasised their community spirit, but the Lewisham Society argued that even 'the quiet red-brick suburb of Hither Green has a much more deep-rooted community than the more dramatic environment of Blackheath.'[67] Community was 'a very delicate thing'; a motorway through Chiswick would drive out 'those people who would plant their oak seeds there', turning it into a second Earl's Court: 'and it is no reflection on the people of Earl's Court that they do not care very much for the environment, and you do not have amenity societies and others in Earl's Court; the people are only there for a couple of years and they cannot care.'[68] The modern American city was depicted as a terrifying spectre. In the GLC's determination to impose an expressway network on London, it would Americanise the capital. Some of the objectors were influenced by Jane Jacobs's *The Death and Life of Great American Cities*, an influential product of US urbanism, first published in 1961.[69] Jacobs asked what sustained and what threatened community life in the modern city. She did not attack US cities so much as conventional planning theory (her subtitle was *The Failure of Town Planning*), but the fear was implanted in British minds that US cities 'show how a community can be destroyed through planning which is not concerned with human values.'[70] The United States, a land of 'choked cities and dead lakes',[71] offered a warning for British planners; indeed, 'the Americans come and see us because we have not spoilt London yet.'[72] If the roads were built, 'the noise, the fumes and the accidents will multiply and the smog now found over cities like Los Angeles, Washington and New York will hang heavily over a bleak, nerve-racking London'; 'tourists will not want to come here if it is simply the Los Angeles of Europe.'[73]

When objectors spoke of 'the American city', they generally meant Los Angeles, a city believed to be cribbed by expressways and smothered by smog. Jacobs had described Los Angeles as 'an extreme example of a metropolis with little public life.'[74] Expressways had not been especially prominent in her argument, but her emphasis on the way in which maladroit physical planning could accentuate social polarisation became the principal component of the opposition case. 'Forced segregation . . . is the antithesis of proper urban life', wrote a Hampstead civil engineer.[75] Urban roads would destroy the inner city while simultaneously providing an escape route for the rich. Blight would destroy the areas immediately surrounding the motorways themselves ('they may however be useful to meths drinkers and those who wish to chop up their professional rivals').[76] As 'no community spirit can exist between people living on opposite sides of a motorway', the Motorway Box would 'emphasise the difference between rich and poor as is seen in America.'[77] An American priest who had moved to Chiswick urged the GLDP's proponents 'to give America a try first. A year in an American city without an automobile or twenty years with one, either experience will certainly convince them that the present course is inadvisable.'[78]

Interrogation

The sheer volume of opposition to the GLDP, and in particular to its road proposals, showed the GLC planners that they faced a political battle. Few of them were political animals. The members of the Planning and Transportation Department were generally technocrats. Stott himself was a civil engineer who had joined the LCC from private industry in 1963.[79] They took the principles of planning to be beyond argument, much as health-service professionals thought socialised medicine uncontentious. By the time of the GLDP's eventual publication, though, the political case for increasing public involvement in the planning process was being pushed with greater urgency, imposing on the GLC planners a degree of accountability to which they were unaccustomed.

Greater public involvement in the planning process had been advocated by the 1965 Planning Advisory Group report. It had been embedded in the 1967 white paper 'Town and Country Planning' and in the 1968 Town and Country Planning Act. The 1969 Skeffington Committee on Public

Participation in Planning had investigated ways of encouraging participation. The GLC was aware of these proposals and wished to accommodate them. When the GLDP was being devised in the mid-1960s, it hoped to encourage 'public interest in the Council's proposals and planning activity',[80] assuming broad public support for its work. In publicising the GLDP, it went beyond the current requirements of the law.

There was, though, a difference between publicity and participation, and the form of any meaningful public participation in the creation of structure plans remained unclear. Abercrombie had consulted instrumentally: he sought out traffic experts, drainage specialists or demographers, but even when his informants were local authority officers, they were consulted as specialists rather than as representatives of their communities. Interest in participation in the 1960s really related to small-scale improvements: its main proponent was Wilfred Burns, city planning officer of Newcastle-upon-Tyne and a member of the Planning Advisory Group. Burns was familiar with US participation initiatives, and he described to the Skeffington Committee the results of Newcastle Corporation's experiments at cooperation with community groups.[81] Such local-level consultation had been the limit of the PAG's ambition, but once the 1968 act generalised the obligation, it became necessary to ask how it could be applied to structure plans. The two principal problems were the difficulty of inducing the public to 'think strategically' and the near impossibility of identifying representative public groups with which to consult at a level above the local. Each problem was acute in London, given the size of the metropolis and the number of its ad hoc community groups.

Burns acknowledged that at the structural level, planning was 'a complicated and difficult process, and to understand it means hard work and real intellectual effort.'[82] The GLC planners agreed and doubted if 'any but the professional and other informed sections of the public would positively criticise strategic policies or make alternative suggestions.'[83] The Council could negotiate with the London boroughs, but it balked at parlaying with innumerable amenity societies, let alone Motorway Action Groups which existed purely to oppose the GLDP. Such consultation in Camden, for instance, would entail dealing with fifteen different, unconnected, societies.[84] 'I never know quite how responsible or representative one of these groups is,' Vigars argued. 'It may really represent public opinion or—for all I know—it may just be a man and his wife.'[85] 'Why should one group of residents get preferential treatment just because they band themselves into a pressure group to shift the line of a road to someone else's road?', asked

Betty Turner, of the GLC's Public Information Branch.[86] The Council was probably overeager to ascribe 'nimbyism' to its opponents, but when a protest group could guilelessly call itself the South Orbital Road Diversion Committee, the suspicion remained.[87] The ideas mooted before the Skeffington Committee—and eventually endorsed by them—for ad hoc community forums conflicted with established principles of representative local democracy. The committee assumed that one reason for the apparent distance between the public and the planners was lack of faith in local government: the GLC unsurprisingly denied that and fell back on a robust defence of the role of the elected member.[88] Betty Turner called for 'the inclusion of civics in the school curricula' to draw the public back to constitutional orthodoxy.[89]

The advocates of participation before Skeffington argued simply that 'local democracy should have the right to produce a bad plan';[90] the GLC was unwilling, though, to risk planning badly on a metropolitan scale. Vigars put the matter characteristically bluntly: 'on major matters such as the planning of the strategic highways network, the GLC had to take policy decisions and then consult.'[91] This was less Orwellian than it sounds: one proposal to facilitate participation at the strategic level was to devise alternative options and then put them to the public. In principle the GLC supported this approach,[92] but it carried the insuperable drawback of exacerbating planning blight. Blight was the debasement of the value of property threatened by a proposed road or other construction, making it impossible for owners to sell until the scheme was approved and compulsory purchase could take place. The GLC understood the corrosive effects of blight and pressed without success for more generous compensation powers.[93] Announcing a multitude of possible routes for the sake of consultation would worsen blight and delay the final choice of route.[94] Skeffington had considered an increase in blight to be an acceptable price for greater public involvement; besieged by irate property owners, the Council could not.[95]

For these reasons, the GLC's engagement with the public never ranged beyond didactic and promotional exercises. The Public Information Branch, formed soon after the Council's creation, spent much of its time promoting transport policy. Early efforts to sell the transport-management strategy employed the black arts of advertising, with dubious results. The GLC paid an agency £200,000 to teach it to preach that antisocial parking was 'the act of a stupid child rather than of a reasoning adult' ('a few interpolated words of one or other of the current popular [television] police inspectors . . . would have real significance').[96] By the time the campaign for the GLDP proper was launched, the techniques were more sophisticated, but the danger of patronising the public remained. An introductory public meeting in the Queen Elizabeth Hall in November 1968 was followed by nine shamelessly promotional local meetings. The Ealing meeting, 'arranged by the slick and efficient operators of the GLC's press and public relations office' in January 1969, 'had the air of a well run television show. There were even girls in mini-skirts to welcome people at the door.'[97] What Abercrombie would have thought of this we can only guess; what the Council's sceptical audiences thought is clear. In reality few of those who attended the meetings were sufficiently open-minded on the roads question to be swayed by such methods: 'the vast majority of those attending tend to be activists of one sort of another', Gerard Vaughan, chairman of the Strategic Planning Committee, told Skeffington.[98] With hindsight, the GLC accepted that 'public presentations by a large organisation will always result in a high proportion of aggressive criticism rather than praise for proposals.'[99]

In a hostile climate promotional sophistication became in itself sinister, reinforcing the impression that the Council was more interested in selling its proposals than in consultation.[100] 'The glib advertising language that is used to sell the plan to the unsuspecting public: improved environment and all that crap',[101] did little good. In any case, whatever educative advantages the promotional campaign brought were soon offset by the public relations disaster of Westway, which prompted the most heated antiroad protests that London has ever seen.[102] Westway, the motorway-standard extension of Western Avenue to join the projected Ringway 1, was an uncouth intrusion into the Ladbroke Grove area, carrying eastbound traffic within feet of inhabited houses at roof level. Even the British Road Federation considered Westway one of 'the insensitive and socially unacceptable examples of motorways.'[103] 'You only have to look at Westway', claimed one of the few council tenants to appear before the public inquiry: 'People who live on that can shake hands with a motorist on the thing. But they expect people to live on it.'[104] Even the GLC's counsel acknowledged 'the failure or the inability ... to resolve properly the local environmental effects' of Westway.[105] Westway scarred London's fabric in the 1960s much as the construction of the Metropolitan Railway had done a century earlier. While the Council mounted its glossy campaign for the plan, Westway showed the reality of urban road-building. As one objector told the inquiry, 'one bases one's experience on the Westway, because we have not got another urban motorway.'[106]

Mrs Terry of Oxford Gardens, North Kensington, looking at the stub of motorway protruding from the Westway and threatening her back garden in March 1969. (PA/Alamy Stock Photo)

All of this strengthened the objectors' demand that the GLDP should be subjected to proper scrutiny, by 'a full Government Commission of Inquiry into the GLC Development Plan as a whole and not a series of local inquiries.'[107] They got their way in December 1969 when the Labour government announced the intention to mount such an inquiry. It was eventually constituted under Sir Frank Layfield, who, with a panel of experts to advise him, was charged with investigating every aspect of the plan. The inquiry held its first session in July 1970. It would sit for 237 working days, until September 1972, making it at that time Britain's longest planning inquiry.

Though the Council claimed to welcome the inquiry, it must, in reality, have viewed it as an unsolicited intrusion. It was already reassessing the philosophy behind the plan. Where initially the case for the Ringways had been based on mobility and personal freedom, by 1969 the GLC's emphasis was shifting to ameliorating the problems created by congestion. The statutory written statement accompanying the plan argued that unchecked congestion would disable business, paralyse vital services and 'lead to more families leaving London.'[108] In November 1969, Stott borrowed the objectors' image of US cities to warn of social polarisation if congestion continued: London would become 'a place where there is no intermediate between the very rich and the rather poor': 'It is not my idea of a city.'[109] This change of emphasis was doubtless primarily tactical, but one major change behind the scenes indicated that it was more than cosmetic. Once it had become clear that the GLDP would be scrutinised by some kind of major public inquiry, a new Strategy Branch had been created within the Planning and Transportation Department, and a new chief planner (strategy) appointed in David Eversley.

Eversley was a historical demographer and the only nonplanner amongst over two hundred applicants for the post. He was also something of a sceptic towards the GLDP, questioning the 'belief in the possibility of physical (land use) planning solving almost every urban problem.'[110] He saw the planner as 'a listener, a researcher, as well as a decision-maker.'[111] His view of 'strategy' included 'a consideration of direct action, pressure, advocacy, community involvement, new legislation, collaboration with neighbouring authorities . . . as a means of achieving a total planning process', which led him to take an interest in Skeffington's community forums, to the alarm of his colleagues.[112] Standing 'well to the left of the Labour Party', Eversley saw planning as political—felt, indeed, that 'planning . . . was essentially redistributive.'[113] He had arrived too late to play any part in shaping the GLDP, and had the plan proceeded smoothly to its anticipated approval by the secretary of state, his heresies would doubtless have been smothered; but the approach of Layfield laid every aspect of the GLDP open for reconsideration.

As Eversley put it, 'the Inquiry became the Plan.'[114] It inevitably produced much crankiness, but two years of probing revealed the GLDP's weaknesses. As Simon Jenkins noted, 'no central department has ever been subjected to the expert cross-questioning in public which officers of the GLC had to undergo before Layfield—which had more in common with an American congressional hearing than with a normal public inquiry.'[115] The Council was criticised for replicating Abercrombie's transport proposals while neglecting his concern for social dynamics.[116] One manifest flaw, actually the reason for Colin Buchanan's hesitancy about endorsing the GLDP, was rapidly brought to light: while claiming flexibility as an advantage of the new system of structure planning, the GLC was boxing London into an inflexible infrastructural cage—as counsel for the London Borough of Greenwich put it, 'there can be few things more immutable than a motorway.'[117] The existence of a demand for orbital journeys was challenged on the basis of the underuse of the Broad Street–to–Richmond railway.[118]

The Council's dismissive view of public transport (it had no power over British Rail and only acquired responsibility for London Transport in 1969) attracted much criticism. Its relaxed attitude towards the problem of pollution was attacked, as vehicle exhaust threatened to undo the work of the Clean Air Act.[119] The panel experts demonstrated the GLC's unclear demographic priorities, its limited comprehension of the London economy and its flimsy housing strategy.[120]

Though the plan's opponents thought themselves disadvantaged by the forensic nature of the public inquiry—'the difficulties of individual objection against a mountain of Background papers ... and in the face of massed professional expertise'[121]—this was a battle within the planning profession as much as between planners and public, and the opposition could invoke much technical expertise. The author of the preceding statement was, in fact, a master of city planning from Harvard, an associate of the RIBA, a member of the Royal Town Planning Institute and the chairman of the Haringey Planning and Development Committee. If anything, the debate with the Council over planning theory was conducted more effectively by such specialist witnesses than by the panel. So was broader discussion of the nature of the city. The Town and Country Planning Association's evidence about the relationship of city and region, Chris Holmes's analysis of gentrification in Islington, the account from the spokesman of the St Pancras Civic Society of the social and ethnic mix in modern Camden, even the aperçu from the Grove Park Group representative that Carnaby Street was a 'place that gained momentum until it was not possible for a local authority to overplan it'—all showed an understanding of urban evolution not always evident in the GLDP.[122] The objectors could assault the plan from all angles without any need to ensure overall coherence, while GLC witnesses had to keep their testimony consistent with the plan as a whole, which became increasingly difficult. By day one hundred, after seventy hours' examination of GLC witnesses, Fitzpatrick was rightly worried that 'it is not possible for witnesses to be certain as to Council policy' as panel questioning became ever more stringent.[123]

This was all the more true because Council policy continued to evolve during the inquiry, as Eversley found his feet. His background paper on the aims of the plan, stressing that the planner was 'deeply involved with the efficient functioning of the economy, the growth of communities, the correct use of scarce resources' and other things that the Planning and Transportation Department was not, in fact, very deeply involved with, was published after internal censorship in 1970.[124] In the uncertain economic climate of

the early 1970s, Eversley formed apocalyptic views of London's future, believing 'not simply that London Bridge was falling down but that London
was dying',[125] as depopulation robbed the centre of its most productive
elements. He had no time for conservation groups,[126] whose conservatism
would create 'a London composed of only five million people, of whom a
high proportion are pensioners, out of a job, [or] too poor to buy much.'[127]
Consequently, his scepticism towards physical planning did not lead him
to disown the Ringways: Eversley saw the car as 'the redundant worker's
passport to a new and better job'.[128] Once the talisman of prosperity, the
Ringways now became a defence against decline.

Eversley's unorthodoxy made enemies within the Council, particularly
amongst those who had been involved with the plan from the start. The
Planning and Transportation staff did not understand Eversley's preoccupation with economic and demographic movements and did not think
that such things lay in the province of the planner. They could not substan-
tiate his concerns about social polarisation and were concerned at the
prospect of 'a complete somersault on the definition of London's problems.'[129] Less predictable was the implosion of Eversley's own section. The
new Strategy Branch was staffed, in Eversley's account, by 'not-so-good
geography graduates' whose 'desks were littered, according to sex, with
copies of knitting patterns and recipes for low-calorie meals, or motor
sports journals and racing papers.' It became the preserve of the public-
sector Left, devoted to 'bureaucratic guerrilla warfare' against capitalism.[130] It was probably inevitable that Eversley's approach to the planning
process would let the political genie out of the bottle. The young planners
in the Strategy Branch voiced a critique of redevelopment—public and
private—fuelled by the property boom that peaked in the early 1970s.
They had more in common with the Westway protestors than the conser-
vationists and amenity-group stalwarts who were so visible at the inquiry.
A new journal, Community Action, appeared in 1972, largely written by
members of the Strategy Branch. It provided an unwavering critique of
redevelopment and gentrification and offered support to 'action groups in
low-income areas.'[131] It advocated 'new kinds of political action that will
combine argument with pressure, lobbying with sanction and direct action':
'remember Watts got burned because the blacks got tired of waiting—then
the money trickled in.'[132] It blamed Eversley himself for 'perpetuating policies
that have the interests of industrialists and developers, rather than London's
workers, at heart.'[133] Caught between the unsympathetic traditionalists of
Planning and Transportation and the 'immature pseudo-revolutionaries'

in his own section, Eversley suffered a nervous breakdown and left the Council in July 1972.[134]

By then Stott had concluded that 'the value of the whole system is becoming very questionable' and that 'nobody is likely to suggest another GLDP . . . for a long time.'[135] Though Layfield had still to report, 'we remain afeared of attempts to cobble up an approval of some GLDP at all costs, because we consider that everybody ought to do a sufficiency of thinking about improving the system of planning, or non-system, which London appears to be saddled with under present arrangements.'[136] In this context the Layfield inquiry's perverse recommendation to build only Ringway 1[137]—the most expensive and unpopular of the three roads—was academic: few at the GLC now expected any of the roads to be built.[138] Eversley's testy reaction to the inquiry report in February 1973 made no mention of the Ringways.[139] Labour's victory in the GLC election six weeks later ensured the Ringways' demise, but it did not cause it. Though the campaign was dominated by motorways, Labour won because a Conservative government at Westminster was beset by growing economic problems. Had Labour been in government, the Conservatives would doubtless have retained control of the GLC, but the roads would still not have been built. The primary road network—the central feature of the GLDP—died because its flaws had been exposed during the public scrutiny process and because the bureaucracy behind it collapsed in the attempt to respond to criticism.

In the early 1970s London thus decided not to follow the path taken by the Victorians—not to sacrifice substantial parts of the urban fabric to the needs of transportation. Londoners resolved not to acquire a road system comparable to the local railway network built in the nineteenth century. This was not acknowledged by all involved—most of the objectors to the motorways persuaded themselves that the solution to London's traffic problem lay in greater investment in public transport—but some understood that they were really arguing for 'restraint by congestion.'[140] The concept is familiar to Londoners today.

Conclusion

In 1970 A. F. Dunning, the Council's director of public information, noted that where town planning had once been characterised by 'a bi-partisan approach', now 'with strategic planning so much involved with economic planning and overall policies this has become another matter.'[141] He presumably regretted this development; certainly the more technocratically minded among the GLC planners felt frustrated that questions which they thought should have been determined by objective analysis had become distorted by politics. Regrettable or not, though, politicisation had always been a likely consequence of the Council's eagerness to carry planning to the next level—the ambitious structure plan involving extensive disruption of the urban environment. Its belief that the objective needs of the city could be determined by extensive empirical analysis was not irrational. The GLC recognised that a large number of individuals would see their lives disrupted by the Ringways and sought a more generous measure of compensation for them than central government was minded to allow. The construction of London's railways in the Victorian period had, after all, affected a larger proportion of the metropolitan population, treating them less tenderly, and had taken still longer than the GLC envisaged for its motorway proposals. Large infrastructural projects in a major city inevitably entail individual dislocation for any general benefit, but by the 1970s such projects could no longer be pushed through with the relative ease evident in the Victorian period. Instead a paternalistic, top-down planning tradition inherited from the war years, by which evidence-based rationalism provided its own justification, clashed with the new vogue for consultation and participation, with the homes and environment of many thousands of people at stake. In such circumstances, the issue was unlikely to remain nonpolitical for long. The Labour Party doubtless was acting opportunistically in taking up the protestors' case, given that a Labour-controlled LCC had nurtured the project in its early stages and a Labour-controlled GLC had proposed the Motorway Box, but it was scarcely conceivable that so large and vocal a protest movement could be ignored indefinitely by the political parties.

Writing shortly after the effective burial of the Ringways scheme, Simon Jenkins concluded that 'the present GLC has become impotent as a strategic authority.'[142] It had, with far-reaching implications. The intention behind the overhaul of London government in 1963–65 had been to assign strategic powers—directing the development of the metropolis as a whole—to the new GLC, and the new Council's adoption of structure planning was in tune with this goal. The modernisation of the road network was central to the eventual plan that the GLC presented in 1966, and although the remnants of the GLDP—shorn of the Ringways—would receive ministerial approval ten years later, without the roads the plan was neutered. In that context, some people began to ask what the GLC was for.

The Labour victory in the 1973 Greater London Council elections made this question more pressing, encouraging some fundamentalist Conservatives to contemplate doing away with a body that was still less than ten years old. In 1974 Geoffrey Finsberg, MP for Hampstead and a former Camden councillor, produced a pamphlet advocating GLC abolition—a piece of blue-sky thinking which Conservative Central Office was, significantly, happy to publish. The abolition campaign would rumble on throughout the decade, even after the GLC reverted to Tory control in 1977.[143] It probably owed more to resentment of the radicalism and supposed extravagance of the 1973–77 Labour GLC than to any scars left by the battle over motorways, but the Tory attack on the GLC would not have been carried to the lengths of proposing abolition had the Council appeared administratively indispensable. The abandonment of its key strategic project reinforced claims that London could live without it.

Less tangibly, the debate over the Ringways contributed to a growing disenchantment with the actions and intentions of the local state in London. The GLC's predecessor, the London County Council, had had its critics, of course—those who saw it as unduly 'nannyish' or who resented its status from the thirties as a permanent Labour fiefdom—but the dominant narrative around the LCC in the welfarist postwar years portrayed it as a practitioner of progressive social policies and a force for public good. In the 1970s, though, the shift from a welfare to a strategic-planning orientation at the metropolitan level diminished public support for the activist local state, just as the boroughs were coming under fire for their performance in their housing and social service roles. Not content with the assaults on Piccadilly Circus and Covent Garden, it was held, 'the planners' had now set their sights on the whole of Greater London, threatening thousands of homes and familiar local environments. In reaction, Simon Jenkins suggested, 'city politics have reached a stage where the sole aim of public involvement in decisions affecting the environment really is the preservation of the physical status quo.'[144] In London, as elsewhere, the ethos of urban modernism never really recovered.

7

The Conservation Consensus

The winter of 1961–62 saw the demolition of two monuments to London's Victorian development, Philip Hardwick's Doric Arch, built in 1838 to frame the entrance to Euston Station, and J. B. Bunning's Coal Exchange (1842), in Lower Thames Street, the interior of which boasted innovative ironwork galleries. The fate of both buildings was discussed in Parliament, and a deputation had called on Prime Minister Harold Macmillan in October 1961 in an attempt to save the Euston Arch.[1] The destruction of these two landmarks coincided with the death sentence pronounced on the Shot Tower on the South Bank, soon to make way for the Hayward Gallery. It followed the widespread regret at the loss of the St James' Theatre for an office block in 1957 and the uproar prompted by the proposal to redevelop part of Piccadilly Circus in the following year. In a House of Lords debate in March 1962, prompted by the threat to the Coal Exchange, Lord Rea asked for a 'satisfactory reassurance about Westminster Abbey and the Tower of London, both of which are frightfully old-fashioned.'[2]

Questioning Urban Renewal

The point was often made in debates over London's largely Victorian urban fabric that the Victorians themselves had shown little compunction in destroying old buildings when they appeared unfit for purpose (as 'old

Demolition of the Doric Portico at Euston Station, March 1961. (Science and Society Picture Library/ Getty Images)

Euston' was deemed to be) or impeded essential improvements (as was claimed of the Coal Exchange). 'I believe in moving with the times', observed London's 'demolition king', Frank Valori: 'there's always something to be knocked down.' Starting from nothing, Valori had built up a business worth £250,000 by the midsixties. He disliked modern architecture, regretted having to destroy the Euston Arch and the Coal Exchange, and incorporated stones from the Arch into his own new house in Bromley but still looked covetously at the Albert Hall: 'I'd love to take that one down. It would be an honour.'[3] The idea that buildings were expendable, and might simply become obsolete well before there was any danger of their physical collapse, survived well into the postwar years. Strikingly, correspondence relating to the proposed redevelopment of Piccadilly Circus in the early

1960s shows that both Sir William Holford, drawing up the scheme, and officials in the Ministry of Housing and Local Government assumed that Reginald Blomfield's Quadrant and other buildings on the west side of the Circus would be replaced anyway by the end of the century, although they were only thirty-five years old and of massive construction.[4]

Demolition was seen as necessary to rejuvenate an urban system. This view was centuries old but had inevitably been reinforced by the random but extensive destruction of London property between 1939 and 1945. Just as the human tragedy of the war was taken as an opportunity to build better welfare and health-care systems for the postwar world, so it appeared to offer scope for replanning and rationalising Britain's older industrial cities. The two major plans produced by Sir Patrick Abercrombie, the *County of London Plan* and the *Greater London Plan*, represented holistic prescriptions for London's postwar recovery, embracing demography, housing, industry, transport and leisure. The generally favourable reception of the Abercrombie plans made their implementation a public desideratum. This would entail substantial disturbance to the built environment, generally justified by reference to the destruction that London had already suffered involuntarily. Urban reconstruction was taken to imply more than the mere patching up of the built environment, and there was little appetite for the faithful reconstruction of buildings destroyed in the bombing, whatever their merits. But while London had suffered extensive damage in the Blitz, it had not been obliterated. In the capital, as in most of Britain's bombed cities, there remained an assessment to be made of the extent to which postwar reconstruction should respect what had survived. As Andrew Saint has shown, the policy of listing buildings of architectural or historical interest, enacted in 1944, was intended to provide an inventory of buildings deserving protection in an age of urban redevelopment, so that 'when the experts came to lay their plans they would know without ambiguity or delay what to incorporate or skirt round.'[5]

Listing was the consequence of a backbench amendment to a Town and Country Planning Bill: although the guidelines compiled to govern the process in 1944 suggest a more sensitive and inclusive approach to the exercise than is sometimes imagined, conservation remained the junior partner of urban planning.[6] It was subject to a fundamental understanding that the retention of historic buildings should not be carried to such lengths as to frustrate the work of reconstruction. This principle was, if anything, reinforced in the late 1950s and early 1960s, when public policy shifted from the reconstruction of bombed cities to the modernisation of town centres to accommodate 'affluence' in general and the motor car in particular, following Colin Buchanan's 1963 report *Traffic in Towns*.[7]

Buchanan had developed his theories while chairing the public inquiry into the future of Piccadilly Circus in December 1959 and January 1960, when he had concluded his report with a powerful argument that the spread of the private car demanded 'radical new thinking on urban forms and arrangements.'[8] The inquiry had been prompted by the clandestine success of the property developer Jack Cotton and his City Centre Properties in acquiring more than a hundred interests in the Monico site, on the north edge of the Circus, during the 1950s.[9] Cotton had submitted to the LCC in 1957 a plan for an office block on the site which exceeded the permitted plot ratio by 25 percent. The Council's architect, Hubert Bennett, had helped Cotton rework the plans, apparently in the hope that cooperation with the developers—by now irremovably installed on the site—would encourage them to join the Council in producing a coordinated redevelopment plan for the entire area to attack the Circus's traffic congestion problem.[10] The result was an inelegant 'square tower' on a podium,[11] which passed the undemanding test of approval from the Royal Fine Arts Commission in February 1958 only to be shot down by much of the architectural profession eight months later, when Cotton presented the scheme at a press conference. The minister of housing, Henry Brooke, had called in the plans and convened the public inquiry. The Civic Trust, leading the opposition to the proposals, suggested that the inquiry would be 'a critical moment in the development of London',[12] and so it was, culminating in Buchanan's rejection of the Cotton block and his call for a more plausible—and comprehensive—scheme for the Circus as a whole.

At first glance, the outcome of the Piccadilly inquiry amounted to a restatement of the wartime faith in rational planning for the community, in opposition to a piecemeal proposal from a profit-seeking private developer, epitomised by architecture of stunning banality. There was truth in this. The Civic Trust, opposing Cotton's proposals, had argued not that the Circus should be left alone but that a comprehensive scheme, devised by 'a single architectural mind',[13] was preferable to a developer's scheme fudged in clandestine collusion with the planning authority. But there were other lessons to be learned from the Piccadilly affair. Despite Cotton's defeat, it demonstrated the power exercised by the property developer—in particular by the small group of men who had had the foresight to buy into London property towards the end of the war and had benefited lavishly from the Churchill government's abolition of building licences in 1954.[14]

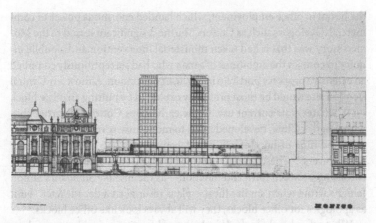

Architect's sketch of the building proposed for the Monico site at Piccadilly Circus, which stirred the anger of both the architectural profession and the general public when it was unveiled in 1958. (London Picture Archive 239452 © London Metropolitan Archives [City of London])

It demonstrated the weakness of the local authority—even a substantial authority like the LCC—in the face of this developer cartel. The Council's deference to Cotton over Piccadilly evoked the kind of sweetheart deal that it had concluded with another developer, Joe Levy, by which it gained the land for what would become the Euston Road underpass in return for granting Levy lucrative planning permission over an unusually extensive area.[15] Less tangibly, the Monico episode suggested that the public enthusiasm for urban modernisation was not unconditional: an existing cityscape might be valued on account of its very familiarity by a citizenry which only fifteen years earlier had been inured to the instant obliteration of London's landmarks. In 1960 it was clear to Buchanan—and doubtless to most public policy makers—that the proper corrective for piecemeal, commercially driven redevelopment was planned, publicly directed redevelopment. Over the next few years, though, many would question the need for redevelopment at all.

Fragile City

The destruction of familiar landmarks such as the Euston Arch touched a nerve because London's built environment was threatened by several— essentially unrelated—pressures in the early sixties. The first of these was the boom in office employment, which handed enormous power to commercial developers such as Cotton. The most significant lesson of the Monico story was that it had taken ministerial intervention and a public inquiry to contain the ambitions of a man who had surreptitiously compiled an extensive property portfolio in the heart of London. Almost any Central London site would be most profitably exploited by putting an office block on it, whatever its current use. In the early 1960s Cotton, in partnership with Charles Clore, developed plans to modernise several West End theatres and nine of London's railway terminals, placing all of them under office towers.[16] These proposals denied both theatres and stations any relationship between form and function—as the *Evening Standard*'s Simon Jenkins wrote when similar theatre plans resurfaced a decade later, 'built as apologies for office blocks, they will always look like office blocks.'[17]

What office blocks looked like in the early sixties was seldom appealing. In recent years, as Paul Cheshire and Gerard Dericks have argued, London developers have been able to win consent for taller blocks by engaging an award-winning architect to design them—a gaming strategy which implies at least some attention to aesthetics, whether or not it actually produces more beautiful buildings.[18] In the 1960s, by contrast, though local authorities had the opportunity to influence design when planning consent was sought, they seldom took it.[19] London's planning authorities concerned themselves primarily with a building's plot ratio—the relationship between its 'footprint' and its floor area—with an eye to those things that it was thought proper for a planning authority to control, in particular the number of new office workers likely to be drawn into the city centre. Maximising the return to given plot-ratio limits became the commercial architect's principal skill: the most successful of the breed, Richard Seifert, prospered under the LCC's planning regime because 'he knew some of the regulations far better than the LCC himself.'[20] Aesthetic considerations were secondary. Cotton responded to his rebuff from the architectural profession by hiring the ageing Walter Gropius to advise on a new Piccadilly proposal,[21] but ultimately he, like his collaborator Clore, did not 'believe in any great architectural triumphs which end up in bankruptcy.'[22] Not all 1960s office developments were banal, but it is safe to say that few developers risked bankruptcy to beautify London.

The second threat to London's built environment came from the upsurge in interest in holistic planning and redevelopment in the late fifties and early sixties, encouraged in particular by the problem of adapting traditional urban configurations to the growth in motor traffic. One unanticipated

Terraced houses in Dame Street, Islington, ca. 1960. Most of the houses in this view would be demolished for Islington Council's Packington Estate. (John Gay/Historic England/Mary Evans)

consequence of the Piccadilly furore was that the resultant public inquiry gave its chairman, Colin Buchanan, the chance to air his evolving views on the relationship between city dwellers and the car.[23] He would develop his views in the ambitious *Traffic in Towns* report of 1963, which sought to adapt Britain's urban topography to accommodate growing car use.[24] He proposed a radical segregation of pedestrians and traffic, to be effected by various measures including pedestrian precincts and walkways and the separation of cars and people on different levels. Effecting all this would require 'a gigantic programme of urban reconstruction';[25] Kenneth Browne's futuristic illustrations to the report made clear just how dramatic a transformation would be required.

The third threat to London's built environment derived from the urgency of London's housing crisis. A tenth of Greater London's dwellings in 1960 were either deemed unfit or held to have a life expectancy of less

Demolition of an unidentified Georgian terrace, probably in Camden, early 1960s. (John Gay/English Heritage NMR/Mary Evans Picture Library)

than fifteen years.[26] The majority of these dwellings predated the stringent building legislation of the 1870s, but these buildings might be Georgian or early-Victorian terraces of some distinction, however dilapidated. It was generally assumed in the early 1960s that once property of this age had fallen into decay, demolition was the only remedy, and public anxiety over London's slum problem in the early sixties made conservationist objections to the demolition of characterful buildings appear self-indulgent. In the controversial case of the destruction of the mid-Victorian terraces of the Packington Estate in Islington in 1965, the housing minister Richard Crossman argued, 'These old houses that you want to preserve have middle-class snob appeal. I am sure that council tenants are happier in new council flats.'[27] Comprehensive redevelopment was a blunt instrument, not least because it was often necessary to expand the redevelopment area

Demolition work in an unidentified North London street, early sixties. (John Gay/English Heritage NMR/Mary Evans Picture Library)

to include neighbouring, less crowded, property, in order to ensure a housing gain from the new scheme. The destruction of historically significant property that was not unfit intensified controversy.

In the Packington case there was much doubt as to whether the property at issue was in poor repair—Islington Council argued somewhat sheepishly that central government's housing subsidy system encouraged redevelopment before refurbishment[28]—but there can be no doubt that the condition of much of London's cheaper property made rehabilitation daunting to local authorities charged with providing decent homes for their electors. In addition, most inner-London buildings had been tainted by up to two centuries of grime, accumulating in the years before the 1956

Clean Air Act made 'clean-ups' worthwhile. Photographs of the Euston Arch shortly before demolition all make clear how grimy the portico—gleaming white in J. C. Bourne's 1839 lithograph—had become. Modern buildings offered a sparkling contrast to the sooty city—invariably in architects' drawings but often also in reality. It was only really in the 1970s that it became clear how far London's dirt had concealed the qualities of even the most deserving buildings. In 1972 the government embarked on a wholesale cleanup of public buildings in London;[29] Simon Jenkins suggested in the following year that the cleaning of Whitehall had changed the public view of the buildings threatened with demolition in 1965: 'it is worth remembering how little people cared for them when they were a dirty black.'[30] Probably the most striking example of this effect came with the cleaning of Gilbert Scott's former Midland Grand Hotel—forming the frontage of St Pancras Station—in 1977. What emerged was the station that the Victorians would have seen, as a dull maroon building was transformed into a salmon-pink one, becoming less forbiddingly 'industrial' in the process.[31]

A decade earlier the debate over the British Transport Commission's proposal to demolish St Pancras had provided the most significant indicator of the changing public view of the nineteenth century's architectural legacy. For all London's Wren churches and Bloomsbury squares, it was essentially a nineteenth-century city, and the listing system remained coy in its approach to nineteenth-century buildings. The 1944 guidelines suggested that 'between 1800 and 1850 listing should be confined to buildings of definite quality and character. From 1850 down to 1914 only outstanding works should be included.'[32] The listing of Victoriana, in particular, was 'more a matter of taste than of fact.'[33] A high-powered committee appointed by the Ministry of Housing and Local Government in 1960 to consider the question of preserving Victorian buildings found that of 153 Victorian and Edwardian buildings listed in the seven boroughs examined, 102 were placed only on the Supplementary List, which afforded no statutory protection. These included Tite's Royal Exchange, Norman Shaw's Frognal and his Albert Hall Mansions, the Albert Hall itself and even Waterhouse's Natural History Museum. The Albert Memorial had been Grade 2 listed before being raised to Grade 1 by the Advisory Committee: the Ministry stressed in its public statements that it was listed on historical rather than aesthetic grounds. 'A building may be "ugly as sin" and still be listed—if it is of historic interest. So the Albert Memorial finds a place', Ivan Yates of the *Evening Standard* wrote in 1957, quoting the Ministry of Housing's

Chief Investigator for Historic Buildings, S. J. Garton. 'They even toyed with including the oldest extant gasometer, but Mr Macmillan, when Minister of Housing, wouldn't wear that.'[34] Macmillan was not alone in believing that the products of industrial architecture were simply not the kind of buildings that the listing system had been devised for.

In addition, the public mind still harboured some of the ethical disdain for the Gothic Revival implanted by the modern movement. When the threat to St Pancras emerged in 1966, the GLC's Historic Buildings officers thought it vulnerable precisely because it was the most unapologetic statement of Gothic Revival principles in London: 'Those who, some forty or fifty years ago, led the inevitable reaction against Victorian ideals and aspirations showed a sure instinct when they singled out the St Pancras Hotel for special attack. Architecturally it epitomises those ideals more effectively perhaps than any other building.'[35] It had made only the Supplementary List at a time 'when it was considered almost a concession to list such a C19th building at all.'[36] The GLC's concern was understandable— even the broadly sympathetic Historic Buildings Council for England thought that 'to raise the building to Grade I status is to exaggerate its importance'[37]—but what is most telling is the Ministry's reaction to the controversy: 'We don't want another case of the Euston Arch where everyone got off on the wrong foot because it had been under-listed.'[38] St Pancras still attracted modernist criticism in the midsixties, but by then it was clear that demolition would repeat the Euston Arch furore for the benefit of British Rail alone.

The gradual rehabilitation of Victoriana in the eyes of the public owed most to growing public disenchantment with modernism. Within any new and unfamiliar architectural style it is difficult for the lay public to distinguish immediately between the mundane and the deserving, with the result that it tends to be judged as a whole. The scale and pace of the office boom and the housing drive, combined with the mass production of many of the residential buildings, ensured that much of the architecture produced was routine and formulaic. What had previously been seen as the virtues of modernism—its clean lines and avoidance of otiose ornamentation—appeared to many people dreary and anonymous when repeated across London. In many parts of the centre the sheer cost of land impelled developers towards 'no-frills' commercial architecture—in much of the City and most obviously in Victoria Street, Westminster, where 'development was shared out between those few monolithic enterprises which can afford such square footage in a central area.' Victoria Street was singled out by the conservationist group SAVE in 1976 to exemplify the ruination of an important locale by the appeasement of commercial developers, enhanced by Westminster City Council's eagerness to strengthen its rate base, regardless of the effects on tourists, local shopkeepers or the public at large.[39] Increasingly, modernism was simply rejected as a genre. Public inquiries prompted by redevelopment proposals or by appeals against Building Preservation Orders frequently produced written or verbal tirades against 'the louring hostile cliffs of concrete' and the threat of the 'concrete forest' or the 'glass-caged tower.'[40] Such generic criticism makes it difficult to gauge the public response to individual buildings, which did, in fact, vary in nature and quality. The *Evening Standard* attempted to do so in 1979, in an unscientific but illuminating canvass of its readers, asking which modern London buildings deserved to be listed. The Post Office Tower (now BT Tower) won support, as did even some of the buildings in Victoria Street, including New Scotland Yard—'a refreshing alternative to the usual glass box.' Most favoured was Jeremy Mackay-Lewis's building for Credit Lyonnais in Cannon Street, a design which deliberately echoed the City's Victorian Gothic commercial architecture. One reader praised its medieval qualities, 'which have long since vanished from the City'; another admired its 'high narrow windows [which] bring an air of cloistered calm instead of the slab glass effect of so much modern architecture.'[41] If one can read anything into this limited exercise, it is that modern buildings were admired to the extent that they did not look modern. When, by contrast, the St Anselm Development Company suggested in 1973 that an office block designed by Basil Spence and proposed for Mayfair might appeal more than the Georgian and Victorian buildings that it would replace, its claim had prompted a mixture of bemusement and ridicule.[42]

Long before then, telling evidence of the public aversion to modernism, and of the difficulties facing its advocates, had emerged in the debate over the fate of three contiguous hotels in Montpelier Row, overlooking Blackheath. The buildings, dating from the 1780s, had been protected by an LCC Building Preservation Order in 1963. The conservation society the Georgian Group described them as 'extremely simple and restrained in design',[43] but made little real attempt to argue for their architectural originality or distinction; at the public inquiry the inspector felt that 'their gaunt mass lacks graciousness and is a slightly forbidding element in the landscape.'[44] The freeholders, the Cator Estate, had engaged the well-regarded modern residential developers Span to design a four-storey block of flats to replace the hotels. The architectural historian Robert Furneaux Jordan had argued that 'scale, colour, height in relationship to space ... are far more fundamentally Georgian than are, say, such things as fanlights or sash-windows' and that recent building on the Cator Estate (much of it by Span) did possess 'those very real Georgian qualities and are in that way far more Georgian than are some of the rather foolish sham Georgian brick boxes nearby.'[45] Such expert opinion cut little ice, though, with local residents, who saw only the angularity of the buildings and the supposed avarice of the Estate, 'whose purpose is to pack the ground in rectangles so that their ground rents multiply' and who would happily redevelop St Paul's Cathedral 'if they could get away with it.'[46] The Preservation Order was revoked, but the Borough of Lewisham issued a new order for the entire street in 1965. The buildings survive today.[47]

So far as residential property was concerned, it was evident even by 1963 that the market for modern town houses was a limited one and that London buyers were more eager to sink money into the renovation and conversion of older houses if they possessed 'character.' Gentrification produced a de facto conservationism in those areas—Chelsea, Camden, Notting Hill, Barnsbury, Canonbury, north Lambeth and the like—which offered early nineteenth-century terraces, 'cottages' or mews, but the demand for what were then disparagingly called 'secondhand' houses went far beyond these classic sites of gentrification and covered much of the Victorian housing stock. Modern design was largely banished to the social housing sector, where it was not always at its best. On occasion, admittedly, councils attempted to deploy innovative design to win over sceptical locals. In 1967 Islington, still smarting from the Packington controversy, engaged the adventurous partnership Darbourne and Darke for the controversial Marquess Road development in Canonbury. 'After many years of council building with little architectural merit', the *Standard*'s Judy Hillman suggested, 'this was a welcome change.'[48] Neave Brown's ziggurat design for the Borough of Camden's Alexandra Road development was intended to assuage local concern at the erosion of the Victorian buildings of the Eyre Estate. It and several other Camden estates were the work of a young in-house team of architects eager to show that social housing did not have to be banal, and their work is now celebrated.[49] In general, though, the economics of building for low-income tenants on expensive London land worked against adventurous design, particularly as central government subsidies for social housing fell from the late sixties. The recurrent spats between gentrifying home owners and local authorities over proposed developments were therefore plausibly characterised as conflicts between beauty and the beast, with elegant terraces pitted against industrial-built boxes. The public inquiries into such schemes frequently resembled a surrogate class war, with academics, media executives and, invariably, architects lining up to protect their newly won nests from the menace of social housing, but owner occupation was not confined to such classic gentrifiers: in reality any significant level of home ownership posed obstacles to comprehensive redevelopment. As early as 1960, Hackney Council's attempt to replace the 1830s houses of De Beauvoir Town with a new development, 'ultramodern in design, layout and amenities', encountered resistance from working-class owners in the area: 'We bought our house 10 years ago for £750. There are hundreds like us who have put every penny they had into their homes—and now this'; 'My place has been in the family 50 years. I've spent hundreds of pounds doing it up.'[50]

The steady growth of owner occupation in the 1960s encouraged the development of a broader understanding of conservation. In the first place, owner occupation in itself offered a more promising basis than private renting for encouraging the protection of deserving buildings, particularly in poor areas. In 1959 the LCC's Historic Buildings officers had stressed the obstacles to conservation evident in places such as Fournier Street in Spitalfields, where eighteenth-century weavers' cottages were now 'in multiple occupation as workrooms for working tailors, milliners, etc. . . . Very few of the owners or occupiers have the slightest interest in the architectural character of the buildings, many of which have been mutilated both internally, by patched up repairs and alterations, and externally, by inappropriate refacing.'[51] Nine years later their GLC successors still considered the parts of London most at risk to be those 'where housing stress and architectural or historic interest are seen to occur in the same areas (for example Barnsbury and Paddington).'[52] By 1968, though, both areas were being floated off the rocks by gentrification, and Barnsbury, in particular, was experiencing a spectacular transformation. In 1965 the GLC had petitioned the Ministry of Housing for the preservation of a number of Barnsbury houses compulsorily purchased under a slum-clearance scheme, arguing that it 'represents one of the most coherent and little altered examples in London of estate development in the early nineteenth century.'[53] Within a few years, the demolition of Barnsbury's Georgiana had become unthinkable. Owner-occupiers, in Barnsbury and elsewhere, possessed rapidly appreciating assets: the pioneer purchasers of the attractive 1790s terraced Houses in Cleaver Square, Kennington, saw a fivefold increase in their properties' value in under a decade, while the price of a three-storey

Georgian terraced house in Camden rose from £900 in 1960 to £10,000 in 1969.[54] The GLC Historic Buildings Board noted of Colebrooke Row and Duncan Terrace in Islington in 1970 that 'although stressed housing conditions are not uncommon, parts of the area . . . are improving rapidly, mainly in the hands of owner-occupiers.'[55] It recognised that 'in general those areas which are of such distinctive character as to merit designation are areas where property is sought after and which therefore tend to attract the more prosperous sections of the community. For this reason the financial implications of conservation need not be unduly onerous to the Council.'[56] In fact the GLC developed the practice of making pump-priming improvement grants to owners, conditional on acceptance of a Building Preservation Order on the property.[57] At the 1963 Montpelier Row inquiry, the Cator Estate had complained that a Preservation Order 'relegated the owner to the role of curator',[58] but within a few years the rise in London property values, most marked in the case of buildings with historical cachet, meant that listing represented a positive asset in owners' eyes. In such circumstances demolition was now seldom a risk, but Preservation Orders did make it easier to prevent the kind of inappropriate alteration of detail that could threaten the integrity of a streetscape.

This concern to protect the visual integrity of attractive ensembles was rooted in the policy developed by the GLC and its predecessor over a decade or more. The notion that groups of buildings might have value in epitomising a locality, even if individually they lacked particular significance, had been understood from the early days of conservation. The 1944 'Instructions to Investigators' had directed their attention to 'buildings which have in their view cumulative group or character value, but which have not that degree of intrinsic architectural or historical interest which would naturally be called special interest', but in the absence of this 'special interest' they were to be included only on the supplementary list.[59] In London, though, this question of 'group value' was critical to the whole conservation issue. Much of the city's visual appeal and its 'character' derived from unpretentious streets or locales which appealed primarily as an ensemble. That appeal might be jeopardised by the kind of piecemeal redevelopment likely to be encouraged by the lack of statutory protection. Above all it was the terraces of Georgian London which stood to lose their aesthetic impact through ad hoc alterations. Recognising this, the LCC's Historic Buildings Sub-Committee had in 1957 resolved to investigate the question of preserving 'single houses, groups or terraces . . . with a view to the provision of a general plan for the preservation of Georgian London.'

The Historic Buildings Board had reported in February 1959, with the result that several significant groups of buildings, including Bedford Square and its vicinity, a clutch of streets in Belgravia, streets and squares in Canonbury and Highbury, Dorset Square and Doughty Street, had been put forward for protection.[60]

This investigation was limited to Georgian London, and the buildings covered had been erected in the years between 1700 and 1840, when existing listing criteria suggested that 'the greater number of buildings should probably be listed, though selection will be necessary.'[61] More delicate was the question of the large mid-nineteenth-century terraces of West and Northwest London, such as the Ladbroke Estate, considered by the LCC's officers 'perhaps the most remarkable piece of garden town planning in London.'[62] They anticipated that in the wake of the breakup of London's great estates with the sale of freeholds after the war, the local authority 'may in future be called upon to exercise the control which was once in estate hands', in order to ensure that group uniformity was not eroded by 'the worst excesses of decoration and mutilation of detail.'[63] Before that sort of control could be contemplated, though, the danger of piecemeal demolition had to be resisted. Ministerial approval for what would become the Royal Lancaster Hotel at Lancaster Gate in 1961 prompted the Historic Buildings officials to recommend bulk listing of 1850s terraces in southern Paddington which had been denied listing 'as a result of the lateness of their construction', while in the same year a Building Preservation Order was sought for several houses in Melbury Road, Holland Park, in view of 'their importance as a group expressing the taste of well known artists of the later Victorian period.'[64] In the following year the LCC's Historic Buildings officers tried unsuccessfully to prevent their own council from scheduling the western end of Cantwell's Royal Crescent, Holland Park (1842–43) for demolition under a road scheme.[65] This was followed in 1965–66 by Preservation Orders for the Ladbroke Estate and for a group of streets near Warwick Avenue.[66] The threat of hotel development in Holland Park in 1963 drew attention to the weakness of the Kensington lists, drawn up when listing was young and consequently deficient in 'the principal groups of Victorian buildings on which the character of the better parts of the Royal Borough is dependent.'[67] In these years new group listings were also recommended for buildings in Finsbury, in Chelsea and—extensively—in Barnsbury.[68]

This emphasis on estate and group listing necessarily entailed issuing Building Preservation Orders for large numbers of buildings which were admitted to be of little individual importance. The Ministry of Housing and Local Government, concerned that listed status might be debased, stressed in 1966 that the statutory requirement remained that listed buildings should be of '*special* architectural or historic interest'.[69] The early years of the policy consequently brought several disputes between the LCC and the Ministry. In November 1961 the Council's Historic Buildings Sub-Committee considered protesting to the Ministry about recent reversals, deciding instead to 'watch for any divergence of policy which may develop'.[70] Two years later it criticised 'the inconsistency of [the Minister's] decision, and the reasons therefor' in failing to protect the whole of Westbourne Terrace.[71] This decision does now seem perverse, but more significant in the long run was the inspector's implicit support to the LCC's approach in an unusually lyrical portrait of 'England's grandest residential street': 'By Georgian standards this street may be over-ornate but it is a composition in stucco, a very different material to the reticent bricks of the Georgians, and it must be judged by different standards. . . . Although Victorian architecture is not now generally admired, and bearing in mind that Georgian architecture was little respected by the Victorians, tastes change and are, in fact, now changing'.[72] Indubitably the value of Westbourne Terrace derived from its appeal as an early-Victorian streetscape.

According to John Delafons, the minister of Housing and Local Government in the 1964 Labour administration, Richard Crossman, was seized by the concept of group value and encouraged the Conservative MP Duncan Sandys to use his success in the Private Members' ballot to introduce a bill to promote the principle.[73] The resultant Civic Amenities Act of 1967 allowed local planning authorities to designate Conservation Areas within their boundaries; the GLC Historic Buildings officers noted that it was 'the first measure to make provision for the preservation or enhancement of complete areas of special architectural or historic interest'.[74] It did not, though, provide group listing of the type that the GLC and its predecessor had pursued, as it gave buildings within the Conservation Areas no greater protection than they enjoyed already. That the Ministry initially envisaged Conservation Areas as a second-order mode of preservation is suggested by an exchange with the GLC over Bedford Park as the bill went through Parliament. The work of Norman Shaw and others at Bedford Park in Chiswick was the late-Victorian, suburban equivalent of the kind of mid-nineteenth-century estate that the LCC had sought to protect in Kensington and Paddington. Comprehensive listing had been considered by the minister's Advisory Committee in 1963, prompted by the proposed demolition of two of the houses but rejected on the ground that most were 'of such indifferent quality that no additions to the lists should be made' and that 'the architecture of the houses was too debased to be worthy of listing.'[75] The two demolitions led to the formation of a residents' society, however, and the GLC once again sought widespread listing in 1966, to be told that the imminent Conservation Area mechanism would instead provide 'an appropriate means of giving recognition to an area of character such as the Estate,'[76] even though it would not prevent a future cull of Shaw's work. The Council asked whether 'any useful purpose is served in designating areas containing buildings to which no protection is offered' and concluded that the designation of a Conservation Area should not preclude 'a careful examination of the area to ensure that all of the existing fabric worthy of preservation is included in the statutory list.'[77] Thirty years later Andrew Saint noted, 'Listed building legislation has strong teeth. Conservation Area legislation has weak ones.'[78]

Nonetheless, Conservation Area status did create a presumption of preservation in the areas covered and, usually, an army of residents eager to defend their local environment. The response of the boroughs was enthusiastic, with more than a hundred proposed Conservation Areas under discussion by the summer of 1968. Moreover, the GLC pursued with vigour its declared intention to reinforce Conservation Area status by seeking protection for deserving buildings in the areas concerned, so that the Ministry faced a blizzard of individual applications for listing. In 1972 'the volume of representations that are coming from the Greater London Council concerning the revised London lists', including two hundred recent suggestions for Southwark and a similar number for Lewisham, induced such listing fatigue in the Department of the Environment that it introduced amending legislation to limit demolitions in Conservation Areas.[79] Two years later it devolved responsibility for compiling the lists for most of London to the GLC.[80]

By the late 1960s, therefore, public policy had travelled far from the postwar assumption that listing served to protect individual gems in the context of widespread urban modernisation. The growing respect for the townscapes created by the Victorians, the de facto conservationism produced by the spread of owner occupation and the profusion of Conservation Areas fostered an assumption that the existing urban environment should be retained unless good reason existed to change it. This was crystallised in the Ministry's Circular 61 of 1968 and in that year's Town and

Country Planning Act, the combined effect of which was that 'policy now favoured the tightening of conservation control to the point of rigidity.'[81]

Arguments for conservation became less academic as they were more widely diffused, particularly after 1967. Whatever emotion underlay the GLC Historic Buildings officials' drive for group listing in the early sixties, each case had been the subject of meticulous research. Proposals for Conservation Area status, though, 'ranging from an extensive nineteenth century estate in Westminster to a small village green in Croydon',[82] were likely to be more impressionistic. The Conservation Area legislation, reliant as it was on local initiative, gave more weight to locals' wishes for their own environment than did the statutory listing process. In this it was consistent both with the late-sixties vogue for popular involvement in planning decisions and with the steady diffusion throughout the decade of Jane Jacobs's arguments for recognition of the psychological value of the familiar in the urban environment. This changing climate ensured a rougher ride than might once have been expected for the more ambitious public proposals for urban redevelopment in Central London.

Three Fiascos: Piccadilly, Whitehall, Covent Garden

Three major schemes for the redevelopment of parts of Central London wound their way through the planning system in these years: the successive proposals to remodel Piccadilly Circus following the 1959 fiasco, the attempted modernisation of the government quarter at the southern end of Whitehall from 1963 onwards and the GLC's 1968 scheme to redevelop the Covent Garden area, prompted by the 1961 decision to move the fruit and vegetable market.

At Piccadilly the lesson drawn from the 1959 episode was that redevelopment should not happen piecemeal under developer pressure but should be under public control, directed by 'a single architectural mind.' The role of the new Wren was assigned to Sir William Holford, regarded as Britain's leading architect-planner after Abercrombie's death in 1957, inaugurating a saga which would continue until the Circus was conservatively remodelled in the 1980s. Holford produced in 1962 a scheme to transform the Circus, with Eros beached on a pedestrian piazza surrounded by office towers.[83] He envisaged a 'very slim vertical feature' to identify the new space, topped by 'a finial in the form of a "ruff"' as an easily recognisable

Piccadilly Circus, 1962. (Mary Evans/Classic Stock/H. Armstrong Roberts)

symbol of the pieces of cloth . . . which gave their name to Piccadilly.'[84] The Ministry of Transport, unmoved by the ruff, protested that the scheme did not allow for the 50 percent increase in traffic envisaged,[85] and it found few friends in the Housing Ministry, where the secretary, Evelyn Sharp, was unimpressed by Holford.[86] For a while the Ministry's Piccadilly Working Party was gripped by Buchanan's urban vision and by a peculiarly exuberant report pointing 'towards a "two-level city"' produced by Freeman, Fox

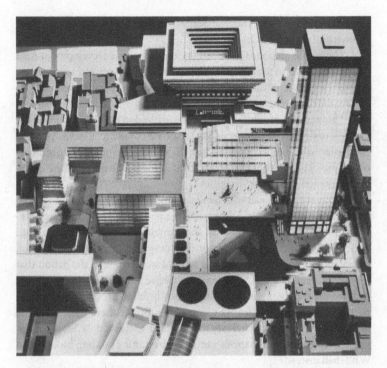

Architectural model of Sir William Holford's second Piccadilly Circus scheme, 1966–68, with Eros relocated to a raised piazza and traffic channelled underneath. (London Picture Archive 239561 © London Metropolitan Archives [City of London])

in 1964.[87] Holford was urged to replan Piccadilly along these lines and did so, returning in 1966 with proposals for a new piazza on the eastern side of the Circus, raised to first-floor level with traffic passing underneath.[88] The GLC revealed this scheme at a public exhibition in 1968, eliciting as little public enthusiasm as the previous Piccadilly proposals, and the redevelopment of the Circus stalled again. When this fantasy was ditched, a less ambitious version of the Holford scheme resurfaced in 1972, though it came no closer to realisation.

The Whitehall scheme grew exponentially from 1963 proposals to redevelop the 'tawdry slum' of the Foreign Office.[89] The 1965 plan produced by Leslie Martin and Buchanan advocated not only the immediate obliteration of the Foreign Office, the Treasury and several neighbouring buildings but also, more distantly, the transformation of Whitehall itself into a

'Grand Axis', running to Trafalgar Square, through the redeveloped Covent Garden and on as far as Bloomsbury.[90]

At Covent Garden the GLC sought Comprehensive Development Area powers to transform the area with a cluster of office towers and a web of new roads. The closure of the market offered 'probably the last opportunity to achieve the comprehensive development of a substantial part of central London',[91] but the cost of rebuilding the heart of London in this way obliged the Council to operate in partnership with several commercial developers—a concession which called into question the scheme's standing as a genuinely public project and exposed it to criticism as the public image of the developer darkened in the early seventies.

All three schemes dealt with familiar landmarks, with an emotional hold on the London public. At a time when the pace of private commercial redevelopment appeared relentless, these public schemes intensified Londoners' sense of dislocation. As one witness cried out to the Whitehall public inquiry in 1970, 'we just like to have somewhere in the nation that we feel will not change.'[92] She would not have known that her sentiment had been shared by members of the recently fallen Labour government: Barbara Castle felt that 'from St James' Park Bridge there was one of the loveliest vistas in any capital city in the world' and asked, 'Were we really going to be guilty of monstrous vandalism by putting modern buildings in Whitehall instead?'[93]

Just as the trend towards group listing and conservation areas was gathering steam, these comprehensive development schemes inevitably implied a return to the stark 1940s approach to historic buildings, singling out those individual gems which it would be hard to destroy and preserving them in isolation. As Adam Sharr and Stephen Thornton write of the Whitehall scheme, the historic buildings which were spared were merely 'treated as isolated objects': 'Even where they stood for most of their history as part of a block, they might nevertheless be detached and set free to be viewed. This is, perhaps, a fulfilment of the art-historical idea of architectural history; idealising the art object, imagined as a thing-unto-itself.' Martin and his team reprieved individual buildings because, they said, 'we liked them', damning the rest;[94] the overriding aim to transform the neighbourhood as a whole was unquestioned. At Covent Garden the GLC, faced by the bulky reality of Inigo Jones's Grade 1–listed St Paul's Church and the certain public opposition to the loss of the Royal Opera House or the market building, drew a 'line of character' embracing these monuments, running from west to east across the proposed CDA area.

Optimistically it designated the line a Conservation Area shortly before the opening of the public inquiry in 1971, in the hope of gaining 'advantages . . . in the public relations field.'[95]

Tellingly it was Piccadilly, with no unquestionable architectural treasures, which evoked the strongest emotional response, purely because the Circus, as symbol of the city and as public gathering ground, stood for London in the eyes of many people. When Holford's 1962 plan was unveiled, a spokesman for the LCC was reported to have said, 'we don't feel that the public really cares what Piccadilly Circus looks like.'[96] If this appears cavalier, it should be remembered that the area was generally accepted to be an architectural mess and a traffic glue pot. Nevertheless, the Monico episode had shown 'the public' to be sensitive to any threat to the Circus, simply because of its status as a national symbol. The minister, Charles Hill, was urged by one correspondent in April 1962 to 'strongly veto this proposed atrocity . . . that, if it is allowed, will entirely wipe out the character of the place; not that it possesses any architectural value from an artist's point of view, but it is familiar, and not hideously American as the proposed plan will make it.'[97] Similar entreaties were produced in reaction to each of the successive proposals to reshape the Circus.

All of this helps explain the strong purchase gained in London by the arguments of the American urban activist Jane Jacobs, whose *The Death and Life of Great American Cities* was published only a few months before the demolition of the Euston Arch and the Coal Exchange. Its arguments would resonate through the debates on London's comprehensive development schemes. Jacobs's classic was a protest against the perceived inhumanity of the redevelopment of US cities since 1945, urging a retreat from the iconoclastic absolutism of modern planning practice and a recognition of the importance of the intimate, the irregular and the familiar in the urban environment. For more than a decade after its appearance, any well-briefed opponent of redevelopment or demolition would come armed with Jacobs's bons mots. Martin felt it necessary to dismiss Jacobs's principal arguments as 'entirely false' in 1971, while in the GLC's submission to the Covent Garden public inquiry in the same year, it stressed with some irritation that it 'was aware of the need to preserve character without the help of Jane Jacobs.'[98]

The 1970 Whitehall and the 1971 Covent Garden inquiries each provided a platform for Jacobs's views on the relationship between the city and its residents. Retaining familiar details of urban life, however apparently inconsequential, became a conservationist refrain. Nicholas Taylor fought

for the souvenir shops around Whitehall, because trinket merchants conferred 'very great value in introducing an element of humanity' in a tourist
city, just as 'one of the things that is most attractive in Rome is that there
are little stalls with people selling images of John XXIII.'[99] Gordon
McLeish, defending the Floral Hall in Covent Garden, advocated 'preserving the coster barrows' once the market had gone, 'for retail selling of flowers, fruit and vegetables where they have always been.'[100] The Joint Committee of conservation groups formed to oppose the Covent Garden
development argued that this quartier was 'one of the very few remaining
areas where small traders and personal service industries can continue to
thrive', precisely because it was 'the only part of the West End and Central
districts of London that has not been vigorously planned at one time or
another.'[101] Even Lord Clark, probably not a Jacobs disciple, used his appearance before the Whitehall inquiry to argue that prewar London had
been distinguished by the organic evolution of its architecture over the
centuries and that postwar rebuilding in the 'steel and glass style which is
indistinguishable from the buildings in any large city in the world' had
sacrificed 'a great deal of the personal character for which people loved and
admired it.'[102] Steadily the eclecticism, irregularity and quirkiness of London's built environment came to be seen as a strength, signifying a plural-
ism inconsistent with the imposition of drawing-board designs by local
or—in the case of Whitehall—central government. 'This is the kind of
capital we have', Taylor told the Whitehall inquiry. 'We do not have great
dictatorial avenues ending with triumphal arches.'[103]

Jacobs's arguments permeated the architectural profession during the
1960s, just as they influenced the general public. Whereas in 1959 a recent
president of the Royal Institute of British Architects, Howard Robertson,
had spoken at the Piccadilly inquiry in support of the Monico proposals,
the president in 1970, Peter Shepheard, spoke against the Whitehall scheme,
arguing in now familiar terms that 'the essential qualities of London architecture [are] first, a human scale; second, a mixture of uses, and styles, of building
giving a constant and delightful variety; third, an admission of accident and
chance, and a rejection of excessive monumentality and pomp.'[104] In the
same year the architect and writer Theo Crosby produced a hymn to the
humane city which displayed—and acknowledged—a 'great debt' to
Jane Jacobs. Crosby attacked the 'elementarism' of modern planning and
the mentality of comprehensive redevelopment: 'A small scale area with
many varied owners and users will always, by its cycle of random clearing,
painting and alteration demonstrate its inner dynamic, and because of the

multiplicity of its parts it is less liable to general blight.' Suggesting that 'one can be almost certain under present conditions that a new building will be a bad building', Crosby called for fresh thinking on the future use of threatened but valued monuments like St Pancras. Buildings of this sort were 'necessary treasures', helping to spread the tourist load away from Westminster Abbey and the Tower. They were 'reminders of our better selves, our communal responsibilities and of our present slavery to the requirements of the production process. It is no wonder that there is so much pressure to replace them with plastic packs for conveniently processed people.'[105]

These movements within the profession were sharpened by the emergence of a new, far more overtly political, radicalism in the schools of architecture in the late 1960s and early 1970s. This strain of thought, which owed more to the general student militancy of the period than to the stylistic debates described earlier, reflected a fear amongst the student body that the profession had sold itself to capitalism and bureaucracy and that its practitioners were separating themselves from the society in which they lived. The architecture student, though aspiring to 'the "free professional" status of the independent small office', was more likely to be employed in 'some large corporation or government bureaucracy', where 'his autonomy and level of responsibility are likely to be low [and] he is unlikely ever to meet or know very much about the people who know his building.'[106] Architecture's New Left expressed itself above all in a hostility to property developers and to the local authorities who gave them planning permission or even direct commissions. Squatting, occupations and demonstrations were prompted by, in particular, the third Piccadilly Circus scheme in 1972, by Stock Conversion's attempts to redevelop Tolmers Square, near Euston, in league with Camden Council, in 1973 and, above all, by the GLC's Covent Garden scheme. The involvement of the junior members of the profession was conspicuous. Nick Wates, leader and chronicler of the Tolmers Square protest,[107] was a product of the UCL Bartlett School of Architecture, while Jim Monaghan, spokesman for the community resistance at Covent Garden, was also an architecture student. Assessing the composition of an open-air protest meeting in the Market area in April 1971, involving around 300–350 people, the GLC's Public Information Branch estimated that 'the average age of 70% of the audience was about 22, mainly young planners, architects, and students of these professions.'[108] Under their influence, the political tone which had arguably always been implicit in Jacobs's arguments became explicit, with development depicted as a conspiracy to destroy working-class communities for the benefit of property speculators—'why should we be moved for the sake of land values?', as one Covent Garden resident asked.[109] The Covent Garden campaign was characterised by its leaders as part of a 'world-wide struggle against giantism and authority', when 'local and national government have lost touch with the people.'[110] In their essentially political fight, the conservationist stance of these groups was often not developed beyond a reluctance to see 'sturdy buildings' give way to office blocks, but their concern to protect working-class communities in situ instilled a protective attitude towards the buildings in which the working class lived, an attitude which appeared excessively conservative to their critics. At the public inquiry in 1971 the GLC complained that the Community Association wished 'to fossilise the area for all time.'[111]

At the very least, the growing links between conservationism and community politics challenged the traditional view of conservation as a bourgeois hobby. Beyond that, Simon Jenkins suggested in 1973, the growth of community pressure groups showed that 'urban renewal can proceed without necessarily destroying the existing fabric of the city.'[112] One by-product of the prolonged and largely fruitless efforts to advance the comprehensive redevelopment proposals for key London sites had been to draw attention to their exorbitant cost, which in turn challenged the assumption underlying the Abercrombiean plans and above all the Buchanan proposals that physical remodelling was essential for a city to flourish economically. As Otto Saumarez Smith has recently argued, the authors of the various town improvement schemes in vogue in the early sixties had been culpably vague about the financing of what were often very substantial projects, assuming they would be funded by the rising national prosperity that was held to have made them necessary in the first place.[113] By the early seventies that prosperity was no longer taken as given, and central government was becoming more sceptical of ambitious public redevelopment schemes, particularly in Central London.

In 1971 the inspector at the Covent Garden inquiry endorsed the GLC's Comprehensive Development Area application in an imperceptive report which hardly enhanced public respect for such investigations. The Department of the Environment, though, was affected more by the range of objections to the scheme, 'both weighty and passionately argued', and by the prominence amongst the objectors of 'elements of the "alternative society."'[114] Unsurprisingly the alternative society's demand that the area's working-class community be preserved in situ even after its main employment source had vanished cut little ice, and there was little prospect of satisfying 'those who pine after the continuing occupation of low-cost premises in decaying buildings, on the fag-end of leases, on land worth £1.5 million or more an acre for redevelopment.'[115] Nonetheless, the department accepted that 'the present GLC proposals would produce over-development and destroy the existing social structure.'[116] By 1972 its officials were questioning their flirtation with Buchanan—a 'rather dated theory that has been under increasing attack for the last eight years', resting on 'the optimistic assumption that we can afford the major restructuring of existing city centres and that we will like the results.' In a trenchant memorandum, O. T. Humphreys argued that the GLC's dependence on private developers to subsidise the scheme would leave it at the developers' mercy even if CDA powers were to be granted: put bluntly, by supping with speculators 'the GLC will be . . . screwed rotten.'[117]

Such disenchantment drew officials steadily to accept conservation as a form of development control. Early in 1972 the environment secretary, Peter Walker, announced the listing of several 1920s buildings around Piccadilly, asserting disingenuously that the new listings would not jeopardise the redevelopment of the Circus.[118] A year later his successor, Geoffrey Rippon, mounted a still more remarkable coup to kill off the Covent Garden scheme. Responding to rising opposition to the GLC plans, the department had already resolved that approval should only be granted subject to 'some very stringent conditions', including conservation outside the existing conservation area.[119] It initially envisaged adding around a hundred buildings to the statutory list, but the eventual total was a startling 250, although, as officials acknowledged privately, 'architecturally few parts of Covent Garden are distinguished, and apart from the general scale of certain areas there is little homogeneity of style.'[120] The GLC's proposals depended for their viability on their developer partners having the free hand that extensive listing would deny them; they were understandably surprised 'that there were so many more buildings of listable quality.'[121] They 'hoped Ministers realised that "more conservation meant more deficit."'[122] In fact more conservation meant the abandonment of the scheme. Whereas once listing had been seen as a means of protecting deserving buildings from the impact of urban modernisation, by the early 1970s listing was being used to stifle modernisation. The idea no longer prevailed that Britain's economic future required the physical transformation of Central London.

1973: 'The Year We Changed Our Minds'

Whatever Walker's and Rippon's private views of architecture, they were politicians, responding to an evolving public mood. Walker was said to have 'leapt on to the environmental bandwagon back in 1970 and picked up the tune with extraordinary facility.' One of his officials suggested that 'it only takes a brief mention of any London controversy in the Press . . . to have the Secretary of State demanding to see the file on it, however trivial.'[123] Rippon had been the energetic advocate of Whitehall redevelopment in 1963 but ten years later described himself as 'a preservationist rather than a conservationist.'[124] The constant public reinterrogation of the Piccadilly and other redevelopment schemes had challenged earlier assumptions that, however disruptive, they would eventually benefit the community. Increasingly, arguments over London's built environment revolved around private, speculative office developments, the debate becoming in the process a more distinctly Manichaean one between public amenity and private profit.

The main reason for that was the decision of the Heath government, on taking office in 1970, to repeal the 'Brown ban' on office building in Central London. For two years or so, little in the centre appeared safe, as developers rushed to satisfy the pent-up demand for office space. Towards the end of 1973 Simon Jenkins counted sixteen major office developments in progress within two hundred yards of Holborn Circus.[125] None was on a bomb site: the main targets of the new office boom were relatively unheralded Victorian buildings. They were unlikely to provoke the kind of stir caused by, for example, British Rail's threat to St Pancras, but, Jenkins argued, they provided 'a lasting reassurance to people who live in cities—who take enough punishment as it is—that everything is not in a permanent state of disruption and upheaval.' For all the recent shift towards protecting characterful areas, whole *quartiers* in Central London were now threatened: Soho's Chinatown, the booksellers of Charing Cross Road, the jewellery quarter of Hatton Garden and Clerkenwell.[126] This surge of development proposals, coming at a time when the public mind had been moving discernibly in the direction of conservation, added new urgency to the question of how much say Londoners could have in the appearance of their city.

It would be the bursting of the property bubble in the autumn of 1973 which tilted the balance decisively against the developers, as Jenkins noted at the time.[127] The secondary banking crisis which followed produced severe liquidity problems for property companies. In March 1974 the *Standard*'s Robert Langton predicted 'a massive shedding of top quality buildings and land by the late spring and early summer.'[128] The deepening of the property crisis into 1975 caused British Land to call time on Biba,[129] Joe Levy to abandon his office block in Tolmers Square[130] and almost all property companies to rein in their more ambitious schemes. Office development did not come to an end in 1973, but the onslaught on London's fabric seen in the previous two years would not be repeated. Instead, property companies turned their attention to the benefits of refurbishment. The initiative shifted from the combative Cottons and Levys to firms like Haslemere Estates, which had pioneered the conservation-minded refurbishment of older office property, coining the slogan 'Doing a Haslemere' to describe their activity.[131] Early in 1975 the industry scheduled a one-day conference in London on the restoration and rehabilitation of office buildings. As one developer put it, 'This is the only patch left where we can actually do something.'[132]

The City as Amenity

A telling exchange occurred in 1964 between Nikolaus Pevsner, writing as chairman of the Victorian Society, and Anthony Dale, the Town and Country Planning Ministry's chief inspector of historic buildings, over the fate of R. L. Roumieu's exuberant Gothic creation at 33–35 Eastcheap in the City, built as a warehouse and offices for the vinegar makers Hill, Evans of Worcester in 1868. 'Of course it is crazy', Pevsner suggested, 'but wouldn't we put a premium on the craziest of 18th century follies as well?' Dale replied that while eighteenth-century follies were private jokes on private land, Roumieu's building, in a public street, could not be taken as a jeu d'esprit: 'he meant it seriously': 'Nineteenth century buildings listed are supposed to have definite character and quality. Character this certainly has. But could you really say it has quality? I can just see the press headlines if such a building were listed & the press got hold of it. . . . In my view it is just the sort of building that we should avoid listing as being likely to do much harm both to the Ministry and to nineteenth century listing as a whole.'[133] In 1964 the listing of Victorian buildings was not to be undertaken frivolously. Seven years later, though, Roumieu's 'folly'—'one of the most remarkable and dramatic examples of Gothic style applied to a commercial building'[134]—was Grade 2 listed.

Gothic survivor. 33–35 Eastcheap, by Robert Lewis Roumieu, 1868, photographed in 2007. (Photo by David Iliff; licence: CC BY-SA 3.0)

The story illustrates more than just the rapid change of heart towards Victorian Gothic in the sixties. The office buildings in Eastcheap stood at the heart of the City, the nation's financial and commercial centre, a block away from the site of the Coal Exchange, on some of the most valuable land in Britain. Hill, Evans & Co had ceased trading in 1965, Roumieu was not a household name, and his building, however dramatic, seemed out of place in the modern City of London, notable for the 'virile philistinism' of its Corporation.[135] If sixties London depended on its service sector, and that sector required suitable modern accommodation, the building should presumably have been demolished. In 1962, after all, Sir Keith Joseph had overturned LCC Preservation Orders for houses in Harley and Wimpole Streets, though acknowledging that these Georgian buildings possessed a 'pleasant architectural unity which retains the character of a simple digni- fied 18th century street', because they were 'not now very convenient for living and working.'[136] Having survived the sixties, though, Roumieu's whimsical piece survives today. This episode in its way illustrates the dis- tance travelled in attitudes towards the urban built environment in the quarter century since the war's end.

When the listing system was introduced in 1944, it appeared as an inci- dental component of a planning system founded on the belief that the ravages of war would allow postwar London to be rationalised in a way that Victorian and interwar London had never been and that a rational city would function more efficiently and be a better city to live in. But the general respect accorded to the Abercrombie plans in the 1940s concealed the fact that the war's psychological effect on Londoners was double- edged. There *was* much support for the idea that conflict had created a blank slate on which a better city could be drawn, but while London had suffered much physical damage, it had not come near obliteration. What had survived of the city's fabric acquired an emotional value on the strength of its survival, regardless of its architectural or historical signifi- cance. The familiar complaint in the fifties and sixties that 'the planners' appeared bent on completing the job that the Luftwaffe had left unfinished showed the durability of that sentiment for a generation or longer.

It is difficult today not to disparage the planning professionals of the postwar years. It is still harder to understand the enthusiastic reception for the 1963 Buchanan report, whose 'logic of demolishing and rebuilding parts of the city to avoid their destruction by traffic appears rather back- to-front today.'[137] But while the planners' approach to the built environ- ment might have been hubristic, it was founded on principles which had applied for centuries: the belief that the urban fabric was essentially malleable and that buildings and even street patterns should be replaced when no longer fit for purpose. What happened in the 1960s and 1970s was the displacement of this orthodoxy by the view that a city's prosperity need not depend on the constant remodelling of its structures. A converted vinegar warehouse might be suboptimal as a modern office, but that did not warrant its destruction if the local environment was diminished in the process. Increasingly the city was seen as an amenity.

In October 1973 the *Evening Standard* published a defence of developers written by Sir Fred Catherwood, managing director of the construction firm John Laing. At the height of their power, few developers would have troubled to influence the reading public, relying instead on backstage lobbying and similar black arts; Catherwood's piece was a sign of changing times. His claim that 'conservation is overdone' was to be expected from the head of a building firm, but he made a lucid case for the former orthodoxy: there was a long-run shift from manual work to office work; London was the commercial centre of Europe, vital to Britain's balance of trade; the London office worker was 'the most skilled and experienced in the world'; obsolete commercial buildings needed replacing—'there are slum offices as well as slum houses.' One clue as to why this sixties orthodoxy was waning was provided, though, by his acknowledgement that 'it is the protruding arrogance and clinical coldness of the tower blocks which makes them unacceptable.'[138]

We will never know how conservation would have developed had London's developers in the 1960s produced modern townscapes that were better received by contemporaries. Much public criticism of modernist architecture was as formulaic as the buildings it attacked, but what mattered was the pervasive assumption that any new building would be worse than whatever it replaced. There was no 'battle of the styles' in 1960s London, merely a crude fight between ancient and modern, weighted in favour of the former. In this context, the attraction of Jacobs's doctrines is evident: during the seventies, they became effectively consensual. An urban activist herself, she naturally appealed both to liberals and to the Left, who shared her commitment to community and her suspicion of the covert manoeuvres of capital. Many on the right were, simply put, conservative by instinct, even if some of their best friends were developers. They had little enthusiasm for the modernist aesthetic and were uncomfortable with disruption to a familiar environment. In 1972, as Westminster City Council tried once again to impose Holford's piazza on an unreceptive public, the chairman of the Piccadilly subcommittee explained to Simon Jenkins why the new plan had jettisoned the redevelopment of the Circus's hinterland once thought essential to the project: 'I just took a walk one day . . . from the London Pavilion round into Coventry Street and through Rupert Street into Wardour Street. I just could not see the whole lot being demolished just like that. It was inconceivable.'[139] It was a Conservative junior minister, Lord Sandford, who declared in January 1973 that policy should 'take account of the growth of public opinion in favour of conserving the familiar and cherished local scene. It should also have care for the conservation of existing communities and the social fabric, wherever public opinion points clearly towards it', the change being crystallised in a circular to local authorities.[140] The two environment secretaries in Edward Heath's growth-fixated Conservative government, Peter Walker and Geoffrey Rippon, did as much as anyone to subvert the assumption that a modern economy required a modernised environment. In the 1980s Thatcher's economic liberalism would prove compatible with a massive increase in listing and in the creation of conservation areas.[141]

Conclusion

Though many of the elements of Britain's postwar settlement were coming under fire by the late 1970s, the welfare state and, particularly, the National Health Service still had determined defenders, as, indeed, did the more restrictive aspects of the 1947 Town and Country Planning system—development control and the protection of green belts. But the core assumption of Abercrombiean town planning—that towns could be effectively redesigned to make them work more rationally and to fit the demands of modern urban life—had been all but abandoned by 1979, at least as it affected the built environment. Discussion of what a city should look like was less directly influenced than welfare or health care by ideological presuppositions, with the result that expressions of public taste tended to be more absolute. In the 1940s, so far as we can tell, there was widespread public approval for the idea of the planned city: the rather forbidding full version of the *County of London Plan* sold ten thousand copies in wartime, justifying the production of a paperback edition.[142] Even in 1963 the favourable reception of Buchanan's *Traffic in Towns* warranted a Penguin Special version.[143] In the following year, though, Penguin published a paperback edition of Jacobs's *Death and Life*, although it was primarily concerned with the United States. In the years that followed, events in London evolved in ways conducive to conservation—the repeated demonstrations of the impracticability of the more ostentatious public projects, the increasing misgivings about local authority high-rise housing, the spread of owner occupation, the bursting of the property bubble in 1973 and the greater willingness of developers to interest themselves in refurbishment as a result—all reinforcing the deepening aesthetic disenchantment with modernism amongst the London public. A new conservationist orthodoxy formed.

8

East End Docklands and
the Death of Poplarism

In the 1880s those who sought London's social fault lines went to the East End. In the 1950s they went to Notting Hill. It was not that the East End had experienced a dramatic social transformation: London's early gentrification passed the area by, and it remained overwhelmingly working class. There was still much poverty to be found east of the City, and it was still an area where 'social workers and journalists come on safari to study the working classes';[1] but the East End had done well out of postwar affluence. David Widgery, the radical '68-er who became a GP in Bethnal Green, described the 1950s East End aptly as 'a vast autonomous ... proletarian city basking in the long economic boom.'[2]

In an age of full employment, the East End working man benefited from labour shortages. Put simply, in the postwar years people left the area more quickly than did jobs. The population of Stepney halved between 1939 and 1961,[3] but the small employers who dominated the borough's traditional tailoring trade tended to stay put in their archaic Victorian premises. Denys Munby's 1951 report to the ad hoc Stepney Reconstruction Group noted that the immediate postwar years even saw houses converted into workshops as ex-servicemen returned to the borough and started up businesses. He accurately predicted future labour shortages in key local industries.[4] Illustrations accompanying the illuminating memoirs of Alfred Gardner, who entered the rag trade in the midfifties, show two Stepney factories in the 1950s, flying banners appealing for dress machinists, finishers, pressers and cutters. Gardner himself effectively chose his employers in these years,

Docklands from the air. The Isle of Dogs, November 1977. (Evening Standard/Hulton Archive/ Getty Images)

spurning those offering insanitary premises, inadequate fire escapes, surly managers or unsociable workmates.[5] Gardner was able to live comfortably, regularly travelling to his various social venues by taxi—until he bought a car.[6] Otto Newman, in his study of East End gambling, noted that after the legalisation of off-course bookmaking in 1960 Tower Hamlets boasted the highest number of betting shops per capita of any London borough.[7] The dockers' leader, Jack Dash, and others commented on the sharp dressing of the East End male, as the area's long-established clothing industry responded to the 1960s fashion revolution.[8] The opening of the menswear shop Boutique in Bethnal Green in 1965, coming shortly after the establishment of a Tower Hamlets hairdressers academy to promote West End styles in the east, suggested that the East End was even beginning to swing a little.[9]

The Docks and Docklands

Docklands was at the heart of this prosperity. As Widgery pointed out, Docklands was effectively a separate territory within the East End—a largely Anglo-Irish community unlike the ethnically complex manufacturing

The docks were still busy in July 1965, as John Gay's photographs show. (Historic England/Heritage Images/Alamy Stock Photo)

areas of Stepney and a notoriously introverted one.[10] Madge Darby, of the Wapping Community Association, suggested in 1973 that 'the least easily assimilated of all groups of newcomers [to Docklands] are people from other parts of East London', pointing out that 'one of the most resented developments in Wapping in recent years was when the GLC brought into the area a large number of problem families from other parts of East London.'[11] It is clear, though, that the buoyancy of the docks in the postwar years lubricated the entire economy of the inner East End: as the social geographer Roger Lee noted in 1972, 'the docks were a powerful form of social and economic multiplier.'[12] Critically the postwar revival of the port had been accompanied by a strengthening of the dockworkers' position following the implementation of the Attlee government's Dock Labour Scheme of 1947, creating a registered dock labour force enjoying job security and a minimum wage. This measure put an end to the oversupply of labour that had made the docks notorious for exploitative employment in the late nineteenth century, and by the 1960s the combination of the port's buoyancy and the industrial strength conferred by job security had propelled dockers nearly to the top of the manual earnings league.[13]

On top of dockers' formal earnings, they enjoyed greater opportunities to benefit from low-level pilfering as the volume of goods passing through the docks grew. This had always been a de facto perk of the job.[14] A concordat had developed by which the Port of London Authority turned a

Dockers waiting for the allocation of work, August 1965. (Mirrorpix/Alamy Stock Photo)

blind eye to the theft of goods consumed within the dock walls—hardly preventable in practice.[15] Such occasional episodes as the death of a docker who fell into the hold of a ship and whose system was found post mortem to contain the alcoholic equivalent of a gallon and a half of beer suggest that such misdemeanours could reach an epic scale,[16] but there were limits to the amounts that even dockers could consume 'on site': the real profits were to be made from smuggling out goods to be sold in the wider world. No licence was given here: the PLA almost invariably prosecuted those who were caught by the dock police and sacked those who were convicted. The loss of a protected job represented a substantial penalty, but it was offset by the relatively low probability of detection: such was the rush to leave the docks at the end of the working day that the smugglers had a reasonable chance of secreting themselves in the crowd.[17] It was a calculated risk, and those who were caught seldom made much effort to contest their prosecutions ('I am sorry I done it, that's all'; 'What can I say? I am unlucky—I got caught and that's that').[18] The sack must, though, have appeared a less daunting sanction in years of full employment, and the early 1960s was evidently the golden age of dock theft.[19]

David Carpenter, dockland apprentice in the 1950s, remembered the phrase 'well of course he works in the docks' used of anyone 'who perhaps had recently acquired a motor car or was going away for a holiday.'[20] He was able to indulge his passion for vintage cars while still an apprentice, turning up for work at the docks in a 1932 Rolls Royce Phantom Two which he had bought in 1959, when he was twenty. He paid £75 for it—a sum equal to thirteen weeks' pay but 'offset by the overtime and bonus that was now coming in on a regular basis.'[21] Similar benefits were enjoyed by workers in the many riverside industries dependent on the docks themselves. Stan Dyson, born at Silvertown in 1945, entered working life at a moment when 'you literally walked up to any of the factories from Tidal Basin right up to North Woolwich and their Personnel Department could sort you out with a job there and then.' A carefree existence as a costings clerk at a metal containers factory left him wondering 'why on earth they didn't just sack' him: the workers had the whip hand in the early 1960s.[22]

They had gained it, though, more from statutory protection and labour shortage than by conventional collective bargaining. Labour organisation in the docks themselves was complex. In the first place, the port's workforce was divided between two main unions, the Transport and General Workers' Union (TGWU) and the National Association of Stevedores and Dockers. In practice, though, the survival of the casual labour system until the 1960s meant that dockland industrial relations operated by their own rules.[23] The TGWU had been incorporated into the management of the docks by the Dock Labour Scheme, with the result that much of the workforce saw union as being hand in glove with the employers: 'the union is useless and Dash is doing the job instead.'[24] Jack Dash, the communist de facto leader of the London dockers, believed the TGWU leadership to be complicit with the Wilson government in the task of betraying the working man.[25] Stephen Hill, interviewing dockers in the mid-1970s, found much scepticism towards the TGWU and the Labour-union alliance, with 40 percent of his interviewees claiming that trade unions were too powerful in Britain. He saw the failure of trade unions to win the trust of their members as the most notable feature of London dock unionism after 1945.[26] Industrial solidarity was real enough, though: even in the 1960s, older men had been marked for life by their roles in the great strikes of 1911–12, with blacklegs still shunned.[27] Seemingly minor disputes could be magnified instantly to paralyse the system; but such action was sporadic, and labour organisation was meaningful only at the 'shopfloor' level. There was little sense that a docker's union was an integral part of his life.

Indeed, one of the aims of the Devlin Committee inquiry into the port transport system in the 1960s was to impose an industrial relations structure more like those existing elsewhere, in the hope of bringing a degree of predictability into the system.

Poplarism and After

East Enders were more likely to look to the agencies of the national or local state than to trade unions to improve their lives. The area was more reliant on public agencies—primarily the local authorities—than any other part of London. Even a cursory reading of the local press shows the locals' readiness to keep their councils up to the mark, if necessary by ad hoc gestures of direct action. The residents of Cardigan Road, Bow, who threatened to dump their children on the Tower Hamlets welfare authorities if conditions there did not improve, the mothers who blockaded Tredegar Terrace in Mile End to protest against the absence of play facilities, the residents of the Samuda Estate in the Isle of Dogs who held GLC rent collectors hostage in their car to protest against the removal of the resident caretaker, the woman who dumped three phials of black beetles from her tenement home in Brady Street Buildings on the desk of the Tower Hamlets Health Department—all testify in their way to a healthy civic awareness.[28]

Harry Brack, examining Tower Hamlets in a ten-part series for the *Evening Standard* in 1968, described an array of public services across the borough: the public baths and laundry in Cheshire Street, the Langley House children's home, the special care unit by Bethnal Green Gardens, the industrial training centre in Stepney, the old people's homes provided by the borough and the GLC, the units for 'problem families' in Wapping and Cable Street and, of course, the council housing that accommodated three-quarters of the borough's population.[29] Most of the services Brack described were statutory: an area which had had its fill of charitable intruders in the past looked at the voluntary sector with some suspicion. John Orwell, the leader of Tower Hamlets Borough Council, told him that 'where volunteer organisations were doing work which could be done by the council, he would prefer the council services to function alone. Jobs would be offered to the voluntary full-time professional staff.'[30] In 1971 the Borough Council terminated its grant to the Tower Hamlets Council of Social Service—the umbrella group for 240 voluntary organisations operating in the borough—in order to bring as much voluntary-sector activity as possible under the wing of its new Social Services Department.[31]

So far as the authorities themselves were concerned, although both Tower Hamlets and Newham Councils lacked young blood, were disproportionately male[32] and barely reflected the presence of ethnic minorities in their areas,[33] they *were* drawn from the population they served. John O'Malley, in a perceptive account of Newham Council for the Newham (Canning Town) Community Development Project in 1973, noted the absence of any 'intervention in local affairs by ambitious, professionally qualified Labour Party careerists'—familiar elsewhere in London Labour circles—which he attributed to 'the shortage of middle-class housing anywhere in the Borough.'[34] Most Tower Hamlets councillors were said to live in council accommodation,[35] like the majority of the borough's population. The councillors and the users of their services shared a straightforward view of the purpose of municipal government, which was to ameliorate the social and environmental disamenities created by industrial capitalism. The roots of that attitude might be traced to the work of the London County Council in the area before the First World War, but it was really crystallised in the immediate aftermath of the war, when the young Labour Party took power in several East London borough councils and thirty Poplar councillors went to prison to defend their view of socialism in local government.

The 1921 Poplar rates rebellion was already inscribed in the local history of Tower Hamlets (which had absorbed the Poplar Metropolitan Borough in 1965), with a statue to its leader, George Lansbury, a memorial clock to his daughter-in-law Minnie Glassman and six housing estates named after rebel councillors. They had been jailed for withholding the payments which the borough was required to make to the London County Council and other London-wide bodies, a gesture designed as a protest against the inadequate equalisation of the local tax burdens between rich and poor areas of London. The Poplar Council's expenditure on raising the wages of its employees, building social housing and implementing various public-health measures had pushed the rates up to levels far higher than applied in areas with wealthier populations and fewer social problems: the councillors argued that their municipal welfarism was socially necessary, that an impoverished borough could not afford such expenditure on its own and that the London community as a whole should contribute to diminish the disparity in resources between the different parts of the metropolis.

The Poplar policy of expanding municipal provision and calling on the rest of London to share the cost was less opportunistic than it might sound.

It was inherent in London's two-tier governmental system that much management should be carried out at the local level: that being so, the attainment of a reasonable uniformity of standards required some redistribution of resources within London. A partial rate equalisation had been enacted in 1894. It was extended after the councillors' release from prison—tacit official recognition that while their methods might have been controversial, their case had force. By the postwar years Poplarism seemed far less controversial. In the first place, the outward movement of population from the East End between the wars and in 1939–45 had carried with it much of the area's middle class, and the Labour ascendancy established on East End councils in 1919 became a hegemony. West Ham Council, incorporated in Newham in 1965, had been under continuous Labour control since the First World War. Stepney and Poplar, absorbed into Tower Hamlets in 1965, were virtual Labour monopolies. Interviewing John Orwell in 1973, Simon Jenkins noted that 'Big Joe', as Orwell was known, had never faced a Tory across the council chamber, opposition coming only from a handful of communists (Orwell had been a councillor in Stepney and Tower Hamlets for fourteen years).[36] The Conservative candidate gamely contesting the Stepney and Poplar seat in the 1977 GLC election noted that his few supporters would invite him into their homes in order not to be seen talking to him.[37] Secondly the London County Council, at odds with the Poplar rebels in 1921, had been captured by Labour in 1934, and County Hall would remain in Labour hands until the second GLC election in 1967. Finally, not only did welfarism become national orthodoxy during and after the Second World War, but it came to be integrated into the movement for comprehensive postwar planning and reconstruction, to be orchestrated by local authorities. The LCC's *County of London Plan* of 1943 projected the postwar reconstruction of a severely bomb-damaged Stepney in a redevelopment which would 'embody the character and vitality of a new East End.'[38] In the event, some 1945 acres of Stepney and Poplar, bounded by the Whitechapel Road in the west and the River Lea in the east, the Mile End Road in the north and the Thames in the south, were identified by the LCC as ripe for holistic replanning. On the last day of 1947 the minister for Housing and Local Government designated 1,312 acres of this land as the Stepney-Poplar Comprehensive Development Area—the largest CDA in the country. The entire area was to be refurbished—its housing, schools, shops, industries, places of worship, open spaces and even pubs rationalised and where necessary rebuilt—and divided into twenty-one 'neighbourhoods', centred on shops and other facilities. The LCC would manage the project, assisted by the Stepney and Poplar Borough Councils.[39]

Contested Renewal

Following a royal visit to the East End in 1962, the LCC was told by the Duke of Edinburgh's office that Prince Philip was unimpressed by the state of Stepney. This produced an introspective acknowledgement at County Hall that 'conditions there are still . . . quite appalling' and an anxiety that the LCC was 'working . . . without any real timetable.'[40] By 1966, almost twenty years after the CDA had been designated, not one of the proposed neighbourhoods had been completely laid out, less than half the intended public open space had been provided and only eleven of the sixty projected schools had been built. On the other hand, more than sixteen thousand houses or flats had been provided by the LCC and the boroughs.[41] As the urban geographer John Hall would comment in 1972, 'so often "comprehensive redevelopment" means "housing schemes with a few shops."'[42]

The emphasis on housing was no accident. Put simply, it indicated that the priorities of the boroughs had prevailed over those of the LCC. Much of the area's housing stock had been poorly built in the first place, and almost all of it had suffered some war damage.[43] At a meeting in 1961 between representatives of Stepney Borough Council and the LCC, Stepney argued that 'the view was strongly held in the Borough that homes were the first need' and urged 'that sites immediately available should be used for housing rather than open space, which could be provided later.' The LCC's Town Planning Committee chair replied that 'it was also necessary to provide for relaxation and recreation. The Borough Council was advocating housing at any price, and this he could not agree to.' He sought to hold the line on the overall residential density planned for the area.[44]

The LCC aimed at the rehabilitation of the whole area, in line with the 1943 model, with a significant amount of open space and with much of the new housing being low-rise, as in the showpiece Lansbury Estate in Poplar, built by the LCC for display in the 1951 Festival of Britain. There was no dispute over the need to provide better accommodation for the residents of the CDA, but Stepney saw slum clearance as a matter of urgency, requiring the rapid transfer of large numbers into high-density and generally high-rise buildings. Similar urgency was evident in what would become Newham, where both component boroughs, East and West Ham, committed to mass housing programmes in the early sixties.[45] The argument pressed by the chief housing officer for East Ham, J. E. Austin, in 1957, was one which would have been echoed by all local authorities in the area: that the borough was losing population because the condition of its housing stock and the length of the council waiting list were driving people away.[46] Although wartime and postwar planning had aimed to decentralise the crowded population of inner London, and the LCC's approach reflected that aim,[47] even crowded boroughs feared that a sharp population fall might threaten local tax revenue, and they generally sought to provide new accommodation locally for those who were evicted by slum-clearance schemes. At a further meeting between Stepney and the LCC in 1962, the borough representatives called for 'land which was being kept vacant for education or open space purposes to be rezoned and made available to the Borough Council to enable them to build units of housing for use by them as a decanting pool.'[48] Several sites were in fact subsequently rezoned for housing.[49] Under this pressure, the wartime aim of producing holistically planned urban neighbourhoods, offering a range of social amenities, yielded to a new variant of Poplarism, placing regeneration firmly in the context of social policy, with a narrow but heavy emphasis on mass, high-rise, housing.

A Dazzling City of Skyscrapers

By the early sixties, the emerging new East End was 'a dazzling city of skyscrapers.'[50] 'For good or evil,' wrote Ashley Smith in 1961, 'they represent what a major part of the East End is going to be.' He suggested, plausibly, that 'nowhere else in England has such a large group of people, leading an easily recognisable, closely integrated, and passionately traditional communal life, been offered on such a large scale, and with such a pressure of urgency, what may be considered a radically different way of living.'[51] The disamenities of high-rise living are familiar enough, and they were reinforced in the East End by concerns over the structural safety of, particularly, industrial-built blocks following the gas explosion which killed four people and destroyed a corner of the tower block at Ronan Point in Canning Town in May 1968. There can be little doubt that Ronan Point intensified a disenchantment with high-rise building that was already setting in. Structural problems alarmed tenants in tower blocks: '[I'm] terrified when I think of what happened at Ronan Point'; 'I don't want to be 14 storeys up in a second Ronan Point.'[52] The GLC initially found it hard to recruit tenants for its twenty-one-storey Barkantine Estate, in the Isle of Dogs, which opened in the year of the Ronan Point tragedy.[53] When Docklands residents

East End social housing. The Samuda Estate, Isle of Dogs, LB Tower Hamlets, shortly after its opening in 1967. The tower block is Kelson House. (John Gay/Historic England/Mary Evans Picture Library)

were asked to state their preferred type of accommodation in 1973 only 2 percent opted for a high flat, conservatively defined as above four storeys.[54] After Ronan Point Newham Council fought a battle with the people on its waiting list seeking reassurance that they would not be moved into high blocks.[55]

The council was able to sit this protest out, though, because it knew that the demand for council housing was strong enough to deter most people from sacrificing their place on the waiting list. Two months after the disaster, the *Standard*'s planning correspondent, Judy Hillman, found those who moved into Merritt Point, Ronan Point's identical sister block, to be impressively sanguine about the prospect: 'it's a million to one chance of it happening again'; 'we wouldn't be allowed to stay here, would we, if it wasn't safe?'; 'we take risks all our lives'; 'thinking there would be another explosion is like waiting for an atom bomb to go off.' 'This is bliss', one resident

East End social housing. Interior of a flat in Robin Hood Gardens, Poplar, designed for the Greater London Council by Alison and Peter Smithson and completed in 1972. Robin Hood Gardens was demolished in 2017, a section being preserved by the Victoria and Albert Museum. (Sandra Lousada/ Mary Evans Picture Library)

told her. 'We were so cramped living with my mother.' Seventy-one-year-old Harry Willig described his new flat this way: 'the kind of home we have always looked forward to, easy to clean, not like the dreadful Dickensian place we've spent most of our lives.'[56] Half of the households on Newham's waiting list were currently living in houses lacking an inside toilet:[57] the opportunity to escape such conditions outweighed whatever risk there might have been of being caught up in another disaster.

Surveys showed that housing remained the principal concern of local residents,[58] and the two Docklands boroughs still struggled to clear lengthy waiting lists—six thousand in Tower Hamlets, seven and a half thousand in Newham.[59] The councils' preoccupation with building social housing was therefore understandable, but the crash programmes pursued by both boroughs produced a relatively poor fit between the housing actually built—overwhelmingly flats rented from the council—and the developing requirements of the local population. Both boroughs saw the provision of social housing simply as what Labour authorities did. These socialist councils were temperamentally disinclined to build for sale and still less enthusiastic about encouraging private development in their areas, fearing with some justification that developers would confiscate desirable riverside sites for gentrification: 'a lot of people come down here wanting to use *our land* for themselves', as John Orwell of Tower Hamlets complained to Simon Jenkins in 1973.[60] Only 2 percent of accommodation in Tower Hamlets was owner-occupied in 1971, and the proportion of council housing rose to almost 80 percent. The effect was put concisely in a GLC critique of the borough's policy: 'The near monopoly of municipal housing ... means that those who do not qualify for council housing cannot live there and for those who do want to live there council housing is the only tenure available.'[61] Council accommodation went disproportionately to those who were evicted by slum-clearance schemes, along with those who had been longest on the waiting list. This effectively favoured older residents, who were indeed most likely to prefer to rent and more likely than other age groups to prefer a flat to a house.[62] Young married couples, who were more likely to wish to buy and to prefer a house to a flat,[63] were generally disadvantaged by allocation policies. Council housing 'tends to be a one-generation affair, since when children grow up and marry they are rarely eligible to go on the housing list.'[64]

Environmental Decay

Many people did not wish to join the waiting list. The prolonged process of modernising the East End had the effect of degrading the local environment for decades, as the apparently unending task of slum clearance added to the dereliction created by war. Tom Pocock's generally optimistic account of the Stepney-Poplar project in 1960 acknowledged that the slow progress of reconstruction meant that 'housewives must walk to their smart new homes down rutted, stony tracks which wreck their shoes. Children still play in bombed slum ruins. A shanty town of 400 squatters' caravans appeared on waste land that should have been ornamental gardens.'[65] Twelve years later, in the view of the urban geographer John Hall, little had changed: 'the area has not even been brought into the 1950s, and redeveloped areas jostle with decayed housing and industries.'[66] In 1970 the Tower Hamlets Council of Social Service estimated that a third of the borough's population was directly affected by redevelopment work; the proportion is likely to have been significantly higher in the Comprehensive Development Area.[67]

The addition of slum-clearance sites to the area's substantial number of bomb sites also had the unwelcome effect of making Tower Hamlets, in

The three seventeen-storey blocks of the London County Council's showcase Stifford Estate, Stepney, on their completion in 1961. The estate replaced some of the most degraded housing in the East End, but as David Granick's photograph shows, the process of redevelopment frequently created a wasteland while it was under way. The Stifford Estate blocks would themselves be demolished in 1997. (David Granick, Stifford Estate, 1969, DG/1/88; reproduced with the permission of Tower Hamlets Local History Library and Archives, London Borough of Tower Hamlets)

particular, a magnet for vagrants and meths drinkers. 'If we could complete the redevelopment of our area and remove the blighted pockets, the environment would discourage their congregation in this borough', the Tower Hamlets medical officer wrote to Stepney MP Peter Shore in 1966,[68] but that day remained distant. Their congregation was believed by locals to have been encouraged by the various charitable agencies set up in the borough to help them: five of London's twelve vagrant hostels in the mid-1970s were located in Tower Hamlets.[69] The Reverend Dennis Downham of Christ Church Spitalfields turned the crypt of his church into a refuge for vagrant meths drinkers in the early 1960s, sure that 'each one of these men is one of God's children . . . as precious as the Archbishop of Canterbury himself.'[70]

Such arguments cut little ice with the locals, who feared that still more vagrants would be drawn to shelters 'as wasps to a jam pot.'[71] Dossers were not good neighbours. Locals were hostile witnesses, of course, but the frequency of tales of 'methy' misdemeanours—tramps hurling bottles filled with urine at people passing by the derelict buildings in Raven Row, Stepney, a vagrant defecating on the doorstep of a man who refused to take him in and 'all manner of public indecency committed by crude spirit drinkers, both men and women, who have completely lost mental and physical control of their faculties'[72]—makes them hard to dismiss. Nearly 80 percent of minor cases handled at Leman Street Police Station in 1974 involved vagrant alcoholics.[73] Gardner wrote laconically of fights between vagrants providing spectator sport for East Enders but also described trenchantly the 'awful, putrid smell' emanating from derelict houses being 'used as latrines or for mentholated [sic] spirit consumption.'[74] Real bitterness was directed at Downham, at the Simon Community, which established a shelter for alcoholics in Sclater Street, Bethnal Green, in 1967, at Christian Action, which set up a centre for woman alcoholics in Settles Street, Stepney, in 1969 and at similar philanthropic agencies.[75] A proposal for a Salvation Army women's hostel in East India Dock Road in 1972 evinced once again the local belief that 'the East End always gets the worst of everything. The authorities use it as a place to get rid of the rubbish that no-one else will take.'[76]

Further environmental disamenity was provided by the so-called bad neighbour industries. As in much of inner-city Britain, the weakness of planning controls when the area was built up, the intermingling of small homes and small workshops and the general sense that an already blighted area had little to lose environmentally had left the residential East End peppered with small-scale industrial sites, and 'the mixture of uses which has evolved results in conflicting activities being located adjacent to one another, causing widespread intrusion of industrial noise and pollution into residential . . . areas.'[77] Much of the garment trade, buoyant as it was in the early 1960s, was carried on in appalling conditions. Gardner spent six weeks of 1960 in a dress factory in Aldgate, where a colony of rats had entered the factory from a sewer next to the cellar. Felled by warfarin, they crawled under the long-cutting table to die: 'the smell was appalling.'[78] Munby had argued in 1951 that 'industry in Stepney is as much in need of slum clearance as are large tracts of housing',[79] and the relocation of ageing local industries was integral to the objectives of the Stepney-Poplar CDA; but, as Patricia Garside has argued, local authorities facing a drop in the area's rateable value through the outward movement of population had no incentive to force out local industries as well, however noxious they were.[80]

Derelict warehouses in Cable Street, LB Tower Hamlets, 1969. (David Granick, Cable Street, 1969, DG/I/I; reproduced with the permission of Tower Hamlets Local History Library and Archives, London Borough of Tower Hamlets)

'Bad neighbour' industries remained prominent in Stepney and elsewhere. Dyson recalled 'animal carcasses stacked up like mountains' at John Knight's soap factory, contributing to 'the general "stink" of Silvertown.'[81] Carpenter likewise remembered horse carcasses piling up in the West India Dock, with 'thick layers of yellow fat running through them.'[82] By 1980 Tower Hamlets and Newham had twice the London average of scrap yards, while the Docklands area as a whole, north and south of the river, could claim a quarter of London's vehicle body builders and repairers, 30 percent of its producers of asbestos products, 46 percent of its waste-paper dealers and 64 percent of its rag dealers.[83] Asked in 1974 'what needs doing first in Docklands?', nearly a quarter of the area's residents answered, 'clean up the area'—taken to imply 'an improvement on present drabness and deterioration.'[84]

'How would you like to live, eat and sleep in conditions that were slums long before this golden era of so-called prosperity struggled into existence?', asked the Dunstan Buildings and School House Lane Tenants' Association in a 1964 pamphlet titled 'Who Cares?'[85] Ashley Smith's description of car marts springing up in East End bomb sites captures neatly the mismatch between the new prosperity of many East Enders and the continuing—or worsening—poverty of their environment.[86] When such conditions combined with the sheer difficulty of obtaining local accommodation, many who could afford to leave the area chose to do so: 'those who can get on get out', as Harry Brack was told in 1968.[87] In the mid-1960s the unusual combination of a rising number of marriages and a falling number of live births in Tower Hamlets provided an early sign that young people were leaving on marriage.[88] Two editorials in the *East London Advertiser* in 1968 drew attention to the stream of young married couples leaving the East End in search of better living conditions and more space—particularly houses with gardens. They moved to Basildon or Debden to rent or to Brentwood or Rayleigh to buy.[89]

To a point the population fall promised to ease the increasingly intractable housing problem. The GLC was apparently given to suggesting to tenants that they stood a better chance of gaining improved accommodation if they were prepared to move out of the area.[90] So, more puzzlingly, were the boroughs, even in the seventies: 'One moment Tower Hamlets Council are telling you to try and find accommodation in a new town and the next minute they are complaining about so many young people leaving the borough', observed nineteen-year-old Lorraine Tucker in 1974.[91] She had a point. Departures from the borough might ease the pressure on housing, but if the exodus came disproportionately from the economically active age groups, it was likely to exacerbate the area's industrial crisis.

The Death of the Docks

Newham's population fell by 12.6 percent between 1961 and 1966, but the number aged between fifteen and forty-four fell by 20.6 percent. In Tower Hamlets the comparable figures were 14 percent and 24 percent.[92] Newham and Tower Hamlets were the only boroughs in London to see a fall in economic activity between 1961 and 1966.[93] The closure of Wall Paper Manufacturers, Ltd, of Bow in 1966, with the loss of 350 jobs, gave an early hint of the paradox that would become very evident in the seventies—the combination of general labour glut with specific skill shortages: 'as skilled people in the factory had become elderly, there were not enough replacements willing to stay long enough to learn the trade.'[94] The likelihood that industry would follow the more productive members of the labour force out of the East End was always high, particularly given the inadequate nature of so many industrial premises, but the situation was exacerbated immeasurably by the unexpectedly rapid run-down of the upriver docks, which had been central to the local economy since the early nineteenth century. The St Katharine's Dock closed first, in 1968, followed by the London Docks and the Surrey Docks in 1969, while the larger Royal Docks in Newham saw their activity dwindle rapidly before eventual closure in 1981. These closures followed hard upon the rationalisation of the dock labour force by the first report of the Devlin Committee of 1965, appointed to bring about the overdue end of casualism.[95] Dock jobs were protected under the 1947 scheme and had to be bought out. Redundancy was consequently softened by generous golden handshakes, which turned the East End briefly into a gold-rush economy. As Dick Hobbs puts it, 'That East London was in decline in the late 1960s is not in dispute; rather the point is that one could hardly detect its decline in a community enjoying regular wages and into which hundreds and thousands of pounds of severance pay was being pumped.'[96] Few mass layoffs can ever have been celebrated as enthusiastically as the rationalisation of the dock labour force following Devlin. In March 1968, 107 employees of the Thames and General Lighterage Company each received £1,250, regardless of age, position or length of service. A voluntary redundancy scheme for dockers, published in the summer of 1968, was more generous still, though it was calibrated to reflect years of service. In September its first beneficiaries, clutching up to £2,000 each, marched behind an Irish piper in orange kilt and green hat to the Old Rose pub in Shadwell, where thirty-seven men drank £187 of their winnings.[97]

Many dockers aspired to start their own businesses. One made redundant by the closure of St Katharine's Dock told the *East London Advertiser* of his intention to 'take a dabble in City finance.'[98] Doubtless many did put their windfalls to good use, but the dock labour force consisted largely of middle-aged men with few transferable skills: 'if I had [a trade] I wouldn't have been a docker in the first place, and that applies to all the lads.'[99] Men with twenty or thirty years of working life to fill were being cast onto a local labour market that was contracting rapidly in the late 1960s and early 1970s.

Dock closures had obvious knock-on effects for shipbuilding and shiprepairing, but there was also a penumbra of East London industry which had been located where it was because of advantages deriving from the proximity of the docks but which was not intrinsically tied to the river. The run-down of the docks led either to the closure of many of these firms or to their relocation to more modern premises elsewhere.[100] The effect was felt most severely in Newham, dependent as it was on heavy industry. Employment in the borough fell by no less than 40 percent between 1961 and 1971, with a further 13 percent fall between 1971 and 1974. The greatest damage was done after 1966 and in the borough's industrial zone around the Royal Docks: Canning Town was said to have lost 17,800 jobs between 1966 and 1972. The withdrawal of P&O from the Victoria Docks cost 3,700 jobs, while the closure of their ship repair subsidiary Green and Silley Weir made a further 1,000 redundant. Harland and Wolff ship repairers closed in the late 1960s with the loss of 1,500 jobs. The decision by Tate and Lyle to end sugar refining at its Plaistow Wharf works brought 1,500 redundancies in 1966, while the 1971 decision by Unilever to end production at the John Knight soap factory, which had contributed so pungently to the smell of Stan Dyson's Silvertown, added another 900. By cruel coincidence, 3,000 more Newham jobs were lost at Beckton gasworks, closed by the advent of North Sea gas in 1970.[101] By 1976 the male unemployment rate in Stepney stood at 11.9 percent, in Poplar at 13.8 percent, against a Greater London average of 5.4 percent.[102]

The East End had not suffered in the way that much of industrial Britain had done in the 1930s: the experience of becoming one of the unemployment black spots of the 1970s was unfamiliar and traumatic. 'One thing that can always be said about Canning Town', the Newham Council leader told the Commons Expenditure Committee in 1975, 'is that whatever is wrong with it you could always get a job. It may have been dirty and industrialised, but the one thing you could say about it is that there were plenty of jobs. It is now reduced to an area which has twice the [London] average of unemployment.'[103] The southern part of Newham was essentially an industrial town which had grown up around the Royal Docks. Many people had left it, of course, as part of the large-scale exodus from the East End already described, but those who remained—those without the skills to gain jobs in the new towns or those simply habituated to living and working in the area—were effectively bound to it. As the Newham (Canning Town) Community Development Project suggested, 'there are few, if any, similar areas anywhere else in London . . . where the pattern of living and working in one place still pervades.'[104] 'The trouble with communities that look down the road for their jobs', David White wrote in *New Society* in 1975, 'is that they become vulnerable and isolated when the jobs move away.' 'There has been little or no fight about the matter of redundancies in this borough', the secretary of the West Ham Trades Council told White:

in its quiescence Newham resembled the single-industry towns devastated by the collapse of a dominant employer in the interwar years.[105]

The End of Poplarism

The combination of population loss and industrial collapse steadily undermined the tradition of municipal welfarism in the East End. Social housing, central to that tradition, came under pressure first. The trigger was an event outside the East End: the election of a Conservative Greater London Council in 1967, ending more than thirty years of Labour rule at County Hall. The conviction that Labour councils routinely subsidised their tenants in order to harvest their votes was a commonplace among Conservatives in local government, and one of the new Council's early initiatives was a comparison of GLC rents with those in the private sector. It concluded that rises of between 60 percent and 100 percent would be necessary to bring GLC rents into line, and in October 1968 the Council embarked on a 70 percent increase, phased over three years.[106] The result was protest across London and uproar in the East End. The financial weakness of the borough authorities had meant that the GLC's predecessor, the London County Council, had become the principal provider of social housing in the East End in the late nineteenth century and between the wars, and it had been the senior partner in the Stepney-Poplar CDA, where the GLC was landlord to some 15,000 households. Although only 5,500 of the GLC's 230,000 tenants withheld their rent, 92 percent of those who did came from the East End.[107] They were encouraged by the local MP, Ian Mikardo; the dockers' leader, Jack Dash, a GLC tenant himself; the port militant Bernie Steer; and other local sympathisers. Tower Hamlets Council held a special protest meeting and considered taking GLC estates into its own stock in order to maintain the pre-1968 rents, until the GLC refused to allow transfer on those terms.[108] The Isle of Dogs community activist and Tower Hamlets councillor Ted Johns saw the increases as the greatest attack on working people since the 1920s, 'when Lansbury went to prison in similar circumstances.'[109]

The GLC's action was clearly politically driven, but there was a structural consideration behind its initiative. As Harry Brack pointed out in the *Evening Standard*, LCC/GLC rents had been rising for a decade or so: he cited a four-room maisonette in Carron Close, Bow, which had seen a 23 percent increase in 1963 and a 25 percent rise in 1965, both applied by

Labour administrations. The furore that the 1968 increases provoked was intensified by the fact that they represented the first Conservative challenge to the local social compact forged over three decades in these Labour strongholds, as well as by the confrontational approach of Horace Cutler, the proto-Thatcherite chair of the GLC Housing Committee, but the increases themselves were not new. The burden of providing subsidised housing at below-market rates while expanding the municipal stock already weighed heavily on many authorities' Housing Revenue Accounts. The GLC anticipated a housing deficit of £10 million by 1970,[110] but it was not alone. Newham was impelled by a £2 million deficit to increase its rents in July 1969.[111] Tower Hamlets Council had been forced in 1967 to raise what were then the lowest council rents in London, after being cautioned by the district auditor for its housing deficit, and imposed another five-shillings rise in 1970, even as they protested at the GLC's increases.[112] All of this somewhat undermined the East End councils' attempts to resist the Heath government's 1972 Housing Finance Act, which obliged all housing authorities to apply 'fair rents', closer to market levels. Tower Hamlets issued the usual threats of noncompliance, only to retreat—along with all London's other would-be rebel councils—in the face of the threat to surcharge dissident councillors and appoint a commissioner to run the borough.[113]

Potent as this threat was, some councillors might also have had in mind the question of whether the borough's tax base could bear for much longer the growing cost of the local welfare state. Between 1965 and 1970 the product of a penny rate in Tower Hamlets increased by only 0.1 percent, while that in Greater London as a whole rose by 6.7 percent. By 1972 the borough's rateable value had actually fallen marginally from its 1965 level; 'if we cannot increase our revenue,' Orwell warned in that year, 'we are going to reach an impossible situation. Either social services will have to be cut or rates will get so high that they will drive everyone out of their business or their homes.'[114] The collapse of the local economy and the exodus of so many wage earners curbed the borough's power to tackle social problems which were already intense and likely to be exacerbated by economic stagnation. The incidence of depressive illness in Tower Hamlets was 75 percent higher than in the rest of London—and three times the national average amongst men in Stepney and Whitechapel. The cluster of vagrant hostels in Tower Hamlets was thought to attract 'problem' patients, and schizophrenia rates in the borough were double the national average.[115] Tower Hamlets had eight times the London average of children in care. The

exodus of working-age residents was already producing a marked rise in
the dependency ratio (the proportion of dependants to wage earners) by
the midsixties,[116] which is certain to have worsened with the dock closures
later in the decade. Paul Beasley, Orwell's successor as leader of Tower
Hamlets Council, told a House of Commons Committee in 1979 of his
concern that the borough 'would be left with a very elderly population and
a large number of families in need of support': 'with the problems—I
almost said "dregs."' He dutifully maintained, 'we welcome the opportunity to look after the elderly and those in need of support',[117] but Tower
Hamlets' social services budget had risen by 460 percent between 1965–66
and 1975–76, at a time when its rate income was stagnating.[118] By the midseventies it was becoming clear that the principal effect of the postwar
boom had been to enable its beneficiaries to leave the area, that the East
End was consequently resuming its Victorian position as one of Britain's
chief centres of deprivation and that local agencies were shackled in their
efforts to improve matters.

A Blank Slate

At the same time the extent and severity of the East End's economic collapse encouraged more speculative approaches to reviving an area that was
rapidly becoming a planners' tabula rasa. At the very least this implied a
return to the kind of holistic spatial planning that had characterised the
schemes for postwar rebuilding. More commonly it also implied active
attempts to regenerate the area's economy by changing its very nature. 'To
assume that the local inhabitants can only be served by using the redeveloped docklands area for the provision of local authority housing', argued
Roger Lee, lecturer in geography at Queen Mary College, 'is to completely
misunderstand the functioning of urban areas.'

> The aim of the redevelopment should be to maximise the local benefits
> and minimise the costs of a development which nevertheless makes full
> use of its locational opportunities. The need is to redistribute income
> to East London by the provision of self-sustaining investment which
> will provide local employment opportunities; encourage the return of
> its young population and increase the attraction of East London for
> outside commercial and private interests; to provide a more viable and
> buoyant local tax-base and to stimulate the provision of local shopping and

entertainment services; to remove the severe physical deprivation and housing shortages, but to provide at the same time a location which will attract private and housing association finance in order to reduce pressure on local authority housing and to provide a social-mixture less weighted towards a very high concentration of local authority tenants.[119]

Previous public action in the East End, from the London County Council in the late nineteenth century onwards, had worked on the understandable assumption that it was and would remain an industrial area with an overwhelmingly working-class population. Population drain and industrial collapse had, though, undermined that assumption, with the result that much new thinking about the East End was founded on the principle that in order to recover, it needed to change its fundamental nature. The extract from Lee's paper just quoted suggests external private investment, the encouragement of private housing and the creation of a more socially mixed community, any of which, if accomplished widely, would have transformed the East End.

Such a transformation was enthusiastically anticipated in an uninhibited exercise in blue-sky thinking prepared by the GLC for a meeting with Peter Walker, environment secretary in the Heath government, in January 1971. 'What the builders of Venice, New Orleans and Amsterdam achieved', Walker was told, 'that is the challenging task before the architects and planners of the new London east of Tower Bridge.' It was imperative to avoid 'the perpetuation of the West End/East End polarisation which should have gone out of the planning map years ago', which meant no longer perpetuating the area's one-class community. 'There is a feeling abroad that the East End is finished, that it is only fit for lower paid workers, for those who cannot afford to get out of it. The idea is never expressed, but it is implicit in some current planning. This must stop.' The GLC questioned 'whether it is best in the long run simply to devote every acre that becomes available to local authority housing', arguing that 'the best solution for the Docklands is a mixture of public and private housing, but also with associated work places, not only in manufacturing industries, but in enterprises new to east London—offices, hotels, educational establishments, perhaps exhibitions and conference facilities, and centres of entertainment.' If private capital was not attracted to a part of London that it had shunned for decades, if private developers did not 'put up housing, shops and entertainment centres, not to speak of offices and hotels, then the area will be just one large council estate—a deprived east end before a single family moves in.' By extension, 'the public and private sectors will have to combine to create a desirable environment' where 'there are now no trees and no fountains, no piazzas and no arcades. The water is dirty and the buildings are drab.' Environmental improvement would need to be underpinned by social mix—a conclusion founded on the GLC's 'observation that both personal and financial pressures for better facilities and services tend to be strongest if there is a middle-income, professional and white collar element in the community. . . . The Docklands must have them from the start.' Overall, Docklands promised 'the extension of London's heart downstream, the creation of vast new areas of life and activity' to revitalise the lower Thames.[120]

Three months later Walker announced that the consultants R. Travers Morgan and Partners had been engaged to produce 'an urgent and comprehensive study of the potentialities for redevelopment of the whole riverside area—from London and Surrey Docks in the west to Beckton in the east', intended to 'lay the foundations for one of the most exciting developments of the century.'[121] When Travers Morgan reported in 1973, it put forward five options for remodelling the Docklands. They varied in their radicalism, but with four including golf courses, three 'equestrian centre[s]' and one a safari park, it was clear that they envisaged a substantial transformation of the old East End.[122]

Docklands was not ready for a safari park, and a consultation exercise demonstrated clearly that 'no one option had substantial appeal to the local people.'[123] The return of a Labour GLC in the spring of 1973, followed by the defeat of the Conservatives nationally in February 1974, effectively killed the Travers Morgan report. In the meantime—doubtless animated by the results of allowing planning consultants free rein—the Docklands councils had expressed their 'strong and unanimous view' to Geoffrey Rippon, Walker's successor as environment secretary, that the redevelopment should be managed by the relevant local authorities rather than the kind of unelected corporation standard in New Town development.[124] In January 1974 Rippon announced the formation of the Dockland Joint Committee (DJC), composed of representatives of the five Docklands boroughs (on both sides of the river), the GLC and nominees of the Department of the Environment.

The DJC produced its own report on Docklands redevelopment in 1976. It reflected the emerging consensus that Docklands needed investment in new industries, new infrastructure—particularly transport infrastructure—and new housing, more than half of it to be owner-occupied or held under

Desmond Plummer, leader of the Greater London Council; Frank Taylor, of the developers Taylor Woodrow; and Andrew Renton, architect, admiring the model of the proposed redevelopment of St Katharine's Dock. This would be the only part of Docklands to be redeveloped during the period covered by this book. (Keystone Pictures USA/ZUMAPRESS.com/Mary Evans)

equity-sharing schemes, to attract skilled workers.[125] It also advocated the cultivation of new local communities, to be based on units of four thousand to six thousand people and focused on local facilities such as shops and pubs.[126] This proposal carried echoes of the 1943 *County of London Plan*, as well as more recent theories of neighbourhood planning. It rested on no clear definition of community[127] and was probably intended as a counterweight to concerns that bringing newcomers into the area would threaten its social cohesion, but it did reflect the increased prominence of the concept of community in discussion of Docklands redevelopment.[128]

The notion of community was particularly evident in the arguments of the various ad hoc Action Groups which sprang up as a defensive response to the proposals to transform the area.[129] They included the East End Docklands Action Group (EEDAG), the Isle of Docks Action Group and, south of the river, the Surrey Docks Action Group and others, grouped under the umbrella of the Joint Docklands Action Group (JDAG).

Federation was clearly necessary: there was no single Docklands 'community' discernible across the entire area from Tower Bridge to Silvertown. Nonetheless, the idea of community in the individual neighbourhoods of the East End Docklands was less spurious than was sometimes the case in the community politics boom of the early seventies. The ethnic homogeneity of most Docklands areas, the 'number of inter-related families who have lived there for generations'[130] and the reproduction of kinship, friendship and socio-religious networks in recruitment for the gangs working in the docks themselves[131] all pointed to a high degree of social solidarity. Much of Docklands was physically difficult for outsiders to penetrate and for residents to escape, on account of the barriers created by the docks themselves, poor road access and a public transport service universally considered appalling. This generated a local introversion most evident in the Isle of Dogs, a peninsula formed by a bend in the Thames rather than a true island but almost severed from the East End 'mainland' by the West India Dock. Residents of the Isle announced a quixotic Unilateral Declaration of Independence in March 1970, in protest at the area's poor bus service, inadequate schools and shops and high rents. Ted Johns, of the Isle of Dogs Action Group, was proclaimed president of the island and appointed two lightermen as joint prime ministers. For two hours the area was sealed off by a cordon composed of eight hundred locals; a bus had its tyres slashed, and a Swedish cargo ship was prevented from entering the Millwall Dock by islanders holding down the bascule bridge at the entrance.[132]

This was a stunt, but it was also evidence that an actually existing community might voice concern about inadequate local facilities and services. Like most community organisations, the Action Groups were suspicious of the area's local authorities, particularly as those authorities interested themselves in prevalent ideas of private housing, social mix and the attraction of newcomers. The Action Groups brought together local residents, instinctively resistant to the threatened transformation of their neighbourhood, and sympathetic radical activists enthused by a nostalgic view of working-class solidarity; they bonded to promote an East End version of pavement politics. They sought to protect existing communities, as they perceived them, rather than to generate new ones through planning. Their approach was consequently unrepentantly conservative. The manager of the World Trade Centre, a gleaming new construction at St Katharine's Dock embodying virtually everything that was anathema to the Action Groups, emerged from a difficult meeting with EEDAG in 1974 convinced that 'these people want nothing to happen to dockland....

They call themselves an Action Group; they are an un-action group.'[133] The docker-turned-lecturer Danny Connolly of EEDAG effectively acknowledged this in his evidence to a Parliamentary committee in 1975: 'We are a conservation group. We view the preservation of the way of life that has gone on and developed in East London ... [as] of much greater importance than the preservation of the osprey, or the golden eagle, or the peregrine, or various other sorts of species of life on which people spend enormous sums of money to preserve.'[134] JDAG's response to the DJC report argued that existing industry should be preserved in situ, that new industry should 'relate to the traditional skills and potential of the area' and that most Docklands housing should continue to be provided by local authorities, with preference given to local residents.[135] Implausible as this was, it had a ready audience. Those who had stayed in the area as its population shrank were likely to be older and more conservative. With redevelopment looming and gentrifiers already claiming riverside sites in Wapping High Street ('they are only 1000 yards from the Tower of London, and therefore ideal for people working in the City'),[136] they feared the erosion of a familiar way of life.

Conclusion

It had been accepted from the late nineteenth century that the social and environmental problems of the East End warranted ameliorative public intervention. However contentious at the time, the case argued by the Poplar councillors in 1920–21 came steadily to be accepted in the decades that followed: that this public intervention should be under largely local management, by authorities in practice under permanent Labour control, but should be extensively subsidised by the metropolis as a whole, through rate equalisation or the involvement of the LCC/GLC, or by the nation, through Exchequer grants for housing and other local functions. In the immediate postwar years, following the extensive bombing of the area, policy focused on holistic reconstruction through planned comprehensive development; but in the late fifties and early sixties a shift of emphasis largely driven by the borough authorities made mass housing the principal concern, and East End Docklands rapidly became 'skyscraper city.'

This happened because the local bodies were understandably less sanguine than the metropolitan or national authorities about the drain of population from their areas. They believed that the lamentable condition of, in particular, the privately rented housing stock was driving from the East End even those who continued to work in it and that only a crash housing programme would stem the flow. The aspiration and the achievement of the high-density, high-rise programmes in Tower Hamlets and Newham were, on their own terms, considerable. Nevertheless, those who were best able to leave the area continued to do so, because they despaired of ever reaching the top of the waiting list, because they wished to be owners rather than council tenants, because they rejected high-rise living, because they sought a house and garden, because they tired of living in an area that had become a permanent building site—or any combination of those views. The disproportionate exodus of the economically active was a concern even in the relatively prosperous early sixties, and the signs were clear that the East End was facing an inner-city crisis even before the closure of the docks from the late sixties onwards. But the dock closures, and the contraction of industries once dependent on the port, made matters infinitely worse.

The rapid collapse of the local economy in the early seventies undermined 'postwar Poplarism' in two distinct ways. First it led to the stagnation—shrinkage in real terms—of the boroughs' local tax base, which curtailed their ability to supply the local services they existed to provide. Secondly it encouraged the metropolitan and national bodies which had previously underwritten local social policy to jettison the assumption that the East End was and would forever remain a working-class industrial area. Population flight and industrial contraction prompted thoughts of gentrification and 'social mix', of the dilution of the council housing monopoly, of the enticement of offices and other service industries—of a wholesale transformation of the area, in fact.

This ensured that the next phase in the endless process of replanning the East End would take the form of a conflict over the area's very identity. The culture wars thus triggered were unresolved by 1979, and it is right to argue that there was no inevitability that they would result in such Thatcherite experiments as the London Docklands Development Corporation of 1981 or the Enterprise Zone designated in the following year. Nonetheless, it had become clearer during the decade that Poplarism and its derivatives were falling from favour with the metropolitan and national authorities which had previously supported them. They had been designed to counteract the social and environmental disamenities produced by industrial capitalism and rested on the assumption that the East End would remain a functioning industrial area indefinitely. Once its industry collapsed, the assertion by the Action Groups and others that public policy and money should be directed towards reviving it, in order to preserve the area's traditional character, appeared fragile. The suggestion that 'large injections of public funds' were 'the only way in which plans of long-term benefit to the area will develop' was optimistic at a time of national economic crisis,[137] when many in Whitehall felt that London authorities already had more than their due share of Exchequer support. The demand to 'bring in new jobs which relate to the traditional skills and potential of the area' sounded like a plea to revive an industrial structure which had failed.[138] The idea that community was something to be preserved for its own sake cut little ice in the Environment Department, which believed unsentimentally that 'the break-up of communities and the forcing out of certain classes from [the] city is nothing new' and had been a regular consequence of urban redevelopment.[139] The department also tended to favour the New Town Corporation model of management for such a large area, rather than the awkward federation of local authorities embodied in the Docklands Joint Committee—a view reinforced by the DJC's largely unimpressive record down to 1979.[140] Finally, the claim that 'the top priority must be for council housing' conflicted with the growing official fear that municipal building had proved a blunt instrument of social policy and, in London, an unduly expensive one.[141]

A tolerably well-informed observer might therefore have inferred by 1979 that future Docklands redevelopment would lean to the right—that it would seek to dilute the area's overwhelmingly working-class character, would be fuelled by private capital, would be steered by a nonelective corporation and would transform the area. So it would prove.

9

The London Cabbie and
the Rise of Essex Man

I n order to understand why Labour never did become the 'natural party
of government' in the postwar years, we should look at those working-
class groups whose support for the Labour Party proved to be conditional—in particular at the working class outside blue-collar industry and
outside the Labour heartlands. They are epitomised by the 'Essex man' of
the 1980s, culturally working class but politically beyond Labour's reach
during the Thatcher years. London's taxi drivers belonged to this group, their
reflectiveness and articulacy making them fruitful research subjects.

The London Cabbie

London's taxi drivers formed a kind of medieval guild in the 'Swinging
City'. Cabbies were free spirits, protective of their status and their rights,
both sheltered and inhibited by elaborate trade regulation. Their trade
originated in the seventeenth century, but it had assumed its modern form
in the mid-Victorian period, the principal subsequent change being motorisation in the 1900s. Many of its regulatory provisions were, though,
remnants of the horse age: the notorious, if unenforced, requirement to
carry a bale of hay, for example, or the rule preventing drivers from leaving
their cab unattended for fear that it might bolt. The regulatory framework
enforced by the Home Office and the Metropolitan Police was reminiscent
in its elaborate nature of the rules governing early railways. The

FX3 taxi negotiating Piccadilly Circus, May 1968. (Atlantic Kid/Getty Images)

dimensions of cabs were prescribed along with, after motorisation, their tight turning circle. Similarly, vehicles were subjected to stringent annual tests and decommissioned after ten years, but these quality controls were augmented by provisions suggesting—at least to those who were touched by them—that the cabbie was still regarded as a coachman without a master, potentially unruly unless firmly controlled. Cabbies had to satisfy a character test to gain their badge, which they had to wear at all times when on duty and during court appearances. They were obliged not merely to demonstrate familiarity with the metropolis and an ability to read a map but to recite by rote, during a notoriously demeaning inquisition, arbitrarily constructed routes across the capital.

Drivers resented much of this regulation and its application by what they considered an overzealous police force, but regulation defined the London taxi fraternity more sharply than was the case in any other city, giving the licensed drivers an esprit de corps lacking amongst their mini-cab rivals. And, as with most guilds, regulation conferred privileges as well as drawbacks. The purpose-built 'black cab' cost roughly as much as a Jaguar, but it offered brand recognition, being as much of a London icon as the Routemaster bus. The right to 'ply for hire' which the badge conferred— the exclusive right to pick up a customer hailing him in the street—was the licensed taxi driver's greatest commercial asset. It *was* a right rather than a duty: a licensed driver was not required to stop when hailed, even if his cab was empty and advertising itself as for hire.[1] Having stopped, however, a driver could not refuse a trip within a six-mile radius of the point of hire.[2] These regulations provided the taxi driver with an element of serendipity in his working day, as he tried to gauge whether a potential customer would request a 'roader'—the lucrative outing to Southampton or Norwich—or demand an irksome trek to a suburb on the other side of London from his garage or home, with little prospect of a return fare.

The pros and cons of the regulatory regime were demonstrated most strikingly by 'the Knowledge'. Only by passing the Knowledge of London test, applied with sadistic rigour by the Public Carriage Office (PCO) examiners since 1843, could a driver gain the green badge allowing him to ply for hire across London (suburban drivers working only in their home area gained a yellow badge from a less exacting test). To pass 'the Knowledge' a driver had to master four hundred theoretical trips devised by the PCO and recite those chosen by the examiner. They might be expected to locate and navigate to 'the Chinese Institute, the Home for Poor Clergymen, the Institute of Ophthalmology, the Society for the Promotion of Christian Knowledge to the Jews' or any one of hundreds of similar destinations.[3] The Knowledge was essentially an extremely demanding memory test, compared by drivers to learning the works of Shakespeare by heart,[4] but it was not just a memory test: examiners might request a description of a building to prove that candidates had not simply prepped by rote. 'Knowledge Boys' therefore learned their routes 'on the ground', making up to five thousand reconnaissance missions by moped,[5] and the majority also had to learn their routes while doing a day job to support themselves. Many found the burden intolerable: the dropout rate in 1969 was 57 percent.[6] Almost all who stayed the course eventually passed, however, but in the 1960s the ordeal took about two years. Drivers nonetheless liked the Knowledge once they had passed it. It was a selling point, reassuring customers that cab drivers—unlike those driving most minicabs—knew their way around an intricate city. Moreover, as the authorities had no power to limit the number of badges issued, the rigours of the Knowledge provided protection against a driver surplus. It was an apprenticeship and valued as such.[7]

The Knowledge inevitably influenced recruitment, ensuring that London's licensed taxi service was never exactly an 'entry trade' like taxi services elsewhere—a first step on the ladder for new immigrants. The Knowledge disadvantaged those who were unfamiliar with London and with the English language. It favoured those from cabbing backgrounds, like Reuben Cohen, whose family produced thirteen drivers from 1889 and who passed the Knowledge in four weeks in 1971.[8] Sixty percent of 'Knowledge Boys' surveyed in 1969 had relatives in the trade.[9] The Knowledge also favoured people with the capital to allow them to study full-time: Alf Townsend, learning the Knowledge in the early 1960s, noted that the Jewish boys 'were subsidised by their dads, many of them already cabmen'.[10]

The strong Jewish presence in the business suggests that cabbing *had* been an entry trade in the late nineteenth century. It explained the location of so much of the industry, before the decline of the major garages after 1960, in London's East End, where 'from the cobbled back streets of Hackney, Bethnal Green and Shoreditch, diesels clattered day and night'.[11] The *Jewish Chronicle* estimated in 1971 that five thousand of London's thirteen thousand drivers were Jewish; 32 percent of Hackney's Jewish population in that year's census worked in transport, most of them as cabbies.[12] The entrepreneurially minded sought to become owner-drivers or garage proprietors, but cabbing was itself seen as a 'good' job for a working-class Jew: a 'fond Jewish grandmother in St John's Wood' would want her grandson to become a doctor or an accountant, but 'if you ask the same question in Ilford or Stamford Hill, the answer is likely to be a taxi-driver'.[13]

Later immigrant groups were less conspicuous. A group of Cossack refugees from the Bolshevik Revolution drove London cabs for the best part of fifty years, dreaming of returning to Russia and their estates,[14] but few of London's postwar immigrants adopted cabbing as an entry trade or established cab dynasties on the Jewish model (even today only 5 percent of cab drivers come from the Black, Asian, or 'other' ethnic minorities comprising a third of the London population).[15]

Cabbies were normally white and male; beyond that, generalisation was dangerous. A survey of 150 'Knowledge Boys' in the trade journal *Steering Wheel* in 1969 found that almost half the 'Boys' were over the age of thirty and that aspirant cabbies came to driving from a variety of other jobs. Many came from the transport industry, driving buses or lorries, but no single occupation accounted for more than 5 percent of respondents.[16] Drivers' life stories confirm this occupational eclecticism. The 'Cabbies of London' interviewed by the *Evening News* in 1961 included a former seller of secondhand tablecloths, a Bevin Boy, a trainee doctor unable to stand the sight of blood, a tailor ruined in the depression, a failed barrister's clerk, three boxers, a film stuntman and wrestler and a violinist who had once performed onstage with a tap dancer but 'found taxi-driving a more secure profession.'[17] Interwar unemployment had driven many to cabbing, but with jobs plentiful in postwar London, it was more likely to be an aversion to industrial routine which drove men onto the Knowledge. A cabman, wrote the chairman of the Owner Drivers Association in 1965, was often a man who 'has sampled industry and cannot fit in.'[18] 'Clocking on and off would get on my nerves', explained William Hull of Roehampton in 1961.[19]

Drivers regularly described themselves as individualists. They were *necessarily* economic individualists. An informal chivalry governed conduct on the road—never overtake an empty cab to reach a fare first and so on[20]—but cabbing was inescapably competitive. '*Every* other taxi on the road is my competitor', wrote driver Roger Annoute in 1970. 'It doesn't do me one iota of good when people ride in other taxis, it doesn't put a brass farthing in my pocket.'[21] Technically, all drivers were freelance. Those working for garages were not the employees of the proprietors but bailees, hiring cabs daily or weekly. None, consequently, had much claim on the welfare state or access to occupational perks: taxi driving was 'a job where there is no promotion, no pension, no workmen's compensation, no overtime pay at weekends.'[22] 'Journeymen' engaged by garages were employed persons for National Insurance purposes and might receive sick pay,[23] but owner-drivers were self-employed and denied such benefits. There was no occupational pension; in fact many drivers appreciated the chance to work beyond retirement age: 'there is not another like the Taxi Trade where an old age pensioner can work for an odd day or two a week', argued 'Jack from Mons' Cohen, a First World War veteran who continued driving into the 1970s.[24] Driver Joe Polski died at the wheel at the age of seventy-five.[25] Like J. S. Mill, cabbies used the term 'individuality' in preference to 'individualism', suggesting that they were free spirits rather than mere economic men.[26] There was truth in the popular view that cabbies' favourite freedom was the freedom of speech. Robert Buckland spoke of '"the full-flowing river of speech" that only a London taxi-driver can command',[27] and the Maxwell Stamp Committee on the taxicab trade noted laconically in 1970 that 'there was no dearth of views for the Committee to consider.'[28] Cabbie aphorisms of the *Private Eye* type can be found in the printed record—'pay policemen well above the average and maybe London will again have a force that will make the toughs think twice';[29] 'I say we should come out, we are throwing good money after bad. I think this Common Market is a bad thing';[30] 'Very straight-faced was Mr Ribbentrop . . . Didn't surprise me a bit when we went to war with that lot'[31]—but it would be misleading to depict cabbies merely as purveyors of unpolished street wisdom. The trade, after all, always sustained at least three journals, written almost entirely by working drivers.

Most cabbies came from working-class backgrounds and had received only limited formal education,[32] but the Knowledge required at least precision and a retentive memory. Many developed an antiquarian interest in London history. Trade journals routinely carried London quizzes, with questions such as 'Why is Piccadilly so called?' or 'Where is London's costliest drinking fountain?'[33] The garage proprietor Harry Baylis established a London Guide School for cabbies in 1973, while in July 1974 London Taxi Guides offered guided tours.[34] The future *Mastermind* winner Fred Housego was named top guide by the London Tourist Board in 1977.[35]

The restless employment history of many drivers perhaps indicated intellectual frustration. Philip Mintz had left grammar school at fifteen because his friends considered it 'sissy' to stay. He drove through London 'knowing full well that had the dice been on his side, he might have been a graduate. . . . It's a fact that sticks hard in the throat'.[36] Buckland suggested that taxi driving attracted 'men whose talents and aspirations range far beyond the job they are doing'.[37] For example, Gary Sherrick, captivated at school by the Romantics, recited his own verses to passengers: 'to make them feel as if they had escaped from the mad rush of London into my world of poetry'.[38] Joe Polski loved languages and chemistry, Fred Whiten mathematics and meteorology, while Michael Freedman conducted Bartók's Concerto for Orchestra at Wembley Town Hall.[39] Several drivers—Herbert Hodge before the war, Maurice Levinson, Robert Buckland, Ron Barnes, Alf Townsend, and Walter Geake—wrote cabbing reminiscences.[40] Barnes and Levinson wrote autobiographies, and Levinson was a published novelist.[41] Sam Raingold compiled an idiosyncratic London tourist guide, and Charles Poulsen wrote London local history.[42]

Cabbies' intellectual independence made them, in Hodge's words, 'philosophical anarchists with a contempt for all law and order imposed from above'.[43] Buckland considered cabbies 'difficult people to fit into a socialistic or totalitarian state'.[44] They encountered authoritarianism only in the dilute form of the Metropolitan Police, but that relationship was antagonistic enough. In 1939, eleven thousand licensed drivers incurred around three thousand summonses a year, coming 'to look on the police-court dock as a normal trade risk'.[45] Things had improved by the 1960s, but drivers felt that the Met still saw the cab trade as a branch of the East End criminal class. Entrapment was frequently alleged, often by 'blue trees'—police officers who hid behind trees to catch taxis jumping lights.[46] Verbatim accounts of police-cabbie exchanges enlivened the London magistrates' courts—'Bugger off. You're power crazy. Don't think you can tell me what to do because you're in uniform. . . . That's why you bastards get shot at', '"You can't treat me like an animal." . . . "I treat all b——cabmen as animals"', and similar.[47]

Sympathy for society's outcasts accompanied this contempt for authority. A driver had to be of good character to gain his badge, but, for Levinson, crooks and cabbies were 'on the same spiritual level, even if one is honest and the other isn't'. Criminals habitually used cabs, tipping well and never inviting police attention by fare-dodging.[48] Levinson also considered homosexuals 'usually good passengers'.[49] With many drivers, he felt an affinity with prostitutes, who likewise plied for hire, suffered police harassment and lived off fleeting encounters with anonymous members of the public.[50]

Prostitutes, moreover, never looked down on taxi drivers.[51] A fear that the trade retained a servile image made cabbies more sensitive to condescension than most groups. Many 1960s cabbies had entered the trade in the 1930s, when the upper classes had provided almost the only custom in a thin market. Buckland remembered living off 'the Clubmen, those denizens of St James's and Pall Mall whose lives seemed to be devoted to driving by taxi from their town houses to their clubs, and back again to their houses'. He recalled, 'I hated [the clubman] in proportion as I needed his patronage'.[52] Jack Cohen remembered being 'looked upon as dirt' by 'the wealthier section of the community' before the war.[53] In the buyers' market of the 1930s cabbies had bitten their tongues, but in the permissive 1960s they could speak their minds: 'You f——people make me sick. You give me, the bloke who does the work, a 6d. piece, and you give the bloody doorman a 2s. piece. I used to get 6d. before the war. What can I spend with 6d. now, you——?'[54] General affluence and a decline in the real level of fares meant that drivers could 'find work . . . in Brixton as well as Kensington'.[55] Taxi slang remained redolent of class warfare—'Rowton House' for the Ritz, 'Den of Thieves' for the Stock Exchange, 'The Cow Shed' for the Ladies' Carlton Club[56]—but with the broadening of the customer base, Levinson suggested, the 1970s cabbie 'on his social rounds . . . might even go to the same places as his passengers'.[57] Dealing with the whole of society rather than just its upper levels, he developed the contempt for his fares that service providers habitually display towards their clients—what one driver described as 'the need-hate relationship that exists between the taxi and its customer'.[58] 'I love my trade', driver Albert Levy told the *Evening Standard* in 1979. 'It's the people I don't like.'[59]

Three-quarters of 'Knowledge Boys' in 1969 thought they had 'good' relations with the public, but Levinson expected the 'butterboy'—taxi slang for a newly qualified driver—eventually to 'wake up to the fact that politeness doesn't pay'.[60] Street hiring implied 'terse instructions barked at the driver in hurried conditions', and the knowledge that driver and passenger were unlikely to meet again produced a 'mutual couldn't-care-less attitude'.[61] So did taxi design. The partition between the driver's cab and the body of the vehicle, along with the noise of the diesel engine, hindered conversation with passengers: 'we carry around 30,000,000 people a year and have very little means of communication with them', argued the Owner Drivers Association in 1970.[62] Cabbing became an oddly solitary business.

Cabbies' dealings with their customers became starkly commercial, and drivers judged passengers according to their generosity. Fare evasion was rare: a driver could expect to be 'bilked' only once every four years.[63] The real point of conflict was the tip. As Hodge put it, 'a "good" rider is one who tips lavishly, though he may have the manners of a pig'. The worst riders were therefore the 'legals', who paid only the metered fare—most prominently Church of England clergymen.[64] Winston Churchill was a hero to the nation but not to the trade, being 'a bit tight when it came to tipping'.[65] Royalty was 'not thought of by cabmen as being conspicuously generous', apart from the Duke of Windsor, a good tipper whose populist repertoire as Prince of Wales had extended to buying drivers breakfast in their shelters.[66] Cab lore held that the poorest fares gave the largest tips— 'Bermondsey nearly always tips better than Belgravia'.[67] London's expanding tourist trade allowed drivers to extend the comparison to most of the planet, producing league tables of visitors ranked by generosity, with Australians invariably at the bottom and Japanese and Chinese at the top.[68] Levinson noted that London's Chinese, many of them restaurateurs, understood the importance of the tip.[69] Other New Commonwealth immigrants were, though, considered bad tippers—'the black person (on average) tips badly, if at all'[70]—explaining drivers' tendency to ignore them and their consequent reputation for racism.

Moreover, the act of tipping was inherently condescending, threatening, Levinson believed, 'to push the London taxi-driver lower down the social scale'.[71] Socialist drivers like Ron Barnes loathed the tip, advocating instead 'a basic wage and a bonus'.[72] The Cab Section of the Transport and General Workers Union (TGWU) campaigned sporadically for a basic wage,[73] which would have made tips less frequent, but gained limited support from drivers. One consideration was that the tip was hard to tax. A driver declaring only his metered fare income would invite 'searching enquiries from his local Inspector of Taxes',[74] but with even the Prices and Incomes Board admitting that 'nothing . . . is known of the true earnings' of most London cabbies, the tax authorities were at a disadvantage.[75] But cabbies also feared that a basic wage 'would mean the loss of the freedom' which they had, in favour of the work discipline that drivers had joined the trade to avoid.[76] It was also unclear how a basic wage could be applied to owner-drivers, whom the TGWU considered regrettable anomalies but who were becoming increasingly numerous. Contained in the issue of the tip were wider questions concerning the trade's organisation and self-image.

Insecurity

'You cannot organise individualists', wrote the chairman of the Owner Drivers Association in 1971. 'Logically, if you could you would cease to have individualists.'[77] A union of London taxi drivers had nonetheless been created in 1894 and absorbed by the Transport and General Workers Union on its formation in 1922. The TGWU's Cab Section had organised a major strike in 1932 and had offered the only defence against appalling trade conditions in the 1930s.[78] That decade cast a long shadow over cabbies. Those who had cruised the streets for £2.10s per week[79]—perhaps as little as 7/6d per week in slack periods[80]—never forgot the experience. The TGWU's response, from 1935 onwards, was to call for limitation of entry to the trade, and for fifteen years or so after the war it made limitation—later called 'stabilisation'—its major objective. It had made no headway, however, either by industrial action or by lobbying government, before the advent of the minicabs made talk of limitation otiose.

In June 1961 Welbeck Motors, run by the private hire operator Michael Gotla, released two hundred red Renault Dauphines onto London's streets, starting the 'minicab war'.[81] Private car hire had previously been a luxury; Gotla aimed to make it an everyday facility by claiming the licensed trade's greatest advantage: the right to ply for hire. Although his vehicles were radio-controlled, would-be passengers were encouraged to hail one, whose driver would hand the customer a telephone enabling them to book a cab—in practice the same cab—through Welbeck's control room.[82] The Home Office thought this trick illegal but showed no eagerness to bring a test case,[83] reinforcing trade suspicion that it favoured Gotla's initiative.[84]

Police taking notes from a minicab driver following a dispute with a licensed cabbie, 6 June 1961. (Keystone USA/Alamy Stock Photo)

The authorities' failure to make difficulties for Welbeck angered licensed drivers. Minicab drivers escaped the Knowledge, the character test, and the advanced driving test faced by cabbies. The ferocious trade reaction reflected both resentment of a competitor and frustration at the authorities' refusal to liberalise regulations from which that competitor was exempt. Much direct action followed Welbeck's arrival, ranging from hoax booking calls to assaults on minicab drivers. Reports of minicabs being boxed in or having their radios torn out—even assaults on minicab passengers—surfaced during Welbeck's first week.[85] This open warfare led to thirty-seven taxi drivers being prosecuted in the autumn of 1961.[86] In November two cabbies were imprisoned for dangerous driving—hemming in a minicab driver who had picked up a passenger—and another for forcing a minicab into the kerb.[87] A six-month sentence in January 1962 for assault on a Welbeck driver underlined the magistracy's impatience with 'jungle law and mob rule.'[88]

The cab war subsided after the High Court decision in *Rose v. Welbeck* in May 1962 reaffirmed the licensed trade's exclusive right to ply for hire. Though rogue minicab drivers continued to ply, minicab firms no longer openly attempted to circumvent the law. Private hire tacitly acknowledged that the two operations were complementary—the licensed trade concentrating on the centre, the minicabs on the suburbs. Casual plying for hire was most profitable in the centre, and, as Sid Pearce, a Richmond cabbie with an LSE economics degree, pointed out, the mandatory initial hiring charge made the return per mile highest for journeys below two miles. Longer journeys within the six-mile limit were appreciably less lucrative, and although the return rose above six miles, the prospect of finding a return fare diminished.[89] In 1974 the GLC established that the average journey by licensed cab covered a mile and three-quarters and lasted twelve minutes. Three-quarters of trips were made in the City and West End, Kensington, or Paddington.[90] As one yellow-badge driver put it, 'Inner London's paved with gold day and night—the suburbs are but a cart track.'[91]

Black cabs consequently neglected the suburbs. It was estimated in 1969 that only seventy licensed cabs worked South London,[92] and minicabs captured the area. Licensed drivers exploited the lucrative City and West End business, while minicabs focused on individual suburbs, where the street map was simpler and lack of the Knowledge mattered less. Welbeck collapsed in 1965, largely because operating a dedicated vehicle fleet at loss-leader rates was uncommercial, but subsequent hire firms succeeded by simply equipping drivers' private cars with radios. By the late 1970s the private hire sector operated 27,000 vehicles, but between 1961 and 1977 the number of licensed cabs had also nearly doubled, from 6,500 to 12,452,[93] sustained by the businessmen, shoppers, theatre-goers and tourists in the central area.

The minicab issue remained, though, an open wound for licensed drivers. The taxi press obsessed over the 'pirates' threatening drivers' livelihood, issuing lugubrious predictions of the death of the black cab.[94] Driver resentment focused on the TGWU. The union had necessarily urged restraint during the violence of 1961–62 but lacked purchase on a Home Office uninterested in limitation. It struggled to retain driver support, and a succession of splinter groups challenged its authority.

In April 1967 the '12,000 Group' staged a protest in which one thousand cabs and four thousand drivers blockaded the House of Commons.[95] In May a meeting at the Festival Hall attended by twenty-five hundred drivers transformed this group into the Licensed Taxi Drivers Association (LTDA), 'dedicated to end the operation of minicabs.'[96] Some forty-five hundred members were soon recruited. Rivalry with the TGWU was immediately evident, reflecting fundamental divisions over the role of a trade body. The LTDA believed that little was gained by being a small part of a large general union.[97] It worked 'for Licensed cab men alone, without the need to consider dockers, busmen, kitchen porters, road sweepers and dustmen'.[98] Unencumbered by TGWU caution, it mounted guerrilla actions like the 1967 boycott of the Park Lane Hilton, which forced the hotel to renounce minicabs. The TGWU, conversely, projected itself as an estate of the realm, with the ear of government and a troop of sponsored MPs. Militancy was beneath it: 'cabdrivers must learn the difference between getting publicity in the House of Commons and getting legislation through the House of Commons.'[99]

Behind these tactical divisions lay deeper questions of status. The TGWU Cab Section considered itself an industrial union, representing the trade's proletariat—the 'journeymen' drivers hiring cabs from proprietors. The LTDA saw itself as a genuine trade association. It included proprietors on its executive, contrary to the TGWU's belief that 'the struggle for improvement in pay and conditions is one against the proprietor.'[100] By 1967 this was a somewhat sectarian view: proprietors and drivers had campaigned together for stabilisation and against the minicabs in the early 1960s. What *was* true was that journeymen and owner-drivers—'mushes' in taxi slang—had different interests. Whereas the journeyman looked to his union to gain from garages a higher percentage of takings, the owner-driver essentially sought protection against the risks involved in running his own business. The LTDA accordingly enhanced its appeal by offering accident, sickness and disablement benefit to its members from the start,[101] courting the charge of being 'a predominantly "mushes" union.'[102]

This rivalry soon acquired a political edge, making reconciliation unlikely. The TGWU accused its competitor of gulling members into believing 'that they don't have anything in common with a working man, but are destined to become tycoons'.[103] The LTDA's public relations officer indeed suggested, 'we have a choice to be classed as workers . . . or in our *own* true perspective of Professional men with our own Professional Association.'[104] The LTDA was apparently advised by Michael Ivens, later director of the free-market lobby group Aims of Industry, and its secretary, Bill D'Arcy, was accused of welcoming the Tory victory in 1970.[105] The TGWU's critics, conversely, alleged that the Cab Section was run by communists.[106]

The LTDA benefited from these turf wars because conventional industrial politics was losing relevance. In the 1950s most drivers had been journeymen, working fixed shifts which allowed their garage to use cabs continuously. They were paid 'on the clock', keeping around 40 percent of metered fares from each shift. This percentage commission system offered a means of regulating the workforce *and* a basis for collective bargaining and was therefore acceptable to proprietors and union alike.[107] The alternative—for those who could not afford their own cabs—was the flat hire system, by which drivers paid a fixed rate to hire a cab for a week, keeping the fares gained. In the 1930s, drivers had disliked 'the flat', as slack trade made it difficult to pay the rental.[108] In the more buoyant 1970s, though, drivers saw 'the clock', with 60 percent of fare income going to the proprietor, as 'the swiftest way to the bun-house ever devised'; it was rejected by 'drivers who wish to earn good money'.[109]

The popularity of 'the flat' also reflected the migration of many taxi drivers, along with much of the East End population, to outer London— one Redbridge street was christened 'Green Badge Alley'.[110] These suburbanites resented commuting to a garage to do a shift. Garages began to offer drivers transport to and from home, hoping to retain their labour force,[111] but they were swimming against a tide carrying drivers away from dependence on garages altogether. Most drivers saw driving on 'the flat' as a step towards owner-driving. In 1961 27 percent of drivers had been mushes. Twenty years later this figure stood at 44 percent.[112] Most of the 'Knowledge Boys' surveyed in 1969 aspired to owner-driving: 'to be my own guvnor'.[113] Facing fixed prices, rising costs and a driver shortage, many garages went under. Their demise hurt the TGWU, which paid the price for remaining a journeymen's union. In 1967 the TGWU Cab Section had claimed thirty-five hundred members, representing 90 percent of garage drivers.[114] Ten years later its membership was estimated at eight hundred.[115]

As the union had feared, owner-driving appealed to cabbies' entrepreneurialism: 'Where else will an investment of £1500 buy you your own independent business?'[116] It was a concomitant of suburbanisation, owner occupation and the escape from proletarian status. Crucially, it offered a means of paying for this improved lifestyle. It was not clear that owner-driving was any more lucrative *per hour* than working as a journeyman. What mattered was that the owner-driver, like the 'flat' driver in the garages, was not restricted by garage shifts. Owner-driver witnesses before Maxwell Stamp described working twelve-hour days.[117] Levinson spoke of fifty-five to sixty hour weeks: he himself had taken only one day off a month when raising his family and paying off his mortgage.[118]

Inflation raised the stakes: Levinson considered it 'the most disturbing feature about the taxi trade.'[119] Maxwell Stamp had noted Whitehall's tendency 'to consider taxi fare increases in the light of the Government's general economic policy',[120] and for several years in the mid-1970s the tariff was frozen, like nationalised industry prices in the same period, in the hope of containing inflation. The real cost of taxi trips fell sharply; Pearce believed that 'the growth in cab utilisation owes more to declining real prices than to any fundamental change in the structure of the market.'[121]

Forty years earlier the cab trade had suffered real poverty, to which trade unionism had been a realistic, if inadequate, response. By the 1970s things were different. The cab trade had shared in the affluence of the postwar years: 'today cabmen do not, as they had ample reason to do in the past, complain over much about the job's financial rewards', as *Taxi Trader* noted in 1972.[122] Many drivers owned their homes and their cabs and paid some income tax at 35 percent,[123] but they considered their relative comfort precarious in an inflationary age, when the price of their services was fixed. They responded in two ways: by pushing themselves harder but also by seeking to maximise their returns. Circumstances allowed this. In the 1930s demand for their services had been inadequate; by the 1970s demand was strong. No 1930s cabbie would have turned away a fare as not worth his while; by the late 1970s drivers were routinely (and illegally) rejecting unrewarding jobs—'"Get one going the other way, will you dear?", they say wearily'[124]—to maximise engaged mileage on lucrative work. This also discouraged collective action: more time spent on the road meant less time on the rank, where union proselytising had been easiest and 'a bond [had been] forged throughout the trade—which today [1979] seems to be disappearing'.[125] 'Only the sick, lame and lazy rank up these days', Pearce noted in 1978.[126] The TGWU's decline has been described, but the LTDA, having failed to kill the minicab, also lost ground after its enthusiastic start. By 1976 it was estimated that only 20 percent of drivers belonged to either organisation.[127] In 1978 driver Peter Schendel urged *Steering Wheel*'s readers to join the National Federation of Self-Employed, at a cost of £12 a year, and the journal printed the federation's application form.[128]

This doubtless supported the charge of class betrayal made by TGWU militants against those who were beyond their ranks, but the self-image of the owner-driver as a successful but hard-pressed entrepreneur was widely accepted. 'As an owner-driver I am doing very well thank you', wrote 'A. Musher' in *Steering Wheel* in 1979: 'I'm not afraid to work in order to pay my mortgage and have two cars plus a good holiday. Yes my wife does go to work so does my neighbours, who is a police super-intendant, as does my bank managers wife. If we want the good things in life we must work for them, without trampling on our fellow citizens.'[129] It is unsurprising that taxi

Whitehall blocked by taxi drivers seeking a 28 percent increase in fare rates to keep pace with inflation, September 1978. (Mirrorpix/Alamy Stock Photo)

drivers proved receptive to the new Toryism of the 1970s. Previously drivers had largely been bred in the East End socialist tradition; Hodge wrote in 1939 that the number of cabbies on London borough councils fluctuated with the strength of the Labour vote.[130] In the mid-1970s, though, the leader of the Conservative minority on the GLC, Horace Cutler, courted the taxi vote, opposing Labour proposals for GLC control of the service[131] and later calling for drivers to be allowed to set their own fares.[132] In the 1977 GLC elections, the Tories ran taxi driver Arnold Kinzley in Ilford South, a constituency containing one thousand cabbie voters.[133] He turned an eleven hundred Labour majority into a fifty-six hundred Conservative one, while the sixteen hundred drivers in neighbouring Ilford North presumably contributed to another Tory gain, with a massive ten thousand increase in their poll.[134] In 1978 a Parliamentary by-election occurred in Ilford North. The Labour candidate, Tessa Jowell, advocated financial support for would-be owner-drivers, but the Tories' Vivian Bendall impressed *Steering Wheel* with 'his grasp of trade matters.'[135] The Conservatives captured a Labour seat, on a swing less spectacular than in recent by-elections but anticipating their national performance in 1979.

Conclusion

'Madam', wrote driver J. M. Marcelle in an open letter to Margaret Thatcher before the 1979 election, 'as self-employed persons, it seems to me that we should believe in enterprise, expansion, and business.'[136] Perhaps it is unsurprising that these self-professed individualists, with their suspicion of officialdom and their arm's-length relationship with the taxman, should have been recruits to Thatcherism, but it remains striking that an outcome which would have appeared unlikely in 1960 appeared natural by 1979. For generations, cabbies' apparently Conservative instincts had been offset by other influences: by their embedding in an East London community—often an East London Jewish community—that was tribally socialist and by their proletarianisation in the larger garages. From the early 1960s, though, they had sought to break out of the garages and flee the East End while becoming increasingly disenchanted with industrial trade unionism and with collective action generally. In these years cabbies' shift from a pointed hatred of the rich to a generalised low-level misanthropy is paralleled by a shift from class-war socialism towards an economic liberalism consistent with the new Conservatism of the 1970s. They became almost stereotypical Thatcherite material, enjoying a prosperity which they could plausibly attribute to their own hard work but, working on a fixed tariff, sensitive to the danger of inflation. Doubtless the cultural elements of Thatcherism—English nationalism, or the no-nonsense approach to crime and punishment[137]—also resonated with this white working-class group, but the roots of their political evolution ran deeper than that, reflecting real material interests and calculations that had developed over a period of at least twenty years. The transformation of Conservatism was also critical: paternalistic, welfare Toryism had cut little ice with these undeferential individualists, but Thatcher did speak to them. One ironic implication was that cabbies' commitment to Toryism was more ephemeral than would have been a conversion based on Pooterism or embourgeoisement: in 1997 New Labour won both Ilford seats.[138] Study of groups like these makes the 'Thatcher moment' easier to understand.

10

Protecting the Good Life

LONDON'S SUBURBS

In August 1969 the *Harrow Observer* published an article containing interviews with around half a dozen residents of Silver Close, Harrow Weald. This was the first of a series titled 'The Street Where You Live', which would run for four years, covering almost the whole of the recently created London Borough of Harrow. Respondents spoke of their lives and their jobs, their families and their hobbies, their satisfaction or dissatisfaction with the area. What emerged was in no sense a systematic survey. This was space-filling journalism in a local paper then publishing twice weekly: the interviewees were probably simply those who opened their doors to the reporter. But the series does provide an extensive cross-section of people and attitudes in the kind of suburban community that had rarely been examined so closely.

The core of the borough was the well-heeled village settlement of Harrow-on-the-Hill; but the area had been connected directly to London by the London and Birmingham Railway in the 1830s, and a working-class area grew up around the mainline station in Wealdstone in the late nineteenth century. The most extensive transformation came in the interwar period, when the previously rural areas of Pinner, North Harrow and Rayners Lane were developed by speculative builders as part of Northwest London's 'Metroland', clustered around the Metropolitan Railway and the link to Baker Street, King's Cross and the City. Like most outer London boroughs, Harrow had its pockets of poverty in the 1970s. It already had the kernel of the South Asian community that is now prominent in the borough. It had Victorian and Edwardian terraces that were slow to gentrify along with the occasional Bohemian oasis like West Street, Harrow Hill, which had 'recently had such an influx of younger artistic people that some have described it as "Little Chelsea."'[1] Harrow displayed diversity, as all outer boroughs did, but a high proportion of its acreage was covered by the characteristic suburban semidetached or detached houses with gardens, whose occupiers ranged from the comfortable to the opulent.

The interviewers took a particular interest in the original residents of the 1920s and 1930s streets, with memories of life on the rural frontier, blackberrying, shooing cattle off the road or dodging the gypsies who lurked in the hedgerows of Rayners Lane. Streets built in the 1930s, occupied then largely by young married couples and displaying a low turn-over rate, were experiencing a natural generational transition by the early 1970s. This is very evident from the *Harrow Observer* articles, which show streets like Holwell Place in Pinner, which was said to have 'no community life because the residents are elderly';[2] others like Cambridge Road in North Harrow, where 'community spirit thrives because so many of the residents are young married couples who moved to Cambridge Road at the same time and their children are growing up together';[3] and several like Wyvenhoe Road, South Harrow, where 'the whole road is altering. . . . Old people are moving out and there are a lot of new people'; or nearby Roxeth Grove, where in 1964 'there were nearly all old people in the road. Since then the young people have been moving in.'[4] One of the original residents of Bellamy Drive, Stanmore, a street of semidetached houses built in 1937, noted, 'the street is coming back to the stage of when we moved in—full of young families.'[5] Some concern was expressed that the influx of younger people was lowering the area's social tone: 'most of the flats were occupied by professional people when we came here [1932], but the road has changed somewhat for the worse, we fear, in our time.'[6] The interwar suburbs had, though, always included their share of people outside the tennis-club milieu, and those once considered below the salt welcomed the dilution of earlier exclusivity. 'You get a different type of person here now', observed Mr Pugh, who had moved to Kenton when his firm had left the East End in 1940: 'They are much more friendly. When we first came here, we thought they were rather snooty.'[7] Westwood Avenue 'was described by one of the older residents as being one of South Harrow's "snob islands", but with the replacement of some older residents by young families the atmosphere has become rather different.'[8]

'Snob islands' were generally becoming rarer. Hillview Gardens, North Harrow, one of the streets most obviously in generational transition, included an engineer for Smiths the watchmakers, an electrician for the Blue Funnel Line, an oboist for the BBC Symphony Orchestra, a buyer in textiles and an academic at Bedford College who was married to a tutor at the Stanmore Orthopaedic Hospital.[9] The residents of Morley Crescent, Stanmore, included a company accountant, the manager of an Angus Steak House who was married to a former Tiller Girl, a lecturer in metallurgy at Southall College of Technology, a home freezer contractor and an auto mechanic for the photographic firm Kodak, Harrow's largest industrial employer.[10] Such variety was not unusual. Harrow obviously included its share of company directors and City men, and there were streets like Buckland Rise, Pinner, dominated by 'teachers, civil servants, accountants, businessmen and insurance officers.'[11] There was no *lumpenproletariat* in Metroland, but this was nonetheless an eclectic community. Skilled manual workers, many though by no means all employed by Kodak, were conspicuous, as were the self-made self-employed—several taxi drivers, the son of Pinner's former village blacksmith who had built up his own coal business, a pastry cook currently working for a builder but aiming to start up a restaurant, an actor learning to become a film stunt driver, a professional trombonist who had accompanied Johnny Dankworth and Engelbert Humperdinck, a Soho strip-club owner, the only English boxer to have knocked out Henry Cooper, even Lord Kitchener's former bugler, aged eighty-three in 1972, who had once started a dance band in Harrow.[12]

The eighteen-foot cabin cruiser in the front garden of a postman in North Harrow and the thirty-foot swimming pool in the back garden of a self-employed central-heating installer in Pinner denoted the impact of postwar affluence.[13] There were other, less ostentatious, signs of material comfort, but the more lasting impression left by the interviews is rather one of satisfaction with the neighbourhood and its environment. The *Harrow Observer*'s subeditors certainly worked hard to convey that impression through the headlines given to the 'Street Where You Live' articles— 'Happy Spirit Reigns among All', 'Contented Air Its Keynote', 'Removal Vans Rare Sight in Contented Road' and so on.[14] In fact, though, the articles themselves highlight the drawbacks as well as the benefits of suburban life, in particular the risk of isolation. Most Harrow dwellers observed the requirements of neighbourliness but did not crave a boisterous communal life. 'We tend to keep to ourselves', one Hatch End resident told the newspaper, the reporter adding the Delphic gloss that 'the people in The

Lawns are community minded but inwardly oriented.'[15] Kathleen O'Shea, moving from Kilburn to Harrow in 1969 ('It's not as rough as Kilburn'), noted that her new neighbours 'don't stop you on your doorstep when you're busy, but they are ready to help you when you are in need.'[16]

Farther out, the larger houses sat in such spacious settings as to be effectively self-contained. 'Looking through the windows of the huge sun-lounge to the well-screened grounds beyond', the wife of an engineering company director, in a seven-bedroom house in Church Lane, Pinner, said, "I don't like living here too much, because you don't really have next-door neighbours': 'it is not a place where one makes friends quickly.'[17] The un-happy of Harrow were those whose personal circumstances meant that the rewards of family, house and garden were lacking or proved inadequate— the widow in Walton Drive ('life can be very lonely in Harrow for a widow because there are no special clubs for widows and it's very difficult to get out on your own')[18] or the young mother not fortunate enough to live in a 'young' street ('says she feels "cut off" and would like to see the Council provide "child minding services" so that young mothers like herself could go back to work part-time, or take up other activities outside the home').[19] Two such mothers in Morley Crescent East banded together 'to stave off "suburban depression" to which many lonely housewives are susceptible.'[20] The first project undertaken by the newly formed Harrow Council of Social Service in 1971 was an investigation of loneliness in the borough.[21] But the space, the detachment and the seclusion that exacerbated such problems were precisely what many people sought in suburban living: 'we have a nice little backwater here and that's the way we enjoy it', as one resident of Hatch End put it.[22] Some of the Harrow interviewees had left the borough once and returned; others asserted that they would never leave 'for all the tea in China.'[23] For most this was an agreeable environment. One couple, newly installed in Morley Crescent West in Stanmore, had christened their house 'Cloud Nine.'[24]

There were good reasons to be happy in Harrow. The crime rate was low: 'we have one or two small-time villains', as Detective Sergeant 'Chalkie' White of the Pinner police station explained in 1971, 'but most of them come from outside.'[25] Transport links to the centre were good. After Kingston, Harrow had the lowest unemployment rate of any London borough.[26] Sixty-eight percent of Harrow households owned a car, against a Greater London average of 53 percent.[27] The 1978 *National Dwelling and Housing Survey* showed 78 percent of Harrow residents to be 'satisfied' or 'very satisfied' with their area.[28] The larger lesson from that survey, though,

Suburban living. Half-timbered, pebble-dashed house, garage, lawn and topiary in West End Lane, Pinner, LB Harrow, 1976. (London Picture Archive 160815 © London Metropolitan Archives [City of London])

was that satisfaction levels were consistently higher in outer than inner London. As the *Evening Standard*'s Simon Jenkins pointed out, 'people who in any other city would be stacked in blocks of flats—see the suburbs of Paris or Stockholm—are here in London living each with his own front door, his own small garden, with somewhere to pamper his car, let his children play and chat with his neighbours.'[29] 'We are lucky who live here', wrote one resident of Oakwood, in Enfield, in 1972. 'Grumbling can become a habit. How about an autumn resolution, "I've had a wonderful summer, I'm jolly glad I live in Oakwood, and I'm not going to wish for anything I haven't already got!"'[30]

The 1978 survey shows a strong positive correlation between respondents' satisfaction with their area, borough by borough, and their satisfaction with their own houses.[31] This is unsurprising, but it does underline the point made by the geographer Peter Hall in 1989, that for all the routine denigration of suburban style, suburbia 'provided good, cheap, basic housing with gardens for people who could never earlier have aspired to anything like it.'[32] There was a still stronger correlation between levels of satisfaction with the house and levels of owner occupation.[33] It was, of course,

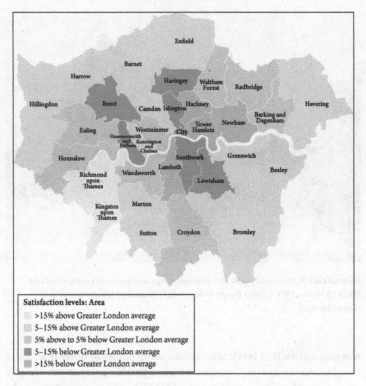

Satisfaction levels: Area
- >15% above Greater London average
- 5–15% above Greater London average
- 5% above to 5% below Greater London average
- 5–15% below Greater London average
- >15% below Greater London average

National Dwelling and Housing Survey, 1978, satisfaction levels: area. Map shows percentage of respondents who professed to be 'satisfied' or 'very satisfied' with their area. Greater London average was 73.1 percent. (Department of the Environment, *National Dwelling and Housing Survey, 1978* [London, 1979], Table 83B, p. 131)

entirely possible to enjoy living in a rented house. The large gardens so treasured by the suburbans ('if one cannot enjoy one's garden one may as well live in an area such as Shepherd's Bush')[34] might have belonged to rented property. A rented house could have provided the space that made it possible to build 'a huge model railway layout in the loft', to store sixty gallons of homemade wine or to provide house room for Sidney the Iguana, to take three Harrow examples.[35]

But owner occupation was the dominant form of suburban tenure. Harrow had the largest proportion of owner-occupiers of any London borough,[36] a privilege enjoyed by the taxi drivers and central-heating installers as much as by the stockbrokers and company directors. Only

Satisfaction levels: Accommodation

- >15% above Greater London average
- 5–15% above Greater London average
- 5% above to 5% below Greater London average
- 5–15% below Greater London average
- >15% below Greater London average

National Dwelling and Housing Survey, 1978, satisfaction levels: accommodation. Map shows percentage of respondents who professed to be 'satisfied' or 'very satisfied' with their accommodation. Greater London average was 77.3 percent. (Department of the Environment, *National Dwelling and Housing Survey, 1978* [London, 1979], Table 82B, p. 129)

owner-occupiers could engage in the frenzy of structural alterations described in the *Harrow Observer* articles, remoulding the interwar fabric to suit 1970s lifestyles, especially by the enlargement of kitchens and the knocking-through of living rooms. The man who invested his army gratuity on a plot in Corbin's Lane in 1920, and waited fifteen years until his house was built, had been animated by the aspiration to own his own home. So had the man transplanted to Harrow when his employers left the East End in 1940, who had stayed put when his firm returned to Stepney: 'we liked it so much and we had the chance of buying the house.'[37] So were the couple who had filmed their Kenton house being built in 1927 and still lived there in 1970: 'we love our house, and we feel that if we did ever move, we would be sorry to leave the bricks and mortar which we regard as home.'[38] So were the young couple who bought a semidetached house in St Ursula Grove in less than twelve hours as the property boom gathered pace in 1972, 'in case the price went up in the next hour.'[39] With the boom nearing its climax in 1973, one local building-society manager commented that 'young people were willing to buy a home and "live in a deckchair" rather than pay rent.'[40] Those who were resistant to deckchair living left the area rather than continue renting, like the young couple interviewed in Gayton Road: 'I am trying to buy a house but the houses around here are too expensive. Between us we earn £6,000 a year but even with that we cannot afford to buy the type of house we want in Harrow.'[41]

Amongst established home owners, though, there was little talk of house prices. Jane Deverson and Katherine Lindsay made the same point in their 1975 study of the unidentified London suburb they called 'Purlbridge'. Whereas in the northern part of this anonymised area, originally built for working-class occupiers, the young gentrifiers spent 'whole evenings talking about nothing but the property market', in comfortable South Purlbridge 'there is no need to join the property race for investment or profit, and a relaxed air of permanence pervades the quiet avenues.'[42] 'They are aware of the value of their property', a local estate agent explained, 'but they never move to make a profit on their houses.' He put this down to their having 'at least second generation wealth—their fathers or grandfathers are the ones who made the money',[43] which may have been true, but across outer London it was the case that the closer one came to the limit of the built-up area, the lower the incentive to move. 'Only a small drive and you are well into the countryside', as one Stanmore resident put it.[44] Leapfrogging the Green Belt would mean passing beyond the tube network and would entail a lengthy and expensive commute. Moving within an outer borough offered little prospect of capital gain, except for 'empty nesters' in a position to trade down. Even they often preferred to stay put: 'their house was, in fact, too big for them, but they would not want to leave', as one Pinner couple told the *Harrow Observer*.[45]

If suburbanites were happy with their neighbourhood, they were as likely to modernise their existing house as to leave it. J. W. M. Thompson noted in his 1962 survey of Sidcup for the *Evening Standard* that some of the houses thrown up by speculative builders between the wars had been built with outside lavatories, while many lacked a bathroom: 'instead there was an awkward contraption in the kitchen which looked like a solid table most of the time, but which could be opened up to disclose a bath when needed.' By 1962, though, 'these houses have generally been modernised. Small extensions have been built to provide a proper bathroom, or one of the bedrooms has been sacrificed.'[46] The numerous structural and decorative improvements described in the 'Street Where You Live' interviews in Harrow were taken, probably rightly, as 'more proof that they [the householders] do not intend leaving the area for quite some time.'[47] Many of the changes made were so idiosyncratic as to suggest that they were not intended to enhance saleability—the mural in Alfriston Avenue depicting a medieval battle scene 'which goes completely round [the] living room wall', the miniature fish pond set into the hearth of a house in Westmorland Road ('another unusual feature to enhance the room') or the 'beautiful Caribbean style bar . . . consisting of mirrors and woodwork' erected in the front room of a house in Fairholme Road.[48] These people saw the house as less a tradeable asset than a treasured possession, to be customised to the owner's satisfaction. The Ratepayers Association at Heston, in the Borough of Hounslow, took up the case of ratepayers who incurred a higher local tax assessment as a result of adding central heating or a garage: 'It is quite true [that] all enhanced the selling price of their property AT THEIR OWN EXPENSE, but none did it for that reason.'[49] Houses were bought to live in. They, and the gardens that came with them, were valued for the pleasure that they gave. Threats to their integrity were resisted vigorously: 'There is no substitute for the loss of homes, and what will replace the beauty of our gardens?'[50] As pressure grew to refashion the suburban landscape, this would place many householders at odds with their local authorities.

Development Dilemmas

If the Harrow interviews are any guide, suburban residents tended to speak of 'London' as somewhere else. One North Harrow resident 'calls herself a "suburban being" and does not want to live in London'; another respondent, living on the edge of the Green Belt in Stanmore, 'agrees with her neighbours on one point—she cannot see Hill Close as part of the *London* Borough of Harrow.'[51] In reality, though, for all the talk of a village atmosphere in parts of suburbia, the suburban appeal rested as much on access to Central London as it did on access to open country. 'What I would really like is to live in a forest in the middle of Mayfair', acknowledged one Harrow resident with compelling candour, 'so Harrow is a compromise.'[52] By containing urban sprawl, the Green Belt had made this compromise feasible: it was still possible to live within easy reach of open country but with relatively speedy access to the centre. Critics of the Green Belt policy in the early 1970s argued that while this dirigiste form of land-use planning had failed to regulate the outward movement of population, it had, by raising land prices on the fringe, proved very effective 'in discouraging the decentralization of offices, shops, cinemas, theatres, hospitals, museums, concert halls and higher educational establishments' in those areas.[53] Whether or not for that reason, there was discernible dissatisfaction with the provision of facilities in the suburbs. Even in the suburb that was apparently best provided with shopping and recreational facilities, it was argued that 'the quality of life in Croydon still owes a lot to London. When Croydon people want a real evening out, a treat, they go to London.'[54] In an unusually acerbic set of interviews in October 1969, one Wealdstone resident complained to the *Harrow Observer* reporter that there was 'nothing to do in the evenings apart from the bingo', while a teenager in the same street expressed the wish to move 'somewhere where there is a bit more life, like Watford. . . . There is dancing there.'[55] A letter writer complained that 'the only way one can guarantee seeing a new movie is to see it in the West End. . . . The reissues keep coming back [to Harrow] again and again.'[56] Other correspondents made the same point, though Harrow at least still had a cinema, unlike many suburban centres. The closure of the Morden Odeon in January 1973 appeared to confirm 'the popular opinion that Morden is not a town—but just the end of the Northern Line.'[57] It was part of a wave of suburban cinema closures in these years.[58]

What worried suburban local authorities most was the shrinkage of many suburbs as shopping centres, eviscerated both by competition from the West End and by a process of economic selection operating within suburbia. Affluence was, ironically, at the root of this—in particular the growth of car ownership. Between 1962 and 1966 the proportion of Richmond households owning a car rose from 28 percent to 52 percent, with immediate effects on shopping habits: 'people say they travel further afield, buy less frequently in greater bulk at centres offering lower prices.'[59] Centres which could offer large, well-stocked shops and easy parking benefited at the expense of those which could not. Put simply, this sharpened the distinction between 'comparison' centres, specialising in nonfood items—clothing and footwear, furniture, white goods—and 'convenience' centres dealing in food and other day-to-day necessities, the former locating themselves in the larger centres like Croydon or Kingston, the latter remaining in the traditional High Street. This distinction was underlined in 1976 by the opening of Brent Cross, an American-style out-of-town mall but within London's built-up area. It made no claim to service the consumer's humdrum needs, providing 'none of the public facilities (such as post office, library or clinic) and few of the service trades (such as laundrette or cobbler) that would normally be present in a shopping centre.'[60]

At the start of 1973 the *Wimbledon News* took stock of the shopping provision in the paper's principal centres—Wimbledon, Mitcham and Morden—all of them squeezed by the retail giants in Croydon and Kingston. 'If I want any clothes I always have to go to Croydon', one teenage respondent put it, 'but when I shop for the family it is O.K. here.' 'Housewives ... admitted to opening their purses well outside the borough boundaries when it came down to it', expressing 'a wistful desire for a Marks and Spencer, as there isn't one in Merton, and Tooting and Croydon branches drew Merton shoppers away from their local centres.'[61] In the same year, the Cole Park Residents Association in Twickenham wrote to Sainsbury's and the fishmonger chain MacFisheries to ask if, having left the area, they would consider returning.[62] In fact food retailers were drawn to the malls of Croydon or Brent Cross just as the fashion chains were, and car-borne consumers preferred to buy food in bulk wherever they could easily park. In many areas, High Street provision dwindled. The London Borough of Wandsworth observed of its own suburban area in 1973 that 'on Upper Richmond Road and, to some extent, in the upper part of the High Street the presence of estate and employment agents, restaurants, second-hand furniture dealers and others indicate [*sic*] a shopping frontage of secondary importance, if not actually in decline.'[63] The proliferation of shoe shops defied economic logic: in Wimbledon there were said to be nine between the station and the town hall.[64] In Wimbledon Village it was observed that the optician, the electrical dealers, the post office, the bakery and other traditional shops had been replaced by eight estate agents and eight restaurants. This was widely regretted, but as a correspondent from the Wimbledon Village Association noted, 'Customers will only come if there is adequate parking and this is one of the major problems of the area. Estate agents require fewer customers and do not have delivery problems; restaurants operate largely at times when parking is uncontrolled.'[65] Merton Council turned down an application from the Leeds Permanent Building Society to use a shop in Wimbledon Broadway as a branch office in 1973, on the grounds that 'another non-retail shop would create "a dead frontage" along the Broadway.'[66]

From the late 1950s suburban local authorities feared that the conventional High Street, often laid out when the settlements were isolated

Sixties suburban development. A car park, shopping arcade and council housing in Ham, LB Richmond, 1960s. (Mary Evans Picture Library)

A characteristic suburban combination of interwar semidetached housing and postwar office development in Kingsbury Road, LB Brent. (John Gay/English Heritage NMR/Mary Evans Picture Library)

villages, was inadequate for the motor age and that a failure to modernise shopping facilities would cause them to suffer in competition with centres elsewhere. In 1966 the *Middlesex Advertiser* expressed the frustration felt in Uxbridge at the repeated delays to a town development scheme first published five years earlier by pointing out the progress being made by the town's neighbours:

> Look in on Slough where the bulldozers are never silent. . . . Large stores have been built, office blocks have risen into the sky. . . . At Ealing two of the town's main stores have been rebuilt and enlarged. . . . Harrow's leading store has also been redesigned and enlarged and considerable building has taken place. At Wembley they're putting the finishing touches to a huge office development over Wembley Central Station and this scheme also includes a most impressive shopping precinct, in which space has been found for not only large multiple stores and supermarkets, but also some of the town's small traders.[67]

As this extract suggests, the London suburbs took a disproportionate part in the urban redevelopment mania of the 1960s.[68] The process was further encouraged by the overhaul of London government in 1965, creating large new boroughs, almost all of them amalgamations.[69] Authorities formed of two or three smaller bodies—in outer London generally Urban District Councils—usually inherited scattered and inadequate offices.[70] In consequence, the incentive entirely to recast the centre of the borough in order to provide larger retail outlets was enhanced by the opportunity such redevelopment gave to build new modern council offices into the scheme. Many councils threw in a library and/or theatre or sports facilities to sweeten the pill.

The model for these initiatives was the expansive redevelopment of Croydon in the 1950s and 1960s. Croydon had been the first part of outer London to attain county borough status under the 1888 Local Government Act, and its Corporation had therefore been a powerful and autonomous local authority before the area was absorbed into Greater London in 1965. The idea of boosting the local economy by creating a new suburban town centre can be traced back to the 1930s, when the Fairfield site was released by the Southern Railway: 'Such an opportunity comes but once. It must not be allowed to pass', as Arthur Lewis, chairman of the Town Planning Committee, urged in 1933.[71] Plans for the new town centre took shape immediately after the war and were implemented under the provisions of private legislation secured in 1956. The Corporation invested heavily in commercial development following the ending of restrictions on office building in 1954, and new offices generated revenue for the construction of new roads and a clutch of public buildings, including a civic centre, council offices, law courts, a new concert venue in the Fairfield Halls and the Croydon College of Art.[72] October 1970 saw the completion of the Whitgift Centre, London's largest covered shopping centre, in an area already well supplied with major stores.

Lewis had noted that 'it was the making of Birmingham when [Joseph] Chamberlain's scheme was carried out.'[73] The burghers of Croydon provided a mid-twentieth-century, suburban analogue to the efforts of Victorian municipal pioneers to provide a civic focus and stimulate the local economy by remodelling the urban environment. In this they were far-sighted: when a metropolis reached the size of postwar London, it was neither necessary nor logical that its suburban centres should remain mere dormitories. They were also successful. There can have been few suburban authorities in the 1960s which did not look jealously at Croydon. Even by 1966, before any of the Whitgift Centre stores had opened, Croydon's retail turnover was 25 percent higher than Kingston's and double those of Brixton, Bromley and even Kensington High Street.[74] With commercial development well under way by the time that the office-building restrictions were reimposed in 1964, Croydon gained a commanding advantage in the commercial office market. Between 1963 and 1973 30 percent of offices and 30 percent of jobs moving out of Central London went to Croydon.[75] Eight million square feet of office floor space and desk space for thirty thousand workers made Croydon the Southeast's largest office centre outside Central London.[76]

Croydon displayed, though, the vices of its virtues. The new developments had been run up quickly and with little coordination. In the view of one architect practising in the town, 'many places have been described as concrete jungles but none more aptly so than Croydon': 'Croydon has quantity but not quality.'[77] It displayed the kind of modern development that modernist architects decried. One of them, Croydon-born Owen Luder, provided a scathing account of the town's dysfunctionality in 1965:

Stand outside the Fairfield Halls and look towards Wellesley Road. You will see examples of virtually every environmental mistake possible. A major road and underpass crash through the town centre, destroying the scale of the buildings, forming a major obstacle to the pedestrian flow from shops and buildings on either side. Traffic funnels into narrow roads at each end of the underpass. Buildings with an indescribable variety of size, height and architectural treatment, few of which deserve more than a second glance and some of which are deplorable examples of the worst commercial architecture of the post-war period. You can see where the planners have changed their minds on densities for office development. The smaller, lower, early office blocks are dwarfed by the later, much larger and higher, monsters.[78]

For a public already sceptical towards modernism, Croydon provided a concrete demonstration of the danger of leaving planners and architects to their own devices—a precedent to be kept in mind when examining the weightless architects' drawings that accompanied redevelopment proposals. Croydon was 'a featureless office centre', a 'chrome and concrete catastrophe' and evidence of the wrongheadedness of 1950s planning which prioritised the car—'how much visual desecration this can cause; how difficult and dangerous this traffic-orientated planning always becomes.'[79] The Strawberry Hill Residents Association, celebrating its tenth year of life, reflected, 'When you consider what has happened to parts of some townships like Croydon, then the fact that we continue to live in relative peace and quiet is no mean achievement!'[80] Objectors to the Ealing Draft Plan in 1968 used a photograph of Croydon on the cover of their protest pamphlet.[81] Any town planner or borough architect hoping to garner public support for redevelopment proposals in the 1970s was well advised to conceal any enthusiasm for Croydon.[82]

In fact no other borough sought to redevelop on anything like Croydon's scale, but it was hard for planners to escape from the abrasive style that so many people found offensive in the Croydon townscape. Architects in the 1960s naturally inclined towards modernist designs for the kind of civic commissions on offer, and some core features of the plans, such as multistorey car parks and road realignments, could only plausibly be rendered in the modernist idiom, however jarring that might be in a suburban setting. Flyovers and pedestrian underpasses were thus presented as indispensable features of the modern urban world: 'we may not like them from the aesthetic point of view, but they are things we have got to come to accept.'[83] There was, in fact, a certain path dependency inherent in development proposals which almost guaranteed that they would alienate many of the people they were intended to benefit. The new shopping centres considered essential to regenerate the local economy would struggle

The Croydon Flyover under construction, June 1968. (PA/Alamy Stock Photo)

without adequate parking for the car-borne shoppers they were intended
to attract, but multistorey car parks were hard to love. The psychologists
consulted by Freeman, Fox & Partners for its 1966 Richmond Study 'de-
tected certain non-articulated reservations and doubts about these structures', and, as one Richmond councillor acknowledged in 1974, 'it was
difficult to make a multi-storey car park look like something else.'[84] The
same was truer still of the high-rise office blocks central to most redevelopment schemes—Croydon boasted fifty of them[85]—which few people
loved for their appearance. Councils occasionally depicted them as '"feature buildings", . . . the town centre's new focal point',[86] but in reality their
purpose was nakedly economic—to stem the flow of white-collar workers
into Central London and provide captive customers to attract retailers into
the new shopping centres.[87] Above all, they would generate rental income
and enhanced rateable value for the council, to offset the unremunerative
theatres or libraries: 'without rating income you can't have fun', as Sutton's
director of engineering put it in 1973.[88] In that year, at the height of the
commercial property boom, the demand for offices appeared insatiable,

and local authorities seemed desperate to feed it. Local amenity groups felt helpless in the face of 'the ever-present menace of the office block which can spring up on any available site to change the character of the town ineradicably.'[89]

For two decades after 1945, there had been an acceptance that some rebuilding was necessary, if only to fill the holes made by the Luftwaffe. The question was whether the process would be handled well or badly. In 1963 the recently formed Kingston Society hired a coach to take councillors and council officials to Coventry so that they should learn by example how to do modern town planning: 'How a pedestrian shopping precinct really works (with all traffic excluded), how people actually like shopping on two levels and how large numbers of cars can be got rid of by tucking them away on the roofs of new buildings. We also saw a new municipal theatre, with a fine square in front of it, where sometimes it is difficult to get a seat and a cathedral where people queue for half an hour to get in.'[90] In 1969, in an exercise in role reversal, the Friends of Old Isleworth, in outer West London, advocated the destruction of the interwar Swan Inn to turn Lower Square into a 'pedestrian precinct with a degree of tranquillity', only to be resisted by the planning officer for Hounslow, who thought the Swan 'a most attractive building worth preserving.'[91]

By the 1970s, though, 'the depressing character of most recently rebuilt town centres' had become a commonplace.[92] Although lip service was paid to the notion that this was due to 'the lack of a coherent and decisive town planning policy',[93] at heart most critics considered town planning more part of the problem than of the solution. Hopes that redevelopment could produce congenial townscapes dwindled, and local amenity groups became preoccupied with resisting change, almost regardless of the merits of whatever was threatened. 'The conservationist movement is not a cause but an effect', declared one member of the Southgate Civic Trust—'the effect of knowing from experience that when something is pulled down, what will replace it will be worse.'[94] Whereas the first issue of the Kingston Society's newsletter in 1962 had warned against 'an uncritical conservatism' concerning architecture and planning—'an inability to have faith in the future'—the society's twenty-fifth-anniversary history measured its achievements purely by its success or failure in saving local landmarks from demolition.[95]

'There is a powerful build-up of strong feeling against those in authority who allow the desecration of our environment', suggested the chairman of the Belvedere Estate Residents Association in Wimbledon in 1973.[96]

Councils were accused of being impervious to the views of their residents and of concealing the deliberations of officers and key committees from them.[97] Outer-London councils were probably no more furtive than most large urban authorities in the period, but that need not suggest a very high level of transparency. By the late 1960s councils understood that redevelopment proposals were unlikely to arouse clamorous enthusiasm and that the growing pressure for public involvement in planning schemes risked further delaying plans that were already delay-prone.[98] With this in mind, officials from Merton Council had asked privately in 1972 'to know the minimum degree of public participation which would be acceptable to the Department of the Environment/Greater London Council' in redeveloping Wimbledon's centre.[99] The loaded terms of a survey question posed by Waltham Forest Council in 1971 suggest that the borough anticipated an uphill struggle to persuade the public to accept office development: 'The shopping centre could contain some offices. Such offices would provide jobs for local people and could reduce the cost of the town centre proposals to the Council. Do you think offices in the town centre is a good idea?'[100] Councils were aware that they were likely to be accused by critics of 'trying to imitate Croydon in a small scale', and they hoped that improved facilities would eventually trump aesthetic opposition—that 'Croydon might look like an abortion—but people enjoy living there."[101]

When Merton Council did eventually consult its public, towards the end of 1973, it discovered little that it cannot have known already: the public wanted bigger and better-known department stores, more leisure facilities, restrictions on office development and a ban on high buildings.[102] How much commercial development suburban residents would *actually* tolerate to gain better shops is hard now to know. In 1973, though, the Hatch End Association in Harrow was in no doubt, opposing a proposed office block above the railway station: 'There *may* be office workers in Hatch End who would find it convenient not to travel to their work . . . but probably few would feel it worth while to spoil the residential nature of their "Village" for such a small privilege.'[103] In a sense, the truth of this claim matters less than that the principle contained in it was universally advocated by residents' groups like the Hatch End Association, for these were the organisations making the running in shaping and voicing opinion in the suburbs. Just as the 1970s saw community and 'pavement' politics emerge in the inner city, these years saw the hardening and sharpening of home-owner politics in outer London.

Protecting Home, Neighbourhood and Environment

It was often assumed that the suburbs lacked associational life—'they've got what they want in life, they're comfortable, and they want to be left alone in privacy to enjoy it.'[104] In fact they displayed no shortage of associationalism. One residents association in Merton counted seven hundred organisations in the borough, 'catering for every possible taste from aero-modelling to wine-making, and from antiques to water-skiing!'[105] They tended, though, to be small-scale, specialised and often rather staid. The journal of the Selsdon Residents Association suggested plausibly in 1974 that the area's associational life had taken shape during and after the war and changed little since: that 'the Townswomen's Guilds, the British Legion, the Selsdon Stagers, the St John's Dramatic Society, etc' risked 'catering too much for the old-timers to the detriment of the new arrivals.'[106]

The residents and ratepayers associations, amenity groups and local history societies that came to embody householder activism in the 1970s displayed many of the same characteristics. They generally had a small active membership and ran on a shoestring. The membership was normally disproportionately middle-aged or retired—the Pinner South Residents Association was affiliated to Age Concern—with officers agonising fruitlessly over recruiting new blood.[107] As their local authority antagonists never tired of pointing out, they could not be considered genuinely representative organisations. As the Harrow interviews show, the suburbs were not peopled entirely by middle-class professionals: Harrow had the lowest proportion of manual workers of any London borough, but they still accounted for 30 percent of the economically active population. In boroughs like Enfield or Hounslow, with more extensive local industry, the figure topped 40 percent.[108] Suburbanites were not all middle-aged antiquarians, disgruntled ratepayers and *Daily Telegraph* readers (in Carshalton, 57 percent of newspaper readers took the *Daily Mirror* or the *Sun*).[109] But in areas with owner-occupation rates of 60 percent or higher, there was a general interest in protecting the home, the neighbourhood and the environment, reinforced by dwindling confidence that local authorities could be entrusted with this task.

Growing concern for the local environment brought together traditional ratepayers and residents associations with the several amenity and conservation groups formed in response to proposed redevelopment. The emergence of the conservation agenda gave a breadth and ballast to conventional ratepayer politics, extending the appeal and the potency of this kind of pressure group. The rates had always hit some individuals with disproportionate force—conventionally non-wage-earners living in large houses—but as the Layfield Committee demonstrated in 1976, the rebated rating system was in general progressive or neutral in its incidence for all but higher earners.[110] The familiar hubbub of ratepayer complaint about council 'extravagance' actually reflected a minority concern, and the steady growth of local authority expenditure in the 1960s generated little real resistance. When, however, the most evident effect of council expenditure appeared to be the desecration of familiar townscapes, the reach of ratepayer groups was significantly extended.

Residential areas tended not to develop the habit of continuous political involvement associated with the workplace but rather displayed a more sporadic activism which, if transient, could be intense. Threats to the local environment could produce a widespread mobilisation of many who were only really stirred by proposals directly affecting their neighbourhood but who, once roused, could display fierce passion. One hapless GLC member deputed to discuss the contentious Crystal Palace Triangle development proposals at a Norwood Society meeting in 1970 had 'never forgotten the controlled fury, the reasoned argument, and the quiet determination of the people of Norwood on that occasion.'[111] The prospect of calling the authorities to account whenever necessary encouraged many residents to see membership of these groups as a kind of insurance policy against unwelcome change, without any necessary intention to get heavily involved. In Harrow the Bishop Ken Road Residents Association could claim eighty-five member families in that road alone, with other members in no fewer than sixty-one neighbouring streets, while in Cuckoo Hill Drive, Pinner Green, 'only one or two of its residents, if any, do not belong to the Pinner Association, that successful society for the preservation of Pinner.'[112]

In the summer of 1970 Pinner was prettified. Fencing was replaced by 'attractive posts and chains', the firemark on Beaumont's cottage, dating from 1760, was repainted in its original colours and an old-style barber's pole was placed outside the men's hairdresser's.[113] Such gestures, visible across outer London, bear witness to a growing eagerness to preserve—or re-create—symbols of the past. The local past became less recherché and more popular. In June 1972 the Sanderstead Residents Association noted that history ceased to be dull when it was local history: 'For some years past it has never been difficult to find an audience from local organisations for any speaker with some knowledge of the subject.' The association appealed for somebody to write a comprehensive history of the area; by the winter the Sanderstead Preservation Society was selling a *History of Sanderstead* at 15p.[114] The Pinner and Hatch End Workers' Educational Association produced a successful volume called *Harrow Before Your Time* in 1973 because 'people wanted to know why a road bent or dipped, or why a hedge had a bank beside it.'[115]

It is hard not to attribute this thirst for a lost past to concern about the apparently irresistible pressure for redevelopment. 'Now that the powers that be are trying to destroy our neighbourhood and community', wrote a member of one Croydon Residents Association in 1974, 'it would seem to be a good time to collect together its history and happenings.'[116] Much of it was unapologetically escapist. In the embittered winter of 1973–74, a member of another Croydon group found that in 'the grave national crisis and the confusion and chaos which seemed to prevail wherever one looked, it was quite soothing to switch off, relax and take a look back instead of worrying about the troubles in this country and the world at large': 'I picked up a book on the history of Croydon and as I turned the pages it seemed as if I was living in a different world. . . . While the cars were speeding up and down Croham Valley Road, I was reading about the pony and trap.'[117] Most people acknowledged that it was 'no good lamenting the disappearance of the polecat, the lark, the field of wheat or the flint cottage' but still thought it 'worth questioning whether future residents will consider that we did better than our predecessors.'[118] Such questions shaped the suburban conservation movement.

The Victorian and interwar developers had left little of real pedigree to protect in outer London. Needless to say, local groups were anxious that 'the few buildings of architectural or historic importance' which existed 'should be preserved',[119] but the emphasis in suburban conservation tended to be placed rather on the protection of the ambience of the existing environment, even if few buildings within it possessed individual distinction. In 1971 the Enfield Preservation Society acknowledged that in its previous solicitude for eighteenth- and early nineteenth-century buildings in the area, it had 'shown little concern for Victorian and Edwardian houses which are well built and well designed' and invited the secretary of the Victorian Society to address its next meeting.[120] In a Victorian suburb like Norwood, it was maintained that the area's 'particular quality lies more in its charm and general character than in the outstanding quality of its individual buildings', even as it was (rightly) acknowledged that if the 'Victorians were alive today they might be far more busy tearing down the past than we are.'[121]

This sentiment reflected understandable anxiety that with the public-sector transformation of town centres now well advanced, private-sector redevelopment posed a growing threat to residential streets. Most at risk were the large mansions in Victorian suburbs like Norwood and Wimbledon, built for an occupier who no longer existed, with more children, more servants and fewer cars than the 1970s client. 'The old house itself is usually very costly to repair and convert to multi-family use and the land it stands on is in fact more valuable than the house itself. The house has become uneconomic for a single family due to its size and condition.'[122] Market logic dictated that it be demolished and replaced by flats. The process was described by one Wimbledon journalist in 1973:

> It's simple. Anyone with the funds can do it. Knock on the door of a large Victorian villa and offer the owner say £50,000. He'll be very unlikely to refuse—after all, to anyone who wants to live in his house, it's only worth £35,000. . . . The next step is to find an architect who will design you a very economical block of say, six flats with car parking spaces. . . . Send in an application to Merton's Planning Department. . . . The Planning Committee will consider your application and almost certainly grant it, providing you agree not to uproot any trees or anything like that. After that, knock down the house. . . . Inside a week there's nothing left but a few bricks and a pattern of tyre marks. Then it's just a question of finding a builder who'll put up your flats for around £42,000 and then get hold of an agent who'll sell them for £18,000 each. What could be simpler. You're left with a profit of around £16,000 out of which to take the incidentals before starting all over again.

Consequently, the uniformity of the Victorian street came regularly to be interrupted by the 'three-storey cube, dazzling with its white paint and picture windows and surrounded by cropped grass and parking spaces neatly painted on the tarmac.'[123] The incongruity of the new developments jarred more than the buildings themselves, which were built with an eye to the planning process. If the local authority did reject them, the developer stood a good chance of a successful appeal to the Minister: 'The inspector would as good as say "You can't expect people to build a replica Victorian mansion when they've just knocked one down. This development before me is not as bad as all that. It's only three storeys, it's built of brick, what more can you ask?"[124] Such considerations inhibited local authorities even as they became conscious of public concern. In November 1973 Merton rejected plans for a four-storey block in Pepys Road, Raynes Park, on the grounds that it was 'unneighbourly.' The decision represented the first success for the local residents association in ten years of lobbying and was taken as 'a pointer towards future policy', but the council subsequently accepted the proposal when it was resubmitted as a three-storey scheme.[125]

The concern was that piecemeal development might proceed to the point at which the whole street appeared tainted, and 'the Council or Ministry might . . . allow wholesale redevelopment on the grounds that the general standard of the district has already been lowered.'[126] This was a consideration which could also apply to unsightly extensions and additions, leading householder groups to adopt an absolutist stance towards almost any visible alterations. They generally took it upon themselves to vet new proposals. At Cole Park, Twickenham, for instance, 'the Committee will keep track of all planning applications affecting the area and will meet to consider its attitude on any which could spoil the area significantly'; ten years of such vigilance at Kingston produced a three-inch-thick file of correspondence with the Planning Committee.[127] The objective could be realised more efficiently, though, by securing Conservation Area status for threatened neighbourhoods. The Copers Cope Residents Association in Southeast London, for instance, sought Conservation Area status for the Cator Estate precisely to avoid having 'to fight continually to try to keep Beckenham an attractive area.'[128] The concept of the Conservation Area had been cast into law by Duncan Sandys's Civic Amenities Act of 1967. The act tilted the scales heavily against development, giving planning authorities power to ensure that any new building accorded with the visual and architectural qualities of an area, introducing an aesthetic dimension otherwise lacking in development control. As one association in Barnet explained to its members, 'The conservation area technique allows . . . streets to be preserved as wholes; this quality is now threatened, as residents know only too well, by piecemeal developments out of character with the villas and family houses of which these pleasant streets are composed.'[129] Within four years of the act coming into force, sixty-four Conservation Areas had been designated in South London, eighteen of them in Richmond alone.[130] By the late seventies, there were more than three hundred Conservation Areas in Greater London, including 123 in the outer boroughs.[131]

Conservationism and the Green Belt

This proliferation of Conservation Areas would have been impossible without the active support of the local authorities, which were required to nominate Areas within their boundaries and to implement the tighter development control involved. At the height of the town development mania, relations between councils and amenity groups had frequently been less than cordial. The proliferation of local groups in these years owed much to the belief that councils simply could not be trusted with the local environment. The founder of the Bexley Civic Society, Peter Barnes, concluded that the task was simply beyond the remit of local authorities and therefore naturally fell within the sphere of voluntary action: 'It is the duty of a Council to see that its citizens have somewhere to live with adequate services but this does not mean that the Borough will be a worthwhile place in which to live. It is the aim of voluntary bodies such as the Bexley Council of Social Service, the Bexley Arts Council and the like to make Bexley a place worth living in, and in this field I am convinced that the Bexley Civic Society has a very important job to do.'[132] At a meeting with the borough's assistant town planning officer in 1973, he asked, 'Why it is that the present generation of architects and town planners who are . . . so assiduously mis-shaping our environment, appear to be recruited, with few exceptions, from the ranks of arrogant philistines?'[133] He was not alone in holding this view. The Richmond Society, addressing the question of 'why an amateur society should think itself competent to pronounce on matters which our elected local government and its officers exist to deal with', explained that 'unfortunately there is little tradition for the politically conscious to be also visually sensitive.'[134] Only householder activism could save the neighbourhood. 'Should we not realise that in 1970 it is informed mass militancy that wins the day?', asked a contributor to the *Sanderstead News*.[135]

Many people looked back wistfully to the days of the pre-amalgamation authorities, supposedly thrifty, concerned only with the interests of their area and uncorrupted by party politics.[136] This was naïve, but the large and increasingly managerial post-1965 boroughs could be accused of creating a democratic deficit in local government. The 1965 amalgamations had been intended to produce areas socially diverse enough to generate political choice, but in practice electoral movements in all of them reflected the ebbs and flows of national politics more than any local influences. Rate-payer groups, in contrast, normally sought to maintain the quaint stance of indifference to party politics. This was a traditional claim of such groups, of course, even when their membership consisted largely of Conservatives. It was adopted either for tactical reasons or in the belief that party labels infringed municipal etiquette.[137] When intrusive redevelopment headed the local agenda, though, it became harder to see ratepayer groups as sur-rogate Tories, at least in Conservative-controlled boroughs. The twenty-three ratepayer candidates who stood for election in Havering in the 1974 council elections (ten of them successfully) were all opposed by official Conservative candidates. The members of ratepayer groups doubtless *were* predominantly Conservative, but their householder Toryism meant that they had little affinity with the other Conservative interests—developers, retail magnates—seemingly directing local policy to the detriment of the area. The 'Bromley Town Plan Action Group', an offshoot of Bromley Ratepayers Association, claimed in 1965 to 'represent the point of view of the ordinary home loving man'[138]—cost-conscious, nostalgic and protec-tive of home and local environment.

In the years down to 1973, when redevelopment appeared irresistible, the apparent unaccountability of local government encouraged guerrilla conservationism by grassroots groups, and much friction developed be-tween the two levels. In the changing context of the midseventies, how-ever, the gap between the two diminished, and householder politics came increasingly to set the tone of suburban Conservatism.

In reality the threat to residential areas had never been as pressing as many people imagined. Whereas local authorities had pursued town-centre redevelopment energetically, out of a conviction that without it their areas would die, no such incentive applied in residential areas. While there were many instances of planning authorities being unnecessarily in-dulgent towards the private developer, most councils understood that in-discriminate development could blight their locale. Many also felt uncom-fortable about their own relative weakness before the determined developer under the existing planning system and were often as keen as the householder groups to create Conservation Areas. Eventually over-coming their instinctive reclusiveness, some councils allowed local groups to scrutinise planning applications as they appeared;[139] indeed, the Old Chis-wick Protection Society 'established cordial relations with Officers of the Borough Council and have been able to discuss many proposals informally before official notification has been received.'[140] 'Planning, once a dirty word, is now seen as an ally to those interested in preserving that which is desirable of preservation', argued a residents association journal in Eastcote.[141]

Meanwhile the frosty financial climate in which councils found themselves in the midseventies, from the pricking of the property bubble in 1973 through the OPEC crisis to Anthony Crosland's curbs on local authority expenditure in 1975, ended the era of local authority boosterism. 'Do we, after all, really need planners when there is little growth in population or the economy?', asked the journalist David Wilcox, assessing the outlook for Greater London in 1976.[142] 'Can we afford £22 million worth of civic pride?', asked one local newspaper in September 1974, as Sutton entertained second thoughts about the parts of its town-centre scheme not already completed.[143] With the conservation movement gaining strength just as the property boom collapsed, the sense that endless redevelopment was inevitable diminished. So did tension between householder groups and local authorities. In the midseventies the threats to the suburbs came increasingly from outside. The related dangers from the relocation of inner-city council tenants to outer London and proposals to build on the Green Belt drew Conservative councils and householders together.

These threats intensified in the early seventies, as the Department of the Environment and the Greater London Council contemplated assertive action to relieve London's housing problem. The department established an Action Group on London Housing in 1971 to propose possible remedies. The group's membership was cross-party and did include representatives from the outer boroughs, but whatever its composition, any activist proposals for new house building in London were likely to be directed at the more spacious parts of suburbia. The group's first report, in 1972, claimed that land for 170,000 homes would need to be found by 1981.[144]

The report's identification of only 499 acres of what it called 'tatty land' within the Green Belt was relatively cautious,[145] but it came at a time when the whole Green Belt concept was coming under attack. The GLC's planners had long worried that the effect of the Green Belt was to strangle London's natural growth, 'like an iron band around an oak tree.'[146] In February 1973 this concern was given weighty backing in the report of the public inquiry into the Greater London Development Plan, which argued that the Green Belt served to inflate land values within London, increasing the cost of building and impeding attempts to relieve London's housing crisis.[147] This criticism was echoed in the same year in an influential academic attack on containment policy by the urban geographer Peter Hall and three collaborators in *The Containment of Urban England*. Hall et al.

attacked the Green Belt for reinforcing existing social divisions within the city and creating 'a civilised British version of *apartheid*.'[148] It was argued that the narrow aim of preventing urban sprawl had been pursued at the expense of the broader social objectives of postwar planning policy: 'the cost of this containment is expensive houses, fewer houses, of smaller size on smaller plots of land.'[149] In similar vein, in September 1973, Hillingdon's director of planning alarmed householders by asking 'if the Green Belt is, in fact, a blessing or not. You can't have a rigid planning policy for all time.'[150]

The conjunction of political pressure to ease inner London's housing problems and intellectual criticism of the Green Belt appeared menacing to suburban residents. Predominantly Conservative voices in the suburbs became fundamentalist defenders of Labour's postwar settlement, at least in its planning aspects: 'The plain fact is that long ago it was decided that haphazard building is not the way to solve London's housing problems. Housing needs were examined in detail and a positive housing policy evolved in which places for houses were nominated, and at the same time it was resolved that there should be a ring of countryside around London into which houses should not go.'[151] 'Before Labour councillors or GLC start earmarking Green Belt land for housing, they should remember that it is the purpose of the new towns to take the London overspill.'[152] 'Although houses have got to be found for people to live in, there are plenty of stinking holes that could be built on', one Harrow resident argued lyrically in 1971.[153] Conscious that 'precedence is a dangerous thing in town planning',[154] defenders of the Green Belt adopted an uncompromising stance towards development, for fear that one concession would so tarnish an area as to encourage future applications and in the knowledge that Green Belt land, once covered, could not easily be reclaimed.[155] 'We must redouble our efforts to defend every square foot of this heritage', argued an Enfield conservationist, 'which, once lost, is gone for ever.'[156]

On this question the borough authorities were generally at one with most of their residents. In 1964 a request to planning authorities from the Ministry of Housing and Local Government to volunteer Green Belt land for possible housing development had yielded only seventy-five acres of dispensable land.[157] Harrow resolved in 1968 to resist *any* Green Belt development which involved the loss of open space.[158] The same applied in Enfield, where, in 1974, the chair of the Housing Committee, while acknowledging that development land in the borough was running out, reaffirmed that 'the council is determined to protect the Green Belt to the bitter end.'[159] Even marginal infringement of the Green Belt was resisted for fear that the expansionary power of the metropolis, if unchecked, would threaten the essence of suburbia. Like 'the industrial revolution, whose needs created the dreadful industrial towns of the north, . . . the administrative machine that is London has created one continuous sprawl. It must be opposed.'[160]

Housing Conflicts

Concern over new building was intensified by the more specific anxiety caused by the threat of overspill housing and the decanting into the suburbs of inner-London residents who could not otherwise have afforded to move there. The fourth report of the Action Group on London Housing, in September 1974, called outspokenly for greater energy to be displayed by suburban councils in this respect. The group criticised five outer boroughs for using barely half the land they had declared available for public housing in 1972; Sutton had built only 170 local authority dwellings since the beginning of that year, which, the group said, 'seems to us a disaster.' The group professed itself 'horrified' by councils' failure to assemble data on land availability, and 'concerned at Outer Borough Council attitudes which claim that the pleasantness of their Borough is at stake and that they are therefore prevented from taking any significant steps to help London as a whole.'[161]

Suburban authorities feared that enclaves of council housing would 'disrupt and polarise the social structure in their Boroughs.'[162] Social distinctions and rivalries within the suburbs were, of course, nothing new. Investigating Sidcup in 1962, J. W. M. Thompson was told by a long-term resident that 'there are more castes here than in India.' Thompson identified five distinct groups: the 'rural rearguard', pining for the country community that had vanished; the 'old villagers', what remained of the agricultural working class; the 'semi-detached settlers', living in Sidcup but working in the centre and focused there; the council tenants; and the 'reluctant exiles', forced to leave Central London flats 'as their families grew faster than their incomes.' Between the wars the tension between different groups had been 'frightful', as one interwar settler remembered: 'you would have thought we were lepers or something.' Almost parodically, the golf club had been the fulcrum of local snobbery: 'it was a real gentleman's club then, just as Sidcup was a gentleman's place.' Significantly, though, Thompson's informant acknowledged that by 1962 the golf club was 'positively cosmopolitan': 'I haven't heard of anyone being rejected for a long time.'[163] Gradually the subtle social distinctions that had once structured suburban society resolved themselves into one major division, between the owner-occupier majority and the rest—particularly council tenants.

Those who had made sacrifices in order to become home owners often saw those with homes provided by a council as free riders. In January 1974 one correspondent told the *Croydon Advertiser* that he had spent two years raising the deposit on a house:

> Now I am established in my house, paying approximately £100 per month in mortgage repayments, rates, maintenance charges, ground rent, etc. Please do not tell me that I should not be bitter if a council tenant were to be moved in next door to me, paying only a tiny fraction of my outlay and having no financial interest in the house. Such a tenant would undoubtedly have a family, while my wife and I, in our desire to become independent, will have to wait several years before even considering having children. While I have no objection whatever to individual council tenants, we know just how unsavoury a neighbourhood can become when large numbers of irresponsible people are housed together.[164]

Ratepayers in Havering were told that on average the rent paid by council tenants in the borough covered only 43 percent of the economic cost of their housing.[165] That was assuming that they paid it at all, tenants being seen as unduly liable to run up arrears of both rent and rates and improperly indulged by councils when they defaulted ('*You* try not bothering to pay *your* rates when they are due. The issue of a summons will follow automatically.').[166] It became the received opinion of householder groups that the 'standard of [GLC] accommodation [is] too high' and that the 'weekly income of Council Tenants often exceeds that of private Tenants and Owner Occupiers.'[167]

Conversely, some of the relatively few instances of discontent in the *Harrow Observer* interviews came from council tenants: 'I don't like living here. It's not a very friendly area and is certainly not as good as it looks'; 'I detest living here. These four years have been four years too long.'[168] In 1973 residents of the new Headstone Lane council estate in Harrow complained of victimisation by locals: 'Some people have made it very clear that we are just not wanted here. . . . Teenagers come around here breaking bottles, shouting and swearing and knocking on our doors and running away late at night. These people live in other parts of the area.'[169]

Such animosities were as old as overspill social housing itself, but tensions were heightened in the seventies, as owner occupation became the dominant form of private tenure in the suburbs and, at the same time, the GLC and some inner boroughs sought more aggressively to relieve inner-London housing pressure by vigorous overspill policies. As the capital's strategic housing authority, the Greater London Council had sought to step up building in the suburbs, even under Conservative control in the early 1970s.[170] With the return of a radical Labour administration at County Hall in 1973 the pressure increased, animated by a conviction that the outer-London boroughs had previously failed to pull their weight in tackling the housing problem. The combative Gladys Dimson, the GLC's Housing Development chair, told Bromley and Richmond that there could be no 'no-go areas' for council tenants in their boroughs, warning that the GLC 'will no longer go cap in hand to the boroughs and say "please may we have some land." We must build and we will build.'[171] In October 1974 the GLC's *Strategic Housing Plan for London* highlighted the difficulties caused by boroughs' tendency to provide social housing only for their own residents, even if their own housing problem was limited: a major obstacle to resolving London's housing problem was 'the unwillingness of many Outer London boroughs to provide either land or dwellings for the wider purpose.'[172]

The boroughs inevitably resisted, confident in the support of the majority of their electorate. 'I'd be failing in my duty if I let Sutton be turned into a massive housing estate', announced Sutton's Housing Committee chairman in 1979 in response to a threatened influx of Lambeth council tenants into his borough: 'the ratepayers don't want it.'[173] In return for agreeing to a 101-flat council block in Hendon, with 70 percent of the occupiers nominated by the GLC, Barnet Council insisted on a six-foot-high fence around the development. The neighbours, who had apparently understood that the building would consist of 'private homes for selected civil servants', still urged the Council to 'take action to protect their interests as citizens seeking to maintain a high value placed on properties in the road and the area.'[174] In Bromley, as Ken Young and John Kramer have shown, the majority Conservative group became steadily more attentive to the views of their residents as the threat of the Liberal revival—evident across London suburbia in 1973—became clear. The borough council outmanoeuvred a succession of GLC housing chairmen, none of whom 'succeeded in placing any more low-income public housing in the borough than its leaders were prepared to accept.' The borough council agreed to build twenty-five hundred units of social housing in five years to stave off the threat of GLC building in the borough, but with a view eventually to selling the council homes to their occupiers. In 1974 it resolved to lift all restrictions on the sale of council houses.[175]

In Havering the ratepayers groups which enjoyed repeated success in borough council elections reversed their earlier opposition to council-house sales in 1967, on the grounds that 'the Council house tenant is no longer the former slum dweller who has obtained accommodation the like of which he had never seen before, but a thriving member of an unsubsidised society.'[176] Their misgivings about selling off municipal assets remained but were increasingly being outweighed by the concern that 'housing finance was going through the roof.' Council-house sales thus came to be seen not just as a step towards a property-owning democracy but also as a means of rate relief. By extension 'it is pertinent to ask whether council housing as such is really a long-term solution to housing problems anyway.'[177] It was argued that 'every encouragement to purchase a home of their own in the private sector as soon as their finances permit should be an accepted part of local housing policy.' By the midseventies, with ratepayer councillors holding the balance of power on the council, Havering's Housing Aid Centre was offering 'sound, unbiased advice' to council tenants as to their potential for home ownership.[178] A Department of the Environment circular of 1976, asking local authorities to explain the slow pace of council house building in London, evinced unabashed resistance from some of the outer boroughs: Havering stressed that 'each new dwelling incurs a considerable loss', with rents covering only a fifth of the cost of new buildings, while Kingston suggested that 'real housing need is not as desperate as it is often made out to be.'[179]

Anti-Socialism

By the mid-1970s, then, tensions between developer Conservatism and householder Conservatism had given way to a shared determination to protect the Green Belt, to resist the intrusion of council tenants into outer London and to challenge the legitimacy of social housing. Suburban politics gained a marked anti-socialist tone as a result, which was sharpened by the startling increases in local taxation following the introduction in 1974 of new methods of calculating central-government support for local authorities. In 1975–76, for instance, outer-London boroughs faced average increases of no less than 62 percent (against 53 percent in inner London), with Waltham Forest ratepayers looking at an 85 percent rise.[180] Conservative councils generally sought to blame the Labour GLC: Bromley included in the council minutes in September 1975 a table showing the rise in the rate burden since 1965, the most visible features of which were the

78 percent increase in the GLC's demands for 1974–75 and the 96 percent hike in 1975–76.[181] At the meeting to determine Havering's rate for 1975–76, the Conservative leader of the council called for the GLC's abolition—a demand echoed by local ratepayer groups, concerned that 'there seems to be developing a determined effort by the GLC to "boss the boroughs about"', especially in outer London.[182]

So far as the rates were concerned, borough councils were indeed at the mercy not only of the GLC but also of Whitehall, which applied an apparently capricious regulation of central-government support under the new arrangements. Conservative suburban authorities were naturally ready to accuse the Labour government elected in February 1974 of deliberately channelling Whitehall's money away from Conservative outer suburbs.[183] The truth was more complex, but their concerns were not entirely baseless. The system had been overhauled in part because it was felt it had previously discriminated against inner-urban areas with declining populations; after 1974, areas with a high rating assessment per head of population were likely to lose grant. The Labour government inevitably *was* more concerned about the worsening inner-city crisis than the woes of the suburban ratepayer: the 1977 white paper on *Policy for the Inner Cities* explicitly advocated the use of the rate support grant in an effectively redistributionary way to alleviate inner-urban problems.[184] On top of all that, the government responded to the financial crisis of the midseventies by reducing central support to local authorities across the board.[185] Suburban councils' claims that the substantial rate rises of the seventies were not entirely their fault were therefore justified. Ratepayer groups and Conservative local authorities drew closer together in the midseventies in a shared opposition to the Labour government and the Labour GLC. Quixotic proposals for rate strikes were rejected.[186] Instead attention shifted to reforming the whole system of local taxation.

The rates were a tax on the home—the embodiment of suburbanity. Home owners saw them as a penalty for the years of thrift undergone to escape the rental sector: as Mrs Kathleen Flanagan of Ealing put it to the *Evening Standard* in 1975, 'We will shortly finish paying off our mortgage so the house will be ours but paying such high rates is almost like living in rented accommodation. We feel almost as though we are paying the rent to Ealing Council for living in the borough.' She had seen a 132 percent increase in her rate burden in five years. Even householder enthusiasm for home improvement faltered in the face of swelling rate demands. 'It's absolutely crazy', complained Reg Smith of Crouch End. 'I am now in the situation where I just cannot afford to carry out improvements to my house. They would only increase the rateable value and thereby increase my rates still further.'[187]

The inequity of the rating system was a familiar preoccupation. Within months of the creation of the new London boroughs in 1965, the Richmond Ratepayers Association had determined that 'local amenities should be paid for by *all* those who enjoy them and not by an irrationally selected few, . . . the householders.'[188] In 1972 one Ratepayers Association in Merton had conducted a level-headed investigation of possible alternatives to the rates in successive issues of its newsletter.[189] In the midseventies, though, resentment intensified towards this 'crude hut tax', 'probably the most unfair and idiotic tax ever devised in modern peacetime.'[190] It was commonly, if implausibly, suggested that ratepayers would soon find themselves simply unable to meet the substantial increases being imposed: 'some of us can no longer scrape any more money for rates, in consequence of which we would be liable for summonses and to have the bailiffs in to collect the rates in kind from our goods and chattels.'[191] In Sanderstead it was asserted, 'The Rating system is rapidly breaking down and this process cannot end happily for anyone. In our Democracy the law, like Government, can only operate by consent.'[192] Even Harrow's controller of financial services accepted that the rating system would be hard pressed to survive successive years of 50 percent increases.[193] His counterpart in Croydon faced a 'capacity audience' at a public meeting in January 1975, urging that 'something must be done, and soon, to relieve the householder of the ever-increasing burden of the outmoded rates levy. Proposals ranged from a local lottery to a transfer of the rates levy to local or national taxation.'[194] One Bromley association considered a proposal for 'a Poll Tax on all wage earners to lessen the burden on ratepayers.'[195] With a general eagerness to broaden the base of local taxation tempered by an acceptance of the difficulties inherent in such solutions as local income tax,[196] the idea of flat-rate per capita levy became seductive. The road to the Community Charge began in suburbia.

Conclusion

In the interwar years, consideration of London's suburbia had been driven by concerns over the threat to the countryside posed specifically by ribbon development along arterial roads and more generally by the capital's

restless expansion. The Green Belt legislation of 1938 had stilled those anxieties, allowing debate to focus on the place of suburbia in a settled metropolitan system. This debate helped determine the political identity of these
areas. With regard to party affiliation, of course, most were instinctively
Conservative, as suggested by Deverson and Lindsay's characterisation of
the worldview of Purlbridge South residents, blaming 'progress' for all they
disliked in the modern world: 'comprehensive schools, violence, traffic
jams, general unrest and the decline in the quality of life.'[197] The question
was rather that of the substance of Conservatism in the mature suburb,
which was settled in these years.

Initially debate revolved around the efforts of councils to pursue economic growth and autarky. These efforts foundered in part because London could not support twenty or thirty Croydons: the GLC envisaged
only six major strategic centres in its Greater London Development Plan
of 1969, and major retailers, already contemplating large out-of-town centres, thought the proliferation of small-scale malls across London 'perhaps
the most expensive exercise in the history of man.'[198] But 'Croydonisation'
also foundered because suburban householders rejected its inherent modernist aesthetic, in favour of conservationism and the protection of the
familiar local environment. From the late sixties, and definitively after
the the bursting of the property bubble in 1973–74, the emphasis shifted to
the question—latent in the 1965 local-government reform—of how far the
outer boroughs should be socially or fiscally integrated with the metropolis
as a whole: how far they should accept overspill housing, sacrifice the Green
Belt or subsidise the inner city.

Environmental arguments had galvanised householder activism, but
pitched small-c conservative residents groups and amenity societies against
their normally Conservative councils. Steadily, though, once councils
moved away from the modernising, managerial, 'Heathite' approach of the
development drive, once the local agenda came to emphasise issues on
which Tories at all levels knew their minds, and once it became easier to
identify external enemies, in the Labour government and the Labour GLC
in the mid-1970s, the interests of grassroots groups and Tory councils
melded, and a more potent and more militant local Conservatism emerged.
Growing grassroots influence brought a discernible shift to the right. The
label 'Thatcherite', with connotations of entrepreneurial dynamism, might
appear inappropriate for these resolutely undynamic groups, but the shift
did promote a Tory fundamentalism that Margaret Thatcher instinctively
shared and whose advocates saw her as a standard-bearer far preferable to

her predecessor as Tory leader. The emerging orthodoxy was protective of the home, home ownership and the green and pleasant land; hostile to planners, the rates and council tenants; defensive, nostalgic and vigorously anti-socialist. In policy terms, it envisaged curtailing social housing, selling off the existing council-housing stock, abolishing the GLC and replacing domestic rates, perhaps by a poll tax. Thatcher's Britain was the product of many influences, but not the least significant of them was the sound of the suburbs.

11

Containing Racism?

THE LONDON EXPERIENCE, 1957–1968

What sort of people are they in Little Rock, Arkansas', asked the *South London Press* as the crisis at Little Rock unfolded in September 1957, 'who look upon Negroes as sub-human—second-class members of the human race who mustn't mix with the white herrenvolk?'[1] The question was not entirely condescending; the editorial was prompted not just by events in Arkansas but also by a letter published in the paper three weeks earlier: 'Every month thousands of immigrants pour into London. Here in Brixton one can see West Indians, Irish, Poles, Cypriots, Maltese, Italians and Pakistanis. I must admit that I have not yet seen an Eskimo but no doubt there are one or two wandering around. Meanwhile the native cockney is slowly but surely disappearing.'[2] Londoners observed the culmination of age-old racial tensions in the United States just as the capital absorbed much of the first wave of postwar immigration from the West Indies. They understood that the implications of racial conflict in the US could not be ignored in a city fast becoming multiracial.

The *South London Press* appeared optimistic about the prospect: 'London is not a closed city, and, as the capital of the greatest European country it has always been a mecca for political refugees, displaced peasantry, persecuted minorities, or the ambitious who gave rise to the saying that our streets are paved with gold.... We need not be jealous of immigrants.'[3] A year later, though, in August–September 1958, the public-order threat posed by racial hostility was made clear when a racially motivated attack on a Swedish woman with a Jamaican husband prompted a week of disturbances in Notting Hill, in which the homes of the area's Black community were attacked by gangs of local whites.[4] Coming days after similar disturbances in Nottingham, the 'Notting Hill riots' advertised unambiguously the danger that Britain's inner cities could produce their own Little Rocks.

Promoting Integration

Concern that the absorption of new, Black, immigrant groups might prove traumatic had already galvanised a network of organisations devoted to easing the entry of the new communities.[5] Immigrant welfare came to preoccupy a voluntary sector whose future role was uncertain in the age of state welfare. The Beveridgean welfare state was 'colour blind', making no allowance for any disabilities encountered by nonwhite immigrant groups, while the casework approach characteristic of voluntary agencies was likely to be more appropriate to the problems of social adjustment faced by ethnic minorities. The Family Welfare Association, which, in its earlier guise as the Charity Organisation Society, had pioneered social casework in Britain, sponsored the creation of a Citizens Advice Bureau in the Borough of Lambeth, containing the immigrant reception area of Brixton, as early as 1954, offering advice on social services to clients of all races but employing 'a coloured West Indian social worker' specifically to deal with the Black community.[6] In 1955 the 'Paddington Project' was launched to advise and support the growing Black community of that part of Northwest London, with the Paddington Overseas Students and Workers Committee—an umbrella group of left-liberal and philanthropic groups interested in race issues—growing out of the project in 1956. Notting Hill provided, though, the main impetus for the expansion of voluntary activity in this field: as the secretary of the London Council of Social Service (LCSS) wrote late in 1958, 'the disturbances have shaken the complacency of many officials and social workers who previously would not recognise the need to encourage active measures to help towards the integration of the coloured population in local communities.'[7]

Within weeks of the riots an emergency meeting had been convened by the mayor of Kensington, the borough in which the events occurred. It convened a Special Committee to consider race relations in London and urged the setting up of consultative committees in neighbouring boroughs to promote racial integration. In early December 1958 the Home Office, alarmed by Notting Hill, 'had come to the conclusion that what was needed was ... the creation of groups of people of goodwill who could help to create an atmosphere in which integration could take place.'[8] A wave of goodwill was consequently released in London, and by September 1960 the Migrant Services Division of the West Indies Federation could identify no fewer than seventy-four local groups in the capital geared to the promotion of better race relations.[9] Nine of them were in North Kensington / Notting Hill, which became a magnet for London's philanthropists— much as the East End had in the late nineteenth century. Race work became the new 'slumming': 'will too many do-gooders pave the path to Notting HELL?', the *Kensington Post* asked in October 1959.[10] Less than a year after the riots, the London Council of Social Service was concerned 'about the position in Kensington and the number of different people who are trying to do something for the West Indian problem, none of whom are in touch with each other, and few of whom really know the borough.'[11]

By the mid-1960s the LCSS was still receiving half a dozen inquiries every week from people anxious to do voluntary work with immigrants.[12] Those involved in this work feared that the tensions generated by the tightening of apartheid in South Africa and by civil rights conflicts and urban unrest in the United States might produce parallels at home. They considered local integration projects 'an urgent necessity if the coloured immigrants are to be assimilated into the ordinary life of the community, and segregation, which is deplored by all, is to be avoided.'[13] They aimed, in the words of the Paddington Council of Social Service, 'to encourage integration by persuading the West Indians to participate more fully [in English social and civic life] and English people to be more tolerant.'[14] Thus they promoted mixed-race associational and advice organisations through which, it was hoped, 'coloured people could be brought into the life of the white community',[15] but they also believed, as the mayor of Kensington told the Kensington Inter-Racial Committee immediately after the disturbances, that 'preventing race riots will be only part of the work': one West Indian member called for the committee to attack 'the ignorance and prejudice which underlies the rioting. For this a great campaign of moral re-education is called for.'[16]

It will not be argued here that integration, as understood by the white liberals involved in antiracist campaigns, was ever realised or likely to be realised. Nor will it be argued that the 'campaign of moral re-education' actually succeeded in removing racism from the cockney mindset. Too many white Londoners had 'no intention of being dragooned or cajoled into joining multi-racial get-togethers, picnics or tea parties to please persons who may wish to turn this country into a polyglot conglomeration of hybrids' for attempts to encourage mixed-race socialising to succeed.[17] The preference of the Black community for all-Black clubs and bars, which white liberals considered pernicious,[18] soon became clear, while a fear of being marginalised fuelled that resentment of white management of Black politics expressed trenchantly in Michael Abdul Malik's autobiography.[19] Above all, although legislation in 1965 and 1968 would make discrimination in pubs and clubs, in housing and in the workplace harder to get away with, it would be difficult to demonstrate that Londoners had been morally reeducated in racial matters by the late 1960s. In February 1965 the advisory officer to the National Committee for Commonwealth Immigrants was writing, 'It has been apparent for some months that the racial situation in Britain has been intensifying in a way that can only be considered as rather alarming, and that all our efforts need to be doubled, indeed trebled. New trends such as the increase in the formation of militant groups at both extremes, the hardening of public opinion, the increasing bitterness of the immigrants and the continual stress on controls, evasions and forged passports rather than the positive work of integration have created a situation totally different from that of even two years ago.'[20] The wave of support for Enoch Powell's 'Rivers of Blood' speech in April 1968 would reinforce these concerns.

The argument here is rather that it would prove possible to 'construct' a narrative of race politics that did not require the capture of Londoners' hearts and minds—that a combination of liberal prompting and political circumstances, enhanced by real concern that London could erupt as Birmingham, Alabama, or Watts erupted, enabled antiracist arguments to become dominant despite the persistence of a truculent but muted racism, with the result that, in these years, no coherent counternarrative emerged.

Shaping Public Opinion

The Afro-Caribbeans were hardly London's first immigrant community, but they were the first major group for whom skin colour was the most distinctive point of difference. Awareness of US precedents engendered a concern that race would become the explanatory variable for any friction caused by the arrival of a new population with unfamiliar customs and attitudes. Initial reaction to Notting Hill was therefore characterised by a strained insistence that the events had not been primarily racially motivated. At an LCSS conference on West Indian integration in October 1958 the social anthropologist Sheila Patterson insisted that it would be 'errone-ous, and indeed harmful, to compare the British situation with that of South Africa or the Southern States, where the colour bar has for genera-tions been fixed in law, custom and the way of thinking of each individual inhabitant.' Drawing on her fieldwork in Brixton, she argued that the prob-lems were those of immigration rather than race and that 'the new West Indian migrants to Britain are passing through the same kinds of process in their relationships with the local population as do all other working-class economic migrants—the same processes as the Puerto Ricans in New York, the East European Jews in London's East End in the last century, or the Poles, Balts and Southern Irish in Britain since the end of the war. . . . If all visible differences were expunged, we should still be facing precisely the same problems of social and cultural differences and frictions.' In a statement as revealing of her fears as of her beliefs, she suggested that 'if we label it as a colour or racial situation now, or allow others to do so, we are half-way to making it into one.'[21]

The belief that racial tension reflected a wider malaise in the inner city was exemplified by the report of the Special Committee appointed by the mayor of Kensington shortly after the 1958 riots. The disturbances were attributed to ingrained social problems characteristic not merely of inner London but of Notting Hill in particular. 'Many social workers', it con-cluded, 'are . . . of the opinion that the "racial riots" were merely one symp-tom of the serious social disintegration which has existed in this district for a long time', namely mental health problems, a high suicide rate, juve-nile delinquency ('there has been extensive adolescent violence—not by any means exclusively against coloured people'), problem families, and so on.[22] Similarly, Ivy Harrison, the social worker appointed by the neigh-bouring Metropolitan Borough of Paddington to work with the area's Black community, argued that working-class hostility to Blacks in her bor-ough 'appears to be largely due to material problems rather than innate prejudice.'[23] It followed, of course, that the underlying problems should be addressed—the Kensington Special Committee called for 'the immediate development of a combined sociological and social welfare operation' in the area[24]—but the more urgent need was to promote a process of public education to guard against the danger that resentment of a deprived social environment would find an outlet in racial hostility.

Patterson's work in South London suggested that 'about coloured people, Brixtonians, like other Londoners, still retain a lot of vague and erroneous notions.' She inferred that 'Britain's colonial past, perpetuated

Run-down housing in North Kensington, photographed by Roger Mayne in 1960. (Roger Mayne Archive/Mary Evans Picture Library)

until recently in outmoded history and geography books, has left the impression that coloured people live in African jungles, and are primitive, savage, promiscuous and inferior' but also that 'the attitudes of South London workers are by no means set hard in hostility.' The public mindset was, if not exactly a tabula rasa, at least open to enlightenment. Patterson saw assimilation and integration as future projects; the realistic aim for the present was the attainment of that modus vivendi which she thought characterised the 'accommodation' stage:

> From the host society we may expect to hear local people saying 'well, there's good and bad in all races', rather than staring and perhaps drawing away at the proximity of a coloured person in the street, the pub or the church. We may look for them to offer new West Indian neighbours the customary welcome and cup of tea and courtesy to worship (if they worship at all) side by side with them; to let their children play together; and to refrain from generalised and prejudiced remarks about the group as a whole. These are the modest indices of adaptation and acceptance in the accommodation stage.[25]

Similarly, Joan Maizels's 1959–60 survey of Willesden residents found a core of around 10 percent who were irreconcileable racists,[26] but she suggested that 'the majority of the residents, while not highly prejudiced, nevertheless have reservations and doubts about the coloured immigrants. . . . The teaching that they have received from school would seem to have left considerable numbers of them with false impressions as to the cultural and social background from which West Indians have come and as to the nature of their ways of life. It is of great importance, therefore, to correct these impressions and to disseminate the correct information in order to strengthen and to support those residents who have the ability to modify their views.'[27]

Interviews with Notting Hill residents just after the riots, when racial hostility might have been expected to be at its peak, suggest that the attitude of the host population was indeed complex. One woman in St Stephen's Gardens complained about the noise from her Black neighbours upstairs and the state of the lavatory but 'vehemently denies having any colour prejudice, and it seems that with some of the previous coloured tenants she was on quite friendly terms'; an unskilled labourer of Faraday Road, running a children's playground, 'raised the question of the colour bar himself, and said most emphatically that we should ignore it', as 'contact with coloured boys and the opportunity for conflict without malice offered by boxing would be very educative'; a man in Wheatstone Road criticised 'this colour-bar nonsense, which was unfair as we're willing to use their services if we need them, even if we don't like them being *here*'; an Irish scrap-metal worker 'when he first came was scared of coloured people (Darkies he called them, but the word was used as pure description, without overtones). But they were very good to him when he was green on the job, better than his own countrymen would have been, so now he says live and let live'; a sixty-year-old woman had 'nothing personal against coloured people as her husband was a coloured man from the West Indies, whom she described as "a man coming from a very good family with a lot of money"', but she thought 'that coloured men should not be allowed to come in this country as it means more unemployment, more dole and overcrowding' ('She feels that given employment, these coloured people behave well. . . . The woman is not prejudicial but opposes immigration in numbers'), while a woman in Lancaster Road 'said she thought those who wouldn't work should be sent back. She didn't mind the ones who stayed here' but asserted that 'the Blacks were not fit to live with White People.' These responses demonstrate the ambiguity in white attitudes, even on London's front line at a time of heightened tension.[28]

A West Indian man crossing the railway bridge at the northern end of Golborne Road, North
Kensington, 1961. (Roger Mayne Archive/Mary Evans Picture Library)

Given the malleability of public sentiment, antiracist activity sought to
ensure that the press not only avoided incendiary coverage of racial situa-
tions but actively promoted racial harmony. In a report presented to the
Kensington Special Committee within weeks of Notting Hill, D. Wallace
Bell of the Council of Christians and Jews advocated counselling the press
'to "play down", rather than "play up" the riots, in interest of preventing
their spread to new areas.' The Rank Organisation was persuaded not to
shoot the film *Sapphire*—a sympathetic account of a Black man's travails
in London—in Notting Hill.[29] Greatest attention was devoted to the local
press. At a National Council of Social Service meeting in September 1958,
'concern was expressed over the attitude of certain local London papers
whose headlines gave the impression that riots were likely to break out in
other areas. It was agreed that if further inflammatory headlines of this sort
were seen by committee members, they would send the paper at once to
the London Council [of Social Service] who would take the matter up
with the Press Council.'[30] Concluding, plausibly, 'that the best method of
inducing the local editors to attend a press conference would be to offer
them lunch',[31] the Paddington Overseas Students and Workers Committee
(POSWC) began in November 1958 a process of lobbying local newspapers

that would last for several years. It focused mainly on papers' readiness to carry adverts for rented accommodation specifying 'Europeans only' or even 'no coloured.' The newly formed Willesden International Friendship Council pursued this issue in its area, with some success; by 1961 the *Kilburn Times* had yielded to the extent that, it explained, 'when an advertisement including phrases like "Europeans only" or "no Irish" is offered to this newspaper over the counter, staff, in accordance with instructions, point out that some people may be offended and the advertiser is invited to amend it. If he is unwilling to do so and the wording is not deliberately offensive, the copy is accepted on the basis that, within reason, the customer is entitled to say what his advertisement shall contain.'[32] James McColl, the Labour MP and Paddington alderman who led the POSWC's campaign on this issue, noted that 'there was evidence that the editors were not happy about these [adverts], but were very much in the hands of their advertising managers': when it came to news coverage, he and his colleagues found themselves pushing at an opening door.

Notting Hill was the catalyst. Two months before the riots, a columnist in the *South London Press* (which circulated in Brixton) responded bullishly to criticism of the headline 'Jamaican in Love with a Girl of Fifteen': 'Why . . . was the fact of his being Jamaican so emphasised? I have no doubt it was to show the colour of his skin, which is an important factor here. The neighbours, for instance, would not fail to mention it. If the reporter said "a 23-year-old man", the reader would not have been given the full facts of the case. It is a pity, of course, that there should be colour prejudice in this country, but no good is done by pretending it does not exist.'[33] Immediately after Notting Hill the *South London Press* claimed that other newspapers were playing down the riots' racial dimension in order 'to show Americans and South Africans that we are not race conscious in this country', asserting fearlessly that 'the truth is that an island race resents immigration more than most other races.'[34] The implication that the *South London Press* was out of line seems, though, gradually to have dawned on its editorial staff, and Patterson noted in 1963 that 'the *South London Press* has increasingly emphasised in editorials its view that the "colour problem" is simply a problem of housing, unemployment, poverty and social evils for which the immigrants are not responsible and should not be blamed.' More generally, she concluded that while 'the local press cannot be said to have played an actively sponsoring role . . . over the years the manner of reporting events . . . involving coloured people, has become more restrained, particularly in the matter of headlines.'[35]

Barely a month after Notting Hill, one correspondent to the *West London Observer* complained that 'the local newspapers have followed the lead of the national newspapers and relegated the subject of racial dissension to the background. It appears from a close study of the local press that editorial policy is being dictated from without.'[36] This was implausible, but the suggestion that local papers were avoiding inflammatory statements on race appears justified. Editorial reactions to Notting Hill had shown genuine alarm that 'racial riots suggestive of the KU-KLUX-KLAN have brought a new and deplorable chapter to West London' and consensual criticism of 'those misguided individuals who tried to sow the seeds of hatred between white and coloured people.'[37] Subsequent editorial comment on race, itself relatively rare, seldom strayed far from uncontentious appeals to harmony. Picture editors in particular responded to the call first issued by Wallace Bell at the 1958 Kensington meeting, urging the press to 'feature instances of harmonious relations between coloured and white people.'[38] Photos of Black and white children playing together in racial innocence, such as that carried by the *Kilburn Times* in May 1959—headed, 'It's a kids' world—one world!'—made good copy. The caption read, 'Their politics stop at "Can we go out to play?" and there's no colour bar among these children of Portnall Road, Paddington. Theirs is a happy world. "Those silly grown-ups should listen to us for a change", they seem to be thinking.'[39]

In June 1959 a correspondent to the *Marylebone Mercury* complained that 'normally the Press is controlled by groups of interests which frequently try to mould public opinion. Since both Conservative and Labour policies are identical as regards the matter under discussion [immigration], we must expect to find this attitude mirrored in the press.'[40] The major parties' positions on immigration may not have been identical, but neither party sought to stir the issue. Intrinsically nationalistic, the Conservatives were inhibited from exploiting concern over immigration by a residual concern for imperial unity and, particularly, Conservative governments' responsibility for the immigration of the mid-1950s. Labour's long-standing internationalism generally held firm, whatever the misgivings of some of its working-class supporters. 'Puzzled', writing to the *Kilburn Times* on the eve of the 1959 general election, affected surprise that 'none of the political parties in this election mentions the grave problems caused by unrestricted immigration into this small overcrowded country from Eire and the Commonwealth', which he blamed on 'the short-sighted, couldn't care less attitude of the politicians in this matter that has caused several of [his] friends to say they will abstain from voting in protest.'[41]

It was this sense of a party cartel which encouraged the Union Movement leader Sir Oswald Mosley to stand for North Kensington—the seat containing Notting Hill—in 1959.[42] As Patrick Keatley put it in the *Guardian*, 'the Mosleyites have the virtue—if that is the word—of putting into blunt, ugly phrases what some people were prepared to think, but not to say out loud.'[43] Mosley's intervention might have been expected to encourage candidates from the major parties to bid for the white racist vote. Indeed, George Rogers, the sitting Labour MP in Kensington North, with a slim three-thousand-person majority, did advocate a limit to future immigration. The obstacle to this electoral strategy, though, was that constituencies where white voters might resent the Black influx were likely already to contain many Black voters. Blacks from Commonwealth countries gained the vote in the same way as white Canadians, Australians, and so, and although Black registration levels were generally lower—in Willesden around half the Blacks eligible to vote were apparently absent from the register[44]—this is likely to have reflected the political inertia often displayed by new immigrant communities rather than the chicanery used to keep Blacks off the rolls in the US South: there was no real 'voting rights' dimension to the race question in Britain. Thus Rogers's decision to play up the immigration issue not only aroused the lasting resentment of his constituency party but also prompted protests from Black constituents and apparently encouraged many Blacks to vote Liberal.[45] Rogers held the seat, but his majority fell below nine hundred.

As the summary by the Institute of Race Relations (IRR) put it, 'the parties did not ignore the coloured vote but it seemed to be difficult to assess.'[46] When this consideration was added to the mixed opinions within the white electorate, optimal political strategy became hard to discern. The political scientist L. J. Sharpe found uncertainty over the issue even at a Conservative Party selection meeting[47] (to choose a candidate to contest Brixton in the first Greater London Council elections in 1964): 'There were questions to the candidates, one of which contained a very hostile reference to immigrants. The first candidate's reply was a vehement and unequivocal plea for racial tolerance, praising the part coloured immigrants were playing in the Health Service. Instead of criticism from the audience, or even silence, this reply was greeted with scattered and polite applause. And it was clear from the somewhat garbled replies of the other candidates to the same question that they too sensed that there was a conflict of emotions and attitudes in the audience.'[48] With no clear-cut party division over the issue, individual candidates contesting seats with a large immigrant presence devised freelance responses to the race question. Robert Taylor, Conservative candidate for Battersea North, asserted that 'it is fundamental to the greatness of our Commonwealth that all its citizens should be able to come to this country. But that right carries with it the obligation to maintain the same living standards as their new neighbours.' He attacked Labour-controlled Battersea Council for neglecting its powers to prevent overcrowding among immigrants.[49] The Tory candidate for Brixton likewise criticised the Labour council for allowing conditions in the borough to deteriorate; this was taken to be a veiled attack on the immigrant community and earned him a vote of censure from the Labour majority in the council.[50] The IRR listed North Kensington, St Pancras North (where a National Labour candidate campaigned on the race issue) and Hampstead (where Labour ran a Black candidate) as the only seats in the country where race was prominent in the campaign. By the time of the 1964 general election Alfred Sherman could speak of a 'general rule that the parties are still strong enough to prevent widespread popular hostility towards immigration and immigrants irrupting directly into party politics.'[51]

In national politics race was indeed a second-order issue in the years after Notting Hill. A handful of individuals obsessed about it, and it could head the political agenda at moments of prominence—the riots themselves, the murder of Kelso Cochrane in 1959, Enoch Powell's 'Rivers of Blood' speech—but it generally lacked staying power. A referendum might have produced a majority for the unfeasible policy of repatriation and very probably would have revealed a majority for controls on future entrants, but no such plebiscite was on the cards. Instead race fought for priority with other more obviously salient issues. Two months after Powell's speech, immigration was considered the most urgent problem facing the country by 27 percent of respondents in a Gallup poll; in May 1970, at the time of a general election in which Powell's views received much attention, the figure stood at 10 percent. Otherwise it hardly ever rose above a low-single-figure percentage.[52] These national figures were presumably deflated by the inclusion of areas untouched by Black immigration, and there is no way of isolating the London returns; but Joan Maizels's 1960 work in Willesden, one of London's principal Black reception areas, is suggestive. Sixty-nine percent of a sample of 312 Willesden residents who were asked to specify social changes in the area in recent years failed to mention immigration, although the Black influx was the most conspicuous recent change in the area.[53] Maizels herself accepted that 'the majority of English people showed a greater antipathy towards coloured immigrants than towards other foreigners', but she found the typical host response to local Blacks to be one of 'avoidance rather than aggressiveness.'[54] Patterson likewise found that 'there have been West Indians in Brixton for over eight years now, and they no longer attract any attention': 'As one Brixtonian said to me: "we didn't fancy them at first, but we've got used to them now."'[55]

In 1965 the National Committee for Commonwealth Immigrants opposed the appointment of special liaison officers in established immigrant areas such as Tower Hamlets, Newham, Haringey, Brent and (North) Kensington on the grounds that 'in these areas, whilst there are of course problems, their [Blacks'] presence has become accepted as part of life, and whilst a great deal of work can be done quietly, to appoint a special officer at this late date specifically to deal with their integration is in fact a retrogressive step.'[56] It is unnecessary to suggest implausible racial harmony in London's immigrant quarters, or to dispute the evidence of daily discrimination, to infer that few people in these areas considered the immigration question their most pressing concern. Race could never shape the politics of inner London—let alone the rest of Britain—as it shaped the politics of South Africa or the US South. Instead the race question was itself refracted by other issues.

'I'm No Racialist, but . . .'

Had late-1950s Britain been as preoccupied with vice as it was with 'Teddy Boy' violence, the alleged involvement of some Notting Hill Blacks with local prostitution rings might have caused the 1958 disturbances to be portrayed in a different light. As it was, in the words of one correspondent to the *Marylebone Mercury*, 'the sudden "discovery" of coloured brothels, etc (so-called but not so-proven), are presenting our white aggressors with the opportunity of parading as crusaders for morality and decent living instead of being unmasked as the vile reality they are—fore-runners of large-scale apartheid practices in this country',[57] and as the sceptical *South London Press* complained, the race riots of Notting Hill and Nottingham were widely represented as 'just a new juvenile crime, a variation on gang fights.'[58] It had a point. The minister of the Congregationalist Paddington Chapel described race rioters as 'mainly hooligans who, if there were not one single coloured resident in London, would still find some excuse for their perverted notion of "fun and games."'[59] Wallace Bell's report for the Kensington Special Committee put 'teen-age hooliganism looking for a new outlet' first in its list of immediate causes of the riots;[60] nine youths were eventually convicted and given exemplary prison sentences for their actions at Notting Hill. Sheila Patterson's claim that 'juvenile ruffianism . . . is a far greater problem in this country than the so-called colour or race problem' obviously squared with her eagerness to play down the racial dimension of the disturbances,[61] but the 1959 interviews with Notting Hill residents suggest that this assumption was widespread. One respondent from Wheatstone Road held that 'the cause of last year's trouble was "the youth element with nothing to do"'; a man from Lancaster Road 'said that he knew some youngsters and their natural inclination was to go out looking for trouble. If they couldn't find motor bikes to pinch they would attack anybody. Whether they were coloured or not made no difference'; a trade unionist from the same street argued that the 'racial disturbances were due to "yoboes" [sic] who came in from other areas, and who were unorganised.'[62]

Organisation being thought beyond 'the simple minds of teddy boys',[63] orchestration by the Union Movement or other fascist sympathisers was widely assumed. The Fulham and Chelsea Trades Council demanded the indictment of people circulating inflammatory leaflets in the area, asking 'that those responsible are punished at least as severely as those who were their dupes.'[64] Two weeks after the riots, the South Paddington Young Conservatives 'agreed that much of the recent troubles in Notting Hill were caused by the more unruly segments of the white population (probably stirred up by the fascists), and eager for any excuse to indulge in violence.'[65] Mosley's intervention in the 1959 North Kensington contest gave the charge weight.

'What is truly shocking is the revelation of the number of socially-resentful young people ready to be exploited by trouble-makers', wrote a correspondent to the *West London Observer* three weeks after the riots. 'There are frightening resemblances to the early days of the Hitler Youth; yet this is not the question that is being discussed.'[66] Fascist attempts to exacerbate racial tension touched a raw nerve. In October 1957 a writer to the *Marylebone Mercury* recalled his experience at Mosley's 1934 Olympia rally: 'As a nursing orderly, of long standing, I attended casualties and dressed wounds. . . . I am appalled to see the appearance of fascists once more. Public halls are let for their meetings and hatred is now spread against coloured workers. Such race hatred is to be deplored.'[67] After Notting Hill a correspondent to the *Marylebone Mercury* described his experience: 'I noticed at the junction of Blenheim Crescent and Portobello Road the men of the type I used to see among the fascists of former days. A few émigrés from Europe were with them. . . . As four harmless negroes with police protection crossed the road and this section of British working men and the sprinkling of foreigners jeered, a rather slight chap said to me "but this is what I saw the crowds doing in Germany. They stood on the corners and jeered the Jews, like this."[68] The evidence of raw hatred evinced at Notting Hill enhanced the riots' impact. The *West London Observer* carried in its first issue after the events an uninhibited interview with a North Kensington resident with the chilling message that a train of urban violence was only just beginning:

> Believe me, mister, we are going to drive the niggers out of this area. First we are going to get them out of North Kensington, then Ladbroke Grove, then "The Town" and finally Westbourne Grove, where it all started. This has been brewing for a long time. Nottingham started it, and we took it up. Brixton will be next, it only needs a spark. People round here have had a lot to put up with. All these niggers live in filthy conditions and as soon as they got hold of a house, white people find life is murder until they get out.... I tell you it won't be long until we get them out. This will go on every night until we do.[69]

The paper, like most witnesses, was convinced that the disturbances had been provoked by white agitators: 'faults have not been confined to one side, but from what *WLO* staffmen saw, it is obvious that most of the aggression has been committed by whites, though in some instances coloured men have retaliated in the same way.'[70]

No fully fledged 'victim narrative' took root in the autumn of 1958, but in an age of welfare and economic management the view emerged that racial tension reflected a poor urban environment that should never have been allowed to develop. 'The coloured people are being made the scapegoats for conditions they did not create', one Camberwell resident wrote to the *South London Press*. 'We had slums, racketeering, landlords and unemployment long before the immigrants arrived.'[71] 'We are all living in the same foul conditions, white and coloured alike', a former Willesden councillor wrote to the *Kilburn Times*: 'there is only one thing we can do, and that is to see, wherever and whenever conditions warrant a change, that we proceed to put the pressure on those who are responsible, not help those responsible by quarrelling among ourselves.'[72] In late September, the Paddington and St Marylebone Trades Council resolved that 'the root evils of unemployment and the housing shortage should be appreciated by us all as the true reason' for racial tension.[73]

This was a left-wing argument, often distinctly partisan, but it did echo a wider concern in London about housing conditions and housing shortage following the partial abolition of rent control in 1957. Maizels found that only 8 percent of her Willesden respondents in 1961 blamed Blacks for the housing shortage: 'More frequently mentioned were difficulties in finding rented accommodation, higher rents and prices. Other reasons included landlords' neglect of property, slow building progress and reduced security under the 1957 Rent Act.'[74] As the Teddy Boy panic subsided, concern over social conditions in general and the housing situation in particular proved more durable, providing a regular context for discussion of the race question: Patterson's suggestion, mentioned earlier, that the *South London Press* tended by 1963 to treat racial problems as symptoms of underlying housing or other social problems exemplifies that precisely.

Significantly, the racism evident at Notting Hill strengthened concerns about casually racialised language. The *South London Press* acknowledged a week after the riots,

> Colonialism created our public image of coloured folk as figures of fun to be tolerated with good humoured contempt as long as they entertain us, from birth as "piccaninnies" to their death as Uncle Tom, Uncle Remus or the coloured evangelists (whose angels are all black). We have not yet outgrown our colonial thinking, and the idea of equality of citizenship in the Commonwealth has yet to reach the backward areas of thought in the slums where race riots occur. . . . The thinking must change, and the climate of popular opinion has to be brought up to date by popular education in the scientific truths on race differences, which is a long process. We could start, at least, by forgetting the "little nigger boy" type of humour, which is out of date anyhow.[75]

This would take time, but a heightened sense of racial etiquette becomes apparent after 1958. Maizels, in constructing her Willesden research strategy in 1960, decided to ask respondents for their impressions of recent social change in the area, fearing that more direct questions about race would elicit insincere replies: 'attitudes which reveal antipathy to colour are beginning to be regarded with some disapproval, and more and more people are anxious that they should not appear hostile.'[76] The *Marylebone Mercury*'s decision, early in 1960, to publish a letter from a Notting Hill resident claiming, 'all coloured people are jealous of our accomplishments, our culture and our looks', brought a rebuke from the leader of the Labour opposition on Marylebone Council, expressing disappointment that the editors 'thought this letter fit for publication in a decent local newspaper.'[77] When the Paddington Labour Party ran two Black candidates for Westbourne Ward in the 1962 local elections, the wife of one of the Tory candidates ham-fistedly drew attention to the men's colour and asked how long they had lived in Paddington. It rapidly became clear that she had transgressed; Labour's political education officer asked whether the woman was suggesting that the two men 'should have stood under the names of (to borrow the idiom of her and her kind) Golly and Sambo, to make quite sure that everyone would know that "these two gentlemen are non-white."'[78]

The suggestion that the public-order legislation passed to curb the Blackshirts in 1936 be extended to cover incitement to racial hatred had been discussed at the LCSS's Caxton Hall conference on West Indians in London in October 1958 and was aired by an all-party deputation of London MPs which sought to draw the attention of Home Secretary R. A. Butler to the parlous situation in Notting Hill in June 1959.[79] Butler was reluctant to curb freedom of speech, but the case for incitement legislation continued to be aired in the local press. 'There should be some legislation against racial intolerance', one correspondent argued in the *Kilburn Times* in January 1960, again invoking the fight against fascism: 'Public opinion would be given a stronger lead and the psychological influence in the home, education and law would give heart to many who by now must be depressed by recent events. Western Germany is to legislate. We who fought for such fundamental freedoms have as much right to defend these and furthermore to honour those millions who were killed by the swastika.'[80] A month later a left-wing Labour councillor argued in the same paper, 'without such a clear stand we are open to retaliation when we protest against apartheid in South Africa and segregation in the Southern States of the USA', and the leader of the Labour minority on Paddington Council advocated fresh legislation against 'inflammatory propaganda.'[81] The Tory leader thought such legislation unnecessary, and it would never gain cross-party support; but the sustained call for legislation on the left does help explain the relative lack of controversy in London over the incitement provisions of the 1965 Race Relations Act.

However effective this legislation, the climate which produced it inhibited racist statements in public, and this was reflected in the way in which those who were critical of immigration and its consequences framed their comments. This was most obvious in the use of such disclaimers as 'I am no racialist, but . . .' to preface any comment on race matters, however intolerant: 'I've nothing against them, but I don't think I would entertain them in the house'; 'Nothing against them, but I wouldn't let rooms'; 'I'm not prejudiced against them, but I don't think they should share the same house as white people.'[82] The sincerity of such claims is irrelevant: what matters is their ubiquity. Thus counsel for the landlord of the Milkwood Tavern in Herne Hill, whose license was challenged in 1959 by five Jamaicans incensed by the pub's colour bar, dutifully maintained that his client 'has no prejudice against any man on the ground of colour or religion.'[83] A former coal miner who informed the readers of the *Marylebone Mercury* in 1962 that 'civilised men cannot compete with people who are accustomed to maintain themselves on a tin of cat food and a handful of rice' nonetheless made clear that his remarks had 'no particular bearing on colour, race or creed': 'I naturally included the members of the Commonwealth, but with no reference to any peculiarities they may be afflicted with, in feature or complexion.'[84]

The National Committee for Commonwealth Immigrants feared that the events of 1968—new restrictive immigration legislation and Enoch Powell's 'Rivers of Blood' speech—meant that 'for the first time opinion in this country appeared to accept as socially respectable the use of blatantly hostile language in public utterances on the subject of race and minority ethnic groups.'[85] Certainly the light-headedness engendered by Powell's speech in April caused several people temporarily to neglect the usual etiquette. In May 1968 Jock Cowan, secretary of the Paddington branch of the postal workers' union, shared with his members the aperçu that 'people from India, Africa, Greece, Malta and other countries' left lands of sunshine in order to come to 'a country with one of the worst climates in the world' because 'Great Britain is a gigantic Benevolent Fund for all and sundry who wish to be resident here.' Nonetheless, a week later, this insight having been leaked to the *Marylebone Mercury*, he wrote to 'make it quite clear' that he did not back Enoch Powell: 'I never have and never will. . . . I would also add that I represent coloured workers employed in the Post Office, and while they are the members of our union, they shall be represented to the full. . . . I would like to make it quite clear that I have nothing against the colour of a man's or woman's skin. These people cannot help where they were born, and, may I add, quite a number of them would not change their colour even if it were possible, as they are proud to be what they are.'[86] Powell's speech was in fact generally handled with caution by the local press in immigrant areas. The principal exception was the *South East London Mercury*, which went for broke with a front-page comment piece beginning, 'Let's face it, Enoch Powell was right.' With inner-London unemployment rising sharply in 1968, the article was accompanied by a photograph of two Black men scanning job adverts at the Greenwich employment exchange, though the paper still felt required to add, in captioning the photo, that 'many others [Blacks] are settled in regular work.'[87]

The *Mercury's* editorial was headed, 'Colour. Why Should We Hush It Up?' Shortly after Notting Hill, a letter in the *South London Press* had complained, 'whenever there is a burst of correspondence in your journal with regard to the vexed questions of relations between the British people and imported Afro-Asian migrants any white person who opposes such racial miscegenation is promptly denounced as a "race-hater."'[88] Over the ten years since the riots, it had become routine for opponents of immigration to allege that 'the present bad situation is one that has been imposed upon the electorate by a minority of politicians' anxious to enforce toleration: 'racial integration isn't wanted in Britain because aside from the opinions of the minority of intellectual cranks in Hampstead, a multi-racial society wasn't desired in the first place!'[89] A correspondent to the *West London Observer* in September 1958 alluded to the 'curious fact that most of those who talk loudest about racial tolerance do not themselves live among "shanty town coloureds"', while a writer to the *Marylebone Mercury* in January 1960 advocated moving all recent immigrants 'into Park Lane, or Belgravia, in those quiet squares': 'Who would not get something done then, I wonder.'[90] Another *Marylebone Mercury* correspondent asked, 'How many of our political hierarchy would react favourably to mixed marriages in their own families?', suggesting that 'if a national referendum were taken amongst British parents as to whether they would like their daughter to marry a coloured man, the answer would be a resounding "No!"' The government would never hold a race referendum, though, as one writer to the *Stratford Express* alleged, because 'it already knows the strength of public opinion.'[91] Much public reaction to Powell's speech expressed exhilaration that an élite taboo had been challenged—that Powell had 'said what no politician has had the courage to say for the past two decades', that 'he only said what an awful lot of people are thinking', that 'he had the guts to say what most of us are thinking': 'I agree with him completely and only wish I had the courage to voice my opinions as he did.'[92]

Complaints about conspiracies of silence generally indicate that the complainers feel excluded from debate. The core argument of this chapter has been that this feeling was justified, in that there were discernible reasons why public discussion of the race issue did not reflect the likely balance of public opinion. The aim has not been to applaud this, still less to lament it, but rather to point out its effect on the construction of the race debate. In short this was to ensure that no significant corpus of 'intellectual racist' thought evolved in this period. Laboured attempts to demonstrate white superiority on historical grounds or denunciations of mixed marriage and miscegenation were never lacking, though they tended to become less frequent—or to be published less frequently—in the years after Notting Hill. But there was little in the way of reasoned policy on offer in opposition to a liberal orthodoxy which, however criticised, was articulate and coherent. By May 1967 one correspondent to the *Hornsey Journal* was ready to throw in the towel: 'I fail to see why it is so necessary to put forward a rational defence for racial prejudice. . . . I dislike anyone, racially as opposed to individually, who is not of a similar ethnic grouping as myself. I don't have to be rational about it. If we were rational about everything we would never achieve anything emotionally. I don't want to mix with them, and I object most strongly to anyone telling me who I will accept or who I won't.' Tellingly, though, after being chosen as a Conservative council candidate five months later, the writer explained that his earlier effusion was 'not against immigrants as such.'[93]

At the time of Little Rock in 1957, defences of segregation could still be read in the London press, asking, for instance, 'Is it absolutely necessary to force the black peoples to live, cohabit or inter-marry with the white peoples? . . . Surely there is something radically wrong in the governments of a "democracy" that would legislate to compel a people to do so against their will. This seems to be the case at Little Rock, Arkansas, USA,'[94] or maintaining, 'The racial integration programme does not issue from manhood suffrage, which is the heart of the democratic ideal. Give the individual, of whatever race, the right to choose, and integration will collapse.'[95] But no template for a British apartheid was ever produced, and the likelihood of one diminished after the Sharpeville Massacre in South Africa in 1960. In the late 1950s a surprising amount of weight had been given to the suggestion that immigration could be slowed by stepping up the long-neglected economic development of the Caribbean: 'If we do not like the coloured people among us, let us carry out the policy I advocated in these columns a couple of years ago—create employment in their country of origin so that they will have no desire to emigrate. What we are paying out in National Assistance and other benefits would be better spent in such an investment.'[96] Such arguments gained traction on the left, reflecting feelings of colonial guilt, but they were little more than an insubstantial echo of interwar colonial development policy. The hope that revived Caribbean economies might encourage voluntary repatriation appeared more plausible in the early years of immigration, when most migrants professed the wish to return home, than subsequently, but it was as close as the opponents of immigration ever came to formulating a repatriation policy. By the mid-1960s it was impossible to ignore the reality of a multiracial Britain.

The only proposal to take concrete form was that of restricting future Black immigration. This would, of course, be the purpose of legislation by a Tory government in 1962 and its Labour successor in 1968. It was nonetheless hardly consensual—one *Marylebone Mercury* correspondent compared Butler to Hitler when the 1962 bill was introduced[97]—but some people had long argued that restricting future immigration offered the best way to ensure good race relations at home. Shortly after the riots, the North Kensington Labour Party—which would later censure George Rogers for advocating restriction—had called for dispersal of the area's Blacks (to prevent ghetto formation) and, failing that, a slowdown in the future rate of immigration.[98] A letter to the *Marylebone Mercury* in September 1965, against the backdrop of deteriorating public order in US cities, voiced the argument clearly:

> It is one thing to ask an immigrant to "When in Rome do as the Romans do", and another thing to treat him as a fifth-class "Roman" when he does. If this is what is going to happen in Britain they will soon realise that they cannot "win" which ever way the game is played. It is then that the most explosive situations will occur. Most people feel that it was time that the brake on unrestricted entry into Britain was applied. On the other hand they realise that immigrants already here should be assimilated as quickly and as fairly as possible.[99]

There was no apartheid, no plausible argument for repatriation, no 'cricket test', no anticipation of recent European controversies over the veil or minarets.

Conclusion

In August 1965 the rector of St Mary Magdalene, Bermondsey, wrote of a 'subtle colour bar' operating in Britain: 'too often the general attitude towards coloured people is one of mild hostility, combined with a wish to avoid too close a contact with them.' In Willesden Joan Maizels asked her respondents 'if they would attend a specially arranged social evening where white and coloured residents would meet each other. This was to test the responses of white residents to the idea of mixing socially with coloured people. The majority did not wish to meet coloured people socially. Two thirds said they would not attend; just over a quarter said they would; a small proportion were uncertain.'[100] This was, after all, a city in which Woolworth's—presumably responding to customer prejudice—'under no circumstances will allow ... immigrant girls to serve loose biscuits.'[101]

The hard evidence of house prices supports this impression: the *London Property Letter*, an unsentimental guide to people seeking to speculate in London residential property, made no attempt to conceal the reality that streets or areas occupied by Blacks were bad investment risks.[102] Significantly, though, the *London Property Letter* was privately circulated. But however substantial the degree of mute racism existing in 1960s London, the 'steer' provided by the spokespeople for antiracist sentiment, the caution enjoined by them on the local press in handling race questions, the reticence of the political parties over race issues, the consequent subordination of race to matters such as youth crime and rent decontrol on London's political agenda, the cultivation of an etiquette which proscribed overtly racist sentiments and required opponents of immigration to foreswear prejudice to get a hearing in polite company all contributed to the creation of an orthodoxy of tolerance. Anti-immigrant sentiment remained inchoate, finding a public outlet only in crude assertions of racial superiority and largely confined to the unappetising tribunes of the Union Movement, the British Movement and the National Front. As a result it could prescribe little in the way of policy proposals beyond the restriction of future immigrant numbers. Strikingly, even Powell, whose reputation as a rapier-sharp logician has surely beguiled historians for too long, produced little more in his 1968 speeches than an airing of English cultural values, a call for further immigration control and an unrealistic proposal for assisted voluntary repatriation. Powell became the mouthpiece of all those who were convinced that liberal stage management had suppressed the true voice of white Britain, but he could not change the parameters of debate. Only the sea change of the 1970s—the coming of age of a British-born radical Black youth coinciding with the collapse of the inner-city economy— could do that.

12

Unquiet Grove

THE 1976 NOTTING HILL CARNIVAL RIOT

On 30 August—Bank Holiday Monday—in 1976 occurred London's worst race riots since the Notting Hill disturbances of 1958. Again they occurred in the flashpoint area of Notting Hill, on the second day of the annual Carnival. The trouble began in the late afternoon, when police sought to deal with a fracas prompted by the theft of a woman's handbag. Police reinforcements, ploughing into the crowd, were greeted with 'a barrage of beer cans, stones, rubble and bricks' from an adjacent building site, thrown by youths who were not involved in the original incident.[1] More missiles came down from the elevated Westway motorway. In the crowded streets, both police and Carnival-goers were static targets, and many were injured. The police improvised their own defence, using dustbin lids, traffic cones and bottle crates as makeshift shields.[2] By the early evening it was clear, in the words of one eyewitness, that 'the police and particularly the black youth population were to be engaged in what was to become a bloody battle of violence and of desperation.' That observer, Paul Stephenson, recorded that 'the missile throwing youths . . . were now gaining the sympathies of large sections of the adult community, both black and white':

> All around me youths were picking up bottles and bricks and stones from the wasteground and hurling them at the police who were standing in a long line with truncheons drawn in one hand and dustbin lids in the other. As they faced this hostile crowd they were attacked from the

rear from the Portobello Road. As they turned to their rear, so those missile throwing youths on the wasteground where I stood, opposite Acklam Road, began to throw with a ferocity of missiles [*sic*] at the police who then had to retreat. As they retreated, under the hail of bricks, stones, bottles and cans, they were reinforced and returned behind a baton charge and the ferocity of police in moving persons from that wasteground was such that no mercy was spared.

Stephenson felt that 'if this was to go on, people would now be killed.'[3] Further violence erupted in Ladbroke Grove, where a police car was set on fire, and in Westbourne Park Road, where two police coaches had their windows shattered. Police responded with concerted baton charges. The Co-op and other shops were looted, the looters in Ancel Kardon's menswear shop apparently trying on the gear before taking it.[4]

By the time that the disturbances fizzled out, around midnight, almost 250 people had been the victims of theft. Over 400 police officers had been injured, along with 188 civilians. Stephenson, a British-born Black community worker, feared with some reason that he had witnessed 'a situation in which police credibility is questioned and lasting damage done to community and race relations.'[5] The tension that had long been developing between London's Afro-Caribbean youth—largely British-born—and the Metropolitan Police had come into the open.

Young Blacks in London

The problems faced by the second generation of any ethnic minority group, struggling for acceptance in the country of their birth, are familiar enough. In the case of London's Afro-Caribbeans, though, they gained added force from the conjunction of the coming of age of the first British-born West Indians and the rapid deindustrialisation of inner London from the mid-1960s. As London's inner-city problem deepened in the 1970s, a new dimension was added to its already delicate racial politics. Race-relations legislation in 1968 had outlawed discrimination in employment, but it was impossible in practice fully to protect the interest of already vulnerable groups as the labour market tightened.

As early as the summer of 1970, well before the oil shock and the consequent collapse of inner-city employment in the mid-1970s, a suggestion of the underlying problem was provided by a freelance survey of just over two hundred West Indian men in North London aged between sixteen and twenty-four, carried out by Peter Wallis and Dennis Stevenson, which found that 22 percent of respondents were unemployed.[6] The authors worked for the market-research firm Conrad Jameson Associates, and their approach, based on interviews by West Indian men of the same age as the respondents, had more in common with market research than quantitative economic analysis. Intensive study of the problem in the decade that followed, however, reinforced the general impression. The Community Relations Commission's 1974 report *Unemployment and Homelessness* calculated an unemployment rate in the Southeast of 15.8 percent for West Indian–born boys aged sixteen to twenty, more than double the rate for whites of the same age.[7] The discrepancy between Black and white employment rates owed something to Blacks' lower attainment levels at school, but the effects of discrimination were inescapable. A Lewisham social worker emphasised in response to the report that the unemployed there were 'educationally quite well qualified'—a conclusion supported by the 1978 survey of that area of the Commission for Racial Equality, which showed that West Indian school leavers with O-Levels were almost four times as likely to be unemployed as similarly qualified whites.[8] In fact young Blacks—men at least[9]—were increasingly removing themselves from the labour market in protest at employers' assumption that they were fit only for manual work. Courtney Laws, the Jamaican-born director of the Brixton Neighbourhood Community Association, attributed much of the frustration experienced by Black school leavers to employer stereotyping, which meant that 'brilliant boys sometimes find themselves in dead-end factory jobs.'[10] The Trinidadian radical Darcus Howe, who had himself worked as a postman in Catford after abandoning his legal studies in 1963,[11] suggested that the next Black generation had decided, 'I don't want to be a bus conductor like my old man, or sweep the floor like my old lady.' His interviewer attributed London Transport's perennial staff shortages to the refusal of young Blacks to take the same jobs as their parents.[12]

Those parents had arrived in Britain at a time of labour shortage, and many enjoyed relative job security in public-sector employment. If their children scorned that employment, they might be impatient at their children's failure to find work at all and their readiness to reject work they thought beneath them. Some bridled at the burden of carrying an unproductive adult family member in an already difficult environment. 'When the pressure of living four in one room got too much for my father, he would get on at me for not keeping a job', eighteen-year-old Tony Joseph

Two residents of Harambee, 'The Black House', Holloway Road, LB Islington, photographed by Colin Jones in 1973. Harambee was one of several self-help hostels established in the seventies for young Blacks who had left—or been evicted from—home. (Colin Jones/topfoto)

told the Black South African journalist Lionel Morrison in 1973. 'Since I was eating his food, in his house, I reckoned it best to leave and spare his lecturing.'[13] Joseph took his chance on the streets: young Blacks were part of London's burgeoning homelessness crisis in the early 1970s.[14] An estimated three hundred young Blacks were living rough in Notting Hill in 1972,[15] and the issue became a short-lived media concern. Several ad hoc voluntary centres and hostels for young homeless appeared across Black London in the early 1970s.[16]

The manager of one such hostel, Ashton Gibson, of the Melting Pot in Brixton, concluded that 'the West Indian family structure has collapsed in this country.'[17] Intergenerational relations were certainly strained in these years. David Dodd claimed in 1978 that 'parents have stopped talking to their children' in Brixton.[18] Conversely, Peter Wallis inferred from the attitudes conveyed in his 1970 survey that 'this latest generation despise their fathers for not objecting to discrimination. They hate the way their parents have tried to be as English as possible.'[19] Speaking after the 1976 riot, Junior Telfer, Trinidadian club manager and leading light of the early Carnivals, attributed Black teenage restlessness to a kind of double alienation: 'not only are they not accepted as English or British ... but they are seen as not having worth in their own right as West Indians.'[20]

The adoption of autonomous cultural symbols was the most obvious consequence. The London patois known loosely as 'Jamaican' or 'Dialect' became, as the radical activist Tony Soares believed, 'a form of nationalism': 'Language allows us to stand unique and separate, and to be understood by others only when we want to be.'[21] Rastafarianism was, though, the most visible feature of this youth-cultural autonomy, embodying both the rejection of the host culture and the rejection of parental values. The social anthropologist Sheila Patterson had discerned small and inconspicuous Rasta groups in Brixton in the 1950s,[22] but the creed was really taken up by young Blacks in the 1970s as a means of explaining their subjugation and as a generational emblem. The Ethiopian World Federation took root in Portobello Road in 1972; the Ethiopian Orthodox Church opened in Ladbroke Grove in 1974, while the London branch of the Jamaican Twelve Tribes of Israel was formed in Brixton in 1972.[23] Rastafarianism comprised not only a creed but also a worldview and a lifestyle. It was not necessary to subscribe to the divinity of Haile Selassie and his imminent second coming to accept its analysis of exploitation, let alone to adopt its cultural accoutrements—clothes in the Ethiopian national colours of red, green and gold, dreadlocks, Dialect, reggae music. The Jamaican writer Len Garrison identified three categories of Ras Tafari adherents: the religious, 'who hold fervently to the faith', the more pragmatic 'secularists', and the 'sympathetic followers.'[24] Stephen Small, in his participant-observation study of twenty-two young Black men in a London hostel, found that five of them subscribed to Rastafarian doctrine, but most of the others showed clear signs of association with Ras Tafari in language, dress or lifestyle. The common currency of reggae helped 'create and reinforce an ethnic identity.'[25] Some of Small's interviewees believed in the white appropriation of Black cultural achievement ('Blacks invented the telephone, the television and electricity. White people would never admit that'; 'Did you know that Beethoven was part black? Nobody ever told me that.').[26] All thought Blackness and English identity entirely antithetical, and several aspired to move to Africa: one was trying to learn Swahili.[27]

By extension, Black youth were more receptive to militant Black nationalism than were their white contemporaries to the Trotskyism propagated by white radicals in the late 1960s. This first became obvious to the wider public in the summer of 1970, with the violent Mangrove protests in Notting Hill, described later in this chapter. Morrison identified then 'a

A Rastafarian community in Notting Hill, 1975. (Janine Wiedel/Alamy Stock Photo)

militancy among blacks hitherto unknown', nurtured by the complete breakdown of communications between the area's Black community and its public authorities. He also noted that 'it was young blacks who are in the majority of the protestors.'[28] Wallis and Stevenson argued that 'only the extreme minority tended to admit to militancy' but that 'the contrast between an external appearance of passivity and strong internal resentment . . . is quite amazingly clear.'[29] Only one in three of their respondents—and fewer than a fifth of those who were unemployed—had any faith in racial integration. Only a quarter of their sample declared themselves prepared to complain to the Race Relations Board if excluded from a public place on grounds of colour.

The race-relations machinery had been devised to cope with individual cases of discrimination. It was not equipped to remedy the collective disadvantage faced by Blacks in a contracting labour market, but the failure to do so damaged the Board and the Community Relations Commission in the eyes of many Blacks, particularly as these agencies remained largely run by whites. In a four-part series in the *West Indian World* in 1971, Lionel Morrison condemned 'the race industry' as a job-creation scheme for white liberals, which, having failed to promote real racial equality, devoted itself to repetitious research projects producing ever less surprising evidence of racial discrimination.[30] Writing in the *Observer* after the 1976 riot, the *Washington Post*'s urban-affairs correspondent, William Raspberry, attributed the absence of any autonomous civil rights movement in Britain to what Morrison had called the 'spongelike genius' of the race-relations machinery for absorbing Black moderates into the British state. Had Martin Luther King Jr. lived in London, Raspberry suggested, he would have become chairman of the Community Relations Commission and, by implication, would have been politically emasculated: 'it simply isn't possible, in the long term, to work for the Government and at the same time lead a civil rights movement whose target could quite possibly be the Government.'[31] As the machinery devised by the British state to defuse racial tension in the 1960s appeared unable to solve the problems emerging in the 1970s, so the appeal of direct action to an embittered Black generation increased. In particular, London's Black Power organisations drew strength from resentment of the actions of the one public agency enjoying a ring-fenced exemption from the attentions of the race-relations agencies: the Metropolitan Police.

Conflict with the Met

In a memorandum to the House of Commons Select Committee on Race Relations and Immigration in 1972, Pansy Jeffrey, a Guyanan-born member of the Citizens Advice Bureau (CAB) in North Kensington, remembered that in the years after the 1958 disturbances, '[the CAB had] found it difficult to believe the behaviour of the police which appeared from stories told to us by callers who came to us for advice. Then it began to seem that there must be some substance to these stories.'[32] By 1965 the West Indian Standing Conference felt that there was enough truth in allegations of police harassment of Blacks in Brixton to recount many of them in an arrestingly titled pamphlet, *Nigger-Hunting in England*.[33] In July 1968 the BBC, after some hesitation, broadcast *Cause for Concern*, a documentary detailing allegations of corruption and brutality in the treatment of Blacks by the Metropolitan Police.[34] Local observers believed that the situation in Notting Hill—always the epicentre of tension between police and Blacks—worsened in the late 1960s.[35]

Certainly by the time that the Select Committee held hearings to the area in 1972 relations were very bad indeed. At a tense meeting between committee members and local Black youngsters in February 1972, the MPs were left in no doubt of Black resentment:

'They search us straight away without asking any questions. We are just walking along the street and they stop us.'

'When you want to talk about police harassment, I am the one for you to talk to, because I have been kicked in the seat, my ribs busted, my head busted against the glass. I have come here to say something, let me get it said, don't tell me to shush.'

'They knocked on my door. The policeman came along and took me to the station. They tried to book me on four charges, taking £20 off this chap. I have never seen him before. They said I had stolen a car, was driving without a licence, tax or insurance.'

'The police came into our house last week, they broke down the door and took almost everybody inside down to the station and beat them up and charged some of them. This girl was three months pregnant and they beat her up and now she has lost the baby.'

'The police have got to go and find someone to provoke and get into trouble. You would not understand that, of course, I don't expect you to.'[36]

'The prevailing mood among young black people', the committee was told, 'is of resentment and hostility towards the police.'[37] Terry Leander, an Inner London Education Authority (ILEA) youth worker working with Blacks in Notting Hill, produced for the Select Committee an ad hoc survey of his clients suggesting that 60 percent of them had been arrested at least once and that almost all the remainder expected to be arrested sooner or later.[38]

The litmus test lay in recruitment of Blacks to the Met, which had only eleven Black constables by 1973. One of them, Clayton Nesbitt, admitted that 'when you join the force you keep your friends and lose your acquaintances' in the Black community.[39] Antiguan-born David Mussington, of the Met's B Division in Notting Hill, accepted that 'a black cop . . . will always be viewed with suspicion—unfounded though it may be, there is always the feeling that this nigger boy is trying to infiltrate for "the man" [Black slang for the Met].'[40] Special Constable Luscombe of Brixton recalled being approached in Stockwell by 'a West Indian youth who told him that it made him sick to see his "brothers" in police uniform.'[41] 'I would not do it', one young Black told the Select Committee at its public meeting: 'I would be hated by my own people.'[42]

The committee concluded that 'allegations of "nigger-hunting" are difficult to prove, impossible to disprove.'[43] The historian is little better placed—at least to judge the actual extent of prejudicial treatment. Episodes of police brutality, harassment or corruption, by their nature, seldom left a clear paper trail, but it would take a heroic effort of will to discount all such charges. The authoritative study of Black-police relations in the 1960s, by James Whitfield—himself a former Met officer—depicts an organisation in which a combination of pervasive prejudice and a lack of effective correction from senior officers or the Home Office allowed grievances to proliferate without challenge. One inspector remembered being shown how to 'fit up' Blacks on his arrival at Harrow Road police station in 1968, as if it were part of his training, yet not one of the forty-one complaints of racial discrimination against the Met in the following year was upheld.[44]

The demonstrators who protested against the Notting Hill police in the 1970 Mangrove march identified a group of individual officers as being particularly brutal or corrupt; it was suggested to the 1972 Select Committee that younger police officers were generally worse than those with more experience.[45] All police officers did not victimise Blacks, but a pervasive culture of racism apparently licensed individual transgressions. As one young Black told the 1972 Select Committee at its public meeting, 'The way I see it, there is the bad copper, the indifferent copper and the good copper, but really and truly there can not be good coppers, because if the good copper knows what the bad copper is doing and does nothing about it, he cannot be a good copper.'[46] Ten years later, the Policy Studies Institute (PSI) researchers investigating police attitudes noted of their own observations, 'Where someone in a group of police officers started on a line of racialist talk we never heard a member of the group explicitly oppose his views or saw the person made to feel that he was being a bore, speaking out of turn or erring against unspoken conventions or inhibitions.'[47] Attitudes may well have been sharpened by the fractious racial politics of the seventies, but this charge is consistent with the allegations made repeatedly against the police since the 1958 riots. As Whitfield points out, the Met drew most of its recruits from outside London—from areas containing no immigrants.[48] W. A. Belson found in 1972 that 32 percent of his sample of a thousand Met officers believed Blacks to be less intelligent than whites.[49] The officers who policed immigrant areas tended not to live in them,[50] and, of course, there were very few Blacks in the force. As one chief superintendent told Whitfield in 2000, 'We were only involved with black people up against the law. The fact that West Indians, black people, were working on our buses, in our hospitals or in our factories was, to some extent, lost on us.'[51] The idea that Blacks were habitually criminal might easily take root even with those who were not necessarily driven by racial hatred.

As the PSI report pointed out, Blacks were disproportionately represented in social categories which received little deference from the police whatever their ethnicity: the lower working class, the rootless, the alienated. They were also disproportionately young: the PSI investigators found that young people of all ethnicities were more likely to have been arrested in the previous five years than their elders were. Strikingly, they also found that fifteen- to twenty-four-year-olds were the only Black age group to have been in trouble with the police more often than whites of the same age, but that the difference in that age group was significant.[52] Stephen Small's participant-observer study of a group of twenty-two Blacks in a London hostel, carried out as part of the PSI project, found that most had had recent contact with the police and that such contact had always been antagonistic.[53] The embittered tone of the Select Committee's public meeting with young Notting Hill Blacks in 1972 suggests that this hostility was long entrenched.

Certainly the sense of a gathering crisis had been sufficiently pressing even in the late 1960s to induce the Met's leadership to create a new Community Relations branch—'A7'—in 1968. The motivation, as the commissioner Sir Joseph Simpson openly acknowledged, was 'to avoid having a situation develop which resembles that already existing in large American cities.'[54] His successor, Sir John Waldron, reminded the rank and file in the Met's house journal to mind their language in dealing with ethnic minorities— 'the burden of nearly every complaint from coloured people is that a racist remark has been used'—and suggested that the day might be approaching when a community liaison officer would be installed in every police station 'who will have as part of his duty the correlation of all aspects of our increasing effort in the field of social welfare.'[55]

Senior officers understood that such advice might not be welcome in the ranks. The late 1960s was a period in which the Met was coming under attack not merely for individual episodes of misconduct but collectively, as an arm of the state—the imperialist state in the eyes of antiwar demonstrators, the white racist state in the eyes of Black radicals. In a force which was, throughout the postwar period, undermanned and overstretched,[56] individual officers found themselves targets of political attacks which they felt they had done nothing to provoke but which might place them in personal danger and certainly made their job more difficult. In response many developed a defensiveness of their own: 'Don't forget we're a tribe. We're a minority', one senior officer at Notting Hill told Peter Evans of the *Times* in 1971.[57] As Whitfield puts it, 'in the 1950s and 1960s one alienated group,

London's West Indian community, was policed by another alienated group, the Metropolitan Police.'[58] In response to political 'complications', many police officers retreated into a reductionist view of their role: their job was simply to enforce the laws that Parliament had passed, without having to make allowances for any particular category of offender. Deep as were the effects of Notting Hill's social deprivation, these were 'problems which are not of the making or curing by police',[59] who should not be expected to act as social workers. Two-thirds of Belson's sample of Met officers in 1972 endorsed the proposition that 'immigrants should be forced to adopt the British way of life.'[60] This was a stronger formulation than the more obvious proposition that immigrants should obey British laws, but the former clearly implied the latter. So even if Caribbean practice endorsed the sale of alcohol in unlicensed basement shebeens or the social smoking of ganja, the law was the law. It might be the case, as David Pitt, the Grenadian chair of the Campaign Against Racial Discrimination, argued in the Met's house journal, that people 'automatically congregate in the streets in the West Indies and if a policeman appears it is usually to join in the conversation',[61] but in Britain obstructing the pavement was an offence; and, as one policeman replied, 'if I were to come across such a gathering and it constituted an obstruction I would move them on and certainly not join them to pass the time of day.' 'Is *all* the "give" to fall to the policeman and all the "take" to the immigrant?', the constable went on to ask. 'It would be nice if the police also could feel that they, one day, may be treated as human beings.'[62]

How far the architects of the Met's community-relations initiative shared these sentiments we cannot say, but they certainly had to take note of the rank-and-file view that 'this issue is being magnified out of all proportion. . . . Even in the West Indies policemen have to enforce the law.'[63] The approach adopted by A7's commander, Frank Merricks, in explaining community relations to the regular officer was to argue, 'in our relationship with coloured persons we face the additional problem that to them anything unpleasant, unfamiliar or unwelcome—and police action too often can be all of these—is regarded as prejudice against their colour.' This produced 'a tendency to believe every tittle of rumour regarding alleged police misbehaviour which is told to them; in particular that we brutalise coloured persons and plant drugs on them.'[64] This mattered, Merricks argued, because politically motivated Blacks were eager to propagate such rumours, and 'although the vast majority [of immigrants] are law-abiding and reasonably content, there exists among the remainder a small minority of agitators and extremists who seek to promote discord, and who see and even search for, evidence of discrimination at every turn.'[65] This interpretation was designed to remind officers of the need for tact in routine law enforcement in immigrant areas and perhaps to counter any assumption that most Blacks were innately criminal. It was certainly true that the years after Stokely Carmichael's visit to London in 1967 had seen the formation of a clutch of radical Black nationalist groups.[66] But the suggestion that those who did not belong to such groups would remain 'reasonably content' unless their minds were turned by extremists was strained. It underestimated the extent of Black discontent, and, still more damagingly, it encouraged police attempts to root out those malcontents supposedly poisoning community relations, producing the repeated—and disastrous— police efforts to suppress the Mangrove restaurant in Notting Hill.

The Mangrove Affair

The Mangrove had been established by the Trinidadian Frank Crichlow in 1968.[67] Crichlow had arrived in Britain in the early 1950s and, after a period as a bandleader later in the decade, had opened the Rio coffee bar in Westbourne Park Road in 1959. The Rio offered Caribbean music and food: Crichlow later explained, 'West Indians in London felt a little like Englishmen in Africa. They wanted to club together—especially after the race riots.'[68] The Rio was indeed the centre for the various West Indian organisations formed in the wake of the 1958 attacks, with the result that its habitués included—as well as the Black hustlers on the fringe of the Profumo episode and many of Notting Hill's sixties Bohemians—some of the leading lights of Black radicalism. This made it the focus of consistent police interest throughout its decade of life until, in March 1968, Crichlow wound it up in order to open a Caribbean restaurant, the Mangrove, in All Saints Road.[69]

The new restaurant was a more smartly appointed venue than the Rio and was less of a magnet for the Rio's criminal fringe. Its clientele in its early years was composed of 'the black working class, black intellectuals and the radical whites.' In particular, the Mangrove became a base for the emergent British Black Power movement in the late 1960s,[70] which guaranteed that Crichlow—who by the early 1990s claimed to have been arrested fifty times since his arrival in Britain[71]—would remain the object of police interest. A succession of raids in the early months of 1970, each founded on unsubstantiated allegations of drug use on the premises, culminated in May in the arrest of Crichlow and his brother, Victor, on a charge of assaulting the police officers involved in one raid. Nine raids followed in the next six weeks,[72] but in fact the police presence was said to have been almost continuous in the course of the summer: according to one employee, 'They just come in and walk around looking at the people eating. . . . They are scaring off a lot of our business.' If the objective was to drive the restaurant out of business, it appeared likely to succeed, as nightly takings fell from up to £100 to only £12 or so.[73] This was the background to the Black counterattack in August 1970, in the form of a mass demonstration in protest at the persecution of Crichlow and the Mangrove in particular and local police actions against the Black community in general.

It was apparently Darcus Howe who advocated a direct-action protest rather than the use of the regular complaints procedure, seeking to emulate the tactics of Black radicals in the United States and the 'Black Power Revolution' against the Williams government in Trinidad earlier in 1970.[74] The protestors, some in Black Panther berets, dark glasses and leather jackets,[75] marched from the Mangrove to Notting Dale and Notting Hill police stations. Before they could reach Harrow Road police station, though, they found their way blocked by a line of police five deep. A pitched battle between marchers and police broke out, in which police attacks on the demonstrators were countered with bottles, bricks and other ammunition gathered from building skips on the street. Seventeen police officers were hurt and nineteen demonstrators arrested. Seven men, including Crichlow and Howe, and two women were later charged with riot, incitement to riot and affray. The incitement charges were withdrawn by the prosecution, and an unusually free-spirited magistrate struck out the riot charges, only for them to be reinstated by the director of public prosecutions, with the result that the defendants faced an Old Bailey trial and the prospect of ten-year sentences.[76]

The twelve weeks of judicial theatre that began at the Old Bailey in October 1971 became, in effect, a continuation of the protest. The defence sought to bring 'the long history of slavery and colonial exploitation into the courtroom' and mounted a sustained criticism of police conduct towards Notting Hill's Blacks,[77] putting the prosecution on the back foot from the start. Howe and Althea Jones-Lecointe, conducting their own defence, and Ian Macdonald, acting for the other seven defendants, augmented their attacks on the police with a critique of the entire judicial system as it dealt with Blacks, Macdonald even attacking the judge for exercising a 'naked judicial tyranny.' In all probability, though, the outcome was determined by the assiduous use of the seven challenges allowed to each defendant to shape the composition of the jury. Borrowing

US Black Power tactics and invoking the Magna Carta right of trial by one's peers, Howe had initially called for an all-Black jury. When this was rejected, the defendants exploited as systematically as they could the chance to gauge the political views of prospective jury members. The eventual favourable outcome—all nine were acquitted on the most serious charge of riotous assembly, all but two were acquitted of affray and only three were convicted on assault charges—suggested that they played the game of jury selection with some skill. Invoking the spirit of Christmas, Judge Edward Clarke imposed only suspended sentences on those who were convicted.[78]

This outcome made the reinstatement of the riot charges and the consequent protracted and expensive Old Bailey trial appear vindictive. Some loose-tongued jurors made their feelings known to a reporter for *Time Out*: 'the police are wankers'; 'there should be an inquiry into the whole police force'; 'what a waste of public money.'[79] Clearly the whole episode amounted to a defeat for the Met. On several points of fact, the jury had decided simply not to believe the police witnesses, while Judge Clarke, generally considered a hard-liner, had observed in his closing remarks that the proceedings had 'regrettably shown evidence of racial hatred on both sides'—a remark which, as one senior officer noted, 'will be used as a stick to beat the police with for years.'[80] Even before the trial concluded, there were suggestions that senior officers in Notting Hill had accepted the need to reduce the level of racial tension in the area.[81] The Carnival appeared to offer one means of doing so.

Carnival

After a decade or so of being stigmatised as London's leading twilight zone, Notting Hill had, by the midsixties, spawned a number of community self-help initiatives. One of these was the London Free School, the brainchild of the hippie figurehead John 'Hoppy' Hopkins. Modelled on the Free University of New York and intended to operate outside the formal education system, it was designed to allow local creatives to 'make whatever skills' they had, 'such as painting or photography, available to kids in the neighbourhood.'[82] The idea of holding a local festival was broached at the school's inaugural meeting in March 1966, at which point it emerged that a similar proposal was being developed by Rhaune Laslett, a community figure of Native American and Russian parentage who had lived in the area since 1958. Laslett operated an ad hoc social advisory service for 'the Grove's' many troubled residents, turning her home in Tavistock Crescent into 'the scene of fantastic activity, a centre for social work, and particularly legal work of every kind.'[83] After one attempt to resolve a landlord-tenant dispute, she 'had this sort of vision' that the community 'should take to the streets in song and dance, to ventilate all the pent-up frustrations born out of the slum conditions that were rife at the time.'[84] The Notting Hill Fayre—or Festival or Carnival—was first staged over a week in September 1966.

It was clearly a local celebration, ostensibly evoking the Notting Hill Annual Fair of Victorian times.[85] Many of the figures portrayed in the first Carnival were stereotypically English: Good Queen Bess, characters from Dickens.[86] The Carnival was not initially intended to be an exclusively Afro-Caribbean affair but rather to reflect the area's kaleidoscopic ethnic composition.[87] West Indians were, though, already the predominant ethnic minority group, and Trinidadians were the predominant group among the West Indians. Trinidad had the most developed tradition of Carnival in the Caribbean, centred on the 'mas'—masquerade—and the steel band, and Russ Henderson's steel band had been amongst the performers in 1966. By 1969, at least, the Carnival was visibly Caribbean in nature, and after Laslett stepped down as organiser in 1970, management passed to the local Trinidadian community leaders. The Carnival Development Committee formed in 1971 took its name directly from the organisation set up in Port of Spain in 1956 to manage Carnivals in Trinidad.[88] The Carnivals of 1971 and 1972 were transparently Trinidadian in nature, with steel bands at their heart.

In that respect the Carnival was still local, Notting Hill being the largest Trinidadian centre in London, but with the waning of the area's hippie/Bohemian identity, its nature changed, becoming less white and more distinctively Afro-Caribbean.[89] Even in 1969 Laslett had notified the police, 'we understand that this year's Carnival will be attracting many people from all parts of London.'[90] Carnival was already becoming an outlet for the metropolitan—rather than merely the Notting Hill—Black community. Given the tense racial politics of Notting Hill in these years, this made the event potentially sensitive. Laslett actually sought to cancel the 1970 Carnival, scheduled for only three weeks after the Mangrove demonstration, after hearing that a Black Power protest was planned, but the event was taken over by the Notting Hill Social Council and passed off peacefully.[91]

More than Black Power, it was the Metropolitan Police that saw the Carnival's potential as a platform. Despite the 1970 scare, the early

Carnivals were largely unproblematic for the police, even as numbers rose from eight hundred in 1967 to thirty-five hundred in 1969 and ten thousand in 1973.[92] These Carnivals showed police-immigrant relations at their most benign—in 1972 the first photograph appeared in the press of a white policeman smiling with a West Indian woman[93]—and the Metropolitan Police files in the National Archives show the eagerness of the Met to propagate this image of amity to an increasingly critical public, particularly in the aftermath of the Mangrove trial. In 1970 the Commander of B Division noted that 'the only regrettable feature [of the Carnival] is that the proliferation of press and television reporters gave no publicity to an event which was carried out with the utmost cordiality between the coloured participants and the police, except for the local newspaper.' In 1972 Chief Superintendent Marshall recorded that the Carnival 'provided yet another opportunity for the residents of Colville and Golborne Wards to see the police of the "B" Division in a different light to that usually presented by the local anti-establishment minority.' The commander of the A7 branch considered the 1973 Carnival 'probably the best event yet. . . . Police received a good press for its public relations.'[94] Indeed it did: the *Kensington News* reporter described one policeman waltzing 'an enthusiastic West Indian girl' the length of Swinbrook Road as onlookers cheered, while another 'exchanged his helmet for a tufted, Death's Head tribal headpiece, to more applause.' He believed that 'August Bank Holiday 1973 may go down with the summer of 1958 as a turning point in the history of race relations in Notting Hill.'[95]

The corollary of all this was that the actual policing of the event had to be low-key and unobtrusive; the question which the 'laughing policeman' image suppressed was how far it was feasible to apply light-touch policing to an event of this scale. This question became more pressing as the Carnival continued to grow, and changed its nature, in the midseventies. Its evolution reflected the emergence of an autonomous Black British culture in London in these years, with the result that Carnival ceased to be a predominantly Trinidadian event.

The change was engineered by Leslie Palmer, organiser of the Carnivals from 1973 to 1975. Palmer believed that Carnival had lost momentum after the problems of 1970 and that the 1972 festival had been 'a non-event.'[96] Though a Trinidadian himself, he attributed the event's waning to the limited appeal of the Trinidadian Carnival model to London's younger Blacks: 'Carnival was dying a natural death—there were no costumes at all, no food at all, it was just the Trinidad guys reliving their youth and

A kiss for PC Alan Phillips on the harmonious Sunday of the 1977 Carnival, 28 August 1977. The Metropolitan Police had sought to use the Carnival to mend fences with the Afro-Caribbean community after the low point of the Mangrove trial. On the following day violent clashes erupted between Blacks and police. (PA/Alamy Stock Photo)

having a bit of a dance in the streets.'[97] Observing that many of the Blacks present took no part as a result ('it was because they didn't feel part of it—you see, it was really a Trinidad thing'), he argued, 'over here we are all West Indians, so we must involve the other West Indians.'[98] The 1973 Carnival, as one local reporter noted, was the first to 'involve all cultures and peoples from the West Indies—not just Trinidadians. It combined music from Jamaican "sound systems" (giant discotheques) playing from under the Westway flyover in Acklam Road, with live reggae and over a dozen steel bands.'[99]

Between 1973 and 1975 Palmer created a pan-Caribbean Carnival, combining steel bands, masquerades and sound systems. The sound system was the most significant addition. It was not simply a 'giant discotheque' but rather a composite network for music production, involving a DJ, assorted soundmen, reggae music, amplification equipment and a group of followers which might number thousands. It was a long-established import from Jamaica which, like the Trinidadian steel band, came to be refined in London to a level which could match or surpass its Caribbean prototypes.[100] Palmer's invitation to sound systems to join the 1973 Carnival

Musicians in the streets of Notting Hill before the 1976 Carnival descended into violence, 30 August 1976. (Tim Ring/ Alamy Stock Photo)

amounted to an appeal to Black youth and to the Jamaican majority amongst London's Blacks. It succeeded spectacularly. By 1975 youth predominated in the Carnival crowd, and the crowd itself had grown from the 3,000 or so in 1972 to around 150,000 in 1974 and 1975.[101]

Initially the Met saw no need to depart from the unobtrusive policing methods developed to promote what one former officer calls its 'eternal quest to ensure that it was always represented in a positive light.'[102] Despite the much enhanced numbers in 1974, Inspector French noted that 'those taking part in the procession were good natured. All Officers entered into the spirit of the occasion and the afternoon passed well.' As the next Carnival approached, Chief Inspector Craven reiterated, 'Local officers have earned a considerable reputation in the Community and with the organisers arising from their tact, good humour and forebearance [sic] in the past. The occasion is one of friendly high spirits and I am sure that the low profile adopted by police is correct. Any show of force or strict control would undoubtedly result in undesirable confrontations and the necessity of employing about 20 times the number of officers.'[103] Palmer had acknowledged as much in thanking the police after the successful 1973 Carnival: 'they were not out in force, and it made all the difference.'[104]

Nonetheless, large gatherings attract criminals, and the expansion of the Carnival crowd to a size half as large again as a Wembley Cup Final attendance called into question the Met's 'light-touch' approach. Press photographs of policemen kissing Black women did little to erase the suspicion of police power that had built up over fifteen years, making conventional police work more difficult in the Carnival. Assessing the 1975 event, Chief Superintendent A. J. Tenten recorded that 252 items of personal property had been handed in to the police over the two days, 'mostly wallets and purses, devoid of cash': 'The difficulties in combating this type of crime is [sic] obvious because most of the offences took place in the dense crowds dancing with the bands and white plain clothes officers would be very noticeable. Even if the culprits were seen, another difficulty would be to get through the crowds, and the possibility of a major disturbance if any arrests were effected by plain clothes officers in these circumstances.'[105] Palmer himself told the Black press that 'the [Carnival Development] Committee were totally disappointed with the small minority of the crowd who tried to defend the young pick-pocketers when the police tried to apprehend them.'[106] The logical answer, as the *Evening Standard*'s Simon Jenkins argued after the 1976 riot, lay in enhanced self-policing—stewarding—by the event organisers.[107] At the time, though, the signs are that the organisers themselves had become fearful of their ever-growing creation. Given the widespread criticism of the Met for overpolicing the 1976 Carnival, Palmer's warning to the Notting Hill police before the 1974 event is striking:

I do not accept responsibility and neither should any other member of the Committee for any acts of terrorism, burglary, vandalism or any other criminal acts committed by any participants of the Carnival. It is the responsibility of the forces of law and order to protect all sections of the community from any criminal acts & if the Police feel, as expressed, that they do not have the man-power to cope sufficiently with the Carnival, the Carnival Committee does not seek to set-up any alternative police force and consequently cannot accept any liabilities for acts which might not have occurred if adequate police were available.[108]

Palmer sent a similar disclaimer to Sir Robert Mark, the Metropolitan Police commissioner, as the 1975 Carnival—the last which he organised—approached.[109]

Frank Bynoe, a Notting Hill Trinidadian and one of many would-be organisers of the 1976 Carnival, was apparently tasked with cleaning up the event by 'the West Indian establishment', who 'were not pleased at the way the Notting Hill Carnival was developing.'[110] Apart from specific criminality, the swelling size of the event inevitably disturbed the locals. Today those residents of Notting Hill who do not participate in the Carnival themselves are at least likely to have moved into the area knowing that it was an ineradicable feature of the locality, but the rapid growth and change in nature of what had once been an unobtrusive local celebration had a major disruptive impact on Notting Hill's long-term residents—several of whom, inevitably, had not welcomed the Caribbean influx in the first place. In 1974 Chief Inspector Wells could appease a forty-year resident distressed by the noise of the sound systems by describing the police's 'active attempts to guide the direction and style of the Carnival',[111] but the more anarchic conditions of 1975 made it harder to convince locals that the police were in control. One former resident of Cambridge Gardens claimed to have moved house to escape 'this dreadful night-mare of misery and tension, caused by the intolerable non-stop pop-groups and steel bands, the stench of urine and being called a white b. . . . by black people drunk with the feeling of power at being allowed to run riot on our Streets with no restrictions whatsoever.'[112] Within a week of the 1975 Carnival a local committee was formed under the vicar of St Michael, Ladbroke Grove, to press for the Carnival to be moved to a venue such as Hyde Park.[113] 'There is no doubt that a lot of local residents are annoyed', as Chief Superintendent Tenten put it cautiously. He was horrified by the possibility that he might have to enforce an injunction brought by residents to prevent a future Carnival: it threatened to provoke 'massive disobedience, and police would inevitably be involved in serious confrontations involving very large numbers of officers.' The low-key policing deployed since 1970, he observed, 'relies very much on good will.'[114]

This was the background to the ill-fated attempt to transfer the Carnival to a fixed venue. Three months after the 1975 Carnival, Chief Superintendent Ronald Paterson, who had been responsible for Carnival's policing on and off since 1967, sent to the chief executive of the Royal Borough of Kensington and Chelsea a lengthy account of the problems posed in a 'noisy, disorganised and potentially explosive' occasion. He argued that few of those who attended had been locals, that despite attempts to prescribe the procession route, bands had 'meandered almost as they wished', that pedestrians were unable to move and local residents were 'virtual prisoners for the weekend', that the amplified music was 'deafening' and 'the noise, dirt and litter were almost insufferable.' The 'so-called Committee seemed completely overwhelmed by the event to which they had given birth and organisation as such barely existed': 'once having done the minimum of organisation, [the Committee] collects money from the traders and sits back hoping other organisations will be responsible for control and any incidents which may arise.' Carnival had 'completely outgrown its venue': if moved to an enclosed location—Paterson favoured the White City athletics stadium—it would be possible to preserve Carnival's 'West Indian spirit' but 'allow for containment and thus satisfy local residents.' 'Amplified music would be controlled, admission could be charged, profit put to a proper purpose and accounted for, and the litter be cleared adequately and at the cost of the Carnival Committee. The bands would have easy progress, the traffic would be unhindered and the local residents be allowed to live in peace. Furthermore it would be self-supporting, the money would be accounted for and the Carnival itself become even more celebrated and be of real cultural significance.' While direct confrontation between police and revellers had so far been 'studiously avoided by both sides . . . had any incident occurred requiring firm police action, it would have been physically impossible to have moved policemen in any numbers quickly through the crowds and any such movement would, I feel, certainly have been strenuously resisted.' He concluded, ominously, that 'a repetition of this year's events in 1976 might well have repercussions which would give rise to public disorder on one hand or increasing contempt for law on the other.'[115]

As a policing solution to an emerging public-order problem this made sense, though Paterson's attempts to identify an actual venue for the 1976 Carnival fell flat after not only White City but also the GLC parks, Wormwood Scrubs and Chelsea FC's Stamford Bridge ground proved unobtainable. But the proposal failed to recognise that the type of Carnival that Palmer had created had provided London's Black community for the first time with a large-scale public celebration of its culture and identity and would not be lightly abandoned. As Peter Minshall, organiser of the Mas's events in the 1975 Carnival, put it, 'The most important aspect of the carnival is a social one. It must bring us together. We must get out of our heads this bus conductor image, we're a very capable people, a very talented people, and this gives us the opportunity to express that capability and to express that talent.'[116] Palmer himself believed that the 1975 Carnival—his third and last as organiser—justified his belief 'that it was possible to harness the "latent positivity" of the annual event and shape it into a West Indian Festival organised by the community for all Londoners to enjoy.'[117] His vision was not uncontested within the Black community. Some objected to the commercialism of the new Carnival ('Carnival is joy and gaiety, at least that's how I know it in Trinidad. But here money is everything').[118]

Divisions surfaced over whether Carnival should be promoted as a political or as a purely cultural event and how far Jamaican and other Caribbean influences should be allowed to distort the original Trinidadian model—divisions which would afflict the Carnival organisation for the rest of the decade[119]—but none of the organisers wished to have the event homogenised and confined at the behest of the police. Location mattered. Notting Hill was revered in the kind of sentimental terms reserved by some whites for the East End:

> I have heard more than one tough black man say they would not live anywhere except in the Grove or in the West Indies. It has its heroes in a wide variety of spheres—men are respected for toughness, strength, capacity for work, sharpness and intellect. There are complex ties of friendship and family. Men and women are old-timers who came here decades ago and survived the hardships together; who go to church or gamble together; who have brothers, sisters, cousins, aunts, uncles, even grandmothers on streets close to where they themselves live. Kids are known, protected, talked about in terms of who their fathers or mothers are. A black woman may walk home over fairly long distances [with little] by way of protection because she is the sister, daughter, mother, woman, of this or that friend or hero.[120]

Moving Carnival even to White City (Shepherd's Bush), let alone Battersea Park—another of Paterson's targets—was unacceptable, while turning it into a stadium event would jeopardise the 'atmosphere and spirit which would be achieved by a spontaneous street carnival',[121] as well as limiting

Police in action during the disturbances at the 1976 Notting Hill Carnival. (Kypros/Hulton Archive/ Getty Images)

the crowd to a level well below the attendance achieved in 1974 and 1975.[122] Even such attempts at compromise as the proposal to crown the Carnival king and queen in a stadium while keeping the main event on the streets left the members of the committee open to attack from rivals in the increasingly divided organisation.[123]

The intractability of the problem became clear. There was no chance of persuading the Carnival organisers to move to an enclosed venue, but they had not shown the willingness or capacity to police the event themselves. Any attempt to cancel the event altogether would produce the kind of uproar that senior officers had professed themselves anxious to avoid. Paterson therefore fell back on implementing the threat that he had issued during his negotiations with the committee, of 'severe policing . . . to ensure the safety of residents if the Carnival was to be in the street.'[124] Deploying a larger number of officers than in the days of 'light-touch' management was not difficult but did not in itself determine how they were to act: one of the arguments for moving to a stadium venue had been the difficulty faced by officers trying to arrest pickpockets and the like, who could melt into the crowd and rely on its protection. One constable's account of the instructions issued to the officers on duty at the 1976 Carnival suggests that the officers themselves were none the wiser: 'First, I was among officers employed on duty at the carnival who were told to be very careful of who we arrested and, if we did make an arrest, to go in ten-handed—or, if necessary, twenty-handed, so that we had plenty of help if needed. Second, we were told to keep "a low profile", this being a well-known phrase when dealing with the coloured community.'[125] The number of officers deployed in 1976—over fifteen hundred on the Monday[126]—represented a sharp increase from the years of deliberately unobtrusive policing and made it more difficult to keep 'a low profile', while the instruction to make arrests 'twenty-handed' would inevitably appear provocative. As Simon Jenkins wrote on the day after the riot, 'No reasonable person could doubt that pockets were being picked in Notting Hill at the weekend—nor that black youths were doing it; nor that a certain amount of threatening was being done to assist it. But what earthly chance was there, at the height of an always emotional Carnival, that a full-blooded police charge into the tightly-packed streets of Notting Hill was going to stop it?' 'Pickpocketing', he concluded, 'will not be cured by massive police presence on the day, wading, truncheons at the ready, into West Indian crowds.'[127]

Conclusion

Clearly the 1976 disaster had been the result of several miscalculations, but as Abner Cohen wrote in 1993, it was not an accident. Rather it indicated the point at which pressures produced by the changing context of London's race relations became impossible to contain. In chapter 11 I argued that the conciliation measures and efforts to curb the overt expression of racist sentiments by the host community had had some success in containing racial tension in the 1960s, but they were geared towards preventing a repetition of the 1958 attacks by whites on the Black minority. They could not solve the problem emerging from the late 1960s of an English-born or English-raised Black generation, coming of age at a time of inner-city deindustrialisation and burgeoning unemployment from which it suffered disproportionately and against which it appeared powerless, inducing a deep sense of alienation. In this context, some form of mass protest, incapable of being defused by the existing race-relations machinery, was always likely. It was also likely that it would be directed against the Metropolitan Police—the state agency with which young Blacks had most contact and the one most impervious to earlier efforts to ameliorate racial tension.

In evidence presented to the 1972 Select Committee, Louis Chase, a Barbadian member of the London Committee of the Race Relations Board, criticised the kind of tokenistic attempts that the Met was given to making in order to defuse criticism of its record on race, 'for example, "Let us have a football match between your black club and the police"': 'I am not saying it is wrong. What I am saying is that the police should not be in a position where they have to forge relationships, relationships should be spontaneous. . . . It is difficult for me to suggest to a black youngster who alleges that he has been accosted by the police that he should take action to improve his relationship with the police.'[128] The suspicion engendered in the 1960s was too heavy to be alleviated by such initiatives. Police attempts to use the Carnival to advertise their ability to coexist with the Black community, at a time when it was becoming the most visible expression of that community's cultural self-confidence, merely launched a sequence of events by which individual decisions, explicable in themselves, combined to produce a catastrophic outcome. What 1976 advertised was the sheer distrust on both sides. The police officers on duty would have been well aware that it should not have taken ten or twenty men to arrest a pickpocket, but they were not confident of operating alone. PC Robinson, quoted earlier, was convinced that the instruction to make arrests 'twenty-handed' was 'an excellent policy as it turned out on the day', but to the fifteen-year-old Blacks interviewed by Barry Troyna in the wake of the Carnival riots, such heavy-handedness only encouraged confrontation: 'when there's lots of them people get tense.'[129] The vast majority of the people in the crowd would have had a low view of young petty criminals but were not willing to hand them over to police officers operating mob-handed, particularly given their understanding of the treatment they would receive in custody. Not only did the crowd impede attempted arrests, as in 1975, but, as police told one looted shopkeeper, 'even some of the victims of the pickpockets turned on [the police] when they tried to take suspects away.'[130]

In turn, this mutual suspicion was reinforced by the events of 1976. Black opinion across the ideological spectrum concluded that the troubles had been engineered by the police, as part of 'the campaign now waged for years to label all black youth as muggers, thieves and petty criminals' and in order to generate 'enough evidence to commit the Notting Hill Carnival to its grave for good.'[131] Conversely, many rank-and-file police officers felt reinforced in their conviction that their high command's enthusiasm for light-touch policing of the Carnival had been proved misguided, privileging one section of the community and preventing the ordinary copper from doing their job. After PC Robinson's firsthand experience of the riot, he asked, 'Why do we persist in saying that we have no colour problem in London when it is quite plain to every officer who was at the carnival, or who patrols the streets of this capital, that there is a colour problem, and an immense one at that? Why don't the senior officers of this job admit this and stop trying to make the usual excuses—or are they afraid to admit what every PC knows?'[132] Subsequently the police charge would become 'a ritual which is built into the structure of the carnival.'[133] Most disturbingly, the inevitable decision to provide those who were policing the 1977 Carnival with riot shields visibly equated Black protest with the incontestable breakdown of public order in Ulster. Police-Black relations would get worse before they could get better. The battle lines were being drawn for the still more serious confrontations of 1981 and 1985.

13

Reshaping the Welfare State?

VOLUNTARY ACTION AND COMMUNITY IN LONDON, 1960–1975

Poverty was 'rediscovered' between the late 1950s and the late 1960s, brought to the public eye by academics like Brian Abel-Smith and Peter Townsend, by the researchers at the Institute of Community Studies, by campaigning voluntary organizations like Shelter and the Child Poverty Action Group, even by the makers of the homelessness TV drama *Cathy Come Home*.[1] The 'rediscovered' poor tended to be those who had not been the principal objects of Sir William Beveridge's attention in his 1942 report—the elderly, the disabled or mentally ill, single mothers, the homeless[2]—and the overall conclusion reached was unsurprising: that there were some forms of poverty resistant to the economic growth enjoyed since 1945 and inadequately supported by Beveridge's welfare system. But because the welfare state had been built on a foundation of universalism, with social security seen as an entitlement pertaining to citizenship, residual poverty was treated as an indictment of the postwar settlement. Whereas the late Victorians, 'rediscovering' poverty in the 1880s, had questioned whether Britain was really a Christian country, the New Elizabethans asked whether Britain was really a welfare state.

In reality the combination of affluence and welfare *had* largely solved the poverty problem as it had been understood in the 1930s—as the intractable effect of mass unemployment in traditional industrial centres. The poverty that was rediscovered in the 1960s, in its focus on marginal groups, more closely resembled the poverty examined by Charles Booth in the East End of London eighty years earlier. Once again the big cities—and particularly the metropolis—became the focus of the poverty problem. In a country as highly urbanised as Britain was, the most conspicuous deprivation was inevitably urban, but now the locus was less the collapsed single-industry centres of the interwar years than the poorest parts of the larger conurbations—less Wigan or Jarrow than the inner city.

There were several reasons why big cities should display what Honor Marshall called 'the phenomenon of poverty in affluence.'[3] In the first place, a dynamic economy placed strain on a comparatively static urban infrastructure, emphasising underlying weaknesses—particularly the inadequacy or obsolescence of the housing stock. Secondly, changes in social composition and stability might accentuate the problems of anomie so often attributed to urban society in contrast to supposedly more settled rural communities. The weakening or the absence of supportive social networks might harm the elderly, the mentally ill or the suicidal or might remove constraints on rootless youth. Thirdly, cities might draw in people attracted by precisely this absence of social constraint, anxious to escape the stigma and the coercion manifested in tighter communities: young runaways, addicts, single mothers, meths drinkers or simple drifters. Finally, as is familiar, the city became home for the vast majority of immigrants from overseas arriving in Britain in the 1950s: race-relations problems were overwhelmingly urban. London displayed all these effects more obviously than any other British city: London was the setting for most of the social causes célèbres of the period—the 1958 race riots, the Rachman scandal and the housing crisis, homelessness and squatting—and, of course, was the focus of much of the research carried out by the East London–based Institute of Community Studies.

This renewed emphasis on big-city poverty produced two major effects. The first was to make the social question so diffuse as to be almost beyond simple administrative solution, as the potential dislocations in city life were so much more varied than the earlier problems of industrial sclerosis had been. One consequence of this was the proliferation of new voluntary agencies to deal with new social problems, augmenting but also frequently challenging the existing statutory services and making the pattern of social provision more complex and less stable than before.[4] The second was to highlight a spatial component to welfare questions that had been largely absent from Beveridge, with his holistic approach and his emphasis on universality. The period sees an increasing concern with urban twilight zones as areas of *multiple* social breakdown and a concomitant interest in the revival of the inner-city community as a prerequisite for urban regeneration. The task of reinventing the welfare state assumed a complexity which would defeat the best efforts of those who were anxious to pursue it, even before the attacks on welfare and dependency that would come from the New Right.

Beyond Beveridge

The City Parochial Foundation (CPF) noted in its quinquennial policy review in 1971,

> Notwithstanding the social revolution which had taken place since the end of the Second World War, and which was continuing to take place, there remained deficiencies in the provision made by the State for the poorer classes of the Metropolis with whom the Foundation is concerned. Some of these deficiencies are by circumstance, since it has come to be recognised that the State is not always the best agency to purvey shelter and relief to the needy; some have arisen as fresh problems, because the meaning of poverty has been widened to include many other things besides a lack of material means; and some exist because not enough resources are made available by Society to remove or alleviate them. In short the belief that a charity no longer has a place or role in Society is without foundation. Exactly where its place is and what its role should be in the Welfare State is properly a matter of continuing debate.[5]

The foundation (now the Trust for London) had been established in the 1890s to organise the distribution of the substantial revenue from parochial charities in the City of London. Grants could only be made to London organizations, and the CPF normally avoided subsidising statutory agencies. In any turf war between public and voluntary sectors it might have been expected to side with the voluntary agencies, but the judgement above was an objective one, reflecting the pattern of grant applications.

The minutes of the CPF—an organisation with no real equivalent outside London—therefore provide a detailed guide to the voluntary revival in London. With the nature of each application recorded in elaborate detail, they make it possible to measure the aspirations of 1960s voluntarism.

Some applications were made in response to those vicissitudes of urban life outlined earlier. In October 1967, for instance, the Lady Margaret Hall Settlement based its appeal for funds for a new community unit on the grounds that 'life in a modern urban society engenders problems and tensions which often lead to the breakdown of the physical and mental health of individuals or of the unity and cohesion of families.' The Golborne Rehabilitation Centre had been established in 1957 for 'the care of the socially inadequate, ranging from drug addicts and ex-prisoners to the ordinary down-and-out, the inept immigrant, and those who are unadaptable to normal living in a normal household. The majority are rootless, without homes or families, some are mentally unstable, many require prolonged psychiatric treatment.' Seventeen years later the Crisis—BIT Trust appealed for funds for a shelter 'to accommodate people who would otherwise be on the street, and anyone non-violent—young, old, black, white, new arrivals in London from the provinces, families who do not qualify for local authority assistance, addicts, unmarried mothers and their children, pregnant women, people released from prison and mental hospitals—but mainly single homeless people.' Most important in this category were, perhaps, the Samaritans, founded by the Reverend Chad Varah at St Stephen's Walbrook, in the City of London, in 1953 to provide a helpline for the suicidal, which had dealt with 14,250 cases by 1965.[6]

More systematically, urban conditions provided the setting for the reinvention of the face-to-face approach associated with Victorian philanthropy but largely abandoned by the bureaucratic twentieth-century welfare state. The casework approach of the Charity Organisation Society (COS) in the nineteenth century had been condemned as judgemental, but this reflected more the COS's desire to curb indiscriminate giving than any lack of sympathy intrinsic to the technique; and by the 1960s, with a greater concern to engage with the underprivileged, there was a casework revival. By 1965 the Family Welfare Association, as the COS had become, noted that 'for the first time in many years the number of caseworkers on the staff has equalled the number the Association can afford to employ.'[7] The face-to-face approach was most evident in work with the young, largely passed over as a category by the Attleeian welfare state but a highly visible, often disaffected, part of the postwar city. 'Much recent thinking in Youth Work', John Edginton wrote in his 1979 study of Avenues Unlimited, a youth project in Tower Hamlets, 'has concentrated upon the theme "*if they won't come to us—we must go to them.*"'[8] Similarly, the Portobello Project, centred on a Portobello Road coffee bar, aimed to 'make contact with anti-social and potentially anti-social young people in North Kensington and to endeavour to provide them with some form of care, interest and a feeling of being wanted. . . . The [Project] Leader was to have a roving commission to seek out the youngsters in the cafes, pubs, dance halls, and streets of Notting Hill, and from them to discover their real needs as seen by themselves.'[9] In Notting Hill, as throughout inner London, much youth work dealt with immigrants, potentially more disaffected than the host young. The London Union of Youth Clubs formed an Immigrants Joint Committee to make young Blacks more aware of local services and pioneered such projects as the establishment of a club for Indian girls in Southall.[10]

The Beveridge report had been colour-blind; but the question of immigrant entitlement to benefits was sensitive, and immigrant groups often avoided public authorities. Members of the Bengali, Chinese and several other communities often lacked the command of English needed to deal with the inescapable technicalities, while after 1962 those who were unconfident of their right to remain in Britain feared that contact with the authorities might lead to expulsion. The problem was not, though, confined to immigrants: the Girls Alone in London Service, which sought to provide this kind of individually oriented assistance to young girls arriving in the capital 'without money, job, or anywhere to stay', noted that 'unfortunately many who most need guidance avoid any service with an "establishment" image', including all the statutory agencies.[11]

'New needs arise, and voluntary action springs up to meet them', wrote a working party of social workers investigating social services in the London Borough of Islington in 1965–66, capturing the ad hoc expansion of the voluntary sector.[12] Several voluntary agencies emerged as responses to new or intensified urban problems: Release, for instance, dealing with drug users, or those charities—most prominently the Reverend Dennis Downham's Spitalfields Crypt—prompted by the burgeoning crude-spirit-drinker problem in the early 1960s.[13] Some CPF applicants exemplified Sidney Webb's 'extension ladder' role of voluntary organizations, taking social provision further than could bodies subject to statutory constraints. The medical officer of health for the London Borough of Hackney, for instance, established a private charity 'to provide poor patients with minor necessities or comforts which could not be charged to statutory funds', specifically the rehabilitation of problem families. More quaintly, the principal youth officer of the London Borough of Waltham Forest won £1,250 to rehabilitate two houses in Leyton for use by a group of local bikers, who 'because they move about in a large group and because their movement is attended by a great amount of noise . . . are unwelcome in the more conventional clubs and cafés.'[14]

In a similar vein, the Mulberry Housing Trust, founded in 1965 under the chairmanship of the Conservative free-marketeer Sir Keith Joseph,

A homeless man accommodated by the Cyrenians in their hostel in Barons Court. The Cyrenians were an offshoot of the Simon Community, founded by Anton Wallich-Clifford in 1963 to combat homelessness in London. They typified the numerous ad hoc voluntary sector responses to new or worsening social problems in the capital. (Mary Evans Picture Library/Moyra Peyralta)

argued that 'Local Authorities, in considering applications for houses, are bound to deal with people on the waiting lists in strict rotation whereas charitable bodies are not similarly tied and can pay much greater regard to urgency.' Other voluntary bodies were, though, less benign towards local authorities' performance. 'It is clearly the duty of the Welfare State to provide adequate, suitable accommodation for all its citizens and particularly for decent, hard-working people who prize home life', announced the Housing the Homeless Central Fund, founded in 1963 in the belief that this duty was being neglected. The housing crisis in 1960s London was, indeed, the principal driving force behind voluntary-sector growth in the capital. The National Federation of Housing Societies noted in 1964 that there were 183 charitable housing societies in the Metropolitan Police Area alone, of which thirty-two had been founded in the previous twelve months.[15]

The state of London's housing stock, and the emergence of the homelessness issue during the 1960s, caused more public anger than any other social concern. It galvanized the guerrilla wing of the Anglican Church in London, in particular the organisation Christian Action (CA), founded

Homeless man and bonfire, Spitalfields, 1976. (Mary Evans Picture Library/Moyra Peyralta)

by the peace campaigner Canon John Collins in 1946. CA aimed 'to infuse all Christians with the burning intention to revolutionise the heart of society and to purify it with the fire of the living Gospel', specifically by 'pricking the social conscience of the nation or the locality where there is a falling short of Christian standards.'[16] Three years before the first screening of *Cathy Come Home*, Collins sought to launch a public appeal on behalf of the homeless. Recognising that their plight was a political problem beyond simple charitable solution, he sought to 'face the political parties with the fact that such a national appeal is necessary, despite all the benefits of the welfare state.'[17] In the event CA dropped its plans for a national campaign in favour of specific schemes such as the shelter for homeless women established near Waterloo Station in 1967 and twelve other housing associations set up under CA auspices by the end of 1966.[18]

Christian Action also aided the establishment of the Notting Hill Housing Trust (NHHT), established by the Reverend Bruce Kenrick, one of the Group Ministry in Notting Hill, which aimed to buy houses in this archetypal twilight zone to let them to local families at low rents. This evolved into Shelter—'The National Campaign for the Homeless'—in 1966.[19] Shelter was a more clearly secular organization, particularly after Kenrick lost a struggle for control of the charity to Des Wilson, but it adopted much of the drive and many of the evangelising methods of Christian Action and the NHHT. Kenrick, like Collins, had been an early advocate of new methods of publicity to convey the urgency of social problems. In 1963 he had proposed to launch the NHHT in a suitably modern, performative, manner: '[stage] a Press Conference; advertise in the Press; appeal by post to a large number of individuals; perhaps have a torch light procession and perhaps a television documentary' whenever London's housing crisis was next raised in Parliament.[20] By 1966 the NHHT was versed in modern advertising techniques, accepting that 'charities which are continuously in the news (Oxfam is an obvious example) tend to attract opportunities and "windfalls" which do not come the way of less-known organisations.'[21] Shelter, above all others, developed the techniques of aggressive publicity, Wilson arguing that the organization's aim was to put pressure on people with political muscle: 'Invaluable though our rescue operations were—and they need no defence—they were inadequate. The real, long-term answers to problems of exploitation and inequality lay with the priorities and policies of the politicians.'[22] He justified an expensive headquarters in the Strand on the grounds that it placed Shelter 'in an ideal position, near to Fleet Street, Whitehall and Westminster, radio and television headquarters. . . . SHELTER has been built by and around the communications world, and it owes a lot to its close proximity to the media.'[23] With its campaigning ethos, a young, radical membership and a modern approach to communications, Shelter, along with other new, campaigning charities like the Child Poverty Action Group,[24] sought to distance itself from a traditional image of philanthropy.

Twilight Zones

The second effect of 'urbanising' discussion of welfare was to restore a spatial dimension which had been visible in Victorian discussion of social problems but had dwindled as social debates had focused on the relationship between the individual and the state. In the 1960s, though, discussion of areas of deprivation moved from the journalistic fixation with 'Twilight London' to become the focus of official inquiries. The 1965 Milner Holland Committee on Housing in Greater London called for the identification of areas of concentrated substandard housing and for special powers to deal with the problem in those areas.[25] Similarly, the 1967 Plowden report on primary education envisaged Educational Priority Areas, requiring targeted assistance.[26] Linked with this awareness of the shortcomings of particular services in particular areas was an understanding that such areas often displayed a comprehensive failure of social provision, creating entire blighted zones in cities. 'Modern urban conditions tend to concentrate social deprivation geographically', explained the Oxford sociologist A. H. Halsey, outlining the rationale behind the Wilson government's Community Development Programme (CDP) in 1969, 'especially in the decaying inner ring of conurbations, in such a way as to reduce the quality of environmental service and opportunity. All local institutions are consequently defective—the family, the school, the welfare agencies, the job market and the recreational organisation.'[27] In London this approach can be traced back to the Notting Hill race riots of 1958. The special committee set up by the Royal Borough of Kensington to investigate the problem cited with approval the view of social workers that 'the "racial riots" were merely one symptom of the serious social disintegration which has existed in this district for a long time'—a problem also manifested in levels of mental illness, the suicide rate, the proportion of residents with prison records, levels of juvenile delinquency and the concentration of problem families in the area. It called for a combined sociological and social-welfare-based approach in North Kensington.[28]

The housing crisis similarly encouraged holistic, area-based approaches. Shelter's Neighbourhood Action Project in the late 1960s extended the charity's original activities by suggesting that 'the comprehensive, social, physical, and economic rehabilitation of a deteriorating residential area' would achieve more than the piecemeal restoration of individual houses.[29] In November 1971 a discussion paper from the London Council of Social Service stressed the centrality of housing to the malaise of deprived areas, arguing that 'poor housing is an important contributory factor in problems such as emotional disturbance, delinquency and truancy, and is often in the background of the break-up of families.'[30] A 1967 survey of London youths admitted to borstal in 1960–62 identified the capital's entire inner ring as a delinquency black spot, noting that 'a high incidence of crime ties in with the boundaries of the Victorian manufacturing belt—with a concentration of industry, overcrowded housing and sparse parks and open spaces as common environmental factors.'[31] Likewise in 1969 the Drug Dependency Unit of the Tower Hamlets youth project Avenues Unlimited pointed to the connection between social conditions, juvenile delinquency and drug addiction. It thought this 'a fresh approach which has not been followed up by anyone else', but by the late 1960s the tendency to connect a poor social environment, anomie and various forms of antisocial behaviour had become commonplace.[32] The concept of 'multiple deprivation', by which specific social problems interacted with one another in particular deprived areas, was well established by the close of the 1960s. It was reinforced, though, by the rapid contraction of London industry from the mid-1960s, which bore heavily on almost all of those inner-city quarters already identified as areas of concern.

Policy

By the late 1960s, then, a rediscovery of disadvantage in urban Britain had emphasized problems beyond the remit or competence of the statutory welfare agencies to tackle, prompting an ad hoc expansion of the voluntary sector. At the same time, there was a growing awareness that different problems might sit side by side, and reinforce one another, in specific deprived areas: 'localities which have a profusion of pressing social problems, offer only a dismal and squalid physical environment, are inadequately served by social services and are considered to justify special attention.'[33] The Wilson government produced a twofold response to this twin problem, though more by accident than design. The executive response was to appoint a committee under Frederic Seebohm ostensibly to implement the 1965 white paper *The Child, the Family and the Young Offender* but in fact to investigate personal social services across the board. It reported in 1968, recommending the creation of an enhanced social service department in every appropriate local authority, to deal with the problems of children, the young, the elderly, the mentally ill and others who were lightly touched by Beveridge. Its proposals were enacted by the Local Authority Social Services Act of 1970. At the same time, though, a separate inner-city initiative was announced in the spring of 1968—an experimental Community Development Programme focusing on a handful of inner-city areas, reflecting the widespread belief in the late 1960s that urban problems reflected a failure of civil society as much as the failure of executive action. The intention was to encourage civic awareness and involvement in the areas chosen, so that the inner-city population would no longer be passive recipients of welfare. Two of the areas chosen for CDPs were in London: Canning Town in the Borough of Newham and Newington in Southwark.

This combination of executive rationalization and community development represented, however accidentally, an apparently coherent approach to the urban problem. Few people in the late 1960s believed unquestioningly that social problems could be solved merely by state action, and Seebohm had devoted a whole chapter to the role of the community.[34] In reality, though, a tension between the two approaches would soon become evident. To understand why, it is necessary to look at the development of the community movement to that point.

The Rise of Community Action

Efforts to encourage community self-help in London predated the official Community Development Programme by several years. They had been a feature of the new voluntarism described here, which had always seen bureaucratic approaches to social problems as inadequate. Following the 1958 disturbances and the furore over exploitative landlordism and slum housing in the 1963 Rachman scandal, the Notting Hill–North Kensington area became London's first community laboratory. In 1963 the North Kensington Project described to the CPF work at the micro level to involve local residents in such activities as rubbish disposal and the provision of playgrounds for the under-fives. It regarded 'as a major achievement the involvement of residents themselves in these experiments' and planned to employ two social workers 'for experimental group action, *always involving the local resident*.' Two years later the North Kensington Family Study received a grant to enable Ilys Booker, the social worker in charge of community projects in the area, to visit the United States: 'the Americans not only have much longer experience of the problems of such mixed communities as that of North Kensington but their social work has concentrated much more than ours on community and group development.' Likewise, the National Institute of Social Work Training (NISWT) sent a staff member, David Jones, to the US to study community development. On his return, the NISWT inaugurated a pilot project in Southwark, promoting 'the participation of people and organisations in the area and the fostering of initiative, community responsibility and self-help. The [social] workers would not aim to organise particular activities or services but to assist people in the community to articulate their own needs and objectives and to take collective action about them.'[35]

David Thomas, in his 1976 study of the Southwark project, described the range of activity that resulted: though prioritising housing and playspace issues, the project also busied itself with 'redevelopment of the riverside, the level of health care, community newspapers, the early detection and prevention of homelessness, the preservation of local gardens and the library, pedestrian crossing provision, parent-teacher associations, support for flat-bound mothers, welfare rights, the level of employment opportunities, and the erosion of shopping and transport facilities.'[36] The pitch made by the Centre '70 Community Association in West Norwood in applying for a CPF grant in 1970 was characteristic: 'This is an area which already has problems, and the indications are that in the next few years those problems will greatly increase. Centre '70's aims are to help people to find solutions to the problems themselves; to stimulate local leadership; to develop a sense of responsibility; in short to build a real community.'[37]

When the Notting Hill Summer Project was formed in 1967 to coordinate the many ad hoc agencies in the area, one local newspaper saw it as 'the first major attempt to bind together the strands of an effective civil rights movement.'[38] Asserting and claiming social rights—tenancy rights, benefit rights, and so on—became an integral part of this kind of community activity, with specialist advice centres providing an outlet for the concerned professionals who frequently found their way into community work. By 1971 the Child Poverty Action Group was running a 'Welfare Rights Advocacy Course' in Camden, including sessions such as 'Tenant Rights and the Prevention of Homelessness', 'Supplementary Benefits', and the like.[39] The neighbourhood law centre—again based on US precedent—was pioneered in Notting Hill. By 1973 such law centres existed in ten boroughs, seeking to demystify the law in the eyes of working-class clients, to propagate an awareness of legal rights and to put pressure on public agencies where necessary.[40]

The law centres were generally supported by their local authority, but as the Notting Hill activist Jan O'Malley pointed out, such advice centres and law centres diminished the traditional mediating role of the local MP or councillor.[41] Most local authorities viewed the community movement, which in many respects trespassed on the regular municipal sphere, with some suspicion. Labour councils—and most inner-city councils were Labour controlled—often believed that they understood their working-class community's needs better than radical lawyers, social workers or altruistic students did.[42] Increasingly, though, local authorities found themselves on the back foot as their record as service providers was attacked by community activists and by the campaigning charities. Honor Marshall, researching her 1971 book *Twilight London*, found council officials 'visibly disturbed' by her request for an interview; some who did agree to talk 'arranged clandestine meetings, pointing out that their jobs were at risk.'[43] They had doubtless been shaken by the attacks on the council sector in discussion of the housing question from the mid-1960s. Social housing had once been the means by which Labour councils, with much central-government support, could demonstrate their socialism and reward their supporters, but as the focus of the housing question switched to the intractable problem of homelessness, councils were attacked for their perceived underperformance and bloody-mindedness. Des Wilson wrote, 'all our experience of dealing with the authorities suggests that there are still far too many people in local authorities whose attitude to the homeless is, at best, moralistic, and at worst, heartless.'[44] In *Cathy Come Home*, fictional but plausible, the 'villain' was less landlordism than officialdom.

In this context the Seebohm Report, apparently advocating 'nationalising' the personal social services by creating local authority superdepartments, seemed rather gauche. Seebohm was not, in fact, oblivious to the work of the voluntary sector, but as the National Council of Social Service commented, 'the idea of working through a voluntary organisation seems to be regarded as a *pis-aller* until the full force of the local authority's own reorganisation can be developed.'[45] In any event, Seebohm's lip service to voluntarism had little effect on the eventual legislation. As Hilary Rose pointed out, although 'scarcely a blue book or white paper discussing the social services can be published without a ritual genuflection in the direction of "rights" and "participation"', the 1970 act 'did not bother even to genuflect to community involvement.'[46]

An already adversarial relationship with local authorities became positively confrontational as the community movement radicalized in the early 1970s. O'Malley suggested that Notting Hill community activism provided a training ground for student politicians in the late 1960s;[47] conversely, student politicians took their activism into the community after 1968. Peter Hain, then a Young Liberal activist who was an early chronicler of the 1970s community politics movement, believed that the anticlimactic Vietnam protest at Grosvenor Square in October 1968 'marked a turning point in radical politics. It represented the exhaustion of a tactic around which the whole movement had been mobilised: the mass, symbolic demonstration.'[48] A shift towards community activism was the consequence; tracing the history of the 'radical turn' in community work in 1977, Peter Baldock described urban community activism as a natural next step for radicals leaving the universities.[49] Claimants' unions,[50] militant tenants' organizations and squatters

Lambeth, 1978. Corrugated iron given a political message, expressing criticism of the treatment of the socially disadvantaged by the Borough Council and the GLC. (Marx Memorial Library/Mary Evans Picture Library)

groups gained direction and leadership—not always solicited—from former *soixante-huitards*. Disenchanted themselves with the Wilsonian Labour Party, they sought through community action a remedy for what they saw as the political passivity of the working class. Thus the middle-class professional and ecclesiastical involvement which Jan O'Malley considered a brake on the wheel in Notting Hill was spurned in the community organizations of the early 1970s,[51] where an assumption of the pervasiveness of social conflict supplanted earlier hopes for a class-neutral approach to community problems. The radicalised community movement remained 'directly about people in deprived areas looking at their own problems and seeking their own solutions', but it doubted that 'the solutions are to be found in the resources of the people themselves. Instead they look to those who at present have power ... and try to find ways either to influence them or to take some of the power away from them.' In particular, local government was considered susceptible to community pressure.[52]

The '68-ers displayed a suspicion of bureaucracy characteristic of the New Left. They criticised the new, enlarged, London borough councils created in 1965 for being managerial, technocratic and designed 'to serve the interests of big business.'[53] Cynthia Cockburn's Marxist study of the 'managerial revolution' in Lambeth argued,

> We have been taught to think of local government as a kind of humane official charity, a service that looks after us 'from the cradle to the grave', protects us from the misfortunes of life, hardships such as poverty and homelessness that fall on us by fate—or are perhaps even our own fault. If the town hall doesn't seem to work in our interest we put it down to 'inefficiency' or 'red tape.' It is by no means obvious that a local council is part of a structure which *as a whole and in the long term* has other interests to serve than our own.[54]

Many local-authority actions in the 1960s strengthened the claim that councils cared little for the communities they served. In particular, a policy error of Stalinist proportions was committed by several inner-London borough councils in the housing field. Following a 1967 survey of London's housing stock by the Greater London Council, many inner-London boroughs resolved to eradicate the slums. Large tracts of slum housing were acquired for clearance, regardless of the squeeze on central support for local capital projects following the 1967 devaluation crisis and anxiety over high-rise industrial building following the Ronan Point disaster in 1968.[55] Many local authorities consequently found themselves with large numbers of poor but useable homes, kept empty at a time of housing shortage, awaiting redevelopment or refurbishment which was, in the straitened 1970s, endlessly deferred.[56] The several tenants' co-operatives that emerged in these years hoped to provide 'a neighbourhood-based movement for homes which offers an alternative to the constant demolition and concrete rebuilding that scars our cities and costs years of pain and upheaval to families with least defences.'[57] As the Sumner House Tenants' Co-operative in Poplar put it, 'if they had waited for the bureaucracy to produce another piecemeal solution to the problem of young families, the Co-operative would probably never have got off the ground.'[58]

The most visible of these ad hoc responses to the housing crisis was, though, the squatting movement which erupted across London from 1969.[59] It was driven by a resentment of local-authority incompetence that was hard to refute: at Arbour Square in Stepney, one of the early squats, sixty out of seventy units in a block awaiting demolition were being kept empty by Tower Hamlets Council, in an area with the most inadequate housing stock in London.[60] Some boroughs, beginning with Lewisham, accepted their effective powerlessness by striking a deal with squatters' representatives to legitimize the action. Redbridge, in contrast, created a public relations catastrophe by engaging bailiffs to evict homeless families from empty property. Either way, the spread of the movement, which embraced perhaps thirty thousand squatters in London at its peak, vindicated the claim of its leader, Ron Bailey, that 'direct action worked where individual campaigns failed.'[61]

Hain agreed.[62] He had led the successful campaign to stop the 1970 cricket tour of England by apartheid South Africa, which 'showed that the protest politics of direct action could flourish where the symbolism and rhetoric of Vietnam-type protests had floundered.' He saw direct action as 'the other side of the coin of direct democracy'; in the most articulate statement of the new community politics, he described the emergence of a new form of grassroots politics, in which 'the experience of direct action and the awareness that this brings will unite the powerless against the powerful, the governors against the governed.' 'The spread of rent strikes, tenants' struggles, information and advice services, welfare groups and all the other examples of community action which we see around us', he argued, 'constitute the reservoir from which an unstoppable radical tide could flow. The essence of radical community action is a recognition of the need for the politics of confrontation, rather than the politics of negotiation.' With this in mind, he stressed what he saw as the limitations of the radical charities of the sixties—Shelter, the National Council for Civil Liberties, the Child Poverty Action Group, and the like—which 'cast themselves in a role which, however valid and necessary in its own terms, essentially *complements* the existing system' rather than confronting it. Invoking Herbert Marcuse's concept of repressive tolerance, he warned of the danger that the disadvantaged poor could be emasculated by dependence on the welfare-state bureaucracy. Instead, participatory democracy would bring 'community control of social services and resources' in 'a society with an infinity of centres of power, expressing the principles of mutual aid and mutual co-operation, rather than competition and authoritarianism.' Decentralisation and participation would empower 'those groups in society who have fallen by the wayside and who do not have even a bargaining *entrée* to the power structure: the poor, the black community, the minorities', in alliance with shop-floor movements, women's liberationists and radical protest groups. Betraying little of his New Labour future, he envisaged a new form of democracy, 'fusing Trotsky's notion of "permanent revolution" with Mao's notion of the "cultural revolution."'[63]

Meanwhile the Community Development Projects were being steered in a Marxist direction hardly envisaged by Home Office when it created them in 1968.[64] The original aim of the project—to revive community solidarity in deprived areas as a means of combating the corrosive effects of deprivation—was dismissed as patronising. The Southwark CDP disparaged 'the former idea of community as a locality in which a set of supportive social relations was sustained, at least partly, by the lack of any alternative resources' and sought to move away from 'the fruitless task of seeking to recreate what some commentators believe were the life styles of traditional working-class neighbourhoods.'[65] The 1973 CDP Inter-Project report parodied the original premise of the project, which was said to have derived from the belief that failing neighbourhoods failed because of the shortcomings of their residents, to contrast it with its own emphasis on the structural nature of inner-city problems. The claim appeared plausible, as the leftward shift of the community movement coincided with the crushing effects of deindustrialization in inner London in the wake of the 1973–74 oil shock. The architects of the CDP had always acknowledged that community development could not be expected to 'secure the provision of a new comprehensive school, or the rehousing of the whole neighbourhood',[66] but by the mid-1970s the kind of civic consciousness-raising that CDP had originally sought appeared inadequate in the face of deepening economic malaise in the inner city. By 1975 the national CDP executive was calling for 'community based strategies for stimulating political demands for the form and quantity of local authority service provision' and for local authorities to be given greater powers to bolster industry and employment in their areas.[67]

Conclusion

'There must be a second revolution in the welfare state, a second revolution', Derek Morrell, principal architect of the Community Development Project, had argued.[68] In the event his aspiration to promote this revolution by enhancing civic awareness in deprived areas was undermined in London by the economic collapse of the inner city. Policy for the twilight zones dichotomized into the choice exemplified in Docklands: a choice between holistic redevelopment proposals devised with little reference to the resident community and quixotic attempts to keep the old industrial economy alive through public expenditure and public-sector job-creation programmes. The second option would become central to the strategy of the emergent New Left on the GLC and some inner-London borough councils in the 1980s, but the shift of national policy in that decade soon snuffed out that form of local boosterism.

In the meantime, the disputed boundary between public and voluntary agencies became little clearer. The new local-authority social services departments were obviously permanent, but they did little to gain public recognition, let alone affection. The resurgent voluntary sector was also clearly durable—at risk of bureaucratization but retaining much of its early campaigning energy. Over time it would become evident that both the 'reach' of the public agencies and the financial capacity of the voluntary bodies were limited. The compromise by which local authorities provided much of the funding for voluntary activity duly emerged and would provide a modus vivendi until 2010, but in the late 1970s it was by no means obvious what the best balance between public and voluntary activity in the welfare field should be. What *was* obvious by the late 1970s was that two decades spent rediscovering poverty had failed to produce a workable blueprint for welfare reform.

In the 1940s Beveridge's core objective of devising a mechanism to provide universal social security, however ambitious, had been relatively easily defined. The public agencies on which he would have to rely were not subject to regular questioning of their goodwill or their competence. He enjoyed a broad-based, cross-party support for the bulk of his proposals. He was also swimming with the tide of public policy in cognate areas, notably full employment and health-care reform. To state these advantages is to underline how difficult the next steps in welfare would be in the 1960s and 1970s. The shift from an industrial to an urban focus, most obvious in London, made the concept of poverty more variegated and harder to tackle, a fact reflected in the explosion of ad hoc voluntary initiatives. Increasingly, urban poverty came to be equated with the failure of individual neighbourhoods, but this understanding did not in itself prescribe any policy options. The executive solution proposed by Seebohm failed to reflect a public mood swing away from top-down social administration and public disenchantment with local authorities. The call for grassroots action to tackle the problems of twilight zones was far more in tune with the times, but under scrutiny 'community' proved an ambiguous and contested concept. Taken up by radical urban activists from the late 1960s, it evolved into a doctrine that was hard-edged and partisan rather than consensual and one which moved progressively out of line with national economic policy during the 1970s.

In the immediate postwar years there had been a broad public faith that the welfare state provided cradle-to-grave social security of the kind clearly lacking in the 1930s, and it was valued in much the same way as the National Health Service—'the closest thing that the English people have to a religion'[69]—continues to be today. During the sixties that understanding of the social security state was weakened in large cities and above all in London, first by repeated exposés of forms of poverty beyond its reach, secondly by the appearance of nonstate agencies to deal with those specific problems and finally by the increasingly frequent attacks—often trenchant and often valid—on the efficacy and benevolence of the statutory agencies. By the late seventies the urban welfare state in practice had come under sustained and damaging attack from people who were unequivocally committed to the use of public resources to combat deprivation. Then came Mrs Thatcher.

14

Strains of Labour in
the Inner City

In 1962 the political journalist Anthony Howard examined the Islington Labour Party for the *New Statesman*. He found the headquarters of the East Islington constituency party, in St Paul's Road, 'surrounded by garbage, dirty milk bottles and even with last year's LCC [election] posters still stuck to its peeling pillars.' The membership of the North Islington party had fallen by more than 80 percent since its Attleeian heyday in 1951. The party had nonetheless controlled the council continuously since 1934: since the war the Conservatives had had a presence on the council only briefly, in 1949–52 when a dozen were returned. Labour control was almost absolute.[1]

Four years later, Ruth Butterworth examined Islington in greater depth, looking at the old metropolitan borough council in its last years, before amalgamation with Finsbury Borough to create the modern London Borough of Islington in 1965.[2] She found that while the turnover of councillors was higher than might have been inferred from this picture of stagnation, the leadership, both in the constituency parties and in the council, tended to be monopolised by people who had served decades in the movement (Howard had cited a prominent member of the party who claimed with pride 'that he himself had been in the party for 30 years, that the chairman had been in it for 40 and the treasurer for 50').[3] In the last council to be elected before enlargement, the leader had been a member for twenty-seven years, as had the chief whip, while the leader of the Labour Group had clocked up twenty-four years. The principle that an apprenticeship in the movement was a prerequisite for preferment in party or council was firmly held. It did not in itself imperil the conduct of local affairs—it was generally agreed that Islington's Labour 'old guard' were competent local managers—but the drawbacks were evident. Most clearly, it encouraged a generational wave effect. Islington Labour had been a relatively young party in 1934; by the midsixties it had become a relatively old one. The effects of the 'buggins turn' principle had been compounded by the outflow of younger skilled labour from inner London, so that even had the 'old guard' been more ready to step aside, the next generation of potential working-class leaders was becoming depleted. Constituency party membership was dwindling, consisting of 'multiple office-holders or non-participating card-carriers with little gradation between these extremes.'[4] Then as ever, Islington had its share of middle-class radicals to draw on: Howard had noted, before 'gentrification' became a term of art, that a 'middle-class invasion' was making parts of Islington 'madly smart', but Butterworth found that 'graduates, professional men, white-collar workers' were more likely to leave the council after one or two terms.[5] Social change in the area, in other words, was not reflected on the council. Nor, by extension, was the evolution of the progressive agenda. Butterworth noted that the top brass of the local party were 'fundamentally apolitical. They identified an interest in national and international affairs with belonging to the left-wing, which was by definition ... irresponsible.'[6]

Islington was far from unique as a virtual Labour monopoly. The twenty-eight metropolitan boroughs within the LCC area had been created in 1900. They roughly reflected the distribution of population at the end of the Victorian era, with several relatively small authorities clustered in the densely populated inner city. By the postwar years, after decades of outward movement by the better-off but before deindustrialisation and gentrification disrupted London's industrial areas, most of the inner city was overwhelmingly working class in composition. Small areas and social homogeneity combined to produce impregnable Labour monopolies. In an analysis of London local authorities produced for submission to the Herbert Commission on London's local government in 1960, the Greater London Group of the London School of Economics (LSE) showed that twenty-two of the twenty-eight metropolitan borough councils had been in single-party control since at least 1937. In seventeen of them the single party was Labour.[7]

The LSE team concluded, reasonably enough, that such conditions 'present[ed] a serious threat to the democratic working and future of local government.'[8] They were acceptable—or at least accepted—in areas where a working-class Labour council could reasonably claim to mirror the industrial community which had elected it. In contrast to the censorious tone of the descriptions of Islington, John E. Turner's work on Bermondsey, published in 1978 but based on research conducted in 1961–62, looked more analytically at Labour's local operations in the borough with the highest proportion of semiskilled and unskilled workers in London in 1951.[9] Turner found that Bermondsey's Labour Party members were overwhelmingly either working class or identifying as working class. Bermondsey Labour had maintained its local profile by such associational initiatives as 'evenings of bingo, dances, theatre parties, day-long outings, a sports day for children and activities for the older folk.'[10] It had run successful recent recruitment drives. Of the party activists, a far higher proportion were interested in gaining election to the local council and a far smaller proportion in getting into Parliament than in the other two constituencies that Turner studied (Fulham and South Kensington). Discussion of national and international politics was not frowned upon in General Management Committee (GMC) meetings, as Butterworth alleged in Islington, despite the fear of some local leaders that the unilateralism issue might split the party. The MP—Robert Mellish—was active and attentive to constituency concerns.

Turner stressed that the Bermondsey party 'certainly did not fit the stereotype of a Labour organisation in an impregnable constituency undergoing a process of decay',[11] but his sympathetic portrait still demonstrates many of the structural weaknesses highlighted by Howard and Butterworth in Islington. Older members dominated the key positions in the local party. If not in decay, the party was 'so stable that its veterans were able to routinise their procedures and virtually convert them into traditions.'[12] Decision-making by the Labour Group in camera meant that the full—public—council meetings were 'stereotyped and dull.'[13] Despite the recruitment drives, its membership had fallen by more than a third in eight years. Party members had to wait almost a decade before securing election to the GMC, significantly longer than in Fulham or South Kensington. As a result, although the age profile of the GMCs in those two seats resembled that of the population as a whole, Bermondsey was appreciably older, with 72 percent of the GMC aged forty-five or over, against 47 percent of the local population. A decade later, John O'Malley reached similar conclusions in his analysis of Newham Council, conducted for the Newham Community Development Project, noting that Labour

Old Labour at play. The Poplar Labour Party Women's Section wheelbarrow race, early 1960s. Standing second from the right is Nellie Cressall, one of the rebel Poplar councillors imprisoned in 1921 and the last of the group to die, in 1973. (Island History Trust, IHT/p.0248; reproduced with the permission of Tower Hamlets Local History Library and Archives, London Borough of Tower Hamlets)

had run the area's local authorities continuously almost since the First World War and that most of the current council's leaders had clocked up at least twenty years' service.[14] In 1974 the American political scientist Andrew Glassberg, researching a study of three London boroughs, interviewed a serving Tower Hamlets councillor who had first been elected to one of the borough's predecessor councils in 1928.[15] In many inner-London boroughs 'Old Labour' really was ageing.

In consequence, even where the charge of stagnation could not be levelled at a local Labour organisation—and Islington was not alone in inviting it—an elderly and entrenched party leadership was likely to respond slowly if at all to changes in the progressive agenda. Solidly working-class parties, with a preponderance of ageing members, were prone to socially conservative attitudes—Turner noted the Bermondsey GMC's support for capital punishment and for immigration restriction, which it felt sufficiently strongly about to submit a resolution to the annual party conference in 1961.[16] As the Left's agenda evolved over the decade, blue-collar councillors showed themselves either bemused by or actively hostile to middle-class radicalism, feminism and the other elements of the emerging identity politics. Though more responsive to the worsening problem of unemployment, they tended to keep claimants' unions, generally under far-left leadership, at arm's length.

Inner-London parties were attuned to a limited model of social service provision—particularly the provision of social housing—which had developed as Labour gained control of many inner-city boroughs in the interwar years. An inherent 'council-knows-best' paternalism had long been justified on the grounds that Labour authorities could claim plausibly to be drawn from the communities they served: 'working-class themselves, "we know what people want" was their frequent claim', as Florence Rossetti, of the Southwark Community Development Project wrote of that borough's Labour leaders in 1978.[17] Consistent electoral success appeared to validate this claim ('Let's face it—what we have here, without beating about the bush, is an electoral machine. . . . What more can be asked of us?', as the deputy leader of the Islington Labour group put it to Howard),[18] but Rossetti believed that 'the [Southwark] Labour group's unbroken period in office may have dulled members' political sensitivity to their working-class supporters, towards whom the traditionalists tended to be highly paternalistic.'[19] In any case, Labour's traditional base was becoming weaker, as deindustrialisation and gentrification diluted the blue-collar identity of inner London. Sue Goss noted in her study of Southwark that even in that apparently solid working-class borough, manual workers accounted for only 31 percent of the population by 1981: 'the rest were white-collar workers, professionals, unemployed, economically inactive or pensioners.'[20]

Outside London's industrial core, the changing social composition of local Labour groups was evident even in the early sixties. The interviews with activists in Putney conducted by the former MP for the constituency Hugh Jenkins in 1980 described a party in which postwar dominance of 'fat trade unionists' yielded to the emergence of 'graduates on quite good incomes', the tipping point coming around 1962–63 when such middle-class activists were radicalised by the Campaign for Nuclear Disarmament (CND).[21] More profound transformation came, though, when the old guard were dislodged from their council fiefdoms by the massive Conservative gains in the borough-council elections of May 1968. The Tories benefited from general disenchantment with the Wilson government's economic record in the wake of the 1967 devaluation of sterling but also, almost certainly, from the airing of the immigration issue by the Tory shadow minister Enoch Powell in his 'Rivers of Blood' speech three weeks earlier. This resonated with many regular Labour voters, and the party was humiliated in many of its regular inner-city strongholds. Having gained no seats on the seventy-strong Hackney Council in 1964, the Tories now took control with thirty-eight councillors and six aldermen. In Hammersmith and Fulham, also seventy strong, Tory numbers rose from eight to fifty-nine. Having held all seventy seats in Islington in 1964, Labour was reduced to ten elected councillors and five aldermen. In Lambeth Labour's 1964 tally of fifty-one councillors and aldermen fell to seven—four of them aldermen chosen in 1964 on six-year terms. Labour also lost Camden, Greenwich, Lewisham and Wandsworth. Its only outright victories in inner London were in their fortresses of Southwark and Tower Hamlets.[22] In all Labour retained only 212 of its 520 elected councillors in inner London, 90 of them in those two boroughs.

Inevitably, several of the 'old guard' leadership fell victim to this cull. This came as a shock to most of them. Butterworth had noted in 1966 that for such figures in Islington death was more likely than retirement to bring council service to an end, with leaving the area a poor third.[23] Electoral defeat had not entered into the matter, and its unanticipated incidence in 1968 hastened the retirement of many in this generally elderly category. The figures who emerged to lead inner-London councils in or shortly after 1971, when Labour recaptured all the inner-London boroughs it had lost in 1968, differed markedly from their predecessors.[24] Lambeth Council was led by Charles Dryland, an economics teacher, from 1971–73 and subsequently by David Stimpson, who worked in insurance. Gerry Southgate, who led Islington from 1972, was office manager for a firm of solicitors.[25] Still more symbolic of Labour's changing municipal image, perhaps, was the emergence in Camden of Millie Miller as London's first female council leader.[26]

Pat Haynes, elected to Islington Council for the first time in 1971 and counting himself on the 'slightly idiosyncratic centre-left', recalled in 1994 that 'I have seen my local party change in the early 1960s when I was a CND member and my local Labour Party [was] dominated by right-wing racist, self-proclaimed working-class champions and I was among a small minority.' Islington's 'new guard' of 1971 included 'a great many new faces. . . . Some were young and educated, many were owner-occupiers and served in professional capacities for a living.'[27] They were, clearly, gentrifiers, in one of the principal sites of London gentrification. Obviously left-leaning, they were likely to have been involved already in some form of voluntary organisation, whether an amenity or residents' association, CND or the anti-apartheid movement, or one of the welfare-oriented pressure groups described in chapter 13. 'The professional middle-class types who came onto the council very recently', explained Bill Bayliss, one of the 'self-proclaimed working-class champions' that Haynes decried, 'themselves were originally all members of pressure groups: that's how they took over, ... consumers associations, so-called, residents associations, so called, amenity groups, and so forth, and they just moved over and took over at the nomination time.'[28] Bayliss's tone was disparaging— 'old Labour' councillors generally distrusted such groups as middle-class ramps[29]—but the sclerosis afflicting constituency Labour parties in much of inner London had meant that left-of-centre local politics had developed in the sixties within a diaspora of voluntary groups emerging outside formal municipal structures. Many were more explicitly political in intent than consumer associations or amenity groups, and many sought to influence policy in their local authorities. Council responses varied. Stimpson in Lambeth, following the current 'managerial' approach to local government, sought to run his borough through a centralised group of committee chairs and senior officers.[30] Southgate in Islington, by contrast, considered voluntary organisations more 'legitimate' than the Labour Party because of their wider reach.[31] He sought to involve them in council business as part of a policy of encouraging civic participation that had been central to Labour's 1971 manifesto in Islington: by 1973 committee agendas were being sent to 150 local voluntary organisations.[32] What was clear was that the days were ending when a local Labour party and a Labour council could be run on the basis of iron discipline and 'Buggins' turn', could depend on the kind of loyalty and solidarity instilled by trade-union membership and could prefer, in Anthony Howard's words, 'the ease of machine politics to the difficulties of democratic participation.'[33] The wider movement could not be ignored. Events would show that it was not easily accommodated.

Alternative Politics

Ruth Butterworth noted that, given the atrophy of the East Islington constituency party and its complete failure to integrate younger members in its processes, the East Islington Young Socialist section became synonymous with CND.[34] Jan O'Malley, both prime mover and chronicler of the community politics movement in Notting Hill, served her political apprenticeship in CND in the early sixties, meeting her husband, John—himself a community activist in Notting Hill and Newham—on a CND march. The pattern of young socialists being galvanised and mobilised by internationalist movements—CND and later the Vietnam Solidarity Campaign—before turning to the domestic reform issues pursued by similar grassroots groups, would become familiar in the late sixties. Just as gaps in the welfare state prompted the emergence of numerous ad hoc pressure groups, described in chapter 13, so the inertia and apparent conservatism of local Labour in London encouraged the formation of quasi-political grassroots organisations, in the form of squatters' groups, claimants' unions, the various women's groups, community action groups and the like, seeking to occupy a vacuum which they did not trust local Labour to fill. There was, inevitably, a substantial overlap between the two categories: Shelter and the Child Poverty Action Group, for example, were effectively political campaigners, while the explicitly political squatters' or women's groups were drawing attention to holes in the welfare safety net by their actions. A new form of socially oriented direct-action politics was emerging.

Notting Hill provided the most fertile soil for this community politics: the area was unusually suitable for an issue-oriented grassroots alternative to conventional local Labourism. The archetypal twilight zone of postwar London, Notting Hill was paradoxically contained before 1965 within two Conservative-controlled metropolitan boroughs: Kensington and Paddington.[35] Labour did hold the Parliamentary constituency of Kensington North, site of the racial disturbances of 1958, but the local party had been in the hands of the old guard since the war. The MP, George Rogers, appeared unresponsive to the social problems of the area and unsympathetic to its ethnic minorities. Arriving from Ulster in 1967, the community activist Sean Baine 'knew that Notting Hill had its fair share of local injustices, and expected, therefore, that the local Labour Party might be that more radical and involved in righting local wrongs, even if it felt more frustrated at the government's performance nationally.' What he found was political inertia. Once again, 'the party overall was controlled by a small group of people which had perpetuated its control over many years', and 'the position was worst in the safest Labour ward, which had the most intractable housing problems, where the ward organization was virtually defunct, occasionally spluttering into a poor imitation of life.'[36] Lacking a campaigning outlet in the local authority, the Constituency Labour Party or the MP,

social activists had formed ad hoc groups even before the 1958 disturbances. A network of organisations emerged in the area during the 1960s,
including the Notting Hill Housing Trust,[37] the Notting Hill Social Council, the Notting Hill Community Workshop and the Notting Hill People's
Association. As Jan O'Malley put it, 'We wanted to change the political
nature of the normal political parties because they seemed so ossified and
non-reactive to the genuine problems people had and we wanted to build
a bottom-up politics.'[38] O'Malley's CND background had fostered the belief, widespread among antinuclear activists, that the disregard of their
protest in the early 1960s demonstrated the inability of the conventional
political system to respond to popular feeling. Accordingly, 'they developed a real scepticism of the type of political organising which relied
heavily on ritualised leafleting, and on meetings of the converted. They
developed a growing conviction of the need to work at the grass roots level,
with all political activity growing out of the needs experienced by working
people.'[39]

Baine had likewise concluded that for the task of righting social wrongs
'the Labour Party was dead as a possible organizational form.'[40] The emergent feminist groups in London inevitably took the same view, not just
because many constituency Labour parties were controlled by ageing men,
though they were, but also because Labour's often formalistic structures
could not offer the fluidity, solidarity and cooperation that the women's
movement sought to foster through its organisations.[41] The radical—and
feminist—editors of the *Islington Gutter Press*, the most prolific of the
many newspapers generated by the London community movement, explained their reluctance to join the Labour Party: 'We do not think it will
ever be turned into a real organisation of working-class power. The main
goal of the Labour left is nationalisation of land and industry. But anyone
who lives in a council flat or works for the Gas Board will know that it
makes precious little difference.'[42]

At the height of the community movement's confidence, in the midseventies, there was much loose talk of new modes of grassroots politics sup-
planting conventional political organisations—including the Labour
Party—altogether. But the limitations of community politics were already
evident. It tended to be episodic and often reactive in nature and prone to
tunnel vision. Cynthia Cockburn's account of Lambeth politics, while accepting that 'this "community" militancy had particular meaning as an
expression of working-class militancy in a situation where industrial militancy was slight', pointed out that community action over schools or the

health service was conspicuously absent, despite problems in both areas.[43] Further, a movement dominated by the radical Left could not ignore the argument put by Irene Binns in the *Community Action* journal in 1973:

> While it is possible to win small scale gains, which are not to be scoffed at, the main problems communities face are outcomes of a class society and need to be seen as such if anything of value is to be achieved. For it is the poor wages, the long hours of work, unemployment and poor opportunities summed up in lack of political power, which make for many community problems. . . . We need to get away from the assumption—implicit in much community action—that pressure group type politics, used so successfully by middle class communities, can be used to alter the allocation of resources in favour of the deprived.[44]

In the event, the broadening of the agenda that Binns advocated would be encouraged by the intensification of London's economic problems in the months after her article was published. The oil shock of 1973 quickened the pace of deindustrialisation in inner London, posing an existential threat to established working-class communities. Between 1973 and 1978 inner London suffered a 26 percent decline in full-time employment.[45] The East End, already struggling to cope with the effects of the closure of the docks, suffered most. Manufacturing employment in Stepney and Poplar fell by 29 percent in only four years, 1971–75, with depopulation to match; outmigration was concentrated heavily in the prime working-age groups.[46]

The suggestion that public policy should seek to prevent the destruction of industry and preserve working-class communities became central to the London Left's agenda. In Docklands and across inner London efforts to preserve a community indefinitely after the loss of its principal source of employment were highly optimistic, but most community activists instinctively sympathised with the objective. It embodied their own reverence for the traditional industrial community, which they saw as the victim of a predatory late capitalism, shifting investment across the globe without concern for the impact on localities. Some targeted research, particularly from the two London Community Development Projects, exposed the collapse of inner-London industry. In the process it made the case for cooperation between all parts of communities whose very survival was threatened: indeed, Binns had praised the cooperation between the Canning Town (Newham) CDP and the opponents of Docklands redevelopment as an example of the kind of wider community activism that she advocated.[47] During 1975 the journal *Community Action* stressed the need to take the community's fight to the workplace—'people forget that whether they are fighting about bad housing conditions or bad workplace conditions the root cause of these problems is the *same*. It is the control of wealth by a minority'—and in February 1976 the journal interviewed the Australian trade unionist Jack Mundey, orchestrator of the 'green bans' which had coordinated environmental and industrial action in Sydney.[48] In 1975 a one-day conference on the East End's unemployment problem brought the formation of a Newham Action Committee comprising trade unions, tenants' groups, councillors and Labour constituency activists.[49] The worsening economic situation in the midseventies emphasised the limitations of the first wave of community politics, which had largely been defensive in nature, aiming to protect communities against evictions or redevelopment but necessarily, given the organisations' lack of statutory powers, stopping short of more constructive policy.

Exactly how to deploy direct action against deindustrialisation remained, though, unclear. The methods used successfully to rehouse homeless families or block an office development could not be relied on to deter a firm from moving from an obsolete Victorian factory to a purpose-built industrial unit outside London.[50] The Newham Action Committee advocated 'occupations, work-ins, pickets and forging new forms of struggle appropriate to the particular circumstances.'[51] Factory occupations and work-ins had been the favoured direct-action method of job protection since the success of the work-in at Upper Clyde Shipbuilders in 1971–72, but such initiatives achieved little in London: Tom Clarke's upbeat 1979 account of successful 1970s occupations included no London examples.[52] Such guerrilla action as the blockade of the Standard Telephones and Cables factory in North Woolwich (in order to prevent the removal of equipment and thwart the company's move to Newport) was unlikely indefinitely to prevent firms from leaving London if they felt that future growth depended on relocation.[53] It became clear that job protection, if it was possible at all, would require intervention by public authorities. At a public meeting in Newham in 1975 the radical economist Stuart Holland attributed the crisis to '1) Capitalist economy 2) Capitalist economic policies', offering such tasters of Labour's later Alternative Economic Strategy as compulsory planning agreements for local industry.[54] The remedy advocated most frequently, though, was the expansion of local-authority direct labour operations to counter unemployment. 'As industry is shedding jobs nationally', one Islington study concluded, 'expanding the labour intensive public service sector seems a good way of increasing employment.'[55]

Such an approach implied a less hostile view of local authorities than had previously prevailed and, by extension, a commitment to steering council Labour groups and Labour-controlled authorities to the left. 'It is still difficult to ignore the council or reject it totally if you need something', the editors of the *Islington Gutter Press* had observed in 1974: 'after all, they could one day play a more useful role.'[56] Bob Colenutt described a similar change of approach in Southwark, prompted by the Labour council's attempts to gentrify the riverside.[57] As one Southwark community worker told Sue Goss, 'people . . . decided that they ought to join the Labour Party—they were banging their heads against a brick wall and there was a door they could open and walk through.'[58] What would later be stigmatised as entryism reflected this change of approach. Gaining a presence in a ward party and subsequently on a local authority was seldom difficult: 'frankly you could take over the Party by accident and in a way that's what happened', the future member of the Livingstone GLC George Nicholson told Goss: 'it wasn't a hugely premeditated thing—just by half a dozen people joining the ward you changed the politics of the ward—you couldn't help it.'[59]

As the politics of individual wards changed, so the politics of constituency parties and Labour councils became more complex and more fractious. Inner-London Labour parties contained, in varying proportions, dwindling but often vocal groups of old blue-collar Labourites, usually socially conservative in outlook, middle-class professionals, instinctively managerial and modernising, and New Left radicals, with a taste for participatory democracy and direct action. This was an unstable mixture.

Culture Wars

Labour was a party in a state of flux, with evident potential for internal culture wars. Sarah Hough's 1977 analysis of local GMCs in Waltham Forest found that while more than half the manual workers questioned believed that immigration should be halted and two-fifths thought the Race Relations Acts to have done more harm than good, the percentage of non-manual workers—disproportionately represented on local GMCs—holding those views was 8 percent and 4 percent, respectively. Only one-third of manual workers supported the abolition of corporal punishment in schools, against three-quarters of nonmanuals.[60] Pat Haynes's fraternal description of the old working class in his own party as 'our neo-fascist right-wingers' gives some sense of the gulf between old and new Labour councillors in Islington.[61]

What Ken Livingstone called the 'dinosaur bloc' of old working-class rightists was probably more vocal in Islington than in many councils: 'in boroughs like Newham, Hillingdon, Brent or Camden this element has shrunk or disappeared.'[62] It did not disappear overnight, though, and remained potent in the two inner-London boroughs which had not experienced the clean sweep of 1968, Tower Hamlets and Southwark—particularly the latter, where the Labour group was controlled by a Bermondsey-centred 'old guard' under John O'Grady, a hard-nosed practitioner of 'Herbert Morrison's style of borough bossdom.'[63] Elsewhere the retreat of the old guard merely increased the scope for conflict amongst their successors.

The squatting issue demonstrates the complex tensions developing within Labour councils. The explosion of squatter numbers in the early seventies caught many authorities off-guard. Traditionally housing was what Labour councils did—'once you've given people a council house you've satisfied them', as Glassberg was told by one of his working-class councillor interviewees[64]—and the sudden popularity of squatting as an ad hoc remedy for the housing shortage appeared to be an indictment of local-authority failure in a key area. The communitarians on the left generally supported squatting as one means of 'bargaining, persuading and cajoling those in power' to mend their ways.[65] The first issue of the *Islington Gutter Press* stressed that squatting was 'not just an activity for derelicts and junkies [but] a positive move that people can make to show that their needs are not being satisfied by present housing schemes.'[66] Many on the left were already concerned about the traditional basis of council housing allocations, which Livingstone considered 'biased in favour of the "respectable" working class, so that new council housing was usually filled by white, skilled, working-class and lower-middle-class families.'[67] Old Labour councillors, on the other hand, felt that they had been elected to represent precisely those people and worried that their interests were being neglected. In Islington Bill Bayliss feared that the new leadership, composed largely of philanthropic professionals, favoured the disadvantaged over the settled working class; his more outspoken colleague Fred Johns criticised the leadership in the local press for 'rehous[ing] squatters from outside the borough, so-called homeless from everywhere but Islington.'[68] They saw squatters as unkempt young radicals set on establishing alternative communities in houses fit only for demolition, cheating the waiting list in the process.

Given these tensions, it is unsurprising that Labour councils found it hard to respond to the squatter problem. It was actually Conservative-controlled Lewisham which forced the pace in 1969, reaching an agreement with Ron Bailey's Family Squatters Association by which houses purchased for redevelopment or rehabilitation could be assigned to squatter groups on condition that they were released when needed. Old Labour Southwark explicitly rejected following the Lewisham scheme in 1971, concerned that it would mean that they had been 'pushed into it by the militants', and pressed ahead with the eviction of nine families who had moved into empty properties in Peckham.[69] The middle-class leaders of other Labour councils might, as alleged, have been more solicitous towards the homeless, but they still sought a more systematic way of dealing with the problem than squatting offered. To Margaret Watson, chair of the Islington housing committee, squatting was simply 'the worst form of queue-jumping.'[70] Over the course of the decade many Labour councils simply lost patience with squatter groups that showed little willingness to move unless coerced. In 1978 the squat at Huntley Street, in Bloomsbury, was cleared by the police at the behest of Camden Council, using bulldozers and grappling hooks in 'a paramilitary operation.'[71] The heavy-handed attempt to clear St Agnes Place, Kennington, in the previous year, when houses were demolished around the remaining squatters before an injunction was obtained to block the operation, suggested that Lambeth Council's conception of social service was becoming strained.[72] It was said to have contributed to the leftward shift within the Labour Group which led to Stimpson's removal by the Left, under Ted Knight, in 1978.[73]

What these episodes demonstrate is that while the gulf in outlook between the dwindling blue-collar Right and those who were replacing them was enormous, there was also little love lost between new Right and new Left. The former tended to be modernisers, exemplified by Paul Beasley, employed by a firm of City solicitors, who narrowly defeated John Orwell to become leader of Tower Hamlets Council in 1974, at the age of twenty-nine and after only four years' council service. He favoured reform of the council's structures in the direction of 'the corporate idea', to make local government less 'amateurish.' Arguing that Tower Hamlets' long-standing housing mission could now be declared accomplished (plausibly, given that almost 80 percent of the borough's housing stock was now socially rented), he believed that the time was ripe to prioritise economic development. Unlike most on both the new and the old Left, he called for mixed development in Docklands.[74] Rightist council leaders, conscious of their strained rate base, were more likely to be sympathetic to commercial development in previously industrial areas: Camden's readiness to break bread with Stock Conversion, the commercial property vehicle of the developer Joe Levy, led to a long-running and ultimately damaging battle with residents and squatters in Tolmers Square, north of the Euston Road.[75]

The new Left saw property developers as social parasites and opposed strenuously any project which, like Tolmers Square, sacrificed housing to offices. They were likely to favour the municipalisation of privately rented property and the freezing of council rents. As the depth of the inner-London employment problem became clear, they called for councils to use such job-creation powers as they possessed, particularly through the expansion of direct labour organisations: as Livingstone argued in 1978, 'if a Labour Council can't build up its own D[irect] L[abour] O[rganisation], it can't do anything. Expansion of its own employment is the only worth-while and practically effective strategy for reducing unemployment in a borough.'[76] Wandsworth, where the new Left had established a significant presence on the borough council by middecade, demonstrates the kind of local regeneration advocated by the municipal Left at this point. Faced with a 20 percent fall in manufacturing employment in five years and a 35 percent increase in unemployment in the course of just one year, the council concluded in 1976 that 'local authorities have long been seen as the agents of intervention when natural disasters, like fire or flood, strike; it is time to see them as agents to deal with economic calamity as well.'[77] Echoing Bennite arguments in the national party, they called for 'an improved economic planning system, with a major role for local government; and . . . experiments in new forms of industrial ownership and control.'[78] These included power for the council to engage in industrial production itself, as 'much stronger forms of public intervention in the local economy were going to be necessary to restore the vigour of the local economy.'[79]

There was, therefore, a discernible left-right division within many Labour councils, which intensified towards the decade's end. It was not, though, replicated precisely in every authority, and it was not enough, on the face of it, to pull the party apart without the intense social and personal hostility that afflicted Labour's development in these years. The new Left believed that the middle-class professionals at the helm of much municipal Labour were not genuine socialists. 'This is a Council Ramsay MacDonald would be dreaming of, if he were alive today', claimed the *Camden Tenant* in 1974, in what was generally considered the most radical borough in London at the time, 'composed as it is of solicitors, shareholders and other questionable "professions."'[80] Livingstone accused the 'soggy centrists' on Islington Council of aligning themselves with the old Right, which 'makes it virtually impossible to get any radical measures through.'[81] The middle-class leadership of many Labour councils, charged with steering their authorities through a very difficult decade, saw the new Left, who did not exercise full control over any Labour council before 1978, as dogmatic, irresponsible and naïvely fundamentalist in their prescriptions, while the Left objected to the secretive control of council processes exercised by some rightist leaders and considered their 'managerial' approach inadequate to meet the exigencies of the inner-city crisis. Schooled in community action, the Left retained an innate faith in the power of subaltern protest, reinforced by images of Poplar and Jarrow and by recent examples: 'the miners, the dockers and the Upper Clyde shipworkers have shown that bad policies and bad laws can be defeated.'[82]

At the root of much mutual suspicion were memories of the bitter internal battle over the Heath government's Housing Finance Act in 1972. Prompted by Tory concern that Labour authorities used rent subsidies to cultivate a captive voting bloc of grateful tenants in council property, the act required councils to levy 'fair rents' on their properties, assessed by local rent-scrutiny boards with regard to the 'age, character and locality of the dwelling' and its condition. In effect, council rents were to be raised to levels comparable to those of the local private rental market, challenging the concept of council housing as a social service. At least eight of the twenty-one London councils in Labour control after the 1971 borough elections considered refusing to implement the legislation,[83] but, faced with central government's armoury of sanctions, including the surcharging—and bankrupting—of noncompliant councillors and their disqualification from future office, all eventually recoiled from confrontation. To the new Left this appeared a craven capitulation. After Islington decided on compliance, the *Hackney Gutter Press* wrote in its inaugural issue, 'Islington Council have already decided to implement the "Fair Rents" Bill ... after all their fine words about fighting against it. We can see from this which side the Labour Party is on—*not ours*! Don't trust them in Hackney either.'[84] Hackney did indeed fall into line shortly afterwards. Camden would be the last London borough to yield, in January 1973.[85]

Acquiescence in the cuts imposed on local authorities by the Labour government from 1975 aroused similar suspicions that local regeneration programmes might be emasculated by supine council leaders. As the authors of the *Socialist Strategy for Wandsworth*, drawn up by the Left for the 1978 borough-council elections, argued, 'It is pointless to have a programme which is abandoned at a nudge by Central Government. We have already defied the government on cuts. We should oppose all legislation either by a Labour or a Conservative Government which is an attack on workers' rights or standard of living, and not give in when the crunch comes as did Wandsworth Council over the Housing Finance Act.' They called for systems of accountability to be imposed on the Labour leadership, seeing 'Labour Councillors as the representatives in the Council of that [wider] movement, fully accountable to it, fully committed to furthering its struggles, and subject to its recall.'[86]

The Left made clear progress in London towards the end of the seventies, gaining a majority on the executive of the Greater London Labour Party in 1977 and taking control of Lambeth's Labour Group, under the leadership of 'Red Ted' Knight, after the 1978 borough elections. The former success paved the way for the Left's takeover of the GLC in 1981,[87] while the latter placed Lambeth Council under unequivocal left-wing leadership. The Left nonetheless remained insecure in its influence over an increasingly fractious party. Demands for constitutional procedures to impose accountability on the Right therefore became a central part of left-wing strategy. This manifested itself most conspicuously in the efforts to remove recalcitrant—or simply right-wing—MPs, which would bring Labour's internal divisions in London to wider public attention, beginning with the explosive events in Newham North-East.

Constituency Unrest

Though Newham was an overwhelmingly working-class dockland area, Labour had retained control of the council in 1968 only by virtue of its majority among the aldermen, and by the early seventies its working-class leadership was ageing. It was clear that, as John O'Malley anticipated in 1973, 'death, age and fatigue suggest that a completely new leadership will arise within the next five or six years.' He noted also, though, that the limited supply of middle-class housing in the borough meant that 'there appears to be no intervention in local affairs by ambitious, professionally qualified Labour Party careerists.'[88] The people who reshaped the Newham Labour Party were not the management consultants and solicitors of North London Labour but rather 'new, young Left-wingers, ... energetic trade unionists, teachers, lecturers and students', seeking to transform a blue-collar party which had changed little in twenty years.[89]

From 1973 the MP for Newham North-East, Reg Prentice, came under fire from activists in the constituency on account of his failure vigorously

Reg Prentice (centre, smiling), Labour MP for Newham North-East and Minister of State for Overseas Development in the Wilson government, surrounded by policemen as he arrives at the special meeting of the constituency party's General Management Committee that would call on him to stand down as an MP at the next election, July 1975. (Keystone Pictures USA/ZUMAPRESS.com /Mary Evans Picture Library)

to oppose the implementation of the Heath government's Industrial Relations Act, his criticism of trade-union militants and his support for European Economic Community (EEC) membership. He was eventually deselected in July 1975. His rejection gained public attention at a time when Labour nationally was widely alleged to be subject to a surreptitious takeover by the far Left. Prentice had represented the area continuously since 1957, winning over 50 percent of the vote in each of his seven Parliamentary contests. His defenestration suggested that the repeated support of a working-class electorate could be overridden by the efforts of a handful of activists. This was literally true, but as Geoff Horn argues, his constituency opponents were acting within the party's rules, and 'in many safe seats, where MPs were re-elected in perpetuity until they retired or died, deselection by the local party was the only method of holding a local MP accountable between elections.'[90]

Hugh Jenkins's 1980 interviews with activists in Putney evinced the widespread conviction that 'something needs to be done about the Labour Party's internal democracy'—and in particular that MPs should be subject to mandatory reselection—in a constituency where there had been no evident friction between a left-wing party and its left-wing MP (Jenkins himself).[91] Where the MP was, like Prentice, outspokenly to the right of the Party or simply appeared to take his tenure for granted, he was likely to come under pressure. Prentice was not the only London Labour MP to come under scrutiny. David Weitzman, MP for Hackney North and Stoke Newington since 1945 and the last MP to have been born in the nineteenth century, was threatened by a leftward shift in his constituency party.[92] Frank Tomney, who supported EEC membership and capital punishment, came under pressure in Hammersmith North and stood down in 1979 (by which time he was over seventy), while one of Prentice's most vocal supporters, Neville Sandelson, MP for Hayes and Harlington, would join the Social Democratic Party in 1981 after prolonged conflict with his constituency left-wingers.[93] The following year, the nomination of the young, leftist gay-rights activist Peter Tatchell to contest the Parliamentary by-election prompted by the imminent retirement of Robert Mellish indicated the waning power of O'Grady's 'Bermondsey mafia.'[94] Activists who had endured the leadership's retreat over the Housing Finance Act in 1971–72, the austerity prescribed by the International Monetary Fund in 1976 and the battle with the trade unions in 1978–79—and noted that none of these concessions prevented electoral defeat in 1979—inferred that the time was ripe for exerting control over both policy making and errant MPs.

This was inevitably contentious outside activist circles. In an open letter supporting Sandelson, Harold Wilson voiced his concern that local activists were seeking to unseat someone who had 'received the approval of the electorate in a parliamentary election.'[95] That the most visible signs of the developing tensions within London Labour were the attempts to deselect sitting MPs gave a sinister aspect to the changes taking place. Whatever the opinions or the competence of the MPs under attack, it was clearly the case that relatively small groups of activists were seeking to negate the choice made by the voters at large. This argument was reinforced by the common assumption that the dissidents were outsiders—interlopers or carpetbaggers invading what were invariably depicted as close-knit working-class communities, with the sole intention of subverting their political processes.[96] 'The activists move in like termites', one unidentified

Labour MP sympathetic to Prentice told the *Daily Telegraph*, 'and sometimes take up accommodation addresses in the constituency.'[97]

How many such 'infiltrators' had moved into Newham cannot be
known, but John O'Malley's 1973 observation, made before the Prentice
affair gathered steam, that the old party leadership was gradually yielding
to younger 'teachers and social workers', who 'seem to be people who will
remain in local politics for a very long time', is pertinent.[98] Horn suggests
that the new, younger members in Newham were the fruits of a recruitment drive following Labour's defeat in the 1970 general election.[99] Older
party members, already uncomfortable with social change in the area,
might resent their involvement (as one 'Labour stalwart' told Michael
Jones of the *Sunday Times*, 'We've had an influx of people from God knows
where. They are more concerned with national issues. If you mention
George Lansbury they don't want to know'),[100] but they were no more
entryists than the gentrifiers who had joined the Islington or Camden
Labour Parties—or, for that matter, the CND-ers who had transformed
the Labour Party in Putney in the sixties. These incomers embodied the
changing nature of Labour's inner-city heartlands, inevitably reflected in
inner-London constituency Labour parties.

Many young radicals had left the Labour Party—or never joined it—in
the late sixties, thinking the party incorrigible. Many rejoined it in the late
seventies, believing that it was now open to change. Some would have
flirted with far-left groups in the meantime, before rejecting them as inadequate vehicles for the social politics that they professed. As a result, the
press image of 'extremists' as a breed apart was misleading. Prentice himself wrote in his apologia that 'the really disturbing aspect of Trotskyist
infiltration into the Labour party is that they are so readily accepted by
other left wingers, whose outlook is not very different.'[101] Boundary lines
within the Labour Left were more fluid than many outsiders believed.

The example of Lambeth is instructive. The principal figures in the Left
opposition to the Stimpson regime between 1973 and 1978 were Ted Knight
and Ken Livingstone. Knight was an entryist by most regular definitions:
expelled from the Labour Party in 1954 for Trotskyist leanings, he had for
several years been an active member of Gerry Healy's Socialist Labour
League (the Trotskyist predecessor of the Workers Revolutionary Party)
before being readmitted to Labour in 1970. He would stand for Labour in
Hornsey in the 1979 general election.[102] Livingstone had been relatively
unusual in joining the Labour Party in 1969 at a time when many leftists of
his generation were leaving it or spurning it—'one of the few recorded

instances', as he put it, 'of a rat climbing on board a sinking ship.'[103] He was described by Eddie Lopez, party agent in Norwood, simply as 'a libertarian socialist', who 'didn't seem to carry all the claptrap that was around Militant or some other Trotskyist organisations.'[104] He rubbed shoulders with Trotskyists throughout his years as a Lambeth councillor from 1971, while seeing 'nothing attractive in being in a disciplined little group that told [him] what to think' and considering revolutionaries 'completely mad.'[105] He worried that the tone of Knight's speeches 'did more to alienate support than to win it over', but the two men formed 'a political relationship which . . . remained extremely useful' to both of them until the mideighties.[106] It remains hard to discern a significant difference in municipal policy between them before the conflict over rate-capping in 1985 which ended their association.

The national Labour Party had, after all, decades of experience of seeing off infiltrators, by means of individual expulsions or the suspension of contaminated constituency parties. If it appeared less resolute in tackling the threat now, that was because what was happening in inner London was not the work of 'termites' but the result of a more general, and more firmly founded, shift to the left in several constituency parties. That shift was at the root of the growing tensions within London Labour. However damaging that shift might have been, it was hardly susceptible to disciplinary action.

Conclusion

In the immediate postwar years Labour had built efficient local party machines across inner London, whose social composition broadly reflected the societies they represented. They acted, in effect, as local agents of the Attleeian welfare state, pursuing a well-defined agenda of social service delivery with slum clearance and rehousing at its core. But resting as it did on firm party discipline, rewards for loyalty and long service and the avoidance or suppression of internal debate, it was a model which proved slow to evolve. Even in 1962 Anthony Howard had warned that Labour could not indefinitely depend on 'its old organisational formula of low polls and general apathy leading to permanent power',[107] and his prediction was vindicated by the spectacular collapse of Old Labour in 1968. Labour was thus pushed into what would prove a prolonged modernisation at exactly the time that its inner-city heartlands were being transformed by the twin processes of deindustrialisation and gentrification. This modernisation was never likely to be a controlled or measured transition; in the event it proved an ad hoc and contested one. As the blue-collar party declined, Labour was required to accommodate large numbers of people who saw themselves as left of centre but who, within that broad definition, might differ radically both socially and ideologically. Whatever personal tensions this engendered were exacerbated by the real difficulties involved in developing plausible municipal policy in the economic maelstrom of the seventies, when the problems of the inner city encouraged expansive regeneration initiatives but the macroeconomic climate dictated retrenchment. In the space of little more than a decade, Labour moved from being a party that was tightly controlled to one that was very hard to control. Its internal tensions were very far from being resolved by the end of the period addressed in this book. All that can be said for certain is that in the London of 1979 Labour was not working.

15

Selling Swinging London,
or Coming to Terms
with the Tourist

The Wilson government, preoccupied with the balance of payments in the midsixties, was alert to the possibility of marketing Britain's new youth culture abroad. The contentious award of MBEs to the Beatles in 1965 had been widely justified on the grounds of their contribution to the export drive; with London becoming the focus of international attention in the spring of 1966, the hope emerged that the 'Swinging City' could be put to similar use. As the nation slid into economic crisis during the summer, though, concern arose that London's new image might prove a mixed blessing, particularly in the United States, where it had been most directly propagated. Two months after *Time*'s 'Swinging City' article, Sir Patrick Dean, British ambassador in Washington, warned that the US press now routinely combined depictions of youthful hedonism and economic crisis to project an image of feckless escapism: 'The Americans are beginning to have a picture of a country whose young people are bent on pleasure and are unwilling to face the realities of the economic situation of the country, and whose senior citizens appear incapable of doing anything about it, . . . a frivolous nation unconcerned about the present or the future.' He advised those who were charged with promoting Britain abroad to concentrate on selling the tangible products of the new fashion trade and to play down the lifestyle connotations of 'Swinging London.'[1] The Foreign Office agreed that promoting fashion was safer than promoting pop music which, however innovative, was tainted by the increasingly licentious behaviour of its performers.[2] The Board of Trade also concurred, concluding, 'fashion shows seem to be better promotion for consumer goods generally than any other gimmick we have yet been able to devise, such as red double-decker buses, London policemen, military bands, sporting events, Royal visits, pop-singers, etc.' They showed Britain to be 'a trend-setter, modern and "with it."'[3] The board hoped 'to use clothing as a spearhead in the lively projection of the British image.'[4] Fashion shows, foregrounding in particular Mary Quant's work, became central features of the promotional 'British Weeks' across the world.

The market appeared promising. The German young-adult magazine *Twen* enthused in March 1966 about the imminent arrival of London fashions in Germany—'in sassy colours, sexy, supershort. And incredibly cheap.'[5] But it rapidly became clear that the small-scale, boutique-centred industry of London's fashion centres did not possess the infrastructure necessary to play the spearhead role envisaged for it. Unanticipated international demand for new London fashion strained designers to the point that production weaknesses soon became evident. New York buyers became quickly disillusioned with 'the cheap Carnaby Street look that has overflooded the American market', the fashion journalist Bill Cunningham reported in October 1966: 'buyers feel most designers haven't learned quality manufacturing, and the public is not accepting any more of the amateur homemade look.' He was told, 'It's all like a child who has been taught to recite one poem before company, adorable the first time, but three years later embarrassingly bad.' As he summarised, 'The general opinion is that the gay London look will die quickly if the designers don't mature, and develop their ideas in a quality product.'[6]

In much of Europe, of course, British exporters were shackled by Common Market tariffs (*Twen* had been wrong to anticipate that English fashion would be 'incredibly cheap': in 1965 it was estimated that duties, taxes and landing charges added 25 percent to the price of British clothes in Germany).[7] In Italy and France, of course, London's promoters were facing competitors at the cutting edge of European fashion while thus hampered. Elsewhere the problem was rather consumer resistance to London's more outré designs. During British Week in Brussels in 1967 the weight of custom in the replica 'Britannia' pub caused its floor to collapse, but 'women's fashions were, as usual, unpredictable due largely to the reluctance of Belgians to accept [Britain's] more daring trends.'[8] John Stephen opened his boutique in the Varner store in Oslo in December 1966 in the knowledge that 'Norwegians are at present more conservative as a market than the British.'[9] And if innovative designs did sell, they could always be copied: 'the whole business is founded on stealing', as a Seventh Avenue manufacturer told Cunningham in 1966.[10] Barbro Mattson, buyer for the Nordiska 'Style 20' boutique in Stockholm, would visit Britain 'four or five times a year both to buy and to collect ideas.'[11] One Munich boutique owner profiled by *Twen* also went to London (and Paris) for inspiration but had 70 percent of his stock made up in his workshops in Schwabia.[12]

It steadily became clear that the real strength of London's fashion exports lay in the 'brand image' of Carnaby Street: 'When will we ever get something like London's Carnaby Street?', asked the German teen magazine *Bravo* in 1966.[13] This lay behind sporadic attempts to re-create the street itself overseas. Two weeks after *Time* magazine's 'Swinging City' article appeared, proposals were mooted to open a British fashion shop in Rome, prompting 'rather breathless prophecies that Rome, first of all Italian cities, is to have its own Carnaby Street.'[14] Ten months later, indeed, Mary Quant launched the attempt to turn Via Margutta, a street favoured by British expatriates, into Rome's own Carnaby Street, the right to use the name in Italy having been legally secured by the project's promoters.[15] By the autumn of 1969, though, the venture was said to be 'going reasonably badly',[16] and Tom Salter's account of Carnaby Street, published in the following year, pronounced it dead. An attempt to establish a similar street in Paris, also mentioned by Salter, now appears untraceable.[17] The concept of a street of boutiques remained a viable one, as proved by the emergence of Barcelona's Calle Tuset—rechristened 'Tuset Street' by the city's youth on account of its 'whiff of Carnaby'[18]—but it was still harder to copyright a street than to copyright individual designs.

In any case, the best way for European youth to gain a 'whiff of Carnaby' was to come to London. The motto adopted for the British Week display in Berlin in March 1968, where Mary Quant appeared in front of an 'olde English pub' accompanied by four uniformed bobbies, was 'England zu Besuch.'[19] Visiting England had, of course, been made easier by sterling's devaluation in November 1967. By the spring of 1969 the Central Office of Information, once nervous about endorsing London's cultural frivolity, had produced a sequence of posed promotional photographs showing 'teenagers in Carnaby Street', 'two young girls shopping in Kings Road', and so on.[20] What had begun as an attempt to market London fashion overseas had turned into an effort to market London itself to potential visitors.

'The Teenagers' Dreamland'

If Americans reacted censoriously to the irresponsible hedonism of 'Swinging London', as Dean suggested, the European response was more tolerant,
emphasising the city's new lifestyle and cultural freedom.[21] A month after
the publication of the *Time* article, Crispin Tickell, at the British embassy
in Paris, collated reports from British consulates in France to produce a
paper titled 'Britain through French Eyes.' From Bordeaux, Marseilles and
elsewhere came the same reaction: though the older generation might still
see Britain as 'a wet, cold, mist-enshrouded country, populated by a phleg-
matic race of bowler-hatted men and badly dressed women who exist on
a diet composed mainly of suet puddings and boiled cabbage', for the
young, it was 'the country of the Beatles, of liberty from parental control,
of everything "with-it"—the teenagers' Dreamland.' Whereas Paris had
once been the place for the Englishman to conquer his various inhibitions,
now 'it is the French teenager who looks across the Channel with admiring
eyes at the exhilarating freedom enjoyed by his English contemporaries'—
indeed Peter Murray reported from the British consulate in Marseilles in
May 1966 that French parents were becoming reluctant 'to expose their
children [through exchange schemes] to the demoralizing influence of
English homes where they may acquire habits of unruliness and insubor-
dination.'[22] A long article by Børge Visby in the Danish newspaper *Politiken* two weeks after the *Time* piece stressed the abandonment of Britain's
sexual conservatism, asking, 'What has happened to old Auntie England?':
'for a young Parisienne who remembers what she learned as a child about
the boring sexless Victorian girls in England it must be a piquant experience when she comes to England and finds that her skirt is too long.'[23]
The French magazine *Réalités*, in an October 1966 article on Carnaby
Street, reiterated *Time*'s emphasis on London's new classlessness, taking
the end of debutantes' presentation at court in 1958 as a turning point
and emphasising that 'no one, just no one, be he the son of a duke or of
a roadsweeper, is excluded if he has his part to play in the spectacle.'[24]
Like many foreign commentators, Visby was struck by the fact that John
Stephen was the son of a Glasgow sweet-shop owner and Mary Quant
the daughter of a Welsh schoolteacher and granddaughter of a miner.[25]
The German commentator Irmgard Lauff, writing in June 1968 against the
background of student revolt on the Continent, described 'another

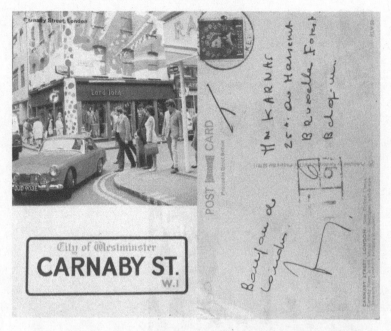

A postcard depicting Carnaby Street, sent to Brussels by a Belgian visitor to London in 1969, bearing the inscription 'Bonjour de Londres.' (In the author's possession. © Kardorama Ltd)

quieter, but no less palpable revolution', centred in 'the small boutiques in the heart of London.'[26]

Visby remarked that the new London had been compared to Weimar Berlin, the Paris of the impressionists and 1890s Vienna.[27] Similarly Silvio Bertoldi in the Italian journal *Oggi Illustrato* in August 1966 invoked the Paris of Hemingway and Fitzgerald, the New York of Capote, the Rome of the dolce vita and, again, Brecht's Berlin.[28] Readers of the German magazine *Twen* were asked to choose between London and Paris in a quiz titled 'How Young Are You?' The 'with it' were expected to prefer London, along with Amsterdam over Brussels and Ibiza over Majorca.[29] Visby noted in 1966 that 'London is attracting as never before visitors from abroad in unheard of numbers and not just the traditional tourists who are interested in historic pomp but to a growing degree the long-haired young generation who find that London is "the place."'[30] In 1967 30 percent of London's visitors were aged between twelve and twenty-four.[31]

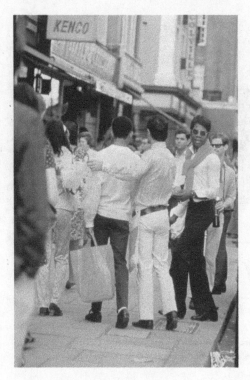

King's Road style, 1966. (Pictorial Press/Alamy Stock Photo)

Carnaby Street was for these visitors the principal magnet, said by one German newspaper even in the summer of 1966 to have been a 'must see' for tourists for some time.[32] A year later, a Dutch paper spoke of entrepreneurs like Stephen ensuring that Carnaby Street pushed the Tower and Big Ben 'ever further into the background' as tourist destinations.[33] Though many overseas visitors clearly did go to Carnaby Street in order to shop, it was already as much an object of the 'tourist gaze' as was the Changing of the Guard.[34] The first edition of the German youth travel guide *Treff Tips* in 1968 suggested that London girls and boys did not take Carnaby Street entirely seriously as a place to shop:[35] most visitors came simply to observe the 'vibrant life and movement' of 'John Stephen Alley' particularly on a Saturday, when 'large and small cars stand bumper to bumper, music blares from every door and each half-open painted shop window, young customers come two or three times, look around the shop, try out the newest shoes—cycling shoes in different colours—and try on crazy wigs.'[36] The King's Road offered a still more elaborate spectacle of hippy dandyism. A report for Kensington and Chelsea Council in 1968 suggested that while its boutiques, restaurants, antique shops and cafés drew the crowds, tourists came mostly 'just to look at the people who have reputedly established its reputation.'[37] Just as Carnaby Street had 'become a promenade as well as a shopping centre' by the summer of 1966,[38] so the King's Road exemplified the performative aspect of tourism described by recent academic observers.[39] In December 1965 Suna Portman, a veteran of the 1950s 'Chelsea Set', described it as 'an institution, even a tourist attraction, judging by the number of foreign languages you hear spoken; people from the continent must see a resemblance to their own weekend ritual of wandering the pavements, eyeing one another.'[40] The 1970 *Grosse Polyglott* guide to London, providing readers with a map of the King's Road detailing every boutique, antique shop and eatery, recommended eleven o'clock on a Saturday morning as the time to watch the young men sporting the newest styles and 'the prettiest girls in the shortest minis and longest maxis.'[41] London's fashion centres turned into sites for people-watching.

The Wrong Kind of Visitor

The number of overseas visitors to the United Kingdom increased by 76 percent between 1966 and 1971,[42] and the rate of increase in London alone was almost certainly greater than that. Some 72 percent of 'bed nights' spent in the UK by overseas tourists in 1970 were said to have been spent in London.[43] Sales of 'go-as-you-please' tickets, allowing unlimited travel on London's buses and underground services and available only to overseas visitors before June 1972, almost quadrupled between 1966 and 1971.[44] Intense pressure was consequently placed on London's tourist accommodation, which had seen little growth since the rash of luxury hotels built in the late 1920s. A quarter of a century of stagnation had followed the completion of the Dorchester in 1931, with no major hotel project finished before the Westbury opened in 1955.[45] Even by 1966, before the scale of the 'Swinging London' tourist boom had become clear, there was said to be a thirty-five-thousand-bed shortfall in the number of hotel beds in London, and for the next three years London's stock of beds in licensed hotels—about sixty thousand—grew only 'at a snail's pace.'[46]

The Wilson government, anticipating tourist growth in the wake of the 1967 devaluation, announced a scheme of incentive grants for hotel development in a 1968 white paper, later enshrined in the 1969 Development of Tourism Act.[47] Grants or loans would be provided by the newly organised

Charles Clore (*right*), chairman of City and Central Investments and one of the principal beneficiaries of the scrapping of the building licensing system in 1954, with the hotelier Conrad Hilton, examining plans for the Park Lane Hilton in 1960. City and Central had spent eight years acquiring the component parts of the site. (Keystone Pictures USA/Alamy Stock Photo)

tourist boards for the construction, extension or improvement of hotels, providing that construction began before March 1971 and was completed by March 1973. The grants amounted to a liberal £1,000 per hotel room or 20 percent of the capital cost of a building. Financial encouragement to satisfy an apparently booming demand proved unsurprisingly attractive to developers, particularly in London, where the 'Brown ban' on office building was still in place, but—perhaps predictably—much of this subsidised effort was misdirected. The cut-off date ensured that a rash of applications came at once. Around one thousand applications for grants had been made in Greater London by the beginning of 1971; Kensington and Chelsea was by then receiving four applications a month for new hotels.[48] Almost as soon as the grants began to be paid, some people in the industry warned that 'there will be burnt fingers' as a result of oversupply.[49] In 1970 Robert Langton predicted in the *Evening News* that 'the capital could have TOO MANY luxury and first-class hotels by 1975–6 but not enough economy class hotels—those in the £2, £3 and £4 a night bracket.'[50] Even with the subsidy, high overheads in Central London meant that the new operators were forced to target the luxury market: the cost of building a London hotel worked out at somewhere between £10,000 and £15,000 per room, putting the room price, by the industry's conventional calculations, at £10–£15 a night. It soon became clear that the demand was not there at that price, and by 1972, when tourist numbers dropped temporarily, London's hoteliers were fighting a price war.[51] In 1973 Kensington and Chelsea's chief planning officer told Simon Jenkins of the *Evening Standard* that developers with planning permission for hotels were seeking consent for change of use.[52] 'The real problem is not that London is attracting fewer visitors', the chairman of a hotel booking agency in Regent Street explained, 'but that it is attracting the wrong kind of visitor as far as hotels are concerned.'[53]

The wrong kind of visitor was young and travelling on a shoestring. The difficulty of accommodating large numbers of young visitors to the capital had emerged as early as the 1951 Festival of Britain, and a standing Conference on Accommodation had been formed in 1956.[54] The LCC had resolved in 1959 to make every effort to provide accommodation for young summer visitors,[55] but this was destined to be a cause generating more hand-wringing than effective action. In 1966, when accommodation was in any case strained by the football World Cup, the French Education Ministry's Comité d'Acceuil brought twenty thousand Parisian pupils to London on day trips for want of anywhere to stay.[56] In response to that summer's crisis, the Inner London Education Authority converted four schools into temporary hostels, being 'aware of the adequate, and often very attractive, facilities made available to [British] young people travelling to the various capitals of Europe' and feeling 'that this was the least [they] could do in return.'[57] The amount of purpose-built hostel accommodation available in the three central boroughs was pitiful—2,885 places in Camden, 1,855 in Westminster and 1,485 in Kensington and Chelsea, at a time when it was estimated that Britain received half a million young visitors a year and that 'for most of them London is the *sine qua non* of their journey to Britain.'[58] British Tourist Authority (BTA) surveys found that in fact more than half of young French visitors to London and a third of Germans and Scandinavians stayed with friends and relatives.[59] The Greater London Council Steering Group on Tourism suggested rather optimistically in 1970 that 'hardship could be avoided if young people could be encouraged to arrange accommodation in advance and not arrive, as so many do, "on spec."'[60]

Britain was unprepared for the kind of independent mass youth tourism that 'Swinging London' unleashed. The assumption had been that most young visitors would come on exchange trips, which did not require bespoke accommodation, though in fact Britain had previously been grudging even in its admission of exchange visitors. While London might have been accessible, it was not very hospitable to young travellers seeking a bed for the night. A 1968 survey for the British Travel Association showed that almost a third of visitors aged sixteen to twenty-four were neither staying in hotels nor with friends or relations.[61] They were forced to use their initiative. 'The lines of camper-vans parked along the Strand, as one cohort of young Australians sold their temporary homes to the next, was perhaps the most conspicuous advertisement of the Australian presence in London' in the sixties.[62] Many on shorter-term visits simply aimed to sleep rough.

In the summer of 1969 the situation became critical. The official response was the opening of Hyde Park and Green Park to rough sleeping, with the result that they immediately hosted hundreds of young visitors. Max Hastings, venturing among them for the *Evening Standard*, counted 250 in the two Royal Parks, though Hugh de Wet reckoned there to be 'hundreds of hairy young people' in Green Park alone.[63] The parks' new residents found them 'a godsend for sleeping in'; 'it is marvellous,' a young German told Hastings: 'No noise, deckchairs to make shields against the wind, right in the centre of everything. We like it here.' He added that 'your youth hostels are unspeakable, . . . dirty, overcrowded and full of rules and regulations.' The tent city continued to enjoy official sanction throughout the year, despite locals' complaints that the parks were littered with 'drug syringes, makeshift tents made with Park deckchairs, rubbish and discarded clothing', while the inhabitants of Green Park would 'bathe in the fountain and . . . make love.'[64] In December John Silkin, minister of public buildings and works, announced that Green Park would be closed at night and fencing erected to keep out 'undesirable elements.'[65]

Deterrence and Acceptance

The right kind of visitor, commentators soon decided, was 'middle aged, mid-Western on a package tour',[66] who did not sleep for free in Hyde Park. Hoteliers began to challenge the received wisdom that support for youth tourism represented an investment in the future. As the director of Inter-Hotel Ltd told the GLC, 'Mention is frequently made that student tourism should be encouraged because the student today will be the wealthy visiter [*sic*] tomorrow. There is little evidence that I know to vindicate this view, my personal and private experience from the few discussions I have had on the matter indicate [*sic*] that international tourists normally choose new countries to visit and therefore once they have visited England would go elsewhere at a future date.'[67] In 1970 the *Financial Times* journalist Arthur Sandles, who specialised in the economics of tourism, asked 'whether the investment in attracting more low-income French and German visitors to Britain is justified in terms of economic gain compared with the much higher-bracket American and Canadian visitors.'[68] When expenditure was systematically measured, later in the decade, the force of the distinction became clear: expenditure per head by North American visitors to London in the summer quarter of 1977 was 73 percent higher than that by European visitors.[69] The efforts of the tourism promoters were soon directed towards recruiting Americans: as early as 1971 a representative of the Association of British Travel Agents told a meeting at County Hall that only 5 percent of Americans travelled and that there was consequently 'a big untapped market for cheaper package holidays.'[70] By 1975, when the oversupply of luxury hotel rooms had become clear and the oil shock had reduced the number of US visitors, the main concern of the director of the London Tourist Board was still 'the problem of how to stimulate the many millions of North Americans into making a trip to Britain.'[71]

Wealthy European visitors were naturally as welcome as wealthy visitors from anywhere else, and a consortium of five European airlines bought into London hotel development in much the same way as the transatlantic airlines did;[72] but the preponderance of young travellers among the European contingent meant that most European visitors were not wealthy. Leaving aside the financial incentive to appeal to the US market, the tourism quangoes had encountered much criticism in the wake of the occupation of the Royal Parks on the grounds that they were attracting visitors indiscriminately, without ensuring that the infrastructure existed to support them. In 1971 the BTA had been forced onto the defensive. Noting that Britain had earned as much from its six million tourists in 1970 as Spain from its twenty-four million, the BTA stressed that it 'was not setting out to attract the hard-up tourists with plans to see Britain on a shoe-string. Its publicity was aimed at the middle and upper-middle class tourist'[73] — particularly Americans, who were more than twice as likely as European visitors to fill London's underused hotel beds,[74] and conference delegates, who were estimated to spend more than four times as much per head per day as the average tourist.[75]

Some people went further, suggesting that *all* tourism was a burden on the capital. In the summer of 1973 the right-wing polemicist Alfred Sherman penned a comprehensive attack on tourism—and particularly London tourism—in the *Daily Telegraph*, questioning the benefits claimed for the balance of payments ('there must surely be better ways of balancing our accounts than Butlinising London') and suggesting that the conversion of residential accommodation into cheap hotels had robbed London of thirty thousand family dwellings. The hotel trade employed a foreign 'coolie labour' workforce, which drew heavily on the social services but sent its wages home, to the detriment of the London economy. 'Why', Sherman asked, 'should North Kensington be turned into a Casbah to house hotel staff so that London can provide a "dirty weekend" for foreign visitors?'[76] Less florid analysis within the GLC underlined the concern that tourists put additional pressure on public services which were already stressed, 'particularly police and fire protection, cleansing services and so on.'[77] Many people complained that in tourist areas useful local shops gave way to boutiques and restaurants, so that 'the local resident who wants to buy a toothbrush often has a very long way to walk.'[78] The growing urban environmental movement also objected to 'souvenir or curio shops' and was reluctant 'to see more tourists encouraged to come here until some real progress has been made on the existing problems of traffic congestion, poor public transport, litter and limited public amenities.' The Greenwich Society, which voiced these views, urged the Greater London Council to 'bear firmly in mind the important principle . . . that the environment of London must prevail over the interests of tourists.'[79]

The most sophisticated critique of the tourism phenomenon came from Sir George Young, future Conservative minister and at this point vice chairman of the GLC's Strategic Planning Committee and one of the Council's representatives on the London Tourist Board.[80] On top of the standard arguments against the repatriation of earnings and the attrition of the housing stock, Young attacked the profligacy of the quango tourist boards, suggesting that the BTA could 'take down the posters of beefeaters they have pinned up in the four corners of the world and save the taxpayer a tidy sum of money.'[81] The core of his case was that London's authorities were acting incoherently by devoting substantial subsidies to the London Tourist Board whilst at the same time protesting that the capital could not accommodate more tourists. In a general study of tourism published in 1973 Young suggested that there was 'a saturation level for tourism in a given locality or region, and if that level is exceeded, the costs of tourism begin to outweigh the benefits.'[82] His argument that tourism 'should be viewed as a planning matter rather than as an export industry' clearly influenced the Greater London Council's pronouncements on the issue during the years of Tory control between 1967 and 1973.[83]

The GLC, as London's strategic authority, began in 1970 seriously to consider what one officer called the 'precious bane' of tourism.[84] Put simply, the Council wanted to cap it: 'a stabilisation in the number of tourists coming to London might well be welcome; perhaps a zero growth rate was desirable.'[85] Discussion was largely nonpartisan, as members on all sides of the Council expressed concern over the impact of the unanticipated tourist invasion on London life.[86] In 1971 the Conservative leader of the Council, Desmond Plummer, listed the main problems as traffic congestion, the depletion of the housing stock by 'creeping conversion' of rental property into cheap hotels[87] and the difficulty of providing low-cost housing for the industry's large but ill-paid labour force.[88] He argued that 'unchecked tourism' would raise demand for unskilled, seasonal and low-paid hotel labour: 'precisely the sort of jobs we do not want to encourage.'[89] His Labour successor, Sir Reg Goodwin, stressed in 1974 that while 'the GLC welcomed tourists in reasonable numbers and recognised their contribution to the country's economy, the GLC's first responsibility was ... to the people who lived and worked in London and it would therefore not wish tourists to come to London in such numbers and at such times as to disorganise London's services, particularly the transport service.'[90] Councillors of both major parties, along with GLC officers, felt that 'the net financial benefit to the public sector [from tourism] accrues mainly to the government in respect of the national economy' and that Londoners should not be asked to suffer congestion and loss of housing stock in order to shore up the nation's finances.[91]

Remedies of varying degrees of plausibility were proposed. It was hoped to spread the number of visitors more evenly across the year, to ease the pressure on services in July and August. 'London in winter has a great cultural vitality and variety, and is a pleasant place to visit then', the GLC argued optimistically in 1974: 'The old image of pea-soup fogs now belongs to history.'[92] Visitors were urged to seek out some of London's less obvious attractions, rather than flocking to Westminster Abbey and the Tower; as Freddie Brampton, one of the founders of the Guild of Guide Lecturers in 1950, pointed out, 'If you went to the National Gallery now you'd see 1500 people ... but you'd only see 50 at the Wallace Collection.'[93] They were encouraged to see London as a staging point, from which they would move rapidly on to Stratford or Edinburgh: while the London Tourist Board accepted that 'most tourists visiting Britain on holiday would inevitably come to London; the general aim should be to pass them through London as quickly as possible and to get them out into the rest of the country.'[94] The principal means of achieving this was intended to be a new London tourist tax—probably a tax on hotel beds—a scheme to which GLC officers devoted much intellectual energy in the mid-1970s.[95] Above all, the GLC hoped to manage tourism by concentrating on attracting the most profitable types of tourist, convincing itself, for instance, that 'in the future it could well be cheaper for a New Yorker to participate at a convention held in London than in Chicago or San Francisco.'[96]

These efforts enjoyed limited success. By 1978 the GLC could report no change in the distribution of London's tourists across the seasons, although the overall number of tourists had increased, meaning that pressure in the summer months was even greater.[97] There were signs that American visitors, at least, became more likely to venture outside London, but hopes of deflecting them from the major sites in London proved misplaced. London tourism had grown so rapidly, and from such a low base, that a high proportion of tourists were first-time visitors, anxious to see major sites rather than minor ones. 'What American is going to go home and confess he didn't see Westminster Abbey?', as the tourist guide John Wittich put it to Betty James in 1971.[98] The tourist tax was the last thing that London's hoteliers wanted as they grappled with the oversupply of rooms; it was strongly opposed by them and by the London Tourist Board. The Department of the Environment showed little apparent interest. Local taxation as a whole was under review in the mid-1970s; while it was probably true, as one GLC officer suggested, that the tourist tax 'hardly goes further into the realms of fantasy than any other proposal for local taxation!',[99] it would relate only to London, and local tax reform, if it happened at all, was unlikely to sanction individual local levies. So far as elite tourism was concerned, London was already establishing itself as one of Europe's principal conference venues, but expansion of this trade appeared difficult. Facilities were lacking for gatherings of more than two thousand delegates unless the Royal Albert Hall or the Royal Festival Hall were to be pressed into an operation for which neither had been designed. 'In London 3000 becomes a big meeting; in world terms it is a medium meeting', the manager of the London Convention Bureau told the *Times* in 1974.[100] More damagingly still, the 1973 oil shock curtailed American tourism. The proportion of London tourists coming from the United States—a market which the authorities and the tourist boards had hoped to see grow—fell from 27 percent in 1972 to 15 percent in 1977.[101]

The real lesson of those years was that the bedrock of London's growing tourist trade remained the young traveller. The most authoritative measurement, the British Tourist Authority's 1975 survey of London tourists, showed that 45 percent of overseas visitors to London were aged between sixteen and twenty-four and that 72 percent were under thirty-five.[102] Little obvious had been done to woo them. The advice sheet produced in three languages by the GLC in 1972, puzzlingly titled *Use It!*, claimed to have been 'written by young people who know what it's like to arrive in a big city without much money.' It was at times savvy and at times condescending but seldom very welcoming. The indispensable warning not to waste time looking for a hotel in the very centre of London was followed by more questionable encouragement to seek out 'the cafes where working people go' ('Look for a Pepsi-Cola sign with the name on it—"Frank's Café" for example—and people with working clothes on'). Adventurously, *Use It!* indicated where *Gay News* could be purchased and, though stressing that possession of classified drugs was illegal, advised readers to 'beware of drugs of poor quality sold to unsuspecting foreigners.' Venereal-disease clinics were identified ('treatment is free, if you explain that you caught the disease in the UK') along with disinfection stations for those who were 'unlucky enough to pick up fleas or any such parasites.'[103] In contrast to the youth-oriented London guides being produced on the Continent, *Use It!* adopted the tone of a survival manual and offered little encouragement to come to London in the first place, but the GLC distributed thirty thousand copies of it in 1972,[104] implicitly acknowledging that the annual backpack invasion had become a fixture.

In 1971 the London Tourist Board had believed that recent rates of tourist growth, attributable to 'the promotion of the "Swinging London" theme' and the 1967 devaluation of sterling, would not be maintained.[105] In the event, youth tourism continued to expand, and the young visitors came more to resemble regular tourists than the hippies who had camped in Green Park in 1969. Carnaby Street continued to draw the crowds, attracting three thousand visitors a week in the summer of 1977, but it was essentially a site to be seen, rather as Haight-Ashbury in San Francisco remains today.[106] The BTA's 1975 survey showed that it was the seventh most visited tourist site in London, attracting 52 percent of European and 38 percent of non-European tourists,[107] although there was little to see there and the surviving boutiques were swimming against the tide of 'denim, cheesecloth and tourist goods.'[108] 'Within cities,' Susan Fainstein and Dennis Judd wrote in 1997, 'spaces or monuments like the Eiffel Tower,

Tower Bridge or the Vatican . . . become identified as official tourist attractions. Such places are "famous for being famous"; the "sacred objects" that make up a circuit of urban tourism.'[109] Carnaby Street became such a sacred place as its original creativity dwindled. Most of London's tourists were, after all, literally strangers in a foreign land. 'In truth, most of them don't know what they are here for', Anne Sharpley wrote in the *Evening Standard* in 1978, 'beyond a short list that runs from the Tower to Buckingham Palace.'[110] Carnaby Street and the King's Road (London's tenth most visited site in 1975) were on that list, but if the *Standard*'s admittedly skimpy interviews with young visitors to London in the summer of 1973 are anything to go by, youth tourists were as anxious to stick to the regular tourist script as any other visitors. 'I visited almost everything tourists are supposed to see', declared one woman from Miami: 'the Tower, Buckingham Palace, Hyde Park, The British Museum, Trafalgar Square.' A twenty-two-year-old Japanese woman lamented missing the Crown Jewels because of the 'interminable queue outside the jewel house' but 'made up for the disappointment with a whistle-stop tour of Westminster Abbey, Buckingham Palace, the Houses of Parliament, Hyde Park.' A young Texan making her second trip to London had likewise missed the Crown Jewels on her earlier trip, 'so this time they were the first thing she wanted to see.' An eighteen-year-old from Toronto felt that 'Trafalgar Square with its pigeons was the one sight not to be missed.'[111]

Rather than seek out London's venereal-disease clinics and disinfection stations, one twenty-three-year-old Canadian 'picked up some local habits and tastes: "Things like afternoon tea with scones, steak and kidney pie, riding in the bus with a newspaper and an umbrella."'[112] The teenager or young adult, both curious and deferential towards British traditions and institutions, was becoming the characteristic London tourist. Despite all entreaties, she would come to Britain in high summer and probably spend all her time in London.[113] She would not be lured to Kenwood House or Hampstead Garden Suburb ahead of Westminster Abbey and would insist on swelling the crowd at that most popular and pointless of ceremonies, the Changing of the Guard, even though that swollen crowd might block her view.[114] She might take advantage of the hotel price war to stay in accommodation intended for someone more opulent than she,[115] or she might stay with friends or relatives;[116] she would probably not attempt to sleep in the parks. The 1979 edition of the French *Guide de Londres en jeans* suggests that while London was not brimming with cheap accommodation, the problem by the end of the decade was not such as to warrant warning young travellers off coming. The authors listed cheap hotels and

recommended the Youth Hostel Association, Young Men's Christian Association and Young Women's Christian Association, along with individual hostels,
lodgings and bedsits, camp sites and even squats and communes (though
there 'commitment has to be total, and as a result is not always easy').[117]

After the best part of a decade's alarmism over the tourist invasion, the
GLC concluded in 1978 that 'what has proved surprising is how well London has met the strains that visitors impose.'[118] The change of tone reflected a rapid realisation over the second half of the decade that tourists
had become indispensable to a London economy which had suffered severe depletion of its traditional industrial base in the 1970s. As London's
economic problems escalated, particularly in the wake of the 1973 oil
shock, policy makers came to accept that the benefits of tourism outweighed the burdens that tourists placed on the capital's infrastructure. At
a meeting with the various tourist boards in the spring of 1975, Illtyd Harrington, deputy leader of the Labour-controlled GLC, described tourism
as 'the one major growth industry in London in the past five to ten years.'
At a local-authority conference four months later, he spelled out that 'it
was difficult to attract (and retain) manufacturing industry in London so
the city had to look for new alternatives, and tourism, along with medicine
and education, were the growth sectors in the London economy.'[119] As if
to demonstrate that the Council's embrace of tourists was as nonpartisan
as its previous suspicion of them had been, the discussion paper issued by
the Conservative GLC in 1978 made the same point with, if anything,
greater vigour: 'The increase in the number of tourists visiting London has
taken place during a period when the traditional inner city activities—
manufacturing industry, warehousing, the Docks, have all declined and the
population living in Inner London reduced dramatically. London has
therefore been fortunate in being able to take advantage of a whole range
of growth activities, focused upon its attractions to the international tourist market, which have helped to sustain its prosperity.'[120] The authors estimated that tourism generated the equivalent of 250,000 full-time jobs in
London at a time of employment decline elsewhere and noted that a quarter of the £1,600 million annual retail expenditure in London was attributed to tourists. They contemplated elevating the Thames river boats to
the standard of the Parisian *bateaux mouches* and creating a Tivoli Gardens
in Docklands. The projected tourist tax was acknowledged to be 'discrimi-
natory' and in any case redundant, given 'the substantial contributions
already made by tourists, directly and indirectly, to the public purse.' Acknowledging that the benefits of tourism could 'only partially offset the
rapid run down of employment and economic activity in other sectors',

they affirmed that 'the acid test is whether London can do without tourists. The answer must be an emphatic "no."'[121] Conversion was complete.

Conclusion

We are familiar today with the idea of cities embracing tourism as a critical part of the postindustrial urban economy. Birmingham has reinvented itself as the largest British conference centre after London.[122] Liverpool, Hull and Coventry have gained European City of Culture status. Post-Troubles Belfast has created a gift shop with a (good) museum attached in order to capitalise on the human tragedy of the *Titanic*. London itself attempted unsuccessfully to win the Olympic Games in 1988 and succeeded in 2012. Civic authorities seek to cultivate 'heritage', including industrial heritage, in what has become a highly competitive market.[123] Failure to find a marketable heritage, or to develop it, can leave a city which has lost its old industries vulnerable to urban blight.

Our present-day experience makes London's approach a generation or two earlier seem all the more anomalous. London possessed abundant genuine heritage along with cultural assets worth travelling to see. These were augmented in the 1960s by the kind of vibrant youth 'scene' that civic boosterism could never have created, drawing young travellers from across the world. The *Evening Standard* captured the contrast between an industrial and a postindustrial city neatly, if perhaps unwittingly, when it suggested that 'the tourist is to modern London what the car is to modern Detroit',[124] yet for a decade or so London treated the tourist as a burden, possibly beneficial to the national economy and the balance of payments but parasitical on the local economy and public services. It embraced tourism only in the late 1970s, when the effects of deindustrialisation were beyond dispute, and even in 1978 the idiosyncratic former GLC chief strategic planner David Eversley could argue that the capital had placed undue faith in the regenerative potential of tourism: 'The problem of London's declining economic base is shared by other cities, and nobody's succeeded in getting manufacturing industries back.... But no city has chosen tourism to replace it. London's unique in that.'[125] It is hard now to understand the reticence of the London Tourist Board in the sixties, declining to advertise the whereabouts of its main Piccadilly office because it 'wouldn't have been able to cope with the vast flow of people wanting the service.'[126] And if the disruptive impact of mass tourism on a city unprepared for it is easily understood, the immediate inference that the authorities' task was not to accommodate but to curb the phenomenon—perhaps substantially—appears surprising today.

To begin to explain this attitude, one needs to recognise that mass urban tourism was an element, albeit a limited one, in the emergence of international or global cities in the late twentieth century and that as such it was hard to reconcile with notions of the managed city which had prevailed since the war. The authorities were disturbed by tourism because it threatened to overload many of the services which they sought to provide. The London Tourist Board worried in its annual report for 1972 that the number of visitors flocking to London might be so large as to deprive Londoners of the facilities and services that they were entitled to expect.[127] Tourists were packing public transport, causing the depletion of the housing stock and even generating the wrong sort of jobs—impeding, in other words, the delivery of the public services which local authorities had been elected to provide. For those who were acclimatised to the production of prescriptive five-yearly development plans and, later, structure plans, such an intrusion was hard to accept.

The story of London's struggle to come to terms with the tourist carries a wider significance than is initially evident. For thirty years the LCC and the GLC had planned for a certain type of city—essentially the mature industrial city—their efforts culminating in the most ambitious attempt to ordain the development of the metropolis in the 1969 Greater London Development Plan. As is argued in chapter 6, the GLDP was initially an attempt to plan for prosperity which mutated into a plan for a city facing decline—at least in the eyes of the GLC's chief planner—but it did so without really changing its essential features. It made only limited efforts to identify such new areas of growth as tourism, and the idea that regeneration of any sort could spring from such unexpected cultural forces as those which produced Swinging London was entirely alien to it. The result was that the rapid expansion of the tourist trade was embarrassingly unplanned for, and what should have been seen as a windfall was treated with suspicion by many people because of the strain it placed on essential services. The reaction of Sir George Young—no Stalinist but a Bow Group Tory—was unambiguously dirigiste:

> The first thing to do . . . is to stop stoking up demand by paying people to advertise London. The second thing is to calculate the maximum number of tourists that the infrastructure of London can take, and work

out how many hotel beds, camp sites, etc, this implies. The third thing is to allocate that supply among the London Boroughs (who must forego their independence in granting planning permission for hotels)—as we do with office and industrial floor space. The fourth thing is to introduce price control so that the surplus of demand does not result in ever-spiralling prices, with the resulting imbalance in the composition of tourists and concentration of profit in the hotel owners' hands. When you have done all that, you will have solved the problem. I reckon it will take ten years.[128]

In practice, though, the lesson of the 1970s was that tourism was beyond such control. At various points the GLC sought to deter tourists or to encourage only the more opulent ones, to deflect them away from London, to divert them to less visited sites within London, to encourage them to come out of season and to tax them—with very limited success. Tourism was, like deindustrialisation, a feature of the emergent forces in the international urban economy over which local bodies could exercise little control. The evolution of the postindustrial city was hard to predict and thus hard to manage. Tourism provided a limited but significant example of the ways in which the new economy of the city would undermine traditional planning methods. The age of the managed city was ending.

16

Becoming Postindustrial

By the midseventies nobody called London the 'Swinging City.' The closure of Biba in 1975—'a sign that the sixties were done for'[1]— and the tenth anniversary of 'Swinging London' in the following year prompted wistful reappraisals of the city's midsixties exuberance. Against a background of national economic crisis, a consensus emerged that the whole thing had been unsustainably light-headed and too good to last. 'The sixties brought colour into everyone's life. But not much more, really', Michael Rainey, who had opened the supremely trendy Chelsea boutique Hung on You in 1965, suggested to Valerie Jenkins of the *Evening Standard* in 1976. Jonathan Aitken told Jenkins that the title of his 1967 study of Swinging London's luminaries—*The Young Meteors*—had been chosen in the expectation that these rapid risers would soon burn themselves out. He concluded, 'My pessimism was not misplaced.'[2]

Some of the more obviously decadent components of the 'Swinging London' collage had indeed been self-negating. The West End casino boom, for example, an element of the collage that has largely disappeared from today's public image of 'Swinging London', began to subside once the easy money on offer attracted the attention of the Inland Revenue. By 1976 'the quick money days have gone', as one unnamed gambler told the *Standard*: 'with the heavy taxation, casinos have become a very good business rather than the little gold mine they used to be.'[3] The rise and fall of the sex trade—another part of the collage—provided an urban morality tale in itself, described in chapter 2. Soho striptease had been presented in the midsixties as a healthy sign that London was shedding its Victorian shackles, but by the midseventies fewer commentators felt willing to indulge the sex trade. As 'the vice' threatened to tawdrify the entire area, public authorities felt compelled to address the ambiguities of policy that had allowed that to happen. The result was, if not exactly a backlash, at least a recognition that commercialised erotic display posed real problems and a retreat from sixties levels of tolerance.

The fashion trade had been as decadent as any component of Swinging London at its midsixties peak, when, as Janet Lyle of Annacat told Jenkins, 'everyone seemed to have plenty of money and there was always a party going on.'[4] Its boutique-based business model proved too delicate to withstand the commercial buffeting that it received in the seventies, and as the fate of Biba showed, attempts to develop that model were risky. It was also risky to attempt to emulate John Stephen's achievement of turning an anonymous back street into a new fashion hub, but at the same time it was becoming increasingly expensive to operate from the established centres. As early as the spring of 1967 concern was being voiced that high rents in the King's Road were driving out the 'oddities and eccentrics' who had created its image, and by the end of the decade freeholds in the street were being snapped up by pension funds and property companies.[5] The cachet of Carnaby Street and the King's Road meant that they effectively became tourist sites almost on a par with the Tower or Westminster Abbey. The John Stephen organisation began to hire shop staff of diverse nationalities: 'because customers are from abroad, they want to be served by a cosmopolitan staff.'[6] The heavy footfall, though rewarding, ensured that Carnaby Street's overheads rose sharply. In 1971 a small shop and basement there cost £4,500 a year to rent, making commercially dangerous the kind of speculative, short-run, innovative designs that had forged the street's reputation.[7] Stephen sold his remaining shares in his business in 1975 and retired. By then Carnaby Street was 'in danger of becoming just another market place for tourists, selling souvenirs, posters and, of course, jeans.'[8] The King's Road also boasted thirty shops or stalls responding to the insatiable demand for jeans and tee shirts, though the nature of Chelsea at least gave King's Road retailers the option of moving upmarket. Jonathan Smith, of the women's-wear store Sidney Smith, told the *Standard*'s fashion correspondent Suzy Menkes in 1976, 'The King's Road has kept its ambience in certain shops. But in the current situation everyone is going to the top end. We are becoming a sort of greater South Molton Street.' He acknowledged that 'it is the rent and rates that killed off the creative talent in the

Carnaby Street as tourist site, 1978. The street had been pedestrianised five years earlier and by the late seventies 'welcomed the world.' 'Carnaby Capers', offering 'Gifts, Watches, Posters', occupied the site of the former Tom Cat boutique. Even this limited view shows three premises to let and one for sale. (Atlantic Kid/Getty Images)

King's Road—or perhaps diversified it.' He was himself diversifying into wine retailing.[9]

Swinging London as a phenomenon proved inescapably transient, but that did not mean that its components were necessarily superficial. What is striking about Valerie Jenkins's piece to the present-day reader is that several of the sixties 'meteors' that she mentioned were still flourishing in 1976 and would continue to flourish—Alan Aldridge, David Bailey, Terence Conran, Terence Donovan, Brian Duffy, David Mlinaric, Mary Quant, among others. Bailey's view that 'all the people of any worth from the sixties are still around. The dross has gone' had some force.[10] The cultural revolution of the sixties had been real, however much 'dross' it attracted.

This concatenation of talent occurred at a time of unusual buoyancy in the capital's economy, producing what I have called London's 'swinging moment.' That moment of economic optimism would, though, soon pass. London was going through the process of becoming postindustrial, an evolution which would bring the expansion of the 'growth services' and the decline of traditional manufacturing industry. In the midsixties the benefits of service expansion had yet to be offset by industrial decline, and

London experienced exceptional prosperity—particularly youth prosperity. Even the limited 'freeze' of the winter of 1966–67 was, though, enough
to curb the city's joie de vivre; the combination of developing structural
unemployment from the late sixties and the national economic turbulence
of the seventies would cause far greater damage. From that point onwards,
the London picture was one of majority affluence offset by often severe
minority deprivation.

Inner-City Malaise

The initial effects of deindustrialisation in London appeared manageable.
The dock closures of the late sixties were actually celebrated by many dockers, who were liberally compensated for the loss of hard and dangerous
work. The Swinging London equivalent of the 1930s hunger marches was
the rumbustious procession to the Rose pub in Shadwell, where dockers
who had taken voluntary redundancy started to part with their windfall.[11]
Few others greeted redundancy with such enthusiasm, but in the early
stages of London's deindustrialisation there was still work to be found.
William Daniel's study of the effects of industrial contraction in Woolwich
in 1968–70 showed that on average workers who were made redundant
found a new job in nine weeks and, remarkably, that more than a quarter
of those who were laid off at the age of sixty-five or older gained new work
within a month.[12] He also showed, though, that the situation had deterio-
rated even during the two years of his research: those who were laid off in
1970 had to wait longer to find work than their predecessors, and to settle
for less rewarding work, with a greater danger of a second redundancy,
when they did find a new job.[13] Within a few years this more pessimistic context had become inescapable. Put simply, between the midsixties and the late
seventies London lost its status as Britain's leading industrial centre. A third
of the capital's manufacturing jobs disappeared between 1961 and 1974, compared with a fall of only 5 percent in England and Wales as a whole.[14]

In 1975 the Conservative peer Lord Trenchard predicted that London
could become 'the Jarrow of the 1980s.'[15] In fact, although 'Jarrow' evoked
in the public mind a simple potent image of mass unemployment, London's situation was more complex. Jarrow in the 1930s had been a single-
industry town which lost its single industry, trapping the workforce in an
area without work. In London the contraction of traditional industrial
employment accelerated—often dramatically—an outward movement

Deindustrialisation. An abandoned lorry at Surrey Commercial Dock, February 1976. The Surrey docks had closed seven years earlier. (E. Milsom/Hulton Archive/Getty Images)

The search for work in a South London job centre, 1976. (Homer Sykes/Alamy Stock Photo)

from the inner city which had been under way for decades. Much of this exodus was voluntary. 'The main reasons why people leave London seem to be environmental in the broadest sense of the word', concluded the South East Strategic Plan team in its 1976 review;[16] the Lambeth Inner Area Study researchers found that the main incentive to leave Stockwell was the simple hope for 'better surroundings' elsewhere, along with 'better housing.'[17] The contraction of inner-city industry prompted others to move who might not otherwise have done so, but they generally moved to new jobs. In 1977 Mary Macpherson of the *Standard* interviewed Jack Cox, a former docker who had been laid off as a supervisor training crane drivers when the London Docks closed. He had taken his £2,000 redundancy money to Ashford in Kent, where he operated cranes for British Rail and lived in a three-bedroomed house with a garden on a council estate. His family had lived in Wapping for two hundred years, though, and he would probably never have moved had the docks not closed. He had seen his pay fall by more than two-thirds and lost the 'abundance of brandy, wangled off the Excise people' which he had enjoyed as a docker. He found Ashford dull, with 'just no closeness' in its society. Having moved, though, he was adamant that he would not return—'could not face Dockland without docks.' He suggested, rightly, that 'all those people who left—you'll never get them going back.'[18]

At the same time, Macpherson interviewed a young couple of council tenants who had moved from Islington to the East End in 1970, under the impression that Wapping 'was somewhere in the country.' The husband had been unemployed for the seven years since the move, with the result that the couple owed £200 in rent arrears to Tower Hamlets Council. They and their five children were consequently trapped in their 'miserable dump', conscious that they were 'regarded by the locals as a problem family.'[19] Tower Hamlets, like most inner-London boroughs in the seventies, feared not just that people were leaving but that the wrong people were leaving and the wrong people staying. When council leader Paul Beasley spoke injudiciously of the danger that the borough's population might come to consist disproportionately of 'the dregs',[20] he voiced a real concern that the area would soon be peopled disproportionately by the economically inactive.

Many observers noted the paradox of a worsening shortage of skilled labour in inner London even as the overall unemployment level rose—too many Jack Coxes were leaving, in other words.[21] Ultimately skill shortages would drive even established firms from the inner city, as they found that 'the major pools of skilled labour lay in other more salubrious areas.' Though most job losses in London were due to straightforward closures, a quarter were the result of firms moving out of the capital.[22] Peter Gripaios's contemporary study of deindustrialisation in Greenwich, Lewisham and Southwark showed a kind of race to the bottom, with the percentage fall in both jobs and resident workers accelerating sharply in the late sixties.[23] It was only in 1968, with the publication of the results of the 1966 Sample Census, that the scale of the dual exodus of jobs and workers became clear.[24] By then the process was well advanced and about to be intensified by the closure of the upriver docks. In the 1970s the evisceration of the inner city became the focus of analyses by the Community Development Projects in Southwark and Newham, by the Environment Department's Lambeth Inner Area Study and, indirectly, by the several investigations into Docklands.

What these and similar studies showed was that the failure of traditional industries was one part of a multifaceted inner-city malaise which afflicted not only the unemployed but also those who were trapped in conditions of structural poverty: pensioners, single mothers, school leavers—especially Black school leavers—the low paid, those living on supplementary benefit. The researchers on the Lambeth Inner Area Study treated deprivation as a matter of quality of life. They identified eight indicators of disadvantage, covering the possession of household amenities, consumer durables, leisure time and holidays as well as job stability, housing space and basic income, and concluded that one in eight of Stockwell's households lived in conditions of multiple deprivation.[25]

For many the quality of life in the inner city depended critically on the support offered by public agencies, even in households which had not suffered redundancy. Virginia Bottomley's 1972 study of low-income families in Bethnal Green—all in work—showed how far the welfare state had travelled from its benign founding ideals:

> The picture was one of unreliable, low-paid jobs with social security playing an essential part in all these families' lives, but in almost all cases one which they said left them with uncomfortable memories. 'I've been once and I'll never go back again'; 'they twist you round their little finger—I'd rather walk the streets' ... 'You can't beat Them: their word is final, there's no way of getting at Them. They pick on certain people and try everything to get you off their books' ... 'You've got to bow down to these people: they look down on you at the Assistance: they

think you're begging and are very sarcastic. They insult you. Sometimes you really want to hit them, but the more you lose your temper, the worse off you are—they just go and put your money down for no reason' . . . Some informants reported waiting six hours to be seen and repeated derogatory remarks by officials. "Oh, go away, you get on my nerves" and "You're classed as dirt" were typical statements quoted.[26]

Staff in the Tower Hamlets Social Services Department were said by one claimant to have alarm buttons under their desks 'which they can press if you get too demanding.'[27] This fractious relationship reflected the strains within the social security system in the inner city. 'The concentration of disadvantaged people puts additional burdens on welfare services', the Lambeth study noted in 1976;[28] in chapter 8 it was argued that the rise in the dependency ratio in the East End boroughs as employment contracted undermined the 'Poplarist' municipal philosophy which had sustained the community for decades.

Inner-city conditions eroded the standard of basic public services. Almost any service could be taken to demonstrate the poverty of social provision in seventies inner London, but the deteriorating health-care system probably makes the point most clearly. Put bluntly, 'the areas with the worst social problems have the least suitable primary care available to them.'[29] The high price of London property even in the poorest areas hindered the purchase or leasing of new premises, with the result that general practitioners (GPs) might practise in 'lock-up shop front premises, poorly decorated, with little or no sanitation or heating.'[30] It also militated against the acquisition of premises suitable for group practice: single-handed practices were twice as common in inner London as in the country as a whole, with the result that fewer practices offered ancillary services such as nurses or health visitors. This was one reason for the failure of health-care providers in inner London to embrace advances in preventative medicine more rapidly.[31] Another was the innate conservatism of a body of GPs who were significantly older than their counterparts elsewhere. Nine percent of inner-London GPs were over seventy, against 3 percent in England and Wales as a whole.[32] The falling population of inner London dissuaded the Medical Practices Committee (the body overseeing the distribution of GPs across the country) from replacing doctors who died or moved, which, combined with the scarcity of group practices, limited the opportunities for any young doctor not already deterred by 'heavy patient demands . . . ; having to work from inadequate premises; and having to live

London disamenities. Commuters pack a delayed rush-hour train at Charing Cross, November 1976.
(Barry Lewis/Alamy Stock Photo)

in an area where housing, schools and community may be unattractive to his family.'[33] The corps of inner London GPs therefore aged in the job. More than a hundred of them were aged over seventy in 1979, including twenty in their eighties and one in his nineties.[34] The income per patient of inner-London GPs was 12 percent lower than that of GPs in England and Wales as a whole, but they soldiered on for fear that their pensions would prove inadequate.[35] Most adopted one of two coping strategies, either limiting their National Health Service (NHS) patients in order to concentrate on private practice or enlarging their NHS lists in order to maximise returns: of the 106 septuagenarian inner-London GPs in 1979 30 had had lists of more than a thousand patients.[36] As one commentator observed, such expedients were 'probably not in the best interests of patients.'[37]

In services such as health care and education, where it was desirable for practitioners to live close to their work, inner-city provision was notably poorer than that in the suburbs, but across the capital the falling population, the costly and inflexible housing market, the high cost of living and the apparent inadequacy of London weighting payments[38] hampered the recruitment and retention of the skilled workers needed to operate routine services.[39] The question of London's public services became a matter of national discussion in the autumn of 1973. The *Evening Standard* ran a seven-part series on the problem in October, under the melodramatic title 'Is London Cracking Up?' In the same month the leader of the opposition, Harold Wilson, worked a lengthy critique of London's shortcomings in transport, education, police and ambulance services into his reply to the Queen's Speech, suggesting that the capital was 'seizing up.'[40] In November the Commons debated a motion by the member for Shoreditch, Ronald Brown, criticising the government for allowing London's services to 'deteriorate to the point where they are now reaching breakdown.'[41] By that point London Transport had 15 percent fewer bus drivers than it needed and 12 percent fewer conductors. The postal service was 15 percent below strength, the Metropolitan Police 20 percent.[42] More than half the teachers appointed by the Inner London Education Authority in 1973 had come straight out of training college; Havering Council, which, as an outer-London borough, ran its own education service, was said to have written to final-year university students with parental homes in the borough to urge them to consider teaching locally.[43] Other, more systematic recruitment drives characterised the decade: the Met's £100,000 'Wear the Badge of Courage' campaign of 1973,[44] the Inner London Education Authority's £1 million teacher-recruitment campaign in the same year,[45] London Transport attempting to recruit 880 drivers and conductors by 'advertising like crazy—as though every Londoner is a bus driver in disguise' in 1979. As the managing director of London Transport buses put it in that year, 'with social change and gentrification there is no longer an adequate pool of homes and labour within reach of the garages'—essential when workers might have to sign on at 4.30 A.M. or sign off at 1.30 A.M.[46] There was no mystery in these shortages. Too many of the types of workers that public services needed had left inner London and perhaps left London altogether. The cost of accommodation and the shrinkage of the private rental sector had made it difficult to remain even for those who were not anxious to leave, creating precisely the problems that the Milner Holland Committee had predicted in 1965.[47]

Declinism

The economic historian Jim Tomlinson has identified a tendency for analyses of deindustrialisation to usher in 'notions of "decline" by the back door, by seeing the loss of industry as evidence of profound economic malaise.'[48] In midseventies London the growing impression of a city simply ceasing to function released a wave of declinist gloom. In March 1974 Sir Reg Goodwin, Labour leader of the Greater London Council, led a deputation to Environment Secretary Anthony Crosland to alert him to London's housing, transport and planning problems.[49] In April 1975 David Wilcox, the *Standard*'s planning correspondent, wrote a front-page story headlined 'London on the Rocks', warning that rising rents, rates and fares were strangling London.[50] This wave of gloom peaked in the summer and autumn of 1977, when the London Chamber of Commerce warned of 'serious social repercussions' in a city 'slowly dying from a lack of new investment'[51] and Thames Television broadcast an evening-long appraisal of London's problems.[52] While the programme's content was not uniformly pessimistic, a survey conducted in conjunction with it spread more gloom by showing that 52 percent of Londoners wished to move.[53] London had 'ceased to be able to deal with the urgent needs of its decaying inner core and maintain the standard of living, public and private, to which most of its citizens have become accustomed', Anne Lapping wrote in a 1977 survey in the *Economist*, warning that 'no city has yet successfully planned for decline.'[54]

Various ad hoc remedies were aired. The London Chamber of Commerce called for the capital to be given Assisted Area status for the next ten years, allowing companies to secure government grants for investment.[55] On the left, the Community Development Projects in Newham and Southwark attributed inner-city ills to footloose capitalism, and those local authorities in which the Left emerged victorious from the Labour Party's internal battles devised new socialist strategies. Ambitious experiments in municipal socialism were contemplated in Wandsworth, Lambeth and other boroughs where the radical Left had gained a foothold.[56] In the meantime the GLC, guided by its gloomy chief planner, David Eversley, called in 1972 for the reversal of the process of dispersing jobs and people from Central London, a national objective since the Barlow report of 1940, in order to allow resources to be trained on regenerating the inner city. 'Unless the nature of metropolitan problems is recognised soon', Eversley suggested, 'we may yet have cause to pay closer attention to the warnings now reaching us from across the Atlantic.'[57]

In 1974 the sociologist Peter Willmott, looking back to his classic study of midfifties Bethnal Green, announced that 'what has happened [in London] over the past 20 years could be described—without too much exaggeration—as the breakdown of community.'[58] He did not say how much exaggeration was too much, but few of the prophets of London's decline showed much restraint in these years. In this climate, the Department of the Environment felt bound to compile its own investigation into 'the future of London.' Its tone was more sanguine. The author, A. S. D. Whybrow, acknowledged the population fall and the 'fairly rapid industrial rundown' but suggested that 'certain small pockets of unemployment . . . tend to reflect lack of jobs in the traditional industries of the area rather than any overall lack of demand for labour.' There were, after all, also skill shortages, and overall it was 'hard to conclude that the average Londoner has so far suffered seriously from the migration of jobs from London.' Public services might become worse and more expensive, but they would not break down. A shift from manual to white-collar jobs was clearly under way, but Whybrow did not envisage London developing the sort of social polarisation which offered 'no chance for the poor to improve their position because everyone who is not poor is a senior manager.' The London of 1981 would have its problems, he acknowledged, but 'most of them will be national rather than local ones, associated with increased prosperity.'[59]

By 1976, when London's future was again assessed as part of the review of the 1970 *Strategic Plan for the South East*, it was harder to be quite so confident, but by setting London's problems in the context of the wider Southeast, the review avoided deriving pessimistic general projections from the difficulties of the inner city. It identified a natural outward movement of both jobs and people from the centre to the periphery of Greater London and the Outer Metropolitan Area, so that 'while manufacturing has declined in London itself, it has expanded (until the last few years) and probably with greater efficiency in the OMA and, more recently in an apparent ripple effect, beyond this.' Losses of population and jobs in the central area were not unique to London but had occurred in most of the world's metropolitan areas through similar centrifugal processes. Inferences as to London's future based on the GLC area alone—let alone inner London—were therefore misleading: 'a static concept of "London" within the GLC boundary can be a blinkered concept.' Addressing directly the demands of the GLC itself, the review concluded that if policy makers faced the 'extreme choice' between 'allocation for redevelopment, rehabilitation and environmental improvements inside London, and for new development and physical growth outside it', greenfield sites on the periphery offered the better option. The Southeast was the most successful part of the British economy, and nothing should be done to impede its growth. That included diverting public resources to the inner city in the hope of reversing a process which the review's authors saw as a natural, evolutionary, one.[60]

The review listed the advantages that London already enjoyed, including most obviously a disproportionate share of support for local authorities—and in particular housing authorities—in England and Wales. The conclusion was brutal: 'Taking together (a) the shift that has already taken place in London's favour as regards distribution of resources between local authorities, (b) the proportion of total resources, particularly in some especially relevant sectors, which London already commands, and (c) the high costs associated with activity in London, it is evident that resources could be shifted towards London only to a limited extent and even to that extent what could be accomplished with them would be even more limited.'[61] Those who were seeking special help for London 'cannot hope to secure much in the way of additional resources.'[62] As if to reiterate the point, the report of the 1976 Resource Allocation Working Party on health-care provision, set up to consider the distribution of funds between NHS regions following the 1973 reorganisation, called for a revision of existing funding patterns which 'tended to reflect the inertia built into the system by history.'[63] Such a rethink could only work against London. Its falling population had already brought the closure of twenty hospitals since 1974; a further eighty-three were under threat by 1977.[64]

Whitehall was generally unmoved by what it saw as special pleading from the most prosperous part of the country at a time of national economic stringency: one unnamed official told Simon Jenkins in 1976 that London could 'go hang itself.'[65] This puts into context the support offered to parts of London under the 1978 Inner Urban Areas Act, by which Lambeth, the Docklands boroughs, Hackney and Islington received enhanced central-government grants and were empowered to promote local industrial development.[66] The Department of the Environment, headed since 1976 by a Docklands MP, Peter Shore, was more ready than it had been at the time of Whybrow's 1974 report to accept the extent and persistence of inner-London poverty, but it also accepted the fundamental argument of the Southeast review that inner London's problems had to be seen in the light of the overall prosperity of the region. Whereas in some provincial cities the decay of the inner city might be taken as a warning sign for the whole urban area, in London this was not the case. In short, Whitehall saw minority deprivation in inner London, intense as it was, as the concomitant of majority prosperity in the metropolis—and the region—as a whole.

Antideclinism

The pessimism of the midseventies surely was overdrawn. The 1977 book based on the Thames TV investigation was titled, pointedly, *London. The Heartless City*, but the urban geographer Peter Hall, in his foreword to the volume, emphasised the capital's strengths. London was unrivalled in Europe as 'a centre for finance, for the media, for entertainment—in short, nearly all the fastest growing tertiary industries.'[67] It was increasingly attractive as a tourist destination.[68] Likewise, John Dunning's 1978 survey of international businessmen for the Department of Trade and Industry found that London was considered the best city in Europe as a business location.[69] Hall's view was that London was simply in 'a state of flux': 'It has strengths and weaknesses. Certain activities grow; others decline. Some kinds of people arrive; others, for equally good reasons, leave. The physical fabric of the city alters to accommodate new jobs, new homes.'[70] The London of the seventies was superficially less enticing than the London of the sixties. Talk of the city as the most exciting place on Earth had yielded to talk of a city in irreversible decline. But while the population flight from the contracting inner-city economy was real enough, the annual rate of inward migration rose by 14 percent between the early sixties and the midseventies, the incomers including 'many young people, and others with varied actual or potential skills.'[71] This was not a city on the ropes.

Thames TV's finding that 52 percent of Londoners wished to move was striking, but on closer inspection it emerged that two-thirds of them envisaged shifting only to the London suburbs or 'a town not too far from the capital'—a result consistent with most actual population movement at the time.[72] In inner-city Stockwell 85 percent of those who wished to move still intended to stay in Greater London.[73] Those who were tired of the inner city were not necessarily tired of London. Similar inertia thwarted attempts to coax commercial firms away from the City and the West End in order to relieve pressure and congestion there. The Location of Offices Bureau, established in 1963 in the hope of diluting the demand for city-centre offices, noted in 1973 that three-fifths of those firms willing to relocate still preferred to stay in Greater London.[74]

As was shown in chapter 5, the trend in London's housing market was towards owner occupation, despite the capital's high prices. Some of those who bought property did so because they saw no acceptable alternative;

but most wanted to own, and nearly all who got onto the housing ladder made a de facto commitment to London in doing so. The Heath government discovered this inadvertently in 1973, during one of Whitehall's recurrent attempts to move civil-service jobs out of London. The Hardman Committee, charged with this task, found that the traditional incentive of easier access to the property market in the provinces no longer operated, as 'the great majority of officers already own their own homes.'[75] It also found that only 20 percent of civil servants were willing to move at all and that more than a third of those who were willing preferred to remain in the Southeast ('I spent four years in Canada. . . . I didn't come back to live in West Cumbria.').[76] This inertia was unlikely to have been confined to civil servants.

It is hard not to suspect that the civil service was being made to compensate for the reluctance of the private sector to leave London. The Location of Offices Bureau acknowledged in 1973 that the firms it had succeeded in moving out of the capital had usually been replaced immediately by new firms moving in; it compared its task to bailing a waterlogged boat.[77] Office rents in the City jumped by 20 percent per year on average in the early seventies, with 50 percent increases coming in the bubble year of 1973. More businesses were already moving into the West End, and 'before long, more firms may move across that other psychological barrier, which is the Thames.'[78] Companies valued London for its 'linkages'—access to networks of expertise, to government departments, to visiting overseas businessmen. They welcomed the fact that 80 percent of trips to business meetings took less than half an hour. They feared losing custom if they left the capital.[79] Many employees believed their career prospects to be better in London. A London School of Economics study of white-collar workers in 1974 found that although almost half said that they would prefer to leave London and just over half found London stressful, 70 percent had spent all their working lives there, and most intended to stay for the sake of the career opportunities that the capital offered.[80] Those who resisted the Hardman Committee's dispersal proposals feared similarly that 'there will be some prejudice to promotion if they are tucked away in some small area.'[81] Beyond that, though, lay lifestyle considerations. The Tavistock Institute for Human Relations, which conducted the committee's survey, noted that few respondents were prepared to be banished beyond the Southeast, a preference attributed to 'what can broadly be described as "London culture."' If it was necessary to leave London at all, the best way to enjoy London culture was not to move too far.[82]

'London culture' was not defined, but it was likely to have embraced more than simply theatres and galleries. One reason why London clearly continued to attract and retain young in-migrants after its swinging heyday had passed was that the kind of lifestyle attractions taken to be exclusive or outré in the midsixties became steadily more widely diffused as the baby-boomer generation matured. The 'Swinging London' stereotype had often been rejected as unreal in the midsixties because it appeared to require a degree of privilege—and an income level—that few people possessed. 'Swinging London' was then represented as a translation of traditional aristocratic libertinism to the West End, and its various venues were portrayed as correspondingly exclusive. 'Real' Londoners, it was said, could not afford to dance at Sibylla's, shop at Bazaar or Blades, eat at Alvaro's or live in gentrified Chelsea. That was true then, but the succeeding years would show that there was little intrinsic to even the most fashionable brands and venues that could not be imitated and diffused.

All the leading names in fashion, for example, were vulnerable to the simple theft of their designs ('one large company copied every dress we put in the shop', Barbara Hulanicki remembered; 'other manufacturers would follow our vans around to see where our things were being made so that they could copy our patterns').[83] They were also open to the more legitimate usurpation of their style and approach by the department stores. 'The problem is that if you start a distinctive trend in fashion', Mary Quant wrote as early as 1966, 'you are digging its grave right from the beginning, because the more people are converted to your way of dress, the less exclusive it becomes and a uniform is born.'[84] By the time the King's Road Bazaar closed in 1969, her 'uniform' was widely worn. Sibylla's discotheque lasted only two years, 'such were the vagaries of fashion among its in-crowd membership.'[85] It had depended almost entirely on its snob appeal: there was nothing inimitable in the disco concept, which, though rare in 1966, had spread across London by the midseventies.[86] Alvaro Maccioni's attempt to create exclusivity by letting it be known that his restaurant was ex-directory was a brilliant gimmick, but it masked the reality that the trattoria fad had already served its purpose of persuading Londoners that there was more to eating out than French haute cuisine. By 1970, indeed, London's growing band of gourmands had decided that there was more to eating out than trattorie and was developing more varied tastes.

The cachet of a Chelsea address proved more durable, because there was a limited supply of endearing early nineteenth-century artisans' cottages in London and no more were being made. Similar property in parts of

Islington, Camden and North Lambeth acquired a similar appeal, which has proved similarly enduring. Nonetheless, the pressure of demand for owner occupation in these years ensured that the improvement vogue was not confined to attractive property. Arundel Square in Holloway, the subject of Jonathan Raban's account of social transformation in the late 1960s, moved upmarket despite what he considered its 'cheapskate style of Victorian architecture.'[87] The displacement of the estate agents' term 'Chelseafication' by the now more familiar 'gentrification' was a sign that the process was no longer parochial and no longer confined to bijou property. It would continue to spread, to the point where it lost its initial peculiarity. When gentrification had been 'discovered' in the early 1960s, it usually entailed the purchase of aesthetically attractive but run-down property in working-class areas by middle-class buyers. The aesthetic appeal justified, to the 'creatives' predominant among early purchasers, both the effort necessary to rescue the building from dereliction and the risk of social isolation. The physical and social transformation of former slum areas was a genuinely striking phenomenon, and contemporaries long continued to portray gentrification in its most extreme form, in which advertising executives or TV producers drove dockers or dustmen from their rented homes to impose a regime of stripped pine and Habitat furniture on their new property, acquired for a song but soaring in value.[88] Reaction to the gentrifiers themselves ranged from mocking parody to outright hostility but generally treated their actions as anomalous, if not antisocial. By the midseventies, though, gentrification—if, indeed, that remained the appropriate term—was more widespread and more mundane and applied even to many of the late-Victorian terraces abundant in London. Renovation of existing property, generally by developers rather than the purchasers themselves, had enabled London's growing numbers of young professionals to be accommodated, funds to be raised for the restoration of the capital's infirm Victorian fabric and much of her private housing stock to pass from renting into owner occupation. The process still excluded many people and provided no more than a partial solution to London's housing problems, but it was no longer unusual. It epitomised the way in which sixties lifestyle chic steadily became commonplace.

Beyond all this was a wider consumerism, doubtless driven by the young professionals but not limited to them. Oxford Street was Europe's premier shopping street by the midseventies, with shop rents rising sixfold in a decade; its Marks and Spencer store was said to have the highest turnover per square foot of shopping space anywhere in the world.[89] Other retail centres less magnetic to tourists than the West End flowered less spectacularly but still prospered. The success of London's first US-style mall, Brent Cross, opening near the peak of midseventies pessimism in March 1976, was instructive. Catering for 'higher-income, car-owning family households', it was 'well patronized and popular' from the start,[90] and by 1979 smaller but similar shopping centres existed or were planned in Wandsworth, Stratford, Wood Green, Harrow, Neasden, Enfield, Brentford, Kingston and Bexley. When the King's Mall in Hammersmith was opened by Diana Dors in April 1979, the *Standard* commented that 'this vast expansion in shopping facilities around London is likely to continue while spending power increases.'[91]

In truth, London contained many higher-income, car-owning households, most of them vigorous consumers. The economic difficulties of the midseventies slowed their spending but did not pauperise them. A bank manager in Becontree interviewed by Max Hastings in 1976 noted that while his middle-class customers might defer the purchase of 'big cars, big fridges', scale down their holiday plans and think twice about private education for their children, and while their wives might take part-time jobs, still 'nobody had had to get rid of their tellies yet, or anything like that.'[92] In fact Londoners generally had more than the average national share of consumer durables by the midseventies.[93] That was unsurprising. What was more telling was the emerging propensity of even the moderately affluent Londoner to carry consumerism to the next level: to indulge in the kind of discretionary spending that only large and prosperous urban areas really allowed. Then as now, big cities offered the kind of attractions encompassed in what has since been christened the 'experience economy.' Access to this economy was not available to all, but by its nature 'the profitable trade [in] experiences requires a mass market',[94] which modern London clearly provided.

Several aspects of London's experience economy have featured in chapters of this book: the proliferating restaurants, the exotic if short-lived emporium that was Big Biba, the tourist trade (experience as invisible export) and the admittedly specialised experiences on offer in Soho. The restaurant trade provides perhaps the best indicator. It was shaken in the difficult midseventies, but the habit of eating out, once established, proved inextinguishable.[95] Many people had anticipated that the antiques trade, a London-centred product of sixties opulence, would wilt in the harsher climate of the seventies.[96] In practice, though, as Dee Wells noted in the *Standard* in 1978, 'from the ephemera of cigarette cards and day-outing tickets to Skegness (circa 1931) through sweatstained *panne* velvet dresses to costly durables like vintage cars and cast iron stoves, nothing lacks for buyers.'[97] For some collectors, antiques might simply have been a hedge against inflation, but Bennie Gray, London's leading antiques entrepreneur, also saw in them a psychological value: 'more and more people want to take refuge in pieces of the past, for they share a horror of the future.'[98] When times were hard, middle-class London sought consolation in *objets*. It did not stop spending.

Winners and Losers

The analysis of real incomes in London in chapter 1 depicted a pronounced change in the late sixties, by which a pattern of general improvement gave way to one where rising median incomes masked a widening gap between the richest and the poorest. The previous two sections have fleshed out this change. London was generally prosperous, and Londoners survived the inflationary shocks of the seventies remarkably well; but people at the sharp end of the inner-city malaise—the unemployed, the elderly, school leavers, ethnic minorities—suffered a serious reduction in their living standards. A wider concern had arisen—exaggerated but not illusory—that the city was ceasing to function properly. Rising inequality and the erosion of public services appeared to some people to raise the question of whether the social compact central to the postwar welfare state was still valid. Deprivation in the midst of plenty was not unfamiliar: it had been central to the 'rediscovery of poverty' in the sixties, much of which had been played out in London. But that 'rediscovery' related largely to perceived gaps in a generally extensive welfare safety net. In a city which had escaped relatively lightly from the troubles of the thirties, a generation which had come to believe that the problem of mass unemployment had been solved by Keynes was unprepared for the scale of the structural problems emerging in inner London. Some of those who had lived life to the full in the sixties began to worry that the solipsistic nature of the counter-culture, preoccupied as it was with challenges to established authority and an emphasis on the creative self, had inadvertently eroded social solidarity and weakened the community. The notion was given academic support in a pessimistic 1982 commentary by the Anglophile American political scientist Samuel Beer, who suggested that the sixties generation's 'hostility to hierarchy' reflected a fundamentally individualistic outlook on their part, which had hastened 'the onset of class decomposition and pluralistic stag-nation.'[99] Experience of the Thatcher decade would give this conjecture a more concrete form. Jenny Diski speculated in her 2009 memoir of sixties London that her generation might have 'caused the greed and self-interest of the Eighties by invoking the self, the individual, as the unit of society and setting up individualism for the Right to pick up and run with.'[100]

Diski did not entirely endorse the suggestion, which does indeed raise more questions than it answers. While individual examples of hippy indi-vidualists evolving into entrepreneurs are relatively familiar, it takes a big-ger leap to imagine the hippy reverence for the self creating a general zeit-geist of economic individualism twenty years later. The most obviously individualistic group studied in this book, after all, were the taxi drivers in chapter 9, few of whom were likely to have had their heads turned by the counterculture. It is true that the more entrepreneurial of the sixties 'Young Meteors' interviewed by Jonathan Aitken openly resented the high taxes of the Wilson years and that some claimed that the tax system made it pointless to expand their businesses.[101] One suspects, though, that such entrepreneurs would have made similar complaints in the fifties. They ap-pear paradoxical only because of an instinctive assumption that the people involved in the youth-cultural revolution of the sixties must ipso facto have been political radicals, when many actually came from Tory backgrounds which they never entirely renounced and directed their satirical fire at the Wilson government.

Most obviously, it is dangerous to read directly from the sixties to the eighties. The troubled seventies intervened, and they were not good years for entrepreneurship. In the spring of 1977 the *Evening Standard* felt im-pelled to launch a hunt for the 'people who are proving enterprise still pays.' It found them where it would have found them in the sixties, in retail-ing and in entertainment—such go-getters as Mel Morris, founder of the Jean Junction chain, who had correctly anticipated that in the seventies 'denim would become a commodity "like bread or butter"', or the concert promoter Mel Bush, who reaped £60,000 a year from staging around 250 events[102]—but they appeared thinner on the ground than a decade earlier.

The taxi drivers were arguably more representative figures. In their edgi-ness and precarity they typified many who had followed a similar trajec-tory from wage labour into small business, having sacrificed much time and effort to secure an independence which they treasured but seldom considered secure. The diverse London economy had always included many such figures, and their plaints were not unfamiliar; but in inflationary times they were genuinely vulnerable. The *Standard* launched a 'small businesses campaign' in 1978, moved by concern that 'golf club professionals, taxi-drivers, greengrocers, Chinese restaurants, . . . all these and many more are joining the army of small businesses going bankrupt.'[103] John Stentiford, the Becontree bank manager mentioned earlier, noted in 1976 that among his customers some small businessmen, particularly in the building trade, had reverted to working for an employer 'because they find they can make enough money that way without the headaches of being your own boss.'[104] They were entrepreneurs in spirit but not risk-takers. Having placed themselves, in practice, beyond the scope of the welfare state, such people associated 'the authorities' more with intrusion, red tape and taxation than with social security. The value-added tax (VAT), then relatively new, was cited by many people in the *Standard*'s survey as a particular irritant. Individualism expressed itself less in any effusion of animal spirits than in the development of an embittered critique of 'the state.'

Disparaging 'the State'

Over the past thirty years our understanding of the urban local state has evolved from an approach treating city authorities as elements of a largely autonomous public sector to one emphasising the interconnectedness of public authorities with economic actors and civil society in their locality, creating 'policy networks': today 'any urban area may have all kinds of governance relations threading through it, around it and over it' as local authorities interact with community groups, residents associations, lobbyists or local businesses.[105] Hints of this development can be identified in some of the preceding chapters. In Soho, for example, the GLC moved from initial attempts to control what audiences could see in clubs and cinemas, anachronistic in a permissive age, to more realistic efforts to reverse the degradation of the local environment by the sex trade, in cooperation with residents' organisations and the local amenity society. The proliferation of Conservation Areas in many London boroughs, described in chapter 7, was frequently the result of cooperation between councils and local amenity groups, and authorities in the outer suburbs often worked with residents' groups to resist incursions into the Green Belt. A new urban micropolitics was taking shape, in which the more ambitious and disruptive schemes nurtured by local authorities appeared out of place. Peter Hall concluded a postmortem on the Ringway scheme in 1980 by suggesting that public aspirations had simply narrowed by the seventies: 'The good future life of the early 1960s consisted in ceaseless mobility in search of an ever widening range of choice in jobs, education, entertainment and social life. The good future life of the early 1970s was seen in almost the reverse kind of life: in a small, place-bounded, face-to face community.'[106] Whatever the reason for this, it implied a less ambitious role for the local state.

Most council officers, particularly in planning departments, remained, though, more comfortable with older traditions of local government—with what might be called municipal philanthropy, dating back to the late Victorian period, and with the Abercrombiean holistic planning creed of the 1940s, updated by the advocates of structure planning in the 1960s. They were not necessarily the megalomaniacs often portrayed, but the process of professionalisation had instilled in many a planner the assumptions described by David Eversley in 1972:

> His whole training, his traditional ideology, make him believe that it is a change in the physical environment which creates health and happiness. . . . He is paternalistic: he knows what is best for the masses. If he has read his planning history, it is the ghosts of Robert Owen, George Cadbury, Patrick Geddes and Ebenezer Howard that dominate him. After all, they *knew* what was best for the people, though it is not recorded that they asked them or subjected themselves to democratic election to find out. The planner automatically assumes that what he is doing is too difficult to understand: the direct involvement of a lay community (let alone a disadvantaged one) in the process is quite foreign to a Royal Town Planning Institute member.[107]

It was always likely that this prescriptive mode of local-authority action would falter in London before anywhere else, given the obstacles it faced: the high costs of land acquisition in the centre, the high levels of owner occupation in the suburbs, pervasive gentrification, the presence of vigorous and articulate residents' groups ready to fight any disruptive redevelopment and the ease with which press campaigns could be mobilised over London issues.

In fact much of this book might be read as a demonstration of the increasing powerlessness of public agencies in London. This was true not only of the more hubristic projects, such as the Ringway motorways, the redevelopment proposals for Whitehall, Piccadilly or Covent Garden, or the efforts—entirely fruitless by the time this book finishes—to plan a future for Docklands but also of much that had previously been assumed to be within the scope of public action. Deindustrialisation in the inner city had stretched the traditional welfare role of local authorities to and beyond the breaking point, leading some policy makers to turn to market-oriented approaches to regeneration.[108] The ambitious slum-clearance programmes of the late sixties had been curtailed by doubts about high-rise construction and, above all, by the sheer cost of building in inner London. The GLC's efforts to act as a strategic housing authority, relocating tenants to outer London to relieve pressure in the inner city, had encountered intense suburban resistance, as had almost every proposed intrusion on the Green Belt. The attempt to extend the welfare state to cover personal social services had proved unpopular and patchy in its realisation. Well-intentioned efforts to ameliorate race relations had been neutered by the sheer scale of the economic disadvantages facing young Blacks and the resentment consequently generated. Attempts by public authorities to stem or channel the tourist wave failed almost completely. This pattern of public-sector impotence emerged even as local authorities engaged in increasingly ambitious exercises of spatial management, in the form of structure plans, development plans or area plans. Seldom can the gulf between the aspirations and the achievements of public authorities ever have been as large as it was in these years.

In the late sixties it became clear that much of the London public was losing its confidence in the ability of public authorities to improve their quality of life. Interviewed by Terry Christensen in 1979, Geoffrey Holland, who had directed the GLC's proposed Covent Garden redevelopment, noted with evident bewilderment, 'In the 1960s change was considered a good thing because it improved the city, providing new facilities, open space, new housing, all the kinds of things people wanted and then profits could be made to pay for all these things. Almost overnight this became a bad thing.'[109] He was right. From the late sixties the London public became more concerned with the threat to treasured landmarks and the urban environment generally from the aspirations of public agencies than they were enthused by the improvements that such change might bring. During the seventies this generalised disenchantment was channelled by more politically focused arguments from both left and right.

On the left, the growing enthusiasm for grassroots activism fed a reaction against what was seen as the dirigisme, bureaucracy and paternalism of the local state in London. It was the Left which advocated the participatory democracy described in chapter 14, in attacks directed at Labour as well as Conservative councils, for breaking up communities with their road or redevelopment schemes, for building themselves grandiose new offices after the 1965 amalgamations, for the compulsory purchase of serviceable houses which were then left empty, for heavy-handed action against the squatters who occupied those empty houses, for the sweetheart deals struck with property developers to fund improvement projects and for many similar crimes against community.

These protests were often directed by activists emerging from the universities in the late sixties looking for communities to nurture. They engaged, though, many people who would never have identified as Far Left but who shared the suspicion of 'council bureaucrats' or 'the planners.' Those interviewed by Ann Holmes in her study of housing stress areas in Islington criticised office blocks deliberately kept untenanted and local authorities' practice of leaving houses unoccupied for years before redevelopment, showing that prevailing critiques of property speculation and of homelessness had taken root outside the radical circles which first propagated them. London's social evolution gradually eroded the faith in public agencies instilled in wartime and in the early years of the postwar welfare state just as many of those agencies were becoming more assertive and more ambitious. Holmes noted that while rent-controlled tenants who had lived through one or both world wars still believed that, given the political will, 'no real obstacle lay in the way of the government making sure that the housing problem was solved', such confidence was much less evident in owner-occupiers *in the same age group*, who 'tended to be much more self-centred.' Strikingly, although most of her tenant respondents had little chance of affording home ownership in the foreseeable future, not only did most of them *wish* to own their homes, but even those who accepted that ownership was unattainable for them still saw it as 'the logical and normal activity.'[110] It is hard not to see this as a reflection of the patchy record of social housing providers in practice. Holmes's respondents had not rejected the local state—they still preferred the idea of a council tenancy to being at the mercy of a private landlord[111]—but they believed, realistically, that their chances of becoming council tenants were scarcely greater than those of buying a house and consequently fixed their gaze on ownership, however distant.

In this climate a generalised trust in public agencies yielded to a more sceptical determination to see that they did their job. A valuable recent article by Emily Robinson et al. has described the emergence of a 'popular individualism' in 1970s Britain, not primarily materialistic in nature but rather concerned to secure both public participation in the processes by which lives were shaped and accountability for the people shaping them.[112] If anything, it was in this way that sixties iconoclasm produced lasting effects. The local law centres in North Kensington and elsewhere which advised benefit claimants or council tenants on their rights were more sophisticated in their methods than were the East Enders who emptied sacks of dead rats in the offices of the Tower Hamlets housing department, but they exemplified a similar determination to keep public authorities up to the mark.

Meanwhile the political Right directed increasingly animated attacks against local-authority extravagance and the system of local taxation thought to encourage it. The rates became a public and press concern throughout the seventies, to a degree unmatched for decades. In the process, the problem's origins in the Heath administration's 1974 local-government reorganisation—never widely understood anyway—slipped from view, leaving the blame to be ascribed to 'spendthrift' authorities, generally under Labour control. In March 1979 the *Standard* ran a week-long series titled 'Rates through the Roof', beginning with an angry attack on council extravagance by the Thatcherite convert Paul Johnson.[113] The second piece in the series pointedly contrasted thrifty Conservative Barnet with high-spending Labour Islington.[114]

As has been shown, the case for abolishing the Greater London Council had been vigorously made by some on the Conservative right, during and even after the years of Labour control of County Hall between 1973 and 1977.[115] In this climate it was always likely that some Tory free thinkers would question the whole concept of local municipal action. The most openly ideological initiative came in Wandsworth. This was a marginal borough, where the challenge to the left-wing Labour council in power since 1971 was mounted by a Conservative group eager to curb the local state and prevent its opponents from imposing 'China's drab uniformity' on Southwest London.[116] After capturing the council in 1978, the Wandsworth Tories pledged to freeze the rates, which they achieved by scrapping Labour's housing municipalisation programme, selling council houses, attacking council tenants' rent arrears, cutting a thousand council jobs, shrinking the direct labour force, raising the cost of meals for the elderly by 50 percent, slimming the children's service by engaging foster parents and generally 'making far greater use of the volunteer, and of voluntary organisations.'[117] In what would become a 'flagship' Tory council in the 1980s and 1990s, London's growing rate burden fostered a Conservative revolution.

It is questionable whether London was a Thatcherite city by 1979, but there can be little doubt that the foundations, the structures and the aspirations of the postwar welfare state had been seriously questioned.

Anticipating 'Thatcher's Britain'

In the run-up to the 1979 general election the polls predicted substantial Conservative gains in London. Margaret Thatcher's 'entourage bubbled with confidence that the capital belongs to Maggie.'[118] The outcome would be more ambiguous. There were very large swings to the Conservatives in an arc of ten seats in the Northeast, stretching from Islington Central to Dagenham—the core of Essex London, in other words, with a mean swing of 14.2 percent. Across the rest of Greater London, though, the swing of 6.2 percent was slightly below the national average.[119] Thatcherite Conservatism had a limited appeal—or none at all—to large parts of the London electorate: traditional Labour voters in the inner city, for instance, liberal-minded gentrifiers, most ethnic minorities. In London, as in much of the country, a vote for the Conservatives was most likely to reflect concerns about inflation or trade-union power—or simply the belief that Labour was not working.

There were many people—suburban householders, working-class individualists—who were active supporters of Margaret Thatcher by 1979, but it would be hard to make the case that the city as a whole had been captured by Thatcherism. What is more plausible is that that erosion of postwar orthodoxies which made Thatcherism possible was well advanced in London by the late seventies. Rapid and severe deindustrialisation brought an end to the period—climaxing in the exuberance of the midsixties—in which almost all Londoners had seen steady improvements in their standard of living. London as a whole continued to thrive, but instead of rising affluence overall it displayed a pattern of majority prosperity and minority deprivation which anticipated the national picture in the eighties. Growing inequality became the norm, however widely it was regretted and however great a departure it represented from the objectives of postwar governance. The decline of London's outmoded industrial base was an inescapable concomitant of the city's evolution into a service-centred economy. Public agencies were largely powerless to resist it, but their impotence strengthened a growing disenchantment with 'the authorities', as significant sections of the metropolitan public—on left and right—rejected welfare-state paternalism. At the same time, those authorities—or many of them—became larger, more bureaucratic, more expensive and more distant from the public they served. They also shifted their policy emphasis from welfarist objectives, which had generally enjoyed broad public acceptance, towards the implementation of long-standing Abercrombiean and Buchananite projects to remodel the urban landscape, which increasingly did not. Deindustrialisation, inequality and increasing scepticism towards the local state were important precursors of Thatcherism, even in a city which was slow to embrace Thatcher herself.

Thus many features associated in the public mind with 'Thatcher's Britain' were evident in London in the 1970s, and many have appeared in this book: the inner-city crisis, associated with intensifying multiple deprivation and even sporadic rioting by young adults in ethnic minority communities; the exodus of the working-age working class to suburban areas where they were likely to slip the associational bonds of labourism; the consequent erosion of established Labour Party organisation in the inner city, exacerbated by generational and ideological conflict when young radicals clashed with the old guard; the dwindling efficacy of traditional municipal socialism in the face of severe inner-city problems and the sidelining of local government generally; the sale of council houses and the contraction of the central-government support which had underpinned local social housing programmes; the calls for the abolition of the GLC and for reform of the local taxation system, perhaps by a poll tax; the attrition of even essential public services through labour shortages and funding problems; the cultural reaction against the perceived hedonism and permissiveness of the 'swinging sixties'; the disavowal of 'sixties planners', of modernity and modernism; the growth of the conservation movement; the evolution of consumerism into something more than the mere demand for 'durables'; gentrification and the drift—sometimes the stampede—into owner occupation; above all, the spread of a majority prosperity which made minority deprivation and growing inequality politically sustainable. All these features would be replicated in Britain as a whole in the 1980s.

In all these ways, the London of 1979 appeared to anticipate 'Thatcher's Britain.' But Margaret Thatcher had had almost nothing to do with it. She had not produced the affluence, and she was not answerable for the deprivation. She had not prompted the move towards owner occupation. She did not initiate the council-house sales, the calls for local taxation reform or the proposals to abolish the GLC. She did not cause the withering of traditional labourism or the stagnation and disintegration of some inner-city Labour parties. She benefited, of course, from the reenergising of suburban Conservatism, and her iconoclastic Toryism undoubtedly appealed to working-class defectors from traditional socialism who would have found a Heath or a Major less magnetic; but it cannot be maintained that she greatly influenced the capital's political direction. Her principal contribution to London's evolution would come later—the liberalisation of the financial markets in the 1986 'Big Bang.' That event provided a distinctively neoliberal coda to the developments described here, transforming the City of London as a financial centre, facilitating London's emergence as a global city and establishing the rapacious banker as a metropolitan type. It was, though, a separate process from those described in this book, which have more to do with the steady, subtle erosion of welfare-state-era orthodoxies.

Margaret Thatcher has inspired much recent work of high quality. It has generally has focused on her political persona and on the revolution in Conservative politics that she led. This is understandable, and nothing in these pages is intended to deny Margaret Thatcher's impact on postwar British politics. But this is not a book about Thatcher. Recent scholarship has, though, thrown light on the extent to which much of what we categorise by the umbrella term 'Thatcherism' had antecedents in the earlier postwar period,[120] and this book seeks to augment that scholarship by showing how, in various, often unrelated, ways, developments in Britain's political and administrative centre, economic hub and principal opinion-former anticipated what would happen nationally in the 1980s. London's evolution prepared the ground for 'Thatcher's Britain' not by encouraging much in the way of entrepreneurial dynamism, still less by instilling any 'gospel of greed' in the metropolitan population, but rather by means of the steady erosion of those orthodoxies which had sustained the postwar settlement. It was necessary, after all, for the ancien régime to crumble before anyone could contemplate a revolution.

NOTES

Chapter 1

1. The claim was attributed to Diana Vreeland, editor of the US *Vogue*, by John Crosby, 'The Most Exciting City', *Weekend Telegraph* 16 April 1965.

2. 'From Britain: the Dash of Bold Bright Tweeds in Narrow Coats, Spanking Suits', *Vogue* September 1964.

3. 'The London Look', *Seventeen* March 1965.

4. M. Bender, 'These Are the Fashion Magazines and the Women Editors Who Run Them', *New York Times* 25 July 1967.

5. 'London: Mods, Rocker, Beatniks, Spießer!', *Star Club News* August 1965.

6. 'So Macht Man Englische Teenager-Mode in der Carnaby Street', *Bravo* 7 February 1966.

7. 'London Charivari 1966', *Esquire* July 1966.

8. Crosby, 'Most Exciting City'.

9. 'You Can Walk across It on the Grass', *Time* 15 April 1966. This account of the construction of the piece is based on Piri Halasz's *A Memoir of Creativity. Abstract Painting, Politics and the Media, 1956–2008* (Bloomington, IN, 2009), ch. 8; quotation p. 119.

10. Halasz, *Memoir of Creativity*, p. 98.

11. 'This was my idea, not from the files', ibid., p. 122.

12. Ibid., p. 120.

13. P. Joffroy, 'L'Angleterre aux Cheveux Longs', *Paris Match* 2 April 1966.

14. W. G. Blair, 'Graham to Give London "Old-Fashioned Gospel"', *New York Times* 28 May 1966.

15. 'Graham Foregoes Glimpse of Soho's Square Mile of Sin', *Washington Post* 18 June 1966.

16. A. Lewis, 'Frivolity in Britain', *New York Times* 8 June 1966.

17. D. A. Schmidt, 'Small Cheer in Britain', *New York Times* 4 October 1966.

18. G. Farmer, 'Shrinking Pains of Mini-England', *Life* 16 December 1966.

19. A. Sherman et al., 'In Search of Swinging London', *London Life* 18 June 1966.

20. M. Cleave, 'Simon Napier-Bell Always Tells the Truth. Especially about Simon Napier-Bell', *Evening Standard* (*ES*) 13 May 1966.

21. M. Shulman, 'D. Frosting the London Scene', *ES* 19 October 1966.

22. A 1963 survey by the Westminster Chamber of Commerce showed 73 percent of retailers still favouring either five- or five-and-a-half-day opening. In 1967 some of the larger Central London stores pressed for the area to be declared a resort under the Shops Act to allow Saturday-afternoon

trading: 'Central London Moves for Trading on Saturday Afternoons', *Drapers Record* 19 August 1967; P. Halasz, *A Swinger's Guide to London* (New York, 1967), p. 115.

23. B. James, *London on a Sunday* (London, 1964).

24. 'No More City Land', *ES* 14 January 1963.

25. E. Blanchet, *Prefab Homes* (Oxford, 2014), pp. 46–47.

26. See chapter 5.

27. Department of Scientific and Industrial Research, *Effects of Polluting Discharges on the Thames Estuary. The Reports of the Thames Survey Committee and of the Water Pollution Research Laboratory* (London, 1964), pp. xx, xxii–xxiii, Table 182, p. 535.

28. J. H. Brazell, *London Weather* (London, 1968), p. 114.

29. C. L. Corton, *London Fog: The Biography* (Cambridge, MA, 2015), pp. 315ff; 'The Worst Fog Is Closing In', *ES* 8 December 1960.

30. P. Fairlie, 'Why Do We Treat Our Air like a Sewer?', *ES* 10 April 1967.

31. W. Davis, 'Is It Worth 1s[hilling] a Head to Clean Up London?', *ES* 18 May 1964.

32. J. Hillman, 'The Dirty Face of London', *ES* 20 December 1966.

33. A. C. McKennell & E. A. Hunt, *Noise Annoyance in Central London. A Survey Made in 1961 for the Building Research Station*, vol. 2 (London, 1966), pp. 3–4.

34. P. Fairlie, 'London Noise Shock Probe', *ES* 21 June 1963.

35. H. R. Jones, 'Modern Emigration from Malta', *Transactions of the Institute of British Geographers* 60, 1973, 103; G. Dench, *Maltese in London. A Case Study in the Erosion of Ethnic Consciousness* (London, 1975).

36. Crosby, 'Most Exciting City.' The Flamingo Club, in Wardour Street, closed in 1967.

37. 'London does import labour on a very large scale. It is easy enough to talk about bus conductors coming from Barbados. I would point out a number of engineers who come from Lancashire, a number of school teachers who come from South Wales, a number of building labourers who come from Dublin', J. Thirlwall before the Committee on Housing in Greater London, 6 January 1964, The National Archives (TNA) HLG 39/65; J. Bugler, 'Ireland in London', *New Society* 14 March 1968.

38. Melanie Phillips, 'People in a House', *New Society* 2 June 1977.

39. J. Reading, 'Clearance in Pimlico', *New Society* 16 June 1977.

40. J. Raban, 'Among Cypriots', *New Society* 24 May 1973.

41. 'Stanley', quoted in Phillips, 'People in a House.'

42. A. McGill, 'Home Is Home, but London Is Where the *Action* Is', *ES* 13 April 1966; J. Reed, *The King of Carnaby Street. The Life of John Stephen* (London, 2010), p. 1.

43. M. Cleave, 'Food, Swearing and the Art of Tom Benson', *ES* 2 June 1965.

44. A. Byatt, 'The First Place I've Lived in I Don't Want to Leave', *ES* 3 October 1964.

45. McGill, 'Home Is Home.'

46. A. Sharpley, ''She Is 18 and Saves £50 a Week—but How Many Girls Would Do a Job like Hers?', *ES* 18 November 1965.

47. A. Sharpley, 'In the Big City—Less Fear, Less Solitude', *ES* 22 July 1964.

48. A. Sharpley, 'Where No Leaves Fall . . .', *ES* 1 October 1964.

49. A. Duncan, 'Hotfooting to London—but There's More to It than Just the Money', *ES* 27 November 1964.

50. M. Cleave, 'The Single Girls. Young, Free and Far from Mum', *ES* 5 October 1964.

51. Duncan, 'Hotfooting to London.'

52. O. Marriott, *The Property Boom* (London, 1967), pp. 3, 155.

53. H. Macmillan to Deputy Secretary, Ministry of Housing and Local Government, 12 January 1954, Harold Macmillan Papers, Bodleian Library, Oxford, MS Macmillan dep.c.290, f.679.

54. See chapter 7.

55. Marriott, *Property Boom*, p. 144; 'Dr Gropius Has a Look at Piccadilly', *ES* 13 July 1960.

56. E.g., the dealings with Stock Conversion over the Euston Road underpass and with Harry Hyams at Centre Point, Marriott, *Property Boom*, pp. 157–58, 112ff.

57. 'It's V-Day for Littler', *ES* 3 November 1960; W. Davis, 'Marylebone Station to Be Rebuilt', *ES* 31 October 1961.

58. See chapter 7.

59. Byatt, 'First Place I've Lived In.'

60. M. Cleave, 'A Big Bed, a Bit of Squalor, and Friends Who Dig', *ES* 9 October 1964.

61. Quotation and statistic from A. Duncan, 'What Happens When You Paint the Walls Blue', *ES* 26 November 1964.

62. This paragraph is largely based on R. Silverstone, 'Just a Sec? . . . Or How I Learned to Stop Worrying and Love the Boss', *Personnel Management* June 1975, pp. 33–36.

63. Duncan, 'Hotfooting to London.'

64. K. Hart, 'The Secretary', *London Life* 25 June 1966.

65. Ibid.; Duncan, 'Hotfooting to London.'

66. J. A. Torode, 'Keeping a Secretary', *New Society* 20 May 1965.

67. Town and Country Planning Association, *The Paper Metropolis* (London, 1962), pp. 49–50; E. Betts, 'Miss Smith, Take a £1000 Pay Cheque', *ES* 29 December 1962.

68. J. Aitken, *The Young Meteors* (London, 1967), p. 19.

69. Karin Hart's estimate, including everyone 'from shorthand-typist to private scribe to glorified personal assistant', 'The Secretary.'

70. M. Cleave, 'Chummeries—Where Six Live Cheaper than One', *ES* 6 October 1964.

71. Duncan, 'Hotfooting to London.'

72. B. Griggs, 'Why Girls Leave Home', *ES* 20 November 1963.

73. 'Unmarried Mothers in Lonely Bedsits', *ES* 21 October 1964.

74. 'Unwed Mothers Flock to London', *ES* 28 October 1963.

75. M. Jeffries, 'Kensington and Chelsea . . . Borough of Unmarried Mothers', *ES* 2 May 1969. During the 1963 moral panic it was pointed out that legal marriage was 'not the normal status' of mothers in the Afro-Caribbean community, which was numerous in North Kensington: 'Refuge for Illegitimates', *New Society* 19 December 1963.

76. London Borough of Redbridge, *Annual Report of the Medical Officer of Health for 1968* (London 1969), p. 5; London Borough of Greenwich, *Report of the Medical Officer of Health, 1971* (London, 1972), p. 52.

77. A. Alvarez, 'The Sweet Smell of Corruption', *Life Atlantic* 4 September 1967.

78. The 'Central Conurbation' comprised the City, Westminster and the inner parts of Tower Hamlets, Hackney, Islington, Camden, Kensington and Chelsea, Lambeth and Southwark. For comparison, women accounted for only 48 percent of the age group twenty-five to thirty-four. General Register Office, *Sample Census 1966. England and Wales. County Report, Greater London* (London, 1967), Table 2A, p. 7.

79. J. Crosby, 'Super Girl', *New York Herald Tribune* 15 January 1964.

80. J. Crosby, 'The Most Exciting City', *Weekend Telegraph* 16 April 1965. Crosby was fifty-three in 1965.

81. M. Cleave, 'The Maureen Cleave Interview', *ES* 16 January 1967.

82. Cleave, 'Chummeries.'

83. Cleave, 'Single Girls.'

84. This paragraph is based on 'Anatomy of the Permissive Society. 3. The Single Girl', *Look of London* February 1968.

85. 'I dislike the attitude of some of the fellows: How do you do, where's your bedroom?' Cleave, 'Chummeries.'

86. J. Norridge, 'Would You Let Your Daughter?', *ES* 11 May 1970. The survey was conducted by Opinion Research Centre, which interviewed a random sample of 1,024 Londoners.

87. Calculated from the table in Town and Country Planning Association, *Paper Metropolis*, Appendix A, p. 74.

88. P. Marshall, 'Bets Shops in London Top 1000 Mark', *ES* 23 January 1964. There were fifty betting shops in Hackney by 1965: J. Barr, 'Betting Shop Dream World', *New Society* 6 May 1965.

89. S. Levy, *Ready, Steady, Go! Swinging London and the Invention of Cool* (London, 2002), p. 124.

90. P. Hanshaw, *All My Yesterdays* (London, 1996), pp. 102–3.

91. T. Steele, 'At 15 I Had My First Argument with an Adult . . .', *ES* 9 December 1960.

92. 'Most Poplar School Leavers Have Now Found Jobs,' *East London Advertiser* 30 August 1963.

93. D. Fagan & E. Burgess, *Men of the Tideway* (London, 1966), p. 183.

94. J. W. M. Thompson, 'You and the Postman—Big Problems Even If Quiet Mr Smith Wins', *ES* 18 January 1962.

95. A. Gardner, *"Watch Your Fingers!" An East End Cutter's Chronicle, 1956–1973* (London, 2006), p. 6 and illustrations after p. 40.

96. See chapter 8.

97. A. McGill, 'Goodbye to the Teddy Boy—Now It's the Smooth Type Tailored to His Fingertips', *ES* 4 April 1962.

98. J. Wilson, 'Teenagers', in L. Deighton, *Len Deighton's London Dossier* (London, 1967), p. 23.

99. Reed, *King of Carnaby Street*, pp. 14, 23.

100. A. McGill, 'It Sounds Silly, but I've Been Shopping in a Boutique!', *ES* 22 July 1964.

101. Reed, *King of Carnaby Street*, p. 101.

102. B. Hulanicki, *From A to Biba* (London, 1983), p. 62.

103. M. Quant, *Quant by Quant* (London, 1966), p. 41.

104. Ibid., p. 40.

105. M. Cleave, 'Quant by Cleave', part 1, *ES* 5 April 1967.

106. M. Cleave, 'Quant by Cleave', part 2, *ES* 6 April 1967.

107. Quant, *Quant by Quant*, p. 40.

108. Quoted in R. Bennett-England, *Dress Optional* (London, 1967), p. 133.

109. Quant, *Quant by Quant*, pp. 43–44; Hulanicki, *From A to Biba*, p. 70.

110. See chapter 3.

111. A. Johnson, *This Boy. A Memoir of a Childhood* (London, 2013), p. 50.

112. J. Wilson, 'Not Much Bottle at the Beat Ball', *London Life* 27 November 1965.

113. E. Rogers (as told to M. Hennessy), *Tin Pan Alley* (London, 1964), pp. 17, 30.

114. M. Cleave, 'Mr Most, Who Can't Wait for Mondays', *ES* 15 August 1964.

115. Reed, *King of Carnaby Street*, p. 244.

116. A. Thompson, 'Another Fantastic Year for the Record Giants', *ES* 19 October 1960.

117. Hugh Blackwell, 'This Is Carnaby Street', *London Life* 14 May 1966.

118. Quant, *Quant by Quant*, p. 153.

119. Ibid., pp. 76, 74.

120. M. Cleave, 'Decline of the Record Tsars', *ES* 15 August 1964.

121. M. Cleave, 'The High Life—and No Back Answers', *ES* 5 June 1965.

122. Cleave, 'Mr Most.'

123. Reed, *King of Carnaby Street*, p. 35; Bennett-England, *Dress Optional*, p. 133.

124. McGill, 'Home Is Home.'

125. A. McGill, 'Look Out. There's a Mod (or Maybe a Rocker) Close Behind You', *ES* 31 July 1963.

126. D. Fowler, *Youth Culture in Modern Britain* (Basingstoke, 2008), p. 174.

127. McGill, 'Goodbye to the Teddy Boy'; McGill, 'It Sounds Silly.'

128. Bennett-England, *Dress Optional*, p. 131.

129. F. Mort, *Capital Affairs. London and the Making of the Permissive Society* (London, 2010), p. 73.

130. For a vivid account of the early Victorian Season see 'The Social Character of the Estate: The London Season in 1841', in F. H. W. Sheppard, ed., *Survey of London*, vol. 39, *The Grosvenor Estate in Mayfair, Part 1* (London, 1977), pp. 88–93.

131. 'The Social Character of the Estate: The Censuses of 1841 and 1871', in Sheppard, *Survey of London*, vol. 39, p. 95.

132. R. Colby, *Mayfair. A Town within London* (London 1966), p. 43.

133. 'The Social Character of the Estate: The Last Hundred Years', in Sheppard, *Survey of London*, vol 39, Part 1, p. 99.

134. D. Pearce, *London's Mansions. The Palatial Houses of the Nobility* (London, 1986).

135. J. Davis, 'Modern London', in P. Waller, ed., *The English Urban Landscape* (Oxford, 2000), p. 138.

136. W. Roland, 'Prestige Address, Mayfair', *ES* 2 March 1960; Roland, 'Mayfair as a Home Is Finished, Says Estate Agent', *ES* 9 September 1965.

137. By 1940 60 percent of the landed aristocracy lacked a London home: P. Thorold, *The London Rich* (London, 1999), p. 326.

138. Ibid., p. 331.

139. Ibid., p. 332.

140. F. Marsden, 'A Bookshop in Chelsea', *West London Press and Chelsea News* 19 February 1965.

141. A. Sharpley, 'Girl Arriving', part 5, *ES* 19 November 1965.

142. R. Douglas-Home, 'The Young Face of Old Chelsea', *Tatler and Bystander* 13 May 1959.

143. 'A New Deal for Artists', *West London Press and Chelsea News* 30 June 1961.

144. For the society's failure to help one artist facing eviction following a rent increase see 'Artist Asks for Housing Help. First Case for Studio Protection Society', *West London Press and Chelsea News* 18 August 1961.

145. See chapter 5.

146. E. O'Brien, 'Turn Right over Putney Bridge', *ES* 30 September 1964.

147. Unnamed friend of the sculptor Loris Rey, quoted in M. Harmsworth, 'The Changing Face of Chelsea', part 2, *West London Press and Chelsea News* 19 May 1961.

148. A. Sharpley, 'The Man from World's End', *ES* 3 March 1960.

149. 'Profile: Paddington', *London Property Letter* July 1963 (2).

150. A. Ince, 'Close Up: David Mlinaric', *London Life* 16 October 1965.

151. M. Boxer, 'My Friend Tony', *ES* 27 February 1960.

152. 'The New Elite', articles by Simon James, John Barber (twice), Donald Edgar and Anne Sharpley, *ES* 29 February to 4 March 1960.

153. R. Wright, 'When You Go to Lunch—It's Hot-Pot in Pimlico', *ES* 27 February 1960.

154. Sharpley, 'Man from World's End.'

155. D. Edgar, 'Young Man, Has Charm, Will Travel (Upwards, Of Course)', *ES* 2 March 1960.

156. Though he pronounced them dead by then, after a three-year existence: A. Haden-Guest, 'The New Class. A Post-Mortem', *Queen* 3 November 1965.

157. A. Duncan, 'The Television Twitch', *ES* 16 March 1967.

158. Ince, 'Close Up: David Mlinaric.'

159. Haden-Guest, 'New Class.'

160. Aitken, *Young Meteors*, pp. 37, 77, 79.

161. M. Cleave, 'Mr Beaumont Fights Off the Brand X Image', *ES* 16 December 1964.

162. D. Kynaston, *The City of London. A Club No More, 1945–2000* (London, 2001), p. 148.

163. Ibid., pp. 151–53.

164. D. Mallory, 'A Snob's Guide to the City', *Queen* 13 February 1963.

165. Aitken, *Young Meteors*, p. 290; Kynaston, *City of London*, pp. 148–49.

166. Aitken, *Young Meteors*, p. 274.

167. M. Pearson, 'Why Solicitors Are up in Arms', *ES* 22 August 1966.

168. Quoted in Kynaston, *City of London*, pp. 149–50.

169. S. Cron, 'The Unseen Women of Television', *London Life* 7 May 1966.

170. J. Wilton, 'Girls like Lucy', *London Life* 8 January 1966.

171. F. MacCarthy, *Last Curtsey. The End of the Debutantes* (London, 2006), p. 216, chapter 10. For debutantes see also L. Gosling, *Debutantes and the London Season* (Oxford, 2013).

172. Margaret Chilton, quoted in MacCarthy, *Last Curtsey*, p. 240.

173. Susan Bishop, quoted in M. Hastings, 'Well, *One* Deb's Determined Not to Marry Hastily', *ES* 5 April 1962.

174. R. Beardwood, 'The Deb Season? "Ridiculous, Idiotic." Who Says So? Why, a Deb', *ES* 29 December 1961.

175. S. Coleman, 'The Deb World Heads Back to the Country', *ES* 20 March 1961. According to Coleman, each cocktail party or deb dance could set parents back by between £1,000 and £5,000.

176. G. Smith, 'Self-Indulgence', in Deighton, *Len Deighton's London Dossier*, p. 113.

177. According to James Hogg, in *The Habits of Good Society* (London, 1859), reproduced in 'Presentation at Court', All Things Victorian, accessed 24 January 2020, http://www.avictorian.com /court.html.

178. D. Topolski, 'The Season', *New Society* 28 June 1979.

179. Haden-Guest, 'New Class.'

180. 'Aristocrats in the Darkroom', *London Life* 8 January 1966.

181. J. Aitken, 'Paying Homage at Sibylla's Shrine', *ES* 28 July 1966.

182. Wilton, 'Girls like Lucy.'

183. T. Jenkins, 'Crisis in Clubland. See How the "In and Out" Has Tackled It', *ES* 26 June 1962, for the Naval and Military Club in Piccadilly; H. Davies, *The New London Spy* (London, 1966), p. 180.

184. Kevin Macdonald, quoted in Aitken, *Young Meteors*, p. 270; A. Haden-Guest, 'Dancing Chic to Chic', *Queen* 22 June 1966.

185. A. S. Sutherland, *The Spaghetti Tree. Mario and Franco and the Trattoria Revolution* (London, 2009), pp. 37ff; and see chapter 4.

186. 'Bird's Eye View of Boutiques', *Queen* 10 July 1962.

187. Bennett-England, *Dress Optional*, p. 68; W. Davis, 'All You Really Need Is Determination', *ES* 30 June 1965.

188. Sutherland, *Spaghetti Tree*, p. 52.

189. N. Cohn, *Today There Are No Gentlemen. The Changes in Englishmen's Clothes since the War* (London, 1971), p. 37.

190. Cleave, 'Simon Napier-Bell.'

191. Haden-Guest, 'New Class.'

192. Steele, 'At 15 I Had My First Argument.'

193. For an account of the coffee bar phenomenon in fifties London see P. Frame, *The Restless Generation. How Rock Music Changed the Face of 1950s Britain* (London, 2007), pp. 118–30.

194. Ibid., p. 365; F. Norman, *Soho Night and Day* (London, 1966), pp. 14–16.

195. Frame, *Restless Generation*, pp. 457, 461.

196. M. Houlbrook, *Queer London. Perils and Pleasures in the Sexual Metropolis, 1918–1957* (London, 2005), pp. 87–88, 56–57.

197. Reed, *King of Carnaby Street*, p. 23.

198. S. Black, 'Carnaby Street. Tourist "Must" in Swinging London', *Financial Times* 24 February 1967.

199. Bennett-England, *Dress Optional*, pp. 83–85, 130–31, 133; C. Breward, 'Fashion's Front and Back: "Rag Trade" Cultures and Cultures of Consumption in Post-war London, c. 1945–1970', *London Journal* 31 (1), 2006, 34–35.

200. Bennett-England, *Dress Optional*, p. 179; Wilson, 'Teenagers', p. 25.

201. A. Sharpley, 'Purple Heart Trip in Soho', *ES* 3 February 1964.

202. For the origins of the Marquee Club see J. Tow, *London, Reign over Me. How England's Capital Built Classic Rock* (Lanham, MD, 2020), Kindle ed., loc. 529.

203. Davies, *New London Spy*, p. 192.

204. Wilson, 'Not Much Bottle at the Beat Ball.' For a different reading of this article, see Fowler, *Youth Culture in Modern Britain*, pp. 175–77.

205. M. Webb, *The Amber Valley Gazetteer of Greater London Suburban Cinemas* (Birmingham, 1986), pp. 60–62.

206. See chapter 10.

207. Bennett-England, *Dress Optional*, pp. 52, 68.

208. D. Edgar, 'An Astonishing New Side to Chelsea Life', *ES* 18 June 1962.

209. 'This Is Chelsea', *London Life* 12 February 1966.

210. W. Mankowitz, 'Yes, but I Knew It When . . .', *ES* 6 May 1963; '"Guns for Sale", Says Hanratty', *ES* 8 February 1962.

211. M. Fogg, *Boutique. A Sixties Cultural Phenomenon* (London, 2003), pp. 22, 25.

212. A. McGill, 'So What Is Le Style Anglais?', *ES* 16 March 1966.

213. J. Moynihan, 'After Saturday Night Comes Sunday Morning', *ES* 10 May 1963; Norman, *Soho Night and Day*, p. 32.

214. Quoted in Sutherland, *Spaghetti Tree*, p. 104.

215. Hulanicki, *From A to Biba*, pp. 88–89, 99.

216. D. Johnson & R. Dunkley, *Gear Guide. Hip Pocket Guide to London's Swinging Fashion Scene* (London, 1967), p. 57; Reed, *King of Carnaby Street*, p. 86.

217. Johnson & Dunkley, *Gear Guide*, p. 47.

218. Reed, *King of Carnaby Street*, p. 216; Cohn, *Today There Are No Gentlemen*, p. 112.

219. Reed, *King of Carnaby Street*, p. 197.

220. Bennett-England, *Dress Optional*, pp. 51, 129.

221. 'Ravers' Map of London', *Rave* April 1966.

222. Johnson & Dunkley, *Gear Guide*, pp. 46, 47.

223. Moynihan, 'After Saturday Night.'

224. Sutherland, *Spaghetti Tree*, p. 118.

225. E.g., Q. Crewe, 'Restaurants', *Queen* 9 November 1966; Sutherland, *Spaghetti Tree*, p. 110.

226. Aitken, *Young Meteors*, pp. 270–71.

227. Wilson, 'Teenagers', p. 29.

228. T. Rawlings, *Mod. Clean Living under Very Difficult Circumstances. A Very British Phenomenon* (London, 2000), p. 40.

229. Preface to Crosby, 'Most Exciting City.'

230. Halasz, *Memoir of Creativity*, p. 119.

231. See chapter 2; and for Raymond, P. Willetts, *Members Only. The Life and Times of Paul Raymond* (London, 2010), Mort, *Capital Affairs*, pp. 263ff.

232. For which see Mort, *Capital Affairs*, pp. 197ff.

233. Mankowitz, 'Yes, but I Knew It When.'

234. 'Clean-Up for the World Cup', *ES* 1 July 1966.

235. 'You Can Walk across It on the Grass.'

236. 'It's no use anybody earning say £2000 a year wanting to join. In fact we don't really want *anybody* on a salary', Tim Holland, manager of Crockford's, quoted in Davies, *New London Spy*, p. 160.

237. E. g., *London Life* 19 February and 5 March 1966.

238. Aitken, *Young Meteors*, p. 10.

239. Between the Beatles' first London performance, at the Romford Ritz in March 1963, and their last, at the Empire Pool, Wembley, in May 1966 they played at Finsbury Park (three times), Lewisham and Walthamstow (twice), Tooting, Woolwich, East Ham and Hammersmith as well as the London Palladium and the Royal Albert Hall. List compiled from H. V. Fulpen, *The Beatles. An Illustrated Diary* (London, 1983), pp. 42ff.

240. 'Boutique Boom!', *Rave* September 1965.

241. Crosby, 'Most Exciting City.'

242. P. R. Myatt, *Carnaby Street Study* (GLC Research Memorandum 466, London, 1975), p. 5.

243. M. Balint, *Greater London's Economically Active Population* (GLC Research Memorandum 441, London, 1975), p. 26.

244. Greater London Council, *Low Incomes in London. Evidence from the Family Expenditure Surveys* (GLC Reviews and Studies Series 20, London, 1983), Table 1.

245. C. Lyte, 'How the Squeeze Hits London', *ES* 6 October 1966.

246. J. Aitken, 'How the Squeeze Has Hit Swinging London', *ES* 22 November 1966.

247. J. Jaroszek, *Earnings in Relation to Employment Changes* (GLC Research Memorandum 500, London, 1975), Table 4, p. 21.

248. Balint, *Greater London's Economically Active Population*, Tables 10–11, pp. 14–16.

249. See chapter 16.

Chapter 2

1. J. Crosby, 'The Most Exciting City', *Weekend Telegraph* 16 April 1965.

2. P. Halasz, *A Memoir of Creativity* (Bloomington, IN, 2009), p. 120.

3. 'You Can Walk across It on the Grass', *Time* April 15 1966.

4. D. Farson, *Soho in the Fifties* (London, 1987).

5. 'Note Regarding Striptease Clubs and Near-Beer Establishments', Memorandum by the Commissioner of the Metropolitan Police, 1963, The National Archives (TNA), HO 300/17.

6. C. Manchester, *Sex Shops and the Law* (London, 1986), p. 31; M. Tomkinson, *The Pornbrokers. The Rise of the Soho Sex Barons* (London, 1982), p. 16.

7. This account is taken from the Joint Report (6 May 1952) by the Solicitor and the Chief Officer of the Public Control Department, in London County Council, Public Control Committee, Presented Papers, 14 May 1952, London Metropolitan Archives (LMA) LCC/MIN/09932.

8. London County Council Minutes, 29 July 1952, ibid.

9. F. Mort, 'Striptease: The Erotic Female Body and Live Sexual Entertainment in Mid-Twentieth-Century London', *Social History* 32 (1), 2007, 30.

10. B. Norman, 'We Never Closed, They Said. And Then the Strip Clubs Blitzed Them Shut', *Daily Mail* 2 October 1964.

11. The Irving Strip Club is described in the autobiography of Victor Spinetti, who sang there: V. Spinetti, with P. Rankin, *Victor Spinetti Up Front . . . His Strictly Confidential Autobiography* (London, 2006), pp. 109–15.

12. P. Willetts, *Members Only. The Life and Times of Paul Raymond* (London, 2010), pp. 80–81.

13. Ibid., p. 101.

14. Quoted in I. Macdonald, 'Stops Girls—Wants Them to Strip', *Reveille* 27 February 1958.

15. Willetts, *Members Only*, pp. 46ff.

16. Ibid., p. 78.

17. Macdonald, 'Stops Girls.'

18. Circular from the Secretary, Raymond Theatre Revuebar Ltd., [1958?], GLC Raymond Revuebar File, LMA GLC/DG/EL/02/058, part I.

19. Quoted in Willetts, *Members Only*, p. 114.

20. Ibid., pp. 116–17.

21. 'Information from Supt Strath's report (lent to Mr Cann informally)', 1 July 1958, and Strath's report (28 May 1958) on the raid of 2 May, GLC Raymond Revuebar File, LMA GLC/DG/EL/02/058, part I.

22. H. Longmuir, '£30? That's Just Chicken-feed Says Mr Striptease', *Daily Mail* 28 November 1958.

23. Ibid.

24. Evidence of Supt King in the Quinn and Bloom case, 'Soho Is "Well Conducted"', *Daily Telegraph* 12 April 1961.

25. P. Forbes, 'This Was Paul Raymond, King of the Filth Merchants', *People* 28 June 1961.

26. 'Eve Lost a Boa Constrictor but They Would Not Believe Her . . .', *Paddington Mercury* 17 October 1958; 'Python in Taxi', *Daily Express* 10 November 1959; 'Mirror Brief', *Daily Mirror* 10 November 1959.

27. 'Acts Not Indecent, Says Clubman', *Times* 13 April 1961.

28. 'Julie and Her (Snake) Family', *Marylebone Mercury* 8 August 1961.

29. 'Paul Raymond's Revue Bar, the Keyhole Club', Memorandum by L. Kelly, Inspector, 25 November 1966, GLC Entertainments Licensing Division, Policy Files, Striptease, LMA GLC/DG/EL/07/050.

30. 'Safeguarding Amusements. How Theatres, Cinemas and Dance Halls Are Licensed', *Times* 21 March 1939.

31. Quoted by Justice Ashworth in the Appeal Court hearing: Regina v. Quinn, *Weekly Law Reports* 1961 (3), 618.

32. Memorandum by Miss M. Hornsby, 24 May 1963, in 'Music and Dancing Licensing. London Government Bill', TNA HO 300/16.

33. 'Paul Raymond's Revue Bar. The Keyhole Club', Memorandum by L. Kelly, Inspector, 25 November 1966.

34. 'Midnight Stewhouse of Vice', *Daily Express* 6 January 1962; 'Keyhole Club Man Jailed for 3 Years', *Daily Mail* 6 January 1962; 'Club a "Vice Stewhouse"', *Daily Telegraph* 6 January 1962.

35. Witness statement by Inspector William Yeoman, West End Central, 13 September 1963, file on 9 Berwick Street, LMA GLC/DG/EL/03/B035.

36. R. Wortley, *Skin Deep in Soho* (London, 1969), p. 11.

37. Ibid., p. 156.

38. Witness statement by Inspector William Yeoman.

39. London Government Act, 1963, ch. 33, Schedule 18, Part II.

40. Joseph Gatt, proprietor of the Keyhole Club in 1972, asked if he was the man who kept the profits, replied, 'what there is after the fines': witness statement by Inspector Ronald Hay, 24 April 1972, Keyhole Club File, LMA GLC/DG/EL/04/036.

41. Wortley, *Skin Deep in Soho*, p. 55.

42. 'Note Regarding Striptease Clubs and Near-Beer Establishments', Memorandum by the Commissioner of the Metropolitan Police, 1963, TNA HO 300/17.

43. Willetts, *Members Only*, p. 124; T. Wiseman, 'Striptease in London', *ES* 19 February 1960.

44. D. Farr, 'Soho—Where Strip Makes a Million a Year', *People* 5 May 1968.

45. Clare, 'Taking Off . . . Thirty Times a Day', *ES* 22 March 1972.

46. Law Report, 'No Assault by Police', *Times* 16 March 1966.

47. Memorandum by W. Tofts, 12 July 1973, Playboy Club File, LMA GLC/DG/EL/04/030.

48. Willetts, *Members Only*, pp. 170–72.

49. 'Acts Not Indecent, Says Clubman', *Times* 13 April 1961.

50. N. Roberts, *The Front Line. Women in the Sex Industry Speak* (London, 1986), pp. 68, 85. I am most grateful to Delyth Scudamore for drawing my attention to this source.

51. Account of police investigation into the Nell Gwynne Theatre, 11 December 1970, Gargoyle Club File, LMA GLC/DG/EL/04/016.

52. R. Durgnat, 'Strippers. A Guide to Soho Clubs', *International Times* 4, 28 November–11 December 1966; 'Passport to Soho', *Sunday Times Magazine*, 21 January 1968.

53. Roberts, *Front Line*, pp. 48–49.

54. Wortley, *Skin Deep in Soho*, p. 7.

55. Roberts, *Front Line*, p. 82.

56. P. Charman, 'The Real Soho Strip Teaser', *ES* 13 May 1977.

57. Yee Seng Kiong to 'The Greater London Council for Public Entertainment', 21 May 1979, in Moulin Rouge File, LMA GLC/DG/EL/04/005. The 'Moulin Rouge 2' turned out to be a booking office for the Moulin Rouge, two doors up the street. The proprietor explained that 'either he or one of his staff escort patrons from the booking office to [number] 34 so they will not be accosted by touts and taken elsewhere and possibly robbed', Report by R. Webster, Inspector, 11 June 1979, ibid.

58. 'No Live "Strip Show" on Sunday', *Marylebone Mercury* 7 March 1969.

59. Farr, 'Soho', for Short; B. Cox, J. Shirley & M. Short, *The Fall of Scotland Yard* (London, 1977), pp. 148–49, for Humphreys.

60. 'Child of Five Will See Striptease Show', *Daily Mail* 28 December 1960.

61. J. Green, 'When the Stripping Has to Stop', *Evening News* 8 January 1969.

62. 'Strippin' off the Ritz', *Sunday Telegraph* 28 April 1968.

63. M. Furlong, 'The Girl with the Most Attentive Audience in Town', *Daily Mail* 9 February 1967; 'Strippin' off the Ritz.'

64. Roberts, *Front Line*, p. 151.

65. Wortley, *Skin Deep in Soho*, p. 4.

66. S. Dalrymple, 'Confessions of a Stripper', *Frendz* 33, 8 July 1971.

67. Roberts, *Front Line*, pp. 50–51.

68. Clare, 'Taking Off'; Roberts, *Front Line*, pp. 51–52.

69. A. Sharpley, 'She Is Eighteen and Saves £50 a Week—but How Many Girls Would Do a Job like Hers?', *ES* 18 November 1965.

70. From the synopsis of *Carousella*, supplied by Mithras Films, 10 February 1965, GLC Licensing Committee Presented Papers, 14 April 1965, LMA GLC/DG/PRE/127/001.

71. Wortley, *Skin Deep in Soho*, pp. 102–3.

72. Clare, 'Taking Off.'

73. Sharpley, 'She Is Eighteen.'

74. Roberts, *Front Line*, p. 54.

75. Clare, 'Taking Off.'

76. For this paragraph, Durgnat, 'Strippers'; Clare, 'Taking Off'; Roberts, *Front Line*, pp. 71, 54, 72–73, 87; Wortley, *Skin Deep in Soho*, pp. 56, 47.

77. 'Note Regarding Striptease Clubs and Near-Beer Establishments', Memorandum by the Commissioner of the Metropolitan Police, 1963, TNA HO 300/17.

78. Farr, 'Soho.'

79. J. Jacobs [Gargoyle Club] to GLC, 7 October 1970, in Sunset Strip File, LMA GLC/DG/EL/02/067.

80. Roberts, *Front Line*, p. 48.

81. Memorandum by J. Howard, 24 March 1972, in file 'Lord Longford Requests Information on Striptease Clubs', TNA HO 302/60.

82. 'Punters and Panties by Soho Stripper', *ES* 20 March 1972, cutting in LMA GLC/DG/EL/04/030.

83. 'Curtain Up—on Strip Censors', *ES* 28 October 1960.

84. E.g., at the Original Geisha Club in Greek Court: 'The girl had stripped off all her clothes and only remained with a piece of sticking plaster covering her private parts. . . . Another girl appeared on stage and began dancing, and stripping until she finished only dressed in sticking plaster

covering her private parts,' statement by PC J. R. Foxley, West End Central, 15 November 1963, Original Geisha Club File, LMA GLC/DG/EL/03/G26.

85. Wortley, *Skin Deep in Soho*, p. 148; N. Nash, *London after Dark* (New York, 1966), p. 31.

86. Durgnat, 'Strippers.'

87. J. Sandford & R. Law, *Synthetic Fun* (London, 1967), p. 83.

88. Clare, 'Taking Off.'

89. Roberts, *Front Line*, pp. 46, 49. There appears to have been no basis for this widely held view. The prohibition of movement at the Windmill and elsewhere on the West End stage had been imposed by the Lord Chamberlain, whose powers extended only to London theatres—not strip clubs—and were ended by the 1968 Theatres Act. The LCC and GLC did not licence striptease at all before 1966 and did not subsequently lay down rules for performance beyond banning underage artistes.

90. Farr, 'Soho.'

91. 'Nobody likes to be reduced to a thing, and strippers are no exception', Roberts, *Front Line*, p. 54.

92. Durgnat, 'Strippers.'

93. Roberts, *Front Line*, pp. 52, 72–73.

94. Report of the Licensing Committee, 7 December 1966, GLC Minutes, 13 December 1966.

95. Report by the Chief Officer of the Licensing Department [E. W. Newberry], 'Prosecutions for Unlicensed Public Dancing (Strip-Tease) and Unlicensed Cinematograph Exhibitions in Soho', 27 October 1966, Striptease Policy File, LMA GLC/DG/EL/07/050.

96. Quotations from D. Gilbert, interviewed by Ch. Insp. D. Thompson, 24 January 1963, and Insp. H. White, 13 February 1963, Original Geisha Club File, LMA GLC/DG/EL3/G026. The Original Geisha does not appear in the list of strip clubs appended to E. W. Newberry's report of October 1966, suggesting that it had indeed gone under by then.

97. Joint Report by the Solicitor and the Chief Officer of the Licensing Department, 'Entertainments Licensing—Powers to Enable the Courts to Make Disqualification Orders', 8 June 1966, Striptease Policy File, LMA GLC/DG/EL/07/050.

98. Memorandum L.C. to Mr Freeman, 18 January 1963, Naked City File, LMA GLC/DG/EL/03/G029.

99. Reports by the Chief Officer of the Licensing Department [E. W. Newberry], 'Prosecutions for Unlicensed Public Dancing (Strip-Tease) and Unlicensed Cinematograph Exhibitions in Soho', 27 October 1966, and 'Prosecutions for Unlicensed Public Dancing (Strip-Tease) in Soho', 28 November 1966, Striptease Policy File, LMA GLC/DG/EL/07/050.

100. M. F. King, 'Grip Tightens on Strip Clubs', *ES* 8 December 1966.

101. J. Jacobs to W. O. Hart, LCC, n.d. [1965], Gargoyle Club File, LMA GLC/DG/EL/4/16. Jacobs claimed to have spent 'at least £1000 in major electrical and building works to ensure [the club's] conformation [*sic*] with [LCC] requirements.'

102. Written statement by PC K. Wharfe, West End Central, 2 June 1975, 11 Greek Street File, LMA GLC/DG/EL/04/005. These premises, previously those of the Carousel Club, were unlicensed in 1975.

103. Memorandum, 25 October 1966, in Striptease Policy File, LMA GLC/DG/EL/07/050.

104. Report by the Chief Officer of the Licensing Department, 'Prosecutions for Unlicensed Public Dancing.'

105. A copy of the letter to Naked City, dated 21 December 1966, survives in that club's file, LMA GLC/DG/EL/23/G029.

106. Memorandum re 28 Wardour Street, 14 February 1967, Playboy Club File, LMA GLC/DG/EL/04/030.

107. List of premises granted or applying for licences by 7 May 1968, Striptease Policy File, LMA GLC/DG/EL/07/050.

108. M. King, 'Strip Clubs Want to Go Straight and Be Licensed', ES 27 February 1967, cutting in LMA GLC/TD/EL/07/050.

109. Mr Boone, of the GLC Architect's Department, quoted in the memorandum 'Striptease Estabs.', 23 April 1968, Striptease Policy File, LMA GLC/DG/EL/07/050.

110. 'Manager of Strip Club Jailed', ES 7 July 1966, cutting in LMA GLC/TD/EL/07/050.

111. Memorandum by R. Veitch, inspector, 24 October 1969, and list of Gardiner's criminal convictions in 9 Berwick St File, LMA GLC/DG/EL/03/B35.

112. H. W. Morgan, for Assistant Commissioner, Metropolitan Police, to Director-General, GLC, 3 April 1968, Carnival Club File, LMA GLC/DG/EL/02/067.

113. Memorandum 'The Carnival Club', 29 May 1968, Carnival Club File, LMA GLC/DG/EL/02/015.

114. F. Norman with J. Bernard, Soho Night and Day (2nd ed., London, 1968), pp. 112–13.

115. Farr, 'Soho.'

116. K. Barisch & P. Sahla, Richtig Reisen. London (Cologne, 1979), p. 156.

117. Memorandum re the Queen's Theatre Club, 37 Berwick Street, 20 February 1968, Striptease Policy File, LMA GLC/DG/EL/07/050.

118. Report by the Chief Officer of the Licensing Department, 29 July 1966, GLC Licensing Committee Presented Papers, 28 September 1966, LMA GLC/DG/PRE/127/007.

119. R. A. Sissons, Talbot Television Ltd, to C. Tugendhat, MP, 15 September 1970, and F. G. West, Director of Architecture and Planning, City of Westminster, to Tugendhat, 22 September 1970, Sunset Strip File, LMA GLC/DG/EL/02/067.

120. GLC Public Services Committee Minutes, 30 November 1970; V. P. Dunbar, Circulation Manager, The Gramophone magazine, 30 Dean St, to Chief Officer, Licensing Department, 7 September 1970; J. Trevor & Sons, Grosvenor St, to C.O.L.D., 30 September 1970, all in Sunset Strip file, LMA GLC/DG/EL/02/067.

121. 'Strip Club Opens to Public—by Permission of the GLC', Daily Express 4 October 1967.

122. 'A. Tennant', Kemp House, to Westminster City Council, 21 October 1969, in 9 Berwick St File, LMA GLC/DG/EL/03/B35.

123. Cox, Shirley & Short, Fall of Scotland Yard, p. 177.

124. For all this see Tomkinson, Pornbrokers, passim but particularly pp. 41–53.

125. 'Former Police Commander Took Nearly £60,000 from London Pornography Dealers, Court Told', Times 1 March 1977.

126. Cox, Shirley & Short, Fall of Scotland Yard, p. 132.

127. Virgo was released after a successful appeal.

128. R. Insall, 'Sex Shops Drive Out the Soho Villagers', Evening News 17 December 1975.

129. G. Walsh, 'Soho Shops in War on Sexploiters', ES 21 June 1977.

130. S. Cook, 'Why Soho Is Naughty, but Not Very Nice', Guardian 30 December 1980; I. Glover-James, '"Cheesecake" Drives Out French Cheese', Daily Telegraph 24 December 1980.

131. I. Glover-James, 'Sex Chain Takes Over Epicerie', Daily Telegraph 27 December 1980.

132. B. Burrough, 'Vicious Circle', *Soho Clarion* 23, Xmas 1978.

133. 'Sex Questionnaire: Report', *Soho Clarion* 17, November–December 1977.

134. 'Another M.P. Speaks Up for Soho', *Soho Clarion* 24, January–February 1979.

135. Bryan Cassidy's phrase, GLC Press Release, 16 May 1978, LMA GLC/DG/PRB/35/031.

136. Mrs A. Webb, Romford, to Brooke-Partridge, 20 February 1981, in Control of Pornography File, LMA GLC/DG/EL/07/016.

137. M. McPherson, 'Anti-Porn Chief: We Expected to Lose', *ES* 16 November 1977.

138. Interview by R. Biddlecombe, 'A Soho Fit for Families?', *New Tomorrow. Unfolding God's Heart to the World* December 1979.

139. 'Report of a Meeting ... 12 July 1977', Cinema X File, LMA GLC/DG/EL/04/005.

140. 'Frankly I would prefer to keep the Festival slightly at arm's length. I don't think it would improve our campaign to be too closely associated with them,' note from B. Cassidy to G. Saxby, on O. R. Johnston, Director, Nationwide Festival of Light, to B. Cassidy, 21 March 1978, Control of Pornography File, LMA GLC/DG/EL/07/016.

141. 'When you legalise a thing you give it respectability. ... I will be very sorry to see any steps taken which give the thing any kind of approval', Rev. E. Stride, Christ Church, Spitalfields, to B. Cassidy, 16 August 1978, Control of Pornography File, LMA GLC/DG/EL/07/016.

142. B. Cassidy to W. Whitelaw, 16 May 1978, Control of Pornography file, LMA GLC/DG/EL/7/16.

143. Manchester, *Sex Shops and the Law*, pp. 94–101, 194.

144. Ibid., p. 202.

145. Three, according to 'Cathy, a Peepshow Dancer', interviewed in Roberts, *Front Line*, p. 153.

146. 'Paul Raymond Buys Another Chunk of Soho', *ES* 6 December 1984, cutting in LMA GLC/DG/EL/07/016 (2).

147. Tomkinson, *Pornbrokers*, p. 121; Manchester, *Sex Shops and the Law*, p. 82. Conegate's Barnsley venture closed after less than three months.

148. Quoted in Mort, 'Striptease', p. 43.

Chapter 3

1. 'Bye-Bye Biba', *Economist* 23 August 1975.

2. S. Arnold, 'Bye-Bye Biba', *Observer* 5 October 1975.

3. '"Moderns" v. "Rockers"', *Evening Standard* (*ES*) 12 March 1963.

4. A. McGill, 'Look Out. There's a Mod (or Maybe a Rocker) Close Behind You', *ES* 31 July 1963.

5. N. Cohn, *Today There Are No Gentlemen. The Changes in Englishmen's Clothes since the War* (London, 1971), p. 45.

6. B. Edwards, 'Swinging Boutiques and the Modern Store: Designing Shops for Post-war London', *London Journal* 31 (1), 2006, 78–79.

7. A. McGill, 'It Sounds Silly, but I've Been Shopping in a Boutique!', *ES* 22 July 1964.

8. Quoted ibid.

9. Both definitions ibid.

10. Cohn, *Today There Are No Gentlemen*, pp. 45–46.

11. M. Quant, *Quant by Quant* (London, 1966), p. 41; B. Hulanicki, *From A to Biba* (London, 1983), p. 62.

12. V. Brittain, 'Success and Carnaby Street', *Investors Chronicle*, Retail Supplement, 28 January 1966.

13. M. Fogg, *Boutique. A Sixties Cultural Phenomenon* (London, 2003), p. 14.

14. R. Bennett-England, *Dress Optional. The Revolution in Menswear* (London, 1967), pp. 133, 85, 80.

15. Quant, *Quant by Quant*, pp. 43–44.

16. F. Green, 'This Is Barbara. Now She's a Dress Manufacturer as Well as a Fashion Artist', *Daily Mirror* 1 May 1964; Hulanicki, *From A to Biba*, pp. 71–73.

17. J. Aitken, *The Young Meteors* (London, 1967), pp. 18–19.

18. Brittain, 'Success and Carnaby Street.'

19. J. Dingemans, 'Watch the Face in the Window for the First Sign of Summer', *ES* 5 May 1965; Foale and Tuffin coats cost between sixteen and twenty-four guineas in 1966: M. Bultitude, *Get Dressed. A Useful Guide to London's Boutiques* (London, 1966), p. 31.

20. Brittain, 'Success and Carnaby Street.'

21. *Financial Times*, 22 May 1967.

22. Aitken, *Young Meteors*, pp. 18, 23.

23. B. Griggs, 'So I Said No More Boutiques!', *ES* 25 April 1966.

24. A. Ince, 'The Boutique Bandwaggon', *London Life* 23 July 1966.

25. Hulanicki, *From A to Biba*, p. 108; F. Green, 'Imagine! 0.53 Half-Undressed Girls per Square Foot, 29 Hatstands, 20 Potted Palms and Princess Anne Just Dropping In . . .', *Daily Mirror* 26 September 1966.

26. 'Togetherness in Fashion', *Drapers Record* 30 March 1968.

27. '"Touchy" About Boutiques', *Drapers Record* 16 November 1968.

28. V. Jenkins, 'For Janet Lyle the Sixties (Remember Them?) Stop Here', *ES* 30 January 1976.

29. 'Suzanne' Boutique, Fortis Green Road, *Drapers Record* 25 May 1968; 'Clothes Peg', Lilley Road, *Drapers Record* 18 May 1968.

30. Harvey Richard, Heath Street, *Drapers Record* 22 July 1972.

31. Cyril and Gillian Bonstein, Bressenden Place, *Drapers Record* 16 November 1968.

32. 'Knew of No Assets to Meet Debts of More than £400,000', *Drapers Record* 12 May 1973.

33. 'Tiny Bit of Capital and a Lot of Hope', *Drapers Record* 20 January 1973.

34. Quant, *Quant by Quant*, p. 141.

35. Bennett-England, *Dress Optional*, p. 79; J. Reed, *The King of Carnaby Street. The Life of John Stephen* (London, 2010), pp. 125–26, 133.

36. Quant, *Quant by Quant*, p. 146.

37. Ibid., p. 141.

38. 'List of Creditors. Vanessa Frye, Ltd.', *Drapers Record* 8 April 1972.

39. Ince, 'Boutique Bandwaggon.'

40. 'Fewer Shop Lights Have Been a Help to Shoplifters', *Drapers Record* 26 January 1974.

41. 'Startling Admissions by London Boys on Stealing from Shops', *Drapers Record* 31 August 1968.

42. A. Sharpley, 'The Confessions of Three Teenage Shoplifters', *ES* 16 August 1966.

43. Hulanicki, *From A to Biba*, pp. 100–101.

44. Bennett-England, *Dress Optional*, pp. 80, 79.

45. Quoted in D. Johnson and R. Dunkley, *Gear Guide. Hip Pocket Guide to London's Swinging Fashion Scene* (London, 1967), pp. 4–5.

46. Cohn, *Today There Are No Gentlemen*, p. 109.

47. M. Bender, 'The Union Jack (Adapted for Bare-Backed Overalls) Waves in London', *New York Times* 13 June 1966.

48. B. Griggs, 'The Battle of the Boutiques', *ES* 18 April 1967.

49. '"Way In" Is Way, Way Out', *Drapers Record* 10 June 1967; 'Point of View. Way In at Last!', *Drapers Record* 6 May 1967; 'Season Barriers "Out" at Way In.' Separate from Harrods with Later Opening and Closing', *Drapers Record* 13 May 1967; '"Way In" Open Until 7 p.m.', *Drapers Record* 20 May 1967.

50. 'How Miss Selfridge Stock Gets Out in Two Hours', *Drapers Record*, 5 April 1975.

51. Bender, 'Union Jack'; Brittain, 'Success and Carnaby Street.'

52. 'What's Kooking', *Drapers Record* 8 April 1967.

53. Brittain, 'Success and Carnaby Street.'

54. R. L. Blaszczyk, 'Doing Business in Transatlantic Fashion: The Experience of Mary Quant', in J. Lister, *Mary Quant* (London, 2019), pp. 110–22.

55. B. Cunningham, 'New York Report', *Diary*, October 1966.

56. S. Black, 'British Fashion Needs Quality to Go with Its Style', *Financial Times* 10 June 1972.

57. See, e.g., the deputation from Henry Moss and Harry Fox, proprietors of Lady Jane in Carnaby Street, to 10 Downing Street in 1967. The Board of Trade was said to have told them that they were 'too small to be helped': 'Carnaby Street Export "Coffin" Goes to the Prime Minister', *Drapers Record* 4 March 1967.

58. Quant, *Quant by Quant*, p. 142.

59. '"Hell of a Lot of Money to Lose" in 12 Months', *Drapers Record* 15 April 1972.

60. Cohn, *Today There Are No Gentlemen*, pp. 149–50; P. Gorman, *Mr Freedom—Tommy Roberts: British Design Hero* (London, 2012).

61. 'The Many Problems of the Mr Freedom Group', *Drapers Record* 10 June 1972.

62. Brittain, 'Success and Carnaby Street.'

63. 'Irvine Sellars Group's Expansion Plans', *Drapers Record* 15 June 1968; 'Mates is Now Located among the Stores', *Drapers Record* 7 December 1968.

64. Hulanicki, *From A to Biba*, p. 125.

65. S. Black, 'A New Bloom on the Dorothy Perkins Rose', *Financial Times* 28 October 1970.

66. S. McLachlan & L. Van der Post, 'The Biba Gamble: Boutique to Department Store', *Financial Times* 11 September 1973.

67. 'Dorothy Perkins Attacks the '70s', *Financial Times* 7 May 1971; K. Gooding, 'Derry and Toms Sold for £4m', *Financial Times* 30 November 1971.

68. J. Rook, 'It's That Old Biba Magic Again', *Daily Express* 7 September 1973.

69. B. Hulanicki, 'Foreword', in S. Thomas & A. W. Turner, *Welcome to Big Biba. Inside the Most Beautiful Store in the World* (London, 2006), p. 5.

70. Thomas & Turner, *Welcome to Big Biba*, p. 15.

71. Illustrated ibid., pp. 40–41, 43.

72. Hulanicki, 'Foreword', p. 5.

73. Ibid.

74. 'Biba Bothers', *Economist* 12 July 1975.

75. Hulanicki, *From A to Biba*, p. 131.

76. 'British Land Loss £0.4m', *Financial Times* 22 August 1974.

77. 'Bye-Bye Biba.'

78. Hulanicki, *From A to Biba*, p. 153.

79. C. Alexander, 'A Cause for Regret', *Drapers Record* 30 August 1975.

80. Ibid.

81. 'Biba . . . What Went Wrong?', *Drapers Record* 30 August 1975.

82. Hulanicki, *From A to Biba*, p. 154.

83. L. Vincent, 'Biba's Rude Awakening', *Observer* 20 July 1975.

84. 'Growing Up', *Economist* 22 July 1972.

85. R. Lester, *Boutique London. A History: King's Road to Carnaby Street* (London, 2010), p. 63.

86. Hulanicki, 'Foreword', p. 5.

87. 'A New Star on the Retail Stage', *Drapers Record* 15 September 1973.

88. S. Lowry, 'Going from Bad to Wurst', *Guardian* 19 July 1975.

89. Fogg, *Boutique*, p. 86.

90. O. Marriott, *The Property Boom* (London, 1967), pp. 30ff.

91. McLachlan & Van der Post, 'Biba Gamble.'

92. Hulanicki, *From A to Biba*, p. 156.

93. A. Neustatter, 'Trimming the Style of Fashion', *Guardian* 8 March 1975.

94. 'Biba's "Extravagant" Era to End—Space Goes to M&S', *Drapers Record* 26 July 1975.

95. Vincent, 'Biba's Rude Awakening.'

96. E. Goodman, 'Disposable as Its Clothes', *Financial Times* 21 August 1975.

97. Ibid.

98. 'London: Safe and Saleable', *Drapers Record* 29 April 1972; L. Foster, ''73. A Changing Pattern', *Drapers Record* 30 December 1972.

99. Lister, *Mary Quant*, p. 177; J. Butterfield, 'A Girl like This Makes You *Want* to Gamble', *Daily Express* 6 November 1963.

100. 'Michael Fish Out of Water—Again', *ES* 2 January 1975.

101. McLachlan & Van der Post, 'Biba Gamble.'

102. A. Lorentzen & C. J. Hansen, 'Introduction,' in A. Lorentzen & C. J. Hansen, eds., *The City in the Experience Economy. Role and Transformation* (Abingdon, 2012), p. 5.

103. B. J. Pine II & J. H. Gilmore, *The Experience Economy* (updated ed., Boston, 2011), p. 3; and see Pine & Gilmore, 'Welcome to the Experience Economy', *Harvard Business Review* 76 (6), 1998, 97–105.

104. B. Hulanicki & M. Pel, *The Biba Years, 1963–1975* (London, 2014), p. 164.

105. P. Norman, 'The Battle for Biba', *Sunday Times Magazine* 28 September 1975.

106. Quoted by Vincent, 'Biba's Rude Awakening'; Pine and Gilmore considered the possibility of charging for admission to shopping malls, 'Welcome to the Experience Economy', p. 101.

Chapter 4

1. 'Pioneer of the Grill—and Still Great', *Where to Go in London and Around* 24 November 1966. The title of this periodical was abbreviated to *Where to Go* at the beginning of 1967. The abbreviated title is adopted in subsequent citations.

2. Ronay quoted in G. H. Bowden, *British Gastronomy. The Rise of Great Restaurants* (London, 1975), p. 102; for Benson, Quentin Crewe, 'The Things They Get Away With Down in the Basement', *Evening Standard (ES)* 25 February 1971.

3. 'Restaurants', *London Life* 26 February 1966.

4. F. Maschler, 'Vive le Bistro—Even When It's Chinese', *ES* 20 February 1974.

5. 'Pioneer of the Grill—and Still Great', *Where to Go* 24 November 1966; R. Postgate, ed., *The Good Food Guide to London* (London, 1968), p. 94.

6. F. Maschler, 'High Speed Feed', *ES* 11 December 1974.

7. A. S. Sutherland, *The Spaghetti Tree. Mario and Franco and the Trattoria Revolution* (London, 2009), pp. 96–97.

8. Q. Crewe, 'Restaurants', *Queen* 12 August 1964; C. Driver, ed., *The Good Food Guide, 1972* (London, 1972), p. 420.

9. M. Gallati, *Mario of the Caprice. The Autobiography of a Restaurateur* (London, 1960), p. 144.

10. S. Cotter, 'Woman behind the Menu' (Simone Prunier), *Hotel and Restaurant Catering* February 1970.

11. Gallati, *Mario of the Caprice*, pp. 165, 166, 167, 161.

12. Customer quoted by John Negri, manager of the Empress, Berkeley Street, in 'The Man behind the Menu', *Hotel and Restaurant Catering* October 1970.

13. The TV presenter Cathy McGowan was ejected from the Savoy in 1965 for wearing Mod trousers. The Ritz and the Dorchester also banned women in trousers. The Mirabelle 'might tolerate really elegant trousers *at lunchtime in the summer.*' The Connaught yielded to female trousers in 1971, but even in 1978 it was observed that 'the modern woman defeats them': 'The Trousers the Savoy Banned', *ES* 31 March 1965; B. Hartland, 'To Dress Up, or Down, for Dinner?', *Daily Telegraph* 21 July 1971; C. Driver, ed., *Good Food Guide, 1978* (London, 1978), p. 403.

14. Q. Crewe, 'Restaurants', *Queen* 12 October 1966.

15. Q. Crewe, *Well, I Forget the Rest. The Autobiography of an Optimist* (London, 1991), p. 155.

16. The Trattoria phenomenon is well described in Sutherland, *Spaghetti Tree*.

17. Ibid., pp. 136, 154, 163.

18. Ibid., p. 174.

19. M. Vestey, 'If Alvaro Likes You, Then He'll Feed You', *London Life* 16 July 1966; Sutherland, *Spaghetti Tree*, p. 110.

20. Postgate, *Good Food Guide to London*, p. 13.

21. 'Boom in Bistros', *Queen* 11 October 1961; F. Maschler, 'Time Capsule to SE13', *ES* 3 September 1975.

22. Q. Crewe, 'Restaurants,' *Queen* 17 June 1964.

23. 'Restaurants', *London Life* 26 February 1966.

24. Maschler, 'Vive le Bistro.'

25. Q. Crewe, 'Eight out of Eight for an Admirable Trio', *ES* 27 October 1971.

26. Postgate, *Good Food Guide to London*, pp. 137–38.

27. F. Maschler, 'Next on the Menu: A Micro-wave Miracle Meal', *ES* 23 January 1974.

28. Q. Crewe, 'Restaurants', *Queen* 27 January 1965; J. Ardagh, introduction to Postgate, *Good Food Guide to London*, 13–14.

29. Q. Crewe, 'Restaurants', *Queen* 16 December 1964.

30. Q. Crewe, 'Restaurants', *Queen* 19 June 1968.

31. 'The Man behind the Menu' (interview with John Stais), *Hotel and Restaurant Catering* November 1969.

32. S. Jenkins, 'Waiter, There's a Brick in My Soup', *ES* 11 June 1974.

33. R. O. Baker, 'The State of the Industry', *Caterer and Hotelkeeper* 8 January 1970.

34. R. Kotas, 'A Study of Labour Costs. VI', *Caterer and Hotelkeeper* 8 October 1970.

35. Letter from M. J. Eynon, *Caterer and Hotelkeeper* 5 February 1970.

36. Cotter, 'Woman behind the Menu.'

37. R. Kotas, 'The Great Price Explosion. IV. Restaurants', *Caterer and Hotelkeeper* 13 January 1972.

38. Q. Crewe, 'Restaurants', *Queen* 16 August 1967; F. Maschler, 'How to Bridge the Price Gap. Cross the River to Battersea before It Gets Too Smart', *ES* 26 September 1973; L. Bareham, 'Food: Eating Out', *Time Out (TO)* 17 June 1977.

39. F. Maschler, 'Don't Let the Kebabs Fool You—Stick to the Homely Kipper', *ES* 15 August 1973.

40. 'Fresh as a Daisy at Borthwicks', *Where to Go*, 7 February 1974.

41. Crewe, 'Things They Get Away With.'

42. Driver, *Good Food Guide, 1972*, p. 430.

43. J. Vaughan, 'Apicella's Opera', *Queen* 17 January 1968.

44. Q. Crewe, 'Restaurants', *Queen* 28 February 1968.

45. L. Blandford, 'Restaurants', *Queen* 31 July 1968.

46. F. Maschler, 'The Place of the Feel', *ES* 5 October 1977.

47. R. Postgate, ed., *The Good Food Guide, 1959–60* (London, 1960), p. 341.

48. F. Maschler, 'The Name of the Game Is the Name', *ES*, 23 May 1973.

49. 'Eating', *TO* 29 June 1973; M. Bygrave & J. Goodman, *Fuel Food. Where to Find Great Meals in London for £1 or as Little as 50p* (London, 1973), p. 65; F. Maschler, 'Lessons in the Language of Food', *ES* 13 June 1973; J. West, 'Something Different and Rather Special', *Where to Go* 11 March 1971; S. Miles, 'Food: Eating Out', *TO* 18 October 1974.

50. F. Maschler, 'Why the Early Bird Gets the Veg', *ES* 5 January 1977.

51. Q. Crewe, 'The Day We Tested the Lager (I Think)', *ES* 29 March 1972.

52. Her name was Lisa de Marinis, 'A Slave Girl at Your Beck and Call and Unique Roman Dishes', *Where to Go* 26 January 1967.

53. Q. Crewe, 'Graffiti Welcomed—but by Invitation Only', *ES*, 23 June 1971; Q. Crewe, 'Restaurants', *Queen* 7 April 1965.

54. J. West, 'The Restaurant with a Plus', *Where to Go* 21 September 1967; 'Restaurant with Artistic Style', *Where to Go* 12 February 1970.

55. Maschler, 'Place of the Feel.'

56. Q. Crewe, 'Restaurants', *Queen* 17 August 1966.

57. R. Postgate, *Good Food Guide to London*, p. 55.

58. Postgate, *Good Food Guide, 1959–60*, p. 364; L. Blandford, 'Restaurants', *Queen*, 14 August 1968. Charco's did, though, survive until the second decade of the present century.

59. Baker, 'State of the Industry.'

60. F. Maschler, 'Confusion Road!', *ES* 26 November 1975.

61. According to F. Maschler, 'Do I Hear £1.25 for a Meal?', *ES* 6 August 1975.

62. 'You make more profit from Country Kitchen canned mushrooms than almost any other vegetable you serve. Fact!', advert in *Caterer and Hotelkeeper* 13 November 1969.

63. F. Maschler: 'The Great Garçon Invasion That Never Happened . . .', *ES* 25 July 1973.

64. R. Kotas, 'A Study in Labour Costs', *Caterer and Hotelkeeper* 6 August 1970.

65. Postgate, *Good Food Guide to London*, p. 63, on Fiddlers Three, Beauchamp Place; P. Rosenwald, 'Eating', *TO* 27 April 1973, on the Private Eye Restaurant, Radnor Walk.

66. Cotter, 'Woman behind the Menu.'

67. S. Blackburn, ed., *James Sherwood's Discriminating Guide. London. Fine Dining and Shopping* (London, 1975), p. 55.

68. F. Maschler, 'A Star Is Shorn', *ES* 13 April 1977.

69. C. Driver, ed., *The Good Food Guide, 1977* (London, 1977), pp. 415, 258, 463, 461. The Savoy responded: 'We don't take a great deal of notice of guides', V. Goldsmith, 'London's Leading Eating Houses Take a Knock', *ES* 3 March 1977.

70. C. Driver, ed., *The Good Food Guide, 1976* (London, 1976), p. ix.

71. Cotter, 'Woman behind the Menu.'

72. Q. Crewe, 'Restaurants', *Queen* 3 January 1968.

73. R. Kotas, 'Of Price and Profit', *Caterer and Hotelkeeper*, 4 December 1969; R. Kotas, *Market Orientation in the Hotel and Catering Industry* (Leighton Buzzard, 1975), pp. 14–15.

74. Restaurant and Caterers Association index of food costs, *British Hotelier and Restaurateur* January 1976.

75. Q. Crewe, 'Restaurants', *Queen* 19 June 1968.

76. Postgate, *Good Food Guide to London*, p. 131; Q. Crewe, 'The Trattoria Tradition', *ES* 26 November 1970.

77. Ardagh, introduction to Postgate, *Good Food Guide to London*, p. 12.

78. 'Fifteen Years of British Eating Out', *Hotel and Restaurant Catering* July 1974.

79. News report, *Caterer and Hotelkeeper* 26 February 1970.

80. Blackburn, *James Sherwood's Discriminating Guide*, p. 8.

81. 'Cette "baby food" sophistiquée, qui aurait pu être inventée par un cuisinier du dimanche, antiquaire-décorateur, a pu passer il y a une douzaine d'années pour audacieuse', H. Gault & C. Millau, *Londres* (Paris, 1977), pp. 57–58.

82. F. Maschler, 'The Day I Had My Chips (and Some of My Husband's Too!)', *ES* 24 November 1976.

83. Quoted in F. Maschler, 'Where the People in the Know Go', *ES* 13 November 1974.

84. F. Maschler, 'Why I've Got the Cordon Bleus', *ES* 19 September 1973.

85. L. Fernandez, 'The Man behind the Menu' (interview with Bernard Walsh, Wheeler's), *Hotel and Restaurant Catering* May 1970.

86. L. Bareham, 'Cheap Eats', *TO* 16 September 1977.

87. S. Campbell with A. Towle, *Cheap Eats in London* (Harmondsworth, 1975), p. 93.

88. M. Bygrave, 'Hamburgers', *TO* 21 October 1977.

89. Ibid.

90. Campbell & Towle, *Cheap Eats in London*, p. 11.

91. S. Hunt, 'Goodbye Mr Chips-with-Everything', *TO* 12 November 1976.

92. R. Postgate, *Good Food Guide, 1959–60*, p. 331.

93. Postgate, *Good Food Guide to London*, p. 111.

94. I. Pylypec, *A Squatter in London* (London, 2018), p. 107. The first London McDonald's appeared in Woolwich in 1974. The first West End outlet was in Haymarket: see S. Miles, 'Food: Eating Out', *TO* 23 April 1976.

95. M. Bygrave, 'Hamburgers', *TO* 21 October 1977.

96. Maschler, 'Why I've Got the Cordon Bleus.'

97. F. Maschler, 'How to Survive the Whims of Change', *ES* 26 February 1975.

98. C. Driver, ed., *The Good Food Guide, 1973* (London, 1973), p. 392.

99. Q. Crewe, 'Restaurants', *Queen*, 23 September 1964; Q. Crewe, 'Restaurants', *Queen* 27 January 1965.

100. C. Driver, 'Crying All the Way to the Bank', *ES* 13 March 1974.

101. H. Lyttelton, 'Restaurants', *Queen* 16 April 1969.

102. J. Walkowitz, *Nights Out. Life in Cosmopolitan London* (New Haven, CT, 2012), pp. 94ff for Leoni's Quo Vadis.

103. V. Gordon, 'Just like Madras—Except You Eat off Plates', *ES* 15 November 1972; M. Bygrave, 'E14—a Decent Meal and Drabble Too?', *ES* 24 April 1974, for Natraj and the Clifton in Brick Lane.

104. Gallati, *Mario of the Caprice*, p. 36.

105. 'Eating', *TO*, 26 January 1973; Postgate, *Good Food Guide to London*, p. 30.

106. Q. Crewe, 'The Real Soho', *Queen* 2 December 1964; P. Fay, 'Anatomy of a Restaurant', *Queen* 30 March 1966.

107. Walkowitz, *Nights Out*, p. 141.

108. S. Jenkins, 'On the Scent of an Outdoor Idyll', *ES* 31 July 1974.

109. Bygrave & Goodman, *Fuel Food*, pp. 11–12.

110. Jenkins, 'On the Scent.'

111. P. Waymark, 'New Chinatown Comes to Soho', *Times* 5 January 1970.

112. Ng K. C., *The Chinese in London* (Oxford, 1968), p. 29.

113. B. Rogers, 'The Strange Community of Gerrard Street', *Daily Telegraph Magazine* 13 March 1970; F. Martin, 'No Future in Mah Jong', *Guardian* 29 May 1972.

114. M. Chow, 'There's Something Fishy about No. 15', *ES* 3 August 1977.

115. F. Maschler, 'Glories of the Past—Like Service', *ES* 20 August 1975; P. Grove & C. Grove, *The History of the 'Ethnic' Restaurant in Britain*, accessed 23 August 2015, www.menumagazine.co.uk/book/restauranthistory.html.

116. Grove & Grove, *History of the 'Ethnic' Restaurant*; W. Frischauer, *Gourmet's Guide to London* (London, 1968), p. 140.

117. Bygrave & Goodman, *Fuel Food*, p. 165.

118. Maschler, 'Glories of the Past'; *Hispanic Britain, or, An Anglo-Spanish Miscellany*, accessed 23 August 2015, https://hispanicbritain.wordpress.com.

119. F. Maschler, 'Go On, Give Your Blinis a Whirl', *ES* 3 December 1975; S. Miles, 'Food: Eating Out', *TO* 13 June 1975.

120. G. Mikes, 'The Gay Hussar', *London Life* 19 February 1966.

121. See the two-part biography of Taylor in *Where to Go*: 'The Mad Millionaire', 28 November 1974. and 'Benny and the Law', 5 December 1974.

122. A. Pottersman, 'Good Eating', *London Life* 16 July 1966.

123. Campbell & Towle, *Cheap Eats in London*, p. 123.

124. Gallati, *Mario of the Caprice*, p. 123.

125. Fay, 'Anatomy of a Restaurant.'

126. L. Kukoy, 'The Pacesetters', *Hotel and Restaurant Catering* January 1970.

127. National Catering Inquiry, *The British Eating Out. A Report from Britain's National Catering Inquiry* (London, 1966), p. 8. Perhaps surprisingly, the figure for London was the same as the national figure.

128. J. West, 'This Will Revise Your Ideas about Chinese Food', *Where to Go* 28 December 1967, on the Lotus House, Edgware Road.

129. Campbell & Towle, *Cheap Eats in London*, p. 15.

130. J. West, 'It's Really Greek, but Very Good Indeed', *Where to Go* 14 December 1967.

131. S. Miles, 'Food: Eating Out', *TO* 29 August 1975, on Nibub Lokanta, Edgware Road.

132. 'Restaurants', *London Life* 12 February 1966.

133. C. Gower, 'It's an Emporium of Oriental Culture', *Where to Go* 4 April 1968.

134. F. Maschler, 'Getting to Know Bhoona, Alu and Tarka the Hotter', *ES* 18 April 1973.

135. Campbell & Towle, *Cheap Eats in London*, p. 139. Georgiou was the father of the singer Cat Stevens.

136. J. West, 'A Long Way in a Short Time', *Where to Go* 4 March 1971.

137. C. Gower, 'I Was Most Impressed', *Where to Go* 25 April 1968.

138. Q. Crewe, 'How to Grow Fat on a Thin Wallet', *ES* 17 November 1971.

139. Advertisement, *ES* 2 March 1977.

140. Quoted in Sutherland, *Spaghetti Tree*, p. 211.

141. Q. Crewe, 'If You Want My Job—Here's Your Chance!', *ES* 6 September 1972.

142. John West suggested that the tandoori oven had been demonstrated at the New York World Fair of 1964 and introduced to Britain shortly afterwards, though the Natraj in Charlotte Street claimed to have started tandoori cooking in 1963: J. West, 'Taking the Plunge', *Where to Go* 31 October 1968, Campbell & Towle, *Cheap Eats in London*, p. 154. See also Gordon, 'Just like Madras.'

143. A. McGill, 'Waiter—There's a Critic in My Soup', *ES* 11 October 1972.

144. Bygrave & Goodman, *Fuel Food*, p. 177.

145. Ibid., p. 178.

146. As Sue Miles lamented, 'Food: Places', *TO* 20 June 1975. For the standardisation of Indian food in Britain see E. Buettner, '"Going for an Indian." South Asian Restaurants and the Limits of Multiculturalism in Britain', *Journal of Modern History* 80 (4), 2008, 881.

147. Ardagh, introduction to *Good Food Guide to London*, p. 11.

148. Bowden, *British Gastronomy*, pp. 153–54. Szechuanese food was slow to take root in London and was not evident in Chinatown at all in this period.

149. Postgate, *Good Food Guide to London*, p. 58.

150. Ibid., on the Dumpling Inn.

151. Bygrave & Goodman, *Fuel Food*, pp. 97–98; F. Maschler, 'Where to Seek a Little Greek Delight', *ES* 6 December 1972; Postgate, *Good Food Guide to London*, p. 58.

152. F. Maschler, 'Where to Seek a Little Greek Delight', *ES* 6 December 1972.

153. Gower, 'It's an Emporium of Oriental Culture.'

154. Bygrave & Goodman, *Fuel Food*, p. 98; J. Palmer in '33 London Lunch Bargains', *ES* 9 December 1972, on Wong Kei, Rupert Street.

155. R. Postgate, ed., *Good Food Guide, 1966* (London, 1966), p. 653.

156. D. Christoff, 'Malaya [*sic*]—Just off the Edgware Road', *Where to Go* 27 December 1973; P. Ingram, 'Come Feast like a Thai King', *Where to Go* 25 November 1971.

157. C. Gower, 'Chinese Food with a Difference', *Where to Go* 29 February 1968, on Singapore, Kensington High Street; J. West, 'Oh, That Wonderful Japanese Style!', *Where to Go* 16 March 1972, on Tokyo, Swallow Street; 'Eating', *TO* 8 August 1970; 'Food; Eating Out', *TO* 25 October 1974.

158. Q. Crewe, 'Restaurants', *Queen* 6 July 1966; Q. Crewe, 'At Last, the Real Pleasures of Peking . . . but Don't Expect Chop Suey', *ES* 20 April 1971.

159. F. Maschler, 'Around the Hot Spots', *ES* 4 October 1978.

160. Bygrave & Goodman, *Fuel Food*, p. 98, on Lee Ho Fook, Gerrard Street; 'Food: Eating Out', *TO* 1 July 1977, on Singapore, Kensington High Street.

161. F. Maschler, 'Snakes Alive! (It's the Chinese New Year)', *ES* 16 February 1977.

162. A. Slinn & M. Benenson, 'Greek Hospitality in Trendy Fitzrovia', *Where to Go* 15 May 1975.

163. R. Postgate, ed. *The Good Food Guide, 1951–52* (London, 1951), p. 193; 'Food: Eating Out', *TO* 1 July 1977.

164. C. Gower, 'A Restaurant Worth Looking For', *Where to Go* 12 November 1970, on the Nguyen, Palace Gate, the Bulgaria, Brompton Road, and Paul's Place, Kensington High Street.

165. Postgate, *Good Food Guide to London*, p. 79; F. Maschler, 'Seventeen of the Best', *ES* 29 December 1976, for the rise of Japanese restaurants during 1976.

166. Interview in 'Man behind the Menu', *Hotel and Restaurant Catering* November 1969.

167. P. Langan, *A Life with Food. Annotated and with a Memoir by Brian Sewell* (London, 1990), p. 75.

168. Bygrave & Goodman, *Fuel Food*, p. 138.

169. 'Food', *TO* 14 May 1971.

170. E.g., 'Food', *TO* 25 June 1971.

171. A. Slinn & M. Benenson, 'Greek Hospitality in Trendy Fitzrovia', *Where to Go* 15 May 1975.

172. F. Maschler, 'Good Food: Have We Really Had Our Day?', *ES* 6 November 1974.

173. V. Jenkins in '33 London Lunch Bargains', *ES* 9 December 1972.

174. National Catering Inquiry, *British Eating Out*, p. 22.

175. F. Maschler, 'A Taste of Tweed and Serve Me Right!', *ES* 12 October 1977.

176. See, e.g., to House of Commons, *Second Report from the Home Affairs Committee, Session 1984–85: The Chinese Community in Britain*, vol. 1 (HC 102-I), p. xiv, and Submission from the London Borough of Camden, Appendix 20, in vol. 3 (HC 102-III), p. 35.

177. 'Dining', *Where to Go* 31 December 1971.

178. 'English Eating in London', *Queen* July 1961.

179. 'Where Has All the Bubble and Squeak Gone?', *TO* 19 October 1973.

180. J. West, 'If You Don't Behave Yourself Here, You Might End Up in the Stocks', *Where to Go* 29 April 1971; 'Jest A Minute', *Where to Go* 20 March 1975; M. Tucker, 'English Fare's Well', *Where to Go* 6 December 1973.

181. F. Maschler, 'Ten Years On. Three of My Golden Oldies', *ES* 9 May 1973, on the Hungry Horse, Fulham Road; Q. Crewe, 'A Rare Find in the City', *ES* 15 April 1971.

182. Crewe, *Well, I Forget the Rest*, p. 158.

183. A. Lorentzen, 'Cities in the Experience Economy', in A. Lorentzen & C. J. Hansen, eds., *The City in the Experience Economy. Role and Transformation* (Abingdon, 2012), p. 16.

184. F. Maschler, 'Secrets of Survival, by the Old Faithfuls', *ES*, 1 October 1975.

185. Maschler, 'High Speed Feed.'

186. B. Weintraub, 'A Real Hamburger a Success in London', *New York Times* 12 August 1970.

187. Peter Eden of American Haven, quoted in R. Miller, 'Instant Eats, or How the Burger Boom Is Biting Britain', *ES* 18 November 1972.

188. 'At a Rainforest Café, for example, diners find themselves in the midst of dense vegetation, rising mist, cascading waterfalls, and evens startling lightning and thunder. They encounter live

tropical birds and fish as well as artificial butterflies, spiders, gorillas, and, if they look closely, a snapping baby crocodile': B. J. Pine & J. H. Gilmore, *The Experience Economy* (updated ed., Boston, 2011), p. 53, and see also pp. 5, 67–68, 89–90.

189. A. McGill, 'Are You One of the Beautiful People?', *ES* 11 September 1968.

190. A. McGill, 'How They Play the Waiting Game', *ES* 14 April 1976.

191. Crewe, 'Restaurants', *Queen*, 12 August 1964.

192. Bygrave & Goodman, *Fuel Food*, p. 137.

193. R. Bourne, 'How the Kebab Conquered', *ES* 4 July 1977.

194. S. Miles, 'Food: Publications', *TO*, 23 April 1976.

Chapter 5

1. P. G. Gray & R. Russell, *The Housing Situation in 1960. An Inquiry Covering England and Wales Carried Out for the Ministry of Housing and Local Government* (London, 1962), Table 27 and analysis, p. 32, Table 80, p. 84.

2. 'Inner London' refers to the London County Council area.

3. 'Home Ownership in the County of London', *Building Societies Gazette* March 1964; and J. C. France, 'Home Ownership in the Home Counties', *Building Societies Gazette* May 1964.

4. G. Shulman, Shulman Investments Ltd, to the Secretary, 11 June 1964, in Milner Holland Committee papers, Landlord Survey, TNA HLG 39/6. The claim, from a property company, was made for effect but was not entirely fanciful. In 1963, when the tenant survey was conducted for the Milner Holland Committee, Radio Rentals Ltd was offering a nineteen-inch TV for 'under 10/- per week' (see, e.g., advert in *Daily Mail* 8 November 1963). One percent of unfurnished houses and 7 percent of flats under rent control in London were let for less than that sum. That said, 6 percent of uncontrolled furnished houses were also rented at less than 10/- per week: P. G. Gray & J. Todd, *Privately Rented Accommodation in London. A Report on Inquiries Made in December 1963 and June 1964 for the Committee on Housing in Greater London*, in Committee on Housing in Greater London, *Report of the Committee on Housing in Greater London*, Government Social Survey (Cmnd. 2605 of 1965) (henceforth cited as Milner Holland Committee, *Report*), Appendix V, p. 352.

5. The 1960 figure is from Gray & Russell, *Housing Situation in 1960*, Table 34, p. 42.

6. P. Child, 'Landlordism, Rent Regulation and the Labour Party in Mid-Twentieth Century Britain, 1950–1964', *Twentieth Century British History* 29 (1), 2018, 87; J. Davis, 'Rents and Race in 1960s London: New Light on Rachmanism', *Twentieth Century British History* 12 (1), 2001, 74–75.

7. 'The Housing Market's Taste of Freedom', *Financial Times* 29 April 1959.

8. Milner Holland Committee, *Report*, pp. 41–42.

9. 'More Tenants Want to Buy', *Financial Times* 8 March 1958.

10. Milner Holland Committee, *Report*, pp. 44, 41.

11. A. E. Holmans, *Historical Statistics of Housing in Britain* (Cambridge, 2006), p. 270 and Table 1.14, p. 284.

12. Memo by Peachey Property Corporation, TNA HLG 39/67.

13. Evidence of J. Thirlwall, 6 January 1964, Milner Holland Committee papers, TNA HLG 39/65.

14. Gray & Todd, *Privately Rented Accommodation in London*, p. 364.

15. Estimate by Gray & Todd, comparing the 1960 and 1963 surveys: ibid., p. 365.

16. Ibid., p. 336.

17. M. Woolf, *The Housing Survey in England and Wales, 1964*, Government Social Survey (London, 1964), Table 2.16, p. 32.

18. J. Greve, D. Page & S. Greve, *Homelessness in London* (Edinburgh, 1971), Table 19, pp. 80–81.

19. For Rachman see S. Green, *Rachman* (London, 1979); Davis, 'Rents and Race in 1960s London.'

20. P. Marshall, 'London's Housing Shock', *Evening Standard* (*ES*) 11 March 1965 (original emphasis).

21. 'Chelsea', *London Property Letter* (*LPL*) 49, 13 February 1965.

22. Ibid.

23. 'Chelsea Prices Amaze Even Estate Agents', *West London Press and Chelsea News*, 7 July 1961.

24. M. Harmsworth, 'The Changing Face of Chelsea', part 2, *West London Press and Chelsea News* 19 May 1961; M. Harmsworth, 'The Changing Face of Chelsea', part 3, *West London Press and Chelsea News* 26 May 1961.

25. U. Bloom, 'Chelsea Goes into the Sixties', *West London Press and Chelsea News* 1 January 1960.

26. A. Bridger, 'The Day I Came to the Village', *West London Press and Chelsea News* 4 September 1959.

27. 'Trends in Property Values', *Financial Times*, 7 October 1950; Bridger, 'Day I Came to the Village.'

28. An auctioneer selling a property in Lincoln Street in 1961 described it as 'one of those very rare things, a freehold in Chelsea': 'Property Deals Make Profit for Council', *West London Press and Chelsea News* 14 July 1961.

29. A. Sharpley, 'Murder Grove, Part V . . . Will the Middle-Class Take Over?', *ES* 2 April 1965.

30. 'Paddington', *LPL* 12, July 1963 (2); 'W11', *LPL* 15, September 1963 (1).

31. A. Powell, 'Living In', *Observer* 12 July 1964 for Kennington; 'Now Southwark's Old Houses Lure the Smart Set', *ES* 21 November 1964.

32. 'Where the Slums Are Paved with Gold', *Financial Times* 27 April 1962; Canonbury was the subject of a case study for the Milner Holland Committee, *Report*, Appendix VI, pp. 422–25; for Barnsbury see P. Hall, 'Out of the Twilight?', *New Society* 17 October 1968.

33. 'Camden Town', *LPL* 16, September 1963 (2), 'Kentish Town', *LPL* 35, 4 July 1964.

34. 'Greenwich', *LPL* 19, November 1963 (1).

35. Denmark Road, Wimbledon: 'Anyone for Wimbledon?', *LPL* 37, 8 August 1964; Thorne Street, Barnes: 'What Price Houses?', *LPL* 37, 8 August 1964; Princes Road, Richmond: Jill Pound-Corner, 'How to Live in a Match-Box', *ES* 28 March 1963.

36. 'Paddington.'

37. 'Good Buys in Gilbert's Bower', *LPL* 4, March 1963 (2).

38. 'Blackheath: Georgian Spic and Span', *LPL* 11, July 1963 (1).

39. 'Camden Town.'

40. 'Greenwich.'

41. 'Paddington.'

42. For Cleaver Square see J. Bastian, 'An Old Square Gets with It', *Ideal Home* June 1964.

43. P. Rawstorne, 'The Lambeth Settlers', *Guardian* 13 May 1963; for Broomhall see Powell, 'Living In.'

44. Quoted in Sharpley, 'Murder Grove, Part V.'

45. B. A. Taylor, 'The Home Page', *ES* 28 January 1965.

46. 'Sweat equity' is the term used by, among other students of gentrification, David Ley, *The New Middle Class and the Remaking of the Central City* (Oxford, 1996), p. 46.

47. 'Holland Park: Back in the Family Way', *LPL* 66, 23 October 1965.

48. Quotation from Pansy Jeffrey, representing the Notting Hill CAB, 17 February 1964, in TNA HLG 39/66. See also, e.g., the evidence of Willesden Borough Council, TNA HLG 39/16, Michael Cliffs, MP, 6 July 1964, TNA HLG 39/67.

49. A. Duncan, 'Public Servant', *ES* 30 November 1967.

50. 'Contemporary Furnishing', *LPL* 104, 27 May 1967; A. Holmes, *Better than No Place* (London, 1971), p. 8.

51. B. Adams, J. Griffin & S. Proudman, *A Study of Rent Tribunal Cases in London* (London, 1971), pp. 30, 36–37.

52. 'Renewal of Residential Areas. Taylor Woodrow's Proposal at Fulham. Note of a Meeting on 18 January 1963', and Memo by J. Delafons, MHLG, 'Fulham Pilot Study', 7 May 1963, both TNA HLG/131/81.

53. 'Renewal of Residential Areas. Note of a Meeting on 18 January 1963', TNA HLG 118/266; Report of Planning Committee (no. 1), 2 December 1963, in Metropolitan Borough of Fulham, *Minutes*, 18 December 1963, Hammersmith and Fulham Local Studies Centre.

54. Unnamed LCC planning officer, quoted in S. Elkin, *Politics and Land Use Planning. The London Experience* (Cambridge, 1974), p. 32.

55. Taylor Woodrow Group, *Urban Renewal: Fulham Study* (London, 1963), pp. 16, 17.

56. Ibid., p. 16.

57. J. Delafons to A. Sylvester-Evans, 9 October 1963, 'Fulham Pilot Study', TNA HLG 131/81.

58. 'Where the Slums Are Paved with Gold.'

59. R. Maugham, *Escape from the Shadows* (London, 1972), p. 215; J.G., 'Fashionable World's End', *West London Press and Chelsea News* 30 March 1962; 'The Battle of Seaton Street', *Sunday Times* 8 April 1962.

60. W. Roland, 'The World's End Has "It" Now', *ES* 23 May 1963.

61. 'When They Pull Down This House I'll Stand and Cheer', *West London Press and Chelsea News* 20 April 1962; 'World's End Hopes and Fears', *West London Press and Chelsea News* 6 April 1962; 'In Fashionable Chelsea: Young Children 4 Years in Condemned Basement', *West London Press and Chelsea News* 30 March 1962.

62. 'The House That Mr Turner Built'; 'World's End? I Hope No-one Touches It'; 'World's End Hopes and Fears', all in *West London Press and Chelsea News* 6 April 1962.

63. E. J. Taylor, 'How CAN They Oppose This Scheme?', *West London Press and Chelsea News* 29 January 1965; J. Brent, 'World's End. I Say Let the Whole Lot Come Down', *West London Press and Chelsea News* 13 April 1962.

64. 'Converting: Ten Commandments', *LPL* 153, 14 June 1969.

65. 'Kennington Comes Clean', *LPL* 144, 25 January 1969.

66. J. Hillman, 'London Homes—Big Step Up', *ES* 20 September 1965.

67. T. E. North, Borough Architect, LB Newham, 'Report to the Housing Committee, 12 September 1966', quoted in P. Dunleavy, *The Politics of Mass Housing in Britain, 1945–1975* (Oxford, 1981), p. 237.

68. J. Hillman, 'Bang on the Homes Target!', *ES* 23 January 1967.

69. J. Hillman, '1000 Skyscrapers—but Is the End in Sight Now?', *ES* 15 August 1968; 'Council Plans Assault on Housing Black Spots', *ES* 8 May 1967.

70. 'Panic in N19?', *LPL* 16, September 1963 (2).

71. A. McGill, 'All That Stands between My Sort of Dump and My Dream House Are Those Beastly Building Society Rules', *ES* 17 April 1963.

72. W. Roland, 'Is Your House Now Worth More than You Paid?', *ES* 9 January 1967.

73. 'Go Catch a Falling Market', *LPL* 66, 23 October 1965.

74. 'Profile for Investor-Occupiers: Islington', *LPL* 97, 11 February 1967.

75. 'Portrait of an Agent: John Birrane', *LPL* 9, June 1963 (1); 'Portrait of a Property Columbus', *LPL* 23, January 1964 (1); 'How to Get Started. Finance for a £500,000 Venture', *LPL* 139, 9 November 1968.

76. 'Portrait of a Property Columbus', *LPL* 23, January 1964 (1).

77. J. Raban, *Soft City* (London, 1974), p. 186.

78. Ibid., pp. 183–84, 189.

79. Shirley Linden, quoted in Sharpley, 'Murder Grove, Part V.'

80. Raban, *Soft City*, p. 185. For a less caustic account of middle-class associationalism, see Martin Wainwright's description of Alma Street in Kentish Town: 'The Way We Live Now', *ES* 19 October 1976.

81. Sharpley, 'Murder Grove, Part V.'

82. J. Ferris, *Participation in Urban Planning. The Barnsbury Case: A Study of Environmental Improvement in London* (London, 1972). A similar scheme was implemented in Battersea in 1975–76: I. Munt, 'Economic Restructuring, Culture and Gentrification. A Case Study in Battersea, London', *Environment and Planning. A* 19 (9), 1987, 1195.

83. 'Kentish Town Capers', *LPL* 186, 14 November 1970.

84. John White, quoted in 'Portrait of a Property Columbus.'

85. 'Canonbury: Shot in the Arm', *LPL* 181, 6 August 1970.

86. 'Fulham Study. London Planning Aspects', appended to Memorandum 'Twilight Areas', 2 January 1963, TNA HLG 118/266.

87. H. Brack, 'London's Twilight Streets', *ES* 15 August 1967.

88. 'Upgrading Highbury', *LPL* 161, 11 October 1969. See also 'Up the Junction', *LPL* 194, September 1971; 'W6', *LPL* 39, 12 September 1964; 'Geography for Converters', *LPL* 150, 26 April 1969.

89. Memo 'Fulham Study', 3 December 1963, TNA HLG 131/81.

90. 'Fulham Revisited', *LPL* 25, 1 February 1964; 'Why Let Sleeping Shops Lie?', *LPL* 4, March 1963 (2).

91. 'Moore Park, Fulham: King's Ransom', *LPL* 140, 23 November 1968.

92. M. Hastings, 'How Britannia Road Went Up in the World', *ES* 4 October 1979.

93. 'Stockwell', *LPL* 5, April 1963 (1), 'Deptford', *LPL* 7, May 1963 (1).

94. 'Better Buys at Barnsbury', *LPL* 170, 28 February 1970.

95. Milner Holland Committee, *Report*, pp. 69–70. Ruth Glass calculated that while 47 percent of households in Greater London consisted of one or two persons, only 8 percent of dwellings were appropriate for that household size: witness evidence to the Milner Holland Committee, 24 February 1964, TNA HLG 39/66.

96. 'Chelsea', *LPL* 49, 13 February 1965.

97. 'Kookie New Cross', *LPL* 174, 25 April 1970; 'Elevating Ealing', *LPL* 176, 23 May 1970.

98. 'Wandsworth: The Common Touch', *LPL* 86, 27 August 1966.

99. Grace Matthews, quoted in M. Macpherson, 'Neighbourly Strife as the Rich Move In', *ES*, 15 August 1977.

100. '"The Days of the Lash-Up Boys Are Numbered"', *LPL* 101, 8 April 1967.

101. Memo 'Fulham Study', 3 December 1963, TNA HLG 131/81.

102. Greater London Council, *The Condition of London's Housing—A Survey* (Department of Planning and Transportation Intelligence Unit Research Report 4, August 1970). For borough figures see Table 4.21, p. 137.

103. Ministry of Housing and Local Government, *Old Houses into New Homes* (Cmnd. 3602, 1968), p. 1, Table 1, p. 16.

104. Ibid., pp. 3–4.

105. B. Crofton, 'The London Problem—Some Solutions', *Housing Review* 22 (5), September–October 1973, 174.

106. S. Merrett with F. Gray, *Owner Occupation in Britain* (London, 1982), p. 32; P. N. Balchin, *Housing Improvement and Social Inequality. Case Study of an Inner City* (London, 1979), pp. 13ff.

107. Housing Act, 1969, ss. 2–6.

108. Holmes, *Better than No Place*, p. 86.

109. 'A Facelift for £875', *ES* 28 April 1972.

110. 'Conversion Grants Whitewash', *LPL* 163, 8 November 1969.

111. R. M. Langdon, St Petersburgh Properties Ltd, 3 April 1973, in House of Commons Expenditure Committee, Environment and Home Office Sub-Committee, *Tenth Report, Session 1972–3, Minutes of Evidence* (HC 349-II), Q. 1773, p. 441; see also E. W. Church, Limerston Securities Ltd, ibid., Q. 1740, p. 439.

112. P. Cousins, Memo, 'Housing Bill', 14 January 1969, TNA T 224/1782.

113. D. Wilcox, 'How to Peg the Cost of a House', *ES* 10 April 1972.

114. 'Conversion Grants Whitewash.'

115. Balchin, *Housing Improvement*, pp. 27–28.

116. 'Balham: Gateway to the South', *LPL* 216, July 1973; 'How Fares Finsbury Park?', *LPL* 210, January 1973; 'A Plug for Peckham', *LPL* 190, May 1971; 'Where Have the Grotty Suburbs Gone?', *LPL* 201, April 1972.

117. E. Pearson, 'Get a "New Home" from the Town Hall', *ES* 28 April 1972.

118. B. Kilroy, 'Improvement Grants Threaten North Kensington', *Housing Review* 21 (3), May–June 1972, 81.

119. J. Norridge, 'Someone Still Lives Here', *ES* 11 July 1972.

120. Balchin, *Housing Improvement*, p. 20.

121. Kilroy, 'Improvement Grants', 80; 'Improvement Grant Mayhem', *LPL* 210, January 1973.

122. Joint Report (29.1.1963) by Architect and Director of Housing, 'Survey on Living in High Blocks', London Metropolitan Archives (LMA) GLC/HG/CHTS/04/13.

123. 'Living off the Ground', *Architects' Journal* 20 August 1969.

124. J. Hillman, 'Today Lambeth, Tomorrow . . .', *ES* 9 November 1965.

125. Dunleavy, *Politics of Mass Housing*, p. 242.

126. H. Brack, 'Are We Building the Slums of Tomorrow?', *ES*, 23 November 1965; J. Hillman, 'Labour Party Kicks Out Mr Brack', *ES* 9 December 1965.

127. E.g., in Newham, Dunleavy, *Politics of Mass Housing*, p. 236.

128. Holmes, *Better than No Place*, pp. 54–55, 80–81.

129. Department of the Environment, Action Group on London Housing, *The Public Sector Housing Pipeline in London* (London, 1976), p. 51.

130. Greve, Page & Greve, *Homelessness in London*, p. 123; R. Bailey & J. Ruddock, *The Grief Report. A Shelter Report on Temporary Accommodation* (London, 1972), pp. 13–15.

131. Greve, Page & Greve, *Homelessness in London*, p. 127.

132. Ibid., Figure 1, p. 57.

133. Community Development Project, *Whatever Happened to Council Housing?* (London, 1976), p. 86.

134. P. Harrison, 'Tower Hamlets: A Social Services Case Study', *New Society* 7 December 1972; J. Morton, 'London's Housing Transfer', *New Society* 5 December 1968.

135. Officials in Barking and Newham, quoted in Bailey & Ruddock, *Grief Report*, pp. 35, 38–39.

136. J. Davis, '"The Most Fun I've Ever Had"? Squatting in England in the 1970s', in F. Anders & A. Sedlmaier, *Public Goods versus Economic Interests: Global Perspectives on the History of Squatting* (London, 2016), pp. 237–54.

137. C. Jackson, *Lambeth Interface. Housing, Planning and Community Action in an Inner London Borough* (Croydon, 1975), p. 30.

138. J. Norridge & V. Jenkins, 'If You're Young and Healthy Find Your Own Place', *ES* 17 September 1970.

139. M. Kinghan, *Squatters in London* (London, 1977), pp. 22, 25.

140. Margaret Watson, Housing Chair, Islington, interviewed in *Islington Gutter Press* 21, June–July 1975.

141. 'Sale of Council Houses, 1967–1979', LMA GLC/HG/HHM/03/A427.

142. Report (3.5.67) by the Treasurer, etc., 'Sale of Council Houses—Circular 24/67', LMA GLC/HG/HHM/03/A427.

143. H. Brack, 'Are GLC Houses a Good Buy?', *ES* 23 May 1967.

144. J. Hillman, 'But What Do the Tenants Say?', *ES* 27 February 1967.

145. Director of Housing and the Valuer and Estates Surveyor, 'Sale of Council Houses. Policy', Joint Report (8.5.1973), LMA GLC/HG/HHM/03/A427.

146. Director of Housing and Valuer and Estates Surveyor, 'Sale of Council Houses', Joint Report (24.9.68), LMA GLC/HG/HHM/03/A427.

147. K. Allen, 'Bingo! It's the Big Boom in Council Houses', *Evening News* 10 August 1972.

148. M. F. King, 'Now—10,000 Council House Owners', *ES* 20 July 1972; Director of Housing and the Valuer and Estates Surveyor, 'Sale of Council Houses. Policy.'

149. King, 'Now—10,000 Council House Owners.'

150. Hillman, 'But What Do the Tenants Say?'

151. J. Morton, 'Raising Council Rents', *New Society* 14 August 1969; H. Brack, 'Pay Up? I'd Rather Pitch a Tent', *ES* 25 August 1969; B. Moorhouse, M. Wilson and C. Chamberlain, 'Rent Strikes—Direct Action and the Working Class', *Socialist Register* 1972, pp. 140ff.

152. M. F. King, 'Council Chief Quits in Row over Rents', *ES* 8 May 1972, for Wandsworth; D. Wilcox, 'Camden Ends War over Fair Rents', *ES* 10 January 1973.

153. M. Harloe, R. Issacharoff & R. Minns, *The Organization of Housing. Public and Private Enterprise in London* (London, 1974), pp. 33–34.

154. Brack, 'Pay Up?'

155. M. Bowley, *Economic Report on Rent Problems*, vol. 3 of London Borough of Camden *Housing in Camden* (London, 1968), p. 6.

156. Department of the Environment, *Housing Policy. Technical Volume*, Part III (London, 1977), pp. 41–42; J. Morton, 'London's Costly Council Housing', *New Society* 9 April 1970.

157. R. Balfe, *Housing in London. A New Socialist Perspective* (London, 1976), pp. 1–2, 4, 6, 8.

158. S. Jenkins, 'The Holes in Shelter's Roof', *ES* 12 August 1976.

159. Department of the Environment, Action Group on London Housing, *Public Sector Housing Pipeline in London*, pp. 38–39; R. Balfe, 'Why It Takes So Long', *Municipal Engineering* 11 March 1977.

160. D. Eversley, 'Collapse of the Council House?', *ES* 26 October 1976.

161. S. Marks, 'In London's Housing Trap', *New Society* 8 September 1977.

162. M. King, 'Tories Ready to Sell Off 500,000 Homes', *ES* 22 June 1978.

163. H. Brack, 'Half Way to Councilville', *ES* 18 December 1978.

164. GLC, Housing Investment Programme, 1980–1984, *London's Housing Needs: An Appraisal of Strategy* (July 1979), LMA GLC/DG/PUB/01/338, pp. 20–22.

165. House of Commons Environment Committee, *Council House Sales*, Minutes of Evidence, 19 June 1980 (HC 535-x), Q. 884, p. 296.

166. J. Barry & P. Knightley, '£826,000,000 a Year Down the Drain', *Sunday Times* 22 August 1976.

167. For the eventual version, G. Shankland, P. Willmott & D. Jordan, *Inner London: Policies for Dispersal and Balance. Final Report of the London Inner Area Study* (London, 1977), pp. 124ff.

168. The two drafts of Henney's memorandum, dated 4 June and 22 June 1976, are in the file 'Reappraisal of London Housing Strategy', TNA HLG 118/2096.

169. Memo by A. Z. Levy, 4 March 1976, TNA HLG 118/2096.

170. 'London Housing Study. Note of Meeting Held in HM Treasury, Thursday 9 November 1978', in 'Finance Housing Policy: Reassessment of the Need for Housing Investment in London', TNA AT 45/42.

171. Memo 'London Housing Issues' by J. A. L. Gunn, Department of the Environment, 14 November 1978, TNA AT 45/42.

172. Memo by Gunn, 11 October 1978; Memo by M. S. Albu, 25 September 1978; P. W. Rumble to Cllr. J. Mills, LB Camden, 'Housebuilding Cost Controls', 16 January 1979, TNA AT 45/42.

173. Memo by Albu, 25 September 1978, TNA AT 45/42.

174. Memo 'London HIPS' by P. W. Wilde, 4 December 1978; Memo by Albu, 25 September 1978, TNA AT 45/42.

175. J. Page, 'The Landlords', *ES* 20 October 1970.

176. C. Gray, 'When a Bad Tenant Just Won't Budge', *ES* 14 August 1974.

177. K. Wheatley, 'Why a Landlord Wishes Her Tenants Would Die', *ES* 20 July 1978.

178. R. Northedge, 'London—the Backdoor City', *ES* 15 May 1978.

179. K. Murphy, 'A Long and Dismal Trail Brings Only Sore Feet', *ES* 17 September 1974.

180. According to Gillian Diamond of After Six: D. Wilcox, 'The Rent Act Mis-fires on Flat-Hunters', *ES* 4 April 1975.

181. S. Godfree, 'Intervention and the Changing Role of the Local Housing Authority: The London Case', *Greater London Intelligence Bulletin* 41, September 1978, 5.

182. G. Tindall, 'Where Have All the Bedsits Gone?' *ES* 6 November 1978.

183. Editorial, *LPL* 9, June 1963 (1).

184. R. Langton, 'The Rent-Hit Young Londoners Go on a Home-Buying Spree', *ES* 27 April 1977.

185. R. Bourne, 'The Rule Is: Keep Looking', *ES* 20 November 1978.

186. 'The Year When Prices Went Crazy', *LPL* 198, January 1972.

187. 'Children Create Friendships in Quiet Grove', *Harrow Observer* 6 October 1972.

188. R. Northedge, 'First Time Unlucky', *ES* 12 April 1979; R. Northedge, 'Homes "Too Dear for First-Time Buyers"', *ES* 2 July 1979; S. Thomas, 'No Welcome for Nigel', *ES* 2 August 1979.

189. L. Murdin, 'Hot Property: It's Mine', *ES* 6 February 1979.

190. J. Marsden, *House Prices in London. An Economic Analysis of London's Housing Market* (Greater London Authority Working Paper 72, London, 2015), Table 3, p. 20.

191. 'Battle against Rachmanism. MP Ben Parkin Answers His Accusers', *Paddington Mercury* 19 March 1965; *Hansard Parliamentary Debates*, House of Commons, 24 July 1963, c. 1474.

192. H. Cutler, *The Cutler Files* (London, 1982), p. 130.

193. Milner Holland Committee, *Report*, p. 24.

194. Holmans, *Historical Statistics of Housing in Britain*, p. 270 and Table 2.14, p. 284.

195. J. Norridge, 'Just Who Can Afford to Buy a House in London?', *ES* 21 August 1970.

196. Holmes, *Better than No Place*, p. 37.

197. Minority Party Report (No. 2)—*GLC Housing Strategy Appraisal, 1981–83—As Suppressed by the Leader of the Housing Policy Committee*, LMA GLC/DG/PUB/01/338.

198. Woolf, *Housing Survey in England and Wales*, p. 25; Milner Holland Committee, *Report*, p. 156.

199. 'Fulham Study', 3 December 1963, in TNA HLG 131/81.

200. 1981 Census, *County Report, Greater London, Part 1* (London, 1982), Table 20, pp. 198ff.

201. A survey of 750 council tenants in Camden, Brent and Harrow in 1973–74 found that if cost was left out of account, 58 percent of them would prefer to own, but of this group only 13 percent expressed themselves dissatisfied with their current accommodation, with no evidence that tenants in modern flats were more eager to move than other respondents were. C. Whitehead with C. Lambert, 'Tenure Preference: What Council Tenants Want', *CES Review* 9, April 1980, 35.

202. M. Swenarton, *Cook's Camden: The Making of Modern Housing* (London, 2017); D. Eversley, 'Collapse of the Council House?'

203. R. E. Pahl, 'Foreword', in Harloe, Issacharoff & Minns, *Organization of Housing*, p. x.

204. Milner Holland Committee, *Report*, p. 224.

205. C. M. E. Whitehead & M. Kleinman, 'Private Renting in London: Is It So Different?', *Journal of Social Policy* 16 (3), 1987, 319–20.

206. Norridge & Jenkins, 'If You're Young and Healthy.'

207. The investigation by the British Market Research Bureau in 1975 found that nearly 70 percent in all tenures wished to be owner-occupiers within two years: National Economic Development Office, *BMRB Housing Consumer Survey. A Survey of Attitudes towards Current and Alternative Housing Policies* (London, 1977), Supplementary Table Volume, Table 75, p. 92. London figures cannot be isolated in this survey, but there are some indicators in A. Harrison & G. Lomas, 'Tenure Preference: How to Interpret the Survey Evidence', *CES Review* 8, January 1980, 20.

Chapter 6

This is a much revised version of the essay published as '"Simple Solutions to Complex Problems." The Greater London Council and the Greater London Development Plan, 1965–1973', in J. Harris, ed., *Civil Society in British History. Ideas, Identities, Institutions* (Oxford, 2003).

1. V. D. Lipman, Assistant Secretary, Planning, MHLG, in 'Meeting of Officers from Government Departments and Officers of the Greater London Council, . . . County Hall . . . 7th June 1966', p. 2, London Metropolitan Archives (LMA) GLC/TD/LU/01/096.

2. Planning Advisory Group, *The Future of Development Plans* (London, 1965), p. 1.

3. Ibid., p. 9.

4. Ibid., pp. 11, 39, 53.

5. Quotations from GLDP Preliminary Report, Autumn 1966, p. 2, and GLC/London Borough Councils, Joint Working Party on Town Planning, 'The Purpose and Nature of the Greater London Development Plan', 31 January 1966, p. 3, both in Stott papers, LMA GLC/TD/CTD/02/020 (1).

6. For which see D. A. Hart, *Strategic Planning in London. The Rise and Fall of the Primary Road Network* (Oxford, 1976), pp. 117–21.

7. From the summary of research material in 'Toward Policies for Central London—Appendix IV', Stott papers, LMA GLC/TD/CTD/02/020(1).

8. H. A. Tripp, *Road Traffic and Its Control* (London, 1938); H. A. Tripp, *Town Planning and Road Traffic* (London, 1942); M. Dnes, *The Rise and Fall of London's Ringways, 1943–1973* (New York, 2019), pp. 12–16; S. Gunn & S. Townsend, *Automobility and the City in Twentieth Century Britain and Japan* (London, 2019), p. 21.

9. Tripp, *Road Traffic and Its Control*, p. 328.

10. P. Abercrombie, *The Greater London Plan, 1944* (London, 1945), p. 67; Hart, *Strategic Planning in London*, p. 75.

11. Tripp, *Road Traffic and Its Control*, pp. 291–92.

12. Ministry of Transport, *Traffic in Towns: A Study of the Long-Term Problems of Traffic in Urban Areas* (London, 1963), p. 7; S. Gunn, 'The Buchanan Report, Environment and the Problem of Traffic in 1960s Britain', *Twentieth Century British History* 22 (4), 2011, 521–42.

13. B. Edwards & D. Gilbert, 'Piazzadilly! The Reimagining of Piccadilly Circus, 1957–72', *Planning Perspectives* 23 (4), 2008, 472ff.

14. Dnes, *Rise and Fall of London's Ringways*, p. 63.

15. London County Council (LCC) and Ministry of Transport, *London Traffic Survey* (London, 1964), p. 159.

16. P. F. Stott, 'Memorandum on the Future of London Communications, with Particular Reference to the Safeguarding of a Motorway Ring', February 1965, p. 3, Stott papers, LMA GLC/TD/CTD/02/028(1).

17. Tripp, *Town Planning and Road Traffic*, pp. 61, 66.

18. S. Jenkins, 'Out of Farce and into Tragedy', *Evening Standard (ES)* 20 February 1973.

19. A detailed description of the proposed or probable Ringway routes is provided by W. Asher, *Rings around London. Orbital Motorways and the Battle for Homes before Roads* (London, 2018), Appendix, pp. 160–69.

20. Dnes, *Rise and Fall of London's Ringways*, pp. 77–78.

21. O. Saumarez Smith, *Boom Cities. Architect Planners and the Politics of Radical Urban Renewal in 1960s Britain* (Oxford, 2019), pp. 58–59; Hart, *Strategic Planning in London*, p. 56.

22. M. F. Collins & T. F. Pharoah, *The Organisation of Transport in a Great City. The Case of London* (London, 1974), Table 45, p. 539.

23. S. Jenkins, 'And *That's* the End of the London Motorway Box', *ES* 18 November 1969.

24. J. Blake, 'The Growth of Traffic in Greater London. Buchanan and London Traffic Survey Too Alarmist?', *Surveyor—Local Government Technology* 19 October 1968, 34–35.

25. LCC and Ministry of Transport, *London Traffic Survey*, p. 159; S. Gunn, 'People and the Car. The Expansion of Automobility in Urban Britain, c. 1955–1970', *Social History* 38 (2), 2013, 234.

26. Robert Vigars, quoted in J. M. Thomson, *Motorways in London* (London, 1969), p. 51; Stott, 'Memorandum on the Future of London Communications', p. 3.

27. P. F. Stott, 'Presenting the Case for the GLDP: A Personal View', 30 July 1969, J. R. Fitzpatrick papers, LMA GLC/TD/DPT/02/002.

28. Memorandum by T. J. Widaker and B. V. Martin on the GLDP Studies Volume, 22 March 1968, p. 1, Stott papers, LMA GLC/TD/CTD/02/020(1).

29. GLDP Preliminary Report, Autumn 1966, p. 4, Stott papers, LMA GLC/TD/CTD/02/020(1).

30. J. R. Fitzpatrick, Memorandum 'The GLC in the Field of Highways and Transportation. The Situation in April 1967', Fitzpatrick papers, LMA GLC/TD/DPT/02/009.

31. S. Dermen, NW5, Obj. 17921, LMA GLC/TD/GLDP/09/175, original capitals.

32. Brief for meeting with members of the Skeffington Committee, 19 December 1968, LMA GLC/TD/PM/PC/01/016.

33. Note by J. R. Fitzpatrick to B. Collins, 'The Form of Inquiry for Structure Plans', 12 December 1971, Stott papers, LMA GLC/TD/CTD/02/062 (2).

34. R. Vigars, 'We Will Build It!', *ES* 20 November 1969.

35. D. Starkie, *The Motorway Age. Road and Traffic Policies in Postwar Britain* (Oxford, 1982), p. 72; Asher, *Rings around London*, p. 54.

36. GLDP Inquiry, Objection 17 (M. Geare, W4), LMA GLC/TD/GLDP/09/001.

37. GLDP Inquiry, Objection 18225 (P. Sherlock, NW6), LMA GLC/TD/GLDP/09/178.

38. GLDP Inquiry, Objection 2247 (A. Hedin, NW3), LMA GLC/TD/GLDP/09/023.

39. At the Camden meeting 54 percent of those present from Camden, 35 percent of those from Islington and 35 percent of those from Westminster were owner-occupiers against 1966 Census figures of 12 percent, 14 percent and 7 percent for those boroughs as a whole. At the Croydon meeting the figures were 82 percent / 55 percent for Croydon and 80 percent / 63 percent for Sutton. M. Harris & M. Myers, 'The Public Meeting as a Means of Participation', GLC, *Quarterly Bulletin of the Research and Intelligence Unit* 9, December 1969, 5.

40. GLDP Inquiry, Inquiry Support S27/92 (Ringway 2 Resistance Group), LMA GLC/TD/GLDP/08/595.

41. GLDP Inquiry, Inquiry Support S27/159 (M. Bayly, Bromley, Kent), LMA GLC/TD/GLDP/08/595.

42. Joint Report of Planning and Transportation Committee and Strategic Planning Committee, 14–15 July 1969, in GLC Minutes, 22 July 1969. This indiscretion was noticed by Mrs M. Grosvenor, GLDP Inquiry, Inquiry Support S27/94, LMA GLC/TD/GLDP/08/595.

43. By extension, one of the very few instances of positive support for the road proposals came from working-class tenants along the West Cross Route (now the M41) who hoped that the motorway would get them rehoused. N. Raynsford, 'Motorway Madness', *Community Action* 2, April–May 1972, on the Townmead Road area meeting.

44. D. Donnison, 'The Micro-Politics of the City', in D. Donnison & D. Eversley, eds., *London. Urban Patterns, Problems and Policies* (London, 1973), pp. 383–404.

45. Hart, *Strategic Planning in London*, p. 157.

46. Collins & Pharoah, *Transport Organisation in a Great City*, p. 125.

47. H. Gilmore, Ealing Residents (Cleveland Ward) Association, GLDP Inquiry, Notes of Proceedings, 68th Day, 12 March 1971, p. 19, LMA GLC/TD/GLDP/08/070. Gilmore had himself been an Ealing councillor for nine years.

48. Harris & Myers, 'Public Meeting', p. 5.

49. Advertisement in *Community Action* 5, November–December 1972; D. Eversley, *The Planner in Society. The Changing Role of a Profession* (London, 1973), p. 210.

50. 'Objections—Situation at 10 A.M.', 10 March 1970', LMA GLC/TD/LU/01/103.

51. E.g., the Federation of Ravensbourne Residents Associations, a collection of twenty-four local groups brought together by the creation of the London Borough of Bromley in 1965: GLDP Inquiry, Notes of Proceedings, 88th Day, 19 April 1971 (G. C. Jenkins, Bromley Residents Association), p. 2, LMA GLC/TD/GLDP/08/090.

52. A. Power, *A Battle Lost—Barnsbury, 1972* (London, 1972).

53. 'Brief History of the Barnsbury Association', with the association's submission to the Skeffington Committee, TNA HLG 136/267.

54. E.g., GLC, *Greater London Development Plan. Statement* (London, 1969), p. 11.

55. Barnsbury Association to A.Skeffington, 8 July 1968, in TNA HLG 136/267.

56. 'Objections—Situation at 10 A.M.'

57. 'Notes on Objections to the GLDP. Section 2: Transport', summary of Thomson by A. M. Voorhees, 23 July 1970, LMA GLC/TD/LU/01/103.

58. Thomson, *Motorways in London.*

59. W. Solesbury, 'The Needs of Environmental Planning', Background Paper, Symposium on Environmental Planning, Churchill College, Cambridge, January 1969, p. 5, TNA HLG 136/278.

60. Mr Ward, Chiswick Motorway Liaison Group, GLDP Inquiry, Notes of Proceedings, 91st Day, 22 April 1971, p. 46, LMA GLC/TD/GLDP/08/093.

61. GLDP Inquiry, Notes of Proceedings, 41st Day, 1 January 1971 (Mrs Jackson, Grove Park Group), p. 31, LMA GLC/TD/GLDP/08/043.

62. S. E. Rasmussen, *London, the Unique City* (London, 1936). Rasmussen was specifically cited by N. Jackson, Grove Park Group, GLDP Inquiry, Notes of Proceedings, 41st Day, 1 January 1971, p. 32, LMA GLC/TD/GLDP/08/043.

63. R. F. Marsh, St Pancras Civic Society, GLDP Inquiry, Notes of Proceedings, 41st Day, 1 January 1971, p. 27, LMA GLC/TD/GLDP/08/043.

64. GLDP Inquiry, Inquiry Support S27/103 (Barnes Motorway Action Group), LMA GLC/TD/GLDP/08/595; Inquiry Proofs E27/57 (Lewisham Society), LMA GLC/TD/GLDP/08/548; E27/93 (Cllr. J. Daly, L. B. Hounslow), LMA GLC/TD/GLDP/08/551; Objection 9163 (Harry Brack, for Tower Hamlets Society), LMA GLC/TD/GLDP/09/087, for Isle of Dogs.

65. GLDP Inquiry, Inquiry Support S27/25 (W. T. Newtold, Highgate), LMA GLC/TD/GLDP/08/592; Inquiry Proof E27/45 (Grove Park Group), LMA GLC/TD/GLDP/08/548.

66. 'The Domesday Book shows that Baddintone manor was then occupied by one Robert de Wateville . . .', GLDP Inquiry, Inquiry Support S27/111 (Beddington & Wallington Ratepayers & Residents Association), p. 5, LMA GLC/TD/GLDP/08/595.

67. GLDP Inquiry, Inquiry Proofs E27/96 (A. Best, Bedford Park), LMA GLC/TD/GLDP/08/551; E27/57 (Lewisham Society), p. 3, LMA GLC/TD/GLDP/08/595, though see the submission of the Blackheath Society, E27/56, p. 12, LMA GLC/TD/GLDP/08/595.

68. GLDP Inquiry, Notes of Proceedings, 91st Day, 22 April 1971 (G. Foley, Chiswick Group), p. 10, LMA GLC/TD/GLDP/08/093.

69. E.g., Neil Jackson, Grove Park Group, GLDP Inquiry, Notes of Proceedings, 41st Day, 1 January 1971, p. 33, LMA GLC/TD/GLDP/08/043, Cleveland Ward, Ealing, Residents Association, Objection 58, LMA GLC/TD/GLDP/09/058. J. Jacobs, *The Death and Life of Great American Cities. The Failure of Town Planning* (Harmondsworth, 1964).

70. GLDP Inquiry, Objection 2247 (A. Hedin, NW3), LMA GLC/TD/GLDP/09/023.

71. GLDP Inquiry Support, S27/169 (Mrs E. Dalton), LMA GLC/TD/GLDP/08/596.

72. D. Beecham, GLDP Inquiry, Notes of Proceedings, 2nd Day, 8 July 1970, p. 13, LMA GLC/TD/GLDP/08/004.

73. GLDP Inquiry, Objection 16923 (D. Wiggins, SW7), Obj. 16900 (P. F. Strawson, Oxford), both in LMA GLC/TD/GLDP/09/165.

74. Jacobs, *The Death and Life of Great American Cities*, p. 83.

75. GLDP Inquiry, Inquiry Support S27/318 (D. E. Hennessy), LMA GLC/TD/GLDP/08/577.

76. GLDP Inquiry, Objection 2693 (G. M. Howell, NW3), LMA GLC/TD/GLDP/09/027. The reference is to the widespread belief that the concrete of the Bow Flyover contained the remains of the Krays' henchman Frank Mitchell, axe man and Dartmoor escapee. See W. G. Ramsey, *The East End Then and Now* (London, 1997), p. 508.

77. GLDP Inquiry, Objection 16841 (A. N. Dalton, Reigate), LMA GLC/TD/GLDP/09/164; Obj. 18081 (P. & R. Facey, Westbourne Park Road), LMA GLC/TD/GLDP/09/176.

78. GLDP Inquiry, Inquiry Proof E27/94 (Rev. J. McCarthy, Chiswick), LMA GLC/TD/GLDP/08/551.

79. Stott's cv is included with his papers in LMA GLC/TD/CTD/02/062 (11).

80. 'GLDP. Progress and Publicity. Joint Report by the Clerk to the Council and the Director of Planning', 7 July 1966, Stott papers, LMA GLC/TD/CTD/02/020 (2).

81. 'Co-operation and the Public', note by Mr Burns, July 1967, Town and Country Planning Bill, 1968, Bill papers, TNA HLG 29/774.

82. 'Participation and All That'. Conference Report of the Standing Conference of Councils of Social Service, Durham, September 1969, p. 33, London Council of Social Service papers, LMA ACC/1888/246/006.

83. Memorandum from J. G. S. Wallace to Mr Bourne, 28 May 1968, LMA GLC/TD/PM/PC/01/016.

84. Notes on meeting with Skeffington Committee, December 1968, LMA GLC/TD/PM/PC/01/016.

85. 'Vigars on the Missing Link', *Times* 24 July 1968.

86. Memorandum 'Public Relations', 4 April 1970, LMA GLC/TD/PM/PC/01/017.

87. GLDP Inquiry, Objection 2625, LMA GLC/TD/GLDP/09/027.

88. 'We pray in aid the role of the elected member in opposition to the idea of community forums, community development officers, etc', note by Dunning, 3 April 1970, LMA GLC/TD/PM/PC/01/017.

89. 'Public Participation in Planning. Observations on the Draft prepared by Mr Lewis', 24 March 1970, LMA GLC/TD/PM/PC/01/017.

90. 'Notes on Views of County and County Borough Planning Officers in Wales', p. 20, Skeffington Committee, Digest of Evidence to 27 June 1968, TNA HLG 136/269.

91. 'Notes of a Meeting with the London Borough Councils . . . 4 July 1968', LMA GLC/TD/PM/PO/022.

92. 'Planning and the Public', Draft Report by the Director General and the Director of Planning, n.d. [1968?], in LMA GLC/TD/PM/PC/01/016.

93. 'Building New Roads: Compensation and Blight', paper read by Kenneth Blessley, Valuer, Greater London Council, Roads Campaign Council, House of Commons, 18 February 1969, pp. 6–7, LMA GLC/TD/CTD/02/004 (3).

94. D. Plummer, 'Homes versus Roads', *ES* 20 January 1969.

95. Memorandum from Dunning to Joint Directors of Planning and Transportation, 2 January 1970, LMA GLC/TD/PM/PC/01/016.

96. Adgroup Organisation, 'The Use of Public Relations and Advertising Techniques in Easing London's Traffic Problems', n.d. [1966], p. 7, LMA GLC/TD/PM/PO/02/021.

97. 'GLC Taken to Task at Mini-Conference', *Acton Gazette and Post* 16 January 1969.

98. Vaughan to Skeffington, 11 February 1969, in Skeffington Committee, correspondence with local authorities, TNA HLG 136/285.

99. J. G. S. Wallace, Draft Report of Strategic Planning, General Purposes and Planning and Transportation Committees on Public Participation in Planning, 11 April 1969, LMA GLC/TD/PM/PC/01/016.

100. E.g., at the St Pancras meeting, J. Hillman, 'Will the New London Put People First?', *Hampstead and Highgate Express* 21 February 1969.

101. GLDP Inquiry, Objection 9880 (P. Ayrton, N5), LMA GLC/TD/GLDP/09/094.

102. Starkie, *Motorway Age*, p. 77; Asher, *Rings around London*, pp. 88–90; Dnes, *Rise and Fall of London's Ringways*, pp. 100–103.

103. GLDP Inquiry, Notes of Proceedings, 94th Day, 27 April 1971 (W. Bor & P. Ahm, BRF), p. 35, LMA GLC/TD/GLDP/08/096.

104. W. J. Piggin, Woodberry Down Tenants' Association, GLDP Inquiry, Notes of Proceedings, 91st Day, 22 April 1971, p. 39, LMA GLC/TD/GLDP/08/093.

105. D. Christy, GLDP Inquiry, Notes of Proceedings, 85th Day, 14 April 1971, p. 83, LMA GLC/TD/GLDP/08/087.

106. M. Armitage, GLDP Inquiry, Notes of Proceedings, 89th Day, 20 April 1971, p. 55, LMA GLC/TD/GLDP/08/091.

107. GLDP Inquiry, Objection 106 (R. W. Russell, W4), LMA GLC/TD/GLDP/09/002. This was the first of 102 identically worded objections.

108. GLC, *Greater London Development Plan. Statement*, p. 22.

109. M. Baily, 'Ringway "Essential to Meet Traffic Growth"', *Times* 1 November 1969, cutting in Stott papers, LMA GLC/TD/CTD/02/004 (4). This piece does not appear in the Times Digital Archive.

110. D. Eversley, 'Three Years at the GLC. 1. Changes in Planning', *Built Environment* February 1973, p.105.

111. GLC, *Tomorrow's London. A Background to the Greater London Development Plan* (London, 1970), p. 44.

112. Eversley, 'Three Years at the GLC. 1'; note from Betty Turner, 21 September 1971, LMA GLC/TD/PM/PC/01/017.

113. Eversley, 'Three Years at the GLC. 1', 106.

114. Ibid., 106.

115. S. Jenkins, 'The Politics of London Motorways', *Political Quarterly* 44 (3), 1973, 260.

116. GLDP Inquiry, Notes of Proceedings, 91st Day, 22 April 1971 (Mr Ward, Chiswick Motorway Liaison Committee), p. 2, LMA GLC/TD/GLDP/08/093.

117. Graham Eyre, GLDP Inquiry, Notes of Proceedings, 61st Day, 3 March 1971, p. 47, LMA GLC/TD/GLDP/08/063; for Buchanan, see his letter to B. Collins, 6 January 1971, LMA GLC/TD/CTD/020/003 ('In a nutshell we are concerned that, in spite of all the protestations in the Consultation Text about flexibility, the GLDP . . . will in fact impose a considerable degree of rigidity on the future development of London'). Hart noted that Abercrombie had similarly been

'relatively unconcerned ... with the impact of unforeseen change on the solutions which he advocated', *Strategic Planning in London*, p. 56.

118. GLDP Inquiry, Notes of Proceedings, 89th Day, 20 April 1971 (Mrs M. Armitage, Strand on the Green Association), p. 48, LMA GLC/TD/GLDP/08/091.

119. 'Who are the GLC trying to kid? You know as well as I do, every stinking rotten motorcar and van that comes through, every time it stops, is belching out—even your GLC ambulances—are belching out smoke and filth', W. J. Piggin, Woodberry Down Tenants' Association, GLDP Inquiry, Notes of Proceedings, 91st Day, 22 April 1971, p. 39, LMA GLC/TD/GLDP/08/093.

120. The Layfield panel found that the GLC's population estimates were 'out of date, based on a dubious methodology', the employment section of the revised written statement contained 'unnecessary descriptive matter, unproductive generalisation and dubious rationalisation of past events' and the housing content of the original written statement was 'thin and unconvincing': *Greater London Development Plan. Report of the Panel of Inquiry* (London, 1973), vol. 1, Report, pp. 627, 127, 633.

121. GLDP Inquiry, Inquiry Proof E111/3 (Cllr B. G. Falk), LMA GLC/TD/GLDP/08/541.

122. These examples from the GLDP Public Inquiry transcripts for 12 November 1970 (TCPA), 3 November 1970 (Holmes), 10 November 1970 (St Pancras Civic Society) and 14 January 1971 (Grove Park Group): LMA GLC/TD/GLDP/08/030, GLC/TD/GLDP/08/024, GLC/TD/GLDP/08/028 and GLC/TD/GLDP/08/050.

123. J. R. Fitzpatrick to R. Vigars, 14 May 1971, Stott papers, LMA GLC/TD/CTD/02/062.

124. GLC, *Tomorrow's London*, p. 44; for authorship and censorship see Eversley, 'Three Years at the GLC. 1.'

125. Letter from Graham Lomas, London Council of Social Service, *Built Environment* April 1973.

126. Eversley, *Planner in Society*, pp. 186–87, 207, 270.

127. Eversley, note, 'GLC. Who Loses?', *Built Environment* May 1973.

128. Ibid.

129. Lomas Letter in *Built Environment* April 1973.

130. Eversley, *Planner in Society*, p. 3; D. Eversley, 'Three Years at the GLC. 2. Inadequate for the Task', *Built Environment* March 1973, 157–58.

131. Editorial, *Community Action* 2, April–May 1972.

132. 'Community Action—What Next?', *Community Action* 3 (P. Marris at Editorial/Advisory Group meeting), July–August 1972; 'A Real Urban Programme', *Community Action* 6, January–February 1973.

133. I. Binns, 'What Are We Trying to Achieve through Community Action?', *Community Action* 6, January–February 1973.

134. Eversley, 'Three Years at the GLC. 2.'

135. 'Structure Plans. Note for Discussion', 4 October 1972, LMA GLC/TD/CTD/02/062.

136. Bernard Collins, Joint Director of Planning and Transportation, to W. R. Cotton, 14 March 1973, Stott papers, LMA GLC/TD/CTD/02/062 (10).

137. Hart, *Strategic Planning in London*, p. 171.

138. D. Wilcox, 'Another Blow for Ringway Plan', *ES* 4 April 1973.

139. D. Eversley, 'Just Let Rip—That's No Logic!', *ES* 20 February 1973.

140. Mr Sherlock, Islington Society, GLDP Inquiry, Notes of Proceedings, 89th Day, 20 April 1971, p. 26, LMA GLC/TD/GLDP/08/091. See also the evidence of Douglas Jay, 82nd Day, 5 April 1971, p. 79, LMA GLC/TD/GLDP/08/084.

141. Note by A. F. Dunning, 3 April 1970, in the file on Public Participation in Planning, LMA GLC/TD/PM/PC/01/017.

142. Jenkins, 'Politics of London Motorways', 269–70.

143. G. Finsberg, *A Policy for London. A Consultative Document* (London, 1974). See also T. Grove, '£1300m—for a Monster London Could Live Without', *ES* 13 March 1975; M. King, 'Campaign to Abolish GLC', *ES* 6 December 1976; M. King, 'Campaign to Axe the GLC Gathers Support', *ES* 7 December 1976; K. Young & P. L. Garside, *Metropolitan London. Politics and Urban Change, 1837–1981* (London, 1983), pp. 324–25; B. Pimlott & N. Rao, *Governing London* (Oxford, 2002), pp. 31–33; T. Travers, *The Politics of London. Governing an Ungovernable City* (London, 2004), p. 29.

144. Jenkins, 'Politics of London Motorways', 270.

Chapter 7

1. Unfortunately for the supplicants, they were heard on the same day as the cabinet discussed the Soviet Union's testing of a thirty-megaton bomb, including the risk that children's milk would be contaminated by fallout. Macmillan saw the deputation as providing a 'ridiculous contrast to all this modern horror' and noted that they had taken forty-five minutes of his time: Harold Macmillan Diary, 24 October 1961, Bodleian Library, Oxford, MS Macmillan dep. d. 44.

2. Hansard, *House of Lords Debates*, vol. 237, col. 1154, 7 March 1962.

3. B. S. Johnson, 'The Demolition Man', *London Life* 11 December 1965; A. McGill, 'Down, Down, Down They Come', *Evening Standard (ES)* 25 October 1972.

4. London County Council, *Piccadilly Circus Future Development. Proposals for Comprehensive Development by the Planning Consultant Sir William Holford, March 1962* (London, 1962), p. 6; for the view that the Quadrant would be redeveloped in the late 1990s when its leases fell in, see J. P. F. Kacirek to J. D. Jones, MHLG, 8. April 1964, TNA HLG 131/271.

5. A. Saint, 'How Listing Happened', in M. Hunter, ed., *Preserving the Past* (London, 1996), p. 121.

6. J. Delafons, *Politics and Preservation. A Policy History of the Built Heritage, 1882–1996* (London, 1997), p. 56 and Appendix B for the 1944 Instructions for Investigators.

7. O. Saumarez Smith, 'Central Government and Town-Centre Development in Britain, 1959–1966', *Historical Journal* 58 (1), 2015, 217–44; S. Gunn, 'The Buchanan Report, Environment and the Problem of Traffic in 1960s Britain', *Twentieth Century British History* 22 (4), 2011, 521–42. See chapter 6.

8. Buchanan's Piccadilly report is in TNA HLG 79/1335; quotation from p. 36.

9. J. Cotton to W. O. Hart, Clerk to the LCC, 2 August 1960, TNA HLG 79/1335. For the Monico saga see O. Marriott, *The Property Boom* (London, 1967), pp. 140ff; and B. Edwards & D. Gilbert, '"Piazzadilly!" The Reimagining of Piccadilly Circus, 1957–1972', *Planning Perspectives* 23 (4), 2008, 455–78.

10. Milner Holland at the Piccadilly Circus Inquiry, day 1, 16 December 1959, p. 18, transcript in London Metropolitan Archives (LMA) LCC/AR/TP/04/134.

11. R. F. Jordan at the Piccadilly Inquiry, day 7, 6 January 1960, p. 49, LMA LCC/AR/TP/04/140.

12. Piccadilly Inquiry, day 11, 14 January 1960, p. 4, LMA LCC/AR/TP/04/144.

13. Elwyn Jones, Piccadilly Inquiry, day 11, 14 January 1960, p. 21, LMA LCC/AR/TP/04/144.

14. Marriott, *Property Boom*, p. 3.

15. Ibid., pp. 157–58.

16. R. Findlater, 'As a Theatre-Lover, I Smell Disaster Near', *ES* 2 November 1960; R. Greig, '"No! It's a Life-Saver, Says Sherek', *ES* 2 November 1960; W. Davis, 'Marylebone Station to Be Rebuilt', *ES* 31 October 1961. The partnership was acting in conjunction with Railways Sites, Ltd, the company set up by the British Transport Commission in 1961 to exploit railway property. In addition to Marylebone, Clore and Cotton hoped to rebuild St Pancras, King's Cross, Euston, Broad Street, London Bridge, Blackfriars, Charing Cross and Victoria.

17. S. Jenkins, 'Stage Set for Destruction—or How Theatreland Can Survive', *ES* 16 October 1973.

18. P. Cheshire & G. Dericks, 'Iconic Design as Deadweight Loss: Rent Acquisition by Design in the Constrained London Office Market', *Spatial Economics Research Centre Discussion Paper* 154, January 2014.

19. Marriott, *Property Boom*, p. 33.

20. Member of the LCC's Town Planning Committee quoted ibid., p. 32.

21. 'The Piccadilly Men', *ES* 8 November 1961; Marriott, *Property Boom*, p. 144.

22. Quoted in Marriott, *Property Boom*, p. 28.

23. Buchanan's report is in TNA HLG 79/1335.

24. Saumarez Smith, 'Central Government and Town-Centre Development'; Gunn, 'Buchanan Report.'

25. Report of the Steering Group, quoted in Gunn, 'Buchanan Report', 531.

26. P. G. Gray & R. Russell, *The Housing Situation in 1960*, Government Social Survey (London, 1962), Table 34, p. 42.

27. Quoted in H. Brack, 'The £90 Houses', *ES* 23 June 1969.

28. Alderman Bayliss, quoted in '"Why Demolish Good Houses?" Get Rid of the Slums First, Says Councillor', *ES* 17 February 1965

29. D. Wilcox, 'The Big Clean-up', *ES* 29 November 1972.

30. S. Jenkins, 'See It All Come Crashing Down!', *ES* 29 March 1973.

31. M. Macpherson, 'Return of Pink Pancras', *ES* 1 August 1977; F. Draper, 'St Pancras Gets a Red Face Again', *ES* 30 November 1977.

32. Delafons, *Politics and Preservation*, Appendix B, p. 195.

33. 'Ministry of Housing and Local Government, Advisory Committee on Buildings of Special Architectural or Historic Interest. Sub-Committee on 19th Century Buildings. Introductory Paper by the Secretary', TNA HLG 126/1253. The subcommittee included Nikolaus Pevsner; S. J. Garton, Chief Investigator for Historic Buildings at the Ministry; Mark Girouard; and the architect John Brandon-Jones.

34. S. J. Garton, quoted in I. Yates, 'It Costs £50,000 a Year to Make a List of Buildings', *ES* 26 August 1957.

35. Joint Report by Architect, Director of Planning and Valuer and Estates Surveyor, 'Proposed Closing of St Pancras Station. Preservation of Historic Buildings', 6 October 1967, Greater London Council (GLC) Planning and Communications Committee (Historic Buildings Sub-Committee), Presented Papers, 13 October 1967, LMA GLC/DG/PRE/143/003.

36. A. Dale, MHLG, to S. C. G. Wilkinson, 23 September 1966, TNA HLG 126/1049.

37. Historic Buildings Council for England, Committee on Buildings of Architectural or Historic Interest, Minutes, 19 December 1966, TNA WORK 94/96.

38. A. Dale, memo to Mr Young, 1 July 1966, 'Camden L.B.: St Pancras Station', TNA HLG 126/1049; GLC Planning and Communications Committee (Historic Buildings Sub-Committee), Minutes, 24 June 1966, LMA GLC/DG/PRE/143/003.

39. M. Binney, T. Cantell & G. Darley, 'One Tree Grows in Victoria Street', in 'The Concrete Jerusalem: the Failure of the Clean Sweep', supplement to *New Society* 23–30 December 1976.

40. Mrs R. S. Jefferies to Chairman, Westminster City Council Planning Committee, 8 August 1973, in the letters concerning Coutts Bank, Strand, GLC Historic Buildings Board Presented Papers, 18 September 1973, LMA GLC/DG/PRE/157/004; Jon Snow, for New Horizon Youth Centre, at the Covent Garden Inquiry, Day 36, 8 September 1971, in the Inquiry Transcripts, LMA GLC/DG/PTI/CG/02/04; R. O. H. Chapman, Ferndown, Dorset, to Department of the Environment, 1 December 1971, in the file of objections to the Whitehall redevelopment, TNA AT 41/113.

41. E. Lucie-Smith, 'Winner That Began in the Bath', *ES* 27 February 1979. The Credit Lyonnais building was listed in 2015.

42. 'Sir Basil "Better than Georgians"', *ES* 2 August 1973.

43. Maria Mathieson, Secretary, Georgian Group, to H. Bennett, LCC, 20 March 1961, in file 'Montpellier [*sic*] Row, Lewisham MBC', TNA HLG 126/881.

44. Inspector's Report on 8–16 Montpelier Row, Building Preservation Order, 1962, in LCC Town Planning Committee, Historic Buildings Sub-Committee, Presented Papers, 12 July 1963, LMA LCC/MIN/12043.

45. Jordan's Proof of Evidence, p. 4, TNA HLG 126/881.

46. F. C. Colman to MHLG, 11 February 1963, and H. Hanning to Inspector, 19 February 1963, TNA HLG 126/881.

47. N. Rhind, *Blackheath Village and Environs, 1790–1970*, vol. 2 (London, 1983), p. 80.

48. J. Hillman, 'New Planning Row Looms at Islington', *ES* 5 May 1967.

49. M. Swenarton, *Cook's Camden. The Making of Modern Housing* (London, 2017).

50. J. Dray, 'De Beauvoir Folk Will Fight the £20m "Vision"', *ES* 4 November 1960; 'Is De Beauvoir Town Doomed?', *Hackney Gazette* 1 November 1960.

51. Report 'Building Preservation Orders on Selected Groups of Buildings', 6 February 1959, LCC Historic Buildings Sub-Committee, Presented Papers, 13 February 1959, LMA LCC/MIN/12032.

52. Report 'Old Houses into New Homes', 12 September 1968, GLC Planning and Transportation Committee (Historic Buildings Board), Presented Papers, 1 October 1968, LMA GLC/DG/PRE/148/001.

53. K. L. Lewis, for Clerk to GLC, to Secretary, MHLG, 19 July 1965, in 'Greater London Council. Retention of Historic Buildings in Slum Clearance Areas', TNA HLG 118/452.

54. 'South London Scene', *London Property Letter* 28 June 1969; 'Camden: Beyond the Fringe', *London Property Letter* 14 June 1969.

55. Report 'Proposed Colebrooke Row/Duncan Terrace Conservation Area in the London Borough of Islington', 9 April 1970, GLC Planning and Transportation Committee, Historic Buildings Board, Presented Papers, 22 April 1969, LMA GLC/DG/PRE/148/001.

56. Report to Historic Buildings Board 'Conservation Areas Policy', 16 May 1969, English Heritage papers, LMA ACC/3499/EH/08/04/012.

57. E.g., at Wilmington Square, where the GLC granted £160 towards the cost of restoration work at no. 35 subject to the acceptance of a BPO on the property: Report by Architect and Treasurer, 7 September 1966, GLC Planning and Communications Committee (Historic Buildings Sub-Committee) Minutes, 7 October 1966, LMA GLC/DG/MIN/143/001.

58. Inspector's Report on Montpelier Row, with R. Ditchfield to Clerk to LCC, 28 June 1963, LCC Town Planning Committee (Historic Buildings Sub-Committee), Presented Papers, 12 July 1963, LMA LCC/MIN/12043.

59. Delafons, *Politics and Preservation*, Appendix B, p. 197.

60. Report 'Building Preservation Orders on Selected Groups of Buildings', 6 February 1959, Historic Buildings Sub-Committee, Presented Papers, 13 February 1959, LMA LCC/MIN/12032.

61. Memo, 'The Principles for Listing', n.d. [1968], LMA ACC/3499/EH/08/04/006.

62. Report 'Ladbroke Estate, Kensington and Chelsea', 16 September 1965, in GLC Planning and Communications Committee (Historic Buildings Sub-Committee) Presented Papers, 24 September 1965, LMA GLC/DG/PRE/143/001.

63. Report 'Conservation Areas Policy', 16 May 1969, in English Heritage papers, LMA ACC/3499/EH/08/04/012.

64. Report 'Preservation of Select Groups of Mid-Victorian Buildings of Southern Paddington', 11 July 1961, in LCC Historic Buildings Sub-Committee, Presented Papers, 14 July 1961, LMA LCC/MIN/12039; for Melbury Road, see R. Ditchfield, Ministry of Housing and Local Government, to the Clerk to the LCC, 30 August 1961, LMA LCC/MIN/12039.

65. Report 'West Cross Route. Holland Park Intersection', 5 March 1962, in LCC Historic Buildings Sub-Committee, Presented Papers, 30 March 1962, LMA LCC/MIN/12040. The subcommittee overturned their recommendation for a Building Preservation Order, but the Crescent survives intact.

66. Report 'Ladbroke Estate, Kensington and Chelsea'; for Warwick Avenue see Sub-Committee Minutes, 24 June 1966, LMA GLC/DG/MIN/143/001.

67. Report '81 and 82 Holland Park, Kensington and 25 and 26 Pembridge Square, Kensington', 9 October 1963, in LCC Historic Buildings Sub-Committee Presented Papers, 18 October 1963, LMA LCC/MIN/12043.

68. Report 'Preservation of Selected Groups, Finsbury', 6 February 1962, Historic Buildings Sub-Committee, Presented Papers, 23 February 1962; Report 'Selected Groups of Buildings in Chelsea', 1 May 1962, 18 May 1962, both LMA LCC/MIN/12040; Report 'Listing of Historic Buildings in the Barnsbury Area, Islington', 29 June 1965, 2 July 1965, LMA GLC/DG/PRE/143/001.

69. Lord Kennet to Mrs I. Chaplin, GLC, 13 December 1966, LMA ACC/3499/EH/08/04/006 (original emphasis).

70. Historic Buildings Sub-Committee, Minutes, 24 November 1961, LMA LCC/MIN/12028.

71. Historic Buildings Sub-Committee, Minutes, 13 December 1963, LMA LCC/MIN/12030.

72. Transcript of Public Inquiry into 'County of London (Westbourne Terrace, Paddington) Building Preservation Order, 1961', Historic Buildings Sub-Committee Presented Papers, 13 December 1963, LMA LCC/MIN/12044.

73. Delafons, *Politics and Preservation*, pp. 90–93.

74. Report by Architect, Director of Planning and Chief Officer of the Parks Department, 'The Civic Amenities Act, 1967', 10 October 1967, Historic Buildings Sub-Committee Presented Papers, 13 October 1967, LMA GLC/DG/PRE/143/003.

75. A. Dale and S. J. Garton in 'Historic Buildings Council for England, Committee on Buildings of Architectural or Historic Interest. Agenda Notes for First Meeting', 19 December 1966 (quoting extract from minutes of June 1963), TNA WORK 94/96. One Voysey building was added to the list.

76. Historic Buildings Council for England, Committee on Buildings of Architectural or Historic Interest, Minutes, 19 December 1966, TNA WORK 94/96; GLC Planning and Communications Committee (Historic Buildings Sub-Committee), Minutes, 3 March 1967, LMA GLC/DG/MIN/143/001.

77. Report by Architect, Director of Planning and Chief Officer of the Parks Department, 'Civic Amenities Act.'

78. Saint, 'How Listing Happened', p. 133.

79. A. Dale, MHLG, to Ashley Barker, GLC, 28 January 1972, English Heritage papers, LMA ACC/3499/EH/08/04/006.

80. H. L. Warburton, D of E, to Ashley Barker, GLC, 10 September 1973, English Heritage papers, LMA ACC/3499/EH/08/01/057.

81. Delafons, *Politics and Preservation*, p. 102.

82. Joint Report by Architect, Director of Planning and Chief Officer of Parks Department, 'The Civic Amenities Act, 1967, Consultations under Section I', 20 June 1968, Planning and Communications Committee (Historic Buildings Sub-Committee) Presented Papers, 2 July 1968, LMA GLC/DG/PRE/143/004.

83. Edwards & Gilbert, 'Piazzadilly!', 464ff.

84. London County Council, *Piccadilly Circus Future Development. Proposals for Comprehensive Development by the Planning Consultant Sir William Holford, March 1962* (London, 1962), p. 17.

85. Memo 'Piccadilly Circus', 9 July 1963, TNA HLG 79/1602.

86. Memo by E. A. S[harp], 'Piccadilly Circus', 12 July 1963, TNA HLG 79/1602.

87. Freeman, Fox, Wilbur Smith and Associates, 'Working Party on Piccadilly Circus. Possibility of a Two-Tier Solution', 27 November 1964, TNA HLG 131/272.

88. The architect's model of the 1968 scheme is illustrated in Greater London Council, *Piccadilly Circus. From Controversy to Reconstruction* (London, 1980), p. 14.

89. A. Sharr & S. Thornton, *Demolishing Whitehall. Leslie Martin, Harold Wilson and the Architecture of White Heat* (London, 2016), p. 46; K. Hamilton, 'Accommodating Diplomacy: The Foreign and Commonwealth Office and the Debate over Whitehall Redevelopment', *Contemporary British History* 18, 2004, 198–222.

90. Sharr & Thornton, *Demolishing Whitehall*, pp. 126ff.

91. Report by the Officers' Group, 'Covent Garden Policy Group. Implementation of the Plan', 3 December 1969, LMA GLC/DG/PTI/P/03/061.

92. Mrs J. Wilson, Whitehall Inquiry transcript, Day 11, 29 July 1970, 59, TNA AT 41/115.

93. Barbara Castle's Diary, 12 November 1969, quoted in Sharr & Thornton, *Demolishing Whitehall*, p. 236.

94. Sharr & Thornton, *Demolishing Whitehall*, p. 89.

95. Consortium of Greater London Council, City of Westminster, London Borough of Camden, Covent Garden's Moving. Covent Garden Area Draft Plan (1968), pp. 20ff., especially 22; Proposed Conservation Area. Report to Covent Garden Officers' Steering Group', n.d. [June 1971], LMA GLC/DG/PTI/P/03/060.

96. Quoted in Edwards & Gilbert, 'Piazzadilly!', 461.

97. V. G. Lewis, Bramley, to Charles Hill, received 16 April 1962, TNA HLG 79/1446.

98. Sharr & Thornton, *Demolishing Whitehall*, p. 270n1; Covent Garden Inquiry Transcripts, Inspector's summary of GLC's opening statement, p. 34, LMA GLC/DG/PTI/CG/02/04.

99. Whitehall Inquiry transcript, Day 10, 28 July 1970, p. 28, TNA AT 41/115.

100. G. McLeish, open letter to Lady Dartmouth, 17 May 1971, in 'Covent Garden General', LMA LRB/PS/EM/04/001.

101. Joint Committee of Society for the Preservation of Ancient Buildings, Georgian Group, Victorian Society and Civic Trust, Proof of Evidence [1971], LMA GLC/DG/PTI/CG/02/004.

102. Whitehall Inquiry transcript, Day 7, 22 July 1970, p. 2, TNA AT 41/115.

103. Whitehall Inquiry transcript, Day 9, 27 July 1970, p. 73, TNA AT 41/115.

104. Piccadilly Circus Inquiry, day 1, 16 December 1959, pp. 41ff., LMA LCC/AR/TP/04/134 (Robertson); Whitehall Inquiry transcript, day 11, 29 July 1970, p. 2, TNA AT 41/115 (Shepheard).

105. T. Crosby, *The Necessary Monument* (London, 1970), pp. 13, 91,65, 79, 70, 85.

106. J. Hurley, 'Towards a Sociology of Architecture', in *A.R.S.E.* [*Architects for a Really Socialist Environment*, aka *Architectural Radicals, Students and Educators*, etc], 5/6, Spring–Summer 1972, 21.

107. N. Wates, *The Battle for Tolmers Square* (London, 1974).

108. GLC, Public Information Branch, 'Covent Garden Public Participation', 30 September 1971, Covent Garden Officers' Steering Group papers, LMA GLC/DG/PTI/P/03/060.

109. John Toomey, printer, quoted in M. Stuart, 'Not So Lovely in Garden', *Guardian* 21 April 1971, cutting in TNA AT 41/144. This article does not appear in the digitised *Guardian Historical Archive*.

110. D. White, 'Protest People', *New Society* 29 June 1972.

111. Inspector's Report, para. 351, p. 60, LMA GLC/DG/PTI/P/03/075.

112. S. Jenkins, 'The Year We Changed Our Minds', *ES* 18 December 1973.

113. Saumarez Smith, 'Central Government and Town Centre Redevelopment', 239–40.

114. Covent Garden Comprehensive Development Area—Interim Report by the Chairman of the Working Party, 18 August 1972, TNA AT 41/144.

115. Memo by F. J. Ward, D of E, 'Covent Garden: Proposed Area of Comprehensive Development', 3 August 1972, TNA AT 41/144.

116. 'Notes on Major Policy Decisions Affecting London', [September 1972?], TNA AT 41/144.

117. Memo by O. T. Humphreys, 'Covent Garden: CDA Reappraisal', 28 July 1972, TNA AT 41/144.

118. D. Wilcox, 'Saved! The 1920s Image in Piccadilly', *ES* 18 January 1972.

119. Memo by P. L. Daniel, 'Covent Garden Enquiry', 11 August 1972, TNA AT 41/144.

120. Press Release 'Covent Garden: Additions to List of Buildings of Special Architectural or Historic Interest', 23 January 1973, TNA AT 41/144; Memo by W. S. Carlow, 'Covent Garden—Notes on Conservation Policy', TNA AT 41/144.

121. Memo by P. S. Waddington to V. D. Lipman, D of E, 'Covent Garden. A Policy for Conservation', 12 January 1973, TNA AT 41/144. In 1968 there had been seventeen buildings on the nonstatutory Supplementary List, and the GLC had considered a further eighteen to be of special architectural or historic interest. With seventeen buildings already on the statutory list, the GLC presumably considered only fifty-two buildings worthy of preservation: GLC, City of Westminster & London Borough of Camden, *Covent Garden's Moving* (London, 1968), Appendix L, pp. 110–11.

122. 'Minutes of Consultation Meeting with GLC on Friday 5th January 1973', TNA AT 41/144.

123. S. Jenkins, 'Mucking About with the Environment', *ES* 14 November 1972.

124. D. Wilcox, 'Covent Garden—the Big Plan', *ES* 15 January 1973. Pendlebury defines the distinction, which emerged during the 1960s, in this way: 'preservation was established as a static concept, applicable to a limited monumental heritage, "preservation as found", whereas conservation was held to be both a broader and more dynamic concept, a process of managing change while sustaining the essential qualities of place': J. Pendlebury, *Conservation in the Age of Consensus* (Abingdon, 2009), p. 33. Whether this is what Rippon meant is unknowable, though his stance at Covent Garden suggests that it was his claim. He had been neither preservationist nor conservationist in 1963: Sharr & Thornton, *Demolishing Whitehall*, pp. 38ff.

125. Jenkins, 'Year We Changed Our Minds.'

126. Jenkins, 'See It All Come Crashing Down!'

127. Jenkins, 'Year We Changed Our Minds.'

128. R. Langton, 'Poor Old Property Men', ES 14 March 1974.

129. See chapter 3.

130. D. Wilcox, 'Developers Quit Tolmers Square', ES 5 June 1975.

131. Haslemere Estates Ltd, Doing a Haslemere (London, 1978). See also the same firm's Something of London Restored (London, 1970) and Something More of London Restored (London, 1974).

132. R. Langton, 'Renewed Interest', ES 19 December 1974.

133. N. Pevsner to A. Dale, 22 June 1964, and A. Dale to N. Pevsner, 25 June 1964, file '33–35 Eastcheap', Victorian Society papers, LMA/4460/01/42/007.

134. 33–35, Eastcheap EC3. List Entry Summary, accessed 24 July 2018, http://historicengland.org.uk/listing/the-list/list-entry/1359154.

135. S. Jenkins, '. . . And Scandal in the City', ES 26 June 1973.

136. M. F. B. Bell, MHLG, to Clerk of LCC, 20 August 1962, Historic Buildings Sub-Committee Minutes, 12 October 1962, LMA LCC/MIN/12041. The buildings were not in fact demolished.

137. Sharr & Thornton, Demolishing Whitehall, p. 189.

138. Sir F. Catherwood, 'I'm All for Developers', ES 16 October 1973.

139. Alderman Sanford, quoted in S. Jenkins, 'The Conversion of Councillor Cubitt', ES 19 December 1972.

140. Delafons, Politics and Preservation, p. 105.

141. Pendlebury, Conservation in the Age of Consensus, pp. 83–85.

142. F. Mort, 'Fantasies of Metropolitan Life. Planning London in the 1940s', Journal of British Studies 43 (1), 2004, 128.

143. Gunn, 'Buchanan Report', 527.

Chapter 8

1. John Wilder, of the Psychiatric Rehabilitation Association, Kingsland High Street, quoted in H. Brack, 'With All Its Other Headaches, the Young People Are Moving Out Now', Evening Standard (ES) 14 May 1968.

2. David Widgery, Some Lives! A GP's East End (London, 1991), p. 7.

3. C. R. Morrey, The Changing Population of the London Boroughs (GLC Research Memorandum 413, London, 1973), Table 2(e), pp. 13–14. Though the Second World War had accentuated population decline, it had not initiated it: Morrey calculated the aggregate populations of the London boroughs created in 1965, projected back to 1851, showing that Tower Hamlets peaked at almost 600,000 in 1901 and Newham (Table 2f, p. 15) at almost 450,000 in 1921.

4. D. L. Munby, Industry and Planning in Stepney (Oxford, 1951), pp. 43, 112, 133, 134, 344–35; Alfred Gardner secured one of his early jobs after noticing that a former air raid shelter in Whitechapel had been converted into a children's dressmaking factory: A. Gardner, "Watch Your Fingers!" An East End Cutter's Chronicle, 1956–1973 (London, 2006), p. 6.

5. Gardner, "Watch Your Fingers", illustrations between pp. 40 and 41.

6. Ibid., pp. 36, 37, 52.

7. O. Newman, Gambling. Hazard and Reward (London, 1972), p. 104.

8. J. Dash, Good Morning Brothers! A Militant Trade Unionist's Frank Autobiography (London, 1970), p. 27.

9. 'Opening of Menswear Shop', *East London Advertiser* (*ELA*) 6 August 1965; P. Strowman, 'Hairdressers in the Tower Hamlets Have Their Own Academy', *ELA* 7 May 1965.

10. Widgery, *Some Lives*, p. 31.

11. M. Darby, 'The Docklands Study Reviewed. IV. A Local Resident's Reactions', *East London Papers* 15, Summer 1973, 34.

12. R. Lee, 'Planning and Social Change in East London', *East London Papers* 14 (1), 1972, 43.

13. D. Wilson, *Dockers. The Impact of Industrial Change* (London, 1972), p. 20; G. Phillips & N. Whiteside, *Casual Labour. The Unemployment Question in the Port Transport Industry, 1880–1970* (Oxford, 1985), p. 263.

14. C. J. Davis, *Waterfront Revolts: New York and London Dockworkers, 1946–1961* (Urbana, IL, 2003), pp. 42–43.

15. N. Watson, *The Port of London Authority. A Century of Service, 1909–2009* (London, 2009), pp. 178–79.

16. 'Man Fell to Death in Ship's Hold', *ELA* 14 January 1966.

17. D. Carpenter, *Dockland Apprentice* (Peacehaven, 2003), p. 46.

18. John Thompson of Stepney, convicted of stealing four bottles of whisky from a ship in the Free Trade Wharf, 'Docker Stole Whisky', *ELA* 12 December 1969; William Lovelock, docker, caught with a plastic dustbin containing twelve whisky and ten gin bottles, '30-Year Docker to Lose Job', *ELA* 17 March 1972.

19. E.g., the comments of the New Zealand Steamship Company, which claimed in 1965 to have lost meat to the value of £50,000 through pilfering, that such larceny had 'got very much more serious in recent years', 'Pilfering of Meat Causes Concern in the Docks', *ELA* 26 February 1965.

20. Carpenter, *Dockland Apprentice*, p. 11.

21. Ibid., pp. 143–44.

22. S. Dyson, *Silvertown Life. A Boy's Story* (Milton Keynes, 2008), pp. 156–57.

23. Wilson, *Dockers*, p. 49.

24. Unnamed docker quoted in J. Bugler, 'Devlin: How the Dockers React', *New Society* 12 August 1965.

25. Dash, *Good Morning Brothers!*, p. 138.

26. S. Hill, *The Dockers. Class and Tradition in London* (London, 1976), pp. 139, 129.

27. Dash, *Good Morning Brothers!*, p. 71.

28. P. Henderson, 'Ceiling Collapses—Mother Threatens to "Dump" Her Children', *ELA* 6 August 1971; 'Mothers Tell Council to "Get Your Fingers Out"', *ELA* 13 December 1974; N. Gansell, 'Fighting Tenants Hold Rent Men "Hostage"', *ELA* 5 October 1973; 'Dustmen Battle with Rats Swarm—And This Family Is Bugged by Beetles', *ELA* 11 February 1972.

29. H. Brack, 'Labour's Last Stronghold', *ES*, series running from 13 to 24 May 1968.

30. Brack, 'With All Its Other Headaches.'

31. P. Harrison, 'Tower Hamlets: A Social Services Case Study', *New Society* 7 December 1972.

32. H. Brack, 'On the Nod: An Evening in the Council Chamber', *ES* 24 May 1968, for Tower Hamlets.

33. C. Forman, *Spitalfields: A Battle for Land* (London, 1989), p. 39.

34. J. O'Malley, 'Political Structures of the Local Authorities in CDP', 8 May 1973, Joint Docklands Action Group (JDAG) papers, Museum of London in Docklands, Box 2.

35. Letter from Mrs M. Fido, *ELA* 3 December 1971.

36. S. Jenkins, 'Big Joe's Last Stand?', *ES* 19 June 1973. I am most grateful to Robert Jones, of Tower Hamlets Archives, for help in tracing Orwell's municipal career.

37. O. Pritchett, 'A Lost Cause in Stepney', *ES* 4 May 1977.

38. J. H. Forshaw & P. Abercrombie, *County of London Plan* (London, 1943), from the caption to the plan between pages 102 and 103.

39. London County Council, *Administrative County of London. Development Plan, 1951. Analysis* (London, 1951), pp. 253–67.

40. 'JS' [J. A. Scott, LCC Medical Officer] to R. E. Cox, Assistant Valuer, 23 July 1962, file 'Stepney-Poplar Comprehensive Development Area, 1960–62', London Metropolitan Archives (LMA) LCC/CL/HSG/01/088.

41. Report of the Planning and Communications Committee, 27 June 1966, Greater London Council Minutes, 5 July 1966.

42. J. M. Hall, 'East London's Future: Visions Past and Present', *East London Papers* 14 (1), 1972, 12.

43. The Milner Holland Committee was told that only one of the twenty-four thousand dwellings in Poplar in 1939 had escaped any war damage: memo by Pilgrim House CAB, Poplar, TNA HLG 39/3.

44. This exchange from 'Note of a Meeting at the County Hall on Wednesday, 4th October 1961,' LMA LCC/CL/HSG/01/088. Quotations from Cllrs Bird and Orwell (Stepney) and Stamp (LCC).

45. P. Dunleavy, *The Politics of Mass Housing in Britain, 1945–1975* (Oxford, 1981), pp. 217ff, 230ff.

46. Ibid., p. 230.

47. The CDA proposals envisaged halving the 1939 population in the area.

48. 'Leader's Conference, MBC Stepney and LCC, 25 September 1962', LMA LCC/CL/HSG/01/089.

49. E.g., Cayley Street, Priscilla Road, Copenhagen Place, Furze Street, Grenade Street, Three Colt Street, all in 1964: LMA LCC/CL/HSG/01/089.

50. T. Pocock, 'Vanishing: The World That Made the Cockney', *ES* 15 November 1960.

51. A. Smith, *The East Enders* (London, 1961), pp. 138–39.

52. Reactions to a hole in the kitchen of a flat in the twenty-four-storey Winterton House, Stepney, and to cracks appearing in the high-rise part of the Samuda Estate, Isle of Dogs: J. Smith, '"Move Us" Plea by 19th Floor Family', *ELA* 27 November 1970; 'Tower Block Cracks Are Not Dangerous—Say GLC', *ELA* 25 May 1973.

53. 'New Island Flats Refused by People Needing Homes', *ELA* 16 May 1969.

54. A. R. Turton, *Analysis of Public Reaction to Development Plans for London Docklands* (GLC Research Memorandum 440, London, 1974), Tables 2.21 and 2.22, p. 26. The figure is deflated by the fact that respondents were also given the option of a house, which they overwhelmingly preferred, but that of a 'low flat' attracted 16.5 percent.

55. Dunleavy, *Politics of Mass Housing*, pp. 244ff.

56. J. Hillman, 'Afraid? No—This Is Bliss', *ES* 26 July 1968.

57. J. S. Chapman, *Sample Survey of London's Housing Waiting List, 1971–2* (GLC Research Memorandum 431, London, 1973), Table A15, p. 22.

58. Turton, *Analysis of Public Reaction*, Table 4.2, p. 55, showed that the keywords 'housing' and 'homes' were mentioned twice as often as any other in respondents' comments.

59. Chapman, *Sample Survey*, Table A16, p. 23.

60. Jenkins, 'Big Joe's Last Stand' (emphasis added).

61. Comments by Simon Gibbs, 4 July 1974, file 'Review of Comprehensive Development Areas—Special Sub-Group—Tower Hamlets', LMA GLC/TD/DP/POL/05/047.

62. F. Skinner, for Tower Hamlets Council of Social Service, *People without Roots: a Study Undertaken in the London Borough of Tower Hamlets 1966–7 and an Appraisal of Services Provided by Voluntary and Statutory Agencies* (London, 1967), pp. 53–54; Turton, *Analysis of Public Reaction*, Tables 2.20 and 2.22, p. 26.

63. In the 1973 Docklands survey 84 percent of seventeen- to twenty-four-year-olds expressed a preference for ownership 'given the chance', and 85 percent preferred a house to a flat: Turton, *Analysis of Public Reaction*, Tables 2.20 and 2.22, p. 26.

64. Darby, 'Docklands Study Reviewed', p. 34. Darby was the secretary of the Wapping Community Association.

65. Pocock, 'Vanishing.'

66. Hall, 'East London's Future', p. 12.

67. Sixth Annual Report of the Tower Hamlets Council of Social Service, 1969–70, p. 8, Peter Shore papers, British Library of Political and Economic Science (BLPES), SHORE 19/49.

68. R. W. Watton to Peter Shore, 24 June 1966, Shore papers, BLPES, SHORE 19/4.

69. *Spitalfields Project News* no. 1, 1975, Avenues Unlimited papers, Tower Hamlets Local History Library and Archives, I/AVU/A/3/1.

70. 'Although the Archbishop of Canterbury isn't an alcoholic', Downham added: 'Helping the "Down and Outs" in Stepney Crypt', *ELA* 3 February 1967; J. W. Coleman, 'The Spitalfields Crypt', *Journal of Alcoholism* 10 (4), 1975, 157–61.

71. Letter from J. B. Alexander, *ELA* 29 November 1974.

72. 'Empty Houses Attract Tramps: Neighbours to See MP', *ELA* 19 August 1966; W. S. Hilton, MP for Bethnal Green, in Hansard, Parliamentary Debates, 'Crude Spirit Drinkers (Treatment)', House of Commons, vol. 756, cols. 1553–61, 21 December 1967.

73. Supt Kenneth Wright: 'Pressure to Rid Area of Vagrant Alcoholics', *ELA* 7 February 1975.

74. Gardner, *"Watch Your Fingers"*, pp. 103, 56.

75. 'Plans to Help Meths Drinkers', *ELA* 10 March; '"We'll Oppose It" Say Local Residents', *ELA* 17 March 1967; 'Stepney Neighbours Oppose Hostel for Women Alcoholics', *ELA* 21 November 1969; A. Lapping, 'The Meths Drinkers Remain', *New Society* 13 July 1967, for the Simon Community and Sclater Street.

76. Unnamed resident of the Lansbury Estate, quoted in 'Special Salvation Army Hostel Plan Still Fought', *ELA* 27 October 1972.

77. GLC Deprived Areas Project, London Borough of Tower Hamlets, Spitalfields Ward, Preliminary Assessment and Proposed Action, 30 May 1974, copy in Avenues Unlimited papers, Tower Hamlets Local History Library and Archives, I/AVU/A/3/1.

78. Gardner, *"Watch Your Fingers"*, p. 30.

79. Munby, *Industry and Planning*, p. 6.

80. P. L. Garside, 'The Significance of Post-war Reconstruction Plans for East End Industry', *Planning Perspectives* 12 (1), 1997, 19–36.

81. Dyson, *Silvertown Life*, p. 24.

82. Carpenter, *Dockland Apprentice*, p. 54.

83. Tym & Partners, *Living by the Yard. A Study of Bad Neighbour Industry in the Inner City* (London, 1981), pp. 44–45.

84. Director, London Docklands Development Team, 'A Docklands Strategy: Setting the Scene', with Docklands Joint Committee report, London Borough of Tower Hamlets, Special Docklands

Development Committee Minutes, 2 January 1975, Tower Hamlets Local History Library and Archives, pp. 22–23.

85. '"Who Cares?" Asks Stepney Tenants', *ELA* 4 September 1964.

86. Smith, *East Enders*, p. 13.

87. Brack, 'With All Its Other Headaches.'

88. Skinner, *People without Roots*, p. 4.

89. 'Multi-Storey Flats Problem', *ELA* 16 February 1968; 'Chance for Residents to Put Their Views', *ELA* 7 June 1968.

90. See the comments of Lou Leighton, Stepney, in 'Five Year Battle for Bigger Flat', *ELA* 2 August 1974.

91. N. Gansell, 'The Hopeless Homeless', *ELA* 7 June 1974.

92. Lee, 'Planning and Social Change in East London', Table 3, p. 35.

93. M. Balint, *Greater London's Economically Active Population* (GLC Research Memorandum 441, London, 1975), p. 26.

94. Company spokesman quoted in 'Old Ford Wallpaper Factory Is Closing Down', *ELA* 6 May 1966.

95. Ministry of Labour, *Final Report of the Committee of Inquiry under the Right Honourable Lord Devlin into Certain Matters Concerning the Port Transport Industry* (Cmnd. 2734, 1964–65).

96. D. Hobbs, *Doing the Business. Entrepreneurship, the Working Class and Detectives in the East End of London* (Oxford, 1989), p. 130.

97. '£1250 "Handshakes" for Dockworkers', *ELA* 8 March 1968; 'Golden Handshakes—Dockers Put Their Names Down', *ELA* 7 June 1968; 'Volunteered for the "Sack." Piper Leads the Singing Dockers', *ELA* 6 September 1968.

98. 'Celebration by Happy Dockers with Big Pay-Off Cheques', *ELA* 20 September 1968.

99. Interview with Dennis Davies, aged thirty-five, Surrey Docks, 'Anger in Dockland', *The Port* 26 May 1967.

100. By 1975 fewer than a third of the firms remaining in Docklands considered themselves dependent on the river, Docklands Joint Committee, *Work and Industry in East London. A Working Paper for Consultation* (London, 1975), p. 4.

101. These figures from the survey 'Industrial Decline in Canning Town', JDAG papers, Box 2.

102. C. Howick and T. Key, *The Local Economy of Tower Hamlets. An Inner-City Profile* (London, 1978), p. 59.

103. W. Watts, in House of Commons Expenditure Committee, *Redevelopment of the London Docklands. Fifth Report from the Expenditure Committee, Together with the Minutes of the Evidence Taken before the Environment Sub-Committee . . . , Session 1974–5*, Parliamentary Papers, 1974–75 (348), 22 January 1975, Q. 103, p. 20.

104. Canning Town Community Development Project, *Canning Town to North Woolwich: The Aims of Industry? A Study of Industrial Decline in One Community* (2nd ed., London, 1977), p. 15.

105. D. White, 'Newham: An Example of Urban Decline', *New Society* 23 October 1975.

106. Joint Report (27.11.67) by Treasurer . . . and Director of Housing, Greater London Council Housing Committee Presented Papers, 7 December 1967, LMA GLC/DG/PRE/088/025; GLC Minutes, 19–20 December 1967; J. Morton, 'Raising Council Rents', *New Society* 14 August 1969.

107. H. Brack, 'Pay Up? I'd Rather Pitch a Tent', *ES* 25 August 1969.

108. '"We Won't Pay GLC Rent Increases"—Island Residents', *ELA* 9 February 1968; 'GLC Rents. Tenants Urge PM to Intervene', *ELA* 16 February 1968; 'Borough Ask to Take Over GLC

Homes', *ELA* 16 August 1968; Dash, *Good Morning Brothers!*, p. 14; Tower Hamlets Borough Council Minutes 14 August 1968, 25 June 1969, Tower Hamlets Local History Library and Archives.

109. '"We Won't Pay GLC Rent Increases"', *ELA* 9 February 1968.

110. GLC Minutes, 19–20 December 1967.

111. 'Council Tenants Face Rents Rises', *ELA* 4 July 1969.

112. Report of the Finance Committee, Tower Hamlets Borough Council Minutes, 11 September 1967, Tower Hamlets Local History Library and Archives; 'Council Divided on Rent Rise Question', *ELA* 22 September 1967; 'Big Rates Jump for Tower Hamlets', *ELA* 13 March 1970.

113. Tower Hamlets Borough Council Minutes, 26 July 1972.

114. Lee, 'Planning and Social Change in East London', p. 38, Table 6; H. Lee, 'Rates Crisis: Plea to Government for Help', *ELA* 29 December 1972; Harrison, 'Tower Hamlets.'

115. Psychiatric Rehabilitation Association (PRA), *The Mental Health of East London, 1966* (Longon, 1968), pp. 9, 12; PRA Report, *Mental Illness in East London* (1964), Shore papers, BLPES, SHORE/19/10; *Spitalfields Project News* 1, 1975, in Avenues Unlimited papers, Tower Hamlets Local History Library and Archives; Skinner, *People without Roots*, p. 50.

116. The ratio in Tower Hamlets rose from 52.9 percent in 1951 to 59.8 percent in 1966: Lee, 'Planning and Social Change', Table 5, p. 37.

117. House of Commons Expenditure Committee, *Redevelopment of the London Docklands. Report of the House of Commons Expenditure Committee (Environment Sub-Committee)*, Parliamentary Papers, 1978–79 (269), 17 January 1979, Q. 104, p. 54.

118. London Borough of Tower Hamlets, 'Unemployment and the Attraction of Industry to the Borough. Meeting to be Held at the Town Hall . . . 14 March 1975', p. 1, Shore papers, BLPES, SHORE/10/48.

119. Lee, 'Planning and Social Change in East London', 43.

120. This paragraph is from the draft 'Green Paper' by P. F. Stott et al., 5 January 1971, file 'Docklands: Consultants' Report on Options', LMA GLC/HG/D/01/001.

121. Hansard, *Parliamentary Debates*, House of Commons, vol. 816, cols. 110–12, 28 April 1971.

122. London Docklands Study Team, *Docklands. Redevelopment Proposals for East London* (London, 1973), vol. 1, pp. 149–224. The Travers Morgan proposals were considered in detail by J. M. Hall, L. B. Ginsburg, J. Eyles & M. Darby in the final issue of *East London Papers* 15, Summer 1973, 'The Docklands Study Reviewed', 5–36.

123. House of Commons Expenditure Committee, *Redevelopment of the London Docklands. Fifth Report*, p. 40.

124. Ibid., p. 43.

125. Docklands Joint Committee, *London Docklands. A Strategic Plan* (London, 1976). The DJC report was reviewed in the same manner as the *East London Papers* assessment of Travers Morgan by J. M. Hall, G. Griffiths, J. Eyles & M. Darby, 'Rebuilding the London Docklands', *London Journal* 2 (2), 1976, 266–85.

126. DJC, *London Docklands*, p. 19.

127. As Eyles argued: 'Rebuilding the London Docklands. 3, Social Implications', *London Journal* 2 (2), 1976, 279–80.

128. In this context—and recognising that Bethnal Green was not Docklands—Jon Lawrence's nuanced account of working-class community in Bethnal Green and Bermondsey (*Me, Me, Me? The Search for Community in Postwar England* [Oxford, 2019], ch. 2), is valuable, as is his earlier dissection of the research base for Young and Willmott's classic construction of traditional working-class community in 1950s Bethnal Green: J. Lawrence, 'Inventing the "Traditional Working Class":

A Reanalysis of Interview Notes from Young and Willmott's *Family and Kinship in East London*, *Historical Journal* 59 (2), 2016, 567–93.

129. 'Docks Campaign', *New Society* 9 August 1973.

130. Darby, 'Docklands Study Reviewed', 33.

131. Hill, *Dockers*, p. 22.

132. 'Human Barriers Seal Off Island', *ELA* 6 March 1970; 'Counter Revolt on the Island', *ELA* 13 March 1970.

133. Peter Drew, quoted in N. Gansell, 'Action Group Hit Back at World Trade Centre Chief', *ELA* 19 July 1974.

134. House of Commons Expenditure Committee, *Redevelopment of the London Docklands. Fifth Report*, Q. 671, 12 March 1975, p. 221.

135. Joint Docklands Action Group, *Docklands. The Fight for a Future* (London, 1976), copy in JDAG papers, Museum of London Docklands, pp. 4, 35–36.

136. J. Rennison, 'Sweet Thames . . .', *Financial Times* 13 November 1971.

137. D. Connolly and D. Jones, East End Docklands Action Group, to the Clerk of the House of Commons Environment Sub-Committee, 3 March 1975, Shore papers, BLPES, SHORE/10/71.

138. JDAG, *Docklands*, p. 4.

139. 'Briefing for Official Working Party on House Improvement in Stress Areas', June 1972, TNA HLG 118/1994.

140. S. Brownill & G. O'Hara, 'From Planning to Opportunism? Re-examining the Creation of the London Docklands Development Corporation', *Planning Perspectives* 30 (4), 2015, 546–48.

141. JDAG, *Docklands*, p. 5.

Chapter 9

This chapter is a slightly amended version of the essay published as 'The London Cabbie and the Rise of Essex Man', in C. Griffiths, J. Nott & W. Whyte, eds., *Classes, Cultures and Politics. Essays in British History for Ross McKibbin* (Oxford, 2011), pp. 102–17.

1. Departmental Committee on the London Taxicab Trade (Maxwell Stamp Committee), *Report* (Cmnd. 4483, 1970), 11.

2. Beyond six miles driver and passenger could negotiate a fare, at least until 1969, when longer trips became chargeable at double the metered rate, largely to end the exploitation of tourists arriving at Heathrow Airport.

3. F. Entwisle, 'Can You Wonder the Cabbies Are Angry?', *Evening Standard* (*ES*) 1 December 1961.

4. M. Levinson, *Taxi* (London, 1963), p. 24.

5. F. Entwisle, 'The Knowledge Boys Face a Hard Road', *ES* 30 November 1961.

6. Maxwell Stamp Committee, *Report*, 24.

7. Transport and General Workers Union, Cab Section, 'Evidence to the Committee on the London Cab Trade', 20 November 1968, p. 2, Transport and General Workers Union (TGWU Archive), Modern Records Centre, Warwick University, MSS. 126/TG/RES/P/16/2.

8. S. Davis, 'Comings and Cohens', *Steering Wheel* (*SW*) 29 May 1971.

9. 'On the "Knowledge"', *SW* 9 August 1969.

10. A. Townsend, *Cabbie* (Stroud, 2003), p. 19.

11. A. Fresco, 'Where Have All the Garages Gone?', *SW* 7 September 1979.

12. C. Field, 'Taxi! The Jews behind the Wheel', *Jewish Chronicle Colour Magazine* 30 April 1971; B. A. Kosmin and N. Grizzard, *Jews in an Inner London Borough. A Study of the Jewish Population of the London Borough of Hackney Based on the 1971 Census* (London, 1975), p. 27.

13. Field, 'Taxi!'

14. 'Should the Lid Go on the Melting Pot?', *Taxi Trader* (*TT*) February 1969.

15. 'Black Cabbies for Black Cabs', *TSSA Journal* December 2007–January 2008, www.tssa.org.uk/ article-259. php3?id_article=3841.

16. 'On the "Knowledge."'

17. 'Cabbies of London', *Evening News* 16, 24, and 25 October, 3, 9, 10, 13, 14, and 15 November 1961.

18. A. Sheehan, 'If', *TT* April 1965.

19. 'Cabbies of London, 17', *Evening News* 31 October 1961.

20. Townsend, *Cabbie*, p. 45.

21. R. Annoute, 'Why DO Taxi Drivers . . . ??', part 2, *SW* 5 September 1970.

22. Levinson, *Taxi*, p. 190.

23. Letter from J. Pilkington, Department of Health and Social Security, *SW* 28 June 1969.

24. Letter from J. Cohen, *SW* 23 March 1968.

25. H. R. Eversfield, 'An Appreciation: Joe Polski', *SW* 24 June 1972.

26. E.g., Levinson for drivers' 'strong streak of individuality': M. Levinson, 'Taximan's Diary', *SW* 9 April 1966.

27. R. Buckland, *Share My Taxi* (London, 1968), p. 82.

28. Maxwell Stamp Committee, *Report*, p. 2.

29. E. Sussman, 'Is Britain Soft?', *TT* January 1960.

30. F. Braverman, 'What Cabmen Think of the Common Market', *Cab Trade News* 29 March 1975, TGWU Archive.

31. Joe 'Rubberface' Wiltshire, 'Cabbies of London, 11', *Evening News* 23 October 1961. Wiltshire had driven von Ribbentrop, German ambassador 1936–38, during the refurbishment of the German embassy.

32. Buckland, *Share My Taxi*, p. 185.

33. 'Historical Quiz', *Cab Trade News* 9 August 1973; 'Ten Teasers', *TT* January 1968; 'Ten Teasers', *TT* February 1968.

34. S. Davis, 'The London Taxi Drivers' Guide Training Course', *SW* 7 July 1973; L. Marlow, 'Praiseworthy', *SW* 18 August 1973; 'Guide Me a Taxi', *SW* 26 July 1974.

35. Letter from T. Smith, *SW* 22 April 1977.

36. P. Moger, '"Carnaby Street" Cabbie', *Acton Gazette* 6 April 1967.

37. Buckland, *Share My Taxi*, pp. 185–86.

38. 'Gerry Sherrick—Poet—Taxidriver', *Cab Trade News* 25 January 1975, TGWU Archive.

39. 'Personality Page', *SW* 16 November 1968; C.Poulsen, 'The Weatherman', *SW* 16 December 1967; M. Levinson, *The Taxi Game* (London, 1973), p. 141; M. Schiman, 'Monty Schiman at Large', *SW* 9 March 1979.

40. H. Hodge, *Cab, Sir?* (London, 1939); Levinson, *Taxi*; Levinson, *Taxi Game*; Buckland, *Share My Taxi*; Centerprise Trust, *Working Lives. A People's Autobiography of Hackney*, vol. 2, *1945–1977* (London, 1977), for Barnes; W. Geake, *What's Next? Incidents Recorded whilst Driving a London Licensed Taxicab* (London, 1999); Townsend, *Cabbie*.

41. R. Barnes, *A Licence to Live: Scenes from a Post-war Working Life in Hackney* (London, 1975); M. Levinson, *The Trouble with Yesterday* (London, 1946), *The Woman from Bessarabia* (London, 1964), *The Desperate Passion of Henry Knopp* (London, 1962), *Greek Street Tragedy* (London, 1964).

42. S. Raingold, *A Taxi Driver's Guide to London* (London, 1973); Charles Poulsen, *Victoria Park. A Study in the History of East London* (London, 1976).

43. Hodge, *Cab, Sir?*, p. 238.

44. Buckland, *Share My Taxi*, p. 86.

45. Hodge, *Cab, Sir?*, p. 238.

46. Barnes in Centerprise Trust, *Working Lives*, p. 156.

47. Hugo Clarke, tried at West London Magistrates Court, 'Cab Owner-Driver before Court. Alleged to Have Assaulted Constable', *Owner Driver* March 1963; V. Gale and an unidentified police constable, Marlborough Street Magistrates Court, 'Cabmen and Animals—Court Statement', *TT* May 1965. Gale was acquitted of driving without due care and attention, but Clarke was imprisoned for driving his cab at PC Sidney Lear.

48. Levinson, *Taxi Game*, p. 100.

49. Ibid., p. 98.

50. Levinson, *Taxi*, p. 106; Buckland, *Share My Taxi*, p. 55.

51. Levinson, *Taxi Game*, p. 73.

52. Buckland, *Share My Taxi*, pp. 21–22.

53. 'Personality Page, No. 1. Jack (from Mons) Cohen', *SW* 13 January 1968.

54. Myer Franks, summoned at Bow Street court for using insulting language to a Belgravia company secretary, 'Cabbie Denies Insulting Language in Question of Values Dispute', *SW* 1 July 1967.

55. Letter from P. Roma, *SW* 12 May 1962.

56. H. Pearman, 'Glossary of Cockney Cabology', *TT* January 1971; Buckland, *Share My Taxi*, p. 25.

57. Levinson, *Taxi Game*, p. 141.

58. G. Bocca, 'Taxi Drivers of the World, I', *SW* 30 December 1967, referring to London, Paris, and Rome.

59. 'Why London's Cabbies Are So Miserable', *ES* 9 November 1979.

60. 'On the "Knowledge"'; Levinson, *Taxi*, p. 69.

61. Editorial, 'Pride or Prejudice?', *SW* 7 August 1971.

62. K. E. Drummond, in 'The Maxwell Stamp Report', *SW* 14 November 1970.

63. Editorial, 'Bilking', *Owner Driver* February 1962.

64. Hodge, *Cab, Sir?*, pp. 78, 89.

65. H. Pearman, 'Call Me Cabby, II', *TT* July 1971.

66. Ibid.; letter from G. Stedman, *SW* 20 September 1974.

67. Hodge, *Cab, Sir?*, p. 95; Buckland, *Share My Taxi*, p. 84.

68. Buckland, *Share My Taxi*, p. 84; R. Annoute, 'Why DO Taxi Drivers . . . ??', part 4, *SW* 19 September 1970; W. J. D'Arcy in D. Orgill, 'Hail and Fare Well', *Daily Express* 15 November 1973.

69. Levinson, *Taxi Game*, p. 107.

70. 'The Taxi Driver and Race Relations', *SW* 6 February 1971.

71. Levinson, *Taxi*, p. 91.

72. Centerprise Trust, *Working Lives*, p. 141.

73. E.g., 'Basic Wage for Journeymen? Revolutionary Union Resolution', *SW* 11 March 1967.

74. Buckland, *Share My Taxi*, p. 88.

75. National Board for Prices and Incomes, Report 87, *Proposed Increase in London Taxicab Fares*, October 1968 (Cmnd. 3796, 1968), p. 12.

76. 'Jack from Mons Cohen', *SW* 7 February 1970. Cohen had been a TGWU member since 1926: see his letter in *SW* 23 March 1968.

77. A. Sheehan, 'On Unity', *SW* 6 February 1971.

78. W. Fox, *Taximen and Taxi-Owners. A Study of Organisation, Ownership, Finances and Working Conditions in the London Taxi Trade* (London, 1935), p. 5.

79. Figures for a journeyman driver in 1938: 'Proposals of the Transport and General Workers Union for the Limitation of the Number of London Taxicabs and Drivers', The National Archives (TNA) HO 45/25256.

80. Alec Weldon in 'Cabbies of London, 4', *Evening News* 12 October 1961.

81. 'Pioneer of Minicabs Exudes Innocence and Ambition', *Times* 19 June 1961.

82. B. Cardew, 'Minicabs Will Start Taxi War', *Daily Express* 6 February 1961.

83. Memorandum by A. Hewins, 28 March 1961, TNA HO 385/7.

84. A. Sheehan, 'The Last Word', *Owner Driver* June 1961.

85. 'Mini Matters', *SW* 8 July 1961.

86. P. Warren, 'Welbeck Minicabs—the Tip of the Iceberg. Part 3', *Cab Trade News* 17 October 1974, TGWU Archive.

87. P. Warren, 'Welbeck Minicabs'; *Daily Mirror* 21 November 1961.

88. Court Report, *TT* January 1962.

89. S. Pearce, 'Fares. Time for a Change?', *SW* 4 July 1975.

90. M. F. Talbot, *Greater London Transportation Survey. A Study of Taxi Trips* (GLC Research Memorandum 307, London, 1974), pp. 17, 43.

91. A. Goldwater, 'Arthur Goldwater's Column', *SW* 13 December 1969.

92. Letter from 'South London businessman and minicab user', *TT* March 1969.

93. Metropolitan Police figures in M. E. Beesley, 'Competition and Supply in London Taxis', in *Privatization, Regulation and Deregulation* (2nd ed., London, 1997), Table 8.1, pp. 112–13.

94. E.g., letter from J. Lovegrove, *TT* September 1970, predicting that the licensed trade would last no longer than five years.

95. A. Goldwater, 'To Set You Thinking', *SW* 22 April 1967.

96. 'London Taxi Drivers "Close Their Ranks"', *Times* 17 May 1967.

97. Levinson, *Taxi Game*, p. 42.

98. J. Toff, 'Joe Toff Replies to Arthur Goldwater', *SW* 16 December 1967.

99. R. Fletcher, 'Taxicabs and Parliament', *SW* 3 June 1967. Fletcher was the TGWU-sponsored MP who spoke for the taxi trade.

100. TGWU Cab Section Bulletin, 23 May 1967, quoted in '"Miracles Sometimes Take Longer", Says Union Bulletin', *SW* 3 June 1967.

101. See Schedule II of the LTDA Rule Book, 1969, in 'Licensed Taxi Drivers Association', TNA NF 2/708.

102. Letter from Mrs M. Kupler, 'A Taxi Driver's Wife', *SW* 13 July 1968.

103. Editorial, 'Disagreement', *Cab Trade News* 10 September 1975, TGWU Archive.

104. Letter from Joe Toff, *SW* 15 July 1967.

105. Letter from H. Bennett, *SW* 31 March 1973; *Cab Trade News* 19 October 1977, TGWU Archive. Both claims refer to articles in taxi journals which have not survived. Both were made by hostile witnesses, but the second cites an article by Ivens himself.

106. 'Taxidermy', *SW* 2 December 1977.

107. M. E. Beesley, 'Regulation of Taxis', *Economic Journal* 83 (1), 1973, 171.

108. Hodge, *Cab, Sir?*, pp. 273–74.

109. Barnes in Centerprise Trust, *Working Lives*, p. 138; S. Pearce, 'On Putting Up or Shutting Up', *SW* 17 December 1976.

110. Maxwell Stamp Committee, *Report*, p. 38; D. Hobbs, *Doing the Business. Entrepreneurship, the Working Class, and Detectives in the East End of London* (Oxford, 1988), p. 178.

111. Beesley, 'Regulation of Taxis', p. 170.

112. Figures from the annual reports of the Commissioner of Police of the Metropolis, taking the number of drivers owning one cab as a proxy, although many with two, three or four cabs would also have thought of themselves as owner-drivers rather than proprietors. By 1986 the figure stood at almost 60 percent.

113. 'On the "Knowledge."'

114. 'Note of a Meeting Held on 23 September [1968]', Working Party on Taxi-Cab and Private Car Hire Trades in London, London Metropolitan Archives (LMA) GLC/DG/GP/01/103.

115. Editorial, *SW*, 28 January 1977.

116. Field, 'Taxi!', p. 15.

117. Maxwell Stamp Committee, *Report*, p. 36.

118. Levinson, *Taxi Game*, p. 20.

119. Ibid., p. 19.

120. Maxwell Stamp Committee, *Report*, p. 29.

121. Pearce, 'Fares. Time for a Change?', *SW* 4 July 1975.

122. Editorial, 'Image', *TT* January 1972.

123. Editorial, *SW* 1 July 1977.

124. K. Whitehorn, 'Spiels on Wheels', *Observer* 29 April 1979.

125. P. Philips, 'As I See It', *SW* 6 April 1979.

126. S. Pearce, 'Minimum Hirings and Maximum Profits', *SW* 7 April 1978.

127. Editorial, *SW* 24 September 1976.

128. P. L. Schendel, 'True Representation', *SW* 5 May 1978.

129. 'A. Musher', 'I'm Doing Very Well', *SW* 9 February 1979 (original spelling and punctuation).

130. Hodge, *Cab, Sir?*, p. 262.

131. Letter from H. Cutler, *Taxinews* March 1977, 'Taxi and car hire', LMA GLC/DG/ADG/05/023.

132. M. Schiman, 'Monty Schiman at Large. Double Talk', *SW* 6 April 1979.

133. 'Ilford South Votes!', *SW* 22 April 1977.

134. M. Irving, 'Storming in After Years in the Cold', *Ilford Recorder* 12 May 1977.

135. Bendall in 'Crucial Bye-Election at Ilford North', *SW* 2 December 1977; J. Craske, 'Double Aid Pledge by Tessa', *Ilford Recorder* 23 February 1978.

136. J. M. Marcelle, 'Cabman's Letter to Margaret Thatcher', *SW* 6 April 1979.

137. E.g., Monty Schiman on Thatcher's support for the death penalty, M. Schiman, 'Monty Schiman at Large. A Slight Case of Murder', *SW* 4 May 1979.

138. Indeed, Labour reclaimed Ilford South in 1992 and recorded a near-twenty-point swing against Bendall in Ilford North.

Chapter 10

1. 'A Street of Memories and Youth', *Harrow Observer* (*HO*) 22 May 1970.

2. 'Where 15 Widows Walk', *HO* 28 October 1969.

3. 'Community Spirit Makes Friends of These Neighbours', *HO* 26 May 1970.

4. 'The School Its Centre', *HO* 20 November 1970; 'Young Families Change Image of Quiet Cul-de-Sac', *HO* 20 January 1970.

5. Stanley Sumption in 'Retreat from Town Bustle', *HO* 5 September 1969.

6. Herbert Gale, Wellesley Road, Harrow, in 'Meters Change Face of Road Where Car Parking Is Free', *HO* 2 June 1970. Wellesley Road was an older street, built ca. 1900.

7. 'Where the Good Companions Can Be Found', *HO* 22 August 1969, on Hughendon Avenue, Kenton.

8. 'Forty Years On: Harrow Road Then . . . And as It Looks Today', *HO* 16 July 1971.

9. 'Where Four Nursery Schools Flourish', *HO* 29 May 1970.

10. 'At Its Best in Blossom Time', *HO* 13 October 1972.

11. 'Ten Years Old and It Still Looks Bright and Fresh', *HO* 7 August 1970.

12. For these examples, see 'Families Who Enjoy a "Close" Relationship', *HO* 19 August 1969; 'Where the Good Companions Can Be Found', *HO* 22 August 1969, 'Behind the Doors of Suburbia: Contentment', *HO* 21 November 1969, 'Some Backstreet Characters Who Link Past and Present', *HO* 12 May 1970, 'A Third Look at Life in Pinner View, Harrow', *HO* 10 July 1970, 'Humdrum? There's a Stunt Driver and a Family of Writers and the "Lady Who Lived in Russia"', *HO* 20 February 1970, 'From Dark Road to Main Road—and Quiet In-between', *HO* 3 July 1970, 'Reserved Spirit Prevails among Busy Neighbours', *HO* 10 February 1970, 'Pangbourne Drive' *HO* 24 February 1970, 'Young and Old Blend in Friendly Circle', *HO* 16 June 1972.

13. 'Change and Maturity Forty Years On', *HO* 1 May 1970, on Priory Way, North Harrow; 'The Family Street into Which a New Generation Has Moved', *HO* 9 June 1970, on Cecil Park, Pinner.

14. 'Happy Spirit Reigns among All', *HO* 18 November 1969, on Beechwood Gardens, South Harrow; 'Contented Air Its Keynote', *HO* 9 December 1969, on Torver Road, Harrow; 'Removal Vans Rare Sight in Contented Road', *HO* 8 January 1971, on Waghorn Road, Kenton.

15. 'Two OBEs Live in This Peaceful Haven', *HO* 21 October 1969.

16. 'Answer to Neighbourliness Seems to Lie in the Soil', *HO* 13 January 1970.

17. 'A Place to Linger and to Take a Second Look', *HO* 12 September 1969.

18. 'Loneliness in a Pleasant, Friendly, Central Drive', *HO* 29 September 1971.

19. 'Where Parents Fear Children Are in Danger', on Harrow View *HO* 14 May 1971.

20. '"Hidden" Half of Morley Crescent', *HO* 20 October 1972.

21. 'Council of Social Service Gets Down to Work', *HO* 12 January 1971.

22. 'Two OBEs Live in This Peaceful Haven', *HO* 21 October 1969, on The Lawns, Hatch End.

23. 'Where the Memories Linger On', *HO* 8 August 1969, on Springfield Road.

24. 'At Its Best in Blossom Time.'

25. Station profile, Pinner, 'The Job', *Job* (Metropolitan Police) 17 December 1971.

26. Department of the Environment, *National Dwelling and Housing Survey, 1978* (London, 1979), Table 96B, p. 157.

27. Ibid., Table 86B, p. 137.

28. Ibid., Table 82B, p. 129.

29. S. Jenkins, 'Come Back Plastic Gnomes, All Is Forgiven', *Evening Standard* (*ES*) 8 May 1973.

30. Editorial, Western Enfield Residents Association *Journal* Autumn 1972, Enfield Local Studies and Archives, Dugdale Centre, Enfield.

31. R = 0.76 for the thirty-two London boroughs (City of London excluded), Department of the Environment, *National Dwelling and Housing Survey, 1978*, Tables 82B and 83B, pp. 129, 131.

32. P. Hall, *London 2001* (London 1989), p. 20.

33. R = 0.91 for the thirty-two London boroughs (City of London excluded), Department of the Environment, *National Dwelling and Housing Survey*, Tables 78B and 82B, pp. 121, 129.

34. Miss M. L. Beer to Mr Hogan, 2 January 1972, Ruislip Residents Association Papers, Hillingdon Heritage, Uxbridge Library.

35. 'Nostalgic Memories of Old South Harrow Farm', *HO* 16 February 1973, on Whitby Road, South Harrow; 'Winemaker and Ant Farmer are Neighbours', *HO* 24 November 1972, on Manor Road, Harrow; 'Sidney the Iguana Settles for Happy Domesticity', *HO* 17 April 1970, on Anglesmede Avenue, Pinner.

36. The proportion of owner-occupiers in Harrow in 1971 was 70.20 percent: Office of Population Censuses and Surveys, *Census 1971, England and Wales. County Report, Greater London*, vol. 3 (London, 1972), p. 6.

37. 'Traffic Hazard in Once Quiet Street', *HO* 5 November 1971; 'Where the Good Companions Can Be Found', on Hughendon Avenue, Kenton.

38. 'Enjoying a Quiet Life', *HO* 4 September 1970, on Briar Road, Kenton.

39. 'Children Create Friendships in Quiet Grove', *HO* 6 October 1972.

40. J. Sherwood, manager of the Harrow branch of the Halifax Building Society, 'House Prospects Better, Experts Think', *HO* 5 January 1973.

41. 'Once It Was Described as London's Prettiest Road', *HO* 9 June 1972, on Gayton Road, Harrow.

42. J. Deverson & K. Lindsay, *Voices of the Middle Class* (London, 1975), pp. 46, 49–50. 'Purlbridge', which was located in Southwest London by the authors in introducing an extract in the *Evening Standard* ('Happy Families', *ES* 28 April 1975) and was said to be five miles from the centre (*Voices*, p. 33), was probably somewhere like Tooting, with a Victorian and Edwardian north and an interwar south. Florence Sutcliffe-Braithwaite analyses Purlbridge and the authors' other survey area, 'Rivermead' in Surrey, in her excellent *Class, Politics and the Decline of Deference in England, 1968–2000* (Oxford, 2018), ch. 2.

43. Deverson & Lindsay, *Voices of the Middle Class*, p. 35.

44. 'Old and New Mix in Harmony', *HO* 23 February 1973, on Old Church Lane, Stanmore.

45. 'These Residents Maintain High Views on Village Amenities . . . Naturally', *HO* 17 December 1971, on High View, Pinner.

46. J. W. M. Thompson, 'The £450 House: Now It Can Change Hands for £3500', *ES* 15 May 1962.

47. 'From Golf Course to Busy Main Road', *HO* 16 March 1973, on the extension to no. 4 Beverley Gardens, Stanmore.

48. 'Heraldic and Portrait Talents Help to Enliven This Area', *HO* 3 March 1970; 'Growing Families Thrive Here', *HO* 17 August 1973; 'International Flavour: Peaceful Co-existence', *HO* 10 December 1971.

49. 'Rates—Always a Sore Point', *Heston Ratepayers Association Magazine* April 1970, Hounslow Local Studies Service, Feltham Library (original emphasis).

50. Anonymous (G. C. Jenkins) to Bromley Town Council, 24 November 1964, Bromley Ratepayers Association Papers, Bromley Local Studies and Archives, Bromley Central Library.

51. 'Where Music Drowns the Noise of the North Harrow By-pass', *HO* 17 October 1969, on Southfield Park; 'Life in New Houses in an Old Setting', *HO* 12 August 1969 (emphasis added).

52. 'Roxborough Avenue', *HO* 17 March 1970.

53. P. Hall, R. Thomas, H. Gracey & R. Drewett, *The Containment of Urban England*, vol. 2, *The Planning System. Objectives, Operations, Impacts* (London, 1973), p. 397.

54. R. Grizell, 'Big, Rich Croydon with a Cold Heart', *Evening News* 7 June 1972.

55. 'Greenway Gardens. A Quiet Place Where Residents Keep to Themselves', *HO* 31 October 1969.

56. Letter from J. Bowden, *HO* 28 May 1971. See also the letter from V. Goldberg in the same issue and Paul Foley's article 'There's One New Film on Release This Week: These Are the Ones You Have Not Seen . . . Yet' in the issue of 14 May.

57. G. Nazer, 'Morden—Nothing There Soon Except the End of the Northern Line?', *Wimbledon News* 19 January 1973.

58. Cinema closures are listed in G. Wharton, *Suburban London Cinemas* (London, 2008).

59. Research Projects Limited, for Freeman, Fox, Wilbur, Smith & Associates, *Richmond Study* (October 1966), pp. 29, 64, copy in London Metropolitan Archives (LMA) GLC/TD/GLDP/08/402.

60. P. Downey, *The Impact of Brent Cross* (GLC Reviews and Studies Series 2, London, 1980), p. 3.

61. 'A Nice Borough to Live In, but It's Thumbs Down for the Shops', *Wimbledon News* 5 January 1973.

62. Cole Park Residents Association *Quarterly Newsletter* March 1973, Richmond Local Studies Library and Archive, Old Town Hall, Richmond upon Thames.

63. L. B. Wandsworth, *Tomorrow's Putney. A Document for Public Consultation, June 1973*, LMA GLC/DG/AE/ROL/02/159.

64. Letter from 'KG', *Wimbledon News* 8 February 1974.

65. S. Howard, 'The Changing Face of Wimbledon Village—a Sad Sign of the Times', *Wimbledon News* 11 May 1973; and letter from P. B. Kenyon, *Wimbledon News* 18 May 1973.

66. 'Dead Shopping Fronts Created by Offices', *Wimbledon News* 2 March 1973.

67. Editorial, 'That Old Flame', *Middlesex Advertiser* 23 September 1966, cutting in file 'Uxbridge Centre Redevelopment. Post-Inquiry Correspondence', The National Archives (TNA) AT 41/40.

68. J. R. Gold, *The Practice of Modernism. Modern Architects and Urban Transformation, 1954–1972* (London, 2007), ch. 6.

69. By the London Government Act, 1963. Harrow was the only London borough to replace a single earlier authority.

70. 'Expensive office equipment—from dictographs to computers—cannot economically be installed in the multitude of offices scattered all over Romford and Hornchurch at the moment': 'Havering's Birth Is a Bit of History—Like It or Not', in Romford Recorder, *Havering. A Recorder Souvenir* April 1965, Havering Local Studies and Family History Centre, Central Library, Romford, LC/914.267.

71. O. Harris, *Cranes, Critics and Croydonisation* (London, privately published, 1993), p. 3. Copy in Croydon Museum and Archive Service, Croydon Clocktower.

72. Ibid., pp. 4–5.

73. Ibid., p.3.

74. Figures from the appendix to the draft memo by Ian Carruthers, GLC, 'Preferred Town Centres for Strategic Development', 21 January 1974, LMA GLC/DG/ISG/06/133(2).

75. Harris, *Cranes, Critics and Croydonisation*, p. 4.

76. Ibid.; D. White, 'The Pleasure of Croydon', *New Society* 29 May 1975.

77. D. Lovejoy, 'Croydon's Road to Chaos', *The Architect* 1, December 1971.

78. O. Luder, 'Croydon—The Lost Opportunity', *Croydon Advertiser* 26 March 1965.

79. Richmond Society, 'The Fight Is Now On to Save Best of Richmond from Destruction', *Richmond and Twickenham Times* 25 May 1973; Cray Action Group *Newsletter* Autumn 1972, Orpington and District Amenity Society Papers, Bromley Local Studies; MS notes, 'Borough Council Traffic Plan', [April 1974?], Kingston Society Papers, Kingston History Centre, Guildhall, Kingston upon Thames.

80. Strawberry Hill Residents Association *Bulletin* 36, October 1974, Richmond Local Studies.

81. Gold, *Practice of Modernism*, pp. 132–33.

82. E.g., J. T. Jobling, Director of Development for L. B. Sutton, E. Lennox & A. Foreman, 'The Shape of Sutton to Come. It's Now in Their Hands', *Wallington and Carshalton Times* 15 February 1973; Nicholas Taylor in Lewisham, D. Wilcox, 'The Changing Face of Greater London. 3: Lewisham', *Investors Review* 84 (22), 11–24 June 1976; Kenneth Beer, Kingston, M. Hanson, 'The Changing Face of Greater London. 6: Kingston', *Investors Review* 85 (5), 15–28 October 1976.

83. R. W. Jenkins, Labour group leader on Sutton Council: 'Sutton's Views on Town Centre Plan, "Big, Bold. Brilliant"', *Surrey County Herald* 13 September 1962.

84. Research Projects Limited, for Freeman, Fox, Wilbur, Smith & Associates, *Richmond Study*, p. 59; Tony Arbour, quoted in 'Waller to Lead Fight against "Over-Development"', *Richmond Herald* 17 January 1974.

85. D. White, 'The Pleasures of Croydon', *New Society* 29 May 1975.

86. E. Lennox, 'The Shape of Sutton to Come, I', *Wallington and Carshalton Times* 23 November 1972, referring to a proposed twenty-eight-storey block on top of Sutton station.

87. E. Lennox, 'The Shape of Sutton to Come, IV: Room at the Top for the Office Brigade', *Wallington and Carshalton Times* 15 January 1973.

88. John Kennedy, quoted in Lennox & Foreman, 'Shape of Sutton to Come'.

89. Richmond Society, 'Fight Is Now On.'

90. D. Ambrose, *Kingston Conserved? A Sketch of the First Twenty-Five Years of the Kingston upon Thames Society* (London, 1988), p. 11.

91. J. H. Webb to R. F. Holman, 13 March 1970, and R. F. Holman to M. H. Penty, 8 July 1969, Friends of Old Isleworth Papers, Hounslow Local Studies, Box 3.

92. Letter from W. E. Fields, *HO* 19 March 1974.

93. Richmond Society, 'Fight Is Now On.'

94. Southgate Civic Trust *Newsletter* September 1976, Enfield Local Studies.

95. Ambrose, *Kingston Conserved?*, pp. 13, 21–22.

96. B. O. Prowse, 'The Conservation of Wimbledon Village', *Wimbledon News* 29 June 1973.

97. E.g., P. Fiddick, 'Local Affairs', *Guardian* 8 August 1972, on Richmond.

98. Gold, *Practice of Modernism*, p. 136, for delay and blight in Ilford.

99. 'Note of a Meeting Held at the Merton Town Hall . . . on Tuesday 27th June 1972', in 'Merton GLB. Development of Wimbledon Town Centre', TNA AT 41/69.

100. London Borough of Waltham Forest, *Walthamstow Town Centre. Who Cares?* (London, 1971), Waltham Forest Archives and Local Studies Library, Vestry House Museum.

101. Michael Wilks, Carshalton Society, quoted in 'Manhattan, Monoliths, or Even Worse—a Sham?', *Wallington and Carshalton Herald* 16 February 1973; Arnold Harris, property surveyor, Wimbledon, quoted in S. Howard, 'Halt the Bulldozers before We Lose All Our Heritage', *Wimbledon News* 16 November 1973.

102. 'Call for More Stores. First Results of Town Centre Questionnaire', *Wimbledon News* 25 January 1974.

103. Hatch End Association, *Hatch End Bulletin* Autumn 1973, Harrow Local History Collection, Headstone Manor.

104. Estate agent in 'Purlbridge South', quoted in Deverson & Lindsay, *Voices of the Middle Class*, p. 36.

105. *Cannon Hill Ward Residents Association Gazette* 38, September 1974, Merton Heritage and Local Studies, Morden Library.

106. Editorial, 'Apathy? Please Not!', *Selsdon Gazette* May 1974, Croydon Museum and Archive Service, Croydon Clocktower.

107. Pinner South Residents Association Minutes, 17 April 1980, Harrow Local History Collection. 'Our Secretary, Soc Secretary and Treasurer are all past retiring age and wish to relinquish their positions to younger members. . . . It would be a shame, if after 35 years of good service, the Assn should fail for lack of a few younger members willing to give some of their time', Queensbury Residents Association, Edgware, Minutes of Extraordinary Meeting, 21 November 1973, Harrow Local History Collection.

108. Department of the Environment, *National Dwelling and Housing Survey, 1978*, Table 97B, p. 159.

109. 'A Report on a Survey of the Parliamentary Constituency of Sutton/Carshalton, February 1976', Conservative Party Archives, Bodleian Library, Oxford, CCO 180/35/1/106, Table 15, p. 28.

110. Committee of Inquiry, Local Government Finance (Layfield Committee), *Local Government Finance. Report of the Committee of Inquiry* (Cmnd. 6453, 1975–76), p. 181.

111. J. Yaxley, 'Chairman's Notes', *Norwood Review* 45, Summer 1971.

112. 'The Street Where You Live', *HO* 16 June 1970, on Cuckoo Hill Drive; 'Residents Maintain Sense of the Past', *HO* 15 September 1972, on Bishop Ken Road, Harrow Weald.

113. Quotation from photo caption in *HO* 21 August 1970; 'Making Pinner Prettier', *HO* 14 August 1970.

114. 'Sanderstead Preservation Society', *Sanderstead News* June 1972; *Sanderstead News* Winter 1972, Croydon Museum.

115. Elizabeth Cooper, quoted in 'Research Reveals the District Really Has a Soul, Says Lecturer', *HO* 19 January 1973.

116. Aileen Turner, letter to Broad Green Residents Association *Newsletter* 3, August 1974, Croydon Museum.

117. 'Looking Back over the Years', Heathfield Residents Association *Newsletter* March–April 1974, ibid.

118. R. W. C. Cox, 'It Is in Our Hands', *Sanderstead News* December 1970.

119. Editorial, *Cannon Hill Ward Residents Association Gazette* 4, October 1971, Merton Local Studies.

120. Enfield Preservation Society *Newsletter* June 1971, Enfield Local Studies.

121. D.Kenyon, 'Norwood Buildings of Special Architectural or Historic Interest', *Norwood Review* 43, Winter 1971; Yaxley, 'Chairman's Notes.'

122. Leo Held, 'Planning Report', *Norwood Review* 41, Summer 1970.

123. John Passmore, 'Desecration? How the Property Developers Are Spoiling Our Heritage and Why We Can't Stop Them', *Wimbledon News* 6 July 1973.

124. Ibid.

125. London Borough of Merton, Town Planning and Development Committee Minutes, 22 November 1973, 25 April 1974, 24 February 1975, Merton Heritage and Local Studies Centre; 'Council Save Victorian House from Developers', *Wimbledon News* 4 January 1974.

126. 'House Extensions', *News and Views of Woodside Park Garden Suburb (Official Journal of the Woodside Park Ratepayers and Residents Association)* Winter 1974, Barnet Local Studies and Archives, The Burroughs, Hendon.

127. E.g., Cole Park Residents Association *Quarterly Newsletter*, June 1972, Richmond Local Studies; Ambrose, *Kingston Conserved?*, 19–20.

128. 'Sure of Success in Keeping Best of Cator', *Bromley Advertiser* 11 April 1974.

129. Dollis Brook Amenities Association *Newsletter* 14 February 1977, Barnet Local Studies.

130. R. Walters, Memorandum, 'Conservation in Greater London South of the River Thames', LMA GLC/RA/D3/01/091.

131. K. Denbigh, *Preserving London* (London, 1978), pp. 220–28.

132. Peter Barnes to Mrs Boyd, 13 April 1971, CS/BCS/B/3/1, Bexley Civic Society papers, Bexley Local Studies and Archives Centre, Central Library, Bexleyheath.

133. 'Meeting with Mr David John', 12 June 1973, CS/BCS/B/3/24, ibid.

134. Richmond Society, 'Fight Is Now On.'

135. Cox, 'It's in Our Hands.'

136. 'Would the old Southgate Borough Council have put a high office block on The Grange site?', letter from Andrew McHallam, *Palmers Green and Southgate Gazette* 24 April 1975. See also *Cannon Hill Ward Residents Association Gazette* 10, April 1972, Merton Local Studies; A. W. Leadbetter, 'Election Special', *Heston Ratepayers Association Magazine* April 1974, Hounslow Local Studies.

137. N. Nugent, 'The Ratepayers', in R. King & N. Nugent, eds., *Respectable Rebels. Middle Class Campaigns in Britain in the 1970s* (London, 1979), 25–26. I am grateful to Harriet Rudden for this reference.

138. Bromley Town Plan Action Group, 'Memorandum on the Draft Proposals for a Town Centre Map of Bromley', June 1965, Bromley Ratepayers Association papers, Bromley Local Studies.

139. E.g., Enfield Preservation Society *Newsletter* Spring 1969, Enfield Local Studies.

140. Old Chiswick Protection Society *Bulletin* 3, June 1979, Friends of Old Isleworth papers, Hounslow Local Studies, Box 2.

141. 'Conservation and Eastcote', *The Aerial. Eastcote Residents Association Journal* Summer 1970, Hillingdon Heritage.

142. D. Wilcox, 'The Changing Face of Greater London. Introduction', *Investors Review* 84 (17), 2–15 April 1976.

143. 'Can We Afford £22m of Civic Pride?', *Wallington and Carshalton Times* 26 September 1974.

144. F. Roberts, 'Action Group Calls for Release of More Land to Meet the Critical Shortage of Houses in London', *Times* 10 August 1972.

145. Memo, 'Dept of the Environment, London Housing Division, "Action Group on London Housing. Meeting with the Secretary of State to Discuss the Release of Green Belt Land", March 1973', LMA GLC/DG/HG/11/052.

146. Report (22.2.66) by the Director of Planning [B. J. Collins], 'The Choice before London—Discussion of Objectives', LMA GLC/DG/TD/03/004.

147. *Greater London Development Plan. Report of the Panel of Inquiry* (London, 1973), vol. 1, p. 216, and 'Recommendations', p. 623.

148. P. Hall, 'The Containment of Urban England', *Geographical Journal* 140 (3), 1974, 406. This article was a distillation of P. Hall, R. Thomas, H. Gracey & R. Drewett, *The Containment of Urban England*, vol. 2, *The Planning System. Objectives, Operations, Impacts*, which examined the social and economic effects of containment policy. See also D. M. Thomas, *London's Green Belt* (London, 1970); and P. Hall, 'Anatomy of the Green Belts', *New Society* 4 January 1973.

149. R. Thomas in the discussion of Hall's paper, *Geographical Journal* 140 (3), 1974, 409.

150. Graham Shaylor, quoted in 'Villages in Green Belt "Are Doomed"', *ES* 12 September 1973.

151. Editorial, *Riddlesdown Recorder* (Riddlesdown Residents Association) 108, April 1971, Croydon Museum.

152. Letter from H. V. Leaning, *Bromley Advertiser* 25 April 1974.

153. Letter from Pat Lewis, *HO* 10 December 1971.

154. 'Local Planning', *The Bulletin. Upminster and Cranham Residents Association Newsletter* January 1972, Havering Local Studies.

155. 'Where Would the Logical "Filling-in" at the Fringes of the Urban Area Cease?', editorial, *Sanderstead News* Winter 1974, Croydon Museum.

156. C. Jephcott, *Enfield Preservation Society Newsletter* Christmas 1973, Enfield Local Studies.

157. See S. Watts, 'Greater London Brief for Planning Inspectors', 27 April 1976, TNA AT 41/15.

158. Reaffirmed in 1969, 'Green Belt "Hard Line" Unchanged', *HO* 1 July 1969.

159. June Watson, quoted in M. Douglas Home, 'Council Housing List: The Facts behind the Figures', *Enfield Weekly Herald* 29 March 1974.

160. Editorial, *Riddlesdown Recorder* 105, December 1969, Croydon Museum.

161. Action Group on London Housing, *Use of Housing Land in Outer London. Fourth Report to the Minister of Housing and Construction* (London, 1974), pp. 26, 23, 24.

162. Ibid., p. 18.

163. J. W. M. Thompson, 'Beneath This Quiet Exterior Are Tensions—Anguish Even', *ES* 18 May 1962.

164. 'Concerned', *Croydon Advertiser* 11 January 1974.

165. G. L[ewis], 'Council Housing', *Bulletin* August 1976, Havering Local Studies.

166. *The Resident. Emerson Park and Ardleigh Green Residents Association Newsletter* November–December 1976, Havering Local Studies. By September 1974 London boroughs' total rent arrears amounted to £6.3 million, rate arrears to more than £43 million: M. Henning, 'London's Boroughs Take a Deep Dive into Red over Rates Chaos', *ES* 14 November 1974.

167. London Ratepayers Alliance, Minutes, 24 February 1970, Bromley Local Studies.

168. Both from 'Greenway Gardens', *HO* 31 October 1969.

169. Resident of Augustine Road, quoted in 'We Are Victimised Say New Residents', *HO* 30 October 1973.

170. K. Young & J. Kramer, *Strategy and Conflict in Metropolitan Housing* (London, 1978), p. 119ff.

171. Ibid., pp. 156–57; 'Fears of Land Grab', *Bromley Advertiser* 31 January 1974; see also Dimson in 'Hall Agrees to Housing Showdown', *Richmond Herald* 2 May 1974.

172. Greater London Council, *A Strategic Housing Plan for London. Consultation Document, October 1974* (London, 1974), p. 6.

173. James Gran, quoted in 'We Will Go into Debt to Keep Out the Tenants', *ES* 9 February 1979.

174. A. Hulls, '£50,000 Blow. "New Estate Will Cut Our Property Value"', *Hendon Times*, 26 April 1974.

175. Young & Kramer, *Strategy and Conflict*, pp. 189–90, 204.

176. 'Sale of Council Houses', *Bulletin* June 1967, Havering Local Studies.

177. L[ewis], 'Council Housing.'

178. L. Sinclair, 'Municipal Housing, Part II', *Bulletin* June 1976, Havering Local Studies.

179. Responses from R. W. J. Tridgell, 12 May 1977, and J. S. Bishop, 10 December 1976, in 'Action Group on London Housing. Follow-up to Fifth Report', TNA HLG 118/2083.

180. J. Munch & L. Forgan, 'Rates Rise Battle Call Goes Out to Resistance Fighters', *ES* 17 February 1975.

181. London Borough of Bromley, Council Minutes, 29 September 1975, Bromley Local Studies.

182. G. L[ewis]', 'The Greater London Council—a Luxury We Can No Longer Afford?', *Bulletin* February and March 1975, Havering Local Studies.

183. 'There seems little doubt that the low grant made by Central Government to Croydon is politically motivated, as similar treatment is given to other Outer London Boroughs, where there is a Conservative parliamentary representation', 'Croydon Rates', Heathfield Residents Association *Newsletter* May–June 1975, Croydon Museum.

184. Department of the Environment, *Policy for the Inner Cities* (Cmnd. 6845, 1976–77), p. 11.

185. T. Travers, *The Politics of Local Government Finance* (London, 1986), pp. 41–46.

186. 'The Association Committee has taken the view that rate strikes are self-defeating and can only add to the rates burden through legal expenses and the cost of money which no doubt the Council has to borrow at high rates of interest to cover the deficiency caused by non-payment of rates', Heathfield Residents Association *Newsletter* September–October 1975, Croydon Museum; editorial, 'Rates', *Sanderstead News* April 1975, ibid.

187. M. King, Growing Cries of Anguish . . ', *ES* 9 May 1975.

188. Richmond upon Thames Ratepayers and Residents Association *Newsletter* 1, August 1965, Richmond Local Studies.

189. 'Is Local Taxation as Fair as It Can Be?', *Cannon Hill Ward Residents Association Gazette* 12, June 1972; 13, July 1972; 16, October 1972, Merton Heritage and Local Studies Centre.

190. Editorial, *Richmond Herald* 20 February 1975.

191. W. H. P. Humphris, 'Chairman's Message', *The Town Crier. The Magazine of the Ruislip Residents Association* February 1976, Hillingdon Heritage.

192. 'Rates', *Sanderstead News* April 1975, Croydon Museum.

193. D. Adams, 'Background to the Rates. An Expert View', *HO* 21 February 1975.

194. *S.P.A.N.—Spring Park Activities News* (Spring Park Residents Association) March 1975, Croydon Museum.

195. Biggin Hill and District Ratepayers and Residents Association Minutes, 10 December 1975, Bromley Local Studies.

196. 'NURA and Rating Reform', *Bulletin* April 1971, Havering Local Studies; *Cannon Hill Ward Residents Association Gazette* 12, July 1972, Merton Local Studies.

197. Deverson & Lindsay, *Voices of the Middle Class*, p. 221.

198. 'Out of Town Centre Shopping. A paper read by Mr J. D. Ridgway [Asda] . . . on Wednesday 20 March 1974', file 'Initial Reactions from Retailers', LMA GLC/DG/ISG/06/136. The GLC's six strategic centres were Croydon, Ealing, Enfield, Kingston, Lewisham and Wood Green: GLC, *Greater London Development Plan. Statement* (London, 1969), Section 8, pp. 42–43. Twenty-two secondary centres were proposed in recognition, as the GLC admitted privately, of 'the political reality that each borough should have at least one centre on the list': I. Carruthers, Draft Memorandum, 'Preferred Town Centres for Strategic Development', 21 January 1974, LMA GLC/DG/ISG/06/133(2).

Chapter 11

This chapter is a slightly amended version of 'Containing Racism? The London Experience, 1957–1968', in R. Kelley & S. Tuck, eds., *The Other Special Relationship. Race, Rights and Riots in Britain and the United States* (Basingstoke, 2015). I am grateful to Rosie Wild, Jed Fazakarley and Joana Duyster Borredà for comments and suggestions, to Queen Mary University of London Archives for permission to quote from the Donald Chesworth papers and to Rachael Takens-Milne and the Trust for London for access to the City Parochial Foundation minutes.

1. Editorial, 'Disappearing Cockneys', *South London Press* 20 September 1957.

2. Letter from A. J. Pyatt, *South London Press* 30 August 1957.

3. Editorial, 'Disappearing Cockneys', *South London Press* 20 September 1957.

4. E. Pilkington, *Beyond the Mother Country. West Indians and the Notting Hill Riots* (London, 1988). Chapters 3 and 4 of K. H. Perry's excellent *London Is the Place for Me: Black Britons, Citizenship and the Politics of Race* (Oxford, 2016) examine the riots and the subsequent mobilisation of Black grassroots organisations. Camilla Schofield and Ben Jones locate the roots of 'New Left' and communitarian antiracism in the local response to the events of 1958 in their '"Whatever Community Is, This Is Not It": Notting Hill and the Reconstruction of "Race" in Britain after 1958', *Journal of British Studies* 58 (1), 2019, 142–73.

5. M. J. Hill and R. M. Issacharoff, *Community Action and Race Relations. A Study of Community Relations Committees in Britain* (London/Oxford, 1971), ch. 1.

6. The scheme is described in the records of the City Parochial Foundation, which sponsored the experiment: City Parochial Foundation (CPF), Minutes of the Central Governing Body, 3 December 1954, application from Family Welfare Association. The City Parochial Foundation was renamed the Trust for London in 2010.

7. 'Welfare of Coloured People in London. Notes on Work Already Undertaken and Plans for Future Development', [November 1958?], 'Policy of Borough Committees', London Council of Social Service (LCSS) papers, London Metropolitan Archives (LMA) ACC/1888/115.

8. 'Report of a Meeting at the Home Office Held on 3rd December 1958', ibid.

9. M. S. Dunn, Migrant Services Division, West Indies Federation, to Nadine Peppard, West Indian Advisory Committee, 26 June 1960, ibid.

10. Quoted in R. Glass, *London's Newcomers. The West Indian Migrants* (Cambridge, MA, 1961), p. 197.

11. N. Peppard to K. Proud, 16 July 1959, file 'West Indians: Racial Disturbances', LCSS papers, ACC/1888/036.

12. K. Proud, LCSS, to K. Lauder, London Boroughs' Committee, 14 September 1965, LCSS papers, LMA ACC/1888/222/34.

13. CPF Minutes, 3 December 1954, application from Family Welfare Association.

14. CPF Minutes, 8 April 1960.

15. 'Report of a Meeting Held at the North Kensington Community Centre on September 5th [1958]', file 'West Indians: Racial Disturbances', LCSS papers, LMA ACC/1888/036.

16. 'Anti-Black Gang Send Threatening Letters', *West London Observer* 12 September 1958.

17. W. R. Nixon, Clapham, letter to the editor, *South London Press* 21 May 1965.

18. E.g., Ivy Harrison: J. Reedy, 'Secret Report to Council on Coloured Immigrants May Be "Disturbing"', *Kilburn Times* 9 September 1960.

19. M. A. Malik, *From Michael de Freitas to Michael X* (London, 1968).

20. N. Peppard to K. Proud, 10 February 1965, 'Immigrants: Miscellaneous Correspondence', LCSS papers, ACC/1888/032.

21. S. Patterson, 'The New West Indian Migration in South London—Some Problems of Adaptation and Acceptance', full text in the file on the Caxton Hall conference, 8 October 1958, LCSS papers, ACC/1888/120.

22. 'Report of the Sub-Committee of the Mayor's Committee on the Problems of North Kensington', 31 October 1958, Donald Chesworth papers, Queen Mary University of London Archives: Chesworth, PP2/46.

23. 'Preliminary Reports on Immigrant Settlements', October 1962, Lionel and Pansy Jeffrey Donated Papers, Eric and Jessica Huntley papers, LMA/4462/P/01/019.

24. 'Report of the Sub-Committee of the Mayor's Committee on the Problems of North Kensington.'

25. Patterson, 'New West Indian Migration in South London.'

26. Gallup's national poll in September 1958 also found one in ten respondents expressing outspoken prejudice: Glass, *London's Newcomers*, p. 125.

27. Summary of 'The West Indian Comes to Willesden', p. 8, file 'Policy of Borough Committees', etc, LCSS papers, ACC/1888/115; E. J. B. Rose, *Colour and Citizenship. A Report on British Race Relations* (London, 1969), p. 384.

28. These interviews are summarised in the Donald Chesworth papers, PP2/49.

29. D. Wallace Bell, 'Preliminary Report on Racial Disturbances', 5 September 1958, file 'West Indians: Racial Disturbances', LCSS papers, ACC/1888/036; Rev. James Fraser to N. Peppard, 14 October 1958, file 'West Indian Advisory Committee', ibid.

30. West Indian Advisory Committee minutes, 17 September 1958, LCSS papers, ACC/1888/222/020.

31. Working Sub-Committee of the Paddington Overseas Students and Workers Committee, minutes, 12 November 1958, file 'West Indians: Racial Disturbances', LCSS papers, ACC/1888/036.

32. Editorial, 'Europeans Only', *Kilburn Times* 31 March 1961.

33. 'Wanderer's Notes and Comments. It's Worse If Father Is Coloured', *South London Press* 24 June 1958.

34. 'Colour Bars Are White', editorial, *South London Press* 5 September 1958.

35. S. Patterson, ed., *Immigrants in London. Report of a Study Group set up by the London Council of Social Service* (London, 1963), p. 13.

36. Letter from A. Loss, Westbourne Park Road, 'Press Freedom and the "WLO"', *West London Observer* 3 October 1958.

37. Editorial, *West London Observer* 5 September 1958; editorial, 'We Disagree', *Kilburn Times* 19 September 1958.

38. Bell, 'Preliminary Report on Racial Disturbances.'

39. 'It's a Kid's World—One World', *Kilburn Times* 1 May 1959.

40. Letter from M. G. Thomas, 'Government Should Back Referendum', *Marylebone Mercury* 5 June 1959.

41. Letter from 'Puzzled', 'Immigration', *Kilburn Times* 2 October 1959.

42. For the 1959 election in North Kensington, North St Pancras and Hampstead, see Glass, *London's Newcomers*, pp. 179ff.

43. P. Keatley, 'The Trumpets Sound in Notting Hill', *Guardian* 5 October 1959.

44. See J. Holland, 'Election Focus on Willesden East. 11,000 Families Who All Want a House . . .', *Evening News* 25 September 1959; for underregistration in Brixton see L. J. Sharpe, 'Brixton', in N. Deakin, *Colour and the British Electorate 1964* (London, 1965), p. 28.

45. For the Liberal Appeal to Black Voters in North Kensington, see Special Correspondent, 'Inactive in Party Politics', *Times* 2 September 1959.

46. Institute of Race Relations, Summary of Press Comment, October 1959, LCSS papers, ACC/1888/120.

47. The 1968 Institute of Race Relations five-borough survey, which included the London boroughs of Lambeth and Ealing, found that 67 percent of Conservative Party members thought Blacks inferior to whites: Rose, *Colour and Citizenship*, p. 559.

48. Sharpe, 'Brixton', p. 22.

49. 'Council Is Accused of Neglect', *South London Press* 25 September 1959.

50. 'Colour Bar Slur Is Alleged', *South London Advertiser* 24 October 1959; 'Dr Warren Will Listen to Debate on Himself', *South London Press* 20 October 1959.

51. A. Sherman, 'Deptford', in Deakin, *Colour and the British Electorate 1964*, p. 119.

52. A. King, *British Political Opinion, 1937–2000. The Gallup Polls* (London, 2001), pp. 264–65.

53. Willesden Borough Council, *The West Indian Comes to Willesden. Report of a Survey Made for the Willesden Citizens Advice Bureau, on Behalf of the Willesden Borough Council, at the Request of the Willesden International Friendship Council, October 1960*, Sivanandan Collection, Warwick University Library, p. 15.

54. 'Coloured and White Can Live in Peace. But Intelligence and Goodwill Are Needed', *Kilburn Times* 22 January 1960.

55. Patterson, 'New West Indian Migration in South London.'

56. 'Report on Voluntary Liaison Committees in the London Area', with K. Proud to K. Lauder, 14 September 1965, National Committee for Commonwealth Immigrants, LCSS papers, ACC/1888/222/034.

57. Letter from E. Ettlinger, *Marylebone Mercury* 12 September 1958.

58. Editorial, *South London Press* 5 September 1958.

59. 'Race Riot Hooligans Wanted Fun and Games', *Marylebone Mercury* 10 October 1958.

60. Bell, 'Preliminary Report on Racial Disturbances.'

61. Patterson, 'New West Indian Migration in South London.'

62. Chesworth papers, PP2/49.

63. Editorial, 'Colour Bars Are White', *South London Press* 5 September 1958.

64. 'Indict Riot Inciters Say Trades Council', *West London Observer* 19 September 1958.

65. 'Coloured Police Might Check Riots—Say Young Tories', *Kilburn Times* 12 September 1958.

66. Letter from D. O. Dixon, *West London Observer* 19 September 1958.

67. Letter from R. E. Williams, *Marylebone Mercury* 18 October 1957.

68. Letter from William Shipp, *Marylebone Mercury* 19 September 1958.

69. 'We're Going to Drive 'Em Out', *West London Observer* 5 September 1958.

70. Ibid.

71. Letter from Mrs J. Goffe, Camberwell, *South London Press* 19 September 1958..

72. Letter from K. Durban, *Kilburn Times* 19 September 1958.

73. 'Racial Discrimination Condemned by Tories and Socialists', *Marylebone Mercury* 26 September 1958.

74. Willesden Borough Council, *West Indian Comes to Willesden*, p. 29; 'No Colour Bar in Willesden', *Kilburn Times* 3 March 1961.

75. Editorial, *South London Press* 5 September 1958.

76. Willesden Borough Council, *West Indian Comes to Willesden*, p. 5.

77. Letter from T. Vernon, *Marylebone Mercury* 15 January 1960, about letter from N. O. Swad, *Marylebone Mercury* 8 January 1960.

78. Letter from J. Fairhead, *Marylebone Mercury* 18 May 1962.

79. 'West Indians in London. Report of a Conference at Caxton Hall, S.W. 1, on 8th October 1958', LCSS papers, ACC/1888/110; 'Note of a Meeting, 9 June 1959', in 'Legislation against racial discrimination: Home Office policy', The National Archives (TNA) HO 342/82.

80. Letter from T. P. Hunt, *Kilburn Times* 15 January 1960.

81. Letter from R. Walsh and report of council meeting, *Kilburn Times* 5 February 1960.

82. Examples from Maizels's Willesden respondents, Willesden Borough Council, *West Indian Comes to Willesden*, p. 45.

83. 'No Colour Bar. It's Peace at the Milkwood Again', *Evening News* 16 February 1959.

84. Letters from Ernest Golding, *Marylebone Mercury* 26 January 1962, 9 February 1962.

85. Report for 1968–69, quoted in Hill and Issacharoff, *Community Action and Race Relations*, p. 24.

86. W. Montgomery, 'Post Office Union Leader Backs Powell', *Marylebone Mercury* 3 May 1968; Montgomery, 'Union Leader and Coloured Workers', *Marylebone Mercury* 10 May, 1968.

87. 'Colour. Why Should We Hush It Up?', *South East London Mercury* 25 April 1968.

88. Letter from N. C. Bealing, *South London Press* 5 September 1958.

89. Letter from A. Harvey, *Stratford Express* 3 February 1967; letter from T. Formby, *Stratford Express* 24 February 1967.

90. Letter from Mrs M. Anderson, *West London Observer* 26 September 1958; letter from G. Hilbinger, *Marylebone Mercury* 22 January 1960.

91. Letter from 'Also Disgusted', *Stratford Express* 3 February 1967.

92. Letter from G. G. Harris, *Marylebone Mercury* 10 May 1968; views of two residents of the Orchard Hill estate, Lewisham 'What the People Said . . .', *South East London Mercury* 25 April 1968.

93. R. J. Atkins, letter to *Hornsey Journal* 12 May 1967; and editorial comment, *Hornsey Journal* 6 October 1967.

94. Letter from E. Orrin, *Marylebone Mercury* 20 September 1957.

95. Letter from Willa Ainsworth, *Marylebone Mercury* 22 November 1957.

96. Letter from Marie Therese, *Marylebone Mercury* 19 September 1958.

97. Letter from R. G. Bevan, *Marylebone Mercury* 19 January 1962.

98. 'Disperse Immigrants to Other Areas, Say Labour, or Flow Must Be Stopped', *West London Observer* 19 September 1958.

99. Letter from Joe Williams, *Marylebone Mercury* 10 September 1965.

100. 'No Colour Bar in Willesden', *Kilburn Times* 3 March 1961; Willesden Borough Council, *West Indian Comes to Willesden*, p. 37.

101. According to Eileen Jones, of the Inter-Racial Council, speaking to the Hammersmith Council for Community Relations: Community Relations Officer's Report, Executive Committee Meeting, 22 July 1969, Hammersmith Council for Community Relations papers, London Borough of Hammersmith and Fulham Local Studies Centre, Hammersmith Library.

102. E.g., 'The Caithness Road [Shepherd's Bush] area will probably need quite a bit of prodding. There's also a nearby immigrant population', *London Property Letter* 147, 8 March 1969. 'Even today, the situation does not at first sight appear too bright. . . . As, with increasing economic prosperity, the artisans have moved increasingly out to commuter suburbs, so the areas they vacated were rapidly occupied by coloured and other immigrants. It's not for nothing that Brixton attracts all the research workers under the sun', *London Property Letter* 154, 28 June 1969. 'Roads to try? Kellett, Mervan, Rattray and Dalberg Roads. But you're likely to find yourself choked by immigrants', *London Property Letter* 155, 12 July 1969. 'But West Kensington needs careful casing. It's still full of pitfalls for the unwary. . . . West Ken has also got a high immigrant population', *London Property Letter* 188, 9 January 1971.

Chapter 12

1. T. Moore, *Policing Notting Hill. Fifty Years of Turbulence* (Hook, 2013), ch. 8.

2. Ibid., p. 173.

3. For Paul Stephenson's account, see his 'The Notting Hill Carnival 1976: A Personal Assessment and Analysis', The National Archives (TNA) CK 3/38, p.4.

4. 'The Two Faces of Notting Hill', *Evening Standard* (*ES*) 31 August 1976.

5. Stephenson, 'Notting Hill Carnival 1976', p.6.

6. P. Wallis & D. Stevenson, 'Unemployment among West Indian Youths', p. 2. The text of the report appears to survive only in the Race Relations Board papers in the National Archives, and there without the appendix containing quotations cited in the report: TNA CK 2/173. The main conclusions were summarised in J. Lawless, 'Race to the Top', *Business Management* 100 (7), July 1970, 26–31.

7. Community Relations Commission, *Unemployment and Homelessness* (London, 1974), p. 18.

8. M. Stellman, 'Sitting Here in Limbo', *Time Out* 23 August 1974; Commission for Racial Equality, *Looking for Work. Black and White School Leavers in Lewisham* (London, 1978), p. 7.

9. Black women were more likely than men to accept inferior terms of employment: N. Buck, I. Gordon & K. Young, *The London Employment Problem* (Oxford, 1986), p. 176.

10. 'Mr Agostini', in 'Note of a Meeting on 23 August 1970 at Messrs Conrad Jameson Associates Ltd', TNA CK 2/173; L. Morrison, 'Growing Problem of Homeless Young Blacks', *ES* 16 February 1973.

11. R. Bunce & P. Field, *Renegade. The Life and Times of Darcus Howe* (London, 2017), pp. 39–40.

12. Stellman, 'Sitting Here in Limbo.'

13. L. Morrison, 'Growing Problem of Homeless Young Blacks', *ES* 16 February 1973.

14. M. White, 'Tell Me How Long My Home's Been Gone', *Guardian* 7 March 1973.

15. Evidence of Rev. D. Mason, Q. 1063, p. 261; G. Clark, Memorandum 'Police/Immigrant Relations in North Kensington', pp. 235–41, both in House of Commons Select Committee on Race Relations and Immigration, *Police/Immigrant Relations*, vol. 2, *Evidence, Session 1971–2*, 471-II.

16. L. Morrison, 'Black Youngsters in Search of Self-Help Dignity', *ES* 19 February 1973; D. Brandon, *Not Proven. Some Questions about Homelessness and Young Immigrants* (London, 1973), p. 16.

17. Quoted in H. L. Gates Jr., 'Black London', *Antioch Review* 34 (3), 1976, 308.

18. D. Dodd, 'Police and Thieves on the Streets of Brixton', *New Society* 16 March 1978.

19. Quoted in Lawless, 'Race to the Top', p. 30.

20. Quoted in W. Raspberry, 'Young, Bitter and Black', *Observer* 5 September 1976.

21. Quoted in Gates, 'Black London', 308; for Dialect see S. Small, *Police and People in London*, vol. 2, *A Group of Young Black People* (London, 1983), p. 71.

22. S. Patterson, *Dark Strangers. A Sociological Study of the Absorption of a Recent West Indian Migrant Group in Brixton, South London* (London, 1963), pp. 354, 358.

23. F. J. Van Dyck, 'Chanting down Babylon Outernational', in N. S. Murrell, W. D. Spencer & A. A. McFarlane, eds., *Chanting Down Babylon. The Rastafari Reader* (Philadelphia, 1998), p. 181.

24. L. Garrison, *Black Youth, Rastafarianism and the Identity Crisis in Britain* (London, 1979), pp. 29–30.

25. Small, *Police and People in London*, pp. 18, 63.

26. Ibid., pp. 80, 85.

27. Ibid., p. 97.

28. L. Morrison, 'I Say the Police Are to Blame', *ES* 10 August 1970.

29. Wallis & Stevenson, 'Unemployment among West Indian Youths', pp. 11–12.

30. L. Morrison, 'The Race Industry Is Weak, White and Wasteful', *West Indian World* 12 November 1971; L. Morrison, 'What Is the Race Board Up To?', *West Indian World* 19 November 1971; L. Morrison, 'CRC: Black Man's Friend or Foe?', *West Indian World* 26 November 1971; L. Morrison, 'What Is the Answer?', *West Indian World* 3 December 1971.

31. W. Raspberry, 'Why Britain's Blacks Have No Leaders', *Observer* 19 September 1976.

32. 'Memorandum by Mrs Pansy Jeffrey', in Select Committee, *Police/Immigrant Relations*, vol. 2, p. 234.

33. J. A. Hunte, *Nigger-Hunting in England* (Longon, 1965), e.g., pp. 4, 12.

34. D. Howe, *From Bobby to Babylon. Blacks and the British Police* (London, 1988), pp. 27–34; Bunce & Field, *Renegade*, pp. 78–88.

35. E.g., Jeffrey's memorandum for the increased use of loitering charges against Blacks in the late 1960s, in Select Committee, *Police/Immigrant Relations*, vol. 2, p. 234; and George Clark's evidence, ibid., Q. 1006, p. 250.

36. 'Record of a Meeting Held with a Group of Young Immigrants at the Ecumenical Centre, Denbigh Road, Notting Hill, 10 February 1972', ibid., QQ. 1165,1229, 1293, 1234, 1220, pp. 281–91.

37. Memorandum by T. M. Ottevanger, Community Relations Adviser, Royal Borough of Kensington and Chelsea, ibid., p. 276.

38. 'Police/Immigrant Relations in Paddington North and North Kensington. Memorandum by London Council of Social Service Committee for Inter-Racial Co-operation', ibid., p. 232.

39. L. Morrison, 'What It Is Like to be Coloured and on the Beat', *ES* 27 April 1973.

40. Interview in A. Douglas, '"Dem" and "We"', *West Indian World* 6 September 1974.

41. 'Special Way to Bridge Community Relations Gap', *The Job* 9 July 1976.

42. 'Record of a Meeting Held with a Group of Young Immigrants', Q. 1208, p. 284.

43. House of Commons, Select Committee on Race Relations and Immigration, *Police/Immigrant Relations*, vol. 1, *Report*, para. 236, p. 69.

44. J. Whitfield, *Unhappy Dialogue. The Metropolitan Police and Black Londoners in Postwar Britain* (Cullompton, 2004), pp. 51, 106.

45. 'Record of a Meeting Held with a Group of Young Immigrants', QQ. 1290–91, p. 289.

46. Ibid., Q. 1263, p. 287.

47. D. J. Smith & J. Gray, *Police and People in London* (London, 1985), p. 389.

48. Whitfield, *Unhappy Dialogue*, p. 125.

49. W. A. Belson, *The Public and the Police* (London, 1975), p. 42.

50. At least in Notting Hill, according to the MP Bruce Douglas-Mann: Select Committee, *Police/Immigrant Relations*, vol. 2, 9 February 1972, Q. 838, p. 200.

51. Whitfield, *Unhappy Dialogue*, p. 126.

52. Smith & Gray, *Police and People in London*, pp. 390, 112.

53. Small, *Police and People in London*, pp. 103–4.

54. J. Simpson, 'Man to Man', *The Job* 8 December 1967.

55. J. Waldron, 'A Problem of Colour and Character', *The Job* 21 June 1968. Both this article and Simpson's were drafted by Chief Superintendent Merricks of A7: TNA MEPO 2/11238.

56. Whitfield, *Unhappy Dialogue*, p. 114.

57. P. Evans, 'Notting Hill Gate: A Suitable Case for Treatment', *Times* 17 December 1971.

58. Whitfield, *Unhappy Dialogue*, p. 152.

59. 'Police/Immigrant Relations in Notting Hill', memorandum by 'B' Division of the Metropolitan Police, in Select Committee, *Police/Immigrant Relations*, vol. 2, p. 215.

60. Belson, *Public and Police*, p. 42.

61. D. Pitt, 'Little Things Add Up to a Very Big Problem', *The Job* 19 July 1968.

62. Letter from PC G. Courtney-Green, *The Job* 2 August 1968.

63. Letter from PC B. Nudd, *The Job* 2 August 1968.

64. Memorandum 'Race Relations', 4 June 1968, TNA MEPO 2/11238. This memorandum was the basis for Waldron's article in *The Job* on 21 June.

65. F. R. Merricks, 'The Development of Community Relations in the Metropolitan Police', *Police Journal* 1 January 1970, 30.

66. R. Wild, '"Black Was the Colour of Our Fight": The Transnational Roots of British Black Power', in R. D. G. Kelley & S. Tuck, eds., *The Other Special Relationship. Race, Rights and Riots in Britain and the United States* (New York, 2015), p. 29.

67. There is a good account of the Mangrove trial and its ramifications in R. Waters, *Thinking Black. Britain, 1964–1985* (Oakland, CA, 2019), ch. 3.

68. Quoted in Moore, *Policing Notting Hill*, p. 65.

69. Bunce & Field, *Renegade*, ch. 7.

70. Ibid., pp. 150–51.

71. A. Cohen, *Masquerade Politics. Explorations in the Structure of Urban Cultural Movements* (Berkeley, CA, 1993), p. 108.

72. Bunce & Field, *Renegade*, pp. 154–55.

73. J. Norridge, 'Behind the Bitterness of Notting Hill', *ES* 10 August 1970.

74. Bunce & Field, *Renegade* pp. 12, 160.

75. Ibid., p. 163.

76. Ibid., p. 182.

77. Waters, *Thinking Black*, pp. 94, 101ff.

78. This paragraph is based on Bunce & Field, *Renegade*, ch. 10; and Moore, *Policing Notting Hill*, ch. 6.

79. 'The Mangrove: Just a Chapter in a 400 Year Story', *Time Out* 24 December 1971.

80. Bunce & Field, *Renegade*, pp. 208–9.

81. E.g., the suggestion in the memorandum by Terry Leander, generally a critic of the police, that 'police pressure on black youths has definitely fallen off in the North Kensington and North Paddington areas' after the raid on the Metro youth club in May 1971 (Select Committee, *Police/Immigrant Relations*, vol. 2, Evidence, pp. 232–33), the suggestion from several witnesses that Inspector Dean had been willing to consult Black spokesmen (e.g., the evidence of Bruce Douglas-Mann, MP, ibid., QQ.841-2, p. 204) and the statistics in the B Division memorandum for the Select Committee suggesting that Blacks were no more likely to incur criminal charges than whites were in 1971 (ibid., p. 211): regardless of the reliability of one year's figures, it is significant that the division was already collecting statistics indicating the racial origin of those who were charged.

82. John Hopkins, quoted in B. Miles, *London Calling. A Countercultural History of London since 1945* (London, 2010), p. 187.

83. Robin Farquharson, quoted in J. Mash, *Portobello Road. Lives of a Neighbourhood* (London, 2014), p. 115.

84. Rhaune Laslett, quoted ibid., p. 117.

85. Cohen, *Masquerade Politics*, p. 11.

86. Ibid.

87. S. Kloß, *Notting Hill Carnival. Die Aushandlung des Eigenen im multiethnischen Großbritannien seit 1958* (Frankfurt, 2014), pp. 113, 109.

88. Ibid., pp. 120–21, 124–25.

89. A. Cohen, 'Drama and Politics in the Development of a London Carnival', *Man* 15 (1), 1980, 70.

90. R. Laslett to R. Paterson, 15 August 1969, file 'Notting Hill Carnival', TNA MEPO 2/10891.

91. J. Donnelly, 'Notting Hill Carnival Procession, 30.8.1970', 21 August 1970, and R. Radford, 'Notting Hill Carnival Procession, Sunday 30 August. Revised Arrangements', TNA MEPO 2/10891; Kloß, *Notting Hill Carnival*, p. 122.

92. Police estimates: Ch. Insp. G. Parry, 'Notting Hill Festival—Procession and Pageant', 18 September 1967, and A/Ch. Supt. G. Rush, 'Notting Hill Festival', 3 September 1969, TNA MEPO 2/10891; M. McKee, 'Dancing in the Streets', *Kensington News and Post* 31 August 1973.

93. According to Kloß, *Notting Hill Carnival*, p. 129.

94. Summary Notes on Carnivals, TNA MEPO 2/10891.

95. McKee, 'Dancing in the Streets.'

96. Kloß, *Notting Hill Carnival*, p. 167.

97. Leslie Palmer in 2013, quoted in Mash, *Portobello Road*, p. 124.

98. Ibid.

99. McKee, 'Dancing in the Streets.'

100. For an account of the People's War Sound System, formed in 1975, see 'Constitution of People's War Carnival Band', George Padmore Institute, CVL/2/1/3.

101. Cohen, *Masquerade Politics*, pp. 99, 34; Memorandum by Ch. Insp. W. Craven, 'Notting Hill Carnival—1975', 11 August 1975, TNA MEPO 2/10891.

102. Whitfield, *Unhappy Dialogue*, p. 71.

103. Memoranda by Insp. D. French, 'Notting Hill Carnival—1974', 28 August 1974, and Ch. Insp. W. Craven, 'Notting Hill Carnival—1975', 11 August 1975, TNA MEPO 2/10891.

104. Quoted in Moore, *Policing Notting Hill*, p. 147.

105. Ch. Supt. A. J. Tenten, 'Notting Hill Carnival', 14 October 1975, TNA MEPO 2/10891.

106. 'Carnival '75 Is a Big Success', *West Indian World* 12 September 1975.

107. S. Jenkins, 'Why We Must Not Ban the Carnival', *ES* 31 August 1976.

108. 'Statement to Chief Inspector Wells and Inspector Craven—Notting Hill Police Station . . . on Thursday Evening 22 August', TNA MEPO/2/10891.

109. L. Palmer to Sir R. Mark, n.d. but in envelope postmarked 30 July 1975, TNA MEPO 2/10891.

110. According to Ch. Supt. R. Paterson, 'Note of a Meeting with Mr Frank Bynoe, Chairman of the Notting Hill Carnival, on Thursday 5 February [1976]', TNA MEPO/2/10891.

111. Ch. Supt. R. Wells, 'Complaint of Noise from Carnival Bands', 16 September 1974, TNA MEPO 2/10891.

112. Resident of Oakworth Road, W10, to R. Paterson, 4 February 1976, TNA MEPO 2/10891.

113. Rev. A. B. Andrews, 'Notting Hill Carnival', Pansy Jeffrey papers, Eric and Jessica Huntley papers, LMA/4462/P/01/48A.

114. Tenten, 'Notting Hill Carnival.'

115. R. Paterson to R. L. Stillwell, Royal Borough of Kensington and Chelsea, 25 November 1975, TNA MEPO 2/10891; Kloß, *Notting Hill Carnival*, pp. 193–94.

116. Quoted in S. Clark, 'Mas in the Grove', *Time Out* 22 August 1975.

117. L. Palmer to P. Stephenson, 9 June 1976, file 'Notting Hill Carnival Development Committee', TNA CK 3/38.

118. 'Ziggalee', panman in the first Laslett Carnival, quoted in Clark, 'Mas in the Grove.'

119. Kloß, *Notting Hill Carnival*, p. 203.

120. 'Notting Hill: The Battle Ground', *West Indian World* 10 September 1976.

121. The arguments of Bynoe, Palmer and Junior Telfer, summarised by Paterson in 'Notting Hill Carnival', 30 January 1976, TNA MEPO 2/10891.

122. The management of the White City stadium could not commit to hosting a crowd of more than fifteen to twenty thousand, on only one day of the bank holiday weekend: Report of the

Voluntary Organisations Liaison Committee in Royal Borough of Kensington and Chelsea, Council Minutes, 9 June 1976, Kensington and Chelsea Local Studies and Archives. Estimated attendance at the 1974 Carnival had been 150,000: Memo by Chief Inspector W. Craven, 11 August 1975, TNA MEPO 2/10891.

123. Kloß, *Notting Hill Carnival*, pp. 201–2.

124. Paterson, 'Notting Hill Carnival.'

125. Letter from PC Robinson, *The Job* 17 September 1976.

126. Details in 'A. 8 Operation No 137/76, 13 August 1976', TNA MEPO 2/10891.

127. Jenkins, 'Why We Must Not Ban the Carnival.'

128. Select Committee, *Police/Immigrant Relations*, vol. 2, QQ. 1091–92, 1096, pp. 267–68.

129. PC Robinson, *The Job* 17 September 1976; 'Delroy', quoted in B. Troyna, 'The Reggae War', *New Society* 10 March 1977.

130. Ancel Kardon, quoted in 'The Two Faces of Notting Hill', *ES* 31 August 1976.

131. Black Liberation Front, 'Statement on the Police Riot at the Carnival', 31 August 1976, George Padmore Institute, BPM/6/1/2/2; 'Police Carnival', *West Indian World* 3 September 1976.

132. Letter from PC Robinson, *The Job*.

133. M. Phillips, 'The Sullen Carnival', *New Society* 31 August 1978.

Chapter 13

This chapter is a slightly amended version of 'Reshaping the Welfare State? Voluntary Action and Community in London, 1960–1975', in L. Goldman, ed., *Welfare and Social Policy in Britain since 1870. Essays in Honour of Jose Harris* (Oxford, 2019), pp. 197–212.

1. P. Townsend, 'The Meaning of Poverty', *British Journal of Sociology* 13 (3), 1962, 210–27; B. Abel-Smith & P. Townsend, *The Poor and the Poorest* (London, 1965), P. Townsend, *The Family Life of Old People* (London, 1957), A. Harvey, *Casualties of the Welfare State* (London, 1960); M. McCarthy, *Campaigning for the Poor: CPAG and the Politics of Welfare* (London, 1986); S. O'Carroll, '*Cathy Come Home* de Ken Loach: Un déclencheur de la "redécouverte de la pauvreté" des années soixantes?', in D. Frison, ed., *Pauvreté et inégalités en Grande-Bretagne de 1942 à 1990* (Paris, 2000), pp. 271–83.

2. T. Evans, 'Stopping the Poor Getting Poorer: the Establishment and Professionalisation of Poverty NGOs, 1945–1995', in N. Crowson, M. Hilton & J. McKay, *NGOs in Contemporary Britain. Non-State Actors in Society and Politics since 1945* (Basingstoke, 2009), pp. 147–63.

3. H. Marshall, *Twilight London. A Study in Degradation* (London, 1971), p. 172.

4. M. Taylor, 'Voluntary Action and the State', in D. Gladstone, ed., *British Social Welfare. Past, Present and Future* (London, 1995), pp. 223–27.

5. Report of the Policy Committee on Quinquennial Policy, 1972–76, City Parochial Foundation (CPF) Minutes, 29 October 1971. I am grateful to Rachael Takens-Milne of the Trust for London for help and guidance with the CPF material.

6. CPF Minutes, 27 October 1967, 30 April 1965, 26 April 1974, 30 April 1965.

7. Family Welfare Association, 96th Annual Report, 1964–65, p. 7, London Metropolitan Archives (LMA) A/FWA/C/B/03/087.

8. J. Edginton, *Avenues Unlimited. A Research Study of Youth and Community Work in East London* (Leicester, 1979), p. 39.

9. Application from Notting Hill Social Council, Finance and General Purposes Committee Report, CPF Minutes, 27 October 1967; memo 'The Portobello Project', n.d., Donald Chesworth papers, Queen Mary University of London Archives, PP2/49.

10. CPF Minutes, 25 October 1968.

11. CPF Minutes, 4 May 1973.

12. 'The Reorganisation of the Social Work Services. Report of a Group of Social Workers in the Borough of Islington', [1966?], pp. 4–5, London Council of Social Service papers, LMA ACC/1888/180.

13. C. Coon, 'We Were the Welfare Branch of the Alternative Society', in H. Curtis & M. Sanderson, *The Unsung Sixties. Memoirs of Social Innovation* (London, 2004), pp. 183–97; A. Mold, '"The Welfare Branch of the Alternative Society?" The Work of Drug Voluntary Organization Release, 1967–1978', *Twentieth Century British History* 17 (1), 2006, 50–73; Spitalfields Crypt Trust, *The Outcasts of Spitalfields* ([1965?]). I am grateful to Graham Marshall of the Spitalfields Crypt Trust for allowing me to consult the Trust's early publications.

14. CPF Minutes, 25 October 1968, 24 October 1969.

15. CPF Minutes, 8 October 1965, 17 April 1964, 9 October 1964.

16. 'Christian Action. Draft Statement Concerning Problems of Policy and Organisation', n.d. [ca. 1964], pp. 1, 6, Canon L. John Collins papers, Lambeth Palace Archives, MS 3298, ff. 325–31.

17. J. Collins to M. Ramsey, 5 November 1963, Archbishop Michael Ramsey papers, Lambeth Palace Archives, vol. 34, ff. 118–25.

18. U. Lambert to M. Ramsey, 15 December 1966, ibid., vol. 93, ff. 219–23; 'Note for the Archbishop', on the Christian Action Shelter for Homeless Women, 15 June 1967, ibid., vol. 111, f. 341.

19. P. Seyd, 'Shelter. The National Campaign for the Homeless', *Political Quarterly* 46 (4), 1975, 418–19.

20. Notting Hill Social Council Minutes, 30 September 1963, Chesworth papers, PP2/49.

21. Philip Barron Associates, 'Public Relations Proposals for 1966/67 for the Notting Hill Housing Trust', March 1966, Eric and Jessica Huntley papers, LMA/4462/P/01/021.

22. D. Wilson, *I Know It Was the Place's Fault* (1970), pp. 114–15; for Shelter's emphasis on advertising see M. Hilton, J. McKay, N. Crowson & J.-F. Mouhot, *The Politics of Expertise. How NGOs Shaped Modern Britain* (Oxford, 2013), pp. 168–72.

23. Wilson, *I Know It Was the Place's Fault*, pp. 157–58.

24. D. Bull, 'CPAG—What an Amazing Time to Be Involved in This Sort of Politics', in Curtis & Sanderson, *Unsung Sixties*, pp. 116–30.

25. Committee on Housing in Greater London, *Report of the Committee on Housing in Greater London* (Cmnd. 2605, 1965), p. 228.

26. Central Advisory Committee for Education (England), *Children and Their Primary Schools* (London, 1967), ch. 5.

27. A. H. Halsey, 'Government against Poverty', paper delivered at the Anglo-American Conference on the Evaluation of Social Action Programmes, Ditchley Park, October 29–31, 1969, p. 4, The National Archives (TNA) HO 389/1.

28. 'Report of the Sub-Committee of the Mayor's Committee on the Problems of North Kensington', 31 October 1958, Chesworth papers, PP2/46. See chapter 11.

29. Des McConaghy, Director of SNAP, quoted in Wilson, *I Know It Was the Place's Fault*, p. 201.

30. 'Homelessness and Housing. A Discussion Paper for Voluntary Organisations', November 1971, London Council of Social Service papers, LMA ACC/1888/362.

31. Marshall, *Twilight London*, pp. 52–53.

32. CPF Minutes, 11 July 1969.

33. Committee on Local Authority and Allied Personal Social Services, *Report* (Seebohm Report) (Cmnd. 3703, 1968), para. 485, p. 149.

34. Ibid., ch. 16.

35. CPF Minutes, 29 November 1963 (original emphasis), 9 July 1965, 28 April 1967.

36. D. N. Thomas, *Organising for Social Change. A Study in the Theory and Practice of Community Work* (London, 1976), p. 20.

37. CPF Minutes, 10 July 1970.

38. M. Adeney, *Community Action. Four Examples* (London, 1971), p. 27.

39. London Council of Social Service papers, LMA ACC/1888/180.

40. Listed in the grant application from the North Kensington Neighbourhood Law Centre, Report of the Finance and General Purposes Committee, CPF Minutes, 13 July 1973.

41. J. O'Malley, *The Politics of Community Action. A Decade of Struggle in Notting Hill* (Nottingham, 1977), p. 25.

42. E.g., for Southwark, F. Rossetti, 'Politics and Participation: A Case Study', in P. Curno, *Political Issues and Community Work* (London, 1978), p. 150; S. Goss, *Local Labour and Local Government. A Study of Changing Interests, Politics and Policy in Southwark, 1919 to 1972* (Edinburgh, 1988), p. 93.

43. Marshall, *Twilight London*, p. 8.

44. Wilson, *I Know It Was the Place's Fault*, p. 56.

45. National Council of Social Service, 'Comments on the Report of the Interdepartmental Committee on Local Authority and Allied Personal Social Services (the Seebohm Report) sent to the Department of Health and Social Security', 20 December 1968, London Council of Social Service papers, LMA ACC/1888/180.

46. H. Rose, *Rights, Participation and Conflict* (London, [1970?]), p. 7.

47. O'Malley, *Politics of Community Action*, p. 44. See in this respect C. Schofield & B. Jones, '"Whatever Community Is, This Is Not It": Notting Hill and the Reconstruction of "Race" in Britain after 1958', *Journal of British Studies* 58 (1), 2019, 161–69.

48. P. Hain, *Radical Regeneration. Protest, Direct Action and Community Politics* (London, 1975), p. 4.

49. P. Baldock, 'Why Community Action? The Historical Origins of the Radical Trend in British Community Work', *Community Development Journal* 12 (2), 1977, 71.

50. Claimants' unions were attempts to organise people on unemployment and supplementary benefit. For those operating in London see 'London Claimants Unions', *Time Out* 7 January 1972.

51. O'Malley, *Politics of Community Action*, p. 46.

52. S. Baine, *Community Action and Local Government* (London, 1975), pp. 11–12, 14–15, 17.

53. J. Benington, *Local Government Becomes Big Business* (Coventry, 1975), p. 11.

54. C. Cockburn, *The Local State. The Management of Cities and People* (London, 1977), p. 41.

55. For which see chapter 5.

56. For Lambeth see C. Jackson, *Lambeth Interface. Housing, Planning and Community Action in an Inner London Borough* (Croydon, 1975), pp. 11ff.

57. A. Power, *I Woke Up This Morning. The Development of a London Community Project* (London, 1972), p. 12.

58. 'Co-operative Action', *Community Action* 17, December 1974–January 1975.

59. J. Davis, '"The Most Fun I've Ever Had"? Squatting in England in the 1970s', in F. Anders & A. Sedlmaier, eds., *Public Goods versus Private Interests. Global Perspectives on the History of Squatting* (London, 2016), pp. 237–54.

60. R. Bailey, *The Squatters* (Harmondsworth, 1973), p. 143.

61. Ibid., p. 28.

62. 'The overwhelming success of the [squatters'] campaign was due to direct action tactics', Hain, *Radical Regeneration*, p. 15.

63. For this paragraph, ibid., pp. 16, 155, 80, 77, 164–65, 147, 170.

64. M. Loney, *Community against Government. The British Community Development Project, 1968–78* (London, 1983).

65. A. Davis, N. McIntosh & J. Williams, *The Management of Deprivation. Final Report of Southwark Community Development Project* (London, 1977), p. 25.

66. Halsey, 'Government against Poverty', p. 14.

67. National Community Development Project, Submission to the Layfield Committee of Inquiry into Local Government Finance, January 1975, p. 21, TNA AT 10/465.

68. Quoted in Loney, *Community against Government*, p. 195.

69. N. Lawson, *The View from No. 11. Memoirs of a Tory Radical* (London, 1992), p. 613.

Chapter 14

This chapter borrows some material from my 'Community and the Labour Left in 1970s London', in C. Williams & A. Edwards, eds., *The Art of the Possible: Politics and Governance in Modern British History, 1885–1997. Essays in Memory of Duncan Tanner* (Manchester, 2015), pp. 207–23.

1. A. Howard, 'Islington's Last Hurrah', *New Statesman* 17 August 1962.

2. R. Butterworth, 'Islington Borough Council: Some Characteristics of Single-Party Rule', *Politics* 1 (1), 1966, 21–31.

3. Howard, 'Islington's Last Hurrah.'

4. Ibid.

5. Ibid.; Butterworth, 'Islington Borough Council', p. 24.

6. Butterworth, 'Islington Borough Council', p. 31.

7. L. J. Sharpe, 'The Politics of Local Government in Greater London', *Public Administration* 38 (2), 1960, Table VI, p. 168.

8. Ibid., 169.

9. J. E. Turner, *Labour's Doorstep Politics in London* (London, 1978), pp. 116, 122, 158, 245, 315.

10. Ibid., p. 122.

11. Ibid., p. 318.

12. Ibid., p. 315.

13. Ibid., p. 215. According to Butterworth, no division was taken in full council in Islington between 1950 and the abolition of the metropolitan borough in 1965, 'Islington Borough Council', p. 25.

14. John O'Malley, 'Political Structures of the Local Authorities in CDP', 8 May 1973, Joint Docklands Action Group (JDAG) papers, Museum of London Docklands, Box 2. West Ham had been controlled by Labour continuously from 1919 and East Ham from 1929 until their amalgamation to form Newham in 1965.

15. A. Glassberg, *Representation and Urban Community* (London, 1981), p. 107.

16. Turner, *Labour's Doorstep Politics*, pp. 180–81, 323.

17. F. Rossetti, 'Politics and Participation: A Case Study', in P. Curno, ed., *Political Issues and Community Work* (London, 1978), p. 150.

18. Howard, 'Islington's Last Hurrah.'

19. Rossetti, 'Politics and Participation', p. 150.

20. S. Goss, *Local Labour and Local Government. A Study of Changing Interests, Politics and Policy in Southwark, 1919 to 1972* (Edinburgh, 1988), pp. 191–92.

21. H. Jenkins, *Rank and File* (London, 1980), pp. 15, 37, 47, 146, 164.

22. In addition to Southwark and Tower Hamlets, Labour retained control of two working-class outer boroughs, Barking and Newham. In the latter case it retained power in a hung council only by virtue of its majority among the six-year aldermen chosen in 1964. All the remaining twenty-eight boroughs were won by the Conservatives.

23. Butterworth, 'Islington Borough Council', p. 24.

24. Glassberg, *Representation and Urban Community*, p. 50; K. Livingstone, *If Voting Changed Anything, They'd Abolish It* (London, 1987), p. 18.

25. T. Marshall, 'Tributes Paid after Death of 1970s Leader of Islington Council', *Islington Gazette* 13 July 2011.

26. L. Garner, 'Millie Miller—Scourge of Centre Point', *Sunday Times* 17 September 1972.

27. P. Haynes, *An Islington Councillor, 1971–1992* (1994), foreword, pp. i, iii and p. 1.

28. Quoted in Glassberg, *Representation and Urban Community*, p. 70. Bayliss was actually a teacher at Highbury Grove school.

29. Ibid., p. 73.

30. Livingstone, *If Voting Changed Anything*, pp. 25–26.

31. Glassberg, *Representation and Urban Community*, p. 73.

32. Haynes, *Islington Councillor*, p. 19.

33. Howard, 'Islington's Last Hurrah.'

34. Butterworth, 'Islington Borough Council', pp. 30–31.

35. After 1965 the Royal Borough of Kensington and Chelsea and the City of Westminster.

36. S. Baine, *Community Action and Local Government* (London, 1975), p. 9.

37. C. Holmes, *The Other Notting Hill* (Studley, 2005).

38. Jan O'Malley, interview with John Davis for the 'Around 1968' project, 22 April 2010, http://around1968.modhist.ox.ac.uk/.

39. Jan O'Malley, *The Politics of Community Action. A Decade of Struggle in Notting Hill* (Nottingham, 1977), p. 32.

40. Baine, *Community Action and Local Government*, p. 10.

41. E. Setch, 'The Face of Metropolitan Feminism: the London Women's Liberation Workshop, 1969–1979', *Twentieth Century British History* 13 (2), 2002, 171–90.

42. Editorial, *Islington Gutter Press* (*IGP*) 17, December 1974–January 1975.

43. C. Cockburn, *The Local State. The Management of Cities and People* (London, 1977), p. 74.

44. I. Binns, 'What Are We Trying to Achieve through Community Action?', *Community Action* 6, January–February 1973.

45. Figures from the Annual Census of Employment, cited in Greater London Council, *Plant Relocation and Closure in London 1976–80* (Economic Policy Group, Strategy Document 3, May 1983), Appendix 2, Table 4, p. 6.

46. C. Howick & T. Key, *Local Economy of Tower Hamlets. An Inner-City Profile* (London, 1978), pp. 14, 38–39.

47. Canning Town Community Development Project, *Canning Town to North Woolwich. The Aims of Industry? A Study of Industrial Decline in One Community* (2nd ed., London, 1975); J. C. Roberts, *Employment in Southwark. A Strategy for the Future* (London, 1976); Binns, 'What Are We Trying to Achieve', p. 6.

48. 'Tenants and Workers Taking Joint Action', *Community Action* 22, October–November 1975; interview with Jack Mundey, *Community Action* 24, February–March 1976.

49. 'Tenants and Workers Taking Joint Action.'

50. The GLC's 1983 survey of forty-nine firms which had left London showed 'inadequate premises', 'lack of space' and 'inefficient site layout' to be the most common reasons for relocation: GLC, *Plant Relocation and Closure in London*, Appendix 2, Table 15, p. 19. The same was true in Tower Hamlets: C. Howick & T. Key, 'Manufacturing Industry and Inner City Regeneration: an Economic Study of the London Borough of Tower Hamlets', *Progress in Planning* 18 (3), 1982, 172.

51. Newham Action Committee, 'Discussion Notes on Industry', n.d. [1976?], JDAG papers, Box 4.

52. T. Clarke, 'Redundancy, Worker Resistance and the Community', in G. Craig, M. Mayo & N. Sharman, eds., *Jobs and Community Action* (London, 1979), pp. 88–93.

53. C. Dyter, 'War Declared in Bid to Save Jobs', *Newham Recorder* 30 December 1975; Dyter, 'Newsprobe Special. Shutdown at STC', *Newham Recorder* 8 January 1976.

54. Minutes of the Newham Job Conference, 20 September 1975, JDAG papers, Box 4.

55. P. Brimson, *Islington's Multinationals* (London, 1979), p. 37.

56. 'Council Participation', *IGP* 15, June–July 1974.

57. R. Colenutt, 'Community Action over Local Planning Needs', in Craig, Mayo & Sharman, *Jobs and Community Action*, p. 246.

58. North Southwark Community Development Group worker, quoted in Goss, *Local Labour and Local Government*, p. 95.

59. Ibid.

60. S. Hough, 'Labour's Radical Right', *New Society* 17 November 1977.

61. Haynes, *Islington Councillor*, p. 34.

62. 'Talking to Ken Livingstone', *IGP* 48, August 1978.

63. W. Phillips, 'O'Grady Says Do This!', *ES* 18 January 1979; P. Tatchell, *The Battle for Bermondsey* (London 1983), pp. 15–19.

64. Glassberg, *Representation and Urban Community*, p. 108.

65. Baine, *Community Action and Local Government*, p. 20.

66. 'Why Not Squat?', *IGP* 1, n.d. but 1972.

67. Livingstone, *If Voting Changed Anything*, p. 32.

68. Glassberg, *Representation and Urban Community*, p. 63; letter from F. Johns, *Islington Gazette* 7 November 1975. For Southgate's reply see *Islington Gazette* 21 November 1975.

69. Cllr. Ian Andrews, quoted in D. Ball, 'Council and Community', *New Society* 7 January 1971.

70. Interview in 'Exclusive Interview with Margaret Watson', *IGP* 21, June–July 1975.

71. S. Platt, 'A Decade of Squatting. The Story of Squatting in Britain since 1968', in N. Anning et al., eds., *Squatting: The Real Story* (London, 1980), p. 96.

72. Ibid., pp. 82–83; T. Osborn, 'Outpost of a New Culture', in Anning et al., *Squatting*, pp. 186–91.

73. W. Phillips, 'Leftist Lambeth: Last of the Big Spenders', *ES* 26 October 1978.

74. Glassberg, *Representation and Urban Community*, pp. 131, 162.

75. N. Wates, *The Battle for Tolmers Square* (London, 1976).

76. 'Talking to Ken Livingstone'.

77. London Borough of Wandsworth, *Prosperity or Slump? The Future of Wandsworth's Economy* (London, 1976), p. 1.

78. Ibid., p. 2.

79. Ibid., p. 12.

80. 'Labour Lash Homeless. Programme Collapses', *Camden Tenant* 21, December 1974.

81. 'Talking to Ken Livingstone'.

82. 'Text of Deputation to Camden Council', *Camden Tenant* December 1972.

83. 'Fair Fight', *Community Action* April–May 1972.

84. Editorial, *Hackney Gutter Press* 1, n.d. but 1972.

85. D. Wilcox, 'Camden Ends War over Fair Rents', *ES* 10 January 1973.

86. P. Cooper, S. Creighton, J. Moore, H. Richards, C. Stevens & M. Ward, *A Socialist Strategy for Wandsworth. Proposals for the Basis of a Socialist Manifesto for the Labour Party in the Wandsworth Council Elections May 1978* (London, 1978), p. 1.

87. As Livingstone pointed out: *If Voting Changed Anything*, p. 78.

88. J. O'Malley, 'Political Structures of the Local Authorities in CDP', 8 May 1973, Joint Docklands Action Group (JDAG) papers, Museum of London in Docklands, Box 2, p. 2.

89. A. Smith, 'First Swallow of a Long Hot Summer?', *Guardian* 28 June 1975; 'Trials of a Militant Moderate', *Observer* 20 July 1975.

90. G. Horn, *Crossing the Floor. Reg Prentice and the Crisis of British Social Democracy* (Manchester, 2013), p. 97.

91. Jenkins, *Rank and File*, pp. 104, 16, 35–36, 85, 113, 117, 142.

92. G. Kemp, 'Labour Marxists Threaten 12 Moderate MPs', *Daily Telegraph* 3 March 1976.

93. Turner, *Labour's Doorstep Politics*, p. 79; 'Another Labour MP in Danger', *Guardian* 30 August 1975; 'Trouble Brewing?', *Guardian* 29 July 1975.

94. Tatchell, *Battle for Bermondsey*. Mellish had represented Surrey Docklands constituencies since 1946.

95. P. Symon, 'Mr Wilson Intervenes in Prentice Affair', *Times* 22 July 1975.

96. 'Nothing is resented more bitterly amongst the traditionalist old guard of Bermondsey than the fact that the new oppositionists were "outsiders" and in some cases actually "middle-class." This mattered far more than the fact that they were left-wing', N. Murray, 'Carpetbagging in Bermondsey', *London Review of Books* 19 August 1982.

97. G. Kemp, 'Ultra-Leftists Plotting to Increase the Number of Communist MPs', *Daily Telegraph* 15 July 1975.

98. John O'Malley, 'Political Structures', p. 3.

99. Horn, *Crossing the Floor*, p. 106.

100. M. Jones, 'The Coup That Threatens Reg Prentice', *Sunday Times* 13 July 1975.

101. R. Prentice, 'Right Turn', in P. Cormack, ed., *Right Turn. Eight Men Who Changed Their Minds* (London, 1978), p. 7.

102. Phillips, 'Leftist Lambeth.'

103. Livingstone, *If Voting Changed Anything*, p. 11.

104. A. Hosken, *Ken. The Ups and Downs of Ken Livingstone* (London, 2008), pp. 19–20.

105. Ibid., pp. 13–14, 35.

106. Livingstone, *If Voting Changed Anything*, pp. 26–28.

107. Howard, 'Islington's Last Hurrah.'

Chapter 15

1. P. Dean to Sir J. Nicholls, 28 June 1966, TNA FO 953/2407.

2. Memorandum by Littlejohn Cook, 5 August 1966, ibid.

3. 'Clothing Export Council—Fashion Presentations Overseas', Memorandum by C. R. Jupp, 20 December 1967, TNA BT 279/307.

4. 'Basis for Appointment of the Clothing Export Council as Consultants to the Board of Trade', Memorandum by G. M. Abrahams, 4 March 1968, ibid.

5. 'Kleider in frechen Farben, sexy, superkurz. Und enorm billig', 'Rock Hoch. Jetzt Kommen die Engländer', *Twen* (Munich) 3 March 1966, Kunstbibliothek, Berlin.

6. Bill Cunningham, 'New York Report', *Diary* October 1966.

7. 'Fashion into Europe', *Times* 26 April 1965.

8. 'Commercial Results of the British Week, Brussels, 29 September–7 October 1967', Memorandum of 1 May 1968, TNA BT 333/41.

9. 'EFTA Takes Off', *Ambassador* March 1967, p. 35.

10. Bill Cunningham, 'New York Report', *Diary* September 1966.

11. 'EFTA Takes Off', p. 37.

12. 'Boutiquen Boom in Germany', *Twen* 10 October 1967.

13. 'Carnaby Street', *Bravo* n.d. but 1966, cutting in John Stephen papers, AAD/1998/5/16.

14. 'Girls of Rome Can Now Join Beat Set', *Times* 29 April 1966.

15. 'Rome Invaded by Carnaby Street', *Times* March 10 1967.

16. P. Nichols, 'Building a New Rome', *Times* 6 September 1969.

17. T. Salter, *Carnaby Street* (London, 1970), p. 58; for a proposed 'Carnaby Centre' in Israel, see B. Moynahan, 'Carnaby Street, Tel Aviv', *Sunday Times* 2 November 1969.

18. 'Barcelona—mit einem Hauch Carnaby', from the Barcelona section of *Treff Tips. Heiße Tips für junge Leute* (Essen, 1968). This work lacks page numbers.

19. F. Roberts, memorandum 'Sales Promotion of British Consumer Goods by Hertie Waren— und Kaufhaus G.m.b.H.', 5 April 1968, TNA FCO 59/340; 'Mini-Mutter Mary Quant wirbt für den Union Jack', *Berliner Morgenpost* 16 March 1968 (I am most grateful to Holger Nehring for this reference); and see the photo of the pub in *Tagesspiegel* 16 March 1968.

20. The photographs are in TNA INF 14/147–50.

21. 'One would have to be a born pessimist to interpret the whole thing as decadence' (Og man skal vist være fodt sotseer for at kunne fortolke det hele som dekadence), B. Visby, 'Teenage-Imperiet', *Politiken* (Copenhagen) 6 May 1966, cutting in John Stephen papers, AAD/1998/5/16. I am most grateful to Carolyne Larrington and Sunniva Engh for translations from the Scandinavian languages.

22. Reports from D. Mitchell, Bordeaux, and P. Murray, Marseilles, both 17 May 1966, file 'Britain through French Eyes', TNA FO 146/4630.

23. 'Hvad er det, der er sket med gamle tante England?'; 'For en ung pariserinde der husker sin børnelærdom om de kedlige, sexløse, viktorianske piger i England, må det være en pikerende oplevelse, når hun kommer til London og opdager, at hendes kjole er for lang.' Visby, 'Teenage-Imperiet.'

24. 'Et personne, non, personne, fils de duc ou de balayeur, n'est exclu, s'il a son rôle a tenir dans le spectacle', 'Carnaby Street', *Réalités* (Paris) October 1966, cutting in John Stephen papers, AAD/1998/5/16.

25. Visby, 'Teenage-Imperiet.'

26. 'Eine andere, stillere, aber nicht weniger augenfälliger Revolution . . . [in] die kleinen Boutiquen im Herzen von London', I. Lauff, 'Firlefanz clever verkauft. Weltweiter Jugendstil aus London', *Rundschau am Sonntag* 2 June 1968, cutting in John Stephen papers, AAD/1998/5/16.

27. Visby, 'Teenage-Imperiet.'

28. S. Bertoldi, 'Un manipolo di inquietanti guastatori. Fa di Londra la piu giovane citta del mondo', *Oggi Illustrato* 4 August 1966, cutting ibid.

29. 'Der Test, der Sie entlarvt: Wie jung sind Sie wirklich?', *Twen* June 1970.

30. Visby, 'Teenage-Imperiet.'

31. Home Office figures, from the Draft Report of the Steering Group on the Needs of Tourists and Visitors in Central London, Table 1, London Metropolitan Archives (LMA) GLC/DG/PTI/P/03/134; G. Young, *Tourism: Blessing or Blight?* (London, 1973), p. 32.

32. 'Seit einiger Zeit sogar in die Liste der Sehenswürdigkeiten für Touristen aufgerückt.' M. Blatz, 'Dandy-Treff. Carnaby Street—Strasse der Jungen Mode', *Christ und Welt* 22 July 1966, cutting in John Stephen papers, AAD/1998/5/16.

33. 'Uitgekookte zakenlieden, zoals Stephen, zullen er wel voor zorgen, dat de Tower en de Big Ben steeds meer op der achtergrond komen', unidentified Dutch paper, 18 November 1967, cutting ibid.

34. J. Urry, *The Tourist Gaze. Leisure and Travel in Contemporary Societies* (London, 1990).

35. 'Also Londoner Girls und Boys nehmen den "Emporkömmling" unter Londons Einkaufsstraßen schon nicht mehr ganz ernst', 'Die Wahrheit über Carnaby Street', *Treff Tips*, London section.

36. 'Kleine und grosse Wagen stehen Stoßstange and Stoßstange, aus jeder Tür und jeden halboffenen bemalten Schaufenster klingt Musik, die jugendliche Kundschaft kommt zu zweit oder dritt, sieht sich im Laden um, probiert stehenden Fusses die neuesten Schuhmachen an—Radfahrschuhe in diversen Farben—und stülpt sich die phantastischten Perücken auf', 'Mode im Zorn', *Aufbau* 13 September 1968, cutting in John Stephen papers, AAD/1998/5/16.

37. Royal Borough of Kensington and Chelsea, 'Amenities and Attractions', report by Borough Surveyor, 30 May 1968, file 'Tourism, 1968', LMA GLC/DG/PTI/P/03/272.

38. 'Carnaby Street Draws the Tourist Crowds', *Tailor and Cutter* 8 July 1966.

39. E.g., J. M. Rickly-Boyd, D. C. Knudsen, L. C. Braverman & M. M. Metro-Roland, *Tourism, Performance and Place. A Geographic Perspective* (Farnham, 2014).

40. S. Portman, 'The Girls Are Not Called Weirdies Now, but a Man Is Still Judged by His Car . . .', *Evening Standard* (*ES*) 31 December 1965.

41. Der Grosse Polyglott, *London* (Munich, 1970), pp. 74–76; *Treff Tips* similarly recommended the hours from 10.00 to 16.00 on a Saturday for gazing at 'die schönsten Mädchen der Welt' in the Kings Road: *Treff Tips*, London section.

42. From the table in Young, *Tourism*, p. 61.

43. Sir George Young in the GLC debate on tourism in London, 21–22 July 1970, transcription in LMA GLC/DG/PR/04/293.

44. E. R. Ellen, London Transport, to P. G. Radford, Greater London Council, 9 October 1972, file 'Tourism: Short-Term Plans, Consultations', LMA GLC/DG/ISG/09/149.

45. A. Lumsden, 'They're Springing Up Everywhere', *Times* 25 February 1970.

46. 'London's Hotels Problem', GLC Press Release, 19 February 1970, LMA GLC/DG/PRB/010/076.

47. The white paper was *Hotel Development Incentives* (Cmnd. 3633, 1968); the legislation was the Development of Tourism Act, 1969, ch. 51.

48. J. Armytage, 'Hotels: A Boom for Rooms but Hesitancy about Occupancy', *Times* 26 February 1971; M. Hatfield, 'The Boom in Hotel Building', *Times* 1 September 1970; Young, *Tourism*, p. 139.

49. Lumsden, 'They're Springing Up Everywhere.'

50. R. Langton, 'Too MUCH Room at the Inn', *Evening News* 15 May 1970.

51. J. Hall, 'Price War Brewing Up for London Tourist Hotels', *ES* 9 August 1972.

52. S. Jenkins, 'The Scars of London's Hotel Gold Rush', *ES* 24 July 1973; B. Glenton, 'Hotel Glut Hits London—Thanks to £60m State Grants', *Sunday Times* 13 May 1973.

53. Michael Lawrence-Smith, chairman of Hotel Booking Service Ltd, quoted in Hall, 'Price War Brewing.'

54. Memorandum by P. S. Green, London Youth Hotel and Information Service, 21 January 1967, file 'Accommodation for Young Visitors to London', LMA GLC/DG/GP/01/060.

55. See the account of the evolution of the question by the Clerk to the Council, W. O. Hart, 18 October 1962, ibid.

56. Draft portfolio for London International Youth Hotel, produced for the conference of 12 April 1967, section 9, 'The Need from Abroad', ibid.

57. Report (ILEA 195) by Education Officer and Medical Officer, 'Use of Day Schools as Temporary Hostels', ibid.

58. Accounts of 'Hostel Accommodation in the Borough of Camden . . . in the City of Westminster and Student/Hostel Accommodation in the Borough of Kensington and Chelsea', file 'Tourism 1968', LMA GLC/DG/PTI/P/03/272; draft portfolio for London International Youth Hotel, section 9, 'The Need from Abroad.'

59. Cited in Steering Group on the Needs of Tourists and Visitors in Central London, Draft Report, May 1970, p. 12, LMA GLC/DG/PTI/P/03/134, covering age group sixteen to twenty-four.

60. Ibid., p. 16.

61. 'Shelter Plea for Young Tourists', *Times* 16 June 1970.

62. G. Davison, 'Tourists, Expats and Invisible Immigrants. Being Australian in England in the 1960s and 70s', in C. Bridge, R. Crawford & D. Dunstan, eds., *Australians in Britain. The Twentieth-Century Experience* (Clayton, Victoria, 2009), pp. 14.1–14.2.

63. M. Hastings, 'London's Parks a Free Hotel', *ES* 1 August 1969; H. de Wet, 'Green Park as Home for Hippies', *Times* 14 August 1969.

64. E. Chowen, 'Hippy Town Moves to Green Park', *Daily Mail* 12 August 1969.

65. 'Hippy Haven to Close', *Times* 19 December 1969.

66. 'London's Paying Guests', *Architects Journal* 19 August 1970.

67. N. Baird to P. G. Radford, 19 March 1973, file 'Tourism: Short-Term Plans. Consultations', LMA GLC/DG/ISG/09/149.

68. A. Sandles, 'Tourism Not So Invisible', *Financial Times* 14 April 1970.

69. £277 per head, against £160: from Table 27 in the report 'Economic Impact of Tourism', LMA LSPU/PPG/06/012.

70. Mr McLean, in 'Note of a Meeting with Hotel Interests, 3 June 1971', file 'Hotels Policy, II', LMA GLC/DG/PTI/P/03/135.

71. Rodney Scrase, in Minutes of Tourism Conference, 14 July 1975, LMA GLC/DG/PR/04/305.

72. Young, *Tourism*, pp. 100–101.

73. G. Hawtin, 'Publicity "Not for Tourists on Shoestring"', *Times* 26 July 1971.

74. South East Economic Planning Council, 'Tourism in London. Note by the Secretary', 28 March 1968, Annex B, p. 3, 'S.E.E.P.C. Amenities and Tourism Committee. Papers and Briefs, 1968', TNA EW 10/220.

75. Greater London Council (GLC), *Tourism in London. Towards a Short-Term Plan. A Consultation Text, January 1973* (London, 1973), p. 19.

76. A. Sherman, 'Are Tourists Really Worth It?', *Daily Telegraph* 2 June 1973. The North Kensington Casbah jibe (Sherman was then a borough councillor in Kensington and Chelsea) was made in his subsequent letter 'Effects of the Tourist Invasion', *Daily Telegraph* 27 August 1973.

77. P. R. Temple, 'Tourism. A General View', paper in file 'Tourist Tax', LMA GLC/DG/ISG/09/151.

78. Young, *Tourism*, p. 121.

79. J. Birch, Greenwich Society, to P. G. Radford, GLC, 24 March 1973, file 'Tourism: Short-Term Plans. Consultations', LMA GLC/DG/ISG/09/149.

80. Young, *Tourism*.

81. G. Young, 'Who Needs Tourists?', *ES* 19 November 1973.

82. Young, *Tourism*, pp. 111–12.

83. Letter from G. Young, 'Tourists: Doubts on the BTA's Performance', *Times* 14 December 1973.

84. 'I'm the only one who thinks that one of my first ideas for a title for the tourist meeting was a good one—TOURISM—THE PRECIOUS BANE—but perhaps no-one else is old enough to remember Mary Webb': Note from J. Bailey to I. Harrington, LMA GLC/DG/PR/04/305.

85. B. J. Collins, GLC, at the meeting of representatives of the GLC and the London Tourist Board, held at County Hall, 15 December 1971, LMA GLC/DG/PTI/P/03/135.

86. F. Roberts, 'Hotel Development Control Urged', *Times* 19 May 1971.

87. J. Morton, 'Creeping Hotels', *New Society* 25 November 1971.

88. Plummer's remarks at the the meeting of representatives of the GLC and the London Tourist Board, 15 December 1971.

89. Plummer's speech at the launch of the 'Green Paper' *Tourism and Hotels in London*, GLC Press Release 102, 19 March 1971, LMA GLC/DG/PTI/P/03/135.

90. 'Tourism. Note of a Meeting between the Leader of the Council and the Chairman of the London Tourist Board, 1 November 1973', LMA GLC/DG/PR/04/306.

91. 'Tourism—Costs and Benefits', report by the Director-General for the Strategic Policy Board, 24 April 1975, LMA GLC/DG/PR/04/307.

92. GLC, *Tourism in London. A Plan for Management* (London, 1974), p. 6.

93. Quoted in B. James, 'How Not to See London in Three Hours Flat', *ES* 11 August 1971.

94. Sir Anthony Milward, London Tourist Board, at the meeting of representatives of the GLC and the London Tourist Board, held at County Hall, 15 December 1971.

95. Memorandum by P. G. Radford, 'Tourist Tax—Letter from A. Campbell', 28 January 1972, file 'Tourist Tax', LMA GLC/DG/ISG/09/151.

96. Report by Joint Directors of Planning and Transportation, 'Hotels Policy', 18 November 1970, LMA GLC/DG/PTI/P/03/135.

97. GLC, *Tourism. A Paper for Discussion* (London, 1978), p. 4.

98. James, 'How Not to See London.'

99. P. R. Temple to C. T. Bourne, 8 August 1973, file 'Tourist Tax', LMA GLG/DG/ISG/09/151.

100. P. O'Leary, 'London Learns to Live with Its Handicaps', *Times* 18 February 1974.

101. GLC, *Tourism*, p. 5.

102. British Tourist Authority, *Survey among Visitors to London, Summer 1975* (London, 1975), p. 17.

103. GLC, *Use It!*, copy of 1973 version in LMA GLC/DG/PR/04/304.

104. GLC, *Tourism in London. Towards a Short-Term Plan*, p. 41.

105. Leader's Coordinating Committee, Report by the Joint Directors of Planning and Transportation, 'Tourism and Hotels in London', Appendix II, 21 October 1971 LMA GLC/DG/PTI/P/03/135.

106. S. Menkes, 'The Site for Style', *ES* 20 September 1977.

107. British Tourist Authority, *Survey among Visitors to London*, p. 42. The difference is likely to reflect the younger age profile of European tourists.

108. F. Martin, 'Death of a Thousand Cults', *Guardian* 20 January 1976.

109. S. Fainstein & D. Judd, 'Global Forces, Local Strategies and Urban Tourism', in D. Judd and S. Fainstein, eds., *The Tourist City* (New Haven, CT, 1999), p. 7.

110. A. Sharpley, 'But What's Happened to London's Sense of Street Fun?', *ES* 11 August 1978.

111. 'The Abbey Is No. 1 for Carol', *ES* 26 June 1973; Midori Komaki from Kamakura, 'Visitor to London', *ES* 16 August 1973; 'Second Time Round', *ES* 21 September 1973; 'Marianne's Only Here for the Pigeons', *ES* 25 June 1973. The 'Visitor to London' articles were accompanied by photographs of the interviewees. All were young and female.

112. 'Her Cup of Tea', *ES* 14 August 1973.

113. The BTA's 1975 survey showed that 59 percent of visitors to London spent all their time in London.

114. The GLC, concerned by the congestion caused by the Changing of the Guard, hoped to 'reduce the dominance of the changing of the guard as a tourist attraction' by persuading tour operators not to go there. Report of the Strategic Planning Committee, 2 May 1972, Greater London Council Minutes, 9 May 1972.

115. By 1977 the GLC felt that the glut in hotel space had removed the need to provide specialised accommodation for young tourists: I. R. McNeill, 'London Tourist Board. Brief for Meeting with the English Tourist Board, 30 March 1977', LMA GLC/DG/SEC/01/201(1).

116. Half the visitors from France in the sixteen-to-twenty-four age group in 1967 stayed with friends or relatives, as did more than a third of those from Germany and Scandinavia: Steering Group on the Needs of Tourists and Visitors in Central London, Draft Report, May 1970, LMA GLC/DG/PTI/P/03/134.

117. D. Twort & G. Varra, *Guide de Londres en Jeans* (Paris, 1979), pp. 35–47, quotation p.42.

118. GLC, *Tourism*, p. 20.

119. 'Note of a Meeting held on Monday 24 March 1975 at County Hall' and Minutes of a Conference, 14 July 1975, both in LMA GLC/DG/PR/04/305.

120. GLC, *Tourism*, p. 15.

121. Ibid., pp. 16, 32, 34, 35.

122. L. van den Berg, J. van der Borg & A. P. Russo, 'The Infrastructure of Urban Tourism. A Comparative Analysis of Mega-Projects in Four Eurocities', in D. R. Judd, ed., *The Infrastructure of Play. Building the Tourist City* (New York, 2003), p. 313.

123. D. R. Judd, 'Building the Tourist City. Editor's Introduction', ibid., pp. 3–16.

124. Editorial, 'Still the Flower of Cities', *ES* 5 January 1977.

125. David Eversley, quoted in D. White, 'Are Tourists Really a Blight?', *New Society* 23 March 1978.

126. R. Bray, 'Sign of the Times—or of the Future?', *ES* 11 August 1970.

127. P. Atkinson, 'Are London's Tourists a Blessing or an Evil?', *ES* 6 July 1972.

128. Young's views as recounted by Illtyd Harrington: 'The Trouble with Tourism Unlimited', *New Statesman* 6 August 1971.

Chapter 16

1. G. Melly, 'The Way We Live Now', *Evening Standard* (*ES*) 18 October 1976.

2. V. Jenkins, 'Whatever Became of Young Whatsisname?', *ES* 21 October 1976.

3. 'No Longer a Gold Mine', *ES* 31 March 1976.

4. Jenkins, 'Whatever Became of Young Whatsisname?'

5. G. Nuttall, 'Chelsea: Amateur or Professional?', *Sunday Times* 26 March 1967; G. Nuttall, 'The Swinging Cash-In down the King's Road', *Sunday Times* 17 August 1969.

6. J. Hackett, 'Rags to Riches', *New Society* 10 June 1971.

7. Ibid.

8. F. Martin, 'Death of a Thousand Cults', *Guardian* 20 January 1976.

9. S. Menkes, 'King's Road, Where Are You Now?', *ES* 5 January 1976.

10. Jenkins, 'Whatever Became of Young Whatsisname?'

11. See chapter 8.

12. W. W. Daniel, *Whatever Happened to the Workers in Woolwich? A Survey of Redundancy in S.E. London* (London, 1972), Table 15, p. 37.

13. Ibid., pp. 121–22.

14. Department of the Environment, *Development of the Strategic Plan for the South East. Interim Report* (London, 1976), p. 60.

15. 'London "Could Become Jarrow of 1980s"', *ES* 28 April 1975.

16. Department of the Environment, *Strategy for the South East: 1976 Review. Report with Recommendations by the South East Joint Planning Team* (London, 1976), p. 37.

17. Shankland/Cox Partnership, *Inner Area Study: Lambeth. Study of Intending Migrants. Report by the Consultants* (London, 1978), p. 22.

18. M. Macpherson, 'The Crane Drain to Kent', *ES* 12 May 1977.

19. M. Macpherson, 'Back from the Dead', *ES* 12 May 1977.

20. See chapter 8.

21. E.g., Docklands Joint Committee, *Work and Industry in East London* (London, 1975), p. 11; 'Christmas on the Dole for East Enders', *East London Advertiser* 5 December 1975; 'It would seem that there is little reason for any skilled building or engineering worker to join Poplar's dole queues', P. Cross, 'The Day I Went on a Job Hunt', *East London Advertiser* 17 September 1976; for Camden see T. Forester, 'An ABC of Unemployment in the Inner City', *New Society* 6 December 1979; and

for Tower Hamlets, C. Howick & T. Key, 'Manufacturing Industry and Inner City Regeneration. An Economic Study of the London Borough of Tower Hamlets', *Progress in Planning* 18 (3), 1982, 147–48, 175.

22. Department of the Environment, *Strategy for the South East: 1976 Review. Report of the Economy Group* (London, 1976), pp. 36, 32–33.

23. Percentage changes in jobs and resident workers: Southeast London:

Year	Number working (jobs)	Number economically active (resident workers)
1961–66	3.9	–4.0
1966–71	12.5	–9.3
1961–71	15.9	–12.9

P. Gripaios, 'Industrial Decline in London: An Examination of its Causes', *Urban Studies* 14 (2), 1977, Table 3, p. 183.

24. A. Lapping, 'London's Burning! London's Burning! A Survey', *Economist* 1 January 1977, p. 20.

25. Shankland/Cox Partnership, *Inner Area Study: Lambeth. Second Report on Multiple Deprivation. Report by the Consultants* (London, 1977), pp. 5–8.

26. V. Bottomley, *Families with Low Income in London* (London, 1972), pp. 6–7.

27. P. Harrison, 'Tower Hamlets: A Social Services Case Study', *New Society* 7 December 1972.

28. Shankland/Cox Partnership, *Inner Area Study: Lambeth. London's Inner Area: Problems and Possibilities* (London, 1976), p. 33.

29. B. Jarman, *A Survey of Primary Care in London. Report Prepared for the Royal College of General Practitioners* (London, 1981), p. 2.

30. London Health Planning Consortium, *Primary Health Care in Inner London* (London, 1981), p. 32.

31. From the 1978 report on West Lambeth health care conducted by David Morrell and John Wyn Owen of St Thomas's Hospital, 'A Survey of General Practice', London Metropolitan Archives (LMA) H01/WL/A/07/006/1–9.

32. Jarman, *Survey of Primary Care*, Table 4, p. 26.

33. M. Downham, 'Medical Care in the Inner Cities', *British Medical Journal* 1978 (2), 545; Jarman, *Survey of Primary Healthcare*, p. 3.

34. London Health Planning Consortium, *Primary Healthcare*, Table 5, p. 21.

35. Ibid., p. 22; Jarman, *Survey of Primary Care*, Table 4.4, p. 33.

36. Jarman, *Survey of Primary Care*, p. 3; London Health Planning Consortium, *Primary Healthcare*, p. 22.

37. Jarman, *Survey of Primary Care*, p. 3.

38. David Guest et al. calculated that a London allowance of £400 p. a. would be necessary to offset the higher cost of accommodation and travel in London, but found that the actual payments made to their sample of white-collar workers varied between £105 and £207: D. Guest, S. Corby, A. Koo & M. Stirling, 'Turn Again Whittington', *New Society* 16 May 1974.

39. In Stockwell, an area 'among London's worst for unemployment', Shankland/Cox still found a relatively high demand for skilled manual workers alongside very weak demand for the unskilled: G. Shankland, P. Willmott & D. Jordan, *Inner London: Policies for Dispersal and Balance. Final Report of the London Inner Area Study* (London, 1977), pp. 79, 87.

40. Hansard, *House of Commons Debates*, 30 October 1973, vol. 863, col. 26.

41. Hansard, *House of Commons Debates*, 20 November 1973, vol. 864, cols. 1133–1211.

42. J. Rogaly, 'London's Case for "Special Treatment"', *Financial Times* 6 November 1973.

43. M. Macpherson, 'The Term the Teachers Ran Out', *ES* 30 August 1973

44. C. McKnight, 'Getting Worse! Crisis in London's Vital Services', *ES* 22 August 1973.

45. McPherson, 'Term the Teachers Ran Out.'

46. R. Bourne, 'Jobs Nobody Wants', *ES* 21 March 1979.

47. Committee on Housing in Greater London, *Report of the Committee on Housing in Greater London* (Cmnd. 2605, 1965), pp. 224, 227.

48. J. Tomlinson, 'Deindustrialisation: Strengths and Weaknesses as a Key Concept for Understanding Post-war British History', *Urban History* 47 (2), 2020, 218. For recent analysis of the phenomenon in provincial England, see A. Kefford, 'Disruption, Destruction and the Creation of the "Inner Cities": The Impact of Urban Renewal on Industry, 1945–1980', *Urban History* 44 (3), 2017, 492–515, which looks at the destabilising effect of regeneration policies in Manchester and Leeds; and A. Andrews, 'Dereliction, Decay and the Problem of De-Industrialisation in Britain, c. 1968–1977', *Urban History* 47 (2), 2020, 236–56, which shows a similar connection between deindustrialisation and environmental degradation in Liverpool to that described here.

49. 'Top-Level Talks on Capital's Problems', *ES* 22 March 1974.

50. D. Wilcox, 'London on the Rocks', *ES* 23 April 1975.

51. D. Churchill, 'Call for Government Grants to Boost Industry in London', *Financial Times* 25 November 1977.

52. For a sceptical response, see S. Jenkins, 'What Alf Garnett Could Tell the Experts', *ES* 23 June 1977.

53. Compared with 28 percent in other regions: D. Wilcox & D. Richards, *London. The Heartless City* (London, 1977), p. 11.

54. Lapping, 'London's Burning!', p. 17.

55. Churchill, 'Call for Government Grants.'

56. See chapter 14.

57. D. E. C. Eversley, 'Rising Costs and Static Incomes. Some Economic Consequences of Regional Planning in London', *Urban Studies* 9 (3), 1972, 366.

58. P. Willmott, 'Population and Community in London', *New Society* 4 October 1974.

59. A. S. D. Whybrow, paper 'The Future of London', amended version, 23 April 1974, TNA AT 72/148.

60. This paragraph is based on Department of the Environment, *Development of the Strategic Plan for the South East. Interim Report* (London, 1976), pp. 63, 67; Department of the Environment, *Strategy for the South East: 1976 Review. Report with Recommendations*, p. 31.

61. Department of the Environment, *Strategy for the South East: 1976 Review. Report with Recommendations*, p. 38.

62. Ibid., p.39.

63. Department of Health and Social Security, *Sharing Resources for Health in England. Report of the Resource Allocation Working Party* (London, 1976), p. 7.

64. A. Massam, 'Why London Got the Knife', 'The Ones that Have Gone', *ES* 25 October 1977; K. Murphy, '83 That Face the Axe', *ES* 27 October 1977; J. Norridge, 'Wincing under the Surgeon's Knife', *ES* 16 October 1979.

65. S. Jenkins, 'The Job Destroyers', *ES* 14 October 1976.

66. O. Saumarez Smith, 'The Inner City Crisis and the End of Urban Modernism in 1970s Britain', *Twentieth Century British History* 27 (4), 2016, 594; P. Shapely, *Deprivation, State Interventions and Urban Communities in Britain, 1968–1979* (Abingdon, 2018), pp. 293ff.

67. P. Hall, 'Foreword', in Wilcox & Richards, *London*, p. 8.

68. See chapter 15.

69. J. Dunning, 'How Multi-nationals Choose Their Locations', *Trade and Industry. News from the Department of Trade and Industry* 31 (8), 26 May 1978. Supplement, 'Use Our Good Offices', 2–3.

70. Hall, 'Foreword', p. 8.

71. Department of the Environment, *Development of the Strategic Plan*, pp. 61, 63.

72. Wilcox & Richards, *London*, p. 11.

73. Shankland/Cox Partnership, *Inner Area Study: Lambeth. Study of Intending Migrants*, p. 18.

74. Location of Offices Bureau (LOB), *Annual Report, 1972–3* (London, 1973), p. 14.

75. Hardman Committee, *The Dispersal of Government Work from London* (Cmnd. 5322, 1972–73), Appendix 8, p. 90. In July 1974 the Wilson government proposed to move thirty-one thousand civil servants from London, though it anticipated that half might refuse to move, 'Civil Service Will Move 31,000 Jobs to Regions', *Times* 31 July 1974.

76. Hardman Committee, *Dispersal of Government Work*, p. 88; quote from government chemist Ian O'Neill, threatened with relocation to Cockermouth: N. Leith, 'The Reluctant Exodus', *ES* 24 January 1977. See also A. Johnson, '"Let Us Stay in London" Demo', *ES* 20 July 1978, concerning a protest by civil servants due to be moved to Glasgow.

77. LOB, *Annual Report, 1972–3*, p. 9.

78. Economists Advisory Group for the Committee on Invisible Exports, *Office Rents in the City of London and their Effects on Invisible Earnings, Revised to 1974* (London, 1974), pp. 3, 5.

79. LOB, *Annual Report, 1967–8* (London, 1968), pp. 30–31; J. M. Hall, 'Office Growth in London', *New Society* 17 January 1974.

80. Summarised in Guest et al., 'Turn Again Whittington.'

81. Norman Howard, GLC, quoted in G. Walsh, 'A Wrong Solution, Hard to Change', *ES* 17 March 1977.

82. *The Dispersal of Government Work* (Hardman Committee), p. 87.

83. B. Hulanicki, *From A to Biba* (London, 1983), pp. 100–101. See also J. Reed, *The King of Carnaby Street. The Life of John Stephen* (London, 2010), pp. 244–45.

84. M. Quant, *Quant by Quant* (London, 1966), pp. 77–78.

85. S. Levy, *Ready, Steady, Go! Swinging London and the Invention of Cool* (London, 2003), p. 248.

86. For the spread of discos in London by 1974 see 'All Dressed Up and Nowhere to Go', *Time Out* 28 June 1974.

87. J. Raban, *Soft City* (London, 1974), p. 181.

88. For the lifestyle trappings of early gentrification in London, see J. Moran, 'Early Cultures of Gentrification in London, 1955–1980', *Journal of Urban History* 34 (1), 2007, 101–21.

89. R. Langton, 'Oxford St—Top Shopping Centre', *ES* 20 December 1976.

90. P. Downey, *The Impact of Brent Cross* (GLC Reviews and Studies Series 2, 1980), pp. 3, 6, 32–33.

91. 'A Shoppers' Paradise, Ever Closer to Home', *ES* 2 April 1979.

92. John Stentiford, quoted in M. Hastings, 'In the Suburbs the Wives Are Having to Work', *ES* 29 January 1976.

93. By the midseventies telephone ownership was significantly higher in London than in Britain as a whole (67 percent against 53 percent, the British figures including those for London) and a discernibly higher proportion of London households owned refrigerators (92 percent against 86 percent). TV ownership levels were almost identical, and close to saturation point, while car ownership in London was marginally below the national average (42 percent against 44 percent). Only in the possession of a washing machine was London notably deficient (53 percent against 71 percent), a deficiency attributed to the prevalence of laundrettes in London: Office of Population Censuses and Surveys, *The General Household Survey, 1976* (1978), Table 5.37, p. 149.

94. A. Lorentzen, 'Cities in the Experience Economy', in A. Lorentzen & C. J. Hansen, eds., *The City in the Experience Economy. Role and Transformation* (Abingdon, 2012), p. 16.

95. F. Maschler, 'Secrets of Survival, by the Old Faithfuls', *ES* 1 October 1975.

96. V. Jenkins, 'When the Bottom Falls Out of an Old Barometer', *ES* 12 May 1975.

97. D. Wells, 'Look Back in Envy', *ES* 22 November 1978.

98. Quoted in D. Benedictus, 'Big Man in the Stalls', *ES* 3 November 1978.

99. S. H. Beer, *Britain against Itself. The Political Contradictions of Collectivism* (London, 1982), pp. 128, 143.

100. J. Diski, *The Sixties* (London, 2009), p. 136.

101. 'We're not going to make any more money with taxes at 18/3d [91p] in the pound. It's very dispiriting': Mary Quant. See J. Aitken, *The Young Meteors* (London, 1967), pp. 160–61.

102. C. Miller, 'The Men Who Put the Zip into Denim', *ES* 13 May 1977; F. Donnelly, 'The Music Man', *ES* 10 June 1977.

103. 'Suffocated—by an Avalanche of Paper', *ES* 12 October 1978.

104. Hastings, 'In the Suburbs.'

105. P. Healey, *Urban Complexities and Spatial Strategies. Towards a Relational Planning for Our Times* (London, 2007), p. 16.

106. P. Hall, *Great Planning Disasters* (London, 1980), p. 86.

107. D. Eversley, 'What Is London's Future?', *New Society* 5 October 1972.

108. See chapter 8.

109. T. Christensen, *Neighbourhood Survival. The Struggle for Covent Garden's Future* (Dorchester, 1979), p. 96.

110. A. Holmes, *Better than No Place* (London, 1971), pp. 80–81, 68–69.

111. Ibid., p. 74.

112. E. Robinson, C. Schofield, F. Sutcliffe-Braithwaite & N. Thomlinson, 'Telling Stories about Post-war Britain: Popular Individualism and the "Crisis" of the 1970s', *Twentieth Century British History* 28 (2), 2017, 268–304.

113. P. Johnson, 'Hands Up to Stop the Spendthrifts', *ES* 5 March 1979.

114. P. Hounam, 'Why Life Is Better in Barnet', *ES* 6 March 1979. For a deeper analysis of the problems of balancing Islington's books, see S. Weir, 'How Islington Decided Its Rates', *New Society* 22 March 1979.

115. See chapter 6.

116. Dennis Mallam, Tory group leader, addressing Putney Young Conservatives, '"Great Divide" Which Separates Parties', *Wandsworth Borough News* 14 April 1978.

117. Councillor Edward Lister at the launch of the Conservative manifesto, 'Tories Spell Out Their Council Economies', *Wandsworth Borough News* 14 April 1978. See also the report of the special meeting of the Policy and Resources Sub-Committee after the election, 'Labour Policies

Scrapped by the New Council', *Wandsworth Borough News* 26 May 1978; J. M. Lucas, *The Wandsworth Story* (London, 1990), pp. 84–89; L. Murdin, 'How Wandsworth's Good Housekeepers Balanced the Books', *ES* 7 March 1979.

118. R. Carvel, 'Maggie's London', *ES* 20 April 1979.

119. J. Curtice & M. Steed, Appendix, 'An Analysis of the Voting', in D. Butler & D. Kavanagh, *The British General Election of 1979* (London, 1980), p. 396.

120. E.g., Ben Jackson's analysis of the evolution of neoliberal thought in 'Currents of Neoliberalism: British Political Ideologies and the New Right, c. 1955–1979', *English Historical Review* 131 (551), 2016, 823–50; Aled Davies's work on the origins of 'Right to Buy': '"Right to Buy": The Development of a Conservative Housing Policy, 1945–1980', *Contemporary British History* 27 (4), 2013, 421–44; Davies's treatment of the road to monetarism in *The City of London and Social Democracy: The Political Economy of Finance in Post-war Britain, 1959–1979* (Oxford, 2017); Amy Edwards's work on popular capitalism in '"Manufacturing Capitalists." The Wider Share Ownership Council and the Problem of "Popular Capitalism", 1958–92', *Twentieth Century British History* 27 (1), 2016, 100–123; and the exploration of popular individualism by Emily Robinson et al. cited earlier ('Telling Stories about Post-war Britain').

BIBLIOGRAPHY

Archives

The National Archives, Kew

TNA AT/   Department of the Environment files.
TNA BT/   Board of Trade files.
TNA CK/   Community Relations Commission files.
TNA EW/   Department of Economic Affairs files.
TNA FCO/   Foreign and Commonwealth Office files.
TNA FO/   Foreign Office files.
TNA HLG/   Ministry of Housing and Local Government files.
TNA HO/   Home Office files.
TNA INF/   Central Office of Information files.
TNA MEPO/   Metropolitan Police files.
TNA NF/   Registry of Trade Unions and Employers' Associations files.
TNA T/   Treasury files.
TNA WORK/   Ministry of Public Buildings and Works files.

London Metropolitan Archives, Clerkenwell

A/FWA/   Family Welfare Association papers.
ACC/1888/   London Council of Social Service papers.
ACC/3499/EH/   English Heritage papers.
GLC/DG/ADG/   Greater London Council, Director-General's Department, papers of the Assistant Director-General.
GLC/DG/AE/ROL/   Greater London Council, Director-General's Department, Administrative and Establishment Branch, Record Office and Library files.
GLC/DG/EL/   Greater London Council, Director-General's Department, Entertainments Licensing files.
GLC/DG/GP/   Greater London Council, Director-General's Department, General Purposes Committee files.

GLC/DG/HG/ Greater London Council, Director General's Department, Housing Committee files.

GLC/DG/ISG/ Greater London Council, Director-General's Department, Intelligence Unit and Policy Study Group files.

GLC/DG/MIN/ Greater London Council, Director-General's Department, Committee Minutes.

GLC/DG/PR/ Greater London Council, Director-General's Department, Policy and Resources Committee files.

GLC/DG/PRB/ Greater London Council, Director-General's Department, Public Relations Branch files.

GLC/DG/PRE/ Greater London Council, Director-General's Department, Committee presented papers.

GLC/DG/PTI/ Greater London Council, Director-General's Department, Planning Transport and Industry Group files.

GLC/DG/PUB/ Greater London Council, Director General's Department, Publications of the Council.

GLC/DG/SEC/ Greater London Council, Director-General's Department, Secretariat files.

GLC/DG/TD/ Greater London Council, Director-General's Department, Town Development Committee files.

GLC/HG/CHTS/ Greater London Council, Housing Department, Controller of Housing and Technical Services files.

GLC/HG/HHM/ Greater London Council, Housing Department, Management Branch files.

GLC/RA/ Greater London Council, Recreation and Arts Department files.

GLC/TD/ Greater London Council, Transportation and Development Department files.

Ho1/WL/A/ West Lambeth Health Authority files.

LCC/AR/TP/ London County Council, Architect's Department, Town Planning files.

LCC/CL/ London County Council, Clerk's Department files.

LCC/MIN/ London County Council, Committee Minutes and Related Papers.

LMA/4460/ Victorian Society papers.

LMA/4462/ Eric and Jessica Huntley papers.

LRB/PS/EM/ Greater London Council/London Residuary Body, Covent Garden General files.

LSPU/PPG/ London Strategic Policy Unit files.

London Borough Local Studies Collections

Barnet Local Studies and Archives, The Burroughs, Hendon:
 Dollis Brook Amenities Association *Newsletter*.
 News and Views of Woodside Park Garden Suburb (Official Journal of the Woodside Park Ratepayers and Residents Association).

Bexley Local Studies and Archives Centre, Central Library, Bexleyheath:
 Bexley Civic Society papers.

Bromley Local Studies and Archives, Bromley Central Library:
    Biggin Hill and District Ratepayers and Residents Association Minutes.
    Bromley Ratepayers Association papers.
    Cray Action Group *Newsletter*.
    London Borough of Bromley Council Minutes.
    London Ratepayers Alliance, Minutes.
    Orpington and District Amenity Society papers.
City of Westminster Archive Centre, St Ann's Street:
    City of Westminster, Council Minutes.
    Soho Clarion.
Croydon Museum and Archive Service, Croydon Clocktower:
    Broad Green Residents Association *Newsletter*.
    Heathfield Residents Association *Newsletter*.
    Norwood Review.
    Riddlesdown Residents Association, *Riddlesdown Recorder*.
    Sanderstead News.
    Selsdon Gazette.
    Spring Park Residents Association, *S.P.A.N.—Spring Park Activities News*.
Enfield Local Studies and Archives, Dugdale Centre, Enfield:
    Enfield Preservation Society *Newsletter*.
    Southgate Civic Trust *Newsletter*.
    Western Enfield Residents Association *Journal*.
Hammersmith and Fulham Local Studies Centre, Hammersmith Library:
    Fulham Metropolitan Borough Council Minutes.
    Hammersmith Council for Community Relations papers.
Harrow Local History Collection, Headstone Manor:
    Hatch End Association, *Hatch End Bulletin*.
    Pinner South Residents Association Minutes.
    Queensbury Residents Association, Edgware, Minutes.
Havering Local Studies and Family History Centre, Central Library, Romford:
    The Bulletin. Upminster and Cranham Residents Association Newsletter.
    The Resident. Emerson Park and Ardleigh Green Residents Association
        Newsletter.
    Romford Recorder, *Havering. A Recorder Souvenir*, April 1965.
Hillingdon Heritage, Uxbridge Library:
    The Aerial. Eastcote Residents Association Journal.
    Ruislip Residents Association papers.
    The Town Crier. The Magazine of the Ruislip Residents Association.
Hounslow Local Studies Service, Feltham Library:
    Friends of Old Isleworth papers.
    Heston Ratepayers Association Magazine.
    Old Chiswick Protection Society *Bulletin*.
Kensington and Chelsea Local Studies, Kensington Central Library:
    Royal Borough of Kensington and Chelsea, Council Minutes.
Kingston History Centre, Guildhall, Kingston upon Thames:
    Kingston Society papers.

Merton Heritage and Local Studies Centre, Morden Library:
  Cannon Hill Ward Residents Association Gazette.
  London Borough of Merton, *Minutes of the Council.*
Richmond Local Studies Library and Archive, Old Town Hall, Richmond upon
  Thames:
  Cole Park Residents Association *Quarterly Newsletter.*
  Richmond upon Thames Ratepayers and Residents Association *Newsletter.*
  Strawberry Hill Residents Association *Bulletin.*
Tower Hamlets Local History Library and Archives, Mile End:
  Avenues Unlimited papers.
  London Borough of Tower Hamlets, Council Minutes.
  Special Docklands Development Committee Minutes.
Waltham Forest Archives and Local Studies Library, Vestry House Museum:
  London Borough of Waltham Forest, *Walthamstow Town Centre. Who Cares?*

Other Archives

Archiv der Jugendkulturen, Berlin:
  Bravo.
Bodleian Library, Oxford:
  Conservative Party Archives.
  Harold Macmillan Papers.
British Library of Political and Economic Science:
  Brixton's Own Boss.
  Camden Tenant.
  London Free Press.
  Peter Shore papers.
International Institute of Social History, Amsterdam:
  Corrugation Street (West Hampstead and Kilburn Squatters Association).
  Islington Gutter Press.
  Kite. Community Newspaper of West Kentish Town and Gospel Oak.
Kunstbibliothek, Berlin:
  Twen.
Lambeth Palace Archives:
  Canon John Collins papers.
  Archbishop Michael Ramsey papers.
Leipziger Stadtbibliothek, Leipzig:
  Star Club News.
Museum of London Docklands:
  Joint Docklands Action Group papers.
George Padmore Institute, Finsbury Park, London:
  BPM/6/1/2   Carnival Development Committee and Related Material.
  CVL/1–4   Notting Hill Carnival collection.
Queen Mary University of London:
  Donald Chesworth papers.

Trust for London:
  City Parochial Foundation Minutes.
Victoria and Albert Museum:
  John Stephen papers.
Warwick University, Modern Records Centre:
  Cab Trade News.
  Transport and General Workers Union, Cab Section, archive.
Warwick University Library:
  Sivanandan Collection.

Interviews

Interviews conducted by the author (recordings and transcripts at https://around1968.history.ox
.ac.uk):
  Piers Corbyn, Borough, 15 June 2010.
  John Cowley, Camden, 22 July 2010.
  Jan O'Malley, Clapham, 22 April 2010.
  Nick Wates, Hastings, 3 March 2009.

Official Reports

Abercrombie, P., *The Greater London Plan, 1944* (London, 1945).
Board of Trade, *Hotel Development Incentives* (Cmnd. 3633, London, 1968).
British Tourist Authority, *Survey among Visitors to London, Summer 1975* (London, 1975).
Census, 1961, England and Wales, *County Report, London* (London, 1963).
Census, 1966, England and Wales, *County Report, Greater London* (London, 1967).
Census, 1971, England and Wales, *County Report, Greater London* (London, 1973).
Census, 1981, England and Wales, *County Report, Greater London* (London, 1982).
Central Advisory Committee for Education (England), *Children and Their Primary Schools* (London, 1967).
Commission for Racial Equality, *Looking for Work. Black and White School Leavers in Lewisham* (London, 1978).
Committee of Inquiry, Local Government Finance (Layfield Committee), *Local Government Finance. Report of the Committee of Inquiry* (Cmnd. 6453, London, 1976).
Committee on Housing in Greater London, *Report of the Committee on Housing in Greater London* (Cmnd. 2605, 1965).
Committee on Local Authority and Allied Personal Social Services, *Report* (Cmnd. 3703, 1968).
Community Relations Commission, *Unemployment and Homelessness* (London, 1974).
Departmental Committee on the London Taxicab Trade. *Report* (Cmnd. 4483, 1970).
Department of Health and Social Security, *Sharing Resources for Health in England. Report of the Resource Allocation Working Party* (London, 1976).
Department of Scientific and Industrial Research, *Effects of Polluting Discharges on the Thames Estuary. The Reports of the Thames Survey Committee and of the Water Pollution Research Laboratory* (London, 1964).

Department of the Environment, *Development of the Strategic Plan for the South East. Interim Report* (London, 1976).

———, *Strategy for the South East, 1976 Review. Report of the Economy Group* (London, 1976).

———, *Strategy for the South East, 1976 Review. Report with Recommendations by the South East Joint Planning Team* (London, 1976).

———, Action Group on London Housing, *Use of Housing Land in Outer London. Fourth Report to the Minister of Housing and Construction* (London, 1974).

———, *The Public Sector Housing Pipeline in London* (London, 1976).

———, *Policy for the Inner Cities* (Cmnd. 6845, 1976–77).

———, *Housing Policy. Technical Volume*, Part III (London, 1977).

———, *National Dwelling and Housing Survey, 1978* (London, 1979).

Forshaw, J. H., & Abercrombie, P., *County of London Plan* (London, 1943).

General Register Office, *Sample Census 1966. England and Wales. County Report, Greater London* (London, 1967).

Gray, P. G., & Russell, R., *The Housing Situation in 1960. An Inquiry Covering England and Wales Carried Out for the Ministry of Housing and local Government* (London, 1962).

Gray, P. G., & Todd, J., *Privately Rented Accommodation in London. A Report on Inquiries Made in December 1963 and June 1964 for the Committee on Housing in Greater London*, in Committee on Housing in Greater London, *Report of the Committee on Housing in Greater London*, Government Social Survey (Cmnd. 2605 of 1965), Appendix V.

Greater London Council, *Minutes* (London, 1965–86).

———, *Greater London Development Plan. Statement* (London, 1969).

———, *The Condition of London's Housing—A Survey* (Department of Planning and Transportation Intelligence Unit Research Report 4, 1970).

———, *Tomorrow's London. A Background to the Greater London Development Plan* (London, 1970).

———, *Tourism in London. Towards a Short-Term Plan. A Consultation Text, January 1973* (London, 1973).

———, *Tourism in London. A Plan for Management* (London, 1974).

———, *Survey of London*, vol. 39, 'The Grosvenor Estate in Mayfair' (London, 1977).

———, *Tourism. A Paper for Discussion* (London, 1978).

———, *Piccadilly Circus. From Controversy to Reconstruction* (London, 1980).

———, *Low Incomes in London. Evidence from the Family Expenditure Surveys* (GLC Reviews and Studies Series 20, 1983).

———, *Plant Relocation and Closure in London 1976–80* (Economic Policy Group, Strategy Document 3, May 1983).

Greater London Council, City of Westminster & London Borough of Camden, *Covent Garden's Moving* (London, 1968).

Greater London Development Plan. Report of the Panel of Inquiry (2 vols., London, 1973).

Hardman Committee, *The Dispersal of Government Work from London* (Cmnd. 5322, 1972–73).

House of Commons Environment Committee, *Council House Sales*, Minutes of Evidence, 19 June 1980 (HC 535-x).

House of Commons Expenditure Committee, Environment and Home Office Sub-Committee, *Tenth Report, Session 1972–3, Minutes of Evidence* (HC 349-II).

————, *Redevelopment of the London Docklands. Fifth Report from the Expenditure Committee, Together with the Minutes of the Evidence Taken before the Environment Sub-Committee . . . , Session 1974–5*, Parliamentary Papers, 1974–75 (348), 22 January 1975.

————, *Redevelopment of the London Docklands. Report of the House of Commons Expenditure Committee (Environment Sub-Committee)*, Parliamentary Papers, 1978–79 (269), 17 January 1979.

House of Commons, *Second Report from the Home Affairs Committee, Session 1984–85: The Chinese Community in Britain*, vols. 1 (HC 102-I) and III (HC102-III) (London, 1985).

House of Commons Select Committee on Race Relations and Immigration, *Police/Immigrant Relations*, vol. 1, *Report*.

————, *Police/Immigrant Relations*, vol. 2, *Evidence, Session 1971–2* (471-II).

Local Government Finance. Report of the Committee of Inquiry (Cmnd. 6453, 1975–76).

London Borough of Greenwich, *Report of the Medical Officer of Health, 1971* (London, 1972).

London Borough of Redbridge, *Annual Report of the Medical Officer of Health for 1968* (London, 1969).

London Borough of Wandsworth, *Prosperity or Slump? The Future of Wandsworth's Economy* (London, 1976).

London County Council, *Administrative County of London. Development Plan, 1951. Analysis* (London, 1951).

————, *Piccadilly Circus Future Development. Proposals for Comprehensive Development by the Planning Consultant Sir William Holford, March 1962* (London, 1962).

London County Council and Ministry of Transport, *London Traffic Survey* (London, 1964).

Ministry of Housing and Local Government, *Old Houses into New Homes* (Cmnd. 3602, 1968)

Ministry of Labour, *Final Report of the Committee of Inquiry under the Right Honourable Lord Devlin into Certain Matters Concerning the Port Transport Industry* (Cmnd. 2734, 1964–75).

Ministry of Transport, *Traffic in Towns: A Study of the Long-Term Problems of Traffic in Urban Areas* (London, 1963).

National Board for Prices and Incomes, Report 87, *Proposed Increase in London Taxicab Fares*, October 1968 (Cmnd. 3796, 1968).

National Economic Development Office, *BMRB Housing Consumer Survey. A Survey of Attitudes towards Current and Alternative Housing Policies* (London, 1977).

Office of Population Censuses and Surveys, *The General Household Survey, 1976* (1978).

Planning Advisory Group, *The Future of Development Plans* (London, 1965).

Shankland/Cox Partnership, *Inner Area Study: Lambeth. London's Inner Area: Problems and Possibilities* (London, 1976).

————, *Inner Area Study: Lambeth. Second Report on Multiple Deprivation. Report by the Consultants* (London, 1977).

————, *Inner Area Study: Lambeth. Study of Intending Migrants. Report by the Consultants* (London, 1978).

Shankland, G., Willmott, P., & Jordan, D., *Inner London: Policies for Dispersal and Balance. Final Report of the London Inner Area Study* (London, 1977).

Taylor Woodrow Group, *Urban Renewal: Fulham Study* (London, 1963).

Willesden Borough Council, *The West Indian Comes to Willesden. Report of a Survey Made for the Willesden Citizens Advice Bureau, on Behalf of the Willesden Borough Council, at the Request of the Willesden International Friendship Council, October 1960* (London, 1960).

Woolf, M., *The Housing Survey in England and Wales, 1964*, Government Social Survey (London, 1964).

Books and Articles

Abel-Smith, B., & Townsend, P., *The Poor and the Poorest* (London, 1965).

Adams, B., Griffin, J., & Proudman, S., *A Study of Rent Tribunal Cases in London* (London, 1971).

Adeney, M., *Community Action. Four Examples* (London, 1971).

Aitken, J., *The Young Meteors* (London, 1967).

Ambrose, D., *Kingston Conserved? A Sketch of the First Twenty-Five Years of the Kingston upon Thames Society* (London, 1988).

Anders, F., & Sedlmaier, A., eds., *Public Goods versus Economic Interests. Global Perspectives on the History of Squatting* (London, 2016).

Andrews, A., 'Dereliction, Decay and the Problem of De-industrialisation in Britain, c. 1968–1977', *Urban History* 47 (2), 2020, 236–56.

Anning, N., Brown, C., Corbyn, P., Friend, A., Gibson, M., Ingram, A., Moan, P., Osborn, T., Pettit, A., Platt, S., Simpson, J., Ward, C., Watkinson, D., Williams, H., & Wood, T., *Squatting: The Real Story* (London, 1980).

Anson, B., *I'll Fight You for It. Behind the Struggle for Covent Garden, 1966–1974* (London, 1981).

Asher, W., *Rings around London. Orbital Motorways and the Battle for Homes before Roads* (London, 2018).

Bailey, R., *The Squatters* (Harmondsworth, 1973).

Bailey, R., & Ruddock, J., *The Grief Report. A Shelter Report on Temporary Accommodation* (London, 1972).

Baine, S., *Community Action and Local Government* (London, 1975).

Balchin, P. N., *Housing Improvement and Social Inequality. Case Study of an Inner City* (London, 1979).

Baldock, P., 'Why Community Action? The Historical Origins of the Radical Trend in British Community Work', *Community Development Journal* 12 (2), 1977, 68–74.

Balfe, R., *Housing in London. A New Socialist Perspective* (London, 1976).

Balint, M., *Greater London's Economically Active Population* (GLC Research Memorandum 441, London, 1975).

Barisch, K., & Sahla, P., *Richtig Reisen. London* (Cologne, 1979).

Barnes, R., *A Licence to Live: Scenes from a Post-war Working Life in Hackney* (London, 1975).

Beer, S. H., *Britain against Itself. The Political Contradictions of Collectivism* (London, 1982).

Beesley, M. E., 'Regulation of Taxis', *Economic Journal* 83 (1), 1973, 150–72.

——, 'Competition and Supply in London Taxis', in *Privatization, Regulation and Deregulation* (2nd ed., London, 1997), pp. 109–41.

——, *Privatization, Regulation and Deregulation* (2nd ed., London, 1997).

Belson, W. A., *The Public and the Police* (London, 1975).

Benington, J., *Local Government Becomes Big Business* (Coventry, 1975).

Bennett-England, R., *Dress Optional* (London, 1967).

Blackburn, S., ed., *James Sherwood's Discriminating Guide. London. Fine Dining and Shopping* (London, 1975).

Blake, J., 'The Growth of Traffic in Greater London. Buchanan and London Traffic Survey Too Alarmist?', *Surveyor—Local Government Technology* 19 October 1968, 34–35.

Blanchet, E., *Prefab Homes* (Oxford, 2014).

Blaszczyk, R. L., 'Doing Business in Transatlantic Fashion: The Experience of Mary Quant', in Lister, J., *Mary Quant* (London, 2019), pp. 110–22.

Booker, C., & Lycett Green, C., *Goodbye London: An Illustrated Guide to Threatened Buildings* (London, 1973).

Bottomley, V., *Families with Low Income in London* (London, 1972).

Bowden, G. H., *British Gastronomy. The Rise of Great Restaurants* (London, 1975).

Bowley, M., *Economic Report on Rent Problems*, Vol. 3 of London Borough of Camden, *Housing in Camden* (London, 1969).

Brandon, D., *Not Proven. Some Questions about Homelessness and Young Immigrants* (London, 1973).

Brazell, J. H., *London Weather* (London, 1968).

Breward, C., 'Fashion's Front and Back: "Rag Trade" Cultures and Cultures of Consumption in Post-war London, c. 1945–1970', *London Journal* 31 (1), 2006, 15–40.

Bridge, C., Crawford, R., and Dunstan, D., eds., *Australians in Britain. The Twentieth-Century Experience* (Clayton, Victoria, 2009).

Brimson, P., *Islington's Multinationals* (London, 1979).

Brownill, S., & O'Hara, G., 'From Planning to Opportunism? Re-examining the Creation of the London Docklands Development Corporation', *Planning Perspectives* 30 (4), 2015, 537–70.

Buck, N., Gordon, I., & Young, K., *The London Employment Problem* (Oxford, 1986).

Buckland, R., *Share My Taxi* (London, 1968).

Buettner, E., '"Going for an Indian." South Asian Restaurants and the Limits of Multiculturalism in Britain', *Journal of Modern History* 80 (4), 2008, 865–901.

Bull, D., 'CPAG—What an Amazing Time to Be Involved in This Sort of Politics', in Curtis, H., & Sanderson, M., *The Unsung Sixties. Memoirs of Social Innovation* (London, 2004), pp. 116–30.

Bultitude, M., *Get Dressed. A Useful Guide to London's Boutiques* (London, 1966).

Bunce, R., & Field, P., *Renegade. The Life and Times of Darcus Howe* (London, 2017).

Butler, D., & Kavanagh, D., *The British General Election of 1979* (London, 1980).

Butterworth, R., 'Islington Borough Council: Some Characteristics of Single-Party Rule', *Politics* 1 (1), 1966, 21–31.

Bygrave, M., & Goodman, J., *Fuel Food. Where to Find Great Meals in London for £1 or as Little as 50p* (London, 1973).

Campbell, S., with Towle, A., *Cheap Eats in London* (Harmondsworth, 1975).

Canning Town Community Development Project, *Canning Town to North Woolwich. The Aims of Industry? A Study of Industrial Decline in One Community* (2nd ed., London, 1977).

Carpenter, D., *Dockland Apprentice* (Peacehaven, 2003).

Castells, M., *The City and the Grassroots. A Cross-Cultural Theory of Urban Social Movements* (London, 1983).

Centerprise Trust, *Working Lives. A People's Autobiography of Hackney*. Vol. 2, 1945–1977 (London, 1977).

Chapman, J. S., *Sample Survey of London's Housing Waiting List, 1971–2* (GLC Research Memorandum 431, London, 1973).

Cheshire, P., & Dericks, G., 'Iconic Design as Deadweight Loss: Rent Acquisition by Design in the Constrained London Office Market', *Spatial Economics Research Centre Discussion Paper* 154, January 2014.

Child, P., 'Landlordism, Rent Regulation and the Labour Party in Mid-Twentieth Century Britain, 1950–1964', *Twentieth Century British History* 29 (1), 2018, 79–103.

Christensen, T., *Neighbourhood Survival. The Struggle for Covent Garden's Future* (Dorcehster, 1979).

City Parochial Foundation, *Minutes of the Central Governing Body* (London, 1954–74).

Clarke, T., 'Redundancy, Worker Resistance and the Community', in Craig, G., Mayo, M., & Sharman, N., eds., *Jobs and Community Action* (London, 1979), pp. 80–99.

Cockburn, C., *The Local State. The Management of Cities and People* (London, 1977).

Cohen, A., 'Drama and Politics in the Development of a London Carnival', *Man* 15 (1), 1980, 65–87.

———, *Masquerade Politics. Explorations in the Structure of Urban Cultural Movements* (Berkeley, CA, 1993).

Cohn, N., *Today There Are No Gentlemen. The Changes in Englishmen's Clothes since the War* (London, 1971).

Colby, R., *Mayfair. A Town within London* (London, 1966).

Coleman, J. W., 'The Spitalfields Crypt', *Journal of Alcoholism* 10 (4), 1975, 157–61.

Colenutt, R., 'Community Action over Local Planning Needs', in Craig, G., Mayo, M., & Sharman, N., eds., *Jobs and Community Action* (London, 1979), pp. 243–52.

Collins, M. F., & Pharoah, T. F., *The Organisation of Transport in a Great City. The Case of London* (London, 1974).

Community Development Project, *Whatever Happened to Council Housing?* (London, 1976).

Coon, C., 'We Were the Welfare Branch of the Alternative Society', in Curtis, H., & Sanderson, M., *The Unsung Sixties. Memoirs of Social Innovation* (London, 2004), pp. 183–97.

Cooper, P., Creighton, S., Moore, J., Richards, H., Stevens, C., and Ward, M., *A Socialist Strategy for Wandsworth. Proposals for the Basis of a Socialist Manifesto for the Labour Party in the Wandsworth Council Elections May 1978* (London, 1978).

Cormack, P., ed., *Right Turn. Eight Men Who Changed Their Minds* (London, 1978).

Corton, C. L., *London Fog: The Biography* (Cambridge, MA, 2015).

Cox, B., Shirley, J., & Short, M., *The Fall of Scotland Yard* (London, 1977).

Craig, G., Mayo, M., & Sharman, N., eds., *Jobs and Community Action* (London, 1979).

Crewe, Q., *Well, I Forget the Rest. The Autobiography of an Optimist* (London, 1991).

Crofton, B., 'The London Problem—Some Solutions', *Housing Review* 22 (5), September–October 1973, 172–75.

Crosby, T., *The Necessary Monument* (London, 1970).

Crowson, N., Hilton, M., & McKay, J., *NGOs in Contemporary Britain. Non-State Actors in Society and Politics since 1945* (Basingstoke, 2009).

Curno, P. *Political Issues and Community Work* (London, 1978).

Curtice, J., & Steed, M., Appendix, 'An Analysis of the Voting', in Butler, D., & Kavanagh, D., *The British General Election of 1979* (London, 1980), pp. 390–431.

Curtis H., & Sanderson, M., *The Unsung Sixties. Memoirs of Social Innovation* (London, 2004).

Cutler, H., *The Cutler Files* (London, 1982).

Daniel, W. W., *Whatever Happened to the Workers in Woolwich? A Survey of Redundancy in S.E. London* (London, 1972).

Darby, M., 'The Docklands Study Reviewed. IV. A Local Resident's Reactions', *East London Papers* 15, Summer 1973, 30–36.

Dash, J., *Good Morning Brothers! A Militant Trade Unionist's Frank Autobiography* (London, 1970).

Davies, A., '"Right to Buy": The Development of a Conservative Housing Policy, 1945–1980', *Contemporary British History* 27 (4), 2013, 421–44.

———, *The City of London and Social Democracy: The Political Economy of Finance in Post-war Britain, 1959–1979* (Oxford, 2017).

Davies, H., *The New London Spy* (London, 1966).

Davis, A., McIntosh, N., & Williams, J., *The Management of Deprivation. Final Report of Southwark Community Development Project* (London, 1977).

Davis, C. J., *Waterfront Revolts: New York and London Dockworkers, 1946–1961* (Urbana, IL, 2003).

Davis, J., 'Modern London', in P. Waller, ed., *The English Urban Landscape* (Oxford, 2000), pp. 125–50.

———, 'Rents and Race in 1960s London: New Light on Rachmanism', *Twentieth Century British History* 12 (1), 2001, 69–92.

———, '"Simple Solutions to Complex Problems." The Greater London Council and the Greater London Development Plan, 1965–1973', in Harris, J., ed., *Civil Society in British History. Ideas, Identities, Institutions* (Oxford, 2003), pp. 249–74.

———, 'The London Cabbie and the Rise of Essex Man', in Griffiths, C., Nott, J., & Whyte, W., eds., *Classes, Cultures and Politics. Essays in British History for Ross McKibbin* (Oxford, 2011), pp. 102–17.

———, 'Community and the Labour Left in 1970s London', in Williams, C., & Edwards, A., eds., *The Art of the Possible: Politics and Governance in Modern British History, 1885–1997. Essays in Memory of Duncan Tanner* (Manchester, 2015), pp. 207–23.

———, 'Containing Racism? The London Experience, 1957–1968', in Kelley, R., & Tuck, S., eds., *The Other Special Relationship. Race, Rights and Riots in Britain and the United States* (Basingstoke, 2015), pp. 125–46.

———, '"The Most Fun I've Ever Had"? Squatting in England in the 1970s', in Anders, F., & Sedlmaier, A., eds., *Public Goods versus Economic Interests: Global Perspectives on the History of Squatting* (London, 2016), pp. 237–54.

———, 'Reshaping the Welfare State? Voluntary Action and Community in London, 1960–1975', in Goldman, L., ed., *Welfare and Social Policy in Britain since 1870. Essays in Honour of Jose Harris* (Oxford, 2019), pp. 197–212.

Davison, G., 'Tourists, Expats and Invisible Immigrants. Being Australian in England in the 1960s and 70s', in Bridge, C., Crawford, R. & Dunstan, D., eds., *Australians in Britain. The Twentieth-Century Experience* (Clayton, Victoria, 2009), pp. 14.1–14.12.

Deakin, N., *Colour and the British Electorate 1964* (London, 1965).

Deighton, L., *Len Deighton's London Dossier* (London, 1967).

Delafons, J., *Politics and Preservation. A Policy History of the Built Heritage, 1882–1996* (London, 1997).

Denbigh, K., *Preserving London* (London, 1978).

Dench, G., *Maltese in London. A Case Study in the Erosion of Ethnic Consciousness* (London, 1975).

Der Grosse Polyglott, *London* (Munich, 1970).

Deverson, J., & Lindsay, K., *Voices of the Middle Class* (London, 1975).

Diski, J., *The Sixties* (London, 2009).

Dnes, M., *The Rise and Fall of London's Ringways, 1943–1973* (New York, 2019).

Docklands Joint Committee, *Work and Industry in East London. A Working Paper for Consultation* (London, 1975).

———, *London Docklands. A Strategic Plan* (London, 1976).

Donnison, D., 'The Micro-Politics of the City', in Donnison, D., & Eversley, D., eds, *London. Urban Patterns, Problems and Policies* (London, 1973), pp. 383–404.

Donnison, D., & Eversley, D., eds, *London. Urban Patterns, Problems and Policies* (London, 1973).

Downey, P., *The Impact of Brent Cross* (GLC Reviews and Studies Series 2, London, 1980).

Downham, M., 'Medical Care in the Inner Cities', *British Medical Journal* 1978 (2), 545–48.

Driver, C., ed., *The Good Food Guide* (London, 1970–78).

Dunleavy, P., *The Politics of Mass Housing in Britain, 1945–1975* (Oxford, 1981).

Dunning, J., 'How Multi-nationals Choose Their Locations', *Trade and Industry. News from the Department of Trade and Industry* 31 (8), 26 May 1978.

Dyson, S., *Silvertown Life. A Boy's Story* (Milton Keynes, 2008).

Economists Advisory Group for the Committee on Invisible Exports, *Office Rents in the City of London and their Effects on Invisible Earnings, Revised to 1974* (London, 1974).

Edginton, J., *Avenues Unlimited. A Research Study of Youth and Community Work in East London* (Leicester, 1979).

Edwards, A., '"Manufacturing Capitalists." The Wider Share Ownership Council and the Problem of "Popular Capitalism", 1958–92', *Twentieth Century British History* 27 (1), 2016, 100–123.

Edwards, B., 'Swinging Boutiques and the Modern Store: Designing Shops for Post-war London', *London Journal* 31 (1), 2006, 65–83.

Edwards, B., & Gilbert, D., 'Piazzadilly! The Reimagining of Piccadilly Circus, 1957–72', *Planning Perspectives* 23 (4), 2008, 455–78.

Elkin, S., *Politics and Land Use Planning. The London Experience* (Cambridge, 1974).

Evans, T., 'Stopping the Poor Getting Poorer: The Establishment and Professionalisation of Poverty NGOs, 1945–1995', in Crowson, N., Hilton, M., & McKay, J., *NGOs in Contemporary Britain. Non-State Actors in Society and Politics since 1945* (Basingstoke, 2009), pp. 147–63.

Eversley, D., 'Rising Costs and Static Incomes. Some Economic Consequences of Regional Planning in London', *Urban Studies* 9 (3), 1972, 347–68.

———, 'Three Years at the GLC. 1. Changes in Planning', *Built Environment* February 1973, 105–6.

———, 'Three Years at the GLC. 2. Inadequate for the Task', *Built Environment* March 1973, 157–58.

———, 'GLC. Who Loses?', *Built Environment* May 1973, 257–58.

———, *The Planner in Society. The Changing Role of a Profession* (London, 1973).

Eyles, J., 'Rebuilding the London Docklands. 3, Social Implications', *London Journal* 2 (2), 1976, 278–81.

Fagan, D., & Burgess, E., *Men of the Tideway* (London, 1966).

Fainstein, S., & Judd, D., 'Global Forces, Local Strategies and Urban Tourism', in Judd, D., & Fainstein, S., eds., *The Tourist City* (New Haven, CT, 1999), pp. 1–17.

Farson, D., *Soho in the Fifties* (London, 1987).

Ferris, J., *Participation in Urban Planning. The Barnsbury Case: A Study of Environmental Improvement in London* (London, 1972).

Fogg, M., *Boutique. A Sixties Cultural Phenomenon* (London, 2003).

Forman, C., *Spitalfields: A Battle for Land* (London, 1989).

Fowler, D., *Youth Culture in Modern Britain* (Basingstoke, 2009).

Fox, W., *Taximen and Taxi-Owners. A Study of Organisation, Ownership, Finances and Working Conditions in the London Taxi Trade* (London, 1935).

Frame, P., *The Restless Generation. How Rock Music Changed the Face of 1950s Britain* (London, 2007).

Frischauer, W., *Gourmet's Guide to London* (London, 1968).

Fulpen, H. V., *The Beatles. An Illustrated Diary* (London, 1983).

Gallati, M., *Mario of the Caprice. The Autobiography of a Restaurateur* (London, 1960).

Gardner, A., *"Watch Your Fingers!" An East End Cutter's Chronicle, 1956–1973* (London, 2006).

Garrison, L., *Black Youth, Rastafarianism and the Identity Crisis in Britain* (London, 1979).

Garside, P. L., 'The Significance of Post-war Reconstruction Plans for East End Industry', *Planning Perspectives* 12 (1), 1997, 19–36.

Gates, H. L., Jr., 'Black London', *Antioch Review* 34 (3), 1976, 300–317.

Gault, H., & Millau, C., *Londres* (Paris, 1977).

Geake, W., *What's Next? Incidents Recorded whilst Driving a London Licensed Taxicab* (London, 1999).

Gladstone, D., ed., *British Social Welfare. Past, Present and Future* (London, 1995).

Glass, R., *London's Newcomers. The West Indian Migrants* (Cambridge, MA, 1961).

Glassberg, A. D., *Representation and Urban Community* (London, 1981).

Godfree, S., 'Intervention and the Changing Role of the Local Housing Authority: The London Case', *Greater London Intelligence Bulletin* 41, September 1978, 4–8.

Gold, J. R., *The Practice of Modernism. Modern Architects and Urban Transformation, 1954–1972* (London, 2007).

Goldman, L., ed., *Welfare and Social Policy in Britain since 1870. Essays in Honour of Jose Harris* (Oxford, 2019).

Gorman, P., *The Look: Adventures in Pop and Rock Fashion* (London, 2001).

———, *Mr Freedom. Tommy Roberts: British Design Hero* (London, 2012).

Gosling, L., *Debutantes and the London Season* (Oxford, 2013).

Goss, S., *Local Labour and Local Government. A Study of Changing Interests, Politics and Policy in Southwark, 1919 to 1972* (Edinburgh, 1988).

Green, S., *Rachman* (London, 1979).

Greve, J., Page, D., & Greve, S., *Homelessness in London* (Edinburgh, 1971).

Griffiths, C., Nott, J., & Whyte, W., eds., *Classes, Cultures and Politics. Essays in British History for Ross McKibbin* (Oxford, 2011).

Gripaios, P., 'Industrial Decline in London: An Examination of Its Causes', *Urban Studies* 14 (2), 1977, 181–89.

Grove, P. & C., *The History of the 'Ethnic' Restaurant in Britain*, accessed 23 August 2015, www .menumagazine.co.uk/book/restauranthistory.html.

Gunn, S., 'The Buchanan Report, Environment and the Problem of Traffic in 1960s Britain', *Twentieth Century British History* 22 (4), 2011, 521–42.

———, 'People and the Car. The Expansion of Automobility in Urban Britain, c. 1955–1970', *Social History* 38 (2), 2013, 220–37.

Gunn, S., & Townsend, S., *Automobility and the City in Twentieth Century Britain and Japan* (London, 2019).

Hain, P., *Radical Regeneration. Protest, Direct Action and Community Politics* (London, 1975).

Halasz, P., *A Swinger's Guide to London* (New York, 1967).

———, *A Memoir of Creativity. Abstract Painting, Politics and the Media, 1956–2008* (Bloomington, IN, 2009).

Hall, J. M., 'East London's Future: Visions Past and Present', *East London Papers* 14 (1), 1972, 5–24.

Hall, J. M., Ginsburg, L. B., Eyles, J., & Darby, M., 'The Docklands Study Reviewed', *East London Papers* 15, 1973, 5–36.

Hall, J. M., Griffiths, G., Eyles, J., & Darby, M., 'Rebuilding the London Docklands', *London Journal* 2 (2), 1976, 266–85.

Hall, P., 'The Containment of Urban England', *Geographical Journal* 140 (3), 1974, 386–408.

———, *Great Planning Disasters* (London, 1980).

——, *London 2001* (London, 1989).

Hall, P., Thomas, R., Gracey, H., & Drewett, R., *The Containment of Urban England*. Vol. 2, *The Planning System. Objectives, Operations, Impacts* (London, 1973).

Hamilton, K., 'Accommodating Diplomacy: The Foreign and Commonwealth Office and the Debate over Whitehall Redevelopment', *Contemporary British History* 18, 2004, 198–222.

Hanshaw, P., *All My Yesterdays* (London, 1996).

Harloe, M., Issacharoff, R., & Minns, R., *The Organization of Housing. Public and Private Enterprise in London* (London, 1974).

Harris, M., & Myers, M., 'The Public Meeting as a Means of Participation', GLC, *Quarterly Bulletin of the Research and Intelligence Unit* 9, December 1969, 3–7.

Harris, O., *Cranes, Critics and Croydonisation* (London, 1993).

Harrison, A., & Lomas, G., 'Tenure Preference: How to Interpret the Survey Evidence', *CES Review* 8, January 1980, 20–23.

Hart, D. A., *Strategic Planning in London. The Rise and Fall of the Primary Road Network* (Oxford, 1976).

Harvey, A., *Casualties of the Welfare State* (London, 1960).

Haslemere Estates Ltd, *Something of London Restored* (London, 1970).

——, *Something More of London Restored* (London, 1974).

——, *Doing a Haslemere* (London, 1978).

Haynes, P., *An Islington Councillor, 1971–1992* (London, 1994).

Healey, P., *Urban Complexities and Spatial Strategies. Towards a Relational Planning for Our Times* (London, 2007).

Hebbert, M., *London. More by Fortune than Design* (Chichester, 1998).

Hill, M. J., & Issacharoff, M., *Community Action and Race Relations. A Study of Community Relations Committees in Britain* (London/Oxford, 1971).

Hill, S., *The Dockers. Class and Tradition in London* (London, 1976).

Hilton, M., McKay, J., Crowson, N., & Mouhot, J.-F., *The Politics of Expertise. How NGOs Shaped Modern Britain* (Oxford, 2013).

Hispanic Britain, or, An Anglo-Spanish Miscellany, accessed 23 August 2015, https://hispanicbritain.wordpress.com.

Hobbs, D., *Doing the Business. Entrepreneurship, the Working Class, and Detectives in the East End of London* (Oxford, 1988).

Hodge, H., *Cab, Sir?* (London, 1939).

Hogg, J., *The Habits of Good Society* (London, 1859).

Holmans, A. E., *Historical Statistics of Housing in Britain* (Cambridge, 2006).

Holmes, A., *Better than No Place* (London, 1971).

Holmes, C., *The Other Notting Hill* (Studley, 2005).

Horn, G., *Crossing the Floor. Reg Prentice and the Crisis of British Social Democracy* (Manchester, 2013).

Hosken, A., *Ken. The Ups and Downs of Ken Livingstone* (London, 2008).

Houlbrook, M., *Queer London. Perils and Pleasures in the Sexual Metropolis, 1918–1957* (London, 2005).

Howe, D., *From Bobby to Babylon. Blacks and the British Police* (London, 1988).

Howick, C., & Key, T., *The Local Economy of Tower Hamlets. An Inner-City Profile* (London, 1978).

——, 'Manufacturing Industry and Inner City Regeneration. An Economic Study of the London Borough of Tower Hamlets', *Progress in Planning* 18 (3), 1982, 133–87.

Hulanicki, B., *From A to Biba* (London, 1983).

Hulanicki, B., & Pel, M., *The Biba Years, 1963–1975* (London, 2014).

Hunte, J. A., *Nigger-Hunting in England* (London, 1965).

Hunter, M., ed., *Preserving the Past* (London, 1996).

Jackson, B., 'Currents of Neo-liberalism: British Political Ideologies and the New Right, c. 1955–1979', *English Historical Review* 131 (551), 2016, 823–50.

Jackson, C., *Lambeth Interface. Housing, Planning and Community Action in an Inner London Borough* (Croydon, 1975).

Jacobs, J., *The Death and Life of Great American Cities. The Failure of Town Planning* (Harmondsworth, 1964).

James, B., *London on a Sunday* (London, 1964).

Jarman, B., *A Survey of Primary Care in London. Report Prepared for the Royal College of General Practitioners* (London, 1981).

Jaroszek, J., *Earnings in Relation to Employment Changes* (GLC Research Memorandum 500, London, 1975).

Jenkins, H., *Rank and File* (London, 1980).

Jenkins, S., *A City at Risk. A Contemporary Look at London's Streets* (London, 1970).

———, 'The Politics of London Motorways', *Political Quarterly* 44 (3), 1973, 257–70.

Johnson, A., *This Boy. A Memoir of a Childhood* (London, 2013).

Johnson, D., & Dunkley, R., *Gear Guide. Hip Pocket Guide to London's Swinging Fashion Scene* (London, 1967).

Joint Docklands Action Group, *Docklands. The Fight for a Future* (London, 1976).

Jones, H. R., 'Modern Emigration from Malta', *Transactions of the Institute of British Geographers* 60, 1973, 101–19.

Judd, D. R., 'Building the Tourist City. Editor's Introduction', in Judd, D. R., ed., *The Infrastructure of Play. Building the Tourist City* (New York, 2003), pp. 3–16.

Judd, D., & Fainstein, S., eds., *The Tourist City* (New Haven, CT, 1999).

Kandiah, P., 'You Thought That a Really Great Society Was Going to Come Out of All This—North Kensington Law Centre', in Curtis, H., & Sanderson, M., *The Unsung Sixties. Memoirs of Social Innovation* (London, 2004), pp. 155–67.

Kefford, A., 'Disruption, Destruction and the Creation of the "Inner Cities": The Impact of Urban Renewal on Industry, 1945–1980', *Urban Studies* 44 (3), 2017, 492–515.

Kelley, R. D. G., & Tuck, S. eds., *The Other Special Relationship. Race, Rights and Riots in Britain and the United States* (New York, 2015).

Kilroy, B., 'Improvement Grants Threaten North Kensington', *Housing Review* 21 (3), May–June 1972, 79–81.

King, A., *British Political Opinion, 1937–2000. The Gallup Polls* (London, 2001).

King, R., & Nugent, N., eds., *Respectable Rebels. Middle Class Campaigns in Britain in the 1970s* (London, 1979).

Kinghan, M., *Squatters in London* (London, 1977).

Kloß, S., *Notting Hill Carnival. Die Aushandlung des Eigenen im multiethnischen Großbritannien seit 1958* (Frankfurt, 2014).

Kosmin, B. A., & Grizzard, N., *Jews in an Inner London Borough. A Study of the Jewish Population of the London Borough of Hackney Based on the 1971 Census* (London, 1975).

Kotas, R., *Market Orientation in the Hotel and Catering Industry* (Leighton Buzzard, 1975).

Kynaston, D., *The City of London. A Club No More, 1945–2000* (London, 2001).

Langan, P., *A Life with Food. Annotated and with a Memoir by Brian Sewell* (London, 1990).

Lawrence, J. 'Inventing the "Traditional Working Class: A Re-analysis of Interview Notes from Young and Willmott's *Family and Kinship in East London*', *Historical Journal* 59 (2), 2016, 567–93.

———, *Me, Me, Me? The Search for Community in Post-war England* (Oxford, 2019).

Lawson, N., *The View from No. 11. Memoirs of a Tory Radical* (London, 1992).

Lee, R., 'Planning and Social Change in East London', *East London Papers* 14 (1), 1972, 25–43.

Lester, R., *Boutique London. A History: King's Road to Carnaby Street* (London, 2010).

Levinson, M., *The Trouble with Yesterday* (London, 1946).

———, *The Desperate Passion of Henry Knopp* (London, 1962).

———, *Taxi* (London, 1963).

———, *Greek Street Tragedy* (London, 1964).

———, *The Woman from Bessarabia* (London, 1964).

———, *The Taxi Game* (London, 1973).

Levy, S., *Ready, Steady, Go! Swinging London and the Invention of Cool* (London, 2001).

Ley, D., *The New Middle Class and the Remaking of the Central City* (Oxford, 1996).

Lister, J., *Mary Quant* (London, 2019).

Livingstone, K., *If Voting Changed Anything, They'd Abolish It* (London, 1987).

Location of Offices Bureau, *Annual Report, 1967–8* (London, 1968).

———, *Annual Report, 1978-9* (London, 1979).

London County Council, *Minutes of Proceedings* (London, 1951–65).

London Docklands Study Team, *Docklands. Redevelopment Proposals for East London* (London, 1973).

London Health Planning Consortium, *Primary Health Care in Inner London* (London, 1981).

Loney, M., *Community against Government. The British Community Development Project, 1968–78* (London, 1983).

Lorentzen, A., 'Cities in the Experience Economy', in Lorentzen & Hansen, *The City in the Experience Economy*, pp. 13–29.

Lorentzen A., & Hansen, C. J., 'Introduction', in *The City in the Experience Economy*, pp. 1–11.

———, eds., *The City in the Experience Economy. Role and Transformation* (Abingdon, 2012).

Lucas, J. M., *The Wandsworth Story* (London, 1990).

MacCarthy, F., *Last Curtsey. The End of the Debutantes* (London, 2006).

Malik, M. A., *From Michael de Freitas to Michael X* (London, 1968).

Manchester, C., *Sex Shops and the Law* (London, 1986).

Marriott, O., *The Property Boom* (London, 1967).

Marsden, J., *House Prices in London. An Economic Analysis of London's Housing Market* (Greater London Authority Working Paper 72, London, 2015).

Marshall, H., *Twilight London. A Study in Degradation* (London, 1971).

Mash, J., *Portobello Road. Lives of a Neighbourhood* (London, 2014).

Maugham, R., *Escape from the Shadows* (London, 1972).

McCarthy, M., *Campaigning for the Poor: CPAG and the Politics of Welfare* (London, 1986).

McKennell, A. C., & Hunt, E. A., *Noise Annoyance in Central London. A Survey Made in 1961 for the Building Research Station* (London, 1966).

Merrett, S., with Gray, F., *Owner Occupation in Britain* (London, 1982).

Miles, B., *London Calling. A Countercultural History of London since 1945* (London, 2010).

Mold, A., '"The Welfare Branch of the Alternative Society?" The Work of Drug Voluntary Organization Release, 1967–1978', *Twentieth Century British History* 17 (1), 2006, 50–73.

Moore, T., *Policing Notting Hill. Fifty Years of Turbulence* (Hook, 2013).

Moorhouse, B., Wilson, M., & Chamberlain, C., 'Rent Strikes—Direct Action and the Working Class', *Socialist Register* 1972, 133–56.

Moran, J., 'Early Cultures of Gentrification in London, 1955–1980', *Journal of Urban History* 34 (1), 2007, 101–21.

Morrey, C. R., *The Changing Population of the London Boroughs* (GLC Research Memorandum 413, London, 1973).

Mort, F., 'Fantasies of Metropolitan Life. Planning London in the 1940s', *Journal of British Studies* 43 (1), 2004, 120–52.

———, 'Striptease: The Erotic Female Body and Live Sexual Entertainment in Mid-Twentieth-Century London', *Social History* 32 (1), 2007, 27–53.

———, *Capital Affairs. London and the Making of the Permissive Society* (London, 2010).

Munby, D. L., *Industry and Planning in Stepney* (Oxford, 1951).

Munt, I., 'Economic Restructuring, Culture and Gentrification. A Case Study in Battersea, London', *Environment and Planning. A* 19 (9), 1987, 1175–97.

Murrell, N. S., Spencer, W. D., & McFarlane, A. A., eds., *Chanting Down Babylon. The Rastafari Reader* (Philadelphia, 1998), p. 181.

Myatt, P. R., *Carnaby Street Study* (GLC Research Memorandum 466, London, 1975).

Nash, N., *London after Dark* (New York, 1966).

National Catering Inquiry, *The British Eating Out. A Report from Britain's National Catering Inquiry* (London, 1966).

Newman, O., *Gambling. Hazard and Reward* (London, 1972).

Ng Kwee Choo, *The Chinese in London* (Oxford, 1968).

Norman, F., *Soho Night and Day* (London, 1966).

Norman, F., with Bernard, J., *Soho Night and Day* (2nd ed., London, 1968).

Nugent, N., 'The Ratepayers', in King, R., & Nugent, N., eds., *Respectable Rebels. Middle Class Campaigns in Britain in the 1970s* (London, 1979), pp. 23–45.

O'Carroll, S, '*Cathy Come Home* de Ken Loach: Un déclencheur de la "redécouverte de la pauvreté" des années soixantes?', in Frison, D., ed., *Pauvreté et inégalités en Grande-Bretagne de 1942 à 1990* (Paris, 2000), pp. 271–83.

O'Malley, J., *The Politics of Community Action. A Decade of Struggle in Notting Hill* (Nottingham, 1977).

Osborn, T., 'Outpost of a New Culture', in Anning, N., Wates, N., & Wolmar, C., eds., *Squatting: The Real Story* (London, 1980), pp. 186–91.

Patterson, S., *Dark Strangers. A Sociological Study of the Absorption of a Recent West Indian Migrant Group in Brixton, South London* (London, 1963).

———, ed., *Immigrants in London. Report of a Study Group Set Up by the London Council of Social Service* (London, 1963).

Pearce, D., *London's Mansions. The Palatial Houses of the Nobility* (London, 1986).

Pendlebury, J., *Conservation in the Age of Consensus* (Abingdon, 2009).

Perry, K. H., *London Is the Place for Me: Black Britons, Citizenship and the Politics of Race* (Oxford, 2016).

Phillips, G., & Whiteside, N., *Casual Labour. The Unemployment Question in the Port Transport Industry, 1880–1970* (Oxford, 1985).

Pilkington, E., *Beyond the Mother Country. West Indians and the Notting Hill Riots* (London, 1988).

Pimlott, B., & Rao, N., *Governing London* (Oxford, 2002).

Pine, B. J., II, & Gilmore, J. H., 'Welcome to the Experience Economy', *Harvard Business Review* 76 (6), 1998, 97–105.

————, *The Experience Economy* (updated ed., Boston, 2011).

Platt, S., 'A Decade of Squatting. The Story of Squatting in Britain since 1968', in Anning, N., Wates, N., & Wolmar, C., eds., *Squatting: The Real Story* (London, 1980), pp. 14–103.

Postgate, R., ed., *The Good Food Guide* (London, 1951–70).

————, *The Good Food Guide to London* (London, 1968).

Poulsen, C., *Victoria Park. A Study in the History of East London* (London, 1976).

Power, A., *A Battle Lost—Barnsbury, 1972* (London, 1972).

————, *I Woke Up This Morning. The Development of a London Community Project* (London, 1972).

Prentice, R., 'Right Turn', in Cormack, P., ed., *Right Turn. Eight Men Who Changed Their Minds* (London, 1978), pp. 1–13.

Psychiatric Rehabilitation Association, *The Mental Health of East London, 1966* (London, 1968).

Pylypec, L., *A Squatter in London* (London, 2018).

Quant, M., *Quant by Quant* (London, 1966).

Raban, J., *Soft City* (London, 1974).

Radford, J., 'Don't Agonise—Organise', in Curno, P., ed., *Political Issues and Community Work* (London, 1978), pp. 106–19.

Raingold, S., *A Taxi Driver's Guide to London* (London, 1973).

Ramsey, W., *The East End Then and Now* (London, 1997).

Rasmussen, S. E., *London, the Unique City* (London, 1936).

Rawlings, T., *Mod. Clean Living under Very Difficult Circumstances. A Very British Phenomenon* (London, 2000).

Reed, J., *The King of Carnaby Street. The Life of John Stephen* (London, 2010).

Rhind, N., *Blackheath Village and Environs, 1790–1970*, vol. 2 (London, 1983).

Rickly-Boyd, J. M., Knudsen, D. C., Braverman, L. C., & Metro-Roland, M. M., *Tourism, Performance and Place. A Geographic Perspective* (Farnham, 2014).

Roberts, J. C., *Employment in Southwark. A Strategy for the Future* (London, 1976).

Roberts, N., *The Front Line. Women in the Sex Industry Speak* (London, 1986).

Robinson, E., Schofield, C., Sutcliffe-Braithwaite, F., & Thomlinson, N., 'Telling Stories about Postwar Britain: Popular Individualism and the "Crisis" of the 1970s', *Twentieth Century British History* 28 (2), 2017, 268–304.

Rogers, E., *Tin Pan Alley* (London, 1964).

Rose, E. J. B., *Colour and Citizenship. A Report on British Race Relations* (London, 1969).

Rose, H., *Rights, Participation and Conflict* (London, [1970?]).

Rossetti, F., 'Politics and Participation: A Case Study', in Curno, P., *Political Issues and Community Work* (London, 1978), pp. 136–58.

Saint, A., 'How Listing Happened', in Hunter, M., ed., *Preserving the Past* (London, 1996), pp. 115–33.

Salter, T., *Carnaby Street* (London, 1970).

Sandford, J., & Law, R., *Synthetic Fun* (London, 1967).

Saumarez Smith, O., 'Central Government and Town-Centre Development in Britain, 1959–1966', *Historical Journal* 58 (1), 2015, pp. 217–44.

————, 'The Inner City Crisis and the End of Urban Modernism in 1970s Britain', *Twentieth Century British History* 27 (4), 2016, 578–98.

————, *Boom Cities. Architect Planners and the Politics of Radical Urban Renewal in 1960s Britain* (Oxford, 2019).

Schofield, C., & Jones, B., '"Whatever Community Is, This Is Not It." Notting Hill and the Reconstruction of "Race" in Britain after 1958', *Journal of British Studies* 58 (1), 2019, 142–73.

Setch, E., 'The Face of Metropolitan Feminism: the London Women's Liberation Workshop, 1969–1979', *Twentieth Century British History* 13 (2), 2002, 171–90.

Seyd, P., 'Shelter. The National Campaign for the Homeless', *Political Quarterly* 46 (4), 1975, 418–31.

Shapely, P., *Deprivation, State Interventions and Urban Communities in Britain, 1968–1979* (Abingdon, 2018).

Sharpe, L. J., 'The Politics of Local Government in Greater London', *Public Administration* 38 (2), 1960, 157–72.

Sharr, A., & Thornton, S., *Demolishing Whitehall. Leslie Martin, Harold Wilson and the Architecture of White Heat* (London, 2016).

Sheppard, F. H. W., *Survey of London*, vol. 39, *The Grosvenor Estate in Mayfair* (London, 1977).

Silverstone, R., 'Just a Sec? . . . Or How I Learned to Stop Worrying and Love the Boss', *Personnel Management* June 1975, 33–36.

Skinner, F., *People without Roots: a Study Undertaken in the London Borough of Tower Hamlets 1966–7 and an Appraisal of Services Provided by Voluntary and Statutory Agencies* (London, 1967).

Small, S., *Police and People in London*, vol. 2, *A Group of Young Black People* (London, 1983).

Smith, A., *The East Enders* (London, 1961).

Smith, D. J., & Gray, J., *Police and People in London* (London, 1985).

Spinetti, V., with Rankin, P., *Victor Spinetti Up Front. His Strictly Confidential Autobiography* (London, 2006).

Spitalfields Crypt Trust, *The Outcasts of Spitalfields* (London, [1965?]).

Starkie, D., *The Motorway Age. Road and Traffic Policies in Postwar Britain* (Oxford, 1982).

Sutcliffe-Braithwaite, F., *Class, Politics and the Decline of Deference in England, 1968–2000* (Oxford, 2018).

Sutherland, A. S., *The Spaghetti Tree. Mario and Franco and the Trattoria Revolution* (London, 2009).

Swenarton, M., *Cook's Camden: The Making of Modern Housing* (London, 2017).

Talbot, M. F., *Greater London Transportation Survey. A Study of Taxi Trips* (GLC Research Memorandum 307, London, 1974).

Tatchell, P., *The Battle for Bermondsey* (London, 1983).

Taylor, M., 'Voluntary Action and the State', in Gladstone, D., ed., *British Social Welfare. Past, Present and Future* (London, 1995), pp. 221–48.

Thomas, D. M., *London's Green Belt* (London, 1970).

Thomas, D. N., *Organising for Social Change. A Study in the Theory and Practice of Community Work* (London, 1976).

Thomas, S., & Turner, A. W., *Welcome to Big Biba. Inside the Most Beautiful Store in the World* (London, 2006).

Thoimson, J. M., *Motorways in London* (London, 1969).

Thorold, P., *The London Rich* (London, 1999).

Tomkinson, M., *The Pornbrokers. The Rise of the Soho Sex Barons* (London, 1982).

Tomlinson, J., 'Deindustrialisation: Strengths and Weaknesses as a Key Concept for Understanding Post-war British History', *Urban History* 47 (2), 2020, 199–219.

Tow, J., *London, Reign over Me. How England's Capital Built Classic Rock* (Lanham, MD, 2020). Kindle ed.

Town and Country Planning Association, *The Paper Metropolis* (London, 1962).

Townsend, A., *Cabbie* (Stroud, 2003).

Townsend, P., *The Family Life of Old People* (London, 1957).

——, 'The Meaning of Poverty', *British Journal of Sociology* 13 (3), 1962, 210–27.

Travers, T., *The Politics of Local Government Finance* (London, 1986).

———, *The Politics of London. Governing an Ungovernable City* (London, 2004).

Treff Tips. Heiße Tips für junge Leute (Essen, 1968).

Tripp, H. A., *Road Traffic and Its Control* (London, 1938).

———, *Town Planning and Road Traffic* (London, 1942).

Turner, J. E., *Labour's Doorstep Politics in London* (London, 1978)

Turton, A. R., *Analysis of Public Reaction to Development Plans for London Docklands* (GLC Research Memorandum 440, London, 1974).

Twort, D., & Varra, G., *Guide de Londres en Jeans* (Paris, 1979).

Tym & Partners, *Living by the Yard. A Study of Bad Neighbour Industry in the Inner City* (London, 1981).

Urry, J., *The Tourist Gaze. Leisure and Travel in Contemporary Societies* (London, 1990).

van den Berg, L., van der Borg, J., & Russo, A. P., 'The Infrastructure of Urban Tourism. A Comparative Analysis of Mega-Projects in Four Eurocities', in Judd, D. R., ed., *The Infrastructure of Play. Building the Tourist City* (New York, 2003), pp. 296–319.

van Dyck. F. J., 'Chanting down Babylon Outernational', in Murrell, N. S., Spencer, W. D., & McFarlane, A. A., eds., *Chanting down Babylon. The Rastafari Reader* (Philadelphia, 1998), pp. 178–98.

Walkowitz, J., *Nights Out. Life in Cosmopolitan London* (New Haven, CT, 2012).

Waller, P., ed., *The English Urban Landscape* (Oxford, 2000).

Waters, R., *Thinking Black. Britain, 1964–1985* (Oakland, CA, 2019).

Wates, N., *The Battle for Tolmers Square* (London, 1974).

Watson, N., *The Port of London Authority. A Century of Service, 1909–2009* (London, 2009).

Webb, M., *The Amber Valley Gazetteer of Greater London Suburban Cinemas* (Birmingham, 1986).

Wetherell, S., *Foundations: How the Built Environment Made Twentieth-Century Britain* (Princeton, NJ, 2020).

Wharton, G., *Suburban London Cinemas* (London, 2008).

White, J., *London in the Twentieth Century. A City and Its People* (London, 2001).

Whitehead, C., & Kleinman, M., 'Private Renting in London: Is It So Different?', *Journal of Social Policy* 16 (3), 1987, 319–48.

Whitehead, C., with Lambert, C., 'Tenure Preference: What Council Tenants Want', *CES Review* 9, April 1980, 34–38.

Whitfield, J., *Unhappy Dialogue. The Metropolitan Police and Black Londoners in Postwar Britain* (Cullompton, 2004).

Widgery, D., *Some Lives! A GP's East End* (London, 1991).

Wilcox, D., & Richards, D., *London. The Heartless City* (London, 1977).

Wild, R., '"Black Was the Colour of Our Fight": The Transnational Roots of British Black Power', in Kelley, R. G. D., & Tuck, S., eds., *The Other Special Relationship. Race, Rights and Riots in Britain and the United States* (New York, 2015), pp. 25–46.

Willetts, P., *Members Only. The Life and Times of Paul Raymond* (London, 2010).

William, C., & Edwards, A., eds., *The Art of the Possible: Politics and Governance in Modern British History, 1885–1997. Essays in Memory of Duncan Tanner* (Manchester, 2015).

Wilson, David, *Dockers. The Impact of Industrial Change* (London, 1972).

Wilson, Des, *I Know It Was the Place's Fault* (London, 1970).

Wortley, R., *Skin Deep in Soho* (London, 1969).

Young, G., *Tourism: Blessing or Blight?* (London, 1973).

Young, K., & Garside, P. L., *Metropolitan London. Politics and Urban Change, 1837–1981* (London, 1983).

Young, K., & Kramer, J., *Strategy and Conflict in Metropolitan Housing* (London, 1978).

Selected Newspaper and Magazine Articles

'Disappearing Cockneys', *South London Press* 20 September 1957.

'More Tenants Want to Buy', *Financial Times* 8 March 1958.

'Colour Bars Are White', *South London Press* 5 September 1958.

'The Housing Market's Taste of Freedom', *Financial Times* 29 April 1959.

'Is De Beauvoir Town Doomed?', *Hackney Gazette* 1 November 1960.

'English Eating in London', *Queen* July 1961.

'Cabbies of London', *Evening News* 16 October–15 November 1961.

'The Piccadilly Men', *Evening Standard* 8 November 1961.

'Fashionable World's End', *West London Press and Chelsea News* 30 March 1962.

'The Battle of Seaton Street', *Sunday Times* 8 April 1962.

'Where the Slums Are Paved with Gold', *Financial Times* 27 April 1962.

'Why Let Sleeping Shops Lie?', *London Property Letter* 4, March 1963 (2).

'Stockwell', *London Property Letter* 5, April 1963 (1).

'Deptford', *London Property Letter* 7, May 1963 (1).

'Portrait of an Agent: John Birrane', *London Property Letter* 9, June 1963 (1).

'Blackheath: Georgian Spic and Span', *London Property Letter* 11, July 1963 (1).

'Paddington', *London Property Letter* 12, July 1963 (2).

'Camden Town', *London Property Letter* 16, September 1963 (2).

'Greenwich', *London Property Letter* 19, November 1963 (1).

'Refuge for Illegitimates', *New Society* 19 December 1963.

'Portrait of a Property Columbus', *London Property Letter* 23, January 1964 (1).

'Fulham Revisited', *London Property Letter* 25, 1 February 1964.

'Home Ownership in the County of London', *Building Societies Gazette* March 1964.

'Kentish Town', *London Property Letter* 35, 4 July 1964.

'W6', *London Property Letter* 39, 12 September 1964.

'Unmarried Mothers in Lonely Bedsits', *Evening Standard* 21 October 1964.

'Chelsea', *London Property Letter* 49, 13 February 1965.

'London: Mods, Rocker, Beatniks, Spießer!', *Star Club News* (Hamburg), August 1965.

'Holland Park: Back in the Family Way', *London Property Letter* 66, 23 October 1965.

'Aristocrats in the Darkroom', *London Life* 8 January 1966.

'Rock Hoch. Jetzt Kommen die Engländer', *Twen* (Munich) 3 March 1966.

'Ravers' Map of London', *Rave*, April 1966.

'You Can Walk across It on the Grass', *Time* 15 April 1966.

'Wandsworth: The Common Touch', *London Property Letter* 86, 27 August 1966.

'Carnaby Street', *Réalités* (Paris) October 1966.

'Profile for Investor-Occupiers: Islington', *London Property Letter* 97, 11 February 1967.

'"The Days of the Lash-Up Boys Are Numbered"', *London Property Letter* 101, 8 April 1967.

'Sale of Council Houses', *The Bulletin* June 1967.

'Boutiquen Boom in Germany', *Twen* (Munich), 10 October 1967.

'Personality Page, No. 1. Jack (from Mons) Cohen', *Steering Wheel* 13 January 1968.

'Passport to Soho', *Sunday Times Magazine* 21 January 1968.

'Anatomy of the Permissive Society. 3. The Single Girl', *Look of London* February 1968.

'Mini-Mutter Mary Quant wirbt für den Union Jack', *Berliner Morgenpost* (Berlin) 16 March 1968.

'How to Get Started. Finance for a £500,000 Venture', *London Property Letter* 139, 9 November 1968.

'Moore Park, Fulham: King's Ransom', *London Property Letter* 140, 23 November 1968.

'Kennington Comes Clean', *London Property Letter* 144, 25 January 1969.

'Geography for Converters', *London Property Letter* 150, 26 April 1969.

'Camden: Beyond the Fringe', *London Property Letter* 153, 14 June 1969.

'Converting: Ten Commandments', *London Property Letter* 153, 14 June 1969.

'South London Scene', *London Property Letter* 154, 28 June 1969.

'Living off the Ground', *Architects' Journal* 20 August 1969.

'Upgrading Highbury', *London Property Letter* 161, 11 October 1969.

'The Man behind the Menu' (interview with John Stais), *Hotel and Restaurant Catering* November 1969.

'Conversion Grants Whitewash', *London Property Letter* 163, 8 November 1969.

'Better Buys at Barnsbury', *London Property Letter* 170, 28 February 1970.

'Kookie New Cross', *London Property Letter* 174, 25 April 1970.

'Elevating Ealing', *London Property Letter* 176, 23 May 1970.

'Conservation and Eastcote', *The Aerial. Eastcote Residents Association Journal* Summer 1970.

'Canonbury: Shot in the Arm', *London Property Letter* 181, 6 August 1970.

'London's Paying Guests', *Architects' Journal* 19 August 1970.

'The Maxwell Stamp Report', *Steering Wheel* 14 November 1970.

'The Taxi Driver and Race Relations', *Steering Wheel* 6 February 1971.

'A Plug for Peckham', *London Property Letter* 190, May 1971.

'Up the Junction', *London Property Letter* 194, September 1971.

'London Claimants' Unions', *Time Out* 7 January 1972

'Where Have the Grotty Suburbs Gone?', *London Property Letter* 201, April 1972.

'The Many Problems of the Mr Freedom Group', *Drapers Record* 10 June 1972.

'Is Local Taxation as Fair as It Can Be?', *Cannon Hill Ward Residents Association Gazette* 12, June 1972; 13, July 1972; 16, October 1972.

'A Nice Borough to Live In, but It's Thumbs Down for the Shops', *Wimbledon News* January 1973.

'How Fares Finsbury Park?', *London Property Letter* 210, January 1973.

'Balham: Gateway to the South', *London Property Letter* 216, July 1973.

'Docks Campaign', *New Society* 9 August 1973.

'Where Has All the Bubble and Squeak Gone?', *Time Out* 19 October 1973.

'All Dressed Up and Nowhere to Go', *Time Out* 28 June 1974.

[Profile of Benny Taylor], *Where to Go* 28 November and 5 December 1974.

'Co-operative Action', *Community Action* 17, December 1974–January 1975.

'Gerry Sherrick—Poet—Taxidriver', *Cab Trade News* 25 January 1975.

'Rates', *Sanderstead News* April 1975.

'London "Could Become Jarrow of 1980s"', *Evening Standard* 28 April 1975.

'Trials of a Militant Moderate', *Observer* 20 July 1975.

'Bye-Bye Biba', *Economist* 23 August 1975.

'Carnival '75 is a Big Success', *West Indian World* 12 September 1975.

'Tenants and Workers Taking Joint Action', *Community Action* 22, October–November 1975.

Interview with Jack Mundey, *Community Action* 24, February–March 1976.

'The Two Faces of Notting Hill', *Evening Standard* 31 August 1976.

'Police Carnival', *West Indian World* 3 September 1976.

'Notting Hill: The Battle Ground', *West Indian World* 10 September 1976.

'Suffocated—by an Avalanche of Paper', *Evening Standard* 12 October 1978.

'On the "Knowledge"', *Steering Wheel* 9 August 1979.

'Why London's Cabbies Are So Miserable', *Evening Standard* 9 November 1979.

Adams, D., 'Background to the Rates. An Expert View', *Harrow Observer* 21 February 1975.

———, 'How the Squeeze Has Hit Swinging London', *Evening Standard* 22 November 1966.

Aitken, J., 'Paying Homage at Sibylla's Shrine', *Evening Standard* 28 July 1966.

Alexander, C., 'A Cause for Regret', *Drapers Record* 30 August 1975.

Allen, K., 'Bingo! It's the Big Boom in Council Houses', *Evening News* 10 August 1972.

Alvarez, A., 'The Sweet Smell of Corruption', *Life Atlantic* 4 September 1967.

Annoute, R., 'Why DO Taxi Drivers . . . ??', part 2, *Steering Wheel* 5 September 1970; part 4, *Steering Wheel* 19 September 1970..

Baker, R. O., 'The State of the Industry', *Caterer and Hotelkeeper* 8 January 1970.

Balfe, R., 'Why It Takes So Long', *Municipal Engineering* 11 March 1977.

Ball, D., 'Council and Community', *New Society* 7 January 1971.

Barber, J., 'The World of John Cranko', *Evening Standard* 1 March 1960.

———, 'Astonishing—His Way of Making a Glum Girl Glitter', *Evening Standard* 4 March 1960.

Bareham, L., 'Cheap Eats', *Time Out* 16 September 1977.

Barr, J., 'Betting Shop Dream World', *New Society* 6 May 1965.

Barry, J., & Knightley, P., '£826,000,000 a Year Down the Drain', *Sunday Times* 22 August 1976.

Bastian, J., 'An Old Square Gets with It', *Ideal Home* June 1964.

Benedictus, D., 'Big Man in the Stalls', *Evening Standard* 3 November 1978.

Betts, E., 'Miss Smith, Take a £1000 Pay Cheque', *Evening Standard* 29 December 1962.

Biddlecombe, R., 'A Soho Fit for Families?', *New Tomorrow. Unfolding God's Heart to the World* December 1979.

Binney, M., Cantell, T., & Darley, G., 'One Tree Grows in Victoria Street', in 'The Concrete Jerusalem: The Failure of the Clean Sweep', supplement to *New Society* 23–30 December 1976.

Binns, I., 'What Are We Trying to Achieve through Community Action?', *Community Action* 6, January–February 1973.

Black, S., 'Carnaby Street. Tourist "Must" in Swinging London', *Financial Times* 24 February 1967.

———, 'British Fashion Needs Quality To Go With Its Style', *Financial Times* 10 June 1972.

Blackwell, H., 'This Is Carnaby Street', *London Life* 14 May 1966.

Bocca, G., 'Taxi Drivers of the World, I', *Steering Wheel* 30 December 1967.

Bourne, R., 'How the Kebab Conquered', *Evening Standard* 4 July 1977.

———, 'The Rule Is: Keep Looking', *Evening Standard* 20 November 1978.

———, 'Jobs Nobody Wants', *Evening Standard* 21 March 1979.

Brack, H., 'Are We Building the Slums of Tomorrow?', *Evening Standard* 23 November 1965.

———, 'Are GLC Houses a Good Buy?', *Evening Standard* 23 May 1967.

———, 'London's Twilight Streets', *Evening Standard* 15 August 1967.

———, 'With All Its Other Headaches, the Young People Are Moving Out Now', *Evening Standard* 14 May 1968.

———, 'On the Nod: An Evening in the Council Chamber', *Evening Standard* 24 May 1968.

———, 'Pay Up? I'd Rather Pitch a Tent', *Evening Standard* 25 August 1969.

———, 'Half Way to Councilville', *Evening Standard* 18 December 1978.

Brittain, V., 'Success and Carnaby Street', *Investors Chronicle*, Retail Supplement, 28 January 1966.

Bugler, J., 'Devlin: How the Dockers React', *New Society* 12 August 1965.

———, 'Ireland in London', *New Society* 14 March 1968.

Bygrave, M., 'Hamburgers', *Time Out* 21 October 1977.

Carvel, R., 'Maggie's London', *Evening Standard* 20 April 1979.

Catherwood, Sir F., 'I'm All For Developers', *Evening Standard* 16 October 1973.

Churchill, D., 'Call for Government Grants to Boost Industry in London', *Financial Times* 25 November 1977.

Clark, S., 'Mas in the Grove', *Time Out* 22 August 1975.

Cleave, M., 'Decline of the Record Tsars', *Evening Standard* 15 August 1964.

———, 'Mr Most, Who Can't Wait for Mondays', *Evening Standard* 15 August 1964.

———, 'The Single Girls. Young, Free and Far from Mum', *Evening Standard* 5 October 1964.

———, 'Chummeries—Where Six Live Cheaper than One', *Evening Standard* 6 October 1964.

———, 'Food, Swearing and the Art of Tom Benson', *Evening Standard* 2 June 1965.

———, 'The High Life—and No Back Answers', *Evening Standard* 5 June 1965.

———, 'Quant by Cleave', part 1, *Evening Standard* 5 April 1967

———, 'Quant by Cleave', part 2, *Evening Standard* 6 April 1967.

Coleman, S., 'The Deb World Heads Back to the Country', *Evening Standard* 20 March 1961.

Cook, S., 'Why Soho Is Naughty, but Not Very Nice', *Guardian* 30 December 1980.

Cotter, S., 'Woman behind the Menu' (Simone Prunier), *Hotel and Restaurant Catering* February 1970.

Crewe, Q., 'The Real Soho', *Queen* 2 December 1964.

———, 'The Trattoria Tradition', *Evening Standard* 26 November 1970.

Cron, S., 'The Unseen Women of Television', *London Life* 7 May 1966.

Crosby, J., 'Super Girl', *New York Herald Tribune* 15 January 1964.

———, 'The Most Exciting City', *Weekend Telegraph* 16 April 1965.

Cross, P., 'The Day I Went on a Job Hunt', *East London Advertiser* 17 September 1976.

Dalrymple, S., 'Confessions of a Stripper', *Frendz* 33, 8 July 1971.

Davis, W., 'Marylebone Station to Be Rebuilt', *Evening Standard* 31 October 1961.

Dodd, D., 'Police and Thieves on the Streets of Brixton', *New Society* 16 March 1978.

Donnelly, F., 'The Music Man', *Evening Standard* 10 June 1977.

Douglas-Home, R., 'The Young Face of Old Chelsea', *Tatler and Bystander* 13 May 1959.

Duncan, A., 'Hotfooting to London—but There's More to It than Just the Money', *Evening Standard* 27 November 1964.

———, 'Public Servant', *Evening Standard* 30 November 1967.

Durgnat, R., 'Strippers. A Guide to Soho Clubs', *International Times* 4, 28 November–11 December 1966.

Edgar, D., 'Young Man, Has Charm, Will Travel (Upwards, Of Course)', *Evening Standard* 2 March 1960.

Entwisle, F., 'The Knowledge Boys Face a Hard Road', *Evening Standard* 30 November 1961.

———, 'Can You Wonder the Cabbies Are Angry?', *Evening Standard* 1 December 1961.

Evans, P., 'Notting Hill Gate: A Suitable Case for Treatment', *Times* 17 December 1971.

Eversley, D., 'Just Let Rip—That's No Logic!', *Evening Standard* 20 February 1973.

———, 'Collapse of the Council House?', *Evening Standard* 26 October 1976.

Farr, D., 'Soho—Where Strip Makes a Million a Year', *People* 5 May 1968.

Fay, F., 'Anatomy of a Restaurant', *Queen* 30 March 1966.

Fernandez, L., 'The Man behind the Menu' (interview with Bernard Walsh, Wheeler's), *Hotel and Restaurant Catering* May 1970.

Fiddick, P., 'Local Affairs', *Guardian* 8 August 1972.

Forester, T., 'An ABC of Unemployment in the Inner City', *New Society* 6 December 1979.

France, J. C., 'Home Ownership in the Home Counties', *Building Societies Gazette* May 1964.

Garner, L., 'Millie Miller—Scourge of Centre Point', *Sunday Times* 17 September 1972.

Goldsmith, V., 'London's Leading Eating Houses Take a Knock', *Evening Standard* 3 March 1977.

Goodman, E., 'Disposable as Its Clothes', *Financial Times* 21 August 1975.

Gray, C., 'When a Bad Tenant Just Won't Budge', *Evening Standard* 14 August 1974.

Green, F., 'This Is Barbara. Now She's a Dress Manufacturer as Well as a Fashion Artist', *Daily Mirror* 1 May 1964.

Griggs, B., 'Why Girls Leave Home', *Evening Standard* 20 November 1963.

———, 'So I Said No More Boutiques ... !', *Evening Standard* 25 April 1966.

———, 'The Battle of the Boutiques', *Evening Standard* 18 April 1967.

Grizell, R., 'Big, Rich Croydon with a Cold Heart', *Evening News* 7 June 1972.

Grove, T., '£1300m—for a Monster London Could Live Without', *Evening Standard* 13 March 1975.

Guest, D., S. Corby, A. Koo, & M. Stirling, 'Turn Again Whittington', *New Society* 16 May 1974.

Hackett, J., 'Rags to Riches', *New Society* 10 June 1971.

Haden-Guest, A., 'The New Class. A Post-Mortem', *Queen* 3 November 1965.

———, 'Dancing Chic to Chic', *Queen* 22 June 1966.

Hall, P., 'Out of the Twilight?', *New Society* 17 October 1968.

———, 'Anatomy of the Green Belts', *New Society* 4 January 1973.

Hanson, M., 'The Changing Face of Greater London. 6: Kingston', *Investors Review* 85 (5), 15–28 October 1976.

Harmsworth, M., 'The Changing Face of Chelsea', part 2, *West London Press and Chelsea News* 19 May 1961.

———, 'The Changing Face of Chelsea', part 3, *West London Press and Chelsea News* 26 May 1961.

Harrington, I., 'The Trouble with Tourism Unlimited', *New Statesman* 6 August 1971.

Harrison, P., 'Tower Hamlets: A Social Services Case Study', *New Society* 7 December 1972.

Hart, K., 'The Secretary', *London Life* 25 June 1966.

Hastings, M., 'In the Suburbs the Wives Are Having to Work', *Evening Standard* 29 January 1976.

———, 'How Britannia Road Went Up in the World', *Evening Standard* 4 October 1979.

Hillman, J., 'Today Lambeth, Tomorrow ...', *Evening Standard* 9 November 1965.

———, 'But What Do the Tenants Say?', *Evening Standard* 27 February 1967.

———, 'Afraid? No—This Is Bliss', *Evening Standard* 26 July 1968.

———, 'Will the New London Put People First?', *Hampstead and Highgate Express* 21 February 1969.

Hough, S., 'Labour's Radical Right', *New Society* 17 November 1977.

Hounam, P., 'Why Life Is Better in Barnet', *Evening Standard* 6 March 1979.

Howard, A., 'Islington's Last Hurrah', *New Statesman* 17 August 1962.

Howard, S., 'The Changing Face of Wimbledon Village—a Sad Sign of the Times', *Wimbledon News* 11 May 1973.

Hunt, S., 'Goodbye Mr Chips-with-Everything', *Time Out* 12 November 1976.

Hurley, J., 'Towards a Sociology of Architecture', in *A.R.S.E.* [*Architects for a Really Socialist Environment*, a.k.a. *Architectural Radicals, Students and Educators*, etc], 5/6, Spring–Summer 1972.

Ince, A., 'Close Up: David Mlinaric', *London Life* 16 October 1965.

———, 'The Boutique Bandwagon', *London Life* 23 July 1966.

Insall, R., 'Sex Shops Drive Out the Soho Villagers', *Evening News*, 17 December 1975.

James, S., 'The New Elite', *Evening Standard* 29 February 1960.

Jeffries, M., 'Kensington and Chelsea . . . Borough of Unmarried Mothers', *Evening Standard* 2 May 1969.

Jenkins, S., 'Mucking About with the Environment', *Evening Standard* 14 November 1972.

———, 'The Conversion of Councillor Cubitt', *Evening Standard* 19 December 1972.

———, 'Out of Farce and into Tragedy', *Evening Standard* 20 February 1973.

———, 'See It All Come Crashing Down!', *Evening Standard* 29 March 1973.

———, 'Come Back Plastic Gnomes, All Is Forgiven', *Evening Standard* 8 May 1973.

———, 'Big Joe's Last Stand?', *Evening Standard* 19 June 1973.

———, '. . . And Scandal in the City', *Evening Standard* 26 June 1973.

———, 'The Scars of London's Hotel Gold Rush', *Evening Standard* 24 July 1973.

———, 'Stage Set for Destruction—or How Theatreland Can Survive', *Evening Standard* 16 October 1973.

———, 'The Year We Changed Our Minds', *Evening Standard* 18 December 1973.

———, 'Waiter, There's a Brick in My Soup', *Evening Standard* 11 June 1974.

———, 'The Holes in Shelter's Roof', *Evening Standard* 12 August 1976.

———, 'Why We Must Not Ban the Carnival', *Evening Standard* 31 August 1976.

———, 'The Job Destroyers', *Evening Standard* 14 October 1976.

———, 'What Alf Garnett Could Tell the Experts', *Evening Standard* 23 June 1977.

Jenkins, V., 'When the Bottom Falls Out of an Old Barometer', *Evening Standard* 12 May 1975.

———, 'For Janet Lyle the Sixties (Remember Them?) Stop Here', *Evening Standard* 30 January 1976.

———, 'Whatever Became of Young Whatsisname?', *Evening Standard* 21 October 1976.

Johnson, B. S., 'The Demolition Man', *London Life* 11 December 1965.

Johnson, P., 'Hands Up to Stop the Spendthrifts', *Evening Standard* 5 March 1979.

Jones, M., 'The Coup That Threatens Reg Prentice', *Sunday Times* 13 July 1975.

Kotas, R., 'Of Price and Profit', *Caterer and Hotelkeeper* 4 December 1969.

Kukoy, L., 'The Pacesetters', *Hotel and Restaurant Catering* January 1970.

Langton, R., 'Poor Old Property Men', *Evening Standard* 14 March 1974.

———, 'The Rent-Hit Young Londoners Go on a Home-Buying Spree', *Evening Standard* 27 April 1977.

Lapping, A., 'The Meths Drinkers Remain', *New Society* 13 July 1967.

———, 'London's Burning! London's Burning! A Survey', *Economist* 1 January 1977.

Lawless, J., 'Race to the Top', *Business Management* 100 (7), July 1970.

Leith, N., 'The Reluctant Exodus', *Evening Standard* 24 January 1977.

Lennox, E., 'The Shape of Sutton to Come, I', *Wallington and Carshalton Herald* 23 November 1972.

———, 'The Shape of Sutton to Come, IV: Room at the Top for the Office Brigade', *Wallington and Carshalton Herald* 18 January 1973.

Lewis, G., 'The Greater London Council—a Luxury We Can No Longer Afford?', *The Bulletin*, February and March 1975.

———, 'Council Housing', *The Bulletin* August 1976.

Lovejoy, D., 'Croydon's Road to Chaos', *Architect* 1, December 1971.

Lucie-Smith, E., 'Winner That Began in the Bath', *Evening Standard* 27 February 1979.

Luder, O., 'Croydon—The Lost Opportunity', *Croydon Advertiser* 26 March 1965.

Lyte, C., 'How the Squeeze Hits London', *Evening Standard* 6 October 1966.

Macpherson, M., 'The Term the Teachers Ran Out', *Evening Standard* 30 August 1973.

———, 'Back from the Dead', *Evening Standard* 12 May 1977.

———, 'The Crane Drain to Kent', *Evening Standard* 12 May 1977.

———, 'Return of Pink Pancras', *Evening Standard* 1 August 1977.

Mallory, D., 'A Snob's Guide to the City', *Queen* 13 February 1963.

Mankowitz, W., 'Yes, but I Knew It When . . .', *Evening Standard* 6 May 1963.

Marcelle, J. M., 'Cabman's Letter to Margaret Thatcher', *Steering Wheel* 6 April 1979.

Marks, S., 'In London's Housing Trap', *New Society* 8 September 1977.

Marsden, F., 'A Bookshop in Chelsea', *West London Press and Chelsea News* 19 February 1965.

Martin, F., 'Death of a Thousand Cults', *Guardian* 20 January 1976.

Maschler, F., 'Where to Seek a Little Greek Delight', *Evening Standard* 6 December 1972.

———, 'Getting to Know Bhoona, Alu and Tarka the Hotter', *Evening Standard* 18 April 1973.

———, 'The Name of the Game Is the Name', *Evening Standard*, 23 May 1973.

———, 'Lessons in the Language of Food', *Evening Standard* 13 June 1973.

———, 'Good Food: Have We Really Had Our Day?', *ES* 6 November 1974.

———, 'Where the People in the Know Go', *Evening Standard* 13 November 1974.

———, 'High Speed Feed', *Evening Standard* 11 December 1974.

———, 'How to Survive the Whims of Change', *Evening Standard* 26 February 1975.

———, 'Do I Hear £1.25 for a Meal?', *Evening Standard* 6 August 1975.

———, 'Secrets of Survival, by the Old Faithfuls', *Evening Standard* 1 October 1975.

———, 'Seventeen of the Best', *Evening Standard* 29 December 1976.

Massam, A., 'Why London Got the Knife', 'The Ones That Have Gone', *Evening Standard* 25 October 1977.

McGill, A., 'Goodbye to the Teddy Boy—Now It's the Smooth Type Tailored to His Fingertips', *Evening Standard* 4 April 1962.

———, 'All That Stands between My Sort of Dump and My Dream House Are Those Beastly Building Society Rules', *ES* 17 April 1963.

———, 'Look Out. There's a Mod (or Maybe a Rocker) Close Behind You', *Evening Standard* 31 July 1963.

———, 'It Sounds Silly, but I've Been Shopping in a Boutique!', *Evening Standard* 22 July 1964.

———, 'So What Is Le Style Anglais?', *Evening Standard* 16 March 1966.

———, 'Home Is Home, but London Is Where the *Action* Is', *Evening Standard* 13 April 1966.

———, 'Are You One of the Beautiful People?', *Evening Standard* 11 September 1968.

———, 'Down, Down, Down They Come', *Evening Standard* 25 October 1972.

———, 'How They Play the Waiting Game', *Evening Standard* 14 April 1976.

McKee, M., 'Dancing in the Streets', *Kensington News and Post* 31 August 1973.

McKnight, C., 'Getting Worse! Crisis in London's Vital Services', *Evening Standard* 22 August 1973.

McLachlan, S., & Van der Post, L., 'The Biba Gamble: Boutique to Department Store', *Financial Times* 11 September 1973.

Melly, G., 'The Way We Live Now', *Evening Standard* 18 October 1976.

Menkes, S., 'King's Road, Where Are You Now?', *Evening Standard* 5 January 1976.

Merricks, F. R., 'The Development of Community Relations in the Metropolitan Police', *Police Journal* 1 January 1970.

Mikes, G., 'The Gay Hussar', *London Life* 19 February 1966.

Miller, C., 'The Men Who Put the Zip into Denim', *Evening Standard* 13 May 1977.

Miller, R., 'Instant Eats, or How the Burger Boom Is Biting Britain', *Evening Standard* 18 November 1972.

Moger, P., '"Carnaby Street" Cabbie', *Acton Gazette* 6 April 1967.

Morrison, L., 'I Say the Police Are to Blame', *Evening Standard* 10 August 1970.

———, 'The Race Industry Is Weak, White and Wasteful', *West Indian World* 12 November 1971.

———, 'What Is the Race Board Up To?', *West Indian World* 19 November 1971.

———, 'CRC: Black Man's Friend or Foe?', *West Indian World* 26 November 1971.

———, 'What Is the Answer?', *West Indian World* 3 December 1971.

———, 'Growing Problem of Homeless Young Blacks', *Evening Standard* 16 February 1973.

———, 'What It Is Like to Be Coloured and on the Beat', *Evening Standard* 27 April 1973.

Morton, J., 'London's Housing Transfer', *New Society* 5 December 1968.

———, 'Raising Council Rents', *New Society* 14 August 1969.

———, 'Creeping Hotels', *New Society* 25 November 1971.

Munch, J., & Forgan, L., 'Rates Rise Battle Call Goes Out to Resistance Fighters', *Evening Standard* 17 February 1975.

Murdin, L., 'Hot Property: It's Mine', *Evening Standard* 6 February 1979.

Murray, N., 'Carpetbagging in Bermondsey', *London Review of Books* 19 August 1982.

Nazer, G., 'Morden—Nothing There Soon Except the End of the Northern Line?', *Wimbledon News* 19 January 1973.

Norman, P., 'The Battle for Biba', *Sunday Times Magazine* 28 September 1975.

Norridge, J., 'Would You Let Your Daughter?', *Evening Standard* 11 May 1970.

———, 'Behind the Bitterness of Notting Hill', *Evening Standard* 10 August 1970.

———, 'Just Who Can Afford to Buy a House in London?', *Evening Standard* 21 August 1970.

———, 'Wincing under the Surgeon's Knife', *Evening Standard* 16 October 1979.

Norridge, J., & Jenkins, V., 'If You're Young and Healthy, Find Your Own Place', *Evening Standard* 17 September 1970.

Northedge, R., 'First Time Unlucky', *Evening Standard* 12 April 1979.

———, 'Homes "Too Dear for First-Time Buyers"', *Evening Standard* 2 July 1979.

Nuttall, G., 'Chelsea: Amateur or Professional?', *Sunday Times* 26 March 1967.

———, 'The Swinging Cash-In down the King's Road', *Sunday Times* 17 August 1969.

O'Brien, E., 'Turn Right over Putney Bridge', *Evening Standard* 30 September 1964.

Page, J., 'The Landlords', *Evening Standard,* 20 October 1970.

Passmore, J., 'Desecration? How the Property Developers Are Spoiling Our Heritage and Why We Can't Stop Them', *Wimbledon News* 6 July 1973.

Pearce, S., 'Fares. Time for a Change?', *Steering Wheel* 4 July 1975.

———, 'Minimum Hirings and Maximum Profits', *Steering Wheel* 7 April 1978.

Pearman, H., 'Glossary of Cockney Cabology', *Taxi Trader* January 1971.

———, 'Call Me Cabby, II', *Taxi Trader,* July 1971.

Pearson, E., 'Get a "New Home" from the Town Hall', *Evening Standard* 28 April 1972.

Pearson, M., 'Why Solicitors Are up in Arms', *Evening Standard* 22 August 1966.

Phillips, Melanie, 'People in a House', *New Society* 2 June 1977.

Phillips, Mike, 'The Sullen Carnival', *New Society* 31 August 1978.

Phillips, W., 'Leftist Lambeth. Last of the Big Spenders', *Evening Standard* 26 October 1978.

———, 'O'Grady Says Do This!', *Evening Standard* 18 January 1979.

Pitt, D., 'Little Things Add Up to a Very Big Problem', *The Job* 19 July 1968.

Pocock, T., 'Vanishing: The World That Made the Cockney', *Evening Standard* 15 November 1960.

Portman, S., 'The Girls Are Not Called Weirdies Now, but a Man Is Still Judged by His Car . . .', *Evening Standard* 31 December 1965.

Powell, A., 'Living In', *Observer* 12 July 1964.

Pritchett, O., 'A Lost Cause in Stepney', *Evening Standard* 4 May 1977.

Raban, J., 'Among Cypriots', *New Society* 24 May 1973.

Raspberry, W., 'Young, Bitter and Black', *Observer* 5 September 1976.

——, 'Why Britain's Blacks Have No Leaders', *Observer* 19 September 1976.

Rawstorne, P., 'The Lambeth Settlers', *Guardian* 13 May 1963.

Raynsford, N., 'Motorway Madness', *Community Action* 2, April–May 1972.

Reading, J., 'Clearance in Pimlico', *New Society* 16 June 1977.

Rennison, J., 'Sweet Thames . . .', *Financial Times* 13 November 1971.

Richmond Society, 'The Fight Is Now On to Save Best of Richmond from Destruction', *Richmond and Twickenham Times* 25 May 1973.

Rogaly, J., 'London's Case for "Special Treatment"', *Financial Times* 6 November 1973.

Rogers, B., 'The Strange Community of Gerrard Street', *Daily Telegraph Magazine* 13 March 1970.

Sandles, A., 'Tourism Not So Invisible', *Financial Times* 14 April 1970.

Sharpley, A., 'The Man from World's End', *Evening Standard* 3 March 1960.

——, 'Purple Heart Trip in Soho', *Evening Standard* 3 February 1964.

——, 'In the Big City—Less Fear, Less Solitude', *Evening Standard* 22 July 1964.

——, 'Murder Grove, Part V . . . Will the Middle-Class Take Over?', *Evening Standard*, 2 April 1965.

——, 'The Confessions of Three Teenage Shoplifters', *Evening Standard* 16 August 1966.

——, 'But What's Happened to London's Sense of Street Fun?', *Evening Standard* 11 August 1978.

Sherman, A., 'Are Tourists Really Worth It?', *Daily Telegraph* 2 June 1973.

——, 'Effects of the Tourist Invasion', *Daily Telegraph* 27 August 1973.

Sherman, A., et al., 'In Search of Swinging London', *London Life*, 18 June 1966.

Simpson, J., 'Man to Man', *The Job* 8 December 1967.

Sinclair, L., 'Municipal Housing, Part II', *The Bulletin, Upminster and Cranham Residents Association Newsletter* June 1976.

Smith, A., 'First Swallow of a Long Hot Summer?', *Guardian* 28 June 1975.

Steele, T., 'At 15 I Had My First Argument with an Adult . . .', *Evening Standard* 9 December 1960.

Stellman, M., 'Sitting Here in Limbo', *Time Out* 23 August 1974.

Stuart, M., 'Not So Lovely in Garden', *Guardian* 21 April 1971.

Thomas, S., 'No Welcome for Nigel', *Evening Standard* 2 August 1979.

Thompson, J. W. M., 'The £450 House: Now It Can Change Hands for £3500', *Evening Standard* 15 May 1962.

——, 'Beneath This Quiet Exterior Are Tensions—Anguish Even', *Evening Standard* 18 May 1962.

Tindall, G., 'Where Have All the Bedsits Gone?' *Evening Standard* 6 November 1978.

Topolski, D., 'The Season', *New Society* 28 June 1979.

Torode, J. A., 'Keeping a Secretary', *New Society* 20 May 1965.

Troyna, B., 'The Reggae War', *New Society* 10 March 1977.

Vaughan, J., 'Apicella's Opera', *Queen* 17 January 1968.

Vigars, R., 'We Will Build It!', *Evening Standard* 20 November 1969.

Vincent, L., 'Biba's Rude Awakening', *Guardian* 20 July 1975.

Visby, B., 'Teenage-Imperiet', *Politiken* (Copenhagen) 6 May 1966.

Wainwright, M., 'The Way We Live Now', *Evening Standard* 19 October 1976.

Waldron, J., 'A Problem of Colour and Character', *The Job* 21 June 1968.

Walsh, G., 'A Wrong Solution, Hard to Change', *Evening Standard* 17 March 1977.

Waymark, P., 'New Chinatown Comes to Soho', *Times* 5 January 1970.

Weintraub, B., 'A Real Hamburger a Success in London', *New York Times* 12 August 1970.

Weir, S., 'How Islington Decided Its Rates', *New Society* 22 March 1979.

Wells, D., 'Look Back in Envy', *Evening Standard* 22 November 1978.

West, J., 'Taking the Plunge', *Where to Go* 31 October 1968.

White, D., 'Protest People', *New Society* 29 June 1972.

——, 'The Pleasures of Croydon', *New Society* 29 May 1975.

——, 'Newham: An Example of Urban Decline', *New Society* 23 October 1975.

——, 'Are Tourists Really a Blight?', *New Society* 23 March 1978.

White, M., 'Tell Me How Long My Home's Been Gone', *Guardian* 7 March 1973.

Whitehorn, K., 'Spiels on Wheels', *Observer* 29 April 1979.

Wilcox, D., 'Saved! The 1920s Image in Piccadilly', *Evening Standard* 18 January 1972.

——, 'The Big Clean-up', *Evening Standard* 29 November 1972.

——, 'Covent Garden—the Big Plan', *Evening Standard* 15 January 1973.

——, 'London on the Rocks', *Evening Standard* 23 April 1975.

——, 'The Changing Face of Greater London. Introduction', *Investors Review* 84 (17), 2–15 April 1976.

——, 'The Changing Face of Greater London. 3: Lewisham', *Investors Review* 84 (22), 11–24 June 1976.

Willmott, P., 'Population and Community in London', *New Society* 4 October 1974.

Wilson, J., 'Not Much Bottle at the Beat Ball', *London Life* 27 November 1965.

Wilton, J., 'Girls like Lucy', *London Life* 8 January 1966.

Young, G., 'Who Needs Tourists?', *Evening Standard* 19 November 1973.

INDEX

(Italics indicate references to figures and illustrations)

London Amenity and Transport Association, 170

London Bridge, 4, 6, 179

London Bridge station, 473n16

London Chamber of Commerce, 417

London Convention Bureau, 400

London Council of Social Service, 299, 300, 301, 354

London County Council, 124, 172, 182, 213, 223, 239, 365, 366, 395, 405; Historic Buildings Sub–Committee, 197, 199; and entertainments licensing, 50–51, 54–55, 64–65, 446n89; and historic buildings, 194, 196–99, 213; and housing, 6, 138, 143, 149, 236, 243; and Piccadilly Circus, 14, 186–88, 205; planning policy, 14, 161, 181, 224–6; Town Planning Committee, 225

Londonderry House, 26

London Diocesan Council for Moral Welfare, 16

London Docklands Development Corporation, 244

London Docks, 234, 412

London Free School, 333

London Government Act, 1963, 55, 64, 491n69

London Guide School (for taxi drivers), 251

London Labour Party, 125

London Life, 29, 31–33, 44, 79, 115

London Motorway Action Group, 169

London Pavilion, Shaftesbury Avenue, 215

London Property Letter, 130–32, 137–38, 140, 142, 154, 155, 319, 501n102

London Restaurants Training Group, 101

London School of Economics, 82, 170, 256, 366–67, 421

London Season, the, 26, 31–32, 440n175

London Taxi Guides, 251

London Tourist Board, 251, 397–401, 404, 405

London Traffic Survey, 162, 164–66

London Transport, 178, 416

London Union of Youth Clubs, 350

London weighting, 415, 519n38

Look of London, 17

Loon Fung restaurant, Gerrard Street, 113, 116

Lopez, Eddie, Labour Party agent, 385

Lord John boutique chain, 24, 91

Lorentzen, Anne, geographer, 120

Los Angeles, 171–72

Lower Square, Isleworth, 279

Lower Thames Street, EC3, 183

Lucan, John Bingham, 7th Earl of, 40

Lucky restaurant, Gerrard Street, 113

Luder, Owen, architect, 276

Luigi's restaurant, Gerrard Street, 113

Luscombe, Special Constable, 327

Luso restaurant, Beauchamp Place, 94

Lyall, Neil, strip club manager, 52

Lycett Green, Rupert, tailor, 2

Lyle, Janet, boutique proprietor, 80, 408

Lyte, Charles, journalist, 42

Lyttelton, Humphrey, musician, 109

MacCarthy, Fiona, writer, 32

Maccioni, Alvaro, restaurateur, 36, 38, 98, 422

Macclesfield Street, W1, 67

Macdonald, Ian, barrister, 332

Macdonald, James Ramsay, MP, politician, 379

Macdonald, Kevin, club proprietor, 38

Mackay–Lewis, Jeremy, architect, 194

Macmillan, Harold, MP, Minister of Housing and Local Government, 1951–54, Prime Minister, 1957–63, 13, 183, 193, 472n1

Macpherson, Mary, journalist, 412

Madam Cadee's saucepan shop, Soho, 69

'Maggie', striptease artiste, 62

Maison Prunier restaurant, Paris, 96

Maizels, Joan, social observer, 304, 309, 313, 319

Major, John, MP, Prime Minister 1990–97, 434

Malaysian restaurants, 117, 119

Malcolm, Mary, television announcer, 30

Mallory, Diana, journalist, 30

malls, 272–73, 296, 424, 451n106

Maltese community, 9, 56, 59, 64, 298

Man Alive, television programme, 29

Manchester, 97, 520n48

Mandarin restaurant, Gerrard Street, 113

Mangrove restaurant, All Saints Road, 324, 328, 331–33, 334, 335, 336

Printed in the USA
CPSIA information can be obtained
at www.ICGtesting.com
JSHW032234160424
61207JS00020B/215